D0146878

*Bureaucratic Reform
in the Ottoman Empire*

BUREAUCRATIC REFORM
IN THE OTTOMAN EMPIRE

THE SUBLIME PORTE, 1789-1922

Carter V. Findley

PRINCETON UNIVERSITY PRESS

PRINCETON, NEW JERSEY

All Rights Reserved
Library of Congress Cataloging in Publication Data will be
found on the last printed page of this book

Publication of this book has been aided by a grant from the
National Endowment for the Humanities

This book has been composed in VIP Baskerville

Clothbound editions of Princeton University Press books
are printed on acid-free paper, and binding materials are
chosen for strength and durability.

Printed in the United States of America by Princeton
University Press, Princeton, New Jersey

For My Parents

Elizabeth S. Findley
and
John C. Findley

Princeton Studies on the Near East

... lâkin bir devletin böyle
külliyen tebdil ve tecdid-i
nizamatı müceddeden bir
devletin teşkilinden güç
olduğuna binaen ...

... since it is more difficult
thus entirely to change and
renovate the laws of a
state than to found a
state anew ...

Ahmed Cevdet Paşa, *Tarih*, vi, 6

Contents

FRONTISPIECE. *Tuğra* or "Cipher" of Sultan Abd ül-Mecid
(1839-1861)
SOURCE: An original *ferman*, dated El RA 1263/1847, in the
possession of the author

following page 268

1. Façade of the Sublime Porte on the Side Facing the Golden
   Horn, an Ottoman View, c. 1867
   SOURCE: *Tanzimat I: Yüzüncü Yıldönümü Münasebetile* (Istanbul,
   1940), plate I. (The source cited there, *Ayine-i Vatan* of 14
   Kanun-ı sani 1867, does not check against the collection of this
   title in the Library of the School of Oriental and African
   Studies, University of London)
2. The *Bab-ı Kebir*, or "Great Gateway," to the Compound En-
   closing the Buildings of the Sublime Porte, c. 1830s
   SOURCE: Robert Walsh, *Constantinople and the Scenery of the
   Seven Churches of Asia Minor*, plates by Thomas Allom, 2 vols.
   (London, c. 1838), II, opposite p. 67
3. Reception of a European Envoy by the Grand Vezir, c. 1790s
   SOURCE: Topkapı Palace Museum, Istanbul (published by
   permission)
4. Interior Scene in the Residence of an Ottoman Dignitary
   (*Müsellim*) at Alaşehir in Anatolia, c. 1830s
   SOURCE: Walsh, *Constantinople*, plate by Thomas Allom, II, opposite p. 92
5. Mustafa Reşid Paşa (1800-1858)
   SOURCE: Topkapı Palace Museum, Istanbul (published by
   permission)
6. Keçecizade Fuad Paşa (1815-1869)
   SOURCE: Wilhelm Oncken, ed., *Allgemeine Geschichte
   in Einzeldarstellungen*, 46 vols. (Berlin, 1879-1893), 4. Haupt-
   abtheilung, V: *Geschichte der orientalischen Angelegenheit im Zeit-
   raume des Pariser und Berliner Friedens*, by Felix Bamberg
   (1892), 267
7. Mehmed Emin Âli Paşa (1815-1871)
   SOURCE: Topkapı Palace Museum, Istanbul (published by
   permission)

Sublime Porte—there must be few terms more redolent, even today, of the fascination that the Islamic Middle East has long exercised over Western imaginations. Yet there must also be few Western minds that now know what this term refers to, or why it has any claim to attention. One present-day Middle East expert admits to having long interpreted the expression as a reference to Istanbul's splendid natural harbor. This individual is probably not unique and could perhaps claim to be relatively well informed. When the Sublime Porte still existed, Westerners who spent time in Istanbul knew the term as a designation for the Ottoman government, but few knew why the name was used, or what aspect of the Ottoman government it properly designated. What was the real Sublime Porte? Was it an organization? A building? No more, literally, than a door or gateway? What about it was important enough to cause the name to be remembered?

In one sense, the purpose of this book is to answer these questions. Of course, it will also do much more and will, in the process, move quickly onto a plane quite different from that of the exoticism just evoked. For to study the bureaucratic complex properly known as the Sublime Porte, and to analyze its evolution and that of the body of men who staffed it, is to explore a problem of tremendous significance for the development of the administrative institutions of the Ottoman Empire, the Islamic lands in general, and in some senses the entire non-Western world.

The chapters that follow will amplify and substantiate this statement. Before going further, however, it is appropriate to comment more fully than will be possible, once substantive discussion begins, on certain features of the sources and on two principles, formulated in response to these features, that have guided the organization of this study.

Research in Ottoman history is a venture into an ill-charted terrain. Original source materials exist, often in unmanageable bulk, but they are difficult of comprehension and sometimes of access. The state of scholarship in the field, despite the efforts of generations of scholars in many lands, is such that a high proportion of the questions that call for attention in any study cannot be treated adequately by any means other than investigation of the primary sources. Where a given question is only ancillary to the main subject of a study or, however important, is centered elsewhere, a full-scale investigation of the type needed is sometimes not practicable. Nor does such an investigation always answer the researcher's questions. In this as in other societies, it sometimes turns out that important problems either did not attract the attention, or else eluded the comprehension, of contemporaries. Accounts by contemporary observers of different cultural background, when such persons were present, may or may not be of much help. Exploration of certain issues may thus require the painful culling and interpretation of widely scattered fragments of information. At times, the extent to which it is possible to proceed even by this means may be limited.

These are well-known characteristics of the field, and their effects will be apparent at times in the following pages. As we shall note more fully in Chapter Five, for example, Ottoman reformers of the nineteenth century were quicker to proclaim reforms than to regulate exactly how the reforms should be implemented; they were also quicker to regulate than to investigate and record how the regulations were applied. European observers, with a few valuable exceptions, lacked the depth of interest or information that would have enabled them to compensate for this deficiency. In the field of finance, the problems of the sources are even more severe. Their tradition and situation left Ottoman statesmen notoriously ill-equipped to cope with questions of this kind, while Europeans, though more knowing, reacted and commented primarily in terms of their own interests. This situation is particularly unfortunate, as nineteenth-century Ottoman government finance is a topic potentially capable of yielding a study of considerable importance. But little critical scholarship has yet been devoted to the subject, the relevant Ottoman documentation is especially voluminous and difficult to interpret, and the records of the Ministry of Finance for the late nineteenth century were not open to scholars when most of the research for this study was done and presumably still are not. A detailed analysis of one financial issue of particular importance for bureaucrats, the official compensation system, has developed out of the research undertaken for this study. Presentation of the statistical part of this analysis could not be included within this book without expanding it beyond reasonable limits, however, and thus must wait, but for some comments, for a later work.

How should a scholar react to the difficulties of the Ottoman field in designing a program of research? One long-familiar response is to narrow the scope of inquiry, seek a problem as free of impinging uncertainties as possible, and attempt to arrive at a sound interpretation through exhaustive study of the sources and conscientious investigation of the details and technicalities that they present. For thoroughness and attention to specifics, this kind of approach is indispensable in any historical work that is to carry conviction. The research that culminated in the writing of this book made clear, however, that such a method has its potential costs where selection of topic is concerned. There are few subjects, however delimited, in Ottoman history where the scholar does not confront uncertainties that cannot be totally resolved within the framework of a single study. There must also be few topics of significance for which it is humanly possible to locate and use all relevant source materials. This being the case, narrowing the scope of research can hinder more than help the researcher, who must also try to acquire a broad frame of reference in which to interpret his findings and demonstrate their significance. The limited development of the literature on related subjects heightens this danger, creating the risk that the fruit of conscientious scholarship will be idiosyncratic pedantry.

Given this situation, the first principle that has guided the organization of this study is that its scope should be defined as broadly as possible. The study should also be as thorough as possible in the investigation of the sources and the cultural milieu. The situation of a bureaucracy cannot be assessed fully without reference to its relations with its broader political and social setting, however, and it is thus indispensable that the scope of the analysis be large enough to permit appreciation of these relationships, especially as they evolved over time.

For anyone approaching Ottoman bureaucratic institutions of the nineteenth century with these concerns in mind, the ideal subject would be the entire civil bureaucracy, long the most influential and dynamic branch of Ottoman officialdom, and all the institutions it staffed. But this is too much to attempt in any depth in a work of reasonable scale. This study accordingly concentrates on the Sublime Porte, the civil-bureaucratic headquar-

ters of the time, and on the men who staffed it. The following
chapters will examine the development of this complex over the
whole era of reform, paying particular attention to the evolution
of the organizational and procedural apparatus of administration, to the elaboration of the relevant body of laws and regulations, and to change in the corporate state of the branch of the
bureaucracy that staffed the agencies under study. A fuller
treatment of the social, economic, and cultural implications of
reform will be the subject of a later work, which will include the
analysis of the compensation system mentioned earlier.

The wish to achieve a broad frame of reference was decisive
not only in determining the scope of this study, but also in
prompting formulation of the second of the principles that has
guided its preparation. This is that the study should be written
in a way that can be enlightening not only to specialists but also
to a broader audience, including readers who are not historians
of the Middle East but are interested in bureaucracy or the
modernization of traditional societies. It is true that this book is
the work of a historian and deals with the evolution of a bureaucratic system as seen in its own immediate cultural context. Yet
works on bureaucracy and modernization, written by scholars in
a variety of other fields and disciplines, have provided invalu-
able guidance for structuring the present analysis and for
evaluating the phenomena it investigates. This is above all true
of the work of theoretically oriented writers, and especially of
Weber and Eisenstadt. Through the medium of discourse that it
creates, this broader literature has also suggested a way of expressing the conclusions of the present study in terms whose
currency transcends the limits of a particular field of historical
specialization. To pursue the comparisons among different bureaucratic systems or the criticism and refinement of theory,
which are the preoccupations of scholars in some of these other
fields, falls beyond the scope of the present work. One of its
goals, however, is to analyze its subject in a way that both throws
light on the specific cultural setting of that subject and can prove
meaningful to scholars interested in the subject but not in the
cultural setting as such. If this book proves useful to scholars
outside, as well as inside, the field of Middle Eastern history, it
will have achieved one of its most important objectives.

To attempt to recall all those who have contributed to this study is to retrace a path that has wound across much of the world during a period of over ten years. Some scholars have contributed through sustained guidance provided throughout a lengthy period of association. Some have contributed through incisive comments made during brief meetings. Some institutions and individuals have contributed other types of support, material and sometimes moral, as well.

Among scholars, my greatest debts are to Stanford J. Shaw, Roderic H. Davison, Halil İnalcık, and Şerif Mardin. I also owe thanks to Bernard Lewis, S. N. Eisenstadt, Omeljan Pritsak, J. C. Hurewitz, Nermin Menemencioğlu Streater, David S. Landes, Frederick Frey, Richard D. Robinson, L. Carl Brown, Metin Heper, Avigdor Levy, Nejat Göyünç, Halil Sahillioğlu, Mehmet Genç, and Metin Kunt, as well as to the late Gustave von Grunebaum and Uriel Heyd. A number of members of the faculty of Ohio State University, particularly among my colleagues in the History Department, have been of help in various ways. The best tribute in this case is one of collective thanks. Other individuals who have helped in specific matters of detail will be mentioned in the notes.

In the world of librarians, I owe thanks to the staffs of Widener Library, the British Library, the Bibliothèque Nationale, the Municipal Library (Belediye Kütüphanesi) of Istanbul, the Istanbul University Library, the Library of Congress, and the Ohio State University Libraries.

Among archivists, I am indebteded to the personnel of the Public Record Office (London), the Archives du Ministère des Affaires Étrangères (Paris), the Haus- Hof- und Staatsarchiv (Vienna), the U.S. National Archives (Washington, D.C.), the Topkapı Palace Archives, the Foreign Ministry (Hariciye) Archives, and the Prime Ministers' (Başbakanlık) Archives, the last three in Istanbul. The Başbakanlık Archives in particular were my place of work on several occasions, ranging in duration from a few months to a full year, and provided the setting for the formation of many lasting professional friendships as well as for original research without which this study would have been unthinkable. I should here like to express my thanks to the official authorities in Turkey who authorized my research. Among the archivists whom I came to know in Istanbul, it is a pleasure to record my thanks to Midhat Sertoğlu, Fazıl Işıközlü, Ziya Eşrefoğlu, Rauf Tunçay, Turgut Işıksal, Ziya Esrekoğlu, Dündar Günday, Tevfik Temelkuran, İbrahim Sivrikaya, Neptun Erman, Eşref Eşrefoğlu, Hasan Adalı, Nizamettin Yüzbaşıoğlu, Nacı Gönüç, and Nüzhet Ataman. I wish also to thank Cemal Işın, proprietor of the Photographic Workshop attached to the Prime Ministers' Archives, for extraordinary helpfulness in the preparation of photocopies and microfilms.

In material support of my work, I received aid at the predoctoral level through the National Defense Foreign Language Grant and Foreign Area Fellowship programs. During 1971-1972, I held a Younger Humanist Fellowship of the National Endowment for the Humanities and received supplementary grants from the American Research Institute in Turkey and the Social Science Research Council. During 1976-1977, while writing this book, I held a grant from the Joint Committee on the Near and Middle East of the American Council of Learned Societies and the Social Science Research Council. It is a pleasure here to acknowledge my many obligations to two members of the staff of the Social Science Research Council: Dr. Rowland L. Mitchell, Jr., and the late Dorothy Soderlund. Since 1973, my work has also received material support in a variety of forms from Ohio State University.

The Turkish-American Association of Columbus, Ohio, has given assistance by creating the "Atatürk Collection" in the Ohio State University Libraries. Including a wide range of historical materials, this collection provided valuable support for this study, as it no doubt will for others in future.

For help in preparation of this book for publication, thanks are due to Eleanor Sapp for fastidious typing and to Yvonne Holsinger for her painstaking work in preparation of the figures. For help with illustrations I am obliged to Aptullah Kuran, Altemur Kılıç, Michael Rogers, Walter Denny, Howard Crane, Godfrey Goodwin, Victor Ménage, Filiz Çağman, Mary Beeley, Anne Walsh, Lybrand Smith-Mayes, and the staff of the Photography Laboratory of Ohio State University. At Princeton University Press, Sanford D. Thatcher has provided much assistance over a period of several years and Margaret Case has applied great skill and care in editing.

First and last, I owe an inexpressible debt to my wife, Lucia Blackwelder Findley. While pursuing a full life of her own as professional woman, wife, and mother, she has contributed in ways impossible to enumerate to the creation of this book.

1. *Rendering of Ottoman Turkish in Latin Letters.* In transcribing Ottoman terms, names, and expressions from the Arabic script into Latin letters, this study follows the practice, now general among historians of the late Ottoman period, of adhering to the orthographical conventions of modern Turkish. In the transcribed items, as in the citation of modern Turkish names and titles, the reader unacquainted with Turkish will encounter some letters and diacritical marks that are standard parts of the Latin alphabet as used since 1928 in Turkey but that may otherwise be unfamiliar:

c pronounced like "j" in English

ç pronounced like "ch" in "chip"

ğ the "soft g." Depending on the adjacent letters, this is either dropped, pronounced like "y" in English, or treated as lengthening the preceding vowel.

ı Similar sounds exist in English but have no consistent orthographical representation. G. L. Lewis describes this as "a back, close, unrounded vowel. It is not unlike the sound of a in *serial*, but a closer approximation can be achieved by spreading the lips as if to say *easy* but saying *cushion* instead; the result will be the Turkish *kışın*, 'in winter.' . . . Americans will recognize in it the sound of the first vowel of *Missouri* as pronounced by a native of that state." The upper-case form of "ı" is "I." Note, in contrast, that the upper-case form of the front vowel "i" is "İ," pronounced more or less as in English "pit."

ö pronounced like "eu" in French "peur"

ş pronounced like "sh" in "ship"

ü a front vowel sounding much like "ü" in German or "u" in French.

ˆ The circumflex is used chiefly to indicate palatalizing of a preceding g, k, or l. It may also be used to mark long vowels in borrowings from Arabic, especially in otherwise ambiguous cases. For example, the name Âli corresponds to what most Arabists would transliterate as 'Âlî and is to be distinguished from Ali, for which the corresponding transliteration is 'Alî.

ʼ The apostrophe is used in modern Turkish for several purposes. Examples of two of these will appear in this study. The first is to separate proper nouns from grammatical endings attached to them. The second is to represent the Arabic letters " 'ayn" and "hamza," where these are shown at all. In the former case, the apostrophe is purely an orthographical convention and represents no sound at all. In the latter case, educated speakers of Turkish will at most make a slight pause or break between syllables.

For more exact discussion of the sounds of the Turkish language, see G. L. Lewis, *Turkish Grammar* (Oxford, 1967), chapter 1; or Robert Underhill, *Turkish Grammar* (Cambridge, Mass., 1976), chapter 1.

Purists may object that this assimilation of Ottoman to modern Turkish orthography forfeits the unequivocal convertibility between scripts that is the goal of rigorous transliteration systems. For the purely Turkish, as opposed to the Arabic and Persian, elements in Ottoman Turkish, unequivocal convertibility is, however, an elusive goal. The modern Turkish orthography is far less cumbersome to use. And the chief scholarly objection to its use, certainly for late Ottoman texts, has largely fallen by the wayside since the appearance of the *New Redhouse Turkish-English Dictionary*, edited by Bahadır Alkım, Andreas Tietze, et al. (Istanbul, 1968). This shows each term in Arabic script following the main entry in Latin letters and thus makes it possible to verify Arabic-script orthography with convenience. This dictionary has accordingly been adopted as the orthographical standard for this study, except in a few points that should be noted.

Modern Turkish orthography is not so standardized as to exclude a small range of variation, and the entries in the *New Redhouse Dictionary* reflect this fact. Some of the variations amount to inconsistencies in the handling of certain facets of transcription from Arabic into Latin script. In this study, to maintain ease of reference to the dictionary adopted as standard, these inconsistencies have been eliminated only where they would be particularly conspicuous. For example, we have rendered the Arabic plural of the word more or less invariably written in modern Turkish as *memur* ("official," "bureaucrat") as *memurin*, rather than *me'murin* as shown in the dictionary. The latter form is in fact a more accurate transliteration, but it is pointless to use it unless the singular conforms to it.

Some of the historical terms and proper names that appear in the following pages do not appear in the dictionary. This point is of slight consequence, inasmuch as most such terms are derived forms of, or constructs including, terms that do appear there. The Arabic orthography of proper names can also normally be verified from sources such as the English- or Turkish-language editions of the *Encyclopedia of Islam*.

For ease of recognition by nonexperts, a number of Arabic constructs normally written as one word in modern Turkish have been broken down into their component elements. This applies to both terms and proper names. Thus we shall speak of *reis ül-küttab* and *şeyh ül-İslâm*, rather than *reisülküttab* or *şeyhülislâm*, and discuss the reign of Abd ül-Hamid rather than Abd-ülhamid.

Arabic phrases, when quoted totally in Arabic and not incorporated into a syntactically Turkish construction, will be transliterated precisely in a style that normally retains the Arabic-Latin consonantal equivalences of modern Turkish—for example, "c" for "jîm"—but renders the vowels according to an Arabic rather than a Turkish pronunciation. For exact differentiation of the Arabic consonants, added diacritical marks will also be used as needed. For example, when quoting phrases entirely in Arabic, we shall distinguish the " 'ayn" (') and "hamza" ('). These principles will not apply to what are essentially Ottoman historical terms, again such as *reis ül-küttab* or *şeyh ül-İslâm*, but happen to be entirely Arabic from the linguistic point of view. Proper names of Ottomans will also be treated as Turkish irrespective of linguistic provenance.

Final "b" and "d," although converted in Turkish into "p" and "t" except when followed by suffixes beginning with a vowel, will normally be retained as is. Thus we shall prefer Ragıb and Mehmed to Ragıp and Mehmet.

Terms and place names that have acquired wide currency in English will also be rendered as English; for example, Istanbul rather than İstanbul. On the other hand, terms that represent concepts of central importance to this study, such as *vezir*, will be rendered in Turkish fashion instead.

Names of persons alive since the official adoption of the Latin alphabet in Turkey in 1928 will be cited as found in the sources. Citations of books and articles published in modern Turkish will follow the title page.

2. *Translation of Ottoman Terms into English.* The main guideline followed here has been that of intelligibility to the nonexpert reader. A sustained effort has been made to handle Ottoman terminology throughout the text without assuming that the reader understands its meanings or grammatical properties. With few exceptions, Ottoman terms are therefore used in conjunction with their English translations with a frequency which would otherwise be unnecessary and may seem tautological to experts: e.g., "*intisab* connections," or "Tanzimat reforms." For the same reason, given the variety of ways in which plurals were formed in Ottoman, Ottoman terms appearing in conjunction with their English translations will almost invariably be in the singular, even when the context demands that the English be in the plural. The chief exceptions will occur in cases where the sources normally cite only the plural—*hulefa, hacegân*—without ever using the corresponding singular in the same meaning. As a further aid in maximizing the intelligibility of the Ottoman terminology, the figures included in most chapters to illustrate bureaucratic organizational patterns will include the Ottoman as well as the English names of all offices shown. Items included in the index will appear under both their English and their Ottoman names, where appropriate, with cross references from Ottoman to English.

The choice of translations for Ottoman terms has been guided not only by the principle of intelligibility, but also by that of avoiding false analogies. In general, the simplest, most literal translation is preferred, and a careful effort has been made not to make Ottoman offices sound like those of other governments. There were many similarities, of course. But the tradition of Western scholarship on some of these institutions is already centuries old, and full—as the work of Joseph von Hammer demonstrates—of confusing analogies between Ottoman institutions and those of other states, which in some cases no longer even exist.

3. *Conversion of Dates.* The Ottoman sources used in preparation of this study cite dates most often in the *hicrî* (Islamic lunar) calendar, sometimes in the *malî* or *rumî* (solar) calendar used for purposes of financial administration, sometimes in both. Wherever possible, care has been taken to keep the mechanics of date conversion from intruding on the attention of the reader. In

principle, only Gregorian dates will appear in the text. Where necessary to identify a source or indicate its precise location (as in unpaginated archival registers), the *hicrî* or *malî* dates will then appear in the notes with their Gregorian equivalents— unless already indicated in the text—following them after a slash. In converting *hicrî* dates in which no month is mentioned, a single Gregorian year will normally be cited as long as a quick glance at a conversion table makes clear which solar year over- lapped most of the *hicrî* year in question. Since the *malî* or *rumî* year was a solar one, there is never any ambiguity in converting in such cases, although it should be borne in mind that the *malî* year began in March and that its last quarter extended into the Gregorian year following the one which we shall cite. Wherever the original text offers both *hicrî* and *malî* dates, we shall cite only the *hicrî*.

Abbreviations referring to names of archives are followed by an asterisk.

AA*   *Auswärtiges Amt*, papers of the Imperial German Foreign Office; consulted by means of the microfilm collection in the U.S. National Archives, Washington, D.C., whence the inclusion of microfilm roll numbers in the form of citation used in this study.

AAE*   *Archives des Affaires Étrangères*, Paris

A. AMD   Papers of the Office of the *Amedî*, BBA

Ayn.   *Ayniyat Defterleri*, BBA

B   *Receb*, seventh month of the *hicrî* calendar

BBA*   *Başbakanlık* (formerly *Başvekâlet*) Archives, Istanbul

Bd.   *Band* (volume), in citations from AA

Bell.   *Belleten*, Journal of the Turkish Historical Society, Ankara

BEO   *Bab-ı Âli Evrak Odası*, papers of the Records Office of the Sublime Porte, in BBA

Buy.   *Buyuruldu defterleri*, registers of grand-vezirial orders, BBA

C   *Cemazi ül-ahir*, sixth month of the *hicrî* calendar

CA   *Cemazi ül-evvel*, fifth month of the *hicrî* calendar

CD   George Young, *Corps de droit ottoman*

Cev. Har. *Cevdet Tasnifi*, a classification in BBA, subsection on foreign affairs

Conf. Pr. Confidential Print; designates confidential documents found in FO in printed form

deft.   *defter*, register

DSA   *Dahiliye Sicill-i Ahval Tasnifi*, registers containing official biographies, classified in BBA as pertaining to the Ministry of the Interior

Dstr.[1] *Düstur*, collection of legal texts officially published by Ottoman Government, first series, containing texts dating from 1839-1908; cf. bibliography for additional details on the various volumes and appendices.

Dstr.[2] Continuation of the preceding for the years 1908-1922

EI[1]	*Encyclopedia of Islam*, first edition
EI[2]	*Encyclopedia of Islam*, second edition
El	*Evail*, the first ten days of a month
Er	*Evahir*, the last ten days of a month
Et	*Evasıt*, the middle ten days of a month
FO*	Foreign Office Papers, Public Record Office, London
Har.*	*Hariciye* (Foreign Ministry) Archives, Istanbul
Har. Saln.	*Salname-i Nezaret-i Hariciye*, "yearbooks" of the Ottoman Foreign Ministry
HH	*Hatt-ı Hümayun*, collection of imperial decrees, BBA
HHS*	*Haus-, Hof-, und Staatsarchiv*, Vienna
IA	*İslâm Ansiklopedisi*, Turkish edition of the *Encyclopedia of Islam*, with expanded treatment of Turkish subjects
IFM	*İstanbul Üniversitesi İktisat Fakültesi Mecmuası*, Journal of the Economics Faculty of Istanbul University
IJMES	*International Journal of Middle East Studies*
JAOS	*Journal of the American Oriental Society*
JESHO	*Journal of the Economic and Social History of the Orient*
Kal. Niz.	*Kalem Nizamnamesi*, register of regulatory documents for certain offices of the Sublime Porte, BBA
Kanz.	Josef Matuz, *Das Kanzleiwesen Sultan Süleymâns des Prächtigen*
L	*Şevval*, tenth month of the *hicrî* calendar
LO	Grégoire Aristarchi, *Législation ottomane, ou recueil des lois, règlements, ordonnances, traités, capitulations et autres documents officiels de l'Empire ottoman*
M	*Muharrem*, first month of the *hicrî* calendar
Mal. Müd.	*Maliyeden Müdevver*, a classification of financial registers in BBA
MENA	J. C. Hurewitz, ed., *The Middle East and North Africa in World Politics: A Documentary Record*, I
mf.	Microfilm
Müh.	*Mühimme defterleri*, registers of important affairs, BBA
Müt.	*Mütenevvi Tasnifi*, miscellaneous files, Har.
N	*Ramazan*, ninth month of *hicrî* calendar
Niz. Kav.	*Nizamat ve Kavanin*, a collection of laws and regulations, Har.
OT	Enver Ziya Karal, *Osmanlı Tarihi*, V-VIII

OTD	Mehmet Zeki Pakalın, *Osmanlı Tarih Deyimleri ve Terimleri Sözlüğü*
PA	*Politisches Archiv*, a classification in HHS
R	*Rebi ül-ahir*, fourth month of the *hicrî* calendar
RA	*Rebi ül-evvel*, third month of the *hicrî* calendar
S	*Safer*, second month of the *hicrî* calendar
Ş	*Şaban*, eighth month of the *hicrî* calendar
SA	*Sicill-i Ahval*, personnel records, Har.
Sadr.	Mahmud Kemal İnal, *Osmanlı Devrinde Son Sadrıazamlar*
Şair.	Id., *Son Asır Türk Şairleri*
Saln.	*Salname*, yearbooks of the Ottoman government
Şehb.	*Şehbender defteri*, register of consular appointments, BBA
Staats.	Joseph von Hammer, *Des osmanischen Reichs Staatsverfassung und Staatsverwaltung*
Tar. Der.	*İstanbul Üniversitesi Edebiyat Fakültesi Tarih Dergisi*, Historical Journal of the İstanbul University Faculty of Letters
Tar. Ves.	*Tarih Vesikaları*, "Historical Documents," a journal published by the Turkish Ministry of Education
TDvM	*Teşkilât-ı Devair ve Mecalis*, papers on organization of various bureaucratic and conciliar agencies, BBA
TKE	*Tercüme Kalemi Evrakı*, papers of the Translation Office of the Sublime Porte, Har.
TPK*	Topkapı Palace Archives
Z	*Zi 'l-hicce*, twelfth month of the *hicrî* calendar
ZA	*Zi 'l-kade*, eleventh month of the *hicrî* calendar

Bureaucratic Reform
in the Ottoman Empire

INTRODUCTION: THE SUBLIME PORTE AND THE SCRIBAL SERVICE AS ELEMENTS OF STATE AND SOCIETY

Mülk durmaz eğer olmazsa rical
Lâzım amma ki ricale emval

The state cannot stand without statesmen
But the statesmen must have wealth
Nabi, *Hayriye*[1]

In the administrative tradition of the Islamic world, the imperial institutions of the Ottoman Empire hold a place of special importance. The overall continuity of that tradition means that the Ottoman imperial system was the product of a development that had been in progress ever since the rise of Islamic civilization and that drew in notable respects on pre-Islamic roots, as well. The tradition had perhaps passed its classic phase before the Ottoman state emerged, and the Ottomans at their height were not the only contemporary power to preserve it. But preserve it they did, making contributions of sometimes unexcelled importance to its further elaboration. In later centuries, when the two other great empires of the late traditional Islamic world, those of the Safavids in Iran and the Mughals in India, were collapsing, the Ottoman Empire survived to become the longest-lived of the three. Despite the increasingly manifest obsolescence of the imperial form of political organization, the Ottoman Empire also became the only one of those states to continue the evolution of the administrative tradition without break into the era of modernization. The radical reforms through which the Ottomans of the nineteenth century attempted to come to grips with the consequences of their decline and with the altered circumstances of the world they lived in thus form a bridge, unique in its kind,

over which the millennial development of the Islamic administrative tradition continued into the twentieth century.

The final collapse of the state, by sweeping away what was left
of the antiquated superstructure of multinational empire, has
not so much denied as reaffirmed and brought more clearly
into view the significance of the efforts of nineteenth-century
statesmen to reform and revitalize their tradition. This point is
clearest in the history of the Turkish Republic, for decades the
most dynamic and viable of the modernizing Islamic polities of
the Middle East. Despite the traumas attendant on imperial collapse, however, benefits of the late Ottoman reforms also scattered over what are now the other successor states, both Middle
Eastern and Balkan. Examples range from early nationalist
leaders trained in the higher schools of Istanbul[2] to laws and law
codes that were first promulgated by Ottoman reformers and
have in some cases remained in force in the other successor
states after being superseded in the Turkish Republic.[3] Even in
Iran, the one major Middle Eastern state never integrated into
the Ottoman imperium, efforts at reform, both under the Qajars
and under Reza Shah, displayed the marked influence of Ottoman and later republican Turkish example.

The Ottoman reforms of the nineteenth century are thus of
pivotal importance not only for the history of the Ottoman Empire and the Turkish Republic, but also for the entire history of
the administrative tradition of the Islamic world. These reforms
are also significant in a larger sense, as well. If we except Russia,
whose traditional culture had much in common with that of the
West, the Ottomans come to the fore as the first modernizing society of the non-Western world and one of the few such societies
to retain any degree of independence during the nineteenth-
century age of imperialism. In view of the Ottomans' geographic
position and the level of their interaction in all periods of their
history with Europeans, theirs, too, is an exceptional situation.
But their experiences during a century and a third of administrative reform must have implications for the study of the efforts
of other peoples, the world over, who have launched comparable efforts only more recently—at times under even less promising circumstances, and often without any resource equal to the
indigenous tradition that the Ottomans had behind them.

Full appreciation of the Ottoman administrative reforms thus
depends on examining them in a deep chronological perspective

and comparing them with the experiences of other societies. Yet the scale of the Ottoman administrative system and the limited amount of scholarly research thus far devoted to it stand in the way of full realization of any such goal in a single work. The study that follows will therefore take as its goal the explanation and analysis of one quintessentially important phase of these reforms: the development of the most important of the bureaucratic organizations of the later empire and of the branch of the ruling class that staffed it.

The organization in question is that known to generations of Westerners by the exotic title of "Sublime Porte." A gratuitous but long-familiar piece of obfuscation, this term is basically a French translation of an Ottoman Turkish expression, *Bab-ı Âli*, literally meaning "high" or "exalted gateway." The apparent whimsicality of the term diminishes once we recognize that it, like the word "court" as associated with European monarchies, is a way of using a spatial attribute of the center of power as a general designation for the government. Among the Ottomans, indeed, there were terms similar to "Sublime Porte" that did, like "court" in Europe, refer to the Sultan's palace. With the progressive differentiation of governmental institutions, however, the term Sublime Porte came to be used in a loose sense, especially by Europeans, as a designation for the Ottoman government in general. In a more precise way, Sublime Porte referred not to any gateway, but to a specific building, or succession of buildings over time, that housed the principal administrative agencies.

At the beginning of the nineteenth century, the Sublime Porte in this stricter sense was a distinct complex, which was adjacent to the imperial palace and contained the household and office of the grand vezir, the offices of several officials immediately subordinate to him, and the meeting place of the grand vezir's *divan* or council. By 1922, the vezirial household had moved elsewhere, and the internal organization of the Porte had come to consist of the grand vezir and his immediate staff, the Council of Ministers, a body known as the Council of State, and the Ministries of Internal and Foreign Affairs. While this organization seems substantially different from the earlier one, each of the elements in the later pattern is linked in origin to those noted for earlier dates.[4]

The men who staffed these agencies belonged in the vast

majority of cases to a branch of the ruling class that, at the beginning of the nineteenth century, can best be called the scribal
service. Progressively, as a result of changes in the corporate
state of this body, its size, and the roles its members filled, it
assumed the quite different form of what we shall call the civil
bureaucracy.

Our subject, then, is the organizational complex of the Sublime Porte and, viewed in relation to it, the scribal service or,
later, the civil bureaucracy. To study the development of these
institutions, we must first define their place both in the totality of
the governmental system and in the general organizational patterns of Ottoman society. The remainder of this chapter will
pursue this goal by presenting a repertory of organizational
concepts. In subsequent chapters, we shall use these concepts,
first, to reconstruct the developmental patterns of all the
branches of the ruling class and then, in greater detail, to follow
the development of the Sublime Porte and the scribal service
from the late prereform period through the final collapse of the
empire. We shall thus explore the paradoxical and far-reaching
ways in which the politico-bureaucratic tradition continued to
evolve, even as the empire approached its inevitable dissolution.

The Sublime Porte and the Scribal Service as Elements of the Imperial "Center"

In keeping with the length and richness of the political tradition
that lay behind it, the core of institutions, men, and ideas that
composed the ruling system of the Ottoman Empire—what Edward Shils would term the "center"[5]—was a complex entity dis-
playing great variation over time. Radically different in form
from the governmental system of a modern state, this was in
Weberian terms a patrimonial system of a type characterized
both by an extensive development of "patrimonial officialdom"
and by a strong and effective opposition of the state to the
emergence of anything like the social classes or estates associated
with the variant manifestations of the patrimonial tradition
known at the same time in parts of Europe.[6] In fact, the Ottomans did distinguish a ruling class and a subject class, but it will
become clear that these terms, established by convention, designate social classes only in a rather exceptional sense. A general

description of the major organizational elements, first of the imperial "center," then of the larger society, will clarify the meaning of these statements.

The Office of Sultan

The patrimonial character of the system is largely comprehensible from typical, traditional conceptions of the office of the sultan. The sultan's role tended to be conceptualized on the model of that of a patriarch presiding over his household. He was the head of the household, the dynasty was the family proper, the ruling class comprised the slaves who served in the household, the subject classes were the "flocks" (*reaya*) entrusted by God to the care of the family head, and the territory of the state—with theoretically limited exceptions—was the dynastic patrimony. In the sultan, the state found the embodiment of its unity and its one source of legislative authority apart from Islamic law and established custom, while hereditary succession within the dynasty provided the means by which this unity and authority were perpetuated over time.

The powers of the sultan were immense; the governance of the empire was largely dependent on his personal discretion. And yet his powers were far from being without limit. Some of the restrictions were of a practical kind, related to factors such as the capabilities of the administrative and military apparatus under the sultan's command, or the need for him to possess personal strength and acumen if he were to be more than a "cog in a machine."[7] Other limits were ones of principle, derived from the conception of the society as the fulfillment of a divinely appointed and thus invariable plan, and the consequent necessity for the sultan to maintain the legitimacy of his rule through performance of religiously valued functions. In addition to promotion of certain social-welfare policies[8] and respect in practice for the religious-legal tradition, this quest for legitimacy expressed itself in the lives of the sultans most clearly in a progressive accretion of roles and titles—Warrior for the Faith (*Gazi*), Custodian of Sacred Relics, Protector of the Pilgrimage, Servitor of the Two Holy Cities, and finally, if not quite properly, Caliph—through which the sultans sought to establish an unassailable claim to preeminence in the Islamic world.[9] In the era of reform, one of the chief obstacles in the way of efforts to restruc-

ture and broaden the polity would arise from the fact that the
legislative power, the continuity, and the legitimacy of the state
were so thoroughly invested in this one figure.

The Imperial Cultural Tradition

Consideration of the religiously sanctioned roles of the sultans
brings us to the ideals and values associated with the imperial
"center," and thus to the fundamental problem that gave the
roles of the sultan their significance. The Ottoman Empire, like
other sultanates, existed in a permanent state of tension in relation to the Islamic heritage. Shaped by an Iranian tradition of
absolute kingship and a Turkic ideal of quasi-divine monarchy,
both rooted deep in the pre-Islamic past, the very concept of *sultan* was at odds with the Islamic ideal of rule by a caliph in whom
religious leaders acknowledged the legitimate successor (*khalīfa*)
of the Prophet in his capacity as head of the Muslim community.
Exercising a power based on little but military force, no sultan
could gain the acceptance of the pious except as he, in the absence or weakness of a legitimate caliph, devoted himself to the
achievement of religiously valued goals.[10]

The determination with which Ottoman Sultans pursued this
struggle for legitimation is one of the most consistent and in-
triguing themes of Ottoman history. The longevity of the empire, and the measure of seriousness ultimately attributed to
their claims to the caliphate, are a measure of their success. In
fact, however, the struggle to legitimate the imperial system and
assert its claim to a unique position in the Islamic world had
other aspects, which went beyond the office of the sultan and
also helped to shape the imperial cultural tradition.

The stubbornness of the struggle for legitimation is equally
clear, for example, in the field of law. Like other Islamic rulers
from earliest times, the Ottomans had to cope not only with the
need to enforce Islamic law, but also with the fact that the law
was incompletely developed in many respects and thus required
additional enactments based either on the authority of the
sovereign or in custom. The Ottoman approach to striking the
necessary balance was a complex one, including ostentatious
deference in principle to Islamic law and to religious-legal
scholars; unprecedented development of the legislative role of
the state through the promulgation of *kanunname*s, or "codes" of
a sort, and through vigorous use of the sultan's power to issue

decrees; integration of the religious-legal experts into the imperial ruling class; and assignment to the local religious courts of
adjudication in both kinds of law, as well as of a major role in
local administration.[11] It is also significant in this connection that
the school of religious-legal scholarship that the Ottomans espoused was the Hanefi, the most flexible in its methods of the
orthodox four.

The process of creating an imperial tradition and forging
multiple links between it and the religious value system proceeded in other ways, as well. We see this, for example, in the
attempt to identify the state and its ruling class not only with the
religious-legal tradition, but also with the Islamic mystical orders.[12] The same phenomenon appears in the idealized view,
propagated by political thinkers, of state and religion as a single,
undifferentiated whole (*din-ü-devlet*).

The effort to identify the state with established values also
reached beyond the limits of religious tradition as narrowly defined. For example, the Ottomans clearly aspired to create a
composite literary culture that would fittingly express the character of their empire as the preeminent Islamic state. This literary culture was, ideally, to envelop and carry forward not only
the Islamic religious studies (*ulûm*), but also the more worldly
belletristic tradition known in Arabic as *adab*, a term embracing
what Turks ultimately came to refer to as both *edeb*, "good
breeding," and *edebiyat*, "literature." For this worldly literary culture, and for the official uses of the state, to the service of which
the *adab* tradition was always closely linked, a special language
evolved: Ottoman Turkish. In this, distinction of style came to
mean a heavy encrustation of Arabic and Persian and a reduction of purely Turkish elements to little more than a few syntac-
tical devices useful for combining these diverse linguistic elements into sumptuously cadenced and lengthy sentences. The
very texture of the official language clearly tells how the Ottomans saw themselves in relation to the cultural heritage of the
entire Islamic Middle East.

By such means as the accumulation of religiously sanctioned
roles by the sultans, the development of the complex legal system, the identification of the imperial system with as many as
possible of the expressions of orthodox Islam as it then existed,
and the elaboration of a composite literary culture, the Ottomans set about building an imperial cultural synthesis of vast in-

tegrative power. Inevitably, this effort encountered a number of obstacles, some of which are of considerable importance for this study. One arose from the very artificiality of the synthesis. This was and could only be the culture of the palace and ruling class. It could never have a mass basis—not that the Ottomans ever aspired, before the era of modernization, to give it one. Of perhaps greater moment was the uneasiness with which certain elements—sultanate and Islam, religious-legal and mystical traditions, religious studies and worldly *adab*—coexisted within this would-be synthesis. In fact, the imperial cultural tradition was polymorphous, a juxtaposition more than a coherent blending of elements from the traditions out of which it had been forged.

This fact helped to provoke a long series of attacks on the imperial "center" from forces on the "periphery" of Ottoman society or beyond its frontiers, even before the advent of the explosive force of modern nationalism. Predictably, in the context of a traditional society, these challenges tended to express themselves in terms of Islamic religious orientations that the imperial synthesis could not readily accommodate. Such challenges found expression in ways ranging from the rigoristic and antimystical point of view associated with the Hanbali school of legal thought to movements with mystical or heretical orientations too extreme for toleration by the Ottoman "center." The best-known example of the former type is the Wahhabi movement of eighteenth-century Arabia; of the latter type, that which assumed statehood as the Safavid Empire of Iran.

Quite significantly, contrasting responses to the polymorphism of the cultural tradition also appeared, if within a narrower range, among the different services that together composed the ruling class. Among the religious scholars, naturally, the strictest orientation toward the values conveyed through the Islamic religious studies emerged, but with a tendency to polarization between sympathizers and opponents of the mystical orders.[13] Among the military appeared an equally understandable emphasis on holy war for the expansion of Islam, and also, in connections such as that of the Janissaries with the Bektaşi dervish order, inclinations toward mysticism and even heterodoxy. Persons serving in the palace tended to place strongest emphasis on loyalty to the sultan. Those trained in the palace school, in particular, received an education specially aimed at inculcating that loyalty, along with military and vocational skills, polish as cour-

tiers, and a literary culture encompassing a range of "humanis-
tic" studies broader than that encouraged in the colleges of the
religious scholars.[14] The palace school, in fact, served specifically
for the propagation of the *adab* tradition, the "secular" and
"state-oriented" character of which often excited the animosity
of the religious.[15]

This *adab* tradition was also strongly associated with the scribal
officials of the traditional Islamic states. In the Ottoman Empire,
too, it was among members of the scribal service that the purely
literary and intellectual dimensions of this tradition appeared
most strongly. With the decline of the palace school, the scribal
service became, practically speaking, the center for the propagation of this tradition within the ruling class. With the styles of
script and composition, mechanical techniques of document
production, and procedural conventions of the official routine
as its lowest common denominator, this scribal *adab* in its most
evolved form was encyclopedic in scope, as required for the performance of some of the most demanding scribal duties. In this
form, the scribal learning embraced extensive knowledge of
subjects such as Arabic and Persian, the laws promulgated by the
state, geography, and history. However the purists among the
religious scholars felt about it, this was a rich tradition, as the
works of generations of scribal intellectuals attest,[16] and one indispensable to the ongoing life of the state.

Thus, while state and religion were ideally undifferentiated,
the imperial cultural tradition could not, in fact, produce a perfect union of the two. Similarly, while the tradition, though
elaborated over time, was assumed to imply an invariable pattern whose maintenance would assure the legitimation of the
state, this tradition could not blend the elements that it encompassed so as to evoke uniform responses from different social
groups, even within the ruling class. One consequence of this
fact, critically important in the history of the scribal service, is
that the different cultural orientations of the various branches of
the ruling class played a major role in determining the relative
political prominence of each branch as the situation and needs
of the state changed over time. Another consequence, closely
linked to the first, is that the scribal, or by then more aptly civil-
bureaucratic, elite that assumed political preeminence in the era
of reform took a leading role in altering or even abandoning
various elements of the traditional synthesis, and thus in prepar-

ing the way for the cultural revolution that followed on the final
collapse of the imperial order.

Formal Organizational and Procedural Apparatus of Government

Together with the sultan and the imperial cultural tradition, the
Ottoman "center" also included an elaborate mechanism of organizations and procedures through which the business of the
government was discharged. Reflecting earlier Islamic and
non-Islamic patterns, but often used in new ways or refined to
new levels of organization, the various elements of this apparatus are too complex and numerous for easy description.
Any comprehensive account has to reckon with the palace, the
palace school, and the child levy; the *divan*s or councils that de-
liberated on affairs of state, heard complaints, and received ambassadors;[17] the *kadı* courts; the imperial hierarchy of religious
colleges; the Janissary infantry corps; the *tımar* system of landholding, with its important functions in local administration,
revenue collection, and the support of the cavalry corps; the system of land survey and registration required for maintenance of
the *tımar* system; the administrative complex of the Sublime
Porte; and more, besides.

The usual subject matter of the "institutional historiography"
which has long been a favored pursuit of specialists in Ottoman
studies, these institutions are beginning to be well known in
some respects. But there is still much to learn. For example,
greater attention needs to be paid to chronological precision in
treating the relations among institutions; for not all of them
flourished at the same time, and the rise of one and decline of
another often reflected reorientations of far-reaching importance. Most importantly, the study of these institutions needs to
be informed by an awareness of the patterns by which patrimonial political systems characteristically develop out of the household of the ruler.

Weber has given a memorable picture of these patterns in his
discussions of patrimonial officialdom, and the development of
the governmental mechanisms of the Ottoman Empire seems in
general to have progressed along the lines he indicates. In
Ottoman history, we find, for example, the initial assimilation of
tasks falling outside the specifically domestic service of the ruler
to corresponding tasks within; the initial concentration of ad-

ministrative responsibilities in a rudimentary organization headed by a single political official, here the grand vezir; heavy reliance for administrative and judicial purposes on collegial bodies; and early limitation of professional officialdom to little more than a few central bureaus performing secretarial and accounting functions. Here, too, are the complex and variable developmental relationships between the collegial bodies and the bureaus staffed by full-time, professional administrators, as well as the gradual multiplication of bureaus through differentiation of functions.[18]

While there has been much progress in the study of Ottoman governmental institutions,[19] the general reassessment needed to achieve a clearer picture of their developmental patterns will still require the effort of many scholars. A central goal of this study is to contribute to this effort and, as concerns the Sublime Porte and the men who served there, to show how the developmental patterns that Weber outlined continued to operate into the era of modernization.

The Ruling Class

Consideration of the formal organizational and procedural apparatus of the Ottoman government brings us next to the ruling class. Although it was in a sense an aspect of the formal organizational apparatus of government, it requires separate consideration as a social body.

What modern scholars characteristically refer to as the ruling class consisted of men for whom the most characteristic and general Ottoman designations were *Osmanlı* (pertaining to the House of Osman, Ottoman) or *askeri* (military). The members of this group enjoyed a number of distinctions. For example, they were exempt in principle from taxation. With the chief exception of some Christians incorporated directly into the military forces during the first two centuries, members of the ruling class were also set apart by their assimilation of some form of the composite imperial culture. Most importantly, they wielded power. Within the limits traced by factors such as rank, favor, seniority, custom, and law, they enjoyed a discretionary power, derived implicitly or explicitly from that of the sultan, and comparable to his on a reduced scale. One of the clearest signs of their elite status, and one of the clearest differences between them and the officials of most modern states, was the idea that they served the sultan, from whom their power derived, and only secondarily served his subjects.

The elitism of the ruling class was, however, not without serious qualifications related to the patrimonial character of the state. Servants of the sultan indeed, members of the ruling class traditionally stood in the legal status of slaves. When the empire was at its height, many of them were recruited by means that presupposed literal enslavement. This was most notably the case of the Janissary Corps in the era of the child levy (*devşirme*). A technique of slave recruitment drawing on the Christian populations of the empire, this, however foreign to modern ideas, was one of the most significant examples of the evolution of traditional Islamic techniques of government to new levels of elaboration under the Ottomans.[20] But even individuals recruited by means that did not presuppose literal enslavement effectively became slaves of the sultan when they entered his service. The irony of this became more apparent in the later centuries, with the decline of the child levy. The religious scholars alone seem to have formed a sort of exception, thanks to their position as custodians of the religious value system that provided the state with its major source of law and legitimation; but even their relative independence was compromised as the sultans succeeded in bringing them into positions of dependence on the state.[21]

The ruling class was, then, a servile elite. Traditional Islamic ideas of slavery differed enough from those normally assumed by Western observers that this designation is less self-contradictory than it might seem. Yet the juridical fact of absolute subjection to the sultan and absolute subservience to his will remained incontestable. Down to the reforms of the 1830s, and sometimes thereafter, the sultan could punish, execute, or confiscate the estates of his official slaves at will. In principle, he was their heir.[22] For the sultan, the legal principle of servility made it possible to maintain a kind of control that modern bureaucracies, at least as seen by Weber, achieve through the rule of law.[23]

The state-imposed character of this servile elitism had several other important consequences. It meant that the ruling class was in principle deprived of corporate autonomy, and thus was in a position radically different from that of the estates or privileged corporate bodies of medieval or early modern Europe. While assimilation of the imperial culture and access to the material perquisites of high station created in the upper echelons of the ruling class a sort of "grandee mentality" and a style of life to go with it,[24] no member of the ruling class could be sure how long he or his family would enjoy the means to support such a style. Furthermore, while in other societies wealth or status might become the basis for claims to political power, the kind of patrimonial domination seen in the Ottoman Empire made any such claims practically impossible. Wealth and status might to a degree exist in isolation from power, as among the commercial and religious notables of the subject classes; or else they might be secondary attributes of power, distributed along with it by the sultan to the more exalted of his slave officials.[25] With but rare and imperfect exceptions, political power, wealth, and high status could coincide only in the upper echelons of the ruling class, and only on the sufferance of the sultan. The concepts of "ruling class" and "elite" therefore need to be distinguished, as we shall attempt to do from this point on. The former will refer to the servile officials in terms of their state-imposed collective identity; the latter to a relative kind of distinction of which the basis needs to be indicated whenever the term is used.

In addition to these general characteristics of the traditional "Ottomans" or *askeri*s, the ruling class also displayed a division into discrete branches. For reasons partially implicit in the application of the term *askeri* (military) to the whole ruling class, this differentiation is the subject of a controversy that we shall have to reexamine in the next chapter. In any case, we shall ultimately distinguish four branches of the ruling class. These are the military-administrative establishment or "men of the sword" (*seyfiye*); the Islamic religious establishment or "men of religion" (*ilmiye*, or *ulema*); the palace service, the existence of a single Ottoman designation for which is, significantly, problematical; and the scribal service or "men of the pen" (*kalemiye*). For the nineteenth century, it will be more appropriate to refer to the first of these as the military establishment only, its administrative dimension largely having been lost by then, and to the last as the civil bureaucracy (*mülkiye*). Since these branches emerged by processes of differentiation within the ruling class, we shall speak of all of them as "bureaucratic" to the extent that they became distinct from the properly domestic, in the sense of menial, service of the patrimonial sovereign.[26] This should not be taken to imply that they had acquired all the attributes of modern "bureaucracy," as opposed to "patrimonial officialdom," in the Weberian sense. That never happened in the Ottoman period, although the processes that distinguished the various branches within the ruling class and the reforms of the era of modernization were major steps in that direction.

In the nineteenth century, the pattern of ruling and subject classes began to undergo alteration. One of the forces behind these changes was a desire within the ruling class to acquire safeguards against the dangers inherent in its traditional slave status, and, in the process, to take on the privileges typical of a European official aristocracy. The pursuit of this desire in a period of cultural change gave the elitist aspirations of the ruling class a new and, in terms of the underlying legal principles, stronger expression, linked to the emergence of the civil bureaucracy (*mülkiye*). The other main force in transforming the traditional pattern of officially recognized classes was the formal proclamation of something never perfectly realized in practice: the legal equality of all the peoples of the empire. With this went the attempt to create an imperial supranationalism to serve as an antidote to the separatist nationalisms then emerging among various of the subject nationalities.

Since these changes, beginning in the 1830s, contravened basic principles of the traditional order without sweeping away all vestiges of the old patterns, we must treat the old class designations as either obsolete or fundamentally changed in meaning after 1839. The latter is particularly true of the term *Osmanlı*, which subsequently referred not to the official servants of the sultan, but to all his subjects. In some other respects, after 1839 there are no clearcut terms to use in describing social relations. To refer beyond that date to what had previously been the ruling and subject classes, we shall accordingly speak of "officialdom" or of a "bureaucracy" divided into certain branches, or of "subjects of the empire," or the like.

The Political Balance

Having now categorized the component elements of the Ottoman imperial "center," we must note one additional feature of critical relevance to all that follows: this "center" was not simply a matter of disjointed elements; it was a totality uniting all of them. In this totality, depending on the extent to which the imperial "center" had evolved as of any given time from characteristically traditional to modern forms, and on the extent to which the "center" was able to maintain its integrity against hostile peripheral interests, there appeared one of the most important features of the political life of the empire. This is what F. W. Riggs refers to as the political "balance" or "imbalance."

This concept is formally akin to the more familiar and more complex one of "balance of powers" as associated with a political system like that of the United States. As it relates to the bureaucracy of a traditional or modernizing state, the balance or imbalance is basically to be understood in terms of power and legitimacy. We shall use the term in speaking of the relationship between the bureaucracy and that element of the polity in which sovereignty, and thus legitimate control of the power that the bureaucracy wields, is vested, whether directly or by delegation. Even if there is no explicitly articulated system of checks and balances, study of any bureaucratic system requires reference to this larger relationship. For it alone tells whether the bureaucracy operates within the limits of an effective system of control or accountability, and that fact in turn is critical in determining the character of the mixture of functions through which the bureaucracy interacts with all other elements of center and periphery alike.

In the case of a traditional empire beginning to undergo modernization, discussion of the political balance becomes more complicated. Here the polity is in a state of transition from an authoritarian form of organization, in which legitimacy belongs to a more or less autocratic sovereign, to a more broadly based form in which the only definition of the locus of sovereignty that can command ultimate acceptance—certainly in the nineteenth or twentieth century—is the sovereignty, in fact or fiction, of the people. In the traditionalistic pattern, barring the emergence within the state of rival powers that repudiate the control of the center, the polity and the center are practically coterminous, and politics is very much an activity of the bureaucracy. In the modern pattern, the polity is more nearly coterminous with the entire society, and politics and bureaucracy become increasingly differentiated. In the transition between these two patterns, as a number of scholars have pointed out, political systems tend to display a marked loss of balance and a burgeoning of the bureaucracy in both size and power before the controls implied by a balance of the modern kind can develop. Indeed, demand for

the new controls emerges largely in reaction against the bureaucratic preponderance of the transitional period.[27]

In the Ottoman "center"—composed of the sultan and his
family, the imperial cultural tradition, the formal organizational
and procedural apparatus of administration, and the ruling
class—the political balance was constantly threatened by tensions
or incompatibilities built into the component elements of the
"center," and by shifts over time in their importance in relation
to one another, even before the beginning of the reform era.
During that era, the Ottoman system developed a classic case of
the kind of imbalance characteristic of transitional societies. This
was only worsened as doubt about who the "people" really were,
in this as in other multinational empires, compounded the problems of redefining the locus of sovereignty.

In subsequent chapters, we shall draw on the categorization of
the component elements of the "center" presented here in order
to analyze the problems surrounding this imbalance, its significance for the history of the Sublime Porte and its officials, and
the attempts made in the era of reform to achieve a new equilibrium. To prepare for this discussion, however, we must now also
consider the setting of the ruling class in relation to the broader
society.

The Ruling Class as an Element of the Broader Society: Problems of Social Organization

Even before modernization began to create pressures for
broadening the polity, the ruling and subject classes of course
interacted in many ways. Ottoman thinkers evoked one mode of
this interaction through the resonant metaphors that they loved
to use in speaking of the role of the ruling class in the "binding
and loosing" (*akd ve hall*) or, better still, the "rending and mending" (*fatk-u-ratk*), of affairs of state. This was part of what political philosophers conceived as a symbiotic relationship, visualized
in terms of a "circle of justice" (*adalet dairesi*), in which the rulers
provided the justice and protection that the subjects had to have
in order to flourish, while the subjects produced the resources
indispensable for the continued functioning of the state.[28] The
couplet quoted as the epigraph of this chapter alludes to one
element of this schematization.

There were other links between rulers and subjects, as well.

One of these consisted of the mechanisms through which people entered the ruling class. More important for present purposes, there was another, subtle kind of interplay between the two "classes" recognized in the official picture of Ottoman society. This appears in certain models of social organization that originated outside the imperial "center," but found replication in ruling and subject classes alike. To complete our survey of the organizational patterns associated with the officials of the Sublime Porte, we must examine these models and, first of all, attempt to throw some light on the circumstances of their replication within the ruling class.

In describing the official pattern of ruling and subject classes, we have already commented on the extent to which it was imposed and maintained by a state determined to defend its own control over the distribution of political power and the right of access to such power. We have also noted the radical contrast between the Ottoman kind of patrimonialism, which Weber at one point calls "patriarchal," and that found in some other societies characterized by the marked development of privileged classes or estates, or of other types of corporative organizational forms independent in some measure of state control.[29] The Ottomans opposed the development of autonomous organizations intermediary between the individual subject and the state. In this they resembled other Middle Eastern states[30] and found support in the Islamic religious-legal tradition.[31] Where the emergence of such bodies could not be prevented, the state attempted to dominate them and use them to maintain or extend its own power. The emergence of some such organizational forms was inevitable, in fact, given certain fundamental characteristics and aspirations of the populations under Ottoman rule. These features of Ottoman society shaped the organizational models of which we must speak here. The replication of these models within the ruling class shows how basic the forces that shaped them were, and how much those forces did, in spite of all, to determine the character of the state itself.

An exhaustive account of Ottoman social and political history might well turn up a larger number of models of this kind;[32] but a study of the scribal service and later civil bureaucracy brings into view three, on which we shall concentrate for the remainder of this chapter. One of these reflects the ways in which the Ottoman Empire, like all other traditional Islamic polities, had to

respond to the religious diversity characteristic of Middle Eastern society. This can be referred to as the model of the autonomous confessional community. There were also certain persistent forms of voluntary association, which we shall relate to the
model of the guilds, although the importance of this model only
becomes clear in a larger setting that includes organizations of
other types, as well. Finally, there is what we may call the model
of the patrimonial household. We have already mentioned how
this appeared on its grandest scale in the metaphorical integration of the entire state into a single household establishment. In
this concept, a variety of relations extending beyond the range
of kinship proper but still characteristic of the archetypal patriarchal household—the status of the ruling class as slaves and
of the subjects as "flocks"—provided the means by which to link
all the inhabitants of the empire to the sultan. On its smallest
scale, this model, or the social reality underlying it, appeared in
the smaller kinship groups that were the basic building blocks of
imperial society. In an ironic way, then, the official view of the
state as an enormously extended household was both a formal
parallel of the kinds of kinship organization that made up
Ottoman society, and a means of defense against the divisive
tendencies operative within and among those organizations.[33]
Although the models of the autonomous confessional community and the guilds were also influential, we shall find the model
of the patrimonial household to be of particular significance at
all levels of Ottoman social and political life.

The Model of the Autonomous Confessional Community

The development of the system for accommodating religious
diversity under Islamic rule was dominated by the conception of
Judaism and Christianity as coming out of the same prophetic
tradition that culminated in the advent of Islam. There is no
need here to comment on the eventual application of this system
to non-Muslim peoples other than Jews and Christians, the exact
legal terms of the subordinate, protected status (*dhimma*) under
which the "peoples of the Book" were allowed to live within the
Muslim state, or the resulting contrast in official attitudes toward
such peoples living within the "domain of Islam" on one hand
and their coreligionists living in the "domain of war" on the
other.[34]

What does require comment is, first, the traits that distinguished the autonomous confessional communities in practice and, then, the evidence for the replication of the organizational pattern which these traits defined. On the first point, the latest scholarship shows the beginnings of a radical reinterpretation of these communities, or *millets* ("peoples"), as they have long been known. The old interpretation appears to have overestimated the elaboration of communal structures, the scope of communal privilege, and the formalization of the relations that existed between non-Muslim religious leaders and Ottoman officials. The sources of the error lie in self-serving accounts emanating from some of the non-Muslim religious leaders, and in the projection into earlier periods of conditions resulting from reforms of the mid-nineteenth century. As an added irony, the very application of the term *millet* to non-Muslim, as opposed to Muslim, communities of the prereform periods appears mistaken.

The point is not that distinct communities possessing a certain autonomy in their internal affairs did not exist. Rather, they existed at much lower levels of institutionalization, and with much greater interaction between Muslims and non-Muslims, than has commonly been assumed. Each community, of course, had its own religious leaders, who might or might not form a centralized hierarchy. The investiture of these leaders, at least of the more important ones, required the confirmation of the state; but this did not necessarily entail the granting of the extensive powers and privileges assumed in the conventional accounts. The religious leaders of a given community exercised authority in its religious affairs, and in the legal and judicial matters that fell under the scope of its religious law. Indeed, although non-Muslims often appeared, even by choice, in the courts of the Muslim *kadıs*, the Islamic religious-legal tradition was so central to the life of the state that it was necessary for the non-Muslim communities to have courts of their own. In addition, each community had lay leaders who discharged the administrative responsibilities of the community in fields such as taxation. At least in some communities, there might be a series of regular offices held by such figures. From the point of view of the state, this kind of communal organization was not just a way of accommodating non-Muslims within the empire, but also an example of the use of organizational forms external to the administrative system proper in order to extend its capabilities.

With the decline of the imperial system and the resulting

processes of decentralization, both the judicial and the administrative responsibilities of the communal leaders seem to have increased, judging from eighteenth-century documentation that İnalcık mentions. In any case, the distinctiveness of the communities was perpetuated in all periods, not just by legal and administrative needs, but also by the condescending attitude of Muslims toward non-Muslims and the determination of the various communities to perpetuate their identities. Its forms depended in some measure on the community, the locale, and the date; but the autonomous confessional community was a characteristic reality of Ottoman society, and one that the state managed in some respects to adapt to its own ends.[35]

The replication of this pattern of autonomous confessional communities is apparent in a number of respects. Most obviously, there were several communities—Greek Orthodox, Armenian, Jewish—whose affairs and whose relations with official authorities at different levels were organized in terms of this pattern. In the nineteenth century, the same kind of status was officially granted to other religious communities, as well.[36] Replication of the model also appears in the "capitulations" or grants of privileges issued to specify the terms under which non-Muslim merchants of different nationalities might trade within the empire. In the various port cities, the merchants of each capitulatory state were allowed, under the terms of the grants, to organize collectivities to which Ottomans referred as *millet* or *taife*, terms that Europeans translated as "nations." Endowed with internal legal autonomy under the headship of their consuls, these bodies displayed important analogies to the autonomous confessional communities, as well, in other respects, as to the Ottoman guilds.[37] In a more diffuse way, the attitudes that shaped the system of autonomous confessional communities must have left their traces in countless other settings, although, as reports of guilds with religiously mixed membership imply,[38] separation along religious lines did not prevail in every instance.

Within the traditional ruling class, the scope for the replication of the model of the autonomous confessional community was narrow. Once the child levy and the palace school had become fully developed, the role in the Ottoman ruling class—as contrasted with those of some earlier Muslim states—of non-Muslims who had not gone through recruitment processes entailing conversion and cultural assimilation was quite limited. In different periods, there were nonetheless non-Muslims, few in number but sometimes influential, in or on the fringes of the ruling class in a variety of roles, including those of interpreter and physician. Sometimes the roles were no more than quasi-official; often, too, the non-Muslim presence seems to have been strongest in the local administration of certain provinces or tributary regions, such as the vassal principalities of Moldavia and Wallachia.[39] Wherever found, however, these individuals appear to have developed career patterns exclusive to themselves, and to have been, not fully integrated into the ruling class, but rather enclaved into it without loss of status as *dhimmis*.

In the nineteenth century, the formal proclamation of equality among members of the different religions profoundly changed the legal setting of the old system of autonomous confessional communities. Through their efforts to promote concepts of common Ottoman citizenship and patriotism, Ottoman statesmen and intellectuals attempted to actualize the new principle and find in it a new source of strength for the state. As in so many other cases, however, the reforms could not entirely sweep away the preexisting patterns. For a variety of reasons, the system of autonomous confessional communities was not abolished, but rather retained and reformed.[40] This was, in fact, when the term *millet* began to be applied officially to the non-Muslim communities.

Thus began a period in which the pattern of autonomous confessional communities coexisted with the official policy of egalitarian Ottomanism, and both were challenged in turn by the separatist nationalisms that threatened the integrity, not just of the empire, but also, in some cases, of the religiously defined communities. Such circumstances assured that the egalitarian reforms could not produce real social integration. Indeed, the similarities between the social patterns implied in the system of autonomous confessional communities and those found still in some of the most egalitarian and secular sociopolitical systems suggest that complete fusion could hardly have been expected under the best of circumstances. The model of the autonomous confessional community thus never totally disappeared.

Still, the egalitarian reforms made a substantial difference, beginning with the Reform Decree of 1856, which triggered a marked growth in the number of non-Muslims in official service. Indeed, as surely had to be the case if the reforms were to be-

come meaningful anywhere, it was precisely within governmental institutions that the ideals of equality and Ottomanism
produced the most appreciable changes. For the later nineteenth century, this fact forms the background against which the
continuing influence of the tradition of communal separatism
must be assessed in this study.

The Model of the Guilds

The model that we shall identify simply with the guild tradition
was even more widely influential among the ruling class. Full
appreciation of the significance of this model requires that we
recognize its derivation from a rather different institution, characteristic of Anatolia in the early period of Turkish settlement,
at a time when guilds as such had yet to appear in the sources.[41]
This institution is best known under the Arabic name *futuwwa*
(Turkish form, *fütüvvet*), an abstract noun corresponding to
Arabic *fatâ*, "young man." The simplest way to think of the
futuwwa is to adapt Marshall Hodgson's translation and refer to
the *futuwwa* organizations as "young men's clubs."[42] These, in
their turn, were under the influence of the Islamic mystical
brotherhoods or dervish orders. The organization of the guilds,
we shall argue, was based on a model common in general terms
to the guilds, the "young men's clubs" while they existed, and
also the dervish brotherhoods. The widespread replication of
this model must be due in large part to this linkage.

The origins of the "young men's clubs" are obscure. Perhaps
corresponding to a pre-Islamic prototype,[43] they were known in
pre-Ottoman times over a geographical area extending well
beyond Anatolia, and went by a variety of names, including
'ayyârûn ("rogues," "vagabonds"), *runûd* ("debauchees"), *shuṭṭâr*
("tricksters"), as well as *fityân* ("young men," plural of *fatâ*). In
societies typically dominated by what were, or were perceived to
be, establishments of "elders" (*shaykh*), the fact that the members
of these "clubs" often identified the spirit that united them with
young manhood is probably, as Goitein indicates, chiefly emblematic of their anti-establishment orientation.[44] Their other
names convey a similar emphasis.

At any rate, the "clubs" tended to draw their members from
the less favored elements of society. Such men banded together
for the sake of comradeship and for the added conviviality made
possible by the sharing of their resources. In addition, they

characteristically opposed government authority when it was strong, but took the maintenance of local order on themselves when government was weak. This last fact, as much as the natural human inclination to affiliate with groups possessing some such animating spirit (what Ibn Khaldûn calls *'aṣabîya*), goes far to explain the wide diffusion of this organizational pattern and its persistence over a period of centuries when the authority of states was often evanescent.[45]

By the thirteenth century, another important force had begun to influence the development of these associations. This was the tradition of Islamic mysticism. Its history extending back to early Islamic times, the mystical tradition underwent an important development about the twelfth century with the emergence of the organized dervish orders. This event seems to have stimulated various forms of interaction between the "young men's clubs" and the mystics. One celebrated phase of this interaction was an attempt of the Abbasid Caliph al-Nâṣir (1180-1225), in collaboration with a great mystic leader, 'Umar Suhrawardî, to organize the "young men's clubs" under his own auspices and inject into them a "courtly" *futuwwa* ideal linked to and supportive of the caliphate.[46]

One place where this effort had a significant impact was Anatolia, to which Suhrawardî journeyed on the Caliph's behalf. The results appeared not only among the local Turkic dynasts, the Seljuks, but also in more popular settings. These included both the bands of *gazi*s, or warriors for the expansion of Islam, active in the frontier zones, and the urban groups then forming about a kind of religious leaders known as *ahi*s. Lightly Islamized successors of the shamans of the pre-Islamic Turks of Central Asia, the *ahi*s began to be conspicuous in Anatolia in the thirteenth century with the influx of the second wave of Turkish immigration, set in motion by the Mongol invasions. In the disorder left by the Mongols' conquest of the Seljuks, the groups formed by the *ahi*s in the towns and the bands of *gazi*s on the frontiers came to the fore as the most important foci of popular religious life and the most important social organizations in Asia Minor at the time.[47]

While the contribution of the *gazi*s to the formation of the Ottoman imperial system is well known, the *ahi* groups also displayed a combination of traits highly significant for the future development of Turkish society. These groups were the specifi-

cally Anatolian version of the "young men's clubs." As such, they
played the role of vigilante, characteristic of the clubs in periods
of weak governmental authority. They also displayed a mystical
fervor that melded the ideals of the Caliph al-Nâṣir with an ardent if still superficial Islam.[48] Finally, recruiting their adherents
only among craftsmen or merchants, the *ahi* groups appear to
have combined mystical and paragovernmental or paramilitary
characteristics with a progressive evolution toward a guild-like
character. The account of Ibn Battuta, who benefited repeatedly
from the hospitality of the *ahis* while traveling through Anatolia
in the 1330s, indicates no clear articulation of specialized guilds
as of that time. And yet he implies that a consciousness of organization in terms of trade was then emerging in connection
with the *ahi* groups in at least some places.[49]

Subsequently, the *ahis* as such progressively disappeared from
the sources. This very likely reflects a new attempt by established
authority, in this case the Ottoman Sultan Murad I (1362-1389),
to assure control of a popular movement.[50] In addition to recalling the earlier initiative of the Abbasid al-Nâṣir, such an effort
would parallel the contemporary displacement of the *gazi* warrior bands by the highly disciplined slave-military establishment,[51] the fate of *gazis* and *ahis* thus providing two clear illustrations of the determination of the emerging state to assert its
primacy in the regulation of the social order.

As the *ahis* disappeared, however, the organizational elements
that their groups had combined seem to have gone through a
process of differentiation that left common patterns in the successor organizations. On one hand, popular religious life had to
be channeled more into the dervish orders, which had all along
remained distinct from the *ahi* groups to some degree. On the
other hand, specialized guilds began to emerge and proliferate.

That these changes were, in fact, linked to the effort of the
state to assert its dominance over the surviving organizations
seems clear, particularly in the case of the guilds. With the dervishes, there seems to have been a subtler kind of interplay, recalling the policy of the sultans toward the religious establishment and again emphasizing the creation of multiple linkages
between the state and the bodies it sought to control. There
were, to be sure, incidents such as the attempt of Selim I (1512-
1520) to wipe out Safavid sympathizers in Anatolia, or the abolition by Mahmud II (1808-1839) of the Bektaşi order, as well as

of the Janissary infantry corps so closely linked to it. Seemingly more typical, however, were the efforts of the early sultans to use the Bektaşis, then still orthodox, as a force with which to counter the spread of heterodoxy, or the official encouragement of the foundation in the countryside of dervish establishments, which then served as foci for the concentration of Muslim settlers. Paralleling the historical association of the Janissary corps with the Bektaşi order, there was also a link of the palace cavalry regiments with the Melamis, and of many members of the ruling class with the Mevlevis. The sultans, too, had their traditions of affiliation with the dervish orders, often with the Bektaşis through the reign of Bayezid II (1481-1512), but more typically with the Mevlevis in the late period.[52]

In the case of the guilds, state control was more pronounced and direct. Gabriel Baer is certainly right that the picture sometimes painted of a society totally regimented into guilds is exaggerated, and the capabilities of the state for the exertion of that kind of control were, in any case, limited by modern standards. Yet the state was clearly concerned to exert control over commerce and the handicrafts. In an intermittent way, it may even have used guild-like forms to establish certain types of controls over other occupational groups, ranging from the so-called "immoral guilds" of thieves and the like to the religious scholars. To varying extents, the state thus sought to work through the organizational structures of the guilds for purposes such as collecting taxes, controlling prices, policing the market place, outfitting and supplying the army, and eventually limiting the number of shops in a given craft through a kind of licensing system referred to by the term *gedik*.[53]

As economic decline narrowed popular conceptions of trade and commerce more and more to the kind of small-scale operations typically associated with craft guilds, and at the same time confirmed the orientation of popular religious life toward mysticism as a kind of escape, the ideal of young manliness around which the "young men's clubs" grew up metamorphosed, as Ülgener has shown, into an ideal of the wise old man, the *şeyh* or *pir*, whose living embodiments were legion in the bazaars and dervish meeting halls of the later empire. Guildsmen and dervishes were not beyond taking a role in the popular disorders of the later centuries.[54] The original activism of the "young men's clubs" had mostly drained away, however, by the time their tra-

dition assumed its final form under the aegis of the declining
sultanic patrimonialism.

As this transformation progressed, guilds and dervish orders
preserved many common traits. Here we can do little more than
indicate basic points of similarity between two types of organization that could surely support extended comparison. There are,
however, two important sorts of similarity relevant to the study
of conditions in the Ottoman ruling class. These we may group
under the headings of ethics and ceremonial—which are significant for what they imply about behavioral and procedural
patterns—and organizational hierarchy.

In the ceremonial life of these organizations, one of the clearest
signs of links between the guild and dervish traditions appears
in the existence of a special literary genre, found above all in
Turkish, and known as *fütüvvetname*, or *"futuwwa* books." These
include the rules of behavior (which the Turks call *edeb*) appropriate for adherents, as well as the prescriptions for rituals, such
as the girding ceremony of initiation. Given the existence of
similar concepts and rituals in guilds and dervish orders, as well
as the influence of mystics in shaping the "courtly" ideal of the
"young men's clubs," it is particularly significant that the social
bodies that preserved this *futuwwa* literature in the Ottoman period as their ethical and ceremonial guidebooks were not the
dervish orders, which had a rich literature of their own, but
some of the guilds.[55]

In these guidebooks, the rules for behavior are numerous and
minutely detailed. Among them, however, certain concepts
stand out as reflecting significant assumptions fundamental to
both guild and dervish order. One is the novice's or apprentice's
duty of service, in the most varied of senses, to his master.
Another is the concept of the distinctive learning of the group as
esoteric, to be acquired through service and through prolonged
association with the master, rather than as a rationally ordered
body of knowledge that could or should be propagated through
a pedagogical process expressly designed for that purpose.[56]
One of the most serious consequences of the replication of the
model of the guilds and dervish orders would be the diffusion of
this assumption to other fields of endeavor. The significance of
this fact would become particularly clear in the era of economic
decline, under the influence of that altered version of the old
futuwwa ethic that Ülgener so penetratingly evokes.

In organizational terms, meanwhile, there developed various hierarchies characterized by a progressive proliferation of levels and by parallels in nomenclature, and to a degree in purpose, among the grades of the various schemes. Probably the simplest version of the hierarchical scheme is that of disciple (*murîd*) and master (*mürşid*, *şeyh*, *pir*, *baba*), found among the dervishes. Among the *ahi* groups in Anatolia, these grades corresponded to *yiğit* ("youth," "young man," a Turkish translation of Arabic *fatâ*) and *ahi*. Among them, too, this hierarchy acquired a third level, referred to as *şeyh*, perhaps designating a dervish to whom the group acknowledged some attachment.[57] This three-grade scheme may be compared to that which then developed in the guilds, differentiating apprentice, journeyman, and master. The characteristic terms were *çırak* (apprentice) or *şagird* (student) for the first grade, *kalfa* (from Arabic *khalîfa*, but meaning "assistant" in this case) for the second, and *usta* (master) for the last. The hierarchical orderings were variable from guild to guild, and probably also among the dervish orders, and might include fewer grades or more, up to as many as nine. Basically, the designations of the grades indicate differing degrees of initiation, although some of the grades in the extended lists also designate distinction in terms of seniority or officeholding within the group. In any case, the terms appearing in the extended lists give added evidence of borrowing among organizations of the different types. The more extended lists for the guilds include such designations as *ahi* in some cases, or *yiğit başı* ("chief of the young men"), recalling the *ahi* groups, and *şeyh*, recalling the dervish orders.[58] In a dervish order such as the Mevlevis, we find *halîfes* (derived, like *kalfa* as used in the guilds, from the Arabic *khalîfa*), as well as *şeyhs*.[59] One of the distinctive signs of the replication of the model of the guilds and the dervish orders would be the borrowing of such designations and the replication of the relationships that they assumed.

Gabriel Baer has challenged the idea of a "close connection" between the guilds and the dervish orders as unsubstantiated. On the basis of his research on conditions in Egypt, he argues that organizations of the two types "co-existed on different levels," with "many points of contact but no system of connections." Among the Turks, too, there may have been no *system* of direct connections, at least after the disappearance of the old *ahi* groups. The manifestation of traits recalling the *ahi* groups may

also have varied in different guilds, depending on their particular history or degree of organizational elaboration.[60] But the
guilds and dervish orders of the Ottoman Empire do display
noteworthy similarities, which reflect the links between their
traditions in the period of the *ahis*, as well, no doubt, as the fact
that many individuals over the centuries were simultaneously
members of organizations of both types.

Responding to deep-seated human needs and adaptable to
those of the state, the model of the guilds and the dervish orders
also found an extremely wide range of replication, going beyond
anything that the multiplication of organizations of those two
types could alone explain. The extension of elements associated
with this model even into the life of the sultan is apparent not
only from the direct affiliation of some sultans with the orders,
but also from the way in which the ceremony of "girding on the
sword" (*taklid-i seyf*), the Ottoman counterpart of coronation, recalls the initiation ceremony common to the guilds and dervish
orders.[61] Among the Janissaries, the influence of the model appears not only in the close historical link to the Bektaşi order,
but also, Gibb and Bowen assert, in the modeling of the organization of the corps after that of the *ahis*.[62] Guild-like patterns of
hierarchical organization found replication among social groups
as diverse as the women of the imperial harem and school children.[63] Most importantly for our purposes, guild-like patterns
of organization and procedure were strongly entrenched within
the scribal service, especially in its lower echelons, and continued
to exert their influence well into the era of reform, if indeed
they ever ceased to.

The Model of the Patrimonial Household

The last of the models that we must consider is not easy to explain in terms of a historical development. As we have seen,
however, it was operative from the lowest level of Ottoman social
organization, where it reappeared in varying forms in villages
and nomad camps across the empire, to the highest, where it expressed itself in the prevailing conception of the organization of
the state. Correspondingly, this model affected the individual
member of the ruling class in more than one way at once. Generally speaking, some form of it would have characterized the
background out of which he came. Within the ruling class, it affected him inasmuch as he had become a slave in the sultanic

household. As an extension of that fact, the model affected him in another sense; for the sultan's delegation to his official slaves of power and its benefits gave them the means to set up households of their own. Naturally, this was most conspicuously the case in the highest echelons, among what we may term the slave grandees of the ruling class.

It has often been observed that such people tended to pattern their households after that of the sultan. Closer inspection shows that more was involved than mere emulation of sultanic example and that the households represented a particular kind of response to the fact that the grandees were still, in legal terms, no more than slaves. To illustrate these points, we must look at how the grandees organized their establishments and at how these functioned in the political life of the traditional ruling class. We shall do this with particular reference to conditions in the scribal service on the eve of the nineteenth-century reform era. Conditions in other branches of the ruling class and in other periods naturally varied in some respects. Some of the variations are well enough known that it is possible to allude to them; others are still coming to light, particularly through the work of Metin Kunt on the military-administrative elite of the sixteenth and seventeenth centuries.[64]

Imitation of the sultan's palace appears at many points, beginning with the kinds of relationships used by the grandees to put their households together. Until the decline of the child levy, many of these establishments must have had little or no basis in kinship. In the household of any grandee of the old military-administrative establishment who had been recruited through the child levy, there hardly could have been kinsmen, unless there were siblings or cousins also in the slave establishment, or, of course, children. These might be either by wives[65] or by concubines, children of the latter being legitimate when acknowledged by the father.

In other branches of the ruling class, or in periods when the reliance on recruitment systems that involved literal enslavement was less pronounced, the core of any such establishment would have been an extended family. A household of this type would tend to display a dynastic motif, expressed in terms of pride of descent and signaled most conspicuously by the affectation of a familial forename ending in -zade or -oğlu, meaning "son of." Such were the realities of sultanic dominance and official servility, however, that few such families managed in the long run to hold on to more than their name. The chief exceptions would appear in the period of decline among provincial magnates, whose houses, referred to as *hanedan* or *sülâle*, often in fact figured as the self-perpetuating and more or less autonomous dynasties that those terms evoke.

Whether the household was formed about a single individual of slave origin, or whether the head of an extended family was a slave only by virtue of being a member of the ruling class, this individual would use his resources to extend the size of his establishment to the maximum possible extent. To this end, he would make use of a variety of relationships.

Among these, marriage is obviously most important as a means of extending the bonds of kinship. It would be helpful at this point to be able to speak concretely, using the kinds of terminology current among anthropologists, about the characteristic marriage preferences of the Ottoman ruling class. In fact, however, even the relatively rich biographical sources of the later period seldom provide much information on this subject, and there is reason for caution in extrapolating from the growing body of anthropological literature, most of which deals with provincial conditions of the present day. To some degree, members of the ruling class, especially in the later centuries, must have used marriage as a way to interlink families of comparable standing, or perhaps to reinforce already existing kinship bonds. To judge from the seemingly endless kinship ties among present-day descendants of the old elite, we should expect this behavior to have been widespread for a long time, although it would be hazardous at this stage to attempt a more precise definition of customs associated with such marriages in the past.[66]

One reason for this caution is that there are signs indicating that inequality of status, rather than equality, was also sometimes sought between the partners to marriage. One source, referring to the nineteenth century, says that wealthy men selected "their wives from the relatively uneducated or the socially isolated," a custom there interpreted as a way to assure acquiescence of the wife in practices such as polygamy and concubinage.[67] The reasoning was not new: the poet Nabi (1630-1712) advised his son not to marry at all, but only acquire concubines.[68]

As it relates to the daughters of prominent families, who appear often to have been demanding and unruly wives, this pattern of marriage between persons of unequal standing is usually presented in a way that emphasizes the prospective husbands viewed as sons-in-law (*damad*). These were frequently men who had promise, but little else in the way of social assets. In many cases, they were already attached to the household of the prospective bride's father by a kind of clientage, which we shall follow Ottoman usage in terming "connection" (*intisab*), before being chosen for closer integration through marriage. In a society where the emphasis in marriage was, if we may judge from present-day practice in a provincial setting, rather on the integration of the bride into her husband's family, with more or less radical severing of her bonds to her own blood-kin, one trait of the "grandee mentality" thus might be a contrary tendency that emphasized the role of the son-in-law in relation to his father-in-law.[69]

This kind of marriage custom, emphasizing inequality of status among the partners, is in fact simply one more way in which the ruling class imitated sultanic practice. For, ceasing entirely to contract legal marriages after the early sixteenth century themselves, the sultans maintained the custom of marrying their daughters to highly placed members of the ruling class, who thus gained the added dignity, often onerous and dangerous, of being sons-in-law to the sultan at the same time as being his slaves.[70]

Of greater quantitative importance as means of extending the household were other forms of relationship that went beyond the limits of kinship by either blood or marriage. Relationships that might occasionally function in this way included adoption (*evlâtlık*)[71] or "milk-brotherhood" (*süt kardeşliği*), the lifelong bond remaining among persons who had shared a wet nurse in infancy.[72] Another such relationship, much more widely encountered, was slavery. Grand Vezir Husrev Paşa (c. 1756-1855) was reportedly the last major exponent of a long tradition under which members of the ruling class would accumulate large retinues of slaves of their own and train them for government service.[73] Recent research has begun to throw light on the fascinating position in the ruling class of such "slaves of the slaves" of the sultan. In provincial settings, where the households also had a military function, many of the slaves would have had a military role. The household might also include paid mercenaries or, in some settings, consist more or less entirely of military slaves.[74] Both in the accumulation and training of slaves, and in this military dimension, the grandees' emulation of the sultans is again manifest.

In addition, and probably most important in numerical terms, at least among scribal officials of the eighteenth or nineteenth century, there were men who entered the households of patrimonial grandees through the kind of patron-client relationship vaguely referred to as "connection" (*intisab*). If a young man of talent could find a way to bring himself to the attention of a grandee, the formation of such a "connection" might result, and that would mean a place in the grandee's household and—indistinguishable from the household—his official suite. If highly favored, the protégé might be placed at his protector's side in some such role as bearer of the latter's seal (*mühürdar*) or pencase (*divitdar*). From there, it was a well-traveled, if not always easy, path to becoming a son-in-law, then perhaps head of yet another great household. The value of such "connections" is reflected in countless official biographies of the period, and in the difficulties that some of the most outstanding bureaucratic figures endured in order to form the indispensable links.[75]

Behind these formal categories of relationship, certain other principles were also apt to be at work. One might be the attraction of shared geographical, sometimes also ethnic, origin. Metin Kunt has called attention to the importance of bonds of ethnic-regional solidarity among persons entering the old military-administrative establishment as slaves, and has pointed out indications of a kind of rivalry between "Westerners," typically Albanians and Bosnians, and "Easterners," typically Abkhazians, Circassians, and Georgians.[76] The importance of this kind of bond was clearly not limited to slaves or to any specific period. Especially in slave recruitment, another factor that might be decisive was physical appearance, the principle—physiognomy (*kiyafet*) being regarded as a science—on which the child levy operated. Probably, however, what mattered most often for the young man who aspired to form a useful "connection" was to attract attention to himself by a show of talent. In scribal circles, this usually meant a display of proficiency in the Ottoman literary language. An ode submitted voluntarily, perhaps no more than a chronogrammatic couplet or a literary conversation, was enough to launch the career of more than one youthful aspirant who had both skill and luck.[77]

Whatever the basis of the relationship, the patrimonial grandees of the ruling class, like the sultan, viewed relations of personal dependence as the way to assure loyalty and maintain the patron's control over his kinsmen, slaves, and clients.

Contemporary sources, increasingly rich and varied in the late period, convey a vivid picture of life in the great households. The sizes that these establishments could assume are astounding to the modern reader: as high as the low thousands at the height of the empire, in the period of decline they might still include hundreds of people.[78] The sources show the constant comings and goings occasioned in such settings by high rates of birth and death, by polygamy and ease of divorce, by purchase and sale or manumission of slaves, and by the formation and rupture of *intisab* links. Such sources evoke visions of the great wooden mansions in the central quarters of Istanbul and the summer houses along the Bosphorus, with their separate reception rooms for men (*selâmlık*) and private rooms for family life (*haremlik*).[79] In the midst of the city, we see the Sublime Porte, at the start of the nineteenth century still a grandee household as much as a complex of offices,[80] and the even vaster imperial palace.[81]

Particularly fascinating in these settings are the ambiguities and contradictions associated with the "grandee mentality," which coexisted so strangely both with the otherworldliness and fatalism of the popular mentality in its later form, and with the legal principle of official servility. On one hand, there appear among the grandees of the ruling class tendencies toward ostentation and social exclusiveness, as in accounts of the lavish decors and costumes,[82] the studied cultivation of luxury and idleness, the grand scale of hospitality and acts of charity,[83] and sometimes, too, the snobbish insistence (*hadşinaslık*) that others "know their place."[84] On the other hand, there was much behavior of a far less exclusive kind. Various accounts tell of grandees sitting down to dinner with their servants,[85] and of the marriages that such grandees arranged between their clients and their trusted female servants, or even their daughters.[86] In a more casual way, the literary coteries and dervish assemblies that accounted for a great part of the social life of the ruling class created settings for interaction among individuals who differed widely in status. The state-imposed character of the ruler-subject distinction meant

that in all periods, if in differing ways, many members of the ruling class had close familial and other bonds with members of the
subject classes.[87]

Finally, and most importantly for purposes of this study,
sources on the households of the ruling class convey valuable insights into the way they functioned in bureaucratic politics, and
thus into what made replication of the model of the patrimonial
household worthwhile. To assess these factors as they relate to
the scribal service, we may overlook the military function which
might be so important in certain settings, particularly in the
provinces. Obviously, too, we may overlook those elements of
the households—the cooks, stable grooms, and household
stewards—whose functions were purely domestic. We shall
speak only of the part of the household that assumed a role in
the politico-bureaucratic process. Here there are two main
points to emphasize: what we may call the "patrimonial style in
recruitment," and the character of the household as political faction.

One notable consequence of the servile status of the ruling
class and of the state's attempt to dominate the articulation of
social organization was an extreme degree and rapidity of social
mobility.[88] In the heyday of the imperial system, a European observer like Busbecq, his expectations conditioned by the standards of the European aristocracies, was awestruck to find the sultan surrounded by men who had nothing to recommend them
but their abilities and who possessed no claim to power aside
from their status as his slaves.[89] The decline of the child levy and
of the palace school, and the implications of institutional decay
and territorial loss for the possibilities of appointment and promotion, obviously introduced changes into this picture. Still, the
decline of such highly institutionalized recruitment systems as
the child levy and the acquisition by certain elements of the ruling class of some of the attributes of a self-perpetuating elite
kept alive an altered form of the "patrimonial style in recruitment." This emphasized discretional or even capricious use of
patronage and heavy reliance on the kind of relationships
through which the grandee households were put together. A
few examples from the early nineteenth century will illustrate
how this kind of recruitment worked.

While there were often severe problems of overcrowding in
official ranks, it was still striking how abruptly an encounter be-

tween the sultan or a highly placed official and a young man or even a child could lead to the start of the latter's career, or to his enrollment in a school designed to train him for official service. The charmingly naive memoirist Aşçıdede Halil İbrahim, for example, almost began a career when his soldier-father used him, then a small child with long blond hair that had never been cut, to present a petition to the minister of war. The latter reacted by granting the father's request and ordering the boy's enrollment in military school, an idea that the child's mother managed to thwart.[90] The minister of war in question, one Rıza Paşa, had once been an apprentice in the Egyptian Bazaar. Riding through one day, Mahmud II (1808-1839) saw him and, taking a liking to him, asked his name. On being answered with "Rıza," Mahmud responded, "Well, then, follow me Rıza Bey," thus with a word launching the rise of the latter toward the notoriety he acquired as a palace favorite.[91] A not dissimilar incident occurred in the life of Tayyarzade Ata Bey, remembered today as a historian of the palace. Together with his brother and father, who was a palace official, he once encountered the same sultan in the street. The upshot of the meeting was an order for the enrollment of the two boys in the palace service.[92]

Endlessly replicable, these few examples form part of a larger set of promotion patterns that Şerif Mardin has expressively dubbed "Aladdin's lamp mobility."[93] In tribute to the fact that what went up also came down, we shall call it "wheel-of-fortune" mobility.

As the official wheel of fortune carried a young man upward, he would rise not only in formal bureaucratic position, but also in terms of the relationships that characterized the patrimonial household. In order to survive politically, he would have to make the best of opportunities of both these kinds, for bureaucratic life became increasingly politicized and uncertain in proportion as one rose to high station. In a society characterized by the commitment of the state to the maintenance of an ideally changeless cultural pattern and by the supposedly complete subordination of the ruling class to the will of the sovereign, political controversy remained within relatively narrow limits in the articulation of alternative policies or issues.[94] One concomitant of this, however, was a shift of political emphasis to questions of personality and of unconditional personal loyalty, on which the model of the patrimonial household was founded.

Very intense, the political activity that thus surrounded the patrimonial households of the ruling class appears to have taken
two main forms.

One form, used not only by grandees but also by minor officials who might otherwise have had no influence over the great,
was an aspect of the literary life of the traditional ruling class.
Anyone who reads İnal's biographical compendium on the poets
of the late period will be struck by the fact that most were, like
İnal, primarily bureaucrats. The continued association of the
kind of literary skills required for official service with the kind
required for writing verse, while reflecting the still limited intru-
sion of alien ideas and of new media of communication and new
forms of entertainment, signifies the enduring vitality of the
age-old *adab* tradition and the interlinkage to the last of its belletristic and bureaucratic expressions. At the same time, literary
activity had practical political uses. Eulogy and satire were highly
developed genres that also served as means for persons with
sufficient facility in versification to take revenge for a slight or to
establish a claim to the largess of a potential benefactor.[95] Other
genres less explicitly tailored to such ends also served at times
for their achievement.[96] Some of the most amusing incidents in
the social history of the ruling class reflect the patience with
which grandees and even sultans had to endure and reward
literary activity of such kinds. Numerous examples attest the
continuation of this pattern well into the era of reform.[97]

In addition, it was possible, particularly for those in high
office, to pursue political goals not only in verse but also through
intrigue and through appeals to the favor of the sultan. This
could be a very dangerous and competitive activity; for the more
official advancement brought an official into proximity to his
imperial master, the more that official had to contend—whatever the rewards of office—with the dangers implicit in the
sultan-slave relationship. Cevdet Paşa's epic history of the half
century leading up to the destruction of the Janissaries conveys
vivid impressions of what bureaucratic life was like under these
conditions. In his account, the factions, scarcely distinguishable
except in terms of their leaders, pass into and out of the annals
of the empire. Occasionally, particular officials achieve such
prominence that two of them seem to duel for a while for
preeminence,[98] or a single one comes close, as did Halet Efendi
in the years before the outbreak of the Greek Revolution, to a

monopoly on influence.[99] The factions appear short-lived and unstable, however, not only because of the few significant issues by which to distinguish them, but also because factional rivalry compounded the vulnerability of their leaders to the penalties that the sultan could arbitrarily impose on his slave officials.

The model of the patrimonial household thus had greater significance than the mere desire to emulate the sultan's style. Rather, given its structural characteristics and the principles governing the relations of the ruling class to the sultan, the model possessed great political utility. For a prominent official to have the largest possible number of personal dependents trained and placed in strategic positions was as close as he could come to ensuring himself against the intrigue of rivals or the anger of his imperial master. This, presumably, was true in all periods. In the period of decline, however, incentives for the development of household factions were heightened. For one thing, changes in the conditions of access to high office intensified official insecurity and augmented the value of the households as defenses for their heads. Simultaneously, the decline of other systems of recruitment and training made the formation of such households desirable even from the viewpoint of the sultan. These special problems of the period of decline are ones to which we shall return in a later chapter.

In any case, the vulnerability of the slave grandees points again to the principle of state dominance over the differentiation and validation of distinctions of social status, and so to the restriction of possibilities for the emergence of classes, estates, or even smaller types of corporative organizations independent of government control. Within the general framework of a state-imposed dichotomy of ruling and subject classes, a certain differentiation of smaller-scale organizational patterns nonetheless existed. Rooted in ancient tradition and in basic characteristics and needs of the societies under Ottoman rule, these patterns were characteristic not only of the subject classes; they also influenced the formal evolution of the state, as the sultans sought to establish means by which to accommodate and control them, and finally they found replication in varying ways as structuring principles of social life even within the ruling class. Some of the most critical issues of the era of reform would arise over the extent to which these models would continue to exert their influence as the state began to undergo modernization.

Conclusion

In this chapter we have presented a vocabulary of organizational concepts in terms of which to define the setting of the Sublime Porte and of the men who served in it, first as elements of the imperial "center," then as part of the totality of Ottoman society. In the former context, the Sublime Porte was a critical element in the formal organizational and procedural apparatus of the administration, and its officials corresponded in whole or part to a branch of the ruling class that it is appropriate to designate before the nineteenth century as the scribal service, and subsequently as the civil bureaucracy. In addition to the ruling class and the formal organizational and procedural apparatus, the "center" included the office of the sultan and the cultural component of the imperial tradition, all these elements combining to form the vitally important relationship of political balance or imbalance.

In the broader perspective of Ottoman society, the basic distinction, imposed by fiat of the state, was between ruling and subject classes. Within these categories appear the various branches of the ruling class and, among the subject classes, the officially recognized confessional communities. In addition, there were certain organizational forms, smaller in scale, that found replication among rulers and subjects alike. Three such forms, identifiable in terms of the models of autonomous confessional community, guild, and patrimonial household, played a major role in shaping the life of the officials whom we shall study.

In the next chapter, this vocabulary of organizational concepts will provide the means by which to analyze the evolution over time of the entire ruling class and to chart the emergence within it of the scribal service. The same vocabulary will then serve in the remainder of the study for a more detailed examination of the Sublime Porte and the scribal service as they were at the end of the eighteenth century and in each of the successive periods of the era of reform.

Chapter Two

THE EVOLUTION OF THE RULING CLASS
AND THE EMERGENCE OF
THE SCRIBAL SERVICE

Müstağni[-i] tarif olduğu üzere Devlet-i Aliye'de dört tarik
olup.

As there is no need to relate, there are four [official] careers
in the Sublime State.

Mustafa Nuri Paşa[1]

. . . fenn-i kitabet taife-i sanayi ve bedayiin eşref ve akdemi
olup.

. . . the scribal profession is the noblest and oldest of arts.

A grand-vezirial decree of 1824[2]

Even a sketch of the component elements of the Ottoman imperial "center," such as that presented in the last chapter, is
enough to suggest the variability of this system over time. The
governmental system in fact followed a complex life cycle that
included phases, not necessarily well demarcated from one
another, of emergence, florescence, decline, and attempted
modernization. The component parts of the "center" at the
same time followed individual cycles of their own, cycles interre-
lated in origin but differing in length and often out of phase
with one another or with that of the system as a whole. In this
chapter, we shall describe the evolution of the various branches
of the ruling class with reference to these cycles, resolving an
important historiographical controversy in the process. In keeping with the ultimate purpose of this study, we shall give particular attention to the emergence of the scribal bureaucracy and to
introducing the changes attendant on its metamorphosis into
the very different civil bureaucracy of the era of reform.

To discuss the evolutionary cycles of the ruling class in a way that will lead on naturally to the detailed discussion of nineteenth-century developments in subsequent chapters, we shall divide this chapter into separate sections for the prereform and reform eras. We shall define the phases distinguished above as parts of the life cycle of the state so that the phase of emergence corresponds roughly to the years 1300-1350, that of florescence to the years 1350-1600, and that of decline to the years from 1600 to the accession of Selim III in 1789, these three phases together composing the era of traditionalism. The era of reform we shall date more precisely to the interval from 1789 to the fall of the empire in 1922.

While there is an element of arbitrariness in taking 1789 as the watershed between traditionalism and reform, there is no doubt that two major events of the following decade marked new departures in the history of the Middle East. One of these was the Napoleonic invasion of Egypt. Opening an age in which Asiatic and African, as well as European, territories of the empire would fall subject to the direct encroachment of the major European powers, this effectively made it impossible ever to restore the preexisting order in one of the most important of the Arab provinces of the empire.

Disproportionately more important for purposes of this study, the other critical event of the 1790s was Selim III's inauguration of the wide-ranging reform program that became known as the "New Order" (*Nizam-ı Cedid*). This, too, signaled the opening of a new era. The point is not that there had never been attempts at reform before or that everything that could be called traditional vanished at this time. But earlier efforts at reform had, with limited exceptions, had as their goal the restoration of an idealized vision of the traditional order of the state.[3] Those efforts had also been intermittent and had never led to anything like a comprehensive overhaul of the administrative system. Selim's "New Order" was innovative both in some of the specific reforms that it included and, perhaps more importantly, in its comprehensiveness and what this implied about the changing role of the central government.

The history of reform did not become continuous before the second quarter of the nineteenth century. Still, it is logical to regard Selim III's reforms as the symbolic beginning at the Ottoman "center" of transition from a world view oriented toward maintenance of inherited cultural patterns to an outlook that, accepting and even aspiring to change, would increasingly have to turn to reason to regulate and legitimate what tradition could not. In terms of Weber's distinction of traditional, rational, and charismatic authority, here lay the beginning of a movement away from traditionalism and toward a modern system that would be governed by rational plan and specially enacted legislation—in sum, a rational-legal order. Since only the broad approval of the populace, or its politically active segments, could assure ultimate acceptance of policies lacking the transcendental sanction conveyed through perpetuation of traditional norms, here also lay the beginnings of need for that enlargement of the polity that we have already noted as characteristic of modernization.[4]

The accession of Selim III in 1789 serves better than any other single event to mark the beginning of transition in the Ottoman Empire from traditionalism to modernization. Here we shall simply use this date as the dividing line between the two sections of our discussion of the evolutionary patterns of the branches of the ruling class. The significance of this turning point will become clearer in later chapters, as, in some respects, it quickly became to the Ottoman statesmen of the day.

THE EVOLUTION OF THE RULING CLASS IN THE TRADITIONAL STATE: A PROBLEM IN HISTORICAL INTERPRETATION

In characterizing the elements of the imperial "center," we introduced the idea that the ruling class was divided into a number of branches: the military-administrative, or later simply the military, establishment (*seyfiye*); the religious establishment (*ilmiye*); the palace service (the existence of a distinct Ottoman name for which is in doubt); and the scribal service (*kalemiye*) or, later, civil bureaucracy (*mülkiye*). A comprehensive discussion of the Ottoman ruling class, at least as it ultimately came to be, must make use of all these categories. In fact, however, if we confront the literature on the ruling class as it has thus far developed, the four categories appear to be pieces of some vexatious kind of puzzle, in which not only the mutual fit of the pieces, but in some cases also the existence of particular pieces or the propriety of regarding them as parts of the puzzle, are in question. How is it possible to put such a puzzle together?

Conflicting Interpretations and Indifferent Experts

This puzzle has given rise to a controversy among scholars writing about the Ottoman ruling class, at least among those writing in English. Simply stated, the argument is between those who argue that the ruling class was divided into only two branches, a "ruling institution" and a "religious institution," and those who contend that there were at least three branches, or four if the palace service is posited as a distinct entity, the four being named more or less as in the description above.

In the former view, which Albert H. Lybyer introduced in his study on the period of Süleyman the Magnificent (1520-1566), the "religious institution" consisted of born Muslims trained in the religious colleges; the "ruling institution," of slaves recruited from the non-Muslim subject population of the empire through the child levy, the best of these being educated in the palace school.[5] Lybyer's "religious institution" corresponds to our religious establishment, while his "ruling institution" more or less includes all the other branches of the ruling class as we have described it. Writing of the eighteenth century, Gibb and Bowen took Lybyer's classification as their starting point, although they acknowledged that the system by then existed only on paper. They attempted to describe the changes that had occurred, but did not produce an alternative conceptual framework to set in place of Lybyer's dichotomy.[6]

The view that opposes the Lybyer-Gibb-Bowen tradition is the work of Lewis Thomas and Norman Itzkowitz and is a product of further study of seventeenth- and eighteenth-century conditions. This view acknowledges the systems of recruitment and training mentioned above, but correctly cites evidence of movement between those two branches of the ruling class, both in the sixteenth century and at later dates. More importantly, this interpretation argues for a larger number of branches. Itzkowitz, in particular, has attacked the Lybyer-Gibb-Bowen interpretation as incorrect.[7]

The controversy over these two views has generated a certain amount of heat as well as light, but an added peculiarity of the conflict is that some scholars working closely on the ruling class and the imperial administrative system have managed to remain indifferent to such questions. This appears more or less generally true of the Turkish historians; the same applies to various other scholars who have dealt with aspects of the ruling class narrowly delimited in topical or chronological terms.[8]

What to make of this controversy and the curious pattern of responses to it thus emerges as the central question about our historiographical puzzle. Fortunately, if we recall the Weberian conception of the progressive evolution of governmental institutions out of the ruler's household, and bear in mind the links of the opposing interpretations to different centuries, the answer to this question is not far to seek. It will help to distinguish two questions: the character and exclusivity of systems of recruitment and training, on the one hand, and the number of branches of the ruling class, on the other—the latter question being the more important for our purposes. The answer to our central question now presents itself in the form of a schematization that subjects both interpretations to critical scrutiny and assigns each to its chronologically defined place in a larger evolutionary perspective.

The Origins of the Ottoman Ruling Class

As the logical starting point for the development of this schematization, we may take the fact that the entire ruling class was often referred to as *Osmanlı* (Ottoman) or *askeri* (military). The former term obviously identifies the members of this class with the House of Osman; the latter, with the holy war (*gaza*) for the expansion of Islam, the pursuit in which the sultans found their first, and in concept ever primary, means for the legitimation of their rule. Since the holy war was in a sense the foundation of the imperial system, the identification as "military" of the entire ruling class, including judges, professors of the religious colleges, scribes, and eunuchs, as well as soldiers, must not have seemed incongruous to the Ottomans. As late as the beginning of the nineteenth century, indeed, this identification found a tangible expression in the tradition that required much of the central administration, including the scribal officials, to take part in military campaigns, leaving replacements in the capital for the duration, but carrying on the administration chiefly from the field headquarters. By the nineteenth century, this system had become an unworkable anachronism.[9] But in the earliest stage of Ottoman history, when the state was no more than a tiny *gazi* principality, to carry the administration on campaign was no problem. Then there was no bureaucracy distinct from the household of the ruler, still less was there any sense of a ruling class divided into branches, and the administrative needs of the state were of a rudimentary sort that could be handled, so to speak, from the saddle.

The rapid expansion of the state nonetheless quickly began to make a difference, at least in the organization of the ruling class. By the second half of the fourteenth century, cleavages were appearing among the *askeris*, and some of the organizational and procedural elements of the classic imperial system were beginning to take form. On one hand, this period witnessed the phenomenon of the so-called "Turkish aristocracy," representing a phase in the incorporation of the dominant families of the other, once-independent Anatolian *gazi* states into the Ottoman ruling class. On the other hand, in the same period there were two other phenomena of enduring importance. One consisted of the early stages in the institutional elaboration—particularly with the development of the Janissary Corps, the child levy, the palace school, and the *tımar* system of landholding—of the military-administrative establishment. Simultaneously, developments such as the founding of the first Ottoman religious colleges and the organization of a central administrative system, at first staffed largely by men of religious education and administrative experience acquired under other governments, marked the first stages in the emergence of the religious establishment. Leading to the further evolution of the palace organization, the elaboration of a hierarchical order of religious colleges, and the creation of a vast religious bureaucracy headed by the *şeyh ül-İslâm*, the conquest of Constantinople (1453) provided added stimulus to both these lines of development.

The Dichotomous Interpretation Rehabilitated?

These facts suggest that for the period of florescence (c. 1350-1600), there are practical grounds for visualizing the Ottoman ruling class as made up of a "ruling institution" recruited through the child levy and a "religious institution" trained in the religious colleges. This dichotomous classification must be corrected, however, with respect to the identification sometimes made between the "religious institution" (*ilmiye*) and the "men of the pen" (*kalemiye*); indeed, there is a fundamental ambiguity in the way Gibb and Bowen, and their sources, use this latter term. Thomas and Itzkowitz are also right in criticizing the idea, which Gibb and Bowen knew to be inapplicable by the eighteenth century, and which was an exaggeration for any period, that the two "institutions" were hermetically sealed off from each other, one containing only slaves of non-Muslim origin, and the other only free-born Muslims.[10] The discretionary character of the "patrimonial style in recruitment" could hardly have produced such a degree of rigor in any period. In addition, there were elements within the ruling class that did not conform to the typical patterns of either of the two major corps. Still, as a picture of the ruling class at the height of the empire, a modified dichotomous concept cannot be dismissed out of hand or imputed to ignorance of the Ottoman sources.[11]

What, then, happened to the "ruling" and "religious institutions" during the period of decline, and where were the branches of the ruling class not yet accounted for? The answer is that the services prominent in the sixteenth century declined with the empire. Meanwhile, partly as an aspect of the decline of those services, and partly through the continuing processes of differentiation that had given them distinct form in the first place, the pieces of the puzzle not yet accounted for gained increasingly in organizational articulation and importance. This process is particularly linked to the decline of the "ruling institution," or, more specifically, of what we have termed the military-administrative establishment. The religious establishment, too, declined in moral and intellectual standards, but its religious, legal, and educational functions, as also the role of the *kadıs* in local administration, remained essentially in its hands. In some respects, the influence of this branch of the ruling class even increased.[12] In contrast, the military-administrative establishment, which included the Janissary Corps, palace cavalry regiments, and "feudal" cavalry in the provinces, and whose "elite" traditionally rose through the palace school to fill such high positions as provincial governorships and the grand vezirate, declined more drastically. The child levy faded to the point of disappearance by the beginning of the eighteenth century; the various types of military forces declined to the point of more or less complete loss of discipline and effectiveness. As the governmental system continued, even in the face of decline, to differentiate itself more and more from the sultan's household, elements of the ruling class that had been only marginally distinguishable or minuscule in size now emerged with distinct form and unprecedented power.

The Problem of the Palace Service

Searching for the pieces that the dichotomous interpretation excludes from the puzzle of the ruling class, we come back to the question cited earlier: when and whether certain branches of the ruling class can properly be regarded as pieces of the puzzle at all. If we look for a palace service in the period when the military-administrative and religious establishments were at their height, we find that while an elaborately institutionalized imperial household certainly existed,[13] those who served in it could hardly be regarded as forming a distinct and coherent branch of the ruling class. Most of them were actually from the military-administrative establishment. Subsequently, the elements of the ruling class associated with the palace began to change, while a tendency toward bureaucratization—in the sense of the acquisition of administrative responsibilities as well as, or in place of, obligations of personal service—appeared not only among functions that moved out of the household, but even among those that remained within it and were most associated with personal attendance on the sultan and his family. Palace functions traditionally held by members of the military-administrative establishment ultimately gained most from these developments. Since they did so at a time when the child levy was falling into disuse, this phenomenon signified not only bureaucratization in the palace service, but also a fundamental change in its social character.

There was a basic distinction in the palace between the Outside Service (*Birun*), the Inside Service (*Enderun*), and the harem. The first of these was, in the heyday of the empire, the real center of government and was responsible for all functions having to do with the sultan's relations with the outside world. It was the center also of the military-administrative establishment, members of which tended, from the conquest of Istanbul at least through the sixteenth century, to dominate the grand vezirate, then part of this Outside Service. Subsequently, with the further differentiation of services within the ruling class, many of the administrative functions that had been concentrated in the palace, including the grand vezirate, moved out to separate institutional centers and ceased to figure as elements of the palace establishment. In some cases they also passed out of military-administrative and into scribal hands in the process.[14]

What then remained as the quintessential palace service had its center in the imperial harem and the Inside Service. Located in the private quarters of the sultan, the latter included the palace school, the students of which were traditionally recruited through the child levy and waited on the sultan as "pages" before going on to hold military or administrative positions. For a long time, however, the main power in the inner parts of the palace was in the hands of eunuchs, or de facto, of the more favored women of the harem. Originally, the most important of the eunuchs was the chief white eunuch (*bab ül-saade ağası, kapı ağası*), in charge of the palace school, the personal service of the sultan, and the administration of the harem. At the end of the sixteenth century, he lost an important part of his responsibilities thanks to the emergence of a distinct staff of black eunuchs, the chief of which (*dar ül-saade ağası, kızlar ağası*) acquired the role of supervisor of the harem, as well as other duties, including the exclusive right to transmit communications between the sultan and other officials.[15]

Posts originally held by military-administrative personnel became preponderant in the Inside Service only in the eighteenth century with the evolution of the most important part of the old palace school, the Privy Chamber (*Has Oda*), into an organization increasingly devoted to attendance not to the personal needs of the sultan, but rather to his relations with other parts of the administration. With this development, the chief of the pages in the Privy Chamber, known as the *silahdar ağa* or "sword-bearer," emerged as titular head, in place of the chief white eunuch, of the Inside Service. This change entailed the conversion of some of the sword-bearer's subordinates from pages to the sultan into assistants to the sword-bearer and the gradual emergence out of the Privy Chamber of a palace secretariat.

With this, the part of the Inside Service known as the *Mabeyn* (literally, "what is between," in this case between the imperial harem and the remainder of the Inside Service) began to acquire a significant new dimension. In addition to including, as before, those individuals in immediate personal attendance on the sultan, the *Mabeyn* also came to include the new palace secretariat. Much later, at the end of the nineteenth century, the secretariat was in fact known as the "big *Mabeyn*" and the personal servants of the sultan as the "little *Mabeyn*."[16]

Discharging a function for which there had once been no need,[17] the palace secretariat thus surely emerged in response to the evolution of what had formerly been the most important parts of the Outside Service into distinct agencies, mostly headquartered outside the palace precinct. The development of the secretariat clearly challenged one of the prerogatives of the chief black eunuch, and the eighteenth century seems accordingly to have witnessed a struggle between him and the sword-bearer over the control of communications between the sultan and the bureaucracy outside the palace. The sword-bearer apparently gained the upper hand for a while during the reign of Ahmed III (1703-1730), but was not able to consolidate his victory. It is not entirely clear when the sword-bearer's ascendancy became definitive, although he had certainly won control of the flow of communications by the reign of Mahmud II (1808-1839). Since the sword-bearer and his subordinates were by then no longer child-levy recruits, but more likely members of Muslim families long prominent in Ottoman bureaucratic circles, this change represented not only a shift of balance within the palace service, but also the emergence of a new kind of leadership within it.[18]

Ultimately, the palace service would never lose the motley aspect that resulted from its inclusion of personnel categories and career lines as disparate as those of the palace secretaries and the eunuchs. The fact that by the end of the eighteenth century the number of secretaries did not exceed a few tens, that of the eunuchs a few hundreds, or that of the entire palace establishment a few thousands,[19] also kept the palace service from standing out in relation to others, such as the military and religious establishments, far vaster in scale. Still, the simultaneous processes of bureaucratization and partial change in recruitment patterns—changes reflecting the decline of the child levy and the growing differentiation of governmental institutions—had begun to give the palace service a new character and a new place in the balance of power within the ruling class. Evident by the end of the eighteenth century, this trend climaxed at a date so late—at a time when the modernization of the political system was so far launched—that it bore the aspect of an atavistic throwback, ultimately short-lived but redoubtable in effect.

Emergence and Internal Differentiation
of the Scribal Service

Easier in some ways to trace, but again obscured from view by the bulk of the military-administrative and religious establishments, was the early scribal service ("men of the pen," *kalemiye*). Its origins are shrouded by the undifferentiated state of the household of the earliest Ottoman rulers and by the relatively scarce documentation on their reigns. The evidence seems to confirm that the Ottoman principality, for its first half century or so, had no formally organized scribal offices or distinct group of professional scribal officials. Yet the documents surviving from this period, whatever the means for their production, already attest the existence of conventions for their composition, the use of the *tuğra* (a sort of "cipher" of the sultan) as the sign of validation, and thus perhaps the existence of some functionary charged with drawing this complex motif.[20] Within a relatively short time, the growth of the state and the increasing need for written records necessitated a clearer organization and articulation of scribal functions. By the sixteenth century, there had emerged a scribal staff performing a variety of important tasks, but still organized on small scale and still working in large part within the palace and under the grand vezir.

Of these scribal officials, the most prestigious was the *nişancı* or, roughly, the affixer of the cipher, so called because he drew the imperial cipher (*tuğra, nişan*) at the head of the documents that required it. More substantial bases of his importance lay in the fact that he was a member of the imperial Divan and had overall responsibility for the assignment of benefices in land (*tımar, zeamet, has*) and the conduct of land surveys (*tahrir*). He was also the supreme jurisconsult in matters pertaining to the laws promulgated by the state (*kanun*) and enjoyed the right, at least through the seventeenth century, to emend legal enactments and other documents to conform to that law before applying the cipher.[21]

At the high point of the empire, the affixer of the cipher had other officials working under him. These included a figure known as the *tezkereci*, or "memorandum officer," whose role centered, at least at later dates, on the oral presentation in Divan meetings of the matters that required decision there. There was also a figure whose character as some kind of assistant is to be inferred from his title, bearer of the pen-case (*divitdar*).[22] In addition, there were under the affixer of the cipher two other officials, both of whom had staffs of their own. One of these was the *defter emini* or keeper of the registers. His job, perhaps originally one of records conservation in a more general sense, eventually came to center on maintenance of records on land tenure. We shall accordingly call his office the Land Registry Office (*Defterhane, Defter Emaneti, Defter-i Hakani*).[23]

Finally, there was the *reis ül-küttab* or chief scribe, an office evidently created early in the reign of Süleyman the Magnificent as a result of growth in the volume of business on the hands of the affixer of the cipher. The *reis* was chief of the scribes who performed the written business of the imperial Divan. This included making appointments and assigning landholdings, responding to petitions and complaints, and attending to the paperwork related to the "important affairs" (*umur-ı mühimme*) of the state, such as correspondence with foreign governments and registration of all laws (*kanun*) that the state issued concerning nonfinancial matters. Under the headship of the chief scribe, these men would gradually take shape as a bureau organizationally distinct from the Divan itself, an early instance of the evolution of a bureau, staffed by professional specialists and operating on a full-time basis, out of a collegial body.[24]

In addition, there was one other major scribal organization that did not come under the affixer of the cipher. It included the personnel who kept financial records and accounts, was the largest of the scribal departments, and was headed by the chief treasurer (*baş defterdar*), who was a member of the imperial Divan in his own right.[25]

In the period of florescence, then, the subordinates of the affixer of the cipher and the chief treasurer were, in effect, the scribal service proper, for it was chiefly they who conducted the correspondence, kept the accounts on landholding and finance, and conserved the records necessary for the conduct of administration. An exhaustive account of the scribal service in that period would have only to add to them such miscellaneous elements as the translator of the imperial Divan and his assistants, then mostly foreign-born converts to Islam;[26] the master of ceremonies (*teşrifatî*);[27] and a few other scribes working in various posts in the capital, such as the headquarters of the military organizations or the commissionership of the mint, or perhaps in provincial administrative centers.[28]

Despite the manifest importance of its functions, both the size of this scribal bureaucracy and the relatively low level of its institutional development explain how it has been lost to the view of some of the scholars who have attempted to describe the organization of the ruling class in this period. A document of roughly the 1530s, listing scribes serving under the affixer of the cipher and the chief treasurer, includes eighteen secretaries of the imperial Divan (seven of them serving under the treasurer in preparation of correspondence relating to financial affairs), twenty-three other clerks regularly assigned to the Treasury, and twenty-three apprentice clerks, also assigned to the Treasury, followed by nine miscellaneous clerks. This makes a total of fifty clerks and twenty-three apprentices.[29] By comparison, the religious and military-administrative establishments were already organizations of imperial scale, the latter then having some 25,000 members, without counting the provincial cavalry.[30]

Aside from this difference in numbers, the scribal service, while it had come to consist of full-time "professionals,"[31] was still far from having the aspect of a distinct branch of the ruling class. The biographical information that Matuz presents for scribal officials of the reign of Süleyman the Magnificent suggests that most of them were freeborn Turkish Muslims, but with no distinct sense of collective professional identity[32] and no clear-cut or unitary system through which to bring new men into their ranks. The scribal service of the empire's great age tended to draw its personnel, to perhaps varying degrees, from both the other branches of the ruling class which were more highly developed in organization. Already in this period, however, some candidates appear to have been recruited straight into the offices and educated through apprenticeship there, without prior study in either palace or religious college.[33] In the period of decline, reliance on such relatively ad hoc means of recruitment and training became more pronounced, with the result that the scribal service never developed a highly elaborated system like those that served the same purposes for the military-administrative and religious establishments when these were at their height. This is in ironic contrast to the richness of the scribal cultural tradition, its indispensability to the conduct of administration, and the eventual growth of the scribal service in size, organizational distinctness, and political power.[34]

For the sixteenth century, meanwhile, an equally low level of organization and differentiation was apparent in the internal structure of the scribal service. Matuz' findings indicate that in the reign of Süleyman the Magnificent, differentiation of scribal specializations had still not fully hardened. This is apparent in the assignment of scribes subordinate to the affixer of the cipher to serve under the chief treasurer, and in the monopolization by that official—at least if we may generalize from the evidence on which Matuz relies—of the training of apprentice scribes. The scribes of the affixer of the cipher were not yet regarded as forming distinct bureaus; still less was there any evidence of the separate sections that ultimately appeared within the staffs of the keeper of the registers and the chief scribe. While the various types of document that the scribes of the Divan produced were formally distinct, specialization by individual scribes in preparation of documents of one type or another was only beginning to develop at this time.[35]

As in the case of the palace service, there is some reason, then, why scholars surveying the state of the Ottoman ruling class at the height of the empire have tended to overlook the scribal service and concentrate rather on the military-administrative and religious establishments. For the subsequent period of decline, the situation was quite different. Even as the palace service underwent the important changes of role and social character summarized above, the decline in the military fortunes of the empire appears to have affected the position of the scribal service even more significantly, by creating new roles and new possibilities of promotion for its members, as well as by giving a new importance to the "statist-secularist" cultural orientation of which they were increasingly the chief exponents.

The stages of the transformation of the scribal service in the period of decline are not yet fully known. Several recent writers have cited signs of an increase, linked to complex changes in the economy and fiscal system, in the status and power of the chief treasurers as of the end of the sixteenth century and beginning of the seventeenth.[36] In the present limited state of knowledge about this period, the most visible sign of change in the scribal service remains the movement of several of the scribal departments to new locations outside the palace and, in particular, the development in the second half of the seventeenth century of the new grand-vezirial headquarters which history remembers as the Sublime Porte (*Bab-ı Âli*). There, what had been the afternoon *divan* of the grand vezir (*ikindi divanı*), and had previously served for little more than minor business left over from the morning meetings at the palace, began to become the real center of governmental affairs, while the role of the imperial Divan at the palace gradually declined to little more than ceremonial functions.[37]

As the new administrative headquarters emerged, the *nişancı* or affixer of the cipher remained behind in the palace, retaining vestiges of his old honor but losing effective power. The chief treasurer (*baş defterdar*) and keeper of the registers (*defter emini*) acquired new headquarters of their own, separate from but near the Sublime Porte. Although the chief treasurer continued to sit in the *divan* of the grand vezir at the Porte, it is difficult to conceive that spatial isolation from the new executive center, not to mention the general decline of the Ottoman economy, had not already begun to undermine his effective power, which had clearly declined by the eighteenth century.[38] The elements of the scribal service that gained most from the emergence of the Sublime Porte were the scribes of the imperial Divan. Passing out from under the old imperial Divan at the palace, they moved with their head, the *reis ül-küttab* or chief scribe, to the Porte. Perhaps it was at about the same time that they assumed corporate form as the Office of the Imperial Divan, a name anachronistic by then, but reflecting the essential continuity in their functions.

Since a detailed discussion of the Sublime Porte as it existed at the end of the eighteenth century will be the theme of the next chapter, here we need only demonstrate the extent to which the scribal service, specifically as seen at the Porte, and there as quintessentially represented in the staff of the chief scribe, continued to grow in importance up to that time. As will be recalled, the Porte then included a number of organizational elements: the grand vezir's household, his *divan*, and numerous officials. Some of the officials, such as the official historiographer (*vakanüvis*),[39] may have functioned as individuals. For the most part, however, they served under three dignitaries directly subordinate to the grand vezir. Two of these, their origins lying elsewhere, were still in the process of becoming parts of the scribal service in any meaningful sense. These were the *çavuş başı* or chief bailiff, whose duties at the Porte had mainly to do with judicial affairs, and the *kâhya bey* or steward, a former major-domo become a kind of executive assistant to the grand vezir.

In contrast to these two, the central importance of the chief scribe becomes clear. For under his direction, the Office of the Imperial Divan, at first the only properly scribal agency at the Porte, served as the indispensable chancery for the grand vezir. One measure of the chief scribe's consequent growth in importance appears in the development within the Office of the Imperial Divan of three different sections, a change related in turn to the volume of patronage under the grand vezir's control. By the end of the eighteenth century, three other offices had also passed, or developed, under the chief scribe's supervision. As will become clearer in the next chapter, this fact relates to an important qualitative change in the chief scribe's functions. For as head of the office traditionally responsible for correspondence with foreign sovereigns and for the registration of treaties and concessions to foreign powers, he became increasingly occupied with matters of that kind as the diplomatic business of the declining empire grew in volume and seriousness. Evident from the time of the Carlowitz peace negotiations (1698-1699),[40] this fact did not fail to leave its mark on the development of the grand-vezirial chancery.

The chief scribe thus began to take on the character of a foreign minister and, in the process, to grow in prominence within the scribal service. With these changes, the number of men under his supervision rose to some 130 to 200. The total number of scribal officials serving at the end of the eighteenth century, most of them still in the Treasury offices, was 1,000 to 1,500[41]—a contrast indeed to the few score noted in the early sixteenth century.

At the same time, the growth in importance of the scribal service, and especially of that part of it subordinate to the chief scribe, was reflected in the development of new promotion patterns. Thomas and Itzkowitz have argued that in the eighteenth century it became increasingly common for men of scribal background, particularly those rising through the offices under the chief scribe, to go on to high positions such as provincial governorships and even the grand vezirate, positions once filled mainly by members of the military-administrative establishment who had risen through the palace school. Combining titles of address appropriate to the scribal officials on the one hand, and to these high positions on the other, Itzkowitz has designated this phenomenom the "efendi-turned-paşa" pattern.[42]

In the next chapter we shall have to reexamine this pattern in terms of both its novelty and its relative importance. For the moment, the image of the "efendi-turned-paşa" can stand, as that assessment will generally confirm, as a symbol of the extent to which the scribal service had begun to grow in size and prominence as the military-administrative establishment decayed and the needs of the imperial system began to shift.

Resolution of the Historiographical Controversy in an Evolutionary Perspective

Like the contemporary developments in the palace service, though more clearly delineated, this change in the scribal service was a development whose significance would become fully apparent only in the nineteenth century. Before going on to discuss that period, however, we need to note how the changes observable through the eighteenth century affect the historiographical puzzle that has been our preoccupation thus far. In a sense, this is not one puzzle but several. For the earliest period, a ruling class, indeed a political "center" in any sense, existed only in an inchoate and undifferentiated way. By its sixteenth-century heyday, the ruling class and the "center" in general had evolved from the undifferentiated patrimonial household of the early fourteenth century into an elaborately organized example of what Weber would call patrimonial officialdom. At that point, there were two major pieces to the puzzle of the ruling class, the military-administrative and religious establishments. By the eighteenth century, partly as a result of decline in one or both of these, there were at least three—the question of the distinctness and coherence of the palace service being a persistent problem—with the scribal service now appearing as the most important, thanks to its growth in size and range of responsibilities.

In this sense, both interpretations of the now familiar controversy are valid, with suitable emendation of the older view where questions of recruitment and training are concerned and with due care for chronological precision. The indifference of certain experts to the controversy also becomes explicable in the sense that there is no controversy when the different interpretations, as emended, are placed in a larger perspective. Superimposed in chronological sequence, the puzzle-like patterns of all major periods suggest a kaleidoscopic pattern of change over time, beginning with an undifferentiated ruling class, and ending with one divided into four branches.

THE EVOLUTION OF THE RULING CLASS IN THE ERA OF REFORM: WOULD THE SCRIBAL SERVICE REMAIN PREEMINENT?

As the Ottomans began, around the end of the eighteenth century, to undertake reforms that went increasingly beyond the limits of traditional patterns, a central unstated question was whether the trends observable in the development of the ruling class during the preceding period would continue, or whether new pressures would emerge to shift the course of change. Since much of this study will be devoted to analysis of the development of the scribal service through the successive political periods of the nineteenth century, there is no need for detailed comment on it here. But it is worthwhile to take up the question of continuity or change in evolutionary patterns in a more general way, comparing the developmental dynamics of all four branches of service. To do so not only carries our general account of the evolutionary patterns to the fall of the empire, but also provides a basis for differentiating the political periods of the nineteenth century, and thus for elucidating the critical shifts in the political balance during the era of reform.

Why Not Military Politics?

Looking first at what remained of the military-administrative establishment, we encounter a question of a comparative nature, perhaps greater in interest than has commonly been realized by historians working in late Ottoman history. If the Ottoman Empire was the first of the traditional states of the non-Western world to attempt to modernize in the face of the constant threat of Western expansionism, should we not expect the efforts at modernization to have first of all a military thrust? If so, what was there to preclude the emergence of an Ottoman equivalent of the kind of "military politics" so familiar in the Middle East more recently, particularly since the military had once been a dominant force in the administration?[43]

This question is no airy speculation; for in the eighteenth century, when such important developments were occurring at the Sublime Porte, the sultans were simultaneously trying to remake their military institutions. Such attempts began, in fact, in the first half of the century. With the disastrous Russian wars in the last part of the century, Ottoman statesmen renewed and expanded the scope of these efforts.[44] Selim III continued this trend in his "New Order," introduced in the 1790s. While this program went beyond the purely military, its best-known measures lay in that field.[45] After the fall of Selim (1807), a military measure, the abolition of the Janissaries (1826), again opened the way for continued, wide-ranging change by removing the most dangerous single source of opposition.[46] By the death of Mahmud (1839) or soon after, however, the military focus had been lost. The main thrust of reformist energies had begun to go elsewhere, and the real leadership for reform had begun to come from a different quarter.

Why did these changes occur? The answer seems clear, at least in part. Relevant points include the radical change in Ottoman military institutions with the abolition of the Janissaries, and the fact that the old institutions had been in deep decline for so long before then. The old military-administrative establishment having already largely lost its administrative dimension, the new military organizations never fully regained it, although later sultans drew on military men occasionally for governorships, ambassadorships, or other such positions. The discontinuity in the military tradition also extended to the system of military education. Between the decline of the old palace school and the emergence of reasonably effective new military schools in the nineteenth century, the Ottoman military hardly had better educational facilities than did the scribal service. The effort to create new schools for the military did begin earlier,[47] but the task was probably more difficult. For what the military needed was men possessing not just a generalist's grasp of modern European culture, and particularly of the French language, but rather a significant command of more technical subjects, such as medicine, military engineering, or naval architecture, and their applications. How slow the military would be to acquire such men is apparent from the fact that in the 1820s and 1830s the "intellectual-technical elites" of the military and the scribal service still consisted of the same handful of people.[48] The effort to produce a modern school-trained officer corps does not appear to have yielded results on any significant scale before the reign of Abd ül-Hamid II (1876-1909). Even then, while the military schools performed an important function of social mobilization, there was a continuing conflict in the officer corps between the "school men" (*mektepli*) and the "old troopers" (*alaylı*), while both faced the determined efforts of the paranoiac sultan to prevent either from acquiring any real power. The "school men" first emerged as a military elite in little but an educational sense; only through the medium of the Young Turk movement would they produce a power elite as well. By then, the anticipatory tremors of the wars that would destroy the empire were already being felt.[49]

This brings us to another point significant in helping to explain the failure of the military to resume a paramount role in the Ottoman ruling class of the nineteenth century. This was the growing awareness in both the Ottoman Empire and Europe that the survival of the empire depended not solely on its military capabilities, but also, and in the long run primarily, on its ability to pursue its ends effectively in diplomatic relations with the major powers of Europe. Uriel Heyd dates the realization of this fact by Ottoman statesmen as early as 1829, and interprets it as one of the implications of the Peace of Adrianople.[50] In the 1830s, the two disastrous showdowns with Muhammad Ali of Egypt provided clearer proof, especially in 1839, when it was really the collective intervention of the European powers that saved the empire.

As long as the empire remained dependent in this way on the joint support of the European powers and had any hope of getting such support, what the state needed more than military leaders was men skilled in dealing with Europeans and in conceiving and implementing reforms that would—if the two goals could be reached at once—both strengthen the empire and cement relations with those powers. At a time when the military elite could not provide such manpower, developments in the scribal service, and especially in that part of it associated with the chief scribe, meant that it could more quickly supply the need.[51]

Events of 1908 and later would show that the military could not be ruled out once and for all as a major contender for power within the Ottoman and later republican systems. But the vicissitudes of its history, the fact that another branch of the ruling class could adapt more readily to the changing needs of the state, and the peculiar aspect of the international politics of the period combined to keep the military from playing any significant role during most of the nineteenth century.

Eclipse of the Religious Establishment

The eclipse of a once preponderant branch of the ruling class was even more complete in the religious establishment. This fact resulted not just from the bureaucratization of the *ulema* or from the decline of the traditional religious scholarship. It also reflected the inability of men with a traditional religious education to comprehend and comment effectively on the new kinds of problems facing the empire.

Writing from the peculiar vantage point of a nineteenth-century religious scholar turned civil official, Ahmed Cevdet Paşa provides vivid insights into the meaning of these statements. Some of his most mordant passages deal with the corruption, nepotism, and faltering intellectual standards of the religious establishment as of the late eighteenth century.[52] He uses particularly acerbic terms to describe the increasing inability of the religious leaders to advise, as their predecessors had been expected to, on current affairs. He links this inability, in turn, to the changing character and increasing hopelessness of the problems—crushing military defeat, diplomatic helplessness, bankruptcy—then crowding in on the state. In the space of some fifteen years around the time of the Treaty of Küçük Kaynarca (1774) and the Russian annexation of the Crimea (1783), the religious elite seemed to go through a decline, Cevdet says, as if of one or two centuries.[53] This became particularly clear in the consultative assemblies then convoked with increasing frequency to deliberate on each new catastrophe. Never did the incapacity of the religious scholars emerge more dramatically than when a *kadı* of Istanbul turned to the grand vezir in an assembly held in 1784 and said:

We are obedient and subservient outwardly and inwardly to the wishes and commands of our Sovereign (*Padişah*), who is the Commander of the Faithful. It is impossible to obtain from us an explanation of why things have turned out as they have. . . . You are the absolute delegate of our Sovereign.

Deign [to tell us] what is the view of the Sovereign in this matter, and we shall say "we hear and we obey" (*sama'nâ wa ata'nâ*).[54]

Comparison of Cevdet's account with the less highly colored picture that Uriel Heyd paints suggests that Cevdet may have exaggerated the rate and extent of the religious leaders' loss of influence. Yet a crisis was indeed approaching for the religious establishment. In the early nineteenth century, as Heyd shows, religious leaders had still not entirely lost their voice in the making of major decisions. Some of them, in fact, played important roles in support of the reforms of that period. Even as they did so, however, they were working themselves into an impasse from which there would be no escape. For while they may have thought that the reforms would strengthen the empire in its character as an Islamic state, the ultimate impact of those measures was secularization. The beginning of overt legal reform with the Gülhane Decree of 1839 made this fact unmistakable.

Unable any longer to cling to the rationalization that the eternal validity and immutability of Islamic law were being maintained, even if compromises and violations occurred in matters of transitory detail, even the progressive *ulema* then began to abandon their alliance with the reformers.[55] On top of the problems already noted by Cevdet, this alienation and the negative reaction of reformist statesmen to it intensified the decline of the religious establishment and provoked a long series of attacks against it. These included efforts to divert the revenues from pious foundations on which the religious scholars depended,[56] and to deprive religious leaders of their traditional roles in local administration.[57] The attack on the pious foundations accelerated the decline of the religious colleges, while the simultaneous development of new secular educational institutions helped to provoke a "brain drain," as the better minds tended less and less to enter the higher religious schools at all.[58] Not until the reign of Abd ül-Hamid II would any political priority again be given to the promotion of an explicitly religious policy, and then in ways carefully tailored to emphasize the figure of the sultan-caliph, and not the religious establishment as such. The predictable result was further decline and the adhesion of elements of the *ulema* to the Young Turk Movement.[59] By then, the secularization of Ottoman society had progressed to the point of seriously undermining the specifically Islamic elements of the imperial tradition, thereby portending its collapse and reformulation.

Vicissitudes of the Palace Service

While the decline of the religious establishment was thus a kind of opposite to the rise of the scribal service, the palace service followed a course of development competitive with that of the scribal officials, though at odds with the broader political implications of the process of modernization. Indications of what was to come appeared as early as Selim III's "New Order," which was perceived at the time as entailing a reassertion of the power of the palace in relation to the Sublime Porte.[60] While that was a transitory phenomenon, the history of both the palace and the scribal service did pass a critical turning point with a series of reforms that Mahmud II undertook in the 1830s. The goal of these was not just to make the bureaucracy more effective, but specifically to abolish the grand vezirate, subdivide its powers, and centralize the administration to the highest possible degree in the hands of the sultan.

In a later chapter, we shall discuss the details of these changes as they relate to the scribal service, but they cannot be fully appreciated in that connection alone. For they also led to the consummation of the process already apparent in the eighteenth century whereby the old Privy Chamber of the palace school evolved into a sort of palace secretariat, and its head, the sword-bearer, into the director of the entire Inside Service. In the 1830s, this trend culminated in a series of reorganizations and changes of title, out of which the sword-bearer emerged as a marshal of the palace, or more exactly, marshal of the *Mabeyn* (*Mabeyn müşiri*), while one of his subordinates, the former confidential secretary (*sır kâtibi*) of the sultan, emerged as the first secretary of the palace secretariat (*Mabeyn baş kâtibi*). Mahmud intended this new organization to become the means through which he would not just communicate with, but would actively dominate, the rest of a government restructured to facilitate that end.[61]

Mahmud's death in 1839 and the fact that he was succeeded by three weaker sultans has kept later scholars from properly appreciating his intentions. Even during the three succeeding reigns, however, the secretariat continued to exist at the palace, along with a congeries of chamberlains, aides-de-camp, and eunuchs. The civil-bureaucratic dignitaries who dominated the affairs of state during that period never ceased to have reason to fear the opposition of those palace minions or the wrath of the sultan, when he gave vent to it. With the accession in 1876 of Abd ül-Hamid, determined and able to reassert the power of the sultanate, the palace secretariat served as an instrument ready at hand. In its new home at Yıldız Palace, the secretariat grew enormously in size and importance, becoming the hub of a political machine that Abd ül-Hamid built up as a means by which to neutralize and dominate the other branches of government.

Even then, the palace service still did not acquire full organizational coherence or distinctness. It never acquired its own hierarchy of ranks, such as characterized the other branches of the ruling class; nor did it have a single, distinctive name in Ottoman Turkish. But it, and above all the secretariat of the *Mabeyn*, acquired an unequivocally important place in the power equation of the empire. So much was this the case that the first objectives of the Young Turk leadership, when it came to power in 1908, included the dismantling of the mechanisms that Abd ül-Hamid had created for the exertion of control from the palace and the transformation of the palace secretariat into an instrument through which to control the sultan himself.[62]

From Scribal Service to Civil Bureaucracy

The Hamidian system reminds us that the scribal service, to which we now turn, did not dominate Ottoman political life uninterruptedly throughout the nineteenth century. As before, however, this was still the branch of government service that grew most dramatically and was most linked to constructive developments in imperial policy and administration. This fact relates generally to the previous pattern of growth in this branch of service, and particularly to the way in which the relatively "secularistic" and "state-oriented" character of the traditional scribal culture predisposed its exponents to take a leading role in reform and to acquire that knowledge of the world which members of the other services so lacked. The scribal officials of the late eighteenth century may have "lacked complete competence and full knowledge" of political and diplomatic affairs, again to quote Cevdet Paşa, but they "were still superior in these matters as compared with the other classes [that is, other branches of the ruling class]."[63]

As a result, the scribal service grew tremendously during the nineteenth century in size, complexity, and, at times, in power. We shall see this very clearly in the development of the Sublime Porte, but in fact, that is only one part of the process. Whatever modification may ultimately be required in the image of the efendi-turned-paşa for the eighteenth century, by the nineteenth century any such qualifications had largely vanished. Particularly during the period of weak sultans, statesmen of this type dominated the entire government and left an indelible imprint in the reforms (Tanzimat) after which this period is still commonly named. In the process, as the consolidation of the efendi-turned-paşa pattern implies, the domain of this branch of service enlarged considerably. By 1908, it also included nine or ten other ministries located outside the Porte.[64] The civil bureaucracy had expanded overseas through the growth of the consular and diplomatic services, and had institutionalized its role in the provinces by acquiring prime responsibility for the new provincial administration that the nineteenth-century reformers attempted to create. Thanks to this expansion in responsibilities, this branch of official service, which had consisted of a few score men in the early sixteenth century and some 1,000 to 1,500 at the end of the eighteenth, grew to the point that 50,000 to 100,000 were at least nominally affiliated with it during the reign of Abd ül-Hamid II (1876-1909).[65] The range of roles in which these men served had also proliferated beyond the once primary ones of secretary and bookkeeper, to include local-administrative, executive, legislative, judicial, and diplomatic functions.

As if in formal recognition of these changes, the scribal service also underwent fundamental transformations in corporate organization and status. It is about the time of the first series of these changes, concentrated in the 1830s, that it ceases to be appropriate to speak of the scribal service in the sense of the old "men of the pen" or *kalemiye*, a term that could also be translated "men of the offices" and hints at the once more or less exclusive association of these men with the central bureaus in Istanbul. From the 1830s on, we shall speak instead of the civil bureaucracy or *mülkiye*. No such change of nomenclature was ever formally decreed, it seems, nor did it ever become entirely systematic. The emergence of the term *mülkiye*, conveying associations with both landownership and sovereignty, was probably related to the acquisition by the scribal service of responsibility for local administration. Despite continuing inexactitude of usage, however, this became the new name for this branch of the bureaucracy in general and is only erroneously or imprecisely interpreted in any more restrictive sense.[66] In later chapters, we shall investigate in more detail the extent to which nineteenth-century changes justify the identification, which our translation of *mülkiye* conveys, with the civil bureaucracies or civil services of modern Western states.[67]

Pausing first to survey nineteenth-century developments in all branches of government service, we see that trends already in evidence before the beginning of the nineteenth century continued, in interaction with forces bearing on the empire from outside, to exert a decisive influence on the later course of change. This appears in the difficulty with which the military regained either effectiveness in its own field or an important place in the political balance of the empire, as well as in the way in which deliberate cultural change accelerated the decline of the religious establishment. A similar continuity also appears in the development of the palace service and in the continued growth of the scribal service and later civil bureaucracy. Thus, as the state moved from the era of traditionalism into that of culturally innovative reform, the momentum accumulated over the centuries in the development of the imperial "center" continued to be an important determinant in the further development of bureaucratic institutions.

Conclusion: The Developmental Cycles of the Ruling Class and the Political Periods of the Nineteenth Century

To study the evolution of the various branches of the Ottoman ruling class is to gain a new sense of the magnitude of the imperial governmental system, the intricacy of the developmental cycles that characterized it and its component elements, and the importance of long-term continuities, despite the profound changes associated with the beginnings of modernization.

To speak in terms of the comparison, evoked in the introduction of this chapter, between the life cycles of the state as a whole and of the individual branches of the ruling class, we note first that the imperial system displayed little or no internal differentiation during its period of emergence (c. 1300-1350). During the subsequent period of florescence, ending around 1600, the ruling class was dominated by the military-administrative and religious establishments, with distinct palace and scribal services only beginning to emerge. The prominence of the military-administrative and religious establishments in this period is explicable in terms of the strong orientation of imperial policy toward conquest, on the one hand, and toward the institutionalization and legitimation of the state and its administrative system, on the other.

The period of decline (c. 1600-1789) witnessed the decay of the religious and still more of the military-administrative establishments and the concomitant emergence of the palace and scribal services. The emergence of the palace service appears to have been linked to the movement of much of the apparatus of government to loci outside the palace and the consequent need for a secretariat to provide a link between the sultan and the new agencies. The rise of the scribal service, and within it particularly the chief scribe and his staff, seems to reflect a greater variety of factors. One, certainly, is the emergence of the new executive headquarters of the Sublime Porte, the most important product of the increasing differentiation of governmental institutions. Another factor, as the efendi-turned-paşa pattern makes clear, is the new opportunities for promotion created by the decline of the military-administrative establishment. Finally, and perhaps most important, there was the demand for new applications of the scribal culture in an age when the empire found itself less and less able to deal with outside powers from positions of strength and when the religious tradition was beginning to appear insufficient as a guide to a changing world.

Substantially the same developmental trends continued into the nineteenth-century era of reform, varying only slightly with the efforts at reform of the military. In a sense, however, the different services pursued their developmental trends at uneven rates. This is most noticeable in the case of the palace service and civil bureaucracy, the former making gains under strong sultans and the latter under weak, at least down to the time when demands for the broadening of political participation began to produce a restructuring of the traditional polity.

The competitive character of these trends produced a series of shifts in the political balance, allowing us to define distinct political periods within the era of reform: an initial period of strong sultans, spanning the reigns of Selim III (1789-1807) and Mahmud II (1808-1839); a period of civil-bureaucratic hegemony and political imbalance, the Tanzimat (1839-1871); a period of efforts to restore political balance either through the creation of a constitutional system or, more effectively in the short run, through the reassertion of the sultanate (1871-1908); and finally a short-lived and not entirely successful return to constitutionalism (1908-1922).

To follow the development of the Sublime Porte and the transformation from scribal service to civil bureaucracy in the era of reform, we shall now look more closely at the state of those institutions on the eve of reform and then, in subsequent chapters, trace them through the successive political periods that we have just defined.

THE IMPACT OF IMPERIAL DECLINE ON THE EMERGENT SCRIBAL SERVICE: THE SUBLIME PORTE AND ITS OFFICIALS ON THE EVE OF REFORM

Mansıb ve caha heveskâr olma
　Taleb-i izzet için har olma
Ehl-i mansıbda bulunmaz rahat
　Hal-i bi-azildedir emniyet
Zillet-i azline değmez nasbı
　Sarfına ser-be-ser olmaz gasbı

Yearn not for office or for high estate,
　Demean thee not by seeking to be great.
Those in high places know not of repose;
　Peace bides not where sultan may depose.
Appointment is not worth dismissal's pain;
　Oppression pays not back the price again.
Nabi, *Hayriye*[1]

In what has been said thus far about the development of the scribal service of the traditional empire, there are two facts of particular significance. The first is the importance, with reference not just to preexisting tradition, but also to later efforts at reform, of the formulation of the imperial cultural tradition associated with this branch of the ruling class. The other is the extensive growth of the scribal service in both size and importance, even during a period of overall imperial decline. What implications did this decline of the imperial system have for the emergence of the scribal service? And how did decline affect the cultural vitality of the scribes or their readiness to lead, or serve in, movements of reform?

69

These are the questions that this chapter addresses. The best way to answer them is to present an overview, which will also serve as the basis for discussion in subsequent chapters of the changes which followed later, of the Sublime Porte on the eve of the nineteenth-century reform era. We may begin by discussing the patterns of organization and procedure found at the Porte at that time, and then the social state of the scribal personnel who served there. Throughout, we shall emphasize the offices under the *reis ül-küttab* or chief scribe as those which had attained the most advanced state of organization and most fully represented the scribal tradition. Examination of these organizational, procedural, and social patterns will throw additional light on the developmental processes that shaped the scribal service and on the replication within it of the models of social organization presented in Chapter One. In conclusion, to answer the fundamental questions posed above, we shall reexamine the efendi-turned-paşa pattern against the backdrop offered by the general state of the administrative system as of the end of the eighteenth century.

Patterns of Organization and Procedure at the Sublime Porte on the Eve of Reform

Figure III-1 presents the elements that composed the Sublime Porte at the end of the eighteenth century: the grand vezir, his household, his *divan*, and the departments headed by the *çavuş başı* or chief bailiff, the *kâhya bey* or steward, and the *reis ül-küttab* or chief scribe. The one omission is the official historiographer (*vakanüvis*), who was not always of scribal background, and who had no known staff. For reference, the figure also includes the two major scribal agencies located elsewhere in Istanbul, the Treasury (*Bab-ı Defterî*) and the Land Registry Office (*Defter Emaneti*). For purposes of discussion, we shall leave aside those two agencies, as well as the grand-vezirial household, to the extent that it can be distinguished from the other components of the Porte. We shall concentrate first on surveying the general organizational aspect of the other elements of the Porte, as shown in the figure. Then we shall go on to examine more closely the organizational patterns found inside the offices of the chief scribe and, finally, to analyze patterns of procedure characteristic both of those offices and of the Divans of the grand vezir.

Since it is impossible, given the patrimonial discretionalism of the system, to reduce all aspects of its organization or functioning to a consistent system, the picture which we present will in some parts be idealized. It will nonetheless serve to bring out many distinctive traits of the scribal tradition, and thus of the legacy of the traditional scribal service to the reforming statesmen of the later civil bureaucracy.

FIGURE III-1. ORGANIZATION OF THE SUBLIME PORTE, c. 1789

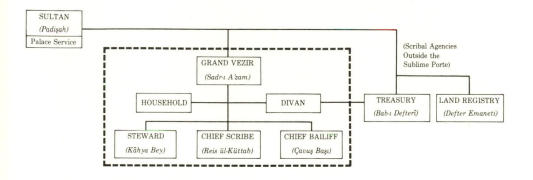

■ ■ ■ ■ Enclosed Organizations are part of Sublime Porte

The Organizational Components of the Sublime Porte

At the head of the organization shown in Figure III-1, but with powers extending far beyond the Porte, was the grand vezir. Traditionally styled the "absolute delegate" (*vekil-i mutlak*) of the sultan,[2] the grand vezir could be described in one sense as exercising as much of the sultan's power as the latter would grant to him. In the period considered here, the grand vezir was the head of both the scribal service and the military establishment.[3] In wartime, he often assumed the role of commander-in-chief (*serdar-ı ekrem*). After the decline of the imperial Divan at the palace and the growth in importance of his own *divan* at the Porte, the grand vezir also served increasingly as the chief functionary in the dispensation of justice, with senior judges from the religious establishment sitting in his council to assist him in this purpose. He had ultimate responsibility for the administration of the capital city and, to the extent that the provinces in fact remained under central control, for provincial administration. In making or approving appointments, finally, his powers extended into all branches of the ruling class.[4]

In terms of the business they discharged, the *divans* of the Porte were in some ways the most important adjuncts of the grand vezirs. While there had historically been several types of these, meeting at different times for various purposes and with different membership, by the late eighteenth century, the grand-vezirial *divans* had come to be of two main types. First, and most directly in continuity with the original afternoon *divan* (*ikindi divanı*), there was a sort of routine *divan* that met on a regular basis, chiefly to serve as a high court of justice. In addition, as the eighteenth century wore on, there began to be more and more extraordinary consultative assemblies (*müşavere*, *meşveret*) convoked to deal with the continuing crises with which the state found itself threatened. These were variable in both membership and place of meeting, including senior officials of all types even if out of office, but they appear normally to have been presided over by the grand vezir. In meetings of this latter type lie the immediate ancestors of the conciliar bodies that proliferated so remarkably during the Tanzimat.[5]

Turning to the three departments subordinate to the grand vezir, we recall that these differed among themselves in that two of them, those of the chief bailiff and the steward, were not yet fully integrated into the scribal service. The internal organization of these two departments was as yet not very clear, either. These agencies provide insights into the developmental processes that shaped the Sublime Porte, however, and may profitably be considered more closely before we go on to the offices of the chief scribe.

The chief bailiff and his men had originally been functionaries of the palace, where they served as heralds and messengers in a variety of circumstances, as bailiffs in meetings of the imperial Divan that served for the disposition of judicial cases, and as agents for the execution of the sentences rendered there. With the transfer of such judicial responsibilities from the old imperial Divan at the palace to the *divan* of the grand vezir at the Porte, the *çavuşes* did not just move from the palace to the Porte. They also began to undergo a change of role, through which they increasingly took on the complexion of the scribal service. At the end of the eighteenth century, this transformation was still incomplete, but the chief bailiff had begun to take over part of the written business related to selection and preparation of cases to be decided in the grand-vezirial *divan*. In this connection, two definitely scribal officials long associated with the imperial Divan, the *tezkereci*s or memorandum officers, whose duty it was to read the petitions submitted to the Divan, appear to have become parts of the chief bailiff's entourage at the Porte.[6] In the nineteenth century, the metamorphosis of the chief bailiff and his staff seems to have culminated in the emergence of a Ministry of Justice separate from the Porte, although in fact the processes that shaped that ministry were complex and are still little known.

The position of the *kâhya bey* or steward was also the product of an unusual evolution, though in a different sense. He had begun as a purely domestic functionary, managing the grand vezir's household and lacking any official character. At the Sublime Porte, he became an official of high status, serving the grand vezir as a kind of deputy, though he was not to be confused with the *kaymakam* or lieutenant appointed during the grand vezir's absences from the capital in wartime. The responsibilities of the steward are usually described as having to do with internal and military affairs. Beyond this, sources on the eighteenth century disagree as to the details of his role or the roster of officials who came under him. Gibb and Bowen list as his subordinates only the *mektubî* or corresponding secretary of the grand vezir, whom we shall follow other writers in placing under the chief scribe; the *kâhya kâtibi* or secretary to the steward; the master of ceremonies (*teşrifatî*); and one or two others. Joseph von Hammer at the turn of the nineteenth century gave a much longer and rather different list, including numbers of functionaries that Gibb and Bowen list only as parts of the grand vezir's domestic staff, as well as the representatives at the Porte of various groups in other parts of the ruling class, especially in the palace service and the military. The disparity clearly evokes an evolutionary process still short of completion. In the nineteenth century, the steward emerged as a minister of the interior. At the end of the eighteenth century, the most important scribal element in the retinue of the steward would have been the Office of the Secretary to the Steward, who had charge of some thirty scribes.[7]

Thanks to the long history of his post and its long-term rise in importance, the situation of the chief scribe is in many ways clearer. In addition to his traditional role as chief of the Office of the Imperial Divan, he figured at the Porte as first secretary to the grand vezir, with responsibility for preparation of the reports and proposals that the latter submitted daily to the palace. While the chief scribe was also acquiring responsibility for the diplomatic business of the empire, and thus for the most sensitive of the ministerial portfolios that would be created in the 1830s, it is important to note that he was not becoming solely or merely a specialist in diplomatic affairs. This is apparent from his prominence in terms of what Itzkowitz has referred to as the efendi-turned-paşa pattern of mobility, as well as from the broad-ranging functions that still fell under the chief scribe's purview.[8]

The best way to appreciate the variety of these functions is to look at the offices under the chief scribe's supervision. Figure III-2 is a graphic portrayal of these, and also includes, for purposes of subsequent discussion, an attempt at reconstruction of the personnel categories found within each.

First in order of emergence among the agencies under the chief scribe was the Office of the Imperial Divan (*Divan-ı Hümayun Kalemi*), under the direction of an official known as the *beylikçi*. By the eighteenth century, this office had been divided into three sections, also confusingly designated as *kalem*. Of these, the first, known as the *Beylik* Section, or sometimes—to make things more confusing—as the Divan Office, had in fact inherited many of the most important functions of the sixteenth-century scribes of the imperial Divan. These included the registration of laws, of provisions pertaining to the legal status of the non-Muslim communities within the empire, and of treaties made with and capitulatory privileges granted to foreign governments, as well as the verification of subsequent measures to see that they conformed to the terms of these commitments.[9]

The other two sections of the Office of the Imperial Divan, the *Tahvil* and *Rüus* Sections, both also under the control of the *beylikçi* but each possessing a supervisory official of its own with the title of purse-bearer (*kisedar*), had to do with the processing of records on appointments of different sorts and took their names from aspects of the procedures used for that purpose. The essential difference in their functions was that the *Tahvil*, also known as *Nişan* or *Kise*, Section issued the brevets of assignment (*tahvil tezkeresi*) required to assign incomes from ben-

FIGURE III-2. THE CHIEF SCRIBE AND HIS STAFF, c. 1789

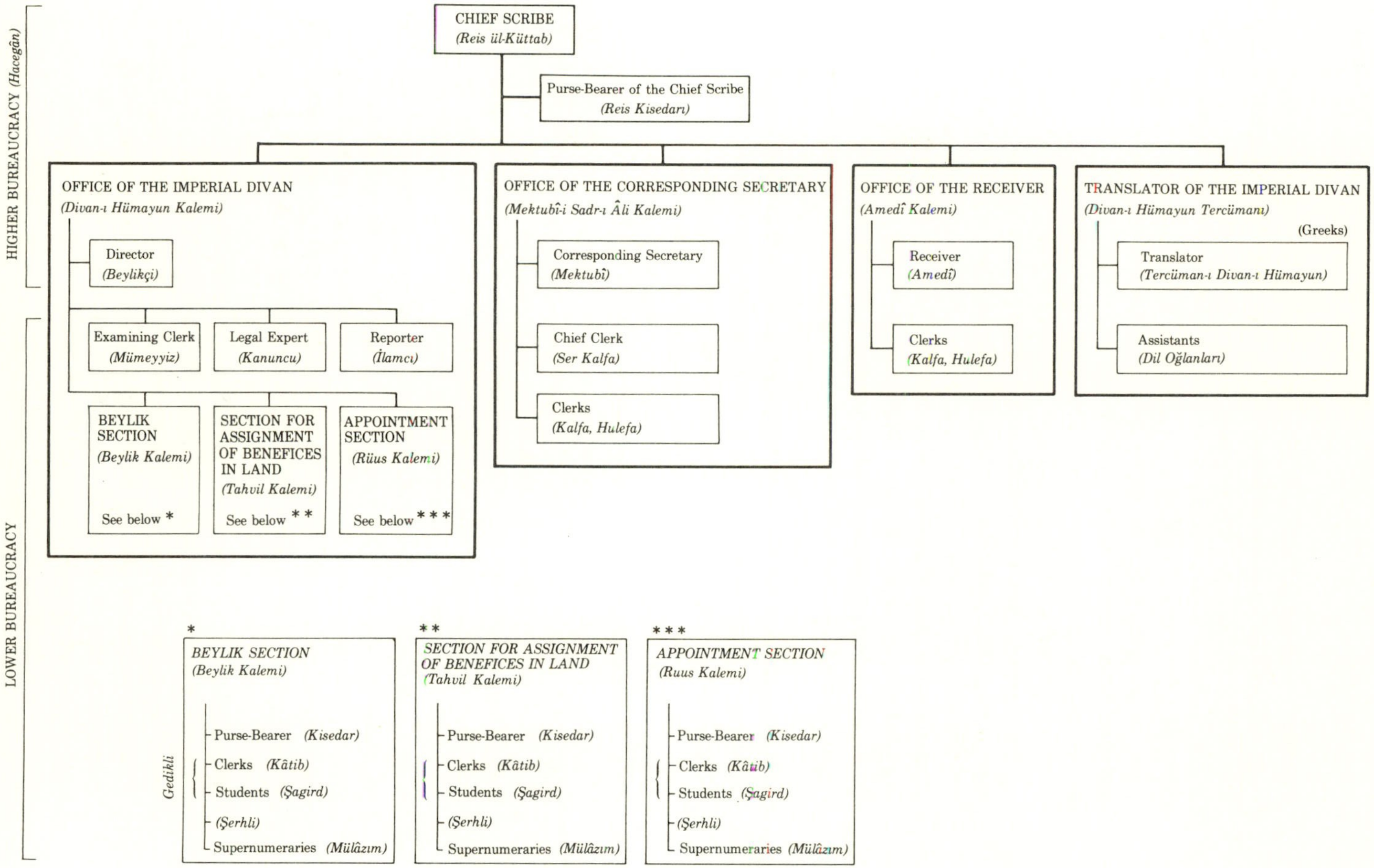

LOWER BUREAUCRACY | HIGHER BUREAUCRACY (Hacegân)

CHIEF SCRIBE (Reis ül-Küttab)

Purse-Bearer of the Chief Scribe (Reis Kisedarı)

OFFICE OF THE IMPERIAL DIVAN (Divan-ı Hümayun Kalemi)
- Director (Beylikçi)
- Examining Clerk (Mümeyyiz)
- BEYLIK SECTION (Beylik Kalemi) — See below *
- Legal Expert (Kanuncu)
- SECTION FOR ASSIGNMENT OF BENEFICES IN LAND (Tahvil Kalemi) — See below **
- Reporter (İlamcı)
- APPOINTMENT SECTION (Rüus Kalemi) — See below ***

OFFICE OF THE CORRESPONDING SECRETARY (Mektubî-i Sadr-ı Âlî Kalemi)
- Corresponding Secretary (Mektubî)
- Chief Clerk (Ser Kalfa)
- Clerks (Kalfa, Hulefa)

OFFICE OF THE RECEIVER (Amedî Kalemi)
- Receiver (Amedî)
- Clerks (Kalfa, Hulefa)

TRANSLATOR OF THE IMPERIAL DIVAN (Divan-ı Hümayun Tercümanı)
- Translator (Tercüman-ı Divan-ı Hümayun)
- Assistants (Dil Oğlanları) (Greeks)

Gedikli

* BEYLIK SECTION (Beylik Kalemi)
- Purse-Bearer (Kisedar)
- Clerks (Kâtib)
- Students (Şagird)
- (Serhli)
- Supernumeraries (Mülâzım)

** SECTION FOR ASSIGNMENT OF BENEFICES IN LAND (Tahvil Kalemi)
- Purse-Bearer (Kisedar)
- Clerks (Kâtib)
- Students (Şagird)
- (Serhli)
- Supernumeraries (Mülâzım)

*** APPOINTMENT SECTION (Rüus Kalemi)
- Purse-Bearer (Kisedar)
- Clerks (Kâtib)
- Students (Şagird)
- (Serhli)
- Supernumeraries (Mülâzım)

efices in land (*tımar*, *zeamet*, *has*) to all members of the ruling class whose positions entitled them to compensation in that form. Hammer, in fact, refers to this as the section for "feudal affairs" (*Lehenssachen*).[10] To avoid any risk of false analogy with European feudalism, we shall translate the Ottoman name as the Section for Assignment of Benefices in Land, or the Assignment Section.[11]

The *Rüus* Section, in contrast, had chiefly to do with issuing brevets of a different type, called *rüus*, used for making appointments that carried compensation in other forms. We shall accordingly call it simply the Appointment Section. Brevets of the same kind were also used to assign pensions to needy individuals, either out of the revenues of certain pious foundations, or from the farms of certain customs duties.[12] Although the *Rüus* Section was a scribal agency, its functions are perhaps best known in connection with the religious scholars. Students who had completed their religious studies would, upon successful passage of a special *rüus* examination, receive brevets from this office for appointment to positions in the religious establishment.[13] This fact is a good indicator of the volume of patronage under the control of the grand vezir.

The distinction between these two sections on the basis of the compensation systems associated with the types of appointments they processed was perhaps not thoroughly systematic,[14] and not enough is yet known about the history of the two to reveal how they emerged. To the extent that it was controlled from the center, the assignment of benefices in land was originally a responsibility of the *nişancı* or affixer of the cipher. This responsibility must have entailed duties for both his major subordinates, the chief scribe and the keeper of the registers (*defter emini*), a title referring specifically to cadastral registers and thus to the basic records of the system of benefices in land.[15] Here, as in so many other details, the later spatial and organizational separation of these three officials appears to have redounded to the benefit of the chief scribe. This fact presumably reflects both the importance of this kind of patronage to the grand vezir and a tightening of central control in the period of decline over the assignment of the benefices.[16]

That the emergence of the *Rüus* and *Tahvil* Offices is linked to a growth in the volume or importance of the business they performed is also apparent from changes over time in the applications of those two terms. At the height of the empire, they referred simply to certain types of records produced by the Office of the Imperial Divan, the term *rüus* designating a daybook in which appointments, without differentiation as to type of compensation, were only the most frequent of a variety of types of entries.[17] With time, the applications of the terms *rüus* and *tahvil* seem to have become more specific and more clearly differentiated, and specialized bureaus appear to have emerged to perform the functions that those terms designated. Ultimately, the decline of the system of benefices in land seems to have limited the range of application of the term *tahvil*; but as the bureaucracy grew in size, the associations of the word *rüus* continued to proliferate, with the result that the term almost survived into the vocabulary of modern Turkish.

By the end of the eighteenth century, then, there were three distinct sections in the Office of the Imperial Divan, and they contained somewhere between 90 and 150 men. Of these, to judge from the one itemized account, two-thirds served in the *Beylik* Section, and the remainder were divided evenly between Benefice Assignments and Appointments.[18]

Outside the Office of the Imperial Divan, probably the first position to become linked with the chief scribe was that of the translator of the imperial Divan (*Divan-ı hümayun tercümanı*). Originally, these translators, too, presumably served under the Divan at the palace, though not as subordinates of the chief scribe.[19] With the rise of the Sublime Porte and the eclipse of the palace Divan by that of the grand vezir, the translators, like the other officers discussed here, moved to the new executive center. There, as the chief scribe became increasingly the man in charge of foreign affairs, the translators began to be regarded as part of his suite. Also at the Porte, this translatorship, previously held by foreign-born converts to Islam, became a virtual monopoly of a coterie of Istanbul Greek families who retained their hold from the mid-seventeenth century until 1821.[20]

At the end of the eighteenth century, the translator of the imperial Divan was responsible for translating all documents submitted to the Porte in foreign languages if not accompanied by translations. In formal audiences, he translated the addresses of European ministers to the sultan or grand vezir. In working sessions, he translated the statements of the chief scribe, the foreign diplomats answering through their embassy translators.

The translator of the Divan also prepared written accounts of these meetings. He was the only Ottoman official to pay formal calls on European diplomats. In sum, he was the most important official after the chief scribe in the conduct of foreign affairs. Given his social marginality to the bulk of the ruling class, this could be a fact of some inconvenience both to the state and to him and his assistants, of which there were eight as of 1764.[21]

Next in order of emergence was the bureau of the *mektubî* or *mektupçu*, the corresponding secretary of the grand vezir, whose full Ottoman title was accordingly *Mektubî-i Sadr-ı Âli*. While various authorities disagree as to whether his formal hierarchical attachment was to the chief scribe or the steward, in practical terms he worked for the grand vezir as a sort of personal secretary, handling incoming and outgoing correspondence. Since the Office of the Corresponding Secretary was strongly linked in terms of promotion patterns to the other offices under the chief scribe and to the position of chief scribe itself, it seems logical to interpret the hierarchical subordination of the office as reflecting those links. We may also hypothesize that this office evolved out of the Office of the Imperial Divan at some point in the late seventeenth or eighteenth century. By the end of the eighteenth, it included about thirty scribes.[22]

Newest of the bureaus of the chief scribe, though again its functions had probably been performed previously within the Office of the Imperial Divan, was the office of the *amedî*, or *amedci*, a curious title that we may render as "receiver." The receiver, the emergence of whose bureau İnalcık dates to about 1777, was a personal secretary to the chief scribe, and his office appears in some accounts as a fourth section of the Office of the Imperial Divan. Noting receipt of fees due the chief scribe from newly invested holders of benefices in land—the duty from which he acquired his name—was but a part of his role. More importantly, he assisted the chief scribe in his written business, including preparation of the documents that the grand vezir submitted to the palace and the correspondence of the grand vezir with foreign governments. The receiver also attended the chief scribe in meetings with foreign diplomats and was responsible for the correspondence of the chief scribe with the foreign diplomatic and consular officials within the empire. At the time of his presumed emergence, then, the receiver's functions also appear particularly linked to foreign affairs. His was a small but important office, with only five to ten scribes at the time here under survey.[23]

On the eve of the nineteenth-century reform period, the organizational pattern presented by the offices of the Sublime Porte thus reflected both the processes of their development and the variety and magnitude of the powers concentrated in the hands of the grand vezir. In the metamorphosis of the chief bailiff from an official of the palace to one of the scribal service, the emergence of the steward from a domestic function under the grand vezir to one of the most powerful offices of state, the apparent differentiation of a series of offices out of that of the imperial Divan, or the accretion of meanings around terms such as *rüus* and *tahvil*, we witness distinct phases of the process, described in the last chapter, that brought the traditional scribal service to the fore within the ruling class. This process displays tendencies at once toward differentiation and specialization, as in the incipient evolution of the bureau chiefships into ministerial portfolios, and toward the continued accumulation of miscellaneous functions, as in the heterogeneous attributions of those same figures or in the generalism implicit in the efendi-turned-paşa pattern. This contrast points to the continuing preponderance of the patrimonial tradition, and to the opposition between its conception of public function as discretional within traditional limits and the more characteristically modern demand for rational definition of jurisdictional lines. The emergence of the various clerical and accounting offices shows that tendencies toward specialization, differentiation, and systematization were operative even within the traditional state.[24] Patrimonialism meant that such tendencies could not be predominant.

Organizational Patterns within the Offices of the Chief Scribe

A survey of organizational traits within the offices of the chief scribe makes this point even clearer. Here, too, the lack of concern for rational systematization means that any attempt to reduce the recorded patterns to a clearcut order has to contend with heterogeneous categorizations, overlapping and conflicting schematizations, and gaps in the data. Significantly, this is nowhere more true than in the oldest part of the system, the Office of the Imperial Divan.

The problems of explaining the organizational patterns are greatest among the scribes and apprentice scribes of that office, thus among those who fell below the level of supervisory officials and bureau chiefs and appear in Figure III-2 as the lowest four categories. The confusion is apparent from the start in the fact that the "scribes" (*kâtib*) and "student scribes" (*şagird*) now appear not as the lowest personnel categories, but as the third and fourth up from the bottom. In the sixteenth century, these two would presumably have been the only categories required for general description of the lower scribal personnel. In terms of the practicalities of entry into the scribal service, they still should have been so. But somehow, with the evolution of the office, the terms seem to have acquired new applications no longer corresponding to their obvious meanings.

This inference gains in probability from the inclusion of both "scribes" and "student scribes" in the category of *gediklis*, which, the sources make fairly clear, must be understood somehow in opposition to the next lower category of the *şerhlis*. Despite the efforts of several recent scholars to produce an explanation,[25] the nature of this distinction remains unclear. The best inference seems to be that the application of these terms reflects two successive attempts made in the period of decline to organize the personnel of this office, and that the organization had to do with regulating the number of officials in each of the two categories, with providing specific forms of compensation for members of each category, and perhaps with maintaining certain differentiations in their obligations.

An eighteenth-century source indicates that the category of *gediklis* (holder of *gediks*) came into being first, dating back at least to the reign of Mustafa II (1695-1703), and that the category of *şerhlis* (holders of *şerhs*) was added later "at the time of the campaigns" (*seferler vukuunda*). In one sense, what the creation of the *gediks* meant may be inferred from the basic meaning of the word: "notch" or "breach," whence "place" in an organization or even "privilege." That the scribal *gediks* also reflected an attempt to regulate the number of scribes is clear from the references to them in the sources as being of specific numbers,[26] a fact recalling the way in which the concept of *gedik* was coming into use in the guilds about the same time.[27]

In the case of the scribal officials of departments in which the *gedik* system was applied, the "privilege" meant, first, the acknowledgment of a right to a "place" as one of a fixed number of clerks and apprentices of the office. The "place," in turn, seems to have been at least partly defined in terms of compensation systems. For with the decline of the ability of the Treasury to pay the salaries that scribes of the central offices had once enjoyed,[28] and with the consequent increase in reliance on prebendal forms of compensation, many incomes from benefices in land, which were then coming increasingly under central control and being diverted to new kinds of beneficiaries because of these very pressures, were assigned to the offices for which the *gedik* system is mentioned. Not by chance, the Offices of the Imperial Divan and Land Registry (*Defter Emaneti*), both of which traditionally had important roles in the assignment of these benefices, appear to have been the only scribal agencies successful in defending their economic interests through the acquisition of such incomes.[29]

In contrast to the *gediklis*, the *şerhlis* (holders of *şerhs*) represented a later addition to the "organization table," apparently made by assigning additional benefice incomes to the same offices. The term *şerh*, usually meaning something like "explanation," "commentary," or "gloss," by itself conveys little more than an allusion to some feature of the records kept on these men.[30] Yet there are hints that their status may have differed from that of the *gedik* holders in ways such as their obligations to go on campaign,[31] or even in terms of whether they really served in the offices to which they were attached, or elsewhere, the link to the office in which they were *şerhli* perhaps pertaining solely to administration of the benefice income.[32] In the present state of the documentation, it is useless to speculate further about two terms that will require little attention beyond this point. It is enough to conclude that while the *gedik* system seems to have represented one attempt to fix the "organization table" of the office and provide for the compensation of its personnel, the system of *şerhs* represented a subsequent increment, analogous in character, but entailing some differences in the roles or statuses of the men in the two categories.

The *mülâzıms*, finally, are probably best understood as a kind of residual personnel category, holding neither *gedik* nor *şerh*, and thus forming the bottom of the scribal heap. In the nineteenth century, the term *mülâzım* normally meant "supernumerary" or "apprentice" and tended in that sense to supplant the terms *şagird* and *çırak* as previously applied to student clerks. For the eighteenth century, the situation is not so clear. Hammer and d'Ohsson do not acknowledge the term *mülâzım* at all, and documentary sources that do apply it to the Office of the Imperial Divan do so in a hopelessly confused way that makes it impossible to distinguish this term clearly from the others we have already discussed. In view of the contrast with the much clearer and more specific sense of *mülâzım* in the following century, it seems reasonable to hypothesize that the term was just coming into use as a designation for a category of scribal personnel, and that it referred to persons who were not provided for through the systems of *gedik* and *şerh*. The *mülâzım*s would thus have been aspirants both in professional terms, as student clerks, and in economic terms, as nonrecipients of benefice incomes. Eighteenth-century documentary references support this hypothesis by referring to the eligibility of the *mülâzım*s to be assigned benefice incomes when scribal officials who had previously received the incomes died without heirs.[33] The presence in the offices of a group of aspirants of this kind is surely one indication of the pressures that the decline of the productive sectors of the economy brought to bear on any attempts, such as the systems of *gedik* and *şerh*, to fix the size of bureaucratic cadres.

By the eve of reform, then, the lowest levels in the Office of the Imperial Divan displayed a heterogeneous set of organizational categories, reflecting successive but uncoordinated and incomplete attempts at the organization of the clerical staff. The terms "student" and "scribe" appear to have become fossilized at the historical core of the office in ways to which the obvious meanings of these terms may have been only marginally relevant. The distinction of *gedik* and *şerh* implies deliberate efforts at organization, but in a sense chiefly apparent in terms of compensation systems. The term *mülâzım* suggests, finally, a continued growth of the office, only incompletely and reluctantly registered as yet in formal organizational terms. Elements of a hierarchical order are implicit in the opposition of "student" and "secretary," and perhaps in that of *şerhli* and *gedikli*, but there is no overall hierarchical articulation, at least none apparent in these categories. Similarly, the real duties of the scribes are, if anything, masked by the terms applied to them. At the lower levels in this oldest of the offices under the chief scribe, fragmentary attempts at systematization, processes of accretion over time, and, in the linkage of the *gedik*s and *şerh*s to the system of benefices in land, the effects of imperial decline appear as the paramount influences on the evolution of organizational patterns.

At the level of supervisory officials of this office, meanwhile, organizational terms begin to reflect the actual duties of the officials more clearly, but within the limits of a significant pattern. At the head of each of the three sections of the Office of the Imperial Divan, and again as a sort of assistant to the chief scribe, came officials known as *kisedar* (purse-bearer), whose duties included filing documents in sacks (*torba*, also *kise*) and collecting the fees charged for the issue of official documents. Some writers attribute the title "purse-bearer" to one of these functions; some, to the other. In addition, the staff of the *beylikçi* also included three other supervisory officials. One of these was the *mümeyyiz* or examining clerk, who scrutinized the documents drafted in the office for correctness of official style and conformity to what Hammer called the "spirit of the constitution." In addition, there was the *kanuncu* or expert on the laws promulgated by the state, who checked each measure for its conformity to those laws, and an *ilamcı* or reporter, who prepared reports on difficult or doubtful subjects as needed.[34] None of these officials appears to have existed in the sixteenth century, and there would hardly have been any need for the *kanuncu* or legal expert before the scribes moved from the palace to the Porte and were separated from their quondam chief, the affixer of the cipher (*nişancı*), in his day the supreme authority in that very field.

In contrast to the confusing organizational patterns apparent among officials at the lower levels in the Office of the Imperial Divan, the duties of the supervisors exhibit a tendency to define official functions in terms of aspects of the processes by which documents were produced. Looking on to the clerks of the other offices under the chief scribe, and then to the bureau chiefs, we encounter the same pattern.

Being smaller and much newer than the Office of the Imperial Divan, the offices of the corresponding secretary (*mektubî*) of the grand vezir and the receiver (*amedî*) should be easier to account for. In fact, however, it is difficult to find information that can be assumed with certainty to depict the state of these offices before the beginnings of reform. The Office of the Corresponding Secretary included a "chief assistant" (*ser kalfa*, *baş kalfa*), a number of clerks usually known in this as in most other offices as *hulefa* (from the plural of the Arabic *khalîfa*, the singular being pronounced "kalfa" in Turkish in this case, as also in the application of the same term in the guilds and in other occupational settings). Significantly, a document of 1797 on the reform of the office identifies the functions of these men only in terms of long-acknowledged aspects of the document-producing process: the making of rough drafts (*tesvid*), of summaries or abstracts (*hulâsa*), and of fair copies (*tebeyyuz*). A document of the same date on the reform of the Office of the Receiver refers to the business treated there only in terms of its confidentiality. Both these offices were, however, small and select in the sense that only persons trained elsewhere—as well, predictably, as well-qualified sons of *vezirs* and scribal officials—were to be appointed to them. This suggests that there was already in this period something more or less approaching a hierarchical ordering of scribal bureaus, with those of the corresponding secretary and the receiver serving the ambitious, as they certainly did later, as way stations on the path to high office.[35] The last of the subordinates of the chief scribe, the translator of the imperial Divan and his assistants, stood outside this pattern, being distinct from the bulk of the ruling class in ethnocultural terms, and had their own *cursus honorum*.

Moving on from the lower scribal personnel and their supervisors to the higher realm of the bureau chiefs, designated by the rank-title of *hacegân*, we again encounter a tendency to define official positions in terms of processes of document production. The term *mektubî*, for example, comes from *mektub*, normally used to refer to "letters" in the sense of written correspondence, whence our translation as corresponding secretary. The term *amedî*, from the Persian verb "to come," reportedly derives from the fact that the receiver wrote the term *amed* ("arrived") in the appropriate registers opposite the names of newly invested holders of benefices in land to indicate receipt of the fees they owed the chief scribe.[36] The term *beylikçi* alone is more obscure—in fact, untranslatable. Some authorities derive it from the word *bey*, and thus see it as having to do with affairs of state as exercises of sovereignty (*beylik*).[37] Probably the more widely accepted explanation traces the title of this official to the word *bitik*, which, though archaic in Ottoman Turkish by this time, meant a written document or inscription, and from which a derived form *bitikçi* ("scribe") is known.[38] Only the title of the *reis ül-küttab* lacks such reference to the phases of document production. He is designated rather in hierarchical terms: the "chief of the scribes."

In sum, then, the patterns of formal organization found in the traditional offices under the chief scribe reflect a variety of developmental processes. Even within the patrimonial system, episodic attempts at systematization obviously could occur. Where they did, they often reflected the way in which the growth in the volume or importance of a given kind of business would lead to the creation of a separate, specialized bureau for precisely that purpose. Alternatively, attempts to cope with personnel problems could give rise to such efforts, as seems to have been the case in the creation of the systems of *gediklis* and *şerhlis*. In addition, processes of differentiation and specialization could create needs for the replication in new settings of official functions—purse-bearers, legal experts—previously performed by perhaps a single individual. Obviously, though, the desire for system could not govern overall in an organizational complex so attuned to reliance on custom and discretionalism in the use of power.

Where efforts at differentiation and systematization did occur, they were typically restricted by a tendency to conceive of official functions only in terms of the internal document-producing processes of the bureaucracy. Indeed, conceptualizations of this kind characterized not only bureaus, such as those for appointments (*rüus*) and benefice assignment (*tahvil*), whose duties were relatively specialized, but also other offices or positions that handled a wide diversity of matters. At times, as in the case of the *beylikçi* or the receiver, the resulting designations necessarily identified the bureau or position only obscurely or incompletely, with the result that direct translation either is impossible, or gives little idea of the responsibilities that went with the title. In the craftsman-like emphasis on document-producing processes, and also in personnel designations such as *şagird* (student), the essentially synonymous *mülâzım* (supernumerary), *kalfa* and its plural *hulefa* (here, clerk), or—we shall argue—even *hacegân* (bureau chiefs), we also begin to notice signs of guild-like traits.

Patterns of Procedure

The procedural patterns of the offices throw light on the way these organizational traits related to the day-to-day operations of the Porte, and begin to show, too, how they were linked to the social realities of scribal life in the late prereform period. We may demonstrate this point by focusing on procedural patterns first in the scribal offices and then in the *divan*s of the grand vezir.

Descriptions of the way the offices operated obviously differ in detail, depending on the specific office in question or the task referred to; yet they do imply an overall pattern. Such descriptions usually deal almost exclusively with the complicated procedures by which documents, before they could be issued, were supposed to pass up through the official hierarchy, being approved at numerous echelons. In the Office of the Imperial Divan, for example, a rough draft would first be prepared by an official of competence and status appropriate for the matter in question. This might mean one of the clerks of the office; or it might mean the *beylikçi* or the chief scribe himself. At whatever level the document originated, it would then pass to higher echelons for approval.

A document drafted by one of the clerks would pass, as necessary, to the reporter (*ilamcı*) and legal expert (*kanuncu*), in any case to the examining clerk (*mümeyyiz*), who would edit it for style, content, and conformity to other measures in force, before passing it on to the *beylikçi* and the chief scribe. The purse-bearer (*kisedar*) perhaps, and certainly the examining clerk, *beylikçi*, and chief scribe would each review the document and signify his approval by writing a conventional term of approbation on the draft. Then, depending on the importance of its subject, the document would either receive approval in the form of an order for execution (*buyuruldu*) from the grand vezir, or it would be referred to the palace in a "summary" version (*telhis*) to receive the commands of the sultan. Once the matter received approval, a fair copy would be prepared and sent to the *nişancı*, whose role of affixing the cipher had by this period become a perfunctory but still requisite formality. Preservation of any drafts or register entries that the office retained, perhaps also the issue of the final fair copy, and certainly the collection of any fees due for its issue were then the responsibility of the purse-bearer (*kisedar*).

Variations of detail would enter into this picture for different types of documents or different offices. Still, conception of official procedure in such terms was typical not only at the Porte, but also in other scribal departments. One contemporary description of how business was done in financial offices, for example, gives only an account of how documents were prepared and issued; this runs to twenty-two stages.[39]

The conception of scribal procedures in terms such as these reinforces the implications, already noted in formal organizational patterns, that the Ottomans conceived of their scribal service above all as a mechanism for the production of documents according to prescribed types. Such a view follows naturally from the original role of the scribes as secretaries to the imperial Divan and is practically a premise of the study of the diplomatics of any traditional state.[40] Document production was the job of the scribes, and they were good at it, so good as to form a startling contrast with the overall condition of the imperial administrative system at the time. As Sir James Porter, an eighteenth-century British ambassador, put the matter after long experience:

> There is no Christian power which can vie with the Porte for care and exactitude in the several offices; business is done with the greatest accuracy, in any important document, words are weighed, and that signification constantly selected, which may most conduce to their own advantage. Papers of the remotest date, if the year of the transaction is but known, may be found at the Porte; every command granted at the time, and every regulation then made, can be immediately produced. . . .
>
> When they feel an inclination to expedite business at the Porte, or it is agreeable to them, no people do it with greater celerity; when the contrary is the case, they will as artfully protract or delay.[41]

Scattered comments of Joseph von Hammer, a better-qualified and hardly over-sanguine observer, confirm this picture, at least in part. The physical aspect of the more formal documents, he said, was of a "splendor . . . which leaves all the elegance of the European Chanceries of State far behind." The role of the examining clerk (*mümeyyiz*) in maintaining correctness and uniformity of style was also one respect in which European governments might well, in his opinion, have followed Ottoman example.[42]

Such proficiency was not without its costs, however. The emphasis on approval of each action at several levels of the hierarchy suggests, for example, a significant limitation of the initiative

left to individual officials. The accounts that we have summarized imply a fixation, craftsman-like in fact, on the documents as ends in themselves. This suggests that many scribal
officials must have been oblivious to the external impact of actions taken within the offices, and that the scribal culture must
have existed, in all but the most vigorous minds, only within narrow limits. The lack of any differentiation between clerical and
professional personnel in the offices, while hardly exceptional
for the period, throws this preoccupation with the official
paperasseries into yet higher relief. The limited scope of initiative
and the strong orientation to the formalistic details of document
production may have served well enough for the old scribes of
the imperial Divan. But how good a preparation would it be for
the efendi-turned-paşa or for the reforming statesmen of a later
age?

Accounts of the meetings of the *divan*s of the grand vezirs deal
with one of the settings in which the efendis-turned-paşa were
active, and thus help us to answer this question, at least as it relates to the period under consideration. The best contemporary
general discussion of procedure in these *divan*s is that of
d'Ohsson.[43] Speaking in particular of the extraordinary consultative assemblies (*müşavere, meşveret*) that the grand vezirs of this
period convoked to deal with urgent problems, d'Ohsson says
that the grand vezir would first present the matters for decision
and then call on the head of the Muslim religious hierarchy, the
şeyh ül-İslâm, to comment first. The latter would normally do so
only vaguely, so as not to inhibit further discussion. Other members of the assembly would then have a turn, but they too would
avoid speaking out for fear of opposing the wishes of the grand
vezir. Were he to press them for opinions, they would answer
evasively that he was wisest, that it was he who had the confidence of the sultan, that it was for him to command and them to
obey. Further urgings to speak would be answered only with the
temenna, the old-fashioned oriental salute made by bringing the
fingers of the right hand first to the lips and then to the fore-
head. Even in the most serious matters, the only point likely to
lead to argument would be the legitimacy of a given project in
terms of Islamic law. Any who disagreed with the grand vezir
on this were likely to find themselves in exile very shortly.

The real purpose of these consultations, d'Ohsson continues,
was not so much policy formulation or even a serious consulta-

tion of opinions, but rather the legitimation of controversial governmental action in the eyes of the populace and the insulation of the sultan and grand vezir from censure. When it became necessary to take decisions that might prove unpopular or harmful to the empire, the clever grand vezir would then, in the most flattering manner possible, refer the difficult decision back to the sultan. At such times, not even the most adroit maneuvering could ensure the grand vezir against loss of his master's favor or a disastrous outburst of public resentment.

D'Ohsson's account should probably not be taken as descriptive of the way business was done in *divan* meetings of more routine kind. It also understates the development of debate in the extraordinary assemblies.[44] Scattered through the "History" of Cevdet Paşa, however, are detailed accounts, presumably drawn from minutes kept by the chief scribe or his assistants, of many such meetings. Already quoted in the last chapter for what they tell about the different branches of the ruling class, these reports generally confirm and amplify what d'Ohsson has to say.

From these accounts, it is a clear inference that the convocation of such assemblies reflected the need not only to spread responsibility for inescapable actions, but also to tap every possible source of solutions for problems that the sultan at times would frankly admit his inability to resolve.[45] The gravity of the issues, together with the servile status of those in attendance, was enough to account for the behavior that d'Ohsson describes, although the sultans and grand vezirs were not sparing in their demands that the officials speak their minds,[46] that the assemblies—however large—maintain absolute secrecy,[47] and that they reach their decision in "unanimity of opinion" (*ittifak-i âra*).[48] This was a phrase that would reverberate through accounts of such meetings for decades to come, its unrealistic character hardly gaining recognition before the late 1830s.[49] Sultans and grand vezirs reacted to the frustrations they experienced with these assemblies by redoubling their demands for secrecy and unanimity and by voicing bitter disillusionment at the quality of the official manpower at their disposal.[50] As we have already noted, Cevdet Paşa associated this kind of deficiency particularly with members of the religious establishment and regarded the scribal officials, whose paper pushing at least gave them some familiarity with the issues in question, in a better light.

In terms of their implications for future developments in the ruling class, these consultative assemblies were of immense significance. But for the late prereform period, their significance lies in what they show about the limited scope of initiative and the tendency toward a kind of bureaucratic formalism, implied both in what d'Ohsson says about the real purpose of the meetings and in the unrealistic demand for unanimity of decision. Formalism and restriction of initiative thus appear at the topmost levels of the ruling class, just as among the clerks of the scribal bureaus. The correspondence of these traits among officials at both upper and lower levels is one of the most significant facts of bureaucratic life in this period and is important for the appreciation of the scribal eminence implied in the efendi-turned-paşa pattern.

The procedural patterns observable in both the scribal bureaus and the assemblies also suggest several additional points of interest. For example, the routines of the offices not only confirm that scribal functions tended to be conceived solely in terms of document-producing processes, but also hint at the pervasive influence throughout Ottoman society of the guild tradition, an influence perceptible in the craftsmanlike approach of the scribes to their work as well as in formal patterns of personnel organization within the offices. The implications of what is often termed bureaucratic formalism are equally far from fortuitous. For the drafting and production of official documents, as well as the subjects with which the documents dealt, were indeed caught up in, and to a degree governed by, patterns of official ritual that served continually to dramatize and reaffirm the character and purpose of a state seen as the expression of a divinely appointed order.[51]

The repression of initiative observable in both the offices and the assemblies, in addition to bespeaking the influence of the guild tradition in the former setting, adds a significant note to what we have seen about the workings of Ottoman patrimonialism. The discretional use of power by those in highest positions had as a necessary concomitant the servility, in practical as well as formal juridical senses, of those who worked in their shadow. The decline of the empire surely compounded both this problem and the bureaucratic formalism. For the progressive loss of control by the central administration over the provinces created a discontinuity between the document-producing proc-

esses of the central offices and the world outside, while the growing hopelessness of many of the issues confronting the state not
only created the need for the special consultative assemblies, but
also conditioned many of the frustrations encountered in them.

What was it like to serve in such a bureaucracy? What could
the eminence of the scribal efendi-turned-paşa have amounted
to in such an age?

SOCIAL DIMENSIONS OF THE LATE TRADITIONAL SCRIBAL SERVICE

To answer these questions, even within the limits of the offices
that fell under the chief scribe, we must begin by acknowledging
the existence there of three distinguishable social groups. The
first, differentiated in ethno-religious terms and thus really
marginal to the Muslim Ottoman ruling class, consists of non-
Muslims in scribal positions. At the Sublime Porte of the eighteenth century, this meant the translator of the imperial Divan
and his assistants. The other two groups may be defined as lower
and upper parts of the scribal service proper, the boundary
between them being most readily identifiable in terms of the
hacelik, or rank of the *hacegân* (approximately, bureau chiefs).

The conditions of service in these groups again illustrate the
organizational and procedural patterns we have just discussed.
More importantly, they illuminate the social context underlying
the operation of those patterns. To be specific, each of the three
groups we have just distinguished displays the influence in particularly marked form of one of the patterns of social organization presented in Chapter One, although the influences are
never unmixed and thus cannot be appreciated simply on a
one-for-one basis.

The Translators of the Imperial Divan

The monopoly of this post by non-Muslims reflects the fact that
while there were many Muslim Ottomans of great learning in
the "three languages" (*elsine-i selâse*) basic to their cultural tradition, few even of the relatively "secular-minded" scribal officials
were capable of the "infidel business" of translating to and from
the languages of the Christian West, while those who were able
were not always willing to accept such duty. The passage of the
translatorship into the hands of Greeks, in place of the foreign-
born renegades who had once filled the post, was a product of

this cultural exclusivism of the Muslims and of the emergence of a sort of Greek "merchant aristocracy." Centered in the Phenar (or Fener) quarter of Istanbul, where the patriarch had his seat, these "aristocrats" used their wealth for the aggrandizement of their families, the acquisition of learning and promotion of Greek culture, and the pursuit of power both in the Orthodox community and—within the limits of the possible—in the Ottoman imperial system.

In Runciman's vivid account of the rise of the great Phenariot families,[52] the tensions implicit between their ambitions, symbolized in their vainglorious claims to Byzantine imperial ancestry, and the practical limitations of the system of confessional autonomy become dramatically clear. The linkage of the Phenariots' story to the history of the Sublime Porte is a by-product of their custom of sending their sons to Italy to study. Acquiring a good Western education, many of the latter took up medicine and returned to become physicians to highly placed Ottoman dignitaries. The first two Greeks to hold the Divan translatorship first served the Grand Vezir Köprülüzade Ahmed Paşa (1635-1676) in this capacity, and their promotion to translator bespeaks his recognition of the political value of the less technical branches of their learning. The career of the second of them, Alexander Mavrocordato, who played a key role in the Carlowitz peace negotiations, is the most brilliant in all the history of the Greek translators and also coincides with a critical moment in the evolution of the office of chief scribe.

Acquisition of a foothold in the governmental system gave the Phenariots added opportunities to increase their wealth, while the value and rarity of their learning placed them in a strategic position to capture other political positions, as well. By the first quarter of the eighteenth century, the Phenariots had developed what amounted to an official *cursus honorum*, consisting of positions in the Ottoman administrative system, distinct from the offices held by laymen within the Orthodox community. According to Cevdet, the lowest positions in this *cursus honorum* were those of the two agents (*kapı kâhyası*) that the tributary princes of Moldavia and Wallachia maintained, as did ordinary provincial governors, to represent them at the Sublime Porte.[53] Above these, in ascending order, came the translatorship of the imperial fleet, then that of the imperial Divan, and finally the two princely thrones of Moldavia and Wallachia. These last were

posts that the Phenariot elite coveted as the only Christian vas-
saldoms then remaining within the Ottoman state and as steps
toward reviving the "Great Idea" of Byzantine imperialism.

Western visitors to the courts of these princes were impressed
by their learning and sumptuous style of life, but also by the
paradox of a Greek prince ruling as the slave of the sultan. At
the Porte, the situation of the *divan* translators was equally paradoxical. These members of what has been called a Phenariot *nob-
lesse de robe*[54] enjoyed privileges of a sumptuary, ceremonial, and
fiscal character comparable to those of the ruling class. In a
sense, they enjoyed a cultural eminence even in relation to the
Ottoman elite. But the ethnoreligious difference separating the
Phenariots from the ruling class proper, combined in the case of
the translators with the doubts and anxieties awakened by their
central role in some of the most sensitive and secret affairs of
state, made their position a particularly dangerous one. In relation to their coreligionists, the Phenariots who had won places in
this *cursus honorum* were patrimonial dignitaries of awesome
scale and even grander aspirations. In relation to the sultans,
they were no more than slaves confined in a sort of bureaucratic
miniature of the Orthodox community, all the more vulnerable
for their powers and their hopes.[55]

The Lower Scribal Service

Muslim scribal officials who fell below the level of the *hacegân*
also displayed the workings of more than one of the organizational patterns described in Chapter One. In this case, however,
the dominant motif seems to have reflected the limited extent to
which mere membership in the ruling class could be equated
with "elitism" in any meaningful sense. While the lower scribal
service displayed traits of the patrimonial motif, its most pronounced characteristic was that of a craft guild. To trace an
imaginary scribe of this period through the career cycle will
demonstrate this fact, leading naturally to the discussion of the
differences found at and above the rank of the *hacegân* or
"bureau chiefs."

Whatever the extent to which the early scribal service had
drawn its personnel from the religious colleges or the palace
school, the normal pattern of the eighteenth century was rather
that the aspiring scribal official would enter an office as a young
boy just out of the elementary mosque school. This might well

mean beginning his official career before the age of ten. Even in
the nineteenth century, there were many who began by the early
teens and some who thus accumulated service records running
into six and seven decades.

The means by which the boys entered the offices reflected the
combined operation of prescribed official procedures and of the
more *ad hoc* patterns characteristic of patrimonial households.
On one hand, to enter central scribal offices, it appears to have
been necessary to obtain some sort of brevet of appointment. In
the Office of the Imperial Divan, the only one of those under the
chief scribe to which a complete novice was supposed to be appointed, this would ostensibly have taken the form of the
şagirdlik rüusü, or brevet of studentship,[56] although the way in
which the term *şagird* (student) actually figured among the personnel designations then used in the office raises questions as to
whether this was in fact invariably the procedure.

In any case, boys of proper age would have needed someone
to complete the formalities, pay the fees, and provide any other
monetary inducements necessary to get such a document. Most
typically, these patrons would have been their fathers, already in
government service. In the case of individuals whose entry depended on the formation of *intisab* connections, and who, to
produce the displays of talent necessary for that purpose, must
have been somewhat older and more experienced, the protector
would have been the head of the patrimonial household to
which the young man had become attached.

In principle, as the system of brevets of appointment implies,
appointment was a matter of centralized official procedures. In
practice, appointment making depended to an important degree on the influence of a patron and meant appointment to a
position in whatever part of the bureaucracy fell under the patron's control or influence. In offices of low status, and probably
in general outside Istanbul, the role of the patron must have
been relatively even greater. There were surely situations in
which appointment was purely discretional, entailing no official
formalities whatever.

Scribal recruitment in the late prereform period thus still displayed only a low degree of formal systematization. In contrast
to the formidable systems characteristic of the military-administrative and religious establishments at their high point, we note
here little more than a reliance on the "patrimonial style in re-

cruitment" and a tendency, which we may think of as guild-like, to follow in one's father's footsteps. Statements have appeared, in fact, to the effect that scribal recruitment in this period was totally hereditary. There was, no doubt, an element of this in recruitment, as in the transmission of the incomes from benefices in land. Yet any conception of scribal recruitment as solely hereditary does not make allowance for the full range of relationships encountered within the patrimonial household, or for the extent to which a concern for the discovery of talent prevailed even there.[57] Nevertheless, the range of recruitment was relatively narrow; and that narrowness, coupled with the distinctive cultural orientation of the scribes and the fact that this culture was hardly propagated anywhere at this time except in the offices themselves, gave the scribal service the inbred, "small-townish" air then characteristic of its members.

Once in the offices, the boys were trained in essential scribal skills through apprenticeship, a function no longer confined, as Matuz believes it was in the time of Süleyman the Magnificent, to the Treasury offices. One eighteenth-century account explains the wisdom (*hikmet*) of training by apprenticeship: "The child who is to become a clerk begins his attendance in the office by being seated facing his 'teacher' (*hace*). Perceiving, thanks to this proximity, everything that his 'teacher' writes or crosses out or says, he observes in which register the affairs of Baghdad are recorded and in which notebook are those of Bosnia, and it remains in his memory as if engraved in stone (*ka'l-naḳş fî 'l-ḥacar*)." Gradually, the "teacher" would begin to entrust tasks of increasing complexity to the boy, until the latter became a master himself of the conventional skills of the scribal profession,[58] that "noblest and oldest of arts."

Implicit in the very concept of apprenticeship, the evocation of the guild tradition is reinforced in the original text by the terms used for the apprentice and his teacher. The passages preceding the one just quoted make clear that the term *hace*, or colloquially *hoca* (singular of *hacegân*), does not here refer to the director of the office, although the latter no doubt had ultimate responsibility for the training of apprentices, as for the other functions performed there.[59] Rather, the term is applied here to one of the clerks of the office (*kâtib*), of the type also referred to as *kalfa* or, in the Turkish version of the Arabic plural, as *hulefa*. As far as we can determine from the text of the document, the term *hace* or *hoca* applies to this official only loosely, in terms of his relation to the boy. In other cases, however, use of this term is a distinctive feature of the application of the basic, three-grade guild hierarchy in the scribal offices. For it is also, and indeed more typically, used both for teachers (*hoca*), such as those maintained even in the offices for subjects like Arabic and Persian,[60] and for the rank commonly borne by the bureau chiefs, the *hacegân*, who stood among the scribal officials in a position comparable to that of the master (*usta*) in the guilds. Neither the terminological substitution nor the history of the term *hace* is easy to explain. But the word *hace*, or the Persian *kh^vâja* from which it comes, had traditionally applied in certain cases, in other Middle Eastern societies as well as among the Ottomans, to merchants, who might also be organized into guilds or even have something like official status. It is thus another term associated with the marketplace, if not with the handicrafts.[61] For the "apprentice" in the account quoted above, the term is *şagird* ("student"), a common synonym for *çırak* ("apprentice") even in the craft guilds, and thus not necessarily to be understood in the peculiar sense that the term seems to have acquired in the formal organizational patterns of the Office of the Imperial Divan.

The influence of the guild tradition thus appears prominently both in the emphasis on training by apprenticeship and in the personnel designations associated with the training process. This helps to explain the scribes' typical predilection for the use of the literary tradition distinctive of their "craft" as if it were not so much a means of simple and straightforward communication as a craft or art, even an esoteric medium, in which what mattered was to demonstrate one's mastery in ways that an outsider would have to marvel at more than comprehend.

Apprentice scribes could, however, also extend their education by means other than apprenticeship. It was not uncommon for them to spend part of the day attending lectures in the religious colleges. Persian poetry could be studied in some of the dervish convents, or in the homes of certain *literati*. Numbers of the latter, who were more or less invariably members of the ruling class, would give instruction to any who came seeking it and, in fact, maintained something like literary salons. Persons of means might retain private tutors (*konak hocaları*). Heads of great households obviously found it in their interest to give considerable attention to the education of their slaves and protégés by such means. Then, too, there were many libraries scattered through Istanbul, numbers of them endowed by celebrated paragons of the scribal culture.[62] The resources available to the scribal official for mastery of his cultural tradition were thus considerable, but hardly well organized for efficient use. They did not compare to the palace school, to the religious educational system at its height, or to the Italian universities frequented by the Phenariot grandees. This fact must have thrown the guild-like traits of the tribal officials into higher relief and helped to limit the numbers of those who developed into really great exponents of the traditional scribal culture.

In any case, when his superiors considered the apprentice scribe to have sufficient mastery in the scribal arts, he would go through a sort of initiation, in which he would be assigned a new name (*mahlas*), usually alluding to some distinction or superior quality, and a seat of his own among the cushions on which the clerks of the office sat (*mindere çıkmak*).[63] No longer an apprentice but now a full-fledged scribe, he would, in accordance with his abilities and connections, begin to progress upward.

Exactly how he did so is not always clear. In some senses, he rose through the social relations assumed in the model of the patrimonial household as much as through the organizational patterns characteristic of the offices. To the extent that the latter were his chief concern, and to the extent that he pursued his career exclusively in the offices of the chief scribe, the young scribe would have begun by moving up through the hierarchically ordered categories within the Office of the Imperial Divan. It would then have been advantageous for him to obtain a transfer into one of the smaller and more select offices, those of the corresponding secretary of the grand vezir or the receiver. To some degree, then, an ambitious scribal official would have to think in terms of rising both through the hierarchical orders within the bureaus and through a hierarchical order of bureaus.

This pattern is too complicated, however, to have prevailed very strictly in a bureaucratic system of this kind. In the biographies of scribal officials who rose to prominence in this period, elements of such a hierarchical pattern do recur.[64] Yet such individuals neither passed through every level of the hierarchical schematization nor spent their entire careers in the offices subordinate to the chief scribe.

Surely what mattered more than the hierarchical pattern per

se was the ability of the individual to establish claims to advancement in ways that his superiors would recognize. In the Ottoman scribal service, this meant giving proof of ability. To make ability count, however, the individual needed connections. Ability without connections would mean frustration; connections without ability might lead to high position, but offered no protection against mockery and reproof.[65] Reasonably combined, however, aptitude and connections would enable the aspiring official to "cut through the stages" (*kat'-ı merahil*—a widely echoed phrase) of the supposed hierarchical ordering and rise quickly to high station.

Meanwhile, where working conditions are concerned, the available information suggests that their status as slaves of the sultan sat but lightly on the lower-level scribal officials of this period. Not only were the facts of their social origin out of consonance with the legal principle of servility, but the conditions in which they served imply that discipline was anything but rigorous. For example, in addition to the apprentices, scribes, supervisors, and bureau chiefs, the offices appear to have been thronged most of the time with other people of the most varied types, including even beggars and peddlars. Many of those standing about were menials—doormen waiting to show the visitor to his destination in return for a tip (*bahşiş*), messengers, guards, and the makers of the innumerable cups of coffee and glasses of tea that provided stimulus for the continual "rending and mending of affairs of state." Others were outsiders who streamed in and out to request favors or appointments, to pay social visits, or to consult scribes who conducted a sort of petty "legal practice" on the side by writing petitions and such as a way to pick up extra income.[66] Some of these visitors posed security risks, of which the beleaguered government was becoming increasingly conscious.

Despite the obvious disadvantages of conducting the most sensitive business amid such a hubbub, many scribes probably found it all congenial and satisfying. Indications are that most scribal officials did not work very hard and never had.[67] While there is evidence to show that there was always a hard core of the serious-minded and ambitious, others no doubt found relief from the boredom of their paperwork, much of it extremely repetitive,[68] in avocations ranging from cutting out and lettering the fancy labels that still grace many of the old registers, to the development of political acquaintance, discussion of literary or mystical interests, or the pursuit of private economic advantage. Not too surprisingly, some abused the prescribed hours, and some simply did not come to work. In 1823, for example, up to a quarter of the clerks of the Offices of the Imperial Divan and the Receiver did not attend at all, and some, while retaining incomes from landholdings assigned to the offices, had taken up other occupations.[69] The guild-like traits of the lower bureaucracy, like the repression of initiative that we noted earlier, were thus associated with underemployment and indiscipline, and so with what sociologists term a "subversion of service goals," an abuse of office for service of personal ends rather than those of the state.[70]

In part, no doubt, this is to be explained in terms of the material rewards for service in the lower scribal offices. Apprentices received no compensation whatever. Even the regular clerks (*hulefa*) no longer received salaries paid from the central Treasury, as had their predecessors of the sixteenth century. Instead, they received their compensation only through a ramshackle series of prebendal systems. The incomes from benefices in land, which we have already discussed in connection with the systems of *gedik* and *şerh*, were only one of these; and since the benefice incomes assigned to the offices of the chief scribe were by now described as "worthless and without yield" (*çürük ve bi-hasıl*),[71] they were perhaps no longer the most important. Other types of prebendal income included fees (*harc*, *rüsum*, *aidat*) collected in the offices for the performance of official functions and divided among the officials in shares, and gifts (*atiye-i seniye*) distributed by the sultan on ceremonial occasions. After retirement, scribes might receive modest pensions assigned through the Rüus Section from the proceeds of the farming of certain customs duties.

It was in these conditions, then, that scribal officials below the rank of the *hacegân* pursued their careers from apprenticeship through clerkship, and on as far as the supervisory positions such as purse-bearer (*kisedar*), examining clerk (*mümeyyiz*), or chief clerk (*ser kalfa, baş kalfa*). The low state of official discipline, the ad hoc character of facilities for scribal recruitment and education, and the regression over time from compensation by salary into prebendalism[72] are all witness to the inhibitive effect of imperial decline on the development of the service. Partly for this reason, the "patrimonial style" was operative in recruitment and promotion to an extent that it probably could not have been, say, in the military-administrative establishment at its height. Even more in evidence, however, is the influence of the guild tradition. The scribal officials in Istanbul, perhaps unlike those in some provincial centers,[73] do not appear to have been formally organized into a guild. Yet guild-like traits appear in the system of training by apprenticeship; in the emphasis, if never exclusive, on following in one's father's footsteps; in procedural patterns; in the application to the scribal offices as well as to the guilds of the *gedik* system; and finally in some of the most important of the terms used to designate the various categories of scribal personnel. In sum, lower scribal life was guild-like in countless details and in its very ethos.

The Upper Scribal Service

The lack of anything like separate career lines for clerical and professional personnel implied that many elements of these guild-like patterns would carry over into the upper scribal echelons. The expectations of high officials about how the business of the offices should be conducted and about how their subordinates would behave, for example, surely came largely from that source. Yet, above the threshold marked by the rank of the *hace-gân*, the relative importance of the influences observable in the lower scribal service shifted markedly. Officials who attained the rank of *hace* or the higher one of *vezir*, which carried the title paşa—these being the only ranks commonly given to scribal officials in this period[74]—were the patrimonial elite of the scribal service, and life for those who joined this elite became quite different from what it had been before. In part, the differences involved advantages for the scribal grandees; to a perhaps larger degree, particularly with the decline of the empire, the differences brought disadvantages.

To begin with some of the more attractive traits, high status entailed a number of conspicuous distinctions, such as rank, occupancy of designated places in the tables of ceremonial precedence (*teşrifat*), receipt of robes of honor (*hil'at*) upon investiture, steeply increased entitlements to compensation, and, increasingly as the official rose in status, the capacity to maintain a large household patterned after that of the sultan. Attainment of the *hacelik* also signified considerable enlargement of the scope of lateral mobility, a distinctive element of the efendi-turned-paşa pattern.[75] The biographies of scribal officials of this type are full of shifts among the higher positions linked to the chief scribe, such other high offices of the Porte as those of chief bailiff and steward, or other scribal positions in the capital, such as the superintendencies (*nezaret, emanet*) of the granaries (*zahire*), cannon foundry (*Tophane*), and naval arsenal (*Tersane*). Even more significant is the inclusion in such biographies of posts traditionally beyond the scribal pale, such as provincial governorships and the grand vezirate.[76]

As we know already, however, status, resources, and an increased range of employment opportunities were not all there was to life in the upper scribal echelons. Rather, those traits were accompanied by a marked politicization of bureaucratic life. Basically, this was a function of proximity to the sultan. The legal principle of slave status may have weighed lightly on the lower officials, who formed the political connections indispensable for the advancement of their careers with persons who were their equals in terms of this principle. But for those who rose to higher status, close contact actualized the dangers of the sultan-slave dichotomy in a way made all the more perilous by the intense competition for favor and office. In the dangers inherent in this situation lay the dark sequel to the "patrimonial style in recruitment," the two together engendering the peculiar pattern of rapid movement, both upward and downward, that we have described as "wheel of fortune mobility."

While the insecurity of high-level officials in relation to the sultan was presumably characteristic in all periods of Ottoman history, at least after the earliest decades, in the period of decline there was an additional problem that compounded these dangers. In one sense, this was actually the mechanism that turned the scribal efendis into paşas, for the mobility of the high-level officials of this period was partly a function of brevity of tenure. This had become institutionalized through a system of annual appointment (*tevcihat*) for all high officials, meaning, in the case of the scribal service, all those who had attained the rank of the *hacegân*. Such officials often obtained reappointment to the positions they already held,[77] but only for a year at a time.

Numerous signs indicate that this practice of annual reappointment, not characteristic of the empire at its height, was a product of imperial decline. References to the holding of office on a rotational basis (*münavebet*) and to the conferment of ranks alone on those for whom there were no appropriate places[78] made clear, for example, that the system operated amid a surplus of aspirants in relation to the number of posts. The economic interests built up around the system are significant in a similar sense. For there were fees to pay, either for appointment or for reconfirmation in place. The fees went into the pockets of the officials who had power to appoint and formed part of the prebendal income of their offices. The grand vezirs of the late eighteenth century received up to 400,000 *kuruş* per year from appointment fees, a sum corresponding at rates of 1797 to about 30,000 English pounds, while various of the grand vezirs' subordinates received proportionate sums.[79] Those who had to pay the fees naturally sought to recoup the outlay during their time in office through demands on their official subordinates or on members of the subject classes who fell under their authority. Referred to by a variety of names such as *caize*,[80] these appointment fees amounted in practical terms to a breach of the supposed tax exemption of the ruling class and appear, if we except the rather different phenomenon of tax farming, to be the sole reality behind talk of sale of office in the Ottoman Empire, at least in the central administration. The history of the *tevcihat* system is unclear in many respects, but its character makes clear how far the fees were from representing a purchase of property rights in office in any lasting sense.[81]

Still, the systems of annual appointment and fee collection were significant in at least two respects. First, in a state that had long allowed collection of fees for performance of certain types of official functions,[82] the annual appointments and the transfers of funds to which they gave rise provided a major stimulus to that proliferation of various forms of extortion and unauthorized taxation which so characterized the decline of the administrative system.[83] In addition, given the personnel needs resulting from the decline of the military-administrative establishment, the system of annual appointments seems to have served as the engine that catapulted the scribal specialists of the central offices into the position of top-level generalists of imperial administration.

The institutionalized uncertainties of the annual appointments may thus have created the efendi-turned-paşa pattern; but the same factor compounded the dangers already inherent

in the sultan-slave dichotomy—arbitrary deposition, exile, expropriation, summary execution—to confront the tribal grandees with uncertainties of which they could never be unmindful.
A series of *causes célèbres* dramatized this fact right up to the
1830s, when conditions of service began to undergo reform. For
example, scribal dignitaries of 1785 were shaken by the overthrow of their colleague, the Grand Vezir Halil Hamid Paşa, the
subsequent expropriation of his estate, and his execution.[84] In
1799, it was the execution in exile of Ebu Bekir Ratib Efendi, not
a paşa but a former chief scribe and once a man of great and
constructive influence.[85] Others of his kind were destroyed by
the troubles attendant on the overthrow of Selim III.[86] In 1823,
a major crisis occurred with the exile, execution, and confisca-
tion of the estate of Halet Efendi, a scribal official and long the
most influential figure at the court of Mahmud II. His fall precipitated the expropriation and the banishment or imprisonment of many of his dependents, including both officials and
household retainers, as well as the release of those whom Halet
had sent into exile.[87] Halet had been much feared and hated,
but the best repute was no guarantee against a similar fate. In
1828-1829, Galib Paşa, a former diplomat and chief scribe become provincial governor, was disgraced unjustly and sent into
exile, where he shortly died.[88] In 1837, a particularly vicious
scribal-bureaucratic rivalry culminated in the overthrow, exile,
and murder of Pertev Paşa. As with Halet, Pertev's fall precipitated that of many of his associates. Pertev's fall did not go un-
avenged.[89] But by then times were changing, and the fruits of
vengeance included not just the liquidation of Pertev's enemies,
but the first fundamental reforms in conditions of service.

An account of these reforms must appear in the next chapter.
Until they occurred, there was little a high-level official could do
to escape the fate of Pertev or the others who had gone before
him. A man of such standing could protect parts of his property
through the abuse of the system of pious foundations (*evkaf*)
known as "family *evkaf*." Property so deeded would in principle
pass beyond the reach of the state, while most or all of the income would remain for the benefit of the family members as
"trustees." In addition, some branches of the ruling class were
considered safer from the insecurities of bureaucratic life than
others. The scribal service was, in fact, regarded as relatively
safe, but the religious establishment was even safer.[90] This im-

plies that a grandee in a particular branch of the ruling class might profit by placing at least some dependents in other branches. Ultimately, though, the inescapable strategy for such a figure was to accumulate the largest possible network of personal dependents, and to acquire for himself the kind of position that would give him sufficient patronage to put his kinsmen and protégés, suitably trained, to political use on the largest possible scale. There are indications, in fact, that government policy had begun as early as the seventeenth century to encourage this kind of behavior, at least in the provincial administration, by favoring heads of "complete" or extensively developed households (*mükemmel kapı*) for promotion.[91]

In any case, the very extremity of the sultan's demands for subservience and the uncertainty of tenure in office meant that the pursuit of household interests would appear to the patrimonial grandees of the period of decline as the most vital issue of political life. In this fact, indeed, lay the upper-bureaucratic counterpart of that "subversion of service goals" observable in the more petty kinds of indiscipline characteristic of the lower officials.

The types and amounts of compensation that the grandees of the ruling class might draw while in favor provide further insights into the stakes of the political struggle and the means available for the maintenance of the households, as well as into the character of the imperial system and the processes of its decline. Upper scribal officials most likely did not receive incomes from benefices in land except in the very highest positions, to some of which incomes from the most valuable category of landholdings, known as *has*, were traditionally assigned. Scribal officials who had held incomes from smaller landholdings before rising to high position were supposed to give up those incomes on leaving the bureaus through which they had been assigned—a rule often honored in the breach.[92] Such officials would then receive compensation in a variety of other prebendal forms.

One of these, evocative of a time when the ruling class was little more than a military retinue undifferentiated from the household of the ruler, took the form of rations (*tayinat*). Even in the early nineteenth century, senior officials were still entitled to startling quantities of such commodities as meat, bread, olive oil, and charcoal, which they presumably used to feed, heat, and light their entourages.[93] Officials also received gifts in customary ways. Some of the most important scribal officials, such as the corresponding secretary of the grand vezir, were said to be dependent for their entire income on gifts (*atiye*) that the sultan distributed once annually.[94] Since most high officials were under obligation to give gifts in certain situations as well as to receive, the economic significance of the gifts as forms of compensation was probably doubtful in most cases. What they do reflect is the preponderance of political criteria in the distribution of economic resources and the emphasis in the traditional economic mentality on patterns of reciprocity and redistribution.[95] Other types of income included the share of the revenues that some high officials received for serving ex officio as supervisors of the large pious foundations created by the sultans.[96] Finally and most importantly, high officials were allowed to collect fees, not only for appointments over which they had control, but also for the services that they or their bureaus performed, lower officials also deriving income from shares of some such receipts.[97] Many of these sources of revenue were surely very lucrative, at least for some individuals. Yet it is difficult to imagine that the mechanics of collecting and disbursing income in such ways did not do as much as the uncertainties of official tenure to concentrate the attention of high officials on personal and household interests.

During the period of decline, then, upper-echelon scribal life increasingly exemplified the model of the patrimonial household, both in the sense that the officials were inescapably slaves in the household of the sultan, and in the sense that they were simultaneously heads of analogous establishments of their own. Their inability to find real security in their own households from the dangers built into that of the sultan points to the continued operation, as in earlier periods, of traditional patrimonial principles. Yet, the decline of the empire had heightened the importance of the grandee households, both because government policy came to assume their existence and because of intensification of the uncertainties of upper-bureaucratic life. The restriction of official tenure through the system of annual appointment, the spread of the fee system, and the effective breaching of the tax exemption supposedly distinctive of the ruling class were key examples of these added uncertainties. Scribal officials of a later generation would tend to view the rudimentary development of a system of ranks for their service, unlike others, as another sign

of the weakness of their position. The status of the scribal officials of the Ottoman Empire was in many respects less different
from that of their counterparts in other states of the time than
comparison with modern-day conditions would imply.[98] Still,
the insecurities built into the situation of Ottoman scribal officials in this period implied a number of important goals that collective self-interest would lead them to pursue in the era of reform, even as they adhered in other ways to the patterns of political activity associated with the patrimonial tradition.[99]

Looking beyond the elite to survey the social state of the late
traditional scribal service overall, we may conclude that the operations of the patrimonial model appeared to varying degrees
in all distinguishable groups, if in conjunction with other patterns. In the case of the Greek translators, the influence of the
patrimonial model, strongly characteristic of the Phenariot elite,
was subordinate to that of the model of the autonomous confessional community. That the official *cursus honorum* of the
Phenariots suggested a non-Muslim enclave in the ruling class is
particularly indicative of this fact. Among the lower scribal echelons, patrimonial traits were ancillary to a strong guild-like pattern. Among the scribal elite, the politicization of bureaucratic
life and the material rewards of power submerged the guild-like
traits in those of the patrimonial household. The decadence of
an imperial system once noted for the vigor and stringent discipline of its ruling class, by thwarting the development of any
consistent policy for the social ordering of the scribal service,
seemed to heighten the manifestations of all these patterns.

The state of the scribal service at the end of the eighteenth
century obviously had critical implications not only for the overall reform of the imperial system, but also for the determination
of the capacity of scribal officials to play a leading role in the reforms. Even before the opening of the era of reform, then, the
condition of the scribal service implied a fundamental question:
how meaningful in fact was the eminence of the scribal efendis
and paşas of the late eighteenth century?

CONCLUSION: THE EFENDI-TURNED-PAŞA IN COMPARATIVE PERSPECTIVE

The eminence of the efendi-turned-paşa had, to return to the
point with which this chapter opened, two essential elements: a
political component expressed in the emergence of the upper

scribal officials as an elite of administrative generalists, and a cultural component identified with the traditional scribal culture. Acquired in a period of decline, this eminence may have been modest by the standards of the Ottoman system at its height, or by those of contemporary Western states, but it was nonetheless there. An attempt at more precise evaluation of the relative significance of its two component elements will make its importance clearer.

To begin with the political component of the scribal eminence, this is most readily appreciable in terms of promotion patterns, on which we have already presented some of the relevant evidence. We have commented, for example, on the decline of the military-administrative and religious establishments and the simultaneous development of the palace and the scribal service. Within the last, we have also noted a shift of balance among its component elements, with the chief scribe and his men emerging to the most prominent position. Considering that the Treasury had reportedly once been the scene for the training of all scribal officials[100] and possibly even the major power center of the scribal service, it was a fact of ironic significance for the future development of reformist policy that by the end of the eighteenth century, Treasury business and the "affairs of the Divan" had come to be regarded as two separate specializations, with the former considered inadequate as preparation for the latter.[101] In any case, the effects of all these long-term shifts in the ruling class were among the influences that converged to shape the pattern of the efendi-turned-paşa.

To have a precise appreciation of the expression of this pattern in terms of lines of promotion, however, it is not enough to say only this. Rather, we must take a closer look at the efendis who turned into paşas by achieving such offices as provincial governorships or the grand vezirate. To assess the relative importance of the kind of mobility that they represent, we must then also go beyond Itzkowitz' discussion of these men to consider them, not in isolation, but in relation to all the other officials who held the same offices they did.

For example, Itzkowitz names eight former chief scribes who served on one or more occasions during the years 1683-1774 as provincial governors.[102] Considering that this kind of promotion was known as early as the time of Süleyman the Magnificent,[103] that the total number of men who served as chief scribe

in the same period was thirty-three,[104] and that the total number
of provincial governors must for the same time span have run
into the hundreds, this does not seem enough by itself to prove
the existence of a strong scribal hold on provincial administrative office.

The same kind of problem appears in the promotion of scribal
officials to the grand vezirate, again a phenomenon with antece-
dents at much earlier dates.[105] Changing his period of reference
somewhat, Itzkowitz cites six officials of scribal origin who rose
to the grand vezirate during the years 1703-1774. Five of these
had served as chief scribe; one had not, although he had been
ambassador to several Western states.[106] Counting one other
grand vezir who had held the rank of *hace* but had never served
in positions associated with the chief scribe would bring the total
of scribal grand vezirs to seven.[107] Yet, the total number of men
who served as grand vezir between 1703 and the conclusion of
the Treaty of Küçük Kaynarca in 1774 was forty. The number
of chief scribes for the same years was twenty-five.

Extending the counts from 1774 all the way to the death of
Mahmud II in 1839 produces two more grand vezirs who had
previously been chief scribe, another who had risen to be corresponding secretary to the grand vezir but then moved over into
the Treasury, plus two *hacegân* who rose to the grand vezirate
outside the offices of the chief scribe, one of them serving en
route as steward (*kâhya bey*), and the other as chief bailiff (*çavuş
başı*).[108] This adds five more scribal grand vezirs, making twelve
for the period 1703-1839, although only seven of the twelve had
served as chief scribe. The total number who held the office of
grand vezir during the same period was seventy-three; and the
total of those who served as chief scribe between 1703 and the
transformation of that office into the Foreign Ministry in 1836
was fifty-three.[109]

In purely quantitative terms, the pattern of promotion from
chief scribe to grand vezir again does not appear strong enough
for its importance to pass without question. To give these figures
the weight they deserve, we have to take account of two other
considerations. Presumably, these apply to the provincial governors as much as the grand vezirs; but it is in relation to the latter,
thanks to their smaller numbers and the greater availability of
biographical information, that these points become most visible.

The first fact, clearly, is the difference in size of the branches of service from which the grand vezirs came. Figures for comparison are not readily at hand, but what was left of the military-administrative establishment certainly was hundreds of times larger than the group of some 130 to 200 who served under the chief scribe at the end of the eighteenth century. The systems of recruitment and training then characteristic of the scribal service also make clear that it was not uniformly an elite corps, and that the number of its members who were serious candidates for the highest offices must at any given moment have been quite small. Closer consideration of who the other grand vezirs of the period were does, however, bring out a factor which makes these few men stand out in a way out of proportion to their numbers.

In fact, it is difficult to detect clear patterns of promotion among the other grand vezirs of the same years. In view of the development of the palace service during the period, one fact that stands out is that eight former sword-bearers (*silahdar ağa*), representing another small group within the ruling class, became grand vezir between 1703 and 1839,[110] as opposed to only seven former chief scribes. Beyond this, there were many grand vezirs with backgrounds in military and provincial positions, although the decline of the military-administrative establishment makes it hard at times to know how to type these men. The best overall description of the backgrounds of the grand vezirs of the late prereform period is perhaps still the "variety" (*tenevvü*) cited long ago by Mustafa Nuri Paşa.[111]

When they are viewed against this variegated backdrop, the factor that gives the scribal officials special prominence, and which also increased their hold on the grand vezirate dramatically after 1839, is their qualifications. These were what made the scribes look good in comparison with officials of other types in the consultative assemblies described by Cevdet Paşa. Similarly, the biographies of the non-scribal grand vezirs of this period make clear how few well-qualified candidates for that office there were. In the last quarter of the eighteenth century, for example, there was one grand vezir who was illiterate.[112] He was not the last. Another figure illustrates our point all the more strikingly in that he was one of the most influential individuals of the day.

A Georgian ultimately known as Koca Yusuf Paşa, he began his career as a slave of the Istanbul harbor master (*liman reisi*).

After manumission and the death of his former master, Yusuf worked as a coffeemaker in the Istanbul harbor district in winter and sailed with the fleet or engaged in trade during the summer. Through his trading partnerships with prominent individuals, including the Grand Vezir Gazi Hasan Paşa, Yusuf formed politically valuable connections, which enabled him to acquire administrative positions. He became known as an opponent of reform, although at times he supported it in the military. In any case, personal links, rather than any concept of policy or ties to any specific branch of service, propelled Yusuf's rise. Selim III disliked him vigorously, however, and Yusuf's appointment as grand vezir in 1791 was proof of the lack of choices. In selecting Yusuf's predecessor, the young Selim had actually been reduced to going into the hall at the palace where the Mantle of the Prophet was kept and choosing by lot among the names of his paşas.[113] As for Koca Yusuf, he ended his career in provincial administrative posts in the Hijaz (c. 1793-1800). These, too, were unwise assignments, if we are to believe Cevdet Paşa; for Yusuf's drinking, lechery, and corruption were hardly the way for the Istanbul government to maintain its influence in the face of the rising Wahhabi movement.[114]

These details are admittedly among the most pronounced indications of disorder and incapacity from this period. Along with the organizational, procedural, and social patterns discussed earlier, however, they provide the context in which the eminence of the scribal officials can be appreciated. There may have been disadvantages implicit in the craftsmanlike approach of the scribal officials to training and the conduct of affairs, in their tendency to harness the interests of the state to personal and familial interests, in their lack of experience in finance, and in their small numbers. Yet the best of the scribal officials were the men who kept alive the ideas of administration of which a Koca Yusuf Paşa was so thoroughly devoid, and they were the ones best prepared, if not in every sense well prepared, to cope with a changing world.

That this scribal elite and its successors in the era of reform would ultimately fail to save the obsolescent, multinational empire, whose decay so trammeled their careers as individuals and their collective development as a branch of the ruling class, can scarcely be cause for wonder. That fact must not, however, be allowed to obscure the revolutionary changes that men of scribal background, more than any others, brought about in the nineteenth century, or the remarkable difference between the legacy that fell to the scribal officials of the late prereform period and that which passed to their republican successors in the twentieth century.

Chapter Four

REASSERTION OF THE SULTANATE AND FOUNDATION OF THE CIVIL BUREAUCRACY

. . . zaman-i Selim-i Hanide her şey taht-ı nizama idhal olunmakta olduğu gibi. . . .

In the time of Selim Han, [it was] as if everything was being brought under order. . . .

Ahmed Cevdet Paşa[1]

. . . kâffe-i memurin haklarında erzan buyurulmuş olan işbu mevâhib-i ulya-yı şahanenin kadr-u-kıymetini ve hidemat-ı Devlet-i Aliye'de usul-ı memuriyet ve mücib-i mükâfat ve mücazatını alâ vechi 'l-küllî bilmek üzere bi-lûtfihi 'l-müstean vaz-u-tesis kılınan kanunname-i ceza-i madelet-ihtivadır ki ber vech-i ati zikr-ü-beyan kılınır.

. . . the penal code, just in its provisions, which has been established by the grace of Him from whom we seek aid in order that all might know the quality and worth of the high imperial benefactions granted all officials and the fundamentals of duty and entitlements to reward and punishment in the service of the Sublime State, is proclaimed as follows.

Penal Code for Officials, 1838[2]

. . . bundan böyle Devlet-i Aliye ve memalik-i mahrusemizin hüsn-i idaresi zımnında bazı kavanin-i cedide vaz-u-tesisi lâzım ve mühim görünerek. . . .

. . . whereas it appears necessary . . . henceforth to establish certain new laws for the good administration of our Sublime State and our well-protected provinces. . . .

Gülhane Decree, 1839[3]

In 1789, in the midst of war and defeat, Selim III succeeded to the Ottoman sultanate. Almost immediately, he began a series of efforts at reform that, once peace had been concluded, blossomed into what became known as the "New Order" (*Nizam-ı Cedid*). Aimed particularly at the creation of a new and more effective military machine and the establishment of the indispensable support services for it, this ultimately affected countless other phases of Ottoman life. A major reassertion of the initiative of the central government, and especially of the sultan, the "New Order" was in effect the first attempt ever made at a general reform of the governmental system. The extent to which certain of Selim's reforms were culturally innovative is sometimes debated.[4] Different ones were to different degrees. But the generality of the drive toward "order," "regulation," or "system," all of which can be used as translations for *nizam*, was an innovation worthy to be taken as marking the symbolic opening of a new age. The very name of Selim's reform program was thus a first explicit evocation of that shift of orientation, away from traditionalism and toward the creation of a rational-legal order, that we have noted as fundamentally distinctive of the era of reform.

After the overthrow of Selim III in 1807 and the abolition of the "New Order," it was not clear during the brief reign of Mustafa IV (1807-1808) or in the early years of Mahmud II (1808-1839) whether either sultanic dominance or the reformist impulse would survive. The early years of Mahmud's reign were, however, ones of preparation, during which he built up his practical political strength.[5] When he felt strong enough to reassert the reformist initiative in unmistakable fashion, as he began to do with the abolition of the Janissaries in 1826, he generally continued along the paths that Selim had earlier begun to explore. This was true of the content and relative importance of the various measures and particularly of the reassertion of the regulatory activity of the central government; it was true, too, of the sultan's dominance over the course of change. In this sense, the reigns of Selim and Mahmud fall together in the history of Ottoman reform as a single period of sultanic leadership.

To appreciate the critically important changes that occurred at the Sublime Porte and in the corporate state of the scribal service under these two sultans, we shall begin by looking at the general way in which Ottomans appear to have perceived their needs for reform as of the opening of this period. We shall then go on to look at the beginnings of reform within the traditional offices of the chief scribe (*reis ül-küttab, reis efendi*) at the Sublime Porte, next at the creation of a series of new organizations and systems related to the transformation of the chief scribe into a foreign minister. This will bring us to the attempt that Mahmud made at the end of his reign to restructure the central administration in general, bringing it more tightly under his own control, but in the process transforming the collective aspect of the scribal service and the traditional conditions of service within it. Throughout the discussion, we shall note the frustrations and failures as well as the successes of the reformers, emphasizing also the progressive contribution of their efforts to the sociocultural transformation of the scribal service. This will help make it possible in the conclusion to evaluate the changes of this fifty-year period and to bring out the distinctive features of a particular approach to modernization, one that became evident in these years and remained so until the end of the empire.

CONTEMPORARY PERCEPTIONS OF THE NEED FOR REFORM

The contrast between the capabilities of the governmental system at the end of the eighteenth century and the problems then facing the empire, obvious to the modern scholar, in many ways was even more cruelly immediate to Ottoman statesmen of the time. To view this contrast as portrayed in Ottoman sources is to appreciate the frame of mind in which Ottoman sultans and statesmen entered the era of reform. Always relating back to the state and its needs, the perceptions of these men provide the natural background for the reforms to be discussed in this chapter.

For contemporary Ottomans, the basic fact in their conception of the need for reform was the continued military defeats they endured. The military was one field in which innovative reform had already begun—in which, indeed, it had always been considered allowable. As Cevdet Paşa points out, however, Ottoman officials had little substantive knowledge of what it would mean to create a modern kind of military system, other than what some of them had gained by fighting armies better than their own.[6] On that account Ottoman efforts at military reform were to remain derivative in inspiration and dependent on obtaining technical assistance from European powers. Military problems nonetheless remained central to the thinking of Ottoman reformers, certainly through the reign of Mahmud, and would do more than anything else to fill any comprehensive account of the reforms of this period.

Any thought of improving military effectiveness raised the equally desperate question of finance. Ottoman statesmen of the 1790s could not escape the fact that the state was practically bankrupt. Selim's predecessor, Abd ül-Hamid I (1774-1789), had been reduced in his last years to lamenting: "This money business is giving me sleepless nights; God help the Sublime State. . . ."[7] The sultan's advisers, too, could think of no solutions more promising than soliciting contributions, further debasement of the coinage, or trying to borrow from foreign states such as Holland or the Sultanate of Morocco.[8]

Of course, none of these efforts worked. In the case of the loans, to judge from later experience, it was just as well. In the case of efforts to raise money internally, the problem was not only the inefficiency of Ottoman fiscal administration, but also the already far-advanced disruption of the Ottoman economy. Unfortunately, Ottoman officials were poorly equipped to address such issues. Their grasp of economic questions was weak by any standard. In the case of the scribal officials, ironically, the relative decline of the Treasury as a path to high office had diminished their preparation to deal with financial problems in the very period when the scribal service was gaining in political importance. So complex were the economic troubles of the period that even modern scholars do not understand them fully.[9] Contemporaries could not have seen them more clearly; yet they could not escape awareness of some of the economic problems of the state. Their inability to raise needed revenue would eventually lead them to think in terms of centralizing the financial administration. They were aware of the evolution of the capitulatory regime toward terms more and more disadvantageous to Ottoman commercial interests.[10] And they could not have failed to sense the linkage between economic disruption and the continuing pressure for expansion of bureaucratic ranks.

In hindsight, military defeat and economic disruption show that the Ottoman Empire was being drawn more and more into a world-embracing system of European hegemony. Ottoman thinkers understood this phenomenon only in part, but their

awareness stimulated their thinking about a broad range of
administrative issues.

They saw, for example, that government business was growing in volume and seriousness every day. This was especially
true of diplomatic affairs,[11] the more so in that many problems
that had once been purely domestic now had diplomatic repercussions. This is apparent in the claims of foreign powers to protect specific religious communities within the empire, in the
abuses of the capitulatory rights of consular protection,[12] and in
a whole galaxy of problems consequent upon loss of territory.

Anxiety about the future and the sense of the growth in volume and gravity of official business led in turn to a new concern
about the state of the governmental apparatus and the ruling
class, as well as to a rise in demands for efficient performance
from them. The influence of this demand on the evolution of
the various branches of the ruling class and on the characteristic
patterns of promotion to high office is already apparent. In the
consultative assemblies that the sultans and grand vezirs of the
eighteenth century convened to deal with problems of particular
gravity, the same demand made itself felt with particular force,
incidentally launching what would prove an unstoppable process of enlarging the basis of consultation. In the demands of the
sultans for solutions, and in the threats they made to officials
who did not meet their expectations, lie the origins of a new kind
of "activism," which became increasingly evident as the nineteenth century progressed. Understanding it in terms that Ottomans of an earlier generation could have appreciated, Cevdet
Paşa described this spirit with the Arabic aphorism "blessing is in
activity" (*al-baraka fî 'l-ḥaraka*).[13]

A kind of dynamic reaction to the trauma of helplessness in
the face of defeat, so widely apparent in the Middle East a half
century later, was thus already in evidence at the topmost echelons of the Ottoman "center." More than that, it had begun to
radiate downward and outward, provoking or preparing the
way for changes in many phases of the administration and in
many phases of its interactions with the subject classes. The concern for military reform and for generating increased levels of
resources are parts of this process. So was the related problem of
reasserting the control of the central government over Janissary
contingents and other disorderly elements in the towns[14] and, in
the countryside, over "notables" (*ayan*) and "lords of the valley"

(*derebey*), who not only enjoyed quasi autonomy locally but also, in the revolt of Bayrakdar Mustafa Paşa (1808), exerted a decisive if temporary influence over events in Istanbul.[15] In the power of the magnates, and in such forces as the Wahhabi movement, the empire building of Muhammad Ali Paşa in Egypt, or the nationalism of Serbs and Greeks, the reformers of the "center" encountered forms of resistance with which they could not effectively cope. In a sense, however, such frustrations only increased the incentives for reform.

As is implicit in the very concept of Selim's "New Order" (*nizam*), another lesson that the reformers quickly began to perceive was that reassertion of the "center" and reform in general would require a new emphasis on law and law enforcement. The fact that the legislative function of the traditional state, limited in any case by modern standards, had fallen to some degree into disuse in the period of decline[16] clearly heightens the significance of this new emphasis. So does the fact that the legislative activity of the reformers quickly became their most important instrument for introducing innovative policies. The culmination of the Bayrakdar Mustafa revolt in the signing of the "Deed of Agreement" (1808) provided a first sign of how readily this legislative reassertion might extend into changes in the fundamental constitutive principles of the state.[17] With the late reforms of Mahmud II, the use of the new legislative function for making such changes became a permanent feature of Ottoman political life.

The success of this legislative reassertion depended, in turn, on enforcement, not only over the subject classes, but also within the administration itself. Recognizing the extent to which the credibility of all their efforts at reform depended on the regularization of the governmental system itself, Selim and Mahmud directed a great part of their regulatory activity toward this objective. Even before the accession of Selim, however, Ottoman statesmen had begun to recognize the need for such improvements. This is clear from vezirial orders to prohibit abuses of official discipline,[18] from high-level complaints about irregularities in preparation of official documents at lower echelons,[19] and from anxiety about the character and purposes of many of the persons then thronging government offices.[20] Problems such as these were to remain objects of concern throughout the period of reform.

Alongside the sense of threat from without that underlay this growing recognition of a need for reform at the imperial "center," a more positive kind of consciousness of the outside world was also emerging. Toward the end of the eighteenth century, while the sense of European menace mounted sharply,[21] a subtler attraction did, too, opening new and larger breaches in the cultural exclusivism and insularity characteristic of traditional Islamic society. The causes of this change are too far-reaching for easy explanation. But it is certainly associated with the decline in the ability of the empire to deal with Europeans from a position of superiority, and thus also with the factors that underlay the growth of the scribal service in relative prominence within the ruling class. In particular, the development of a new outlook is linked to the temporary diplomatic missions that the sultans began to send out with increasing frequency in the eighteenth century, usually under the leadership of scribal ambassadors.[22]

A new degree of positive response to European cultural stimuli had appeared as early as the reign of Ahmed III (1703-1730), in what Berkes has termed the "silhouette of a renaissance."[23] At a later date, it reappeared in the extraordinary efforts of Selim III, even prior to his accession to the throne, to make contact with Louis XVI and gain French assistance for his projects of reform.[24] On the eve of Selim's inauguration of his "New Order," this new interest showed itself in ways especially significant for the development of the ruling class in the reports of the envoys Ebu Bekir Ratib Efendi, in Vienna in 1791-1792, and Ahmed Azmi Efendi, ambassador to Prussia in 1790-1792.

The most important ambassadorial reports of the last decades prior to Selim's institution of permanent embassies in 1793, the accounts prepared by these two men bear testimony to the considerable pains they took at their master's behest to learn about the states to which they were accredited. The unpublished but voluminous reports of Ratib Efendi, to judge from available accounts of them, describe in minute detail the Austrian armed forces, speaking as well of the principal ministries and other features of Austrian government and society.[25] The much briefer published report of Ahmed Azmi Efendi's embassy to Prussia lacks the military emphasis. Yet, it appends to the conventional narrative of the ambassador's journey a topical description of various significant aspects of the administrative system and the economic and social life of that most orderly of kingdoms. From the standpoint of any study of the ruling class, particular importance attaches to Azmi Efendi's laborious but clear description of the ministerial system and the division of portfolios, the concept of bureaucratic professionalism, the system of official salaries and ranks, and the startling facts that officials did not exact fees or bribes and that they were allowed to retain their positions as long as they rendered good service.[26] The implications of these discoveries for the spirit in which the bureaucrats, as opposed to the sultans, of the Ottoman Empire would approach the reform of the ruling class are of the utmost moment; and, while it has been known for some time that Ottoman diplomats were drawing these lessons from the Vienna of the 1830s,[27] this report makes clear that they had already drawn them elsewhere at the very beginning of the era of reform. To the eighteenth-century Ottoman grandee willing to look at contemporary Europe with something other than the traditional contempt, the spectacle could be eye-opening indeed.

As the era of reform opened, then, Ottoman statesmen had an increasing consciousness of Europe as a source both of threats and of ideas that might profitably be applied to improve their own situation. While the sense of threat made them particularly conscious of military issues and thus of fiscal ones, as well, there was also a general sense that administrative problems of all types were making new demands. From this followed a sense of the need to reestablish the control of the central government throughout the empire, to reassert the legislative initiative of the state, and to achieve the improved levels of administrative regularity indispensable for these ends. For reform to succeed, it would, according to this view, have to begin at the "center" and work outward from it.

Obviously unable to verbalize their problems in terms of such modern concepts as integration into a Europe-centered world system, activism, or movement away from a traditionalistic order toward a system of rational-legalism, contemporary Ottomans were nonetheless beginning to formulate essential elements of what modern observers understand by such concepts. Through media such as the memoranda that Selim solicited from leading officials prior to the inauguration of the "New Order,"[28] the ambassadorial reports just mentioned, and the others submitted in increasing volume with the subsequent adoption of a system of permanent, reciprocal diplomatic representation,[29] ideas such as these, and the increasing awareness of the Western world that lay behind them, provided the basic guidance for the reforms to follow. Among these were fundamental changes at the Sublime Porte and in the general corporate state of the scribal service.

REFORM IN THE TRADITIONAL SCRIBAL OFFICES OF THE SUBLIME PORTE

Less conspicuous and narrower in immediate impact than other parts of the "New Order," the reforms that Selim III carried out in the scribal offices have attracted little notice. Nonetheless, it is clear that in addition to creating a special new treasury (known as the "New Income" or *İrad-ı Cedid*) to provide financial services to his new troops, undertaking certain reforms in the preexisting Treasury Offices, and trying to improve the official historiography program,[30] Selim also introduced a series of reforms relating to the core of scribal offices headed by the chief scribe (*reis ül-küttab* or *reis efendi*) at the Sublime Porte. These changes, occurring in the Offices of the Imperial Divan (*Divan-ı Hümayun Kalemi*), the Corresponding Secretary (*Mektubî-i Sadr-ı Âli*), and the Receiver (*Amedî*) can be followed best, although not exclusively, in an archival register, the entries in which begin with several sets of regulations (*nizamname*) dating from the year 1797.[31]

The documents in this register show how Ottoman reformers first applied their perceptions of the general need for reform to specific problems of the scribal offices. For example, signs of mounting pressures for admission into official ranks find confirmation in a variety of prescriptions concerning overcrowding and other related problems. The documents make clear that all three of the offices were overstaffed, and the regulation on the Office of the Corresponding Secretary indicates clearly that the growth in the number of its clerks over the previous three to four decades had outstripped even the needs implied by the growth in the volume of affairs.[32] The fact that many of these unneeded clerks were either untrained or unreliable merely compounded the problems created by their presence. Thenceforth, the backgrounds of candidates for appointment in each of these offices were to be carefully checked. Persons lacking requisite qualifications were not to be admitted, nor were any past "middle age" (*vasat-ı sinni tecavüz edenler*) to be accepted into the Office of the Imperial Divan.[33] No appointments were to be made on the basis of requests or out of deference to men of influence. As the growing pressures on the empire from without and the desire of the sultan to reassert his power against the provincial magnates (*derebey, ayan*) heightened official awareness of the need to maintain the secrecy of government business, this stipulation bore special reference to persons who were in the employ of the magnates or their Istanbul agents and might thus be used to "infiltrate" the central offices.[34] This was one of the chief reasons for the anxiety about the thronging of the offices described in the last chapter.

In the case of the Offices of the Corresponding Secretary and Receiver (*Amedî*), an added concern appears in attempts to keep the main channel of scribal mobility from becoming clogged. The regulations for both these offices, which performed particularly important secretarial services for the grand vezir and the chief scribe, insist that persons employed in them be trained elsewhere, that the qualifications of all candidates for appointment be carefully verified, and that each appointment receive written approval from the sultan. No new clerks were to be taken into the Office of the Corresponding Secretary until the number already there fell within the prescribed limit of thirty, while in the Office of the Receiver, only large enough to accommodate five or six, unqualified persons were to be expelled and worthy ones brought in from other offices.[35]

Some of the same concerns that underlay these rulings on personnel procedures reappear in a regulation of the same year on the drafting and registration of official documents. Acknowledging that certain individuals had succeeded in having documents drawn up specially to facilitate their achievement of corrupt ends, this regulation ordered that due care be taken in reviewing and correcting drafts of orders as they were prepared for issue and forbade the mention in such documents, even by way of example, of anything contrary to law. Similarly, documents were not to be issued by offices other than those properly responsible for their issue, nor were certain matters requiring formal registration in the offices to be so registered without unequivocal order from the sultan.[36] The thought of extreme centralization of the administration seems to have been intoxicating, especially since the headaches that overcentralization could induce were still unknown.

The regulations issued in 1797 for the Office of the Imperial Divan also include a measure of particular significance for Selim's attempts to improve the effectiveness and confidentiality of administration. These regulations begin by describing the variety of matters handled in the office and the way in which the most secret of them had traditionally been drawn up by the *beylikçi*, the director of the office, or by the most trusted and experienced clerks, sometimes taken for the purpose into a separate room. On the supposition that the volume of business in the office would not be great—so the document puts it—those handling such important matters (*umur-ı mühimme*) had not originally been given a separate place, but left for the most part in the same room with the other clerks. This was no longer permissible. A separate room would have to be contrived for the clerks to whom the most confidential business was entrusted, so that they could be separated from the outsiders constantly entering and leaving the office, including not only Ottoman subjects but also the dragomans of the European embassies.[37]

Provision was thus made for the creation of a special Section for Important Affairs (*Divan-ı Hümayun Mühimme Odası*). It was to be staffed initially by fifteen experienced clerks, to whom might be added others of proven ability, to a total of thirty. Whenever incomes from any of the benefices in land assigned to the Office of the Imperial Divan became available, those incomes were to be assigned to the clerks of the new section on a preferential basis.[38] From the start a prestigious place to serve, the Section for Important Affairs was initially under the supervision of the "purse-bearer" (*kisedar*) who also supervised the *Beylik* Section, largest of the three preexisting sections of the Office of the Imperial Divan. The new section grew rapidly in size and acquired a director (*müdür*) of its own in 1837.[39]

The emergence of this new section is noteworthy for several reasons. As may be recalled, the term *mühimme* ("important affairs") was essentially a technical term, referring to matters closely linked to the interests of the state. The creation of a new section to specialize in such business thus appears to be another significant example of the kind of development that had earlier resulted in the emergence within the Office of the Imperial

Divan of the Sections for the Assignment of Benefices in Land
(*Tahvil*) and Appointments (*Rüus*). Precisely as the terms *tahvil*
and *rüus* had been in use before the appearance of those sections
to designate certain types of documents, so the term *mühimme*
had a long history. At least since the 1540s, there had existed a
distinct series of registers for the recording of such matters of
state, and by the end of the eighteenth century, various subseries, such as "secret important affairs" (*mektum mühimme*), had
also developed.[40] The creation of the Section for Important Affairs thus represents another step in the processes of differentiation and specialization already long at work in the scribal offices.
At the same time, it reflects a newer process, one of groping toward a system of stratifying official business in terms of different
degrees of confidentiality and restricting the diffusion of the
most sensitive types. The creation of the new section was only a
single step toward such a system, but it did provide a new model,
which would be followed in later years as a whole series of departments acquired their "Sections for Important Affairs."

In addition to recording the regulations of 1797 for the offices
subordinate to the chief scribe, the same register also includes
later entries indicating the extent to which these measures took
effect. From these entries and other supplementary documentation, it is clear that while the Section for Important Affairs continued to exist, the problems that led to its creation did, too, the
more so as a result of the discontinuity in the reformist initiative
in the years following Selim's fall.

The regulations issued for the Office of the Imperial Divan in
1797 attempted, among other things, to remedy the overcrowding in its older sections by ordering a two-year moratorium on
new appointments and imposing a quota on the numbers of new
clerks, other than sons of men already serving in the office, who
could be taken in thereafter. This quota allowed for only twelve
appointments a year, six in the *Beylik* Section and three each in
the Sections for Appointments (*Rüus*) and Benefice-Assignment
(*Tahvil*).[41] In 1801, an increase in business on account of an approaching campaign became the pretext for admitting all aspirants from whom petitions for appointment were then on hand
and then doubling the quotas.[42] Since there is nothing to indicate that the quotas were subsequently reduced, it is natural to
wonder if things were not again getting out of control. In the
new Section for Important Affairs, this certainly happened.

While the number employed there was initially to be limited to thirty, appointed strictly on the basis of ability, the workings of favoritism and the natural aspiration of the officials to serve in a prestigious office soon shattered this limit. Forty years after its foundation, the staff of this section exceeded one hundred, even though thirty clerks were still, as of 1832, officially considered enough.[43]

As for the attempt to ensure the prior training of persons appointed to the Offices of the Corresponding Secretary (*Mektubî*) and Receiver (*Amedî*), a document dating from some ten years after the original regulations presents it as more or less an oversight that there was no provision for appointment directly into the Office of the Corresponding Secretary of the sons of its employees. Thenceforth, persons whose fathers were already serving there were to be eligible for appointment as supernumeraries (*mülâzım*) without written permission from the sultan, and might become full-fledged clerks as the regular staff fell within its prescribed limit. Supposedly, such candidates would be examined by the supervisory officials of the office, but these examinations were apt to be perfunctory. Rather clearly, the "patrimonial style in recruitment" had prevailed again.[44]

The fact that this concession dates from a few months after Selim's downfall is surely not fortuitous. Indeed, except in the case of the Greek translators, whose situation became untenable with the outbreak of the Greek Revolution, the state of the scribal offices did not arouse any particular concern again before the early 1830s. Then, presumably under the impact of the first, disastrous "round" of the conflict with Muhammad Ali Paşa of Egypt, Mahmud II began to move toward a general reassessment of governmental institutions. As it relates to the Porte, this new approach is clearest in reforms undertaken outside the traditional offices of the chief scribe. Relating to those offices among others, however, a decree of 1832 provides one of the first signs of what was to come.

This document makes clear, though without mention of specific numbers, that overcrowding and the presence in official position of persons of unknown qualifications and intentions were still serious problems. The document promises an investigation of the clerks of both the Sublime Porte and the Treasury Offices to find out "what sort of men [they are] and whose sons, relatives, and dependents"; the presentation of a register containing the findings of the inquiry; the expulsion of the unworthy; and the transfer of qualified but unneeded men to offices short of personnel or to the engineering school (*mühendishane*) or printing house (*tabhane*).[45]

It is not clear how much fruit this promise bore; but the archival register that has been the basic source for this discussion shows this period closing with a measure of tremendous significance both for the traditional scribal offices and for the new institutions that had by then begun to grow up beyond them. This is the founding in 1839 of the *Mekteb-i Maarif-i Adliye*, the first of the new schools set up specifically to train young men for civil-bureaucratic careers, and thus the first element of what would become the imperial network of secular, civil schools.[46]

This document begins with the observation that while attempts to improve the quality of military and naval training had been in progress for a number of years, nothing had yet been done to remedy the ignorance of students emerging from the elementary mosque schools to enter government offices. Before being apprenticed in the offices at age eight or ten, they would at most have learned the Kur'an by rote and traced out a few exercises in a basic script (*sülüs karalayub*), would not have learned any Arabic or Persian (or had any formal instruction in Turkish, for that matter), and perhaps never even have heard the names of such essential subjects as arithmetic or geography. To train them properly in the offices was at last acknowledged as impossible: proper clerks emerging from such material were "rare to the point of nonexistence" (*al-nâdir ka'l-ma'dûm*). The growing demands on the scribal officials required that the educational and clerical functions, traditionally combined in the offices, be separated. Thus occurred one more step toward subdivision of functions, the first clear concession that the guild-like system of training by apprenticeship was no longer functioning adequately for the needs of the scribal service, and the starting point of one of the most important processes through which reform in the central offices would transform the society outside.

Thus, in the traditional scribal offices of the Porte or in direct connection with them, the first of the political periods of the era of reform included a number of important changes. To a degree, these reflected processes of specialization and differentiation already operative in earlier times. In other respects, as in the developing concern for distinguishing different levels of confidentiality, or in the move to separate the training of officials from their service in the offices, the changes were innovative and would, particularly in the case of the school, produce effects extending far beyond the Sublime Porte. Change did not come easily, to be sure. As the difficulties of controlling the numbers and quality of personnel imply, the self-interest and indiscipline of the scribal officials and of those who aspired to join their ranks would survive into the era of reform, and infect the new organizations then created. Similarly, the new school was at best a single breach in the guild-like pattern traditionally characteristic of the lower scribal officials. Nonetheless, the measures here discussed marked first steps in the old central offices toward the administrative regularization that was beginning to assume such a central place in the reformist consciousness.

THE FOUNDATION OF THE FOREIGN MINISTRY AND THE FORMATION OF A MODERNIST SCRIBAL ELITE

Fully to appreciate the changes that Selim and Mahmud made in the part of the scribal service associated with the Porte, we must now examine a sequence of events that occurred chiefly outside the old central offices. These events began in 1793 with what was, in terms of its cultural significance, one of the most innovative of all the reforms of Selim's "New Order": the setting up of a system of permanent embassies in European capitals, and thus the acceptance of the Western concept of permanent, reciprocal diplomacy.[47] Starting with this measure, efforts at reform within old offices and without eventually converged in Mahmud's formal inauguration of a Foreign Ministry. The same sequence of events was also of critical importance in consummating the political emergence of the scribal service. For these events precipitated the formation of a new scribal elite, which not only assumed responsibility for the foreign relations of the empire, but also, thanks to its Westernist cultural orientation acquired through adaptation to the diplomatic role, emerged as the vanguard of modernization in the internal affairs of the empire.

Since the Ottoman Empire had never before sent out embassies on any but a temporary basis and had also applied restrictions that were unconventional by international standards to the permanent embassies of European states in Istanbul, the shift to diplomatic practices of the European type was more complicated than might be expected. In the eighteenth century, for example, European ambassadors in Istanbul were still treated as guests. The Ottoman government paid their expenses while they were within its frontiers and assigned escort officers (*mihmandar*) to them in their travels. In return, the ambassadors had to remain under something like house arrest in their residences, to conform on ceremonial occasions to a demeaning etiquette, and to expect, in time of trouble between the Ottomans and their own governments, to be imprisoned and treated as hostages. After discovering that European governments could not be counted on to pay the expenses of ambassadors accredited to them, the Ottomans began to adapt to international conventions, resisting the process where the old ways favored their interests and encountering European resistance where the advantages fell to the other side.[48]

In fact, the difficulties of adjusting to Western-style diplomatic conventions became a theme of the early history of the Ottoman diplomatic system. Before Selim sent out the first of his permanent embassies, Ottoman officials held detailed discussions with the British ambassador in Istanbul on questions such as which Ottoman officials should, given the disparities of governmental organization, correspond with which European officials, which diplomatic ranks would be best for the new envoys, whether they should travel by land or sea, and other such questions.[49] These were only the first of countless lessons that Ottoman officials would have to learn; the formalism and snobbery common in European diplomatic circles would make many of the lessons unpleasant in the extreme.

Selim's initial plan for sending out his new embassies was that they should go to London, Paris, Vienna, and Berlin for terms of three years each. Each ambassador was to have on his staff young men whose duties would include learning languages and other subjects useful in the service of the state. The first step in implementation of this plan was the sending of Yusuf Agâh Efendi to London in 1793. Within a few years there were missions in all four capitals.[50]

In addition to these attempts to organize a diplomatic corps, Selim appointed consuls to attend to the commercial interests of his subjects abroad. Or rather, it may be more accurate to say that he gave official form to a preexisting consular "system" which had never before had more than a partially official character. As early as 1725, the Grand Vezir Nevşehirli İbrahim Paşa had appointed one Ömer Ağa consul in Vienna.[51] Seemingly an isolated event without sequel, this was perhaps just one more of the velleities of change so characteristic of that time. With or without official appointment, however, "consuls" clearly existed in a variety of places between 1725 and 1802, when their "appointments" began to be recorded officially in a special register. Traian Stoianovich has pointed out that it was traditional by then for Orthodox Balkan merchants trading outside the empire to be "organized into companies or merchant guilds, with a *'consul'* or *'Richter'* [judge] at their head to smooth out discords and promote the business of the entire 'company'."[52] When, apparently in the reign of Selim III, the Ottomans attempted to organize two groups of merchants made up of subjects of the empire, Muslim in one case (*hayriye tüccarı*) and non-Muslim in the other (*Avrupa tüccarı*), who in order to compete more effectively with Europeans would be given privileges analogous to those that the latter enjoyed under the capitulations, the same kind of office appeared among them under the name of *şehbender*.[53] Having originally referred to something like the "mayor" or "provost" of a port town, or by extension to a customs collector, this term was to become in late Ottoman usage the normal one for "consul."[54]

The evolution in meaning of the term *şehbender*, and the terms that Stoianovich uses, provide another significant reflection of the intermingling in Ottoman ideas on the organization of international trade of elements from the organizational traditions of the guilds and the autonomous confessional communities. The issue of brevets of appointment to these "consuls" gave them official status, and the recording of those brevets in a special register makes it possible to trace the gradual development of an official network of consular posts. Beginning in the Mediterranean trade centers in which the disturbances created by the French Revolution had given merchants from Ottoman lands a greatly augmented role, this network extended within a few years to major Western centers such as London and Amsterdam, where such merchants had by this time also long been active.[55]

In the short run, Selim's attempts to establish systems of permanent diplomatic and consular representation were hardly more successful than most other parts of his "New Order." The changeable diplomatic climate of the Napoleonic era and Selim's eventual fall were enough to ensure this. Both systems continued to operate for over a decade after 1807, but even before that time their results had been uneven.

The problems of the early embassies provide insights into the difficulties Ottoman reformers would have to overcome before they could succeed in establishing a new basis of interaction with Western powers. These problems included the transition to the international diplomatic conventions of the times. But a more serious, indeed fundamental, problem was the lack of any well-developed organizational basis for the operation of a system of permanent reciprocal diplomacy. Although the chief scribe had begun to take on some of the attributes of a foreign minister, the agencies under him at the Porte still included none specializing in the coordination and supervision of the foreign relations of the empire. The role of the one partial exception, the translator of the imperial Divan, was essentially limited to relations with the European diplomats in Istanbul. With this lack of organization went the absence of any system for selecting diplomatic personnel and an almost total dearth of officials with real qualifications for diplomatic service, however distinguished some of the early diplomats may have been as exponents of the traditional scribal culture.[56]

The lack of any definable system for making foreign policy was a natural extension of these facts. Indeed, it does not appear that the empire really had a very clear or highly articulated foreign policy at all. The accounts of the embassies abroad show ambassadors striving for alliances or military assistance,[57] or for the impossible goal of getting commercial privileges for Ottoman merchants like those that Europeans enjoyed in the empire under the capitulations.[58] Various ambassadors attempted to influence the European press, or at least reported on it to the Porte.[59] At least one of them attempted to negotiate a foreign loan.[60] On balance, what stands out about their missions is not that they had specific, let alone attainable, policy objectives to pursue, but rather that they and their secretaries were expected, as had been Ebu Bekir Ratib and Ahmed Azmi Efendis, to learn in a general way about the countries to which they had been sent.[61] Understandable in terms of the low level of policy articulation in traditional political systems, as well as in terms of the novelty of permanent diplomatic representation, this fact also bespeaks the position of cultural dependency that the empire assumed in relation to the Western world as the era of westernizing reform began.

It is only natural, then, that the achievements of the early Ottoman ambassadors were limited. Faced with problems such as the necessity of relying on interpreters of questionable qualifications and reliability,[62] poor communications with Istanbul, severe financial hardship,[63] and the nonchalance with which European statesmen could ignore Ottoman interests, some of the envoys seem to have found the strain more than they could bear.[64] At least one, Halet Efendi, became a vociferous and, for a time, extremely influential opponent of westernization.[65] In Istanbul, Selim knew that his diplomatic system was not working well. All too often, however, he could do no more about this than scribble irate comments on the reports he received.[66]

In beginning to add to the traditional scribal culture a new dimension of knowledge about the outside world, Selim's diplomats did, however, make gains that would have long-term significance. To document such gains is difficult, but some evidence has survived. For example, "İngiliz" Mahmud Raif Efendi, who went to London as first secretary to Yusuf Agâh Efendi and learned French there, later became chief scribe and wrote several works in French. Two of these were published in Istanbul, one in French in 1798, one in Ottoman translation in 1804-1805.[67]

A more prestigious member of the first generation of diplomats, the future Grand Vezir Mehmed Said Galib Paşa, made his contributions through his official roles, including an important part in the abolition of the Janissaries, and through personal links as the patron of Pertev Paşa, who in turn was patron of Sadık Rif'at and Mustafa Reşid Paşas.[68] Both of these emerged as leading diplomat-reformers in the mid-1830s, Mustafa Reşid becoming the dominant figure of the reform movement for two decades thereafter.

Another significant figure among the early diplomats was İsmail Ferruh Efendi, Yusuf Agâh's successor in London. Following his return to Istanbul, İsmail Ferruh is known to have been associated with a "scientific society" (*cemiyet-i ilmiye*), which included some of the most broadly learned intellectuals of the day and devoted itself to scientific, literary, and philosophical discussions, as well as to the teaching of individuals interested in such subjects.[69] The educational activities of the society, and the acquisition of İsmail Ferruh's library for the first of the new civil schools at its foundation in 1839, are good indications of the lasting influence that he and his friends exerted.[70]

In the career of İsmail Ferruh there also appears another noteworthy motif, that of official reliance on what were, in terms of the customary social and cultural norms of the scribal service, "marginal men." This motif would reappear with some frequency over the next several decades, until a pool of manpower more adequately prepared for diplomatic roles, and thus endowed with some of the characteristics that had made the "marginal men" useful, had come into existence within the scribal service. A colorful example of these "marginal" types, İsmail Ferruh differed from the typical scribal efendi of the old school in coming from the lands of the former Crimean khanate—the fall of which could hardly have failed to stimulate in him a consciousness of international political problems—and in having made his livelihood more in commerce than in official service. The British ambassador's account of İsmail Ferruh's departure from Istanbul in 1797 records these facts, incidentally providing a memorable indication of how far the Ottomans still were from having adapted to European diplomatic conventions:

Ismael Effendi himself is the son of a reputable merchant at Ozon (Oczakov), where he was born; and has been chiefly bred to trade which gradually led him to the directorship of the public corn magazines in Constantinople; an office of much responsibility, but more emolument than splendor. He can hardly be fifty years of age; and I have already ventured to mention him to your Lordship as a person whose general reputation, and personal expressions, authorised me to consider him as less tinctured with fanatical prejudices, so incompatible with his new career, than many of his countrymen; and perhaps more disposed to identify himself properly with the *Corps diplomatique* than his predecessor. He is so far familiarised with Franks, as to be the only Ottoman of the higher rank, who resides in the village of Boyukdereh, on the Bosphorus, the usual summer resort of the foreign ministers. He is in affluent condition, as your Lordship may judge from the circumstance of his having upon hand at the settlement of his public accompts, when removed from the inspection of the granaries, a stock valued at near 2, millions of Piastres. He has hitherto lived in an opulent stile . . . ; but yet some of the arrangements of his present expedition have rather shewn him liable to be actuated by . . . avarice . . . , perhaps fixed in him by previous mercantile habits. In making his bargain with Captain Castle, which was for 12,000 Piastres (about £900 sterling), he stipulated for the privilege of 800 Quintals stowage, with a view to make a trading voyage by shipping some of his superfluous wheat for sale in Italy: and, having once yeilded to this speculation he could not resist the farther temptation of turning nearly his whole privilege to account in this way so as not only to curtail his sea stores, particularly such an article as water, which the known excess of Mussulman consumption renders most essential, in spite of the best advice; but even to cramp his own comfort, and destroy every advantage to be derived from the hire of a private yacht, by crowding his party into a single indifferent appartment.[71]

Foreign Office officials in London must have been amused at these details. From the Ottoman point of view, it is perhaps unfortunate that there were not more men available with similar qualities.

During the interruption that all aspects of reform underwent after the fall of Selim, efforts to widen the horizons of the scribal service ground more or less to a halt, and the diplomatic and consular systems fell into a state of atrophy. After 1811, none of the diplomatic posts was manned by anything more than a *chargé d'affaires*, the best known being J. Mavroyeni, a Greek who held that post in Vienna.[72] The *chargés* and consuls of the time being Greek, by and large, the outbreak of the Greek Revolution in 1821 led to the abolition of the diplomatic service for the time being.[73] In the case of the consular service, the break may have been less decisive, perhaps only a reversion to the nonofficial status of the eighteenth century.[74] Still, there would be no more diplomatic appointments until the early 1830s; no more consular ones until the middle of that decade.

In Istanbul, meanwhile, the same suspicions about Greeks in official service gave rise at the outbreak of the revolution to a general attack on the Phenariot elite. One phase of this was the overthrow of the last of the Greek translators of the imperial Divan and the creation in his place of a new Translation Office of the Sublime Porte (*Bab-ı Âli Tercüme Odası*). The purpose of the new office was to relieve the state once and for all of the need to rely on Greeks as translators. Since the responsibilities of this office included a typical mixture of educational and bureaucratic roles, it gradually began to yield the desired result, becoming in the process the principal center for the formation of a new type of Muslim scribal official and at the same time the most prestigious place of service at the Sublime Porte. Partly because of the initial lack of qualified Muslims, however, the new office had first to pass through a period of obscurity during which the continued reliance on "marginal men" was one of its most prominent features.

The Translation Office emerged in stages, beginning in the spring of 1821, when Constantine Mourouzi was dismissed from the translatorship of the imperial Divan and executed on grounds of complicity in revolutionary intrigues. To replace him, a teacher from the military engineering school (*mühendishane*), a Bulgarian convert to Islam, known as Bulgarzade Yahya Efendi, and his son, Ruh ul-Din Efendi, were summoned to the Porte to translate Greek and French documents and to train one or two assistants. When it became apparent that this would not yield satisfactory results fast enough, Stavraki Aristarchi, thought to be reliable though still suspect as a Greek, was given the post of translator on an interim basis, with Yahya Efendi to check his work. By April 1822, the supposedly neutral Aristarchi had compromised himself sufficiently that he, too, was dismissed and sent into exile. Never again would a Greek serve as translator of the imperial Divan.[75]

Eventually, Yahya Efendi formally received that title, although he hardly brought to the post all that was desired. The British ambassador said of him that he was "thought to be profoundly versed in the abstract Sciences. But he is not well acquainted with any [*sic*] of the European languages, and even his knowledge of Turkish is said to be limited."[76] Ottomans had doubts about Yahya's occupancy of such a sensitive position on account of his character as a "marginal man." The noted scholar, Şanizade, who was probably better qualified for the post but for whom, as a prestigious member of the religious establishment, it was not thought appropriate, bluntly said that Yahya was left in the job "because a Muslim could not be found."[77]

By the time of Aristarchi's dismissal, Yahya had as his assistant another "marginal" type, an Armenian named Zenob Manasseh, reported to be of European education and a good linguist.[78] The two of them also had a few apprentices to train. A contemporary account shows Yahya Efendi and his associates hard at work:

> M. Chabert [one of the dragomans of the British embassy] called upon him a few mornings ago, and found him surrounded by a number of the young Turks whom the Porte has lately formed into a sort of Collegiate Establishment for the purpose of instruction in the European languages. They had a prodigious pile of the Frankfort Gazettes before them, and were busily engaged in translating indiscriminately, by the sultan's positive order, every Article in which the name or the Affairs of Turkey were to be found. His Highness will, assuredly, be not a little astounded on reading some of the paragraphs dated from Odessa—Augsburgh—and Nuremberg.[79]

Thus began the Translation Office of the Sublime Porte. For the period down to 1833, the office remained very small, and contemporaries, if aware of it at all, seemed to doubt its worth.[80] Most of those associated with the office were still "marginal men," and while several had or acquired importance in one respect or another, none of them ever achieved front-ranking political position in the reformist elite.

Of most immediately perceptible importance was Yahya Efendi's successor as head of the office, İshak Efendi. Resembling Yahya in being of non-Muslim origin, at least according to some accounts, and in having served previously in the military engineering schools, İshak Efendi was in fact a pioneer in the modernization of Ottoman education, especially in technical fields.[81] Of the men who served under him, one, Mehmed Namık Paşa (c. 1804-1892), would discharge several significant diplomatic missions and, shifting to a military career, play a major role in the founding of the new Ottoman Military Academy (*Mekteb-i Harbiye*, 1834) before parting company with the reformist movement.[82] Another is chiefly of interest in this setting as an extreme example of the sociocultural "marginality" of the figures on whom the early reformers had to rely. An English orphan who had apparently been sent to sea and had jumped ship in Istanbul, James Redhouse (1811-1892) was destined to serve the Ottoman government in a variety of sensitive capacities down to the outbreak of the Crimean War and ultimately to distinguish himself as a Turkish lexicographer of unexcelled importance.[83]

The real growth of the Translation Office in size and prestige began only in the 1830s. In the tense interlude between the defeat of the Ottoman armies by the Egyptians at Konya (December 1832) and the conclusion of the Russo-Ottoman Treaty of Hünkâr İskelesi (July 1833), the Translation Office, like the traditional offices discussed in the last section, came under renewed scrutiny. The employees of the office received sizable increases in salary and were joined by three young men from the Important Affairs Section of the Office of the Imperial Divan.[84] These included Âli and Safvet Efendis, each of whom would serve in time as both foreign minister and grand vezir. Within a few years, two more future grand vezirs had joined them: Keçecizade Fuad and Ahmed Vefik Efendis.

Son of Ruh ul-Din and grandson of Bulgarzade Yahya, Ahmed Vefik is a convenient symbol of the way in which service in the Translation Office ceased about this time to be a "marginal" activity and began to appear instead as something highly desirable for the young scribal efendi on the way up. The presence in the office of Âli (1815-1871) and Fuad (1815-1869), who with Mustafa Reşid (1800-1858) would be the leading statesmen of the next political period, is added proof of this change, as is the growth of the office, which acquired a staff of thirty by 1841.[85] With the diplomatic repercussions of the Ottoman-Egyptian crisis, knowledge of French thus clearly began, in Bernard Lewis's phrase, to serve as the "talisman" of preferment, and the main source from which a scribal official could acquire this knowledge was the Translation Office of the Porte.[86]

With this growth in the size and importance of the Translation Office went another response to the same set of underlying pressures: Mahmud's decision to revive the system of permanent diplomatic representation. Since 1832, when on an Austrian proposal Mahmud had reappointed J. Mavroyeni as *chargé d'affaires* in Vienna, the empire had had one, but only one, diplomatic agent permanently resident in the West.[87] Mahmud had also sent out several temporary embassies, including one under Mehmed Namık Paşa, whose mission took him to both London and Saint Petersburg.[88] In 1834, however, Mahmud began to reestablish permanent embassies, starting with the assignment of the then receiver (*amedî*), Mustafa Reşid Bey (Paşa after January 1838) to Paris. With him and the other ambassadors who shortly began to follow him went suites of officials, drawn for the most part from the Offices of the Imperial Divan, the Corresponding Secretary, and the *Amedî*. As translators, Mustafa Reşid took Ruh ul-Din Efendi; the other ambassadors of this period still took Ottoman Greeks, whom Âli and Fuad would only begin to replace a few years later. Soon, too, the appointment of consuls resumed, and with it the extensive growth that characterized the consular service in the following period.

Contemporary documentation suggests that the resumption of diplomatic representation after such a lengthy interval brought with it many of the same problems as in Selim's day. In addition, there is at least one traditional type of problem that surely impinged on Selim's efforts, as well, but is in fact much more readily documented for this period. This is the way in which the patrimonial tradition of politico-bureaucratic life interfered with the rational working of the diplomatic system. The role of personal relationships in determining diplomatic appointments that were otherwise quite foolish is one example of this interference.[89] Another is the impingement on the diplomatic system of factional rivalries. The clearest case of this is the violent wrench given the official wheel of fortune by the fall and death in 1837 of Pertev Paşa, who had been patron to such leading modernists as Mustafa Reşid and Sadık Rif'at, and whose overthrow led to an extensive turnover of personnel in the embassies and in the central offices from which diplomatic appointments were usually made.[90] In the behavior of the sultan, the importance of the patrimonial tradition expressed itself not only in the critical role of the sovereign in determining the outcome of factional clashes, but also in the way in which the long-familiar desire for magnificence and display combined with a newer aspiration to modernity to create a peculiar attitude toward the diplomatic system. An Austrian diplomat characterized this attitude succinctly when he referred to the "sort of *gloriole*" that Mahmud attached to having ambassadors in Europe.[91]

But for certain other circumstances, Mahmud's efforts at diplomacy might thus have produced no greater result than Selim's. The situation of the 1830s differed from that of the 1790s, however, in at least two critical respects. One was the availability within the ruling class of men much better prepared to function in a diplomatic setting. The growth of the Translation Office is symbolic of this development, although in fact the uncertainty of its early history means that some of the new diplomats had to acquire their French elsewhere on a catch-as-catch-can basis.[92] The other major change is that the international situation was vastly different, Middle Eastern affairs being now of much greater interest in Europe than they had been forty years earlier. In particular, the collective European intervention in settling the Ottoman-Egyptian conflict of 1839 showed that there was now a basis, given the danger of what might happen if Muhammad Ali destroyed the empire, for common action by the European powers in support of vital interests of the Porte.[93] Of course, this support had its limits and its costs. The empire had to make concessions in other spheres, such as commercial policy, and it had to demonstrate its capacity for reform in ways that Europeans recognized and appreciated.

Under the circumstances, the position of Mahmud's diplomats proved to be important, if in a paradoxical way. Representatives of a state dependent for its very survival on outside aid, the Ottoman diplomats of the 1830s were again doomed to a role of relative effacement on the international political scene. With goals such as settling the Egyptian and Algerian questions, renegotiating tariffs, influencing the European press, and training additional diplomats,[94] they really could not succeed anywhere, aside from the training function, except where they had European help. Even there, as the Anglo-Ottoman Commercial Treaty of 1838 showed, they succeeded only on European terms.

Where Mahmud's diplomats really produced their impact was not so much as representatives of the Ottoman Empire to the states of Europe as in their unprecedented ability to absorb and respond to their experiences abroad, and in their role in mediating the demands of the major powers to their own people. Thus, in representing the West to the Ottomans, more than the other way round, they quickly acquired an influence that extended in Ottoman official circles far beyond the field of foreign affairs as narrowly defined.

In fact, the competence of the new diplomats to assume this role of expertise in westernization was still in an early stage of development. One sign of this is the contrast between the im-

pression of diplomatic ineptitude that Sadık Rif'at made as ambassador in Vienna on the noted orientalist, Joseph von Hammer, and the reputation that Sadık Rif'at continues to enjoy in
Turkey as one of the pioneers of modernization.[95] The limits of
the diplomats' comprehension no doubt also help to explain the
parochial or short-sighted reasoning that seems at times to lie
behind their espousal of certain concepts. This would appear to
be true in their advocacy of the principles of guaranteed individual rights and legal equality. As Şerif Mardin has plausibly
argued, these ideas must have appealed to scribal diplomats of
this generation primarily as a means by which to strengthen the
position of the servile official class in relation to the sultan and
thus prevent more such catastrophes as the death of Pertev.[96]
Ottomans of the 1830s could not have foreseen the effects that
official adoption of these principles would produce on the traditional social and legal systems of the empire.

And yet, the best of the new diplomats were extremely intelligent men, in direct contact with the most influential European
statesmen of the day, including Metternich and Palmerston.
While the first steps of a Sadık Rif'at or a Mustafa Reşid as diplomats reflected the difficulties of adjusting to a new world, their
writings,[97] and still more their influence on subsequent reforms,
reflect the eagerness with which they responded to the political
lessons to be drawn from the Europe of the 1830s. The vital importance to the empire of the function that they were uniquely
able to perform also provided the diplomats with the political
leverage to translate their ideas quickly into actions of the most
far-reaching significance, a fact that the reforms of the later
1830s began to make clear.

Coming from what was still a relatively small branch of the ruling class, the new diplomatic elite was at this stage only a tiny
band of relatively young men. Those among them who would
play major creative roles in the reform of the empire included
hardly more than Mustafa Reşid, Sadık Rif'at, and the younger
Âli and Fuad. With all their factional hangers-on, irrespective of
merit, they were probably not over one or two score. Nonetheless, they would grow rapidly in numbers, as well as in expertise
and influence. With them, a new elite emerged and a kind of cultural orientation formerly marginal to the norms of the scribal
service assumed a central place within it. Indeed, the scribal tradition began to take on a whole new dimension, if at the cost of

the sociocultural homogeneity once characteristic of Muslim scribal officials. Thus, the processes that over a century and more had brought the scribal service to a position of political preeminence within the ruling class approached their culmination in the era of reform.

As if to provide an organizational basis for this new elite, Mahmud, having strengthened the Translation Office and revived the diplomatic and consular services, went on in March 1836 to transform the chief scribe into a foreign minister (*hariciye nazırı*).[98] While in a sense this was no more than a change of title, Mahmud also began to create other components of what could serve as a Ministry of Foreign Affairs. In November 1836, he instituted the office of *müsteşar* or undersecretary.[99] Slightly over a year later, among a number of important reforms, the traditional Offices of the Corresponding Secretary and the Receiver (*Amedî*) were subdivided into separate sections for internal and foreign affairs, and these in turn were placed under authority of the appropriate ministers.[100] With the Translation Office of the Sublime Porte, the Office of the Imperial Divan, which now included the Section for Important Affairs (*Mühimme Odası*) along with the three traditional sections shown in Figure III-2, and the recently reactivated consular and diplomatic services, this would have been the entire organizational complement of the Foreign Ministry as of 1839.

With the measures which shaped this Foreign Ministry and its diplomats, the Sublime Porte and the scribal service underwent some of the most important changes of the nineteenth century. Not only was a new ministry of critical importance beginning to take shape, but in the process a new elite was forming. In many respects the changes were still far from consolidated. The entanglement of reform in the vicious factional politics of the old style is one witness to this fact. Another is the haste with which new ideas, their implications for Ottoman society still untested, began to be taken up for application. In addition, there was the question, scarcely broached as yet, of the effect that further growth of this new elite would exert on social and political relations within the ruling class.

For his part, Sultan Mahmud gave no heed to doubts such as these. For him, the formation of the diplomatic service and the creation of the Foreign Ministry were part of a larger set of measures governed by a goal distinctly his own. Occurring together in the 1830s, these measures rapidly transformed the organization of the central administration, the corporate state of the scribal service, and thus the context in which the problems implied by the emergence of the new diplomatic elite would continue to develop.

The Later Reforms of Mahmud II: An Autocratic Sultan or a "Patriciate of the Pen"?

Writing in 1835, Joseph von Hammer said that if his book of twenty years earlier on the Ottoman administrative system were to be brought up to date, it would have to be completely revised. If change continued at the same rate, he added, such a revision would also soon be outdated.[101] In the four remaining years of his life, Mahmud proved this prediction to be well founded. Attempting to push centralization and the reassertion of sultanic dominance as far as possible, he launched a frontal assault on the Sublime Porte, dismantled the grand vezirate, and reorganized the scribal service—and the palace service also—to serve as instruments of his personal control. Given his objectives, the changes he made in the scribal service were to be of paradoxically decisive import; for they amounted to giving it, largely at the inspiration of the new diplomatic elite, the much-enhanced organizational forms of what would subsequently become known as the civil bureaucracy (*mülkiye*).

The attack on the Porte is, in fact, the context in which the shift of title from chief scribe to foreign minister occurred. Along with that change, Mahmud also transformed the former steward (*kâhya bey*) of the grand vezir into first the minister of civil affairs (*mülkiye nazırı*) and then in 1837 the minister of the interior (*dahiliye nazırı*), simultaneously giving to the two new ministers and to two treasurers the highest of ranks and enormously inflated stipends.[102] So began the reorganization of the administration along the lines of a European system of ministries. Soon, the chief bailiff (*çavuş başı*) also turned into what is sometimes likened, not too accurately, to a minister of justice (*divan-ı deavi nazırı*);[103] the chief treasurer, into a minister of finance (*maliye nazırı*);[104] and so on.

The central object of these changes became apparent in the spring of 1838, when Mahmud not only abolished the title of grand vezir, but also entrusted the successor post of prime minister (*baş vekil*) as an additional duty to the man then serving as minister of the interior.[105] Attempting thus to wipe out the traditional role of the grand vezir as "absolute delegate" of the sultan, Mahmud went on to parcel out the deliberative functions of the grand vezir's Divan. For example, he reassigned responsibility for the religio-legal cases formerly heard there to the headquarters of the religious establishment (*Bab-ı Meşihat*). Just as the most senior religious judges had formerly attended the *divan*s at the Porte to participate in the decisions on such cases, now the minister of justice had to go to the *Bab-ı Meşihat* for the appropriate sessions.[106] In addition, Mahmud created two new councils, patterned after one that he had already set up to take charge of the legislative process as it related to military affairs.[107] One of the new councils was known as the Consultative Assembly of the Sublime Porte (*Dar-ı Şura-yı Bab-ı Âli*), the other as the Supreme Council of Judicial Ordinances (*Meclis-i Vâlâ-yı Ahkâm-ı Adliye*). The latter was to meet under Mahmud's own direction at the palace.[108]

Ottomans with some knowledge of Western institutions excitedly compared these new councils to the two houses of a European *parlamento*.[109] The real affinities of these institutions lay, however, with the ad hoc consultative assemblies that we have already seen in the eighteenth century. For the future, what the new councils signified was a step toward the more general diffusion of the conciliar form of administration, the emergence of the legislative councils that would assume an important role in the next period, and the shaping of a council of ministers, to which each of the new councils was also sometimes likened.[110] Significantly, however, the history of the Consultative Assembly of the Sublime Porte proved shadowy and brief.[111] That the Supreme Council of Judicial Ordinances survived is another sign that Mahmud was trying to bring the center of deliberation back to its classic locus in the palace, an implication that gains in significance from the contemporaneous reorganization of the palace secretariat, discussed in Chapter Two.

Thus began the general reorganization of the Sublime Porte. While the pattern that Mahmud created was modified soon after his death and was thus ephemeral, it is nonetheless worthwhile for purposes of comparison with the organization charts presented in other chapters to include at this point a graphic representation of this arrangement as he left it. In this and subsequent figures, we shall no longer attempt, as we did in Figure III-2, to show all the personnel categories within each office. Since we have already commented on the internal structure of the Foreign Ministry, and since there is little concrete information for this date on the staffs of the supposed minister of justice or minister of the interior, it will nonetheless be useful to try in the figure to identify the component agencies of these three ministries. Among these components, the two corresponding secretaries and the pair of what we shall, for want of a better translation for *maruzat*, call reports officers are the products of the subdivision of the older Offices of the Corresponding Secretary of the Grand Vezir and the Receiver, a change already noted in commenting on the Foreign Ministry. We shall assume that the grand vezir's, or for the time being the prime minister's, household had also by this time acquired a location outside the premises of the Sublime Porte, although the dating of that event seems to be undocumented. Figure IV-1 thus not only depicts a short-lived arrangement but also, of necessity, is more speculative than our other charts.

Mahmud's apparent success in instituting this rather bizarre rearrangement was, in fact, deceptive. Not only were most of his changes undone after his death in 1839, but even the strongest will to autocratic centralization could not free him from the need for able subordinates, particularly in an age of such urgent needs for reform along lines that others with firsthand experience of the outside world understood better than he. It may be, too, that just as he attached a special importance to having ambassadors in Western capitals, he also wished to see himself surrounded by a bureaucratic elite more like those of contemporary Western states than like the slave-officials of his own tradition. In any case, one aspect of Mahmud's attempt to streamline the administration was a collective reorganization and upgrading of the scribal service, a process directed at least in part by the ideas and elitist aspirations of the new diplomats, not to speak of their desire for self-preservation. Even as he tried to neutralize the Sublime Porte, Mahmud thus also laid a new foundation for the "Patriciate of the Pen" that would become so powerful after his death.[112]

Mahmud's first steps in this direction actually date back to the creation in 1832-1833 of a new hierarchy of civil ranks. These were designated by numbers[113] and inserted between the

FIGURE IV-1. ORGANIZATION OF THE SUBLIME PORTE, c. 1838-39

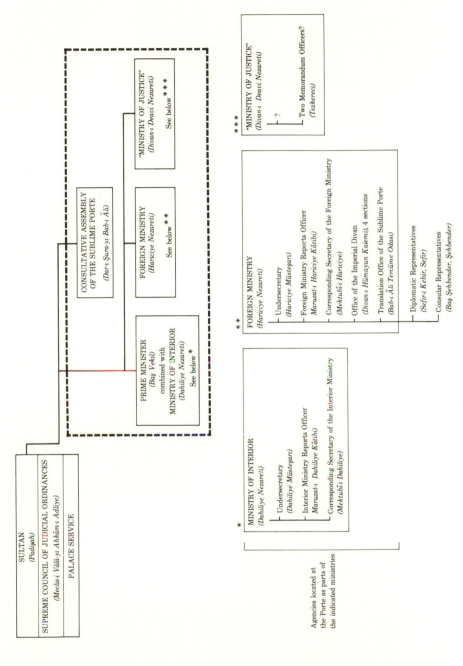

SULTAN
(Padişah)

SUPREME COUNCIL OF JUDICIAL ORDINANCES
(Meclis-i Vâlâ-yı Ahkâm-ı Adliye)

PALACE SERVICE

CONSULTATIVE ASSEMBLY
OF THE SUBLIME PORTE
(Dar-ı Şura-yı Bab-ı Âli)

PRIME MINISTER
(Baş Vekil)
combined with
MINISTRY OF INTERIOR
(Dahiliye Nezareti)
See below *

FOREIGN MINISTRY
(Hariciye Nezareti)
See below **

"MINISTRY OF JUSTICE"
(Divan-ı Deavi Nezareti)
See below ***

* MINISTRY OF INTERIOR
(Dahiliye Nezareti)
├─ Undersecretary
(Dahiliye Müsteşarı)
├─ Interior Ministry Reports Officer
Maruzat-ı Dahiliye Kâtibi)
└─ Corresponding Secretary of the Interior Ministry
(Mektubi-i Dahiliye)

Agencies located at
the Porte as parts of
the indicated ministries

** FOREIGN MINISTRY
(Hariciye Nezareti)
├─ Undersecretary
(Hariciye Müsteşarı)
├─ Foreign Ministry Reports Officer
Maruzat-ı Hariciye Kâtibi)
├─ Corresponding Secretary of the Foreign Ministry
(Mektubi-i Hariciye)
├─ Office of the Imperial Divan
(Divan-ı Hümayun Kalemi), 4 sections
├─ Translation Office of the Sublime Porte
(Bab-ı Âli Tercüme Odası)
├─ Diplomatic Representatives
(Sefir-i Kebir, Sefir)
└─ Consular Representatives
(Baş Şehbender, Şehbender)

*** "MINISTRY OF JUSTICE"
(Divan-ı Deavi Nezareti)
├─ ?
└─ Two Memorandum Officers?
(Tezkereci)

▬ ▬ ▬ Enclosed organizations are part of Sublime Porte

preexisting rank of *vezir*, which thus became superior to the new
"first rank" (*rütbe-i ulâ*), and the *hacelik* (the rank of the bureau
chiefs or *hacegân*). Over the next several years, additional ranks
were inserted into the hierarchy, until by 1846 it included nine
grades, not counting the *hacelik*. As lowest element in the list, the
hacelik began to undergo a devaluation that would presently lead
to the loss of its former character as a rather clear line of division
between upper and lower levels of the scribal service and, indeed, to its obsolescence.[114] Initially, there were attempts to
specify which positions should be held by holders of which rank;
but this degree of systematization soon proved impossible to
maintain. Nonetheless, the continuing issue of tables of equivalence or precedence for the ranks of the civil, religious, and military hierarchies,[115] and the adoption of such related parapher-
nalia as official uniforms[116] or official styles of address (*elkab*)
graded according to rank,[117] gave the scribal service a more
"modern" image and a more sharply delineated collective identity than it had ever before enjoyed. Ultimately, what was most
significant about the table of civil ranks was the way in which it
reflected the growth of this branch of service in relative prominence within the ruling class. Indeed, the civil ranks provided
for the first time a fully elaborated and standardized measure of
equivalence in status between the members of this service and
those of the religious and military establishments.[118]

Meanwhile, in 1834, Mahmud began to alter the old system of
annual reappointment (*tevcihat*) for all officials at or above the
level of bureau chief or equivalent rank in other services. Initially, all he did was shift the month in which the appointments
occurred, without altering the annual limit of tenure or the old
system of appointment fees. The point of this change was simply
to settle all questions about appointments each year before the
beginning of *Ramazan*, the month of fasting, rather than after,
as had previously been the case. In 1838, however, Mahmud
abandoned the system of annual appointment altogether.
Thenceforth, appointments and dismissals were supposed to
occur only as needed.[119]

This change gained in significance from another reform of
the same year. As part of a larger set of measures aimed at centralizing collection and disbursement of revenue,[120] Mahmud
decreed the assignment of salaries to all officials and forbade the
old practices of fee collection and bribe taking, which now be-

came indistinguishable from each other. A needed sequel to other measures such as the abandonment of the annual appointments, which each year had set in motion the exchange of huge sums as appointment fees, or the creation of such new organizations as the embassies, for which the old types of prebendal compensation were unworkable, the salary system in fact functioned poorly from the start. Such contemporary evidence as is now available suggests that the system was inaugurated almost simultaneously with the beginning of the effort at fiscal centralization, with minimal planning as to what requirements the salaries would create or what revenues could be used to cover them.[121] The salaries that Mahmud assigned his top officials were far in excess of those of their European counterparts,[122] and the minister of finance almost immediately declared that he would not be able to produce such sums.[123] Skeptical observers foresaw that Ottoman officials would simply regard their supposed new entitlements as additions to their traditional sources of income.[124] Decades after the institution of the change, the official historiographer, Lûtfi Efendi, a member of the religious establishment, still wrote of it with unwonted vehemence as destructive of the incentives that the old fee system had created for efficient performance of duty, as creating all manner of new needs for record keeping and regulation, and as having a disastrously inflationary impact.[125] In the way the salary system was adopted, Mahmud and his advisers thus revealed their lack of sophistication in economic and fiscal policy. In principle, nonetheless, the shift from prebendalism to payment of regular salaries, and the process of fiscal centralization that the salaries presupposed, were among the most important of the reforms which had to be undertaken if administrative modernization was to become a meaningful reality.

Ultimately most important of the reforms of 1838 was Mahmud's formal reassertion of the tradition of sultanic legislation (*kanun*) with the promulgation of special penal codes (*ceza kanunnamesi*) both for officials (*memurin*) and for the judges (*kadıs*) of the religious establishment. The code for officials, including the scribal service, proclaimed the abolition of "undeserved expropriation" (*müsadere-i gayr-i icabiye*) and nonjudicial, administrative punishment (*siyaset-i örfiye*). Having thus abolished or at least restricted two of the most dreaded sources of the insecurity traditionally characteristic of upper-level bureau-

cratic life, the code added that all offenses by officials, unless subject to penalties specified by Islamic law or to retaliation
(*kısas*), were to be punished under its provisions without deference to the rank of the offender. With this demand for an end to
the customary association of rank and arbitrariness, the code
went on to proscribe violation of the secrecy of government
business, abuses in purchasing and supply, making appointments on a basis of favoritism rather than proven ability, and
finally bribery, penalties being specified for each type of
abuse.[126] While the actual uses to which this and subsequent
codes were put were sometimes another story, the significance of
the code in principle, both for the improvement of the status of
the officials and for the regularization of administration, is self-
evident.

The climax of this series of measures came a few months after
Mahmud's death, with the promulgation of the Gülhane Decree
of 1839. The work of Mustafa Reşid Paşa, this contained legal
innovations of epoch-making importance. Through its guarantee of "perfect security for life, honor, and property," the decree
obliquely implied the complete elimination of the practice of
expropriation, which the code of 1838 for officials had merely
and ambiguously restricted. More explicitly, through a clause
guaranteeing that no accused person should be executed without public trial, the Gülhane Decree reconfirmed the provision
of 1838 concerning nonjudicial punishment. However much the
motives that lay behind the drafting of these clauses may have
involved bureaucratic class interest, the decree no longer bore
the character, as had the code of 1838, of a document addressed
to the ruling class alone. Ignoring the dichotomy of ruling and
subject classes and extending the application of these and all its
other provisions to all the peoples of the empire, Muslim and
non-Muslim alike, the document implied something that it never
quite clearly stated and that few of the sultan's subjects were
ready to comprehend or live with, anyway: the effacement of the
centuries-old dichotomy of rulers and subjects and the opening
of a new age of equality among the various ethnoreligious communities of the empire.[127]

The Gülhane Decree thus opened a vast set of problems pertaining to the general restructuring of Ottoman society. In a
narrower sense, the decree at the same time brought to fulfillment a series of measures which, in less than a decade, caused a

more profound alteration in the collective state of the scribal service than would occur again in any period of comparable brevity. It was not yet clear what the long-term implications of these changes would be. On the one hand, Mahmud had attempted to neutralize the Porte as a power center and reduce it to a mere mechanism for the exercise of a resurgent sultanic domination. At the same time, to make the scribal service into a more effective instrument for the achievement of his purpose, he had drastically altered traditional conditions of service within it. Neither he nor the Gülhane Decree had explicitly renounced the traditional concept of official servility, but he had provided his officials with legal safeguards of a sort that they had never before known.

Whatever its unclear points, this abrupt transformation effectively marked the disappearance of the old scribal service (*kalemiye*) into the new collective forms of what would gradually become known as the civil bureaucracy (*mülkiye*). Only time would tell how much the officials could rely on the newly proclaimed safeguards, or how well the civil bureaucracy and its diplomatic elite would, in fact, serve for the maintenance of the sultanic dominance to which Mahmud aspired.

The Record of a Half-Century of Bureaucratic Reform: Characteristics and Limitations of Modernization in the Ottoman Empire

In the history of the scribal service and the Sublime Porte, the half-century that elapsed between the accession of Selim III and the death of Mahmud II was a time of major changes. To view these in terms of the general perceptions of the need for reform discussed in the first section of this chapter, we note recurrent attempts, as in the reforms that Selim instituted in the old offices of the chief scribe or in Mahmud's later corporate reorganization of the scribal service, to achieve new degrees and new kinds of regularization in the working of bureaucratic systems. The implicit movement away from traditionalism and toward rational-legalism finds confirmation in the reactivation of the legislative role of the state and in the changes of fundamental legal principle conveyed in the Gülhane Decree. Efforts at a reassertion of the central government, indeed at extreme autocratic centralization, mounted to a climax in Mahmud's attack on the grand vezirate. Meanwhile, responding both to the need for new types and levels of official performance and to the combination of menace and attraction apparent in contemporary Ottoman attitudes toward the outside world, the scribal service formed a new elite possessing capabilities and cultural characteristics once hardly found in scribal circles but now supremely relevant to the needs of the state. The emergence of the Foreign Ministry provided the indispensable official mechanism for a new degree of interaction between the empire and the outside world, while the corporate reorganization of the scribal service in the 1830s signified a kind of formal recognition of processes of growth and change already long at work in the ruling class in practical ways.

At the same time, the achievements of this period displayed obvious limitations and left many questions unanswered. Selim's experiments with reform in the traditional offices of the Porte demonstrated the tenacity with which old forms of bureaucratic indiscipline could survive and spread in the face of efforts at reform. The workings of the new diplomatic service, and in a different sense those of the fledgling salary system, offered jarring insights into the ways in which aspects of the patrimonial tradition might interfere with attempts at modernization. The fact that the early diplomat-reformers were themselves only beginning to digest the new Western ideas, and the added fact that those who possessed a Westernist cultural orientation were still a minority even within the ruling class, implied a number of questions about the impact which the new elite would ultimately produce.

There were problems too, about certain implications of the reforms of the 1830s. The old principles of official servility and of the dichotomy of ruling and subject classes were nowhere explicitly abolished, but only overlaid with new measures that ignored or contravened those principles in certain respects; and the extent to which the new measures would, in fact, prevail against tradition remained to be seen. Equally uncertain was the resolution of the conflict, implicit in these same reforms, between reasserted sultanic authority and reformed bureaucracy. Indeed, until the scope of the political process, or at least of the demand for participation in it, began to broaden decisively, this conflict was to govern the shifts in the political balance that distinguished the successive political periods of the era of reform.

Finally, in the association of reform with autocratic centralization, there had emerged a pattern that was to remain characteristic of Ottoman reform throughout the nineteenth century. In an apt if inelegant phrase, S. N. Eisenstadt has designated this pattern "split-up modernization." Certainly where the Ottoman Empire is concerned, this can be regarded as a subcase of what Eisenstadt and others have referred to more recently as neopatrimonialism.[128] As this designation implies, the pattern of "split-up modernization" is a phenomenon of central importance for evaluation of the efforts at reform that are the subject of this study.

In the typology of modernizing societies in which the concept of "split-up modernization" originally appeared, Eisenstadt described it as the principal type observed before the present century in the autocratic states of eastern Europe and beyond. The term "split-up" applies in several senses. On one level, certain elements of such a society push for modernization, while others oppose it. In addition, advocates of change who are in positions of power, their roles still defined and legitimated in basically traditional terms, tend to advocate change in spheres where they think they can control it and use it to buttress the order of which they are a part. Simultaneously, they try to restrict change in the fundamental, constitutive principles of the polity and to keep modernization from becoming a generalized process. As new ideas begin to spread through the society, however, this degree of control proves impossible to maintain. Sooner or later there emerge rival reformist groups that oppose the established leadership and expound alternative concepts of change. While efforts at modernization in such societies display a "split-up" aspect in all these ways, the emergence of such a rival reformist intelligentsia—thus, the "splitting up" of the reformist leadership—is a phenomenon of particular significance. For in the opposition intelligentsia appear most clearly the pressures that force the enlargement in scope of the political process, as the range and intensity of political controversy begin to go beyond the limits of the old factionalism of the ruling class, as a modern kind of issue-oriented political ideology emerges, and as politics and bureaucracy begin to become differentiated from each other.

Faced with mounting pressures for the restructuring of the political balance, the rulers of such societies characteristically use whatever resources are at their disposal to maintain their position. If the resources are great enough, it is not impossible in principle that some new kind of viable order may emerge from this effort. More characteristically, certainly among nineteenth-century cases of "split-up modernization," the sense of contradiction between the demands for change emerging within the society and the traditionalistic foundations of the established order eventually becomes too great. The fact that the reformers presiding over the process of "split-up modernization" are still apt to display a style of political behavior deriving from the patrimonial tradition only heightens the sense of contradiction, helping to bring on eventual political upheaval, which may extend into revolutionary forms of social and cultural change, as well. The new order that then emerges may owe great debts to the reforms of the fallen autocrats and may perpetuate something of their patrimonial style, but will represent fundamentally different principles.

As the nineteenth century wore on, the Ottoman Empire inched its way toward just the kind of multiple transmutation that this pattern envisages. As of 1839, the lines for this conflict were only beginning to be drawn, and it was still not possible, for example, to determine exactly what role the new civil-bureaucratic elite would play in it. Nonetheless, in the use of innovative reform for purposes of sultanic reassertion, Selim and Mahmud had set the fundamental pattern of "split-up modernization." This would provide the context in which the issues aroused by attempts at bureaucratic reform and the struggles over the maintenance and form of the political balance would work themselves out for the remainder of the imperial period.

The transition from a traditionalistic to a rational-legal order had begun. It would gradually become apparent, however, that the patrimonial tradition was far from dead.

Chapter Five

THE CIVIL-BUREAUCRATIC HEGEMONY
OF THE TANZIMAT

. . . Saltanat-ı Seniye'mizin tezyid-i kuvvet ve miknetini ve revabıt-ı kalbiye-i vatandaşî ile birbirine merbut olan ve nazar-ı madelet-eser-i müşfikanemde müsavi bulunan kâffe-i sunuf-ı tebaa-ı şahanemin her yüzden husul-ı tamamî-i saadet-i hal ve memalik-i şahanemizin ma'muriyetini müstelzim olacak esbab ve vesailin anbean ilerilemesi murad-ı merhamet-itiyad-ı mülûkanem iktizasından bulunduğuna binaen hususat-ı atiyet ül-zikrin icrasına irade-i madelet-ifade-i padişahanem şerefsadır olmuştur.

. . . it being the requirement of our benevolent, sovereign intention ever and by all means to promote the increase in power and might of our exalted Sultanate, the prosperity of our imperial lands, and the attainment of full happiness for all classes of our imperial subjects, who are bound to one another by the heartfelt bonds of a common patriotism and are all equal in our equitable and compassionate view, our just and imperial decree for the implementation of the following particulars is hereby issued.
Reform Decree of 1856[1]

Hariciye sadr-ı devlettir masalih andadır.

Foreign affairs are the heart of the state; all business lies there.
Fuad Paşa, from a poem sent to Âli Paşa[2]

Paris'e git hey efendi akl-ü-fikrin var ise
Âleme gelmiş sayılmaz gitmiyenler Paris'e.

Go to Paris, young sir, if you have any wits;
If you haven't been to Paris, you haven't come into the world.
Hoca Tahsin Efendi[3]

With the death of Mahmud II in 1839, the convergence of three major factors determined the resolution of the power conflict between the sultan and his officials, implicit in the reforms of the 1830s, and thus opened a new political period that lasted until 1871. Most basic of these factors was the character of Mahmud's successors: Abd ül-Mecid (1839-1861), who came to the throne in a time of unprecedented danger as an ill-prepared sixteen-year-old;[4] Abd ül-Aziz (1861-1876), who possessed a will to dominate but lacked the comprehension and ultimately the mental stability to do so effectively;[5] and Murad V (1876), whose instability led to his deposition after only three months.[6] The House of Osman was not to produce a real successor to Mahmud before Abd ül-Hamid II (1876-1909).

The second factor in opening this new political period consisted of the changes that the reforms of the 1830s made in the security of tenure in high office. Lowering the rate of bureaucratic mobility, these changes combined with the relative effacement of the sultanate to produce a very clear shift in the locus of power. The chief beneficiary of this shift was the civil bureaucracy. More specifically, thanks to the influence of the third major factor—the political leverage accruing in the circumstances of the times to the officials in the vanguard of westernizing reform—the chief beneficiaries were the new diplomatic elite. Under a triad of great leaders, the last of whom died in 1871, the civil bureaucracy consolidated its hold as the most influential branch of officialdom, both in Istanbul and in the provinces, and the Porte became more than ever the real center of government.

These three factors combined to open a period destined to be remembered as a time of extreme political imbalance—of practically unfettered dominance by the civil-bureaucratic patricians of the Porte over all phases of the life of the state—and, in a sense, as the period of reform par excellence. The very name by which this period is still commonly remembered, *Tanzimat*,[7] a causative form derived from the same Arabic root as the already familiar *nizam* ("order," "regulation," "system") and meaning, simply, "reforms" or "reorganizations," is a subtle witness to the continuation and intensification of reform under the new elite.

In fact, however, this new elite was not able to consolidate its hold immediately. Amounting initially to little more than one faction within the civil bureaucracy, it had to contend both with rival forces within its own branch of service and with a faction-ridden military leadership, among whom those most identified with reform took a different and narrower view of what reforms were desirable. Here the most important opponent of the civil-bureaucratic reformers was the redoubtable Husrev Paşa (c. 1756-1855), who served as minister of war (*serasker*) throughout the years 1827-1837 and assumed for himself the post of grand vezir—no longer "prime minister"—immediately following the death of Mahmud in 1839. Husrev compared to the new civil-bureaucratic diplomats much as Koca Yusuf Paşa had compared to the efendis-turned-paşas of the 1790s. Thanks to the large numbers of slaves that he had trained and placed in sensitive positions, Husrev Paşa was also an extremely difficult man to circumvent.[8]

Mustafa Reşid and his friends were able to do so, largely thanks to the influence that they derived from European intervention in the Ottoman-Egyptian crisis. But other problems awaited them. Their first effort to extend the program of fiscal centralization into local administration produced almost instant failure. Muhammad Ali Paşa used the wealth of Egypt to launch intrigues against them in Istanbul, in opposition to the terms of settlement between the Istanbul and Cairo governments. And the Lebanese crisis of 1840 created continuing difficulties on the diplomatic scene. The fall of Mustafa Reşid in 1841 from the Foreign Ministry, a post that he had held for four years, consequently initiated a short period of reaction.[9] Mustafa Reşid did not again become foreign minister until 1845, following which he received his first appointment as grand vezir the succeeding year. Even after that time, men with backgrounds outside the civil bureaucracy continued to gain the grand vezirate on occasion, down to the Crimean War. Among them were Damad Mehmed Ali Paşa, husband of the sister of Abd ül-Mecid and a palace minion, and Mustafa Naili Paşa, a perplexing figure who had made almost his entire career in Egyptian service and was reportedly illiterate.[10]

As in the past, however, such men could not fill the shoes of the best civil bureaucrats. It is thus not surprising that during and after the Crimean War, the new civil-bureaucratic elite established something of a monopoly on the most important positions at the Porte. After holding the grand vezirate almost continuously from 1846 to 1852, at which time he returned to the

Foreign Ministry, Mustafa Reşid became grand vezir three more
times between 1854 and his death in 1858,[11] although his influence gradually faded before that of his younger associates, now
become rivals, Âli and Fuad. Âli had become foreign minister as
early as 1846 and grand vezir for the first time in 1852, Fuad
following him several years later in each post. Following the
death of Mustafa Reşid, these two men and a small core of civil-
bureaucratic associates—Kıbrıslı Mehmed Emin, Mütercim
Mehmed Rüşdi, and Yusuf Kâmil Paşas[12]—monopolized the
grand vezirate down to the death of Âli in 1871. Meanwhile, Âli
and Fuad, having shared the foreign ministry since 1846 with
only a few other diplomatic colleagues, such as Sadık Rif'at Paşa,
monopolized that post between the two of them from 1857 until
the death of Fuad in 1869, following which Âli combined it with
the grand vezirate until his own demise in 1871.[13] Since the post
of minister of the interior did not exist for most of this period,
its responsibilities being absorbed into those of the grand vezir,
this oligarchical control of the two most important posts of the
Porte provided the means for the domination of almost the
entire administrative system.

The linkage of grand vezir and foreign minister thus became
the central element in a political system that the leaders of the
new elite gradually built up to fill the political vacuum created by
the weakness of the sultans. In fully elaborated form, this system
included a number of other components, as well. There was a
gradually lengthening roster of ministries and councils in Istanbul, located both at the Porte and outside it, which assisted the
reformers in planning and implementing their reforms. Outside
the capital, there was a similarly lengthening list of agencies
manned by civil-bureaucratic personnel, a list that ultimately included a variety of local administrative organs created during
this period, as well as the consular and diplomatic establishments. To govern these agencies, there was also a rapid accumulation of laws and regulations, which record in detail how the
dominant statesmen of the time set about erecting and calibrat-
ing the new bureaucratic system over which they presided. Finally, to fill the organizational strucures and apply the laws and
regulations, there was the social body of the new civil bureaucracy, differing from the old scribal service in a variety of ways,
including size, organizational complexity, sociocultural orienta-

tions, career patterns, and—in part—characteristic modes of political activity.

In this chapter we shall analyze the elements of this system, at least as found at the Porte, and the implications of its workings for the further development of the civil bureaucracy and the "center" in general. Before going on to take up the questions of organizational development, regulation, and social change within the civil bureaucracy, it will, however, be useful to discuss certain critical weaknesses of the civil-bureaucratic hegemony, which seemed so overwhelming to Ottomans at the time.

Structural Weaknesses of the Civil-Bureaucratic System of the Tanzimat

Despite their virtually monopolistic control of the levers of power, the position of the Tanzimat statesmen was far from invulnerable. Before the period ended, they encountered opposition of one sort or another from a number of quarters, and the very character and scope of political controversy began to undergo a profound transformation. Underlying this transformation were a number of general issues that stand out as structural weaknesses in the political position of the Tanzimat statesmen and thus as critical factors in shaping and limiting their achievements in bureaucratic reform. These issues we may identify as the mimetic quality of the reforms, the problems of human and economic resources, the inconsonance of reformist principle and political behavior, and the problems that the westernizing reformers experienced in the legitimation of their power and their policies.

The Mimetic Quality of the Reforms

As the events of the 1830s demonstrated, the new civil-bureaucratic elite emerged with relative abruptness and acquired a broad-ranging influence over the course of reform at a time when the development of its knowledge of Western ideas and institutions was still only beginning. Perhaps this, like the earlier reliance on "marginal men," was simply a phase through which the reform movement had to pass. Ultimately, Mustafa Reşid, and certainly Âli and Fuad, gained acknowledgment from their European counterparts as diplomats of considerable skill.[14] While it was not invariably the case, and while imitation implied pitfalls of its own, some of the reforms also clearly re- flected thorough knowledge of Western prototypes. To varying degrees this was true of the Council of State (*Şura-yı Devlet*) created in 1868,[15] the system of municipal government created for Istanbul,[16] and certain of the legal codes adopted during the period.[17] But certain basic problems inherent in the very con- cept of borrowing from one culture to another, as well as certain peculiarities of this specific historical situation, combined to give even the most carefully planned reforms an air of imitative shal- lowness and incongruity with the Ottoman setting, and thus to generate controversy around them.

In part this was a reflection of the situation in which the Tan- zimat statesmen found themselves in relation to European statesmen and diplomats, on one hand, and to their varied Ot- toman compatriots, on the other. Where the former were con- cerned, the problem of the Tanzimat statesmen was essentially an aggravated version of that mixture of attraction and threat already apparent in the way Ottoman dignitaries of a half cen- tury earlier had viewed the outside world.

As the Middle East became more enmeshed in the evolving, Europe-centered world system, the association of Ottoman statesmen seeking to derive benefits from the West with Western statesmen acting in pursuit of the interests of their governments tainted the Ottomans in a way that the behavior of the Euro- peans seldom did anything to allay. Never did this become clearer than in the career of Stratford Canning, the noted Brit- ish diplomat. Throughout his experience in Istanbul, spanning the half century from the fall of Selim III to the aftermath of the Crimean War, he exerted an influence on Ottoman reform that was surely material, if less nearly exclusive than some of his biographers have implied. But it also did much to make some of the innovations, such as the Reform Decree of 1856, unpalatable to Ottomans, and it tarred some of the Tanzimat statesmen, Mustafa Reşid Paşa most notably, with the brush of subservience to foreign interests.[18] Mustafa Reşid's successors were vulnera- ble to the same charge, if on other accounts. For example, an opponent once attacked Âli Paşa for being, not the foreign minister of the Ottoman Empire, but rather the ambassador of whichever European power had most influence in Istanbul.[19] Reporting Âli's death to London, the British ambassador, Sir H.

Elliot, said of him: "I have never had to complain of his having stopped short of what I had understood him to promise, while I have repeatedly had to thank him for having given way to my wishes further than he had engaged to do."[20] In a way that reflects their cultural formation as much as the international disequilibrium of the times, the Tanzimat statesmen never broke the pattern of dependence on outside powers already apparent in the reforms of the 1830s.

It does not follow that they were unaware of the need to engage the interests of broader segments of Ottoman society in their programs, although in this, too, they faced obstacles that it was impossible to overcome in the short run. It has been argued, in fact, that one of the goals of the local administrative assemblies which the Tanzimat reformers created at the beginning of the period, and which were to include indirectly elected representatives of the local populace, was to link the material interests of broader segments of the population to reform in just this way. No doubt the same could be said of other experiments in representation, cautious though they were, that followed during the remainder of this period.[21] The egalitarian reforms introduced in the Gülhane Decree and the attempt to redefine Ottomanism (*Osmanlılık*) as a supranationalism that would appeal to all the peoples of the empire are clearly significant in the same sense. Such efforts always encountered obstacles, however, either in preexisting vested interests, or in the opposition of principle emerging from the growing sense of cultural cleavage that Berkes evokes[22] or from the self-contradictory character of the imperial supranationalism.

The practically impossible task that the reformers faced in trying to steer a smooth course between European self-interest and interference, on one hand, and the varied sorts of domestic opposition, on the other, complicated a task that would have been awesome even if it could have been pursued in isolation from all such distractions. In purely logical terms, the introduction of new measures and programs seemed to entail a sequence of basic stages, each more demanding than the last. First the concept had to be adopted. Then came two intermediate stages, of which the order varied in Ottoman practice. One was the elaboration of the concept in detail, this being the point in the process where promulgation of new laws and regulations typically occurred. The other was the practical implementation of the concept, whether or not it had yet been worked out fully in regulatory guidelines. Not only did this and the preceding phase occur in variable order, but material restraints often forced the Ottomans to implement new programs on a gradual or piecemeal basis, a method that created additional subphases in the cycle. In any case, the concluding phase of the cycle would be the placing in operation of systems through which to monitor or control the implementation of the concept as elaborated in the laws and regulations.

The reforming statesmen of the Tanzimat were not slow to launch into the first stage of the cycle. Varying the order of the next two, they were usually quicker to create new organizations and programs than to work out how these should operate. As for control and monitoring, in a way that recalls and parallels the lack of effective political controls over the civil bureaucracy itself, the Tanzimat statesmen often seemed not to understand the need for this at all.

On top of the problems of coping with contending interests operating both from Europe and from within the Empire, the inherent difficulty of carrying the reforms through from initial conceptualization to controlled implementation thus did much to give the innovative policies of the Tanzimat an imitative and insubstantial quality. To make matters worse, there were at the same time other obstacles that made it even harder for the reformers to give substance to their programs.

The Problem of Human Resources

The difficulties that the reforming statesmen encountered immediately following the promulgation of the Gülhane Decree of 1839 in their attempts to implement changes in local administration demonstrated how lacking they were in subordinates prepared to understand and support their efforts. Since the social state of the civil bureaucracy at the end of the period will require more detailed consideration later in this chapter, no more need be said about this problem here than to note its seriousness and, in particular, to remark the emphasis which it forced all reformers to lay on reform in the field of education.

In the last chapter we noted the very small size of the modernist segment of the civil bureaucracy at the end of the 1830s and the fact that the Translation Office of the Porte was still, practically speaking, the only place entrusted with the task of inculcating the "talismanic" knowledge of French in civil officials. The school known as the *Mekteb-i Maarif-i Adliye* (1839), and another similar institution, the *Mekteb-i Ulûm-ı Edebiye* (School of Literary Studies, founded about the same time), were supposed to provide a modern kind of education, but appear never to have developed the means to do so.[23] In fact, the development of effective secular civil schools proved disappointingly slow.

The one type of new school most frequently mentioned in official biographies of this period and later, the *rüşdiye*, surely owes its frequency of mention to the fact that it was little better than an elementary school in modern terms, and that a whole system of schools of this type gradually came into existence.[24] The political expediency which the reformers saw in keeping their hands off the monopoly of the religious establishment over the traditional, Kur'anic elementary schools (*sıbyan mektepleri*) and the religious colleges (*medrese*) otherwise hindered the development of a comprehensive system of secular schools, thus limiting efforts to train civil bureaucrats to the development of a series of special institutions. Such, to varying degrees, were the "House of Instruction" (*Dar ül-Maarif*, 1849), the Ottoman School in Paris (c. 1857-1874), and the School of Civil Administration (*Mekteb-i Mülkiye*, 1859, ancestor of the present Faculty of Political Science of Ankara University). Such, also, was something called the "Vestibule of the Offices" (*Mahrec-i Aklâm*, 1862), created in place of the two schools founded in 1839, and the Language School (1864, early history uncertain). Finally, there was the prestigious Galatasaray Lycée (1868).[25]

The existing works on educational history, mostly emphasizing questions of organization and curriculum, provide considerable evidence of the weaknesses of the new schools. From the standpoint of bureaucratic training, there were other problems of at least equal gravity. The fact that the first of these schools were founded expressly for bureaucratic training stamped them with a kind of "trade-school" mentality. This quality comes through with distressing clarity in the name of the "Vestibule of the Offices" and calls attention to the lack of any Ottoman civil school providing the equivalent of a lycée-level education before the foundation of the Galatasaray Lycée in 1868. With this mentality went the projection into the new schools of kinds of indiscipline traditionally associated with lower-level scribal life, and particularly with behavior in matters pertaining to appointment and advancement.

The best indication of this appears in yet another reflection of the extremely close link between school and office: the use of the same kind of brevet, the *rüus*, traditionally required for official appointments, to signify both the admission of students into the earliest of the civil schools and the appointment of the "graduates" from school to office. Records of the bureau responsible for the issue of these brevets, the section for Appointments (*Rüus Kalemi*) in the Office of the Imperial Divan, indicate that during the 1840s, over five hundred persons obtained brevets for admission to the *Mekteb-i Maarif-i Adliye*, the first of the new civil schools, but perhaps fewer than seventy completed the course of study and then obtained brevets once again for appointment to the offices. In some offices, notably that of the imperial Divan, officials continued to be appointed as if the new school did not exist at all. Aspiring bureaucrats who entered the new schools thus resisted the idea that they should complete the course of study, others found ways to get into the offices without going to the schools at all, and the authorities connived in these practices. One document, in fact, says baldly that one purpose of the schools was to make the way into the bureaucracy longer for persons who were not sons of officials.[26]

While the term *rüus* gradually acquired the meaning of "diploma," at least in connection with the new civil schools, in addition to its preexisting significations, changes in records-keeping systems make it impossible to trace the problems here described in a continuous way through the remainder of the period. Nonetheless, it is clear from other sources that in the new schools, as in the offices, disciplinary problems of the type just noted remained as much an issue as did the development of curriculum, texts, and instructional staff. The significance of these problems is apparent in a variety of ways in the sociocultural aspect presented by the Civil Bureaucracy as of the end of the period. The one compensating factor is that the new schools, for all their defects, provided a means for an unprecedented extension of literacy and for the diffusion of new types of cultural stimuli. Like the one-room schoolhouses of nineteenth-century America, these institutions at times exerted an influence to which their modest aspect gives little clue.

The Problem of Economic Resources

Perhaps more significant than anything else in inhibiting the ability of the Tanzimat statesmen to cope with such problems were the difficulties created by the economic situation of the empire. Effectively bankrupt by the end of the eighteenth century, the state stood now under the domination of a new elite that had inherited little if anything from the once impressive Ottoman tradition of financial management and would never succeed in fully comprehending the economic developments then transforming the West. As a result, the economic policies that the Tanzimat statesmen developed tended to be either stillborn or self-defeating, at least in purely economic terms, and the accomplishments of the reformers became a measure of what could and could not be done in the face of a chronic shortage of the material resources indispensable for effective administration.

The crippling effect that financial problems would have on the Tanzimat is clear from two events which occurred prior to the promulgation of the Gülhane Decree. One was the attempt of 1838 to replace tax farming with direct collection and centralized control of revenues and simultaneously to institute a system of salaries, thus providing an alternative form of emolument for the men who had been tax farmers and were now to be integrated into administrative cadres as salaried officials.

The simultaneity of these two measures, and the apparent lack of adequate calculation about how to meet the burdens that the salaries would create, seems to have created a vicious cycle. The salaries could not be covered, in part because revenue collection was not already centralized; and the tax farmers resisted centralization because they suspected that the proposed change would harm them economically. The upshot was that fiscal centralization never became a reality. Both tax farming and a largely nonfunctional salary system continued to exist, while governmental structures continued to expand, partly because of the attempt at bureaucratization of the provincial administration.

These financial difficulties helped to bring on the period of reaction of the early 1840s. In addition, the failure of fiscal centralization led directly, with the help of other problems, to the issuance of paper money (*kaime*), beginning in 1840. Its depreciation helped to necessitate the contracting of the first foreign loan in 1854, while mounting indebtedness in turn led to the official acknowledgment of bankruptcy and the institution of foreign financial controls shortly after the end of this period. Efforts to reform the tax system and raise revenues had by then borne some fruit, but not enough to halt this course of events.[27]

Among the forces propelling this downhill slide was the inauguration, also in 1838, of a fundamental change in the provisions governing international trade. This was the adoption of the Anglo-Ottoman Commercial Convention of Balta Liman. The economic price of British support in the Egyptian crisis, this marked the point at which the traditional system of capitulations, the repeated revisions of which had for a long time been becoming less and less favorable to Ottoman interests, gave way to bilaterally negotiated commercial treaties. The convention of 1838 had the effect of confirming all preexisting capitulatory privileges, setting export and import duties at low rates, abolishing monopolies, and assuring British merchants the same rights as the most favored of local traders. This convention, and the similar ones subsequently concluded with other powers, thus opened Ottoman markets to industrial Europe at a critical moment, effectively giving the coup de grâce to what was left of Ottoman manufactures.[28]

In their ill-planned attempt at fiscal centralization and in this opening of their domestic markets, the Tanzimat statesmen, perhaps irresistibly, became the agents of two critical failures, whose consequences were never fully remedied before the collapse of the imperial system. The effects of these failures on subsequent efforts at bureaucratic reform were to appear at every turn. Indeed, but for two facts, these events might have left little to speak of in the remainder of this study. In a way that the patrimonial tradition of political control over the distribution of economic resources makes more readily understandable, however, the concentration of political power still made bureaucratic growth possible, even without adequate resources to support it. Ultimately more significant is the fact that some of the developments most essential for the modernization of the administrative system—the propagation of new ideas, the modernization of communications, the formation of new concepts of organization and procedure and new attitudes concerning law and legislation—did not always entail substantial economic costs. The material constraints within which Ottoman statesmen operated were very narrow, but not to the point of precluding a drastic transformation of the administrative tradition.

Reformist Principle versus Political Behavior

Interacting with the problems of resources and with the mimetic character of the reforms, another weakness in the political system of the Tanzimat statesmen resulted from the imperfect extent to which they accommodated their political behavior to certain implications of their own reforms.

On an intellectual level and in terms of their own, the reformers seem by the end of the 1830s to have had a rather clear grasp of the extent to which innovative reform implied movement toward a rational-legal order. Their role in the reassertion of the legislative function of the state and the character of the legislation of that decade indicate such an awareness. So does Mustafa Reşid's contemporary perception of European support of the empire against Muhammad Ali as a matter of the entry of the Ottoman state "dans le droit Européen."[29]

Much as George Yaney has found to be the case in nineteenth-century Russia,[30] rational-legalism was coming to exist in the minds of Ottoman statesmen as a myth and an ideal, even if it did not yet exist in the day-to-day workings of the administrative system. From at least as early as 1829, when Chief Scribe Pertev Paşa reportedly angered Mahmud II by insisting that the latter's subjects were "equally possessed of all human rights,"[31] we could cite a long series of often dramatic incidents in which Ottoman statesmen and their republican successors have risked their careers and sometimes their lives for the sake of this ideal.[32] In the nineteenth century, they were sometimes denounced for their pains as excessively Europeanized (*frenkmeşreb*);[33] and one of the things that made them politically vulnerable, as Abd ül-Hamid's persecution of the constitutionalists showed after 1878, was that there was little popular appreciation for the values that lay behind their behavior.[34] Nonetheless, their actions contributed on more than one occasion to the consolidation in fact of the rational-legal ideal.

Among the men of the Tanzimat, however, this was clearly only one variety of political behavior. Much more typically, their political behavior continued to reflect the tradition of patrimonial factionalism. In the period between the fall of Pertev Paşa and the triumph of the new diplomatic elite over Husrev Paşa, with whom the diplomats differed not only because of his policies but also because of his place among Pertev's enemies, this factional activity displayed the intensity of a mortal struggle in which some of the reform measures were used as if they were little more than weapons. For example, Mustafa Reşid and his friends did not stop with securing Husrev's dismissal from the grand vezirate in 1840; they also brought him to trial under the new penal code of the same year and secured his conviction on charges of bribe-taking.[35] Their subsequent efforts at the reform of provincial administration gave rise to many more actions of the same kind.[36]

What makes this use of the new laws more interesting is that the reformers were themselves persistently accused of similar abuses. On and off for the remainder of their careers, reports of venality circulated about the major Tanzimat statesmen and many of their dependents.[37] They were also noted for nepotism and favoritism. The many conciliar bodies founded during the period were often denounced as no more than a form of relief for officials who were out of office,[38] and the evidence on other aspects of favoritism in appointments, though scattered, is quite voluminous.[39]

In terms of the actual political behavior of the leading statesmen, it sometimes seemed to contemporary Ottomans that the era of reform had made no changes in older patterns at all. The two official historians of the day, Lûtfi Efendi and Ahmed Cevdet Paşa, both said as much.[40] Once threatened with being "crushed" if he hesitated to choose between the opposing factions that had grouped around Mustafa Reşid on one hand and Âli and Fuad on the other, Cevdet was speaking from experience.[41] Equally by experience, he knew that whatever the formal structures created for the deliberation of policy, the major questions were still decided by the most influential statesmen in consultation with a few confidants.[42]

Such political behavior had been taken for granted before the beginning of reform, but that could no longer be. The more steps were taken toward erection of a rational-legal order, the more absurd and reprehensible behavior incompatible with such an order inevitably seemed. Since the reforms of the 1830s, eliminating the conditions that had shaped the old pattern of "wheel-of-fortune" mobility, had made it possible for the same few men to hold on to the highest positions in a seemingly unending way, this absurdity was never more apparent than when the offenders were the very leaders of reform, while those slighted by the abuses were subordinates who sensed their chances for advancement to have been diminished by the emergence of this new elite.

The Tanzimat statesmen were not totally unaware of this, and some of the most trenchant descriptions of the discontinuity between practice and principle came, in fact, from statements they made about themselves. For example, Mütercim Mehmed Rüşdi Paşa, one of the grand vezirs of the period, likened the state to a ship in distress. He compared his own position to that of a man who spied this situation from another ship and approached to offer assistance. All those aboard the endangered vessel were drinking and carousing in so frenetic a fashion that Rüşdi Paşa, unable to find anyone to whom to explain why he had come, soon joined in the revelry himself.[43]

An image of imperial decay, this is also an image of the tension between the reformers' promise of a new, rational-legal order and their persistence in patterns of political behavior governed by the patrimonial tradition. Others perceived the Tanzimat statesmen in much the same light. Presently, some of them began to think up other, more effective ways of responding to the situation that Rüşdi Paşa so vividly evoked.

Westernization, Political Imbalance, and Legitimation

This brings us to another weakness of the Tanzimat system, greater in importance than all those discussed thus far: the effect of the Westernist cultural orientation of the reformers on the legitimation of their policies.

As deviations from patterns sanctioned by tradition, the innovations of the era of reform were inherently controversial. With them, the articulation of alternative policies and programs began to assume the prominence and centrality to political activity that is familiar in modern political systems. Each innovative measure was, in effect, a focal point for controversy of a sort differing in both character and intensity from that associated with the personality-centered factionalism of the patrimonial tradition. But the emergence of a more modern type of political activity was not instantaneous. The discontinuity between principle and practice meant that the old and new patterns coexisted during this period, with the Tanzimat statesmen behaving like an enlarged version of a patrimonial household faction, or a set of factions, even as their reforms created a lengthening list of issues for controversy of the new kind.

This increasing articulation of policies, their obviously innovative character, and the new levels and kinds of political conflict that resulted made it more than ever necessary for the reformers to have effective means by which to legitimate the policies they espoused; but the political imbalance of the period turned this into an insoluble problem. In the traditional Islamic state, there had been three sources of legal authority: the Islamic religious-legal tradition, custom, and the will of the sovereign, the last two in theory only ancillary to the first. As long as the initiative for reform remained chiefly with the sultan and it had not become obvious that the reforms would violate fundamental principles of the traditional order, the legitimation of reform was not a major issue. After 1839, those conditions were no longer fulfilled.

For the Tanzimat statesmen, the essential problem was that the orientation of their policies away from the first two of the traditional sources of legitimation inevitably heightened their dependence on the third. However much they manipulated the sultan in practice, however much they sought through the reforms of the 1830s to alter their servile status in relation to him, they still had to respect his office and to cling, sometimes in a purely formalistic way and sometimes in deadly earnest, to conventional concepts of their relation to him if they were to have recognized authority behind their measures. They thus retained the old rhetoric of official slavery at the very time that they tried to suppress the more painful aspects of its reality. They also held fast to the traditional concepts of the delegation of the sultan's power and the "absolute delegacy" of the grand vezir. The only practical alternative to this would have been to effect revolutionary changes in principle, including the redefinition of the bases of sovereignty.

The Gülhane Decree and the promotion of the new, egalitarian concept of Ottomanism (*Osmanlılık*) showed that the reformers were willing to make changes of fundamental principle in certain respects. Yet, to the extent that they understood the implications of the relevant issues,[44] they feared to go further and were, in any case, in no position to attempt a thoroughgoing restructuring of the polity as traditionally conceived. Their power was purely de facto; and, as a number of unpleasant incidents between the sultans and the leading figures of the period made clear,[45] even the supposed safeguards instituted in the 1830s against the arbitrariness of the sultan could not yet be taken for granted.

Even without a revolutionary restructuring of the polity, all it would take to destroy the political system of the Tanzimat would be for its leadership to lose its unity or continuity, or for a sultan strong enough to assert his sovereignty to come to the throne. The death of Âli Paşa in 1871 fulfilled the first of these conditions. Abd ül-Aziz attempted in the five remaining years of his life to fulfill the second; Abd ül-Hamid did so unequivocally.

Thus, the political imbalance of the Tanzimat ended, and another political period opened. Comparable in this respect to the scribal bureaucrats of earlier periods, the Tanzimat elite enjoyed a political eminence that was only relative and that was marked, partly because of the very decrepitude of the imperial system of which they were a part, by critical limitations. The impact of these men on the continuing development of the Ottoman politico-bureaucratic tradition was nonetheless great. Among the measures of this fact are both the growth and reorganization of the bureaucracy under their direction and the pressures for further change that this growth provoked.

The Growth of a Bureaucracy Freed of Outside Control

The transformation of the civil bureaucracy during the Tanzimat was both the culmination of growth patterns apparent in the history of the scribal service from the seventeenth century on and, more immediately, the product of the changes that followed on the shift in the locus of power and the restoration of the grand vezirate in 1839. Partly because the development of new institutions progressed more rapidly than their regulation, not every facet of this growth can be measured with precision. Yet, available information, particularly the government yearbooks published regularly from 1847 until the Young Turk period, provides unmistakable indications of the scale and complexity that governmental institutions acquired in this period, suggesting that the Tanzimat must have accounted for a great part of the numerical growth from the 1,000 to 1,500 who served in the scribal service at the end of the eighteenth century to the 50,000 to 100,000 on its rolls under Abd ül-Hamid.[46] Particularly given the shortage of resources with which the Tanzimat statesmen had to contend, this growth provides impressive evidence of the potential for empire building in a bureaucracy effectively freed of control by other elements of the political system.

As a point of reference for the discussion to follow, Figure V-1 presents a graphic summary of the organizational state of the Sublime Porte as of the death of Âli Paşa in 1871. For the record, the figure also includes other civil-bureaucratic agencies outside the Porte. The organizational developments of the period were such, however, that some bodies that do not show in the figure also require discussion. In addition, it is no longer practicable under conditions of 1871 to include in a single figure details on the internal structure of each agency of the Porte. To give a graphic portrayal of some such structures, which will be discussed in the text, a separate detailed figure for the Foreign Ministry will appear at an appropriate point in this and succeeding chapters. For most, if not all, of the era of reform, the Foreign Ministry continued to be the most highly evolved of the major civil-bureaucratic agencies.

The Grand Vezir and His Staff

Husrev Paşa's peremptory assumption of the grand vezirate following the death of Mahmud not only terminated the latter's experiment with a "prime minister," but also restored full blown the traditional concept of the "absolute delegacy" (*vekâlet-i mutlaka*) of the grand vezir. The decree that the hapless Abd ül-Mecid found himself issuing to Husrev stated this unequivocally, the misrepresentation of the initiative behind the appointment underscoring the fact: "I have of my own good inspiration selected and appointed you with full freedom of action to the exalted station of comprehensive supervisor of all affairs domestic, foreign, financial, or military, to the grand vezirate, and to the great and absolute delegacy."[47]

To the men of the Tanzimat, the high-handed methods by which Husrev assumed office were a shock and a scandal; his conception of the office, not so. For reasons that are by now understandable, they saw to it that formal decrees on at least some subsequent occasions described the office in terms even more

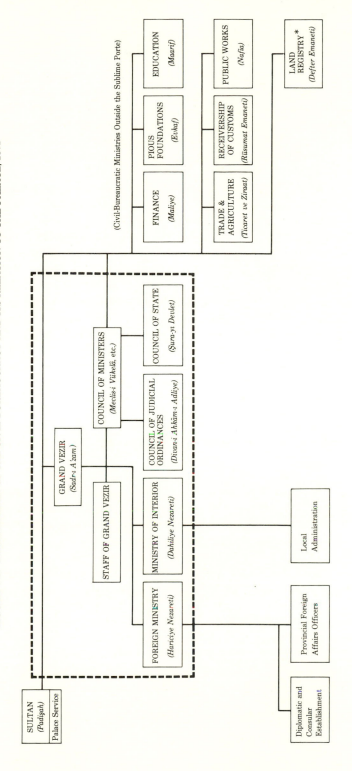

FIGURE V-1. ORGANIZATION OF THE CIVIL BUREAUCRACY AND ITS RELATION TO THE PALACE, 1871

SULTAN
(Padişah)

Palace Service

GRAND VEZIR
(Sadr-ı A'zam)

COUNCIL OF MINISTERS
(Meclis-i Vükelâ, etc.)

STAFF OF GRAND VEZIR

MINISTRY OF INTERIOR
(Dahiliye Nezareti)

COUNCIL OF JUDICIAL
ORDINANCES
(Divan-ı Ahkâm-ı Adliye)

COUNCIL OF STATE
(Şûra-yı Devlet)

FOREIGN MINISTRY
(Hariciye Nezareti)

Local
Administration

Diplomatic and
Consular
Establishment

Provincial Foreign
Affairs Officers

(Civil-Bureaucratic Ministries Outside the Sublime Porte)

FINANCE
(Maliye)

PIOUS
FOUNDATIONS
(Evkaf)

EDUCATION
(Maarif)

TRADE &
AGRICULTURE
(Ticaret ve Ziraat)

RECEIVERSHIP
OF CUSTOMS
(Rüsumat Emaneti)

PUBLIC WORKS
(Nafia)

LAND
REGISTRY*
(Defter Emaneti)

▬ ▬ ▬ = Enclosed organizations are part of Sublime Porte.

* Not included in the Council of Ministers.

bombastic than those addressed to Husrev. The prologue to the Reform Decree of 1856, if we may judge from a French translation, addressed Âli Paşa as "you who distribute the honors of our Caliphal Court" and as the "alter ego" of the sultan.[48] On a day-to-day basis, the men of the Tanzimat exerted continuing vigilance to maintain the grand vezirate on just this footing. Âli Paşa, for example, was noted for insisting that the sultan consult him not only for ministerial appointments, but also for those of secretaries and certain other attendants at the palace. Âli was equally insistent that his ministers have contact with the palace only through him.[49] At his death, Âli was said to have "exercised an authority over every department of the State to a degree that reduced the other ministers to insignificance, and no doubt impeded the independence of action indispensable to their offices being conducted with due vigour."[50] Only after Âli's death did this pattern begin to change.

As differentiation among the organs of the Porte continued, however, the grand vezirate did begin to change in the sense of accumulating a variety of offices directly subordinate to it and not otherwise attached to any ministry. Most important of these was the post of undersecretary (*müsteşar*) to the grand vezir. The history of this post began with the appointment of an "assistant" (*muavin*) to the "prime minister" (*baş vekil*) in 1838, the title being changed to "undersecretary" (*müsteşar*) with the reconversion from prime minister to grand vezir in 1839. From then until 1869, the office of undersecretary, which existed for most but not all of this period, appears to have been a sort of alternate form for that of minister of the interior, a post that existed only when the undersecretaryship did not. More exactly, when the grand vezir assumed responsibility for internal affairs, as was usually the case, the minister of the interior would disappear and an undersecretary to the grand vezir would be appointed.[51]

At the same time, the evolution of the chief scribe (*reis ül-küttab*), traditional head of the grand vezir's chancery, into a foreign minister of relatively specialized functions initiated a process by which most of the offices in the chancery gradually severed their links with the Foreign Ministry and began to assume a new form as a secretarial staff attached directly to the grand vezirate. Since to some degree these offices retained their old, heterogeneous functions, this change is clearer in terms of organizational affiliations than of actual duties. By the end of the

period here surveyed, it had progressed to the point that the
Offices of the Corresponding Secretary of the Grand Vezir
(*Mektubî-i Sadr-ı Âli*) and of the Receiver (*Amedî*), restored to
their old forms in 1839 after their subdivision of a year earlier
into separate sections for internal and foreign affairs, had begun
to be regarded as part of the grand vezir's personal staff.

The logic of this development was obvious in the case of the
corresponding secretary. With growth in business and size of
staff, this office gradually began to go through a process of
internal differentiation, acquiring its own Section for Important
Affairs (*Mühimme Odası*) with fifteen members in 1861-1862.
Later references also mention other sections for matters such as
legal affairs (*hukuk, deavi*) and the preparation of reports and
minutes of meetings (*mazbata*).[52]

In the case of the receiver (*amedî*), the organizational link to
the grand vezir presumably followed from the traditional role of
the office in preparing documents for submission from the Porte
to the palace. In the nineteenth century, the receiver retained
this responsibility, acquiring in addition the related duties of recording the proceedings of the Council of Ministers and registering the imperial commands (*irade*) that came back from the
palace in response to the documents submitted from the Porte.
In consequence, as many traditional offices began to go into
eclipse, this one retained considerable importance. Its staff, no
more than five or ten a half-century earlier, included twenty or
more clerks (*hulefa*) through most of this period.[53]

Also attached to the grand vezir were several other offices that
were smaller in size and importance, or less clearly established in
organizational terms. One traditional function that falls into this
category is that of the master of ceremonies or *chef de protocole*
(*teşrifatî-i Divan-ı hümayun*) and his assistants. Perhaps under him
was a Decoration Office (*Nişan-ı Hümayun Kalemi*), presumably in
charge of issuing the various types of decorations created during
this period.[54] Several agencies dealt with various aspects of official communications and what is now referred to as records
management. Needs in that field led to the creation of new archives (*hazine-i evrak*) for the Porte and the construction in 1846
of a special building to house the records.[55] By 1861, there was a
special Records Office of the Sublime Porte (*Bab-ı Âli Evrak
Odası*), its mission being to supervise the flow of documentation
between the Porte and the other offices in Istanbul and to keep

records that would make it possible to recover documents when needed.[56] The extension into the empire of telegraph lines also led to the creation of a special Telegraph Office of the Sublime Porte.[57]

Thus, while the prevailing conception of the grand vezirate remained practically unchanged, the process of reform precipitated changes in the grand vezir's entourage. Ultimately, of course, the most important adjuncts of the grand vezirate lay not in these offices providing technical and secretarial services, but in the various conciliar bodies and ministries. The differing degrees to which these assumed organizational substance and distinctness are highly indicative of the thrust, and the limitations, of the reformers' efforts during this period.

Conciliar Bodies—The Council of Ministers

As heirs to the *divans* and ad hoc consultative assemblies of the late prereform period, the conciliar bodies have a logical claim to consideration immediately following the grand vezirate. This is true not only on account of the close working relationship between the highest councils and the incumbent of that office, but also on account of the important contributions which the growth of collegial bodies has tended historically to make to the development of more characteristically bureaucratic institutions.[58] Since Mahmud's creation in 1838 of the Consultative Assembly of the Sublime Porte (*Dar-ı Şura-yı Bab-ı Âli*) and the Supreme Council of Judicial Ordinances (*Meclis-i Vâlâ-yı Ahkâm-ı Adliye*) had been an integral part of his efforts to dismantle the grand vezirate and shift the locus of power, the restoration of the grand vezirate in 1839 required immediate changes in those bodies. The sequence of reforms that followed had the effect of replicating the conciliar form of organization much more widely than in the past and regularizing what had been the ad hoc character of earlier consultative assemblies in certain respects. The same reforms also stimulated the organizational growth of many agencies of the civil bureaucracy and furthered the development in certain councils of legislative and representative as well as consultative roles.

While Mahmud had intended his system of dual councils to replace the old *divan* of the grand vezir, it is not surprising that a sort of successor body to the vezirial *divan* reappeared—largely shorn, it seems, of its quondam judicial role—following the restoration of the grand vezirate. Nor is it surprising that this became the most important of all the conciliar bodies. Known by names such as Council of Ministers (*Meclis-i Vükelâ*) or Privy Council (*Meclis-i Has*), this is often compared to the ministerial councils and cabinets of other governments, although it still functioned only in the limited capacity that its transitional state of development and the absolutism of the empire implied.

For example, ministers were chosen in theory by the sultan—a choice usually made during this period at the behest of the grand vezir—and there was no principle of collective ministerial responsibility. Membership in the council was neither entirely fixed nor entirely civil-bureaucratic. Yet, a check through the listings in the government yearbooks shows that there was a more or less permanent core. This consisted of the grand vezir, his undersecretary, the head of the religious establishment (*şeyh ül-İslâm*), the chairmen of the two major councils that Mahmud II had created or their successor organizations, and the ministers of foreign affairs, finance, education, pious foundations, and trade (a portfolio that sometimes also encompassed agriculture and public works). The council also included the officers in charge of the military departments (army, artillery, navy) and police (*zabtiye*), as well, in most years, as the steward of the powerful sultan mothers and various ministers-without-portfolio.[59] Ranging in numbers as high as fifteen or sixteen, the ministers without portfolio began to be listed toward the end of the period as "appointed to the high councils" (*mecalis-i âliye'ye memur*), and indeed their names usually reappear, along with some of those of the ministers with portfolio, among the members of the other conciliar bodies.

The heterogeneous membership of the Council of Ministers in this period suggests that it, like the old ad hoc assemblies, served to a degree as a forum for the creation of consensus, or the appearance of consensus, and thus lends added credence to Cevdet Paşa's indication that the real decisions about matters of policy were arrived at informally by the leading statesmen in discussion with their closest associates. Such a reliance on ad hoc or confidential means of policy making would help to explain the lack of explicit specification of the duties of the Council of Ministers, or of the differences between its attributions and those of the conciliar bodies immediately below it. The same fact would also perhaps explain the shortage of comment in the biographical and historical literature on the inner workings of what should have been one of the most important governmental agencies of the period. Yet the Council of Ministers was not simply a façade. However much it may have differed from the cabinet of a Western European state, the leading statesmen of the period clearly relied on it, at least at times, to respond with comprehension and dispatch to a broad range of policy questions. Indeed, the research of Roderic Davison is beginning to demonstrate that the speed and ingenuity with which the Council of Ministers supported the diplomatic efforts of the leading statesmen was at times remarkable, especially in view of the circumstances in which the empire then found itself.[60]

Major Conciliar Bodies with Legislative, Judicial, and Representative Functions

While the other conciliar bodies of the period were eventually quite numerous, the most important were those that derived directly from the two major councils that Mahmud created in 1838. Following Mahmud's death, one of these, the Consultative Assembly of the Sublime Porte (*Dar-ı Şura-yı Bab-ı Âli*), was abolished or combined with the other, the Supreme Council of Judicial Ordinances (*Meclis-i Vâlâ-yı Ahkâm-ı Adliye*).[61] In a move clearly symbolic of the opening of a new political period, the meeting place of this body, expressly charged under the Gülhane Decree with framing the new laws needed to implement its promises, was transferred from the palace to the Porte. There this council evolved into a permanent institution with a subordinate secretarial bureau (*Meclis-i Vâlâ Tahrirat Odası*) and became the chief center for preparation of the legislation used to institute the reforms of the period. In addition, the council assumed judicial functions in administrative cases and in appeals against decisions rendered under the new secular laws and codes that it gradually began to propound.[62]

Relations between this council and the Council of Ministers were nowhere explicitly regulated, but gradually settled into a pattern governed by the political realities of the time. Particularly as the volume of needed legislation increased, the draft laws prepared in the Council of Judicial Ordinances tended to gain approval without change in the Council of Ministers, and again at the palace. The problems that might have arisen between councils because of the indeterminate allocation of legislative initiative were taken care of in a practical sense by the fact that appointment to and compensation within the Council of Judicial Ordinances depended on the will of the grand vezir and his intimates. Thus, this council became a specialized, second-echelon element in a political machine that included the Council of Ministers, as well.

Over time, the continuing growth in the volume of its business, as well as the complexity of its functions and other political considerations, led to a series of changes in the legislative council. Quite early, it became customary for the council to perform much of its work in small, specialized committees. Between 1854 and 1861, there also existed another council, known as the High Council of Reforms (*Meclis-i Âli-i Tanzimat*). The distinction between its role and that of the older body was to some extent a matter of politics rather than logic. Both councils ultimately discharged a mixture of legislative and judicial functions, but the new one had a greater degree of legislative initiative and gradually became preoccupied in its legislative role with matters of administrative law and regulation. Cevdet Paşa, who was a member of the High Council of Reforms, adds to this that the new council was also to serve as a court for the trial of ministers and to exercise a watchdog role over the implementation of the legislation it prepared. In 1861, however, problems of coping with continued growth in the workload of the two councils led to their recombination into a supposedly improved form, still known as the Supreme Council of Judicial Ordinances. This was divided into separate sections for legislation, administration and finance, and adjudication. According to Cevdet, the watchdog role of the High Council of Reforms was then dropped.[63]

Finally, in 1868, there was another reorganization, resulting in two councils, shown in Figure V-1. The legislative function passed to a Council of State (*Şura-yı Devlet*), consisting of fifty members divided into five specialized departments and having its own secretarial staff. In the limited sense in which the representative principle had already come into use in local administration, the Council of State also had a representative character, both through its inclusion of members chosen from various non-Muslim communities and through the requirement that it meet annually with delegates from the elected general assemblies of the provinces.[64] While this Council of State in fact retained judicial functions as well, those in principle passed to a new Council of Judicial Ordinances (*Divan-ı Ahkâm-ı Adliye*).[65] Of these two bodies, the Council of State continued to exist at the Sublime Porte, if with many ups and downs, until the end of the empire. The Council of Judicial Ordinances, in contrast, appears to have been integrated within a few years into a reorganized Ministry of Justice separate from the Porte, thus providing a particularly notable case of the bureaucratization of collegial institutions.

Smaller Conciliar Bodies

While the details of the subject lie beyond the limits of this discussion, it is relevant to note in general that the development of conciliar bodies of smaller size and more specialized character was also a prominent feature of the bureaucratic growth of the Tanzimat. Where information is available on the early history of these, they often appear to have been little more than special committees that were formed to administer new programs and gradually grew in some cases into regular bureaucratic departments or even ministries.

For example, the Council on Trade and Agriculture was in a curious way an outgrowth of the Foreign Ministry, as well as the first step in the creation of a Ministry of Trade and Agriculture, which emerged later in this period. Reflecting the economic concerns surrounding the negotiation of the Anglo-Ottoman Commercial Convention of 1838, the council was founded under the auspices of Mustafa Reşid Paşa, then foreign minister, with his undersecretary as its first chairman.[66] The Quarantine Board, in turn, evidently came into existence to administer a quarantine system that had already existed for several years. On a practical level, the diplomatic complications arising from the need to gain the compliance of foreign nationals with its measures linked the operations of this board, too, with those of the Foreign Ministry. At the same time, the role of the board, the first governmental agency of consequence in the field of public health, in drafting quarantine regulations provided a good illustration of how these smaller councils could pick up a share of the legislative responsibilities discharged by their larger prototypes.[67] In 1847, the earliest of the government yearbooks listed eight of these smaller, specialized councils. By 1871, their number had surely increased, although their internal subdivisions made the listings so complex that it is difficult to determine an exact count.[68]

In the next period, the smaller conciliar bodies seem by and large to have faded in relative importance, in many cases because they became absorbed into regular bureaucratic agencies. Of course, that was not the only evolutionary route such a body could follow. Just as the Council of Ministers survived, ostensibly as a high-level coordinating and policy-making body, at least one of the small councils was to develop, under the guiding hand of Abd ül-Hamid, into a mechanism for the exertion of his control over bureaucratic appointments. This was a Commission for the Selection of Civil Officials (*İntihab-ı Memurin-i Mülkiye Komisyonu*), first noted in the yearbooks in 1871.[69] Later developments suggest that its mission at the time had to do with staffing the administrative structures called for under the recently enacted laws on provincial administration.

"Ministry of Justice"

As bodies of conciliar form increased in number and developed new functions, the ministries, with the one notable exception of Foreign Affairs, appear to have developed only more gradually, reliance on conciliar bodies remaining most pronounced where the development of bureaucratic organizations was weakest. Nowhere at the Porte was this weakness more pronounced than in what contemporary observers called the Ministry of Justice. In fact, it can be so termed only with reservations and had disappeared by 1871. Consequently, it has no place in Figure V-1, although it requires comment because of the links between its history and that of several others of the institutions we have discussed.

The head of this "ministry" was the successor to the chief bailiff (*çavuş başı*) of the traditional system and was known as the *divan-ı deavi nazırı*. Since for most of this period, the holder of this post was not a member of the Council of Ministers, it is surely better to think of him not as a minister, but as something closer in rank to the various supervisors and intendants known as *nazır* before, and sometimes after, the adoption of that term to designate European-style "ministers." When the title of *divan-ı deavi nazırı* first came into use in 1836, the Austrian ambassador translated the title as "Président de la Cour de Jus-

tice."[70] In fact, there was no distinct court of justice of which this
figure was president, although he was initially assigned to attend
two days a week at appeals courts, then held in the offices of the
şeyh ül-İslâm, at which cases were heard under the new laws
created by the reformers (*nizamî davalar*).[71] Perhaps it will do
just as well, then, to translate *divan-ı deavi nazırı* as "supervisor of
judicial affairs," specifically of those pertaining to the new laws.
Aside from this "supervisor," the yearbooks also mention several
lower-ranking officials recognizable as his subordinates. These
include two assistants (*muavin*), recalling the two scribes known
as *tezkerecis* who worked for the chief bailiff under the old system, and a few others. The numbers of these subordinates grew
slowly until the late 1860s, but never to the point of indicating
the existence of an organization of any size.[72]

This insubstantiality of the supposed Ministry of Justice
appears to provide a particularly strong indication of the difficulties of carrying reform from concept to controlled implementation in the kind of environment in which the Tanzimat reformers had to operate. It was not that the empire had no judicial system. On the contrary, it had more than one, including the
traditional *kadı* courts of the Muslim religious authorities, the
analogous tribunals of the non-Muslim communities, and the
mixed courts trying commercial cases between Ottoman subjects
and foreigners. The councils (*memleket meclisleri*) created in the
course of local administrative reform and the Supreme Council
of Judicial Ordinances at the Porte also performed judicial functions. The problem was rather to create a coherent hierarchy of
civil and criminal courts over which a minister of justice could
assume responsibility. This really only began in the 1860s with
the introduction in the provinces, as part of the general elaboration of a new system for local administration, of what became
known as the *nizamiye* courts.[73]

Paralleling the problems of creating a modern court system
were those of developing a coherent body of secular law for
these courts to enforce. The process was equally gradual. Beginning with the codes of 1838 for officials and *kadıs*, it continued with the successive penal codes of 1840 and later—no
longer drafted, after the egalitarian promises of the Gülhane
Decree, for officials or any other single segment of the population. Then came the land code of 1858, the great *mecelle* of

Ahmed Cevdet Paşa, and a series of codes borrowed more or less from foreign models.[74]

The real beginning of the Ottoman Ministry of Justice lies in the differentiation in 1868 of the Council of State (*Şura-yı Devlet*) from the Council of Judicial Ordinances (*Divan-ı Ahkâm-ı Adliye*). Simultaneously, the "supervisor of judicial affairs" and his subordinates disappeared from the government yearbooks, an accretion of courts and offices began to build up around the new Judicial Council, and it, in turn, metamorphosed a few years later into a Ministry of Justice, which then ceased to figure as an element of the Sublime Porte. The exact course or timing of these events is not totally clear.[75] In an effort to reflect conditions of 1871, Figure V-1 shows only the Council of Judicial Ordinances and neither the "supervisor of judicial affairs" nor the later Ministry of Justice.

Prior to his disappearance, the "supervisor of judicial affairs" (*divan-ı deavi nazırı*) remained so obscure that it is difficult to do more than speculate on his role. It probably involved the presentation of cases and appeals to the higher courts or councils in Istanbul, particularly to the Supreme Council of Judicial Ordinances when functioning in its judicial role, or the enforcement of the decisions there rendered. These functions corresponded to the traditional ones of the chief bailiff and were taken over at the founding of the Council of Judicial Ordinances in 1868 by agencies created within it.[76] Probably the best-known figures to hold this supervisorship were Ahmed Vefik Paşa (1823-1891) and Ziya Paşa (1825-1880), the former in 1857 and the latter in 1863. Since both were politically in Âli Paşa's disfavor, their consignment to the post is presumably an index of its insignificance.[77]

Ministry of the Interior

Discussion of the power position of the Tanzimat statesmen and of the undersecretaryship of the grand vezir has already given an idea of the discontinuities in the history of the Ministry of the Interior, at least as represented by the minister, during this period. Indeed, from 1839 through 1868, there was no titular minister of the interior. Not until the death of Fuad Paşa in 1869 and Âli Paşa's assumption of the office of foreign minister as well as that of grand vezir was a separate Ministry of the Interior

reinstated and provided with regulations. Even so, to judge
from the yearbooks, the central organizational structure of the
ministry developed only slowly. By the end of the period, this
included an undersecretary (*müsteşar*), an assistant to him, and at
least two bureaus. One was headed by a corresponding secretary
for internal affairs (*mektubî-i dahiliye*) and contained several subsections; the other was known somewhat cryptically as the Internal Affairs Office (*Dahiliye Kalemi*).[78] Once again, this hardly
looks like the organization of a ministry with administrative responsibilities over a large empire.

The apparent underdevelopment of the central organs of the
Ministry of the Interior surely reflects not only the determination of the leading men of the Porte to concentrate power as
much as possible in a few hands, but also the concrete problems
of projecting new administrative policies over an empire in
which the power of the central government had been in decline
for so long. The failure of the reformers' first effort at fiscal centralization, an effort that in large part had to take the form of a
change in the methods of revenue collection at the local level,
clearly illustrated the magnitude of these problems.

What survived from that effort, at least through the Crimean
War, was a system of local administration based on several elements. One was the provincial governor general (*vali*), appointed from Istanbul, or other chief administrative official at
the three lower jurisdictional echelons. The provincial governors general exercised rather limited powers, which were increased by a decree of 1852. Nominally in support of the chief
administrative officer, there was a small staff of appointive officials. Part of these were recruited by the chief administrative
officer himself through the mechanisms implied in the model of
the patrimonial household. At least at the provincial level, however, some of the most important—the treasurer (*defterdar*) and
local military commander (*serasker*)—were appointed from Istanbul and represented checks on the governor general's power.
In certain times and places, military commanders were, in fact,
appointed to head the local administration, even at the provincial level. Finally, there was a system of local assemblies. These
included both the appointed officials and other members elected
by an oblique system as representatives of the various ethnoreligious communities of the locality.[79] Relations between the
local authorities and those in Istanbul were assured through

such means as the sending out of provincial inspection missions, the referral of certain types of matters from the local assemblies to the Supreme Council of Judicial Ordinances, and the maintenance by the appointed governors general (*vali*), as in the past, of "agents of the gate" (*kapı kâhyası*) to represent them at the Porte.[80]

The limited extent to which this system differed from that which existed before 1839 may be inferred from the continuing role of the "agents of the gate." Similarly, while the local assemblies were new in form, their elected members were apt to be the same religious dignitaries and other notables who had long dominated local affairs, and these men often managed through the councils to maintain their accustomed influence.[81] While it is true that the assemblies represented a step toward the development of representative institutions, the variety of their powers in fiscal, judicial, and other types of business makes it equally logical to view them as an example of reliance on collegial institutions to supplement the otherwise thinly developed administrative cadres. Considering how rudimentary the central organization of the Ministry of the Interior was, the existence among the various committees of the Supreme Council of Judicial Ordinances, at least after the Crimean War, of a committee specializing in civil-administrative (*mülkiye*) or internal (*dahiliye*) affairs suggests that a similar dependence prevailed even in Istanbul.[82] Underdevelopment of the administrative infrastructure meant that the outreach of the central government into the countryside was still limited; and in fact, the first requirement for implementing reforms in the provinces was often outright pacification.[83]

For most of the period, efforts to improve local administration proceeded on a fragmentary or localized basis. There were occasional redefinitions of the responsibilities of the governors general or other officials. A distinct municipal organization was developed for Istanbul, and special regimes were created for localities which—like Lebanon—were placed in a special status for one reason or another. There was also the major experiment in administrative reform that Midhat Paşa undertook in the province of Nish.[84] But there was no further attempt at general reform of the provincial administrative system until the promulgation of the laws of 1864 and 1871.

These were patterned on the French model of a centralized

system. Again, there were to be four echelons of territorial subdivisions, and there were to be centrally appointed administrative chiefs at all but the lowest. In one sense, the new laws
pointed in the direction of decentralization rather than its opposite; for the power of the provincial governor general (*vali*) was
increased in 1864 and again in 1871. Given the difficulties
experienced earlier in the period with limited gubernatorial
powers, and given the fact that the *valis*,—in contrast to their
predecessors of a generation earlier—were now likely to be
Istanbul-based members of the central bureaucratic elites, this
change must have seemed both indicated on practical grounds
and tolerable in a larger context of centralizing policy. In any
case, to support the chief administrative officers, there was also
to be an expanded cadre of appointive subordinate officials, as
well as a representative collegial body, or now a set of them.
These were the administrative council (*meclis-i idare*) found at
each of the top three administrative echelons; the general assembly set up in each province; the local courts, on which the
inclusion of representatives of the non-Muslim communities was
envisioned chiefly as a way to thwart European complaints about
Ottoman justice; and a series of commissions with responsibilities in fields such as public works, education, agriculture,
and trade. The law of 1864 was first implemented in the single,
specially created Danube province, with Midhat Paşa as governor. In 1867, the law was amended in some points and extended
in its application to a number of provinces. Promulgation of a
revised law then followed in 1871, and application of this law to
virtually all the provinces of the empire occurred over the next
several years.[85]

The law of 1871 remained in force until 1913. It stands out as
a milestone in the development of a modern type of local administrative apparatus, in the expansion of the role of the civil
bureaucracy in administrative positions outside the capital, and
in the broadening of the scope of participation by elements of
the populace in political and bureaucratic processes. At the same
time, the fact that such laws were not even drafted until the very
end of the period is an eloquent witness to the difficulties which
the men of the Tanzimat encountered in pursuit of the long-
espoused goal of reasserting central control over the provinces.
At the Sublime Porte, the rudimentary development of the central organs of the Ministry of the Interior, like the strange his-

tory of the supposed "Ministry of Justice," bore witness to the same fact.

The Foreign Ministry

The state of this ministry as of 1871 forms a marked contrast to those of the two just discussed. Here, the necessity to develop an empire-wide infrastructure was absent, as was the reliance on the collegial bodies that supplemented the gradually developing bureaucratic agencies in other fields. The Foreign Ministry did, of course, require a different kind of network of agencies and representatives outside the capital. But this network was relatively small; and its development, like that of the central organs of the ministry, had already begun in the preceding period in response to some of the most keenly felt necessities of the state. By 1871, the Foreign Ministry thus became the most highly evolved organizational component of the Porte and in some respects the most modern in its structure. These developments gave rise, however, to other organizational problems different from those of the ministries just discussed. For the proliferation of agencies and departments began to imply questions about the relations among them and about the most effective means for coordinating and controlling their efforts. Seemingly of no concern to the men of the Tanzimat, these problems would elicit no response until they became a great deal worse and the political climate underwent a fundamental shift.

At the head of the organization shown in Figure V-2, the foreign minister discharged responsibilities ostensibly much more specialized than those of his predecessor, the chief scribe. At least one of the offices under him, that of the imperial Divan, still retained enough of a traditional assortment of functions, however, to give him powers reaching beyond those implied by his title, particularly where patronage was concerned.[86] In addition, in an age of westernization and foreign encroachment, the head of the agency officially responsible for relations with the states of the Western world naturally retained considerable influence, already apparent in the 1830s, over government policy in many areas. The unusual linkages between the Foreign Ministry and the Board, later Ministry, of Trade and the Quarantine Board are indicative of this fact. The circumstances of the times thus made foreign affairs into a particularly far-reaching category and the foreign minister into the second man at the Porte

FIGURE V-2. ORGANIZATION OF THE FOREIGN MINISTRY, 1871

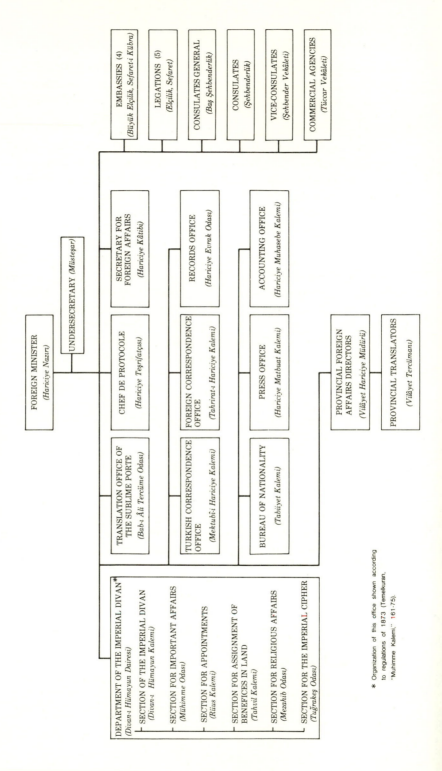

FOREIGN MINISTER
(Hariciye Nazırı)

UNDERSECRETARY (Müsteşar)

SECRETARY FOR FOREIGN AFFAIRS
(Hariciye Kâtibi)

RECORDS OFFICE
(Hariciye Evrak Odası)

ACCOUNTING OFFICE
(Hariciye Muhasebe Kalemi)

EMBASSIES (4)
(Büyük Elçilik, Sefaret-i Kübra)

LEGATIONS (5)
(Elçilik, Sefaret)

CONSULATES GENERAL
(Baş Şehbenderlik)

CONSULATES
(Şehbenderlik)

VICE-CONSULATES
(Şehbender Vekâleti)

COMMERCIAL AGENCIES
(Tüccar Vekâleti)

CHEF DE PROTOCOLE
(Hariciye Teşrifatçısı)

FOREIGN CORRESPONDENCE OFFICE
(Tahrirat-ı Hariciye Kalemi)

PRESS OFFICE
(Hariciye Matbuat Kalemi)

PROVINCIAL FOREIGN AFFAIRS DIRECTORS
(Vilâyet Hariciye Müdürü)

PROVINCIAL TRANSLATORS
(Vilâyet Tercümanı)

TRANSLATION OFFICE OF THE SUBLIME PORTE
(Babı Âli Tercüme Odası)

TURKISH CORRESPONDENCE OFFICE
(Mektubii Hariciye Kalemi)

BUREAU OF NATIONALITY
(Tabiiyet Kalemi)

DEPARTMENT OF THE IMPERIAL DIVAN*
(Divan-ı Hümayun Dairesi)

SECTION OF THE IMPERIAL DIVAN
(Divan-ı Hümayun Kalemi)

SECTION FOR IMPORTANT AFFAIRS
(Mühimme Odası)

SECTION FOR APPOINTMENTS
(Rüus Kalemi)

SECTION FOR ASSIGNMENT OF BENEFICES IN LAND
(Tahvil Kalemi)

SECTION FOR RELIGIOUS AFFAIRS
(Mezahib Odası)

SECTION FOR THE IMPERIAL CIPHER
(Tuğrakeş Odası)

* Organization of this office shown according to regulations of 1873 (Temelkuran, "Mühimme Kalemi," 161-75).

after the grand vezir, a point subtly underscored by the play on the word *sadr* in the verse of Fuad Paşa quoted at the head of this chapter. To assist him, the foreign minister had an undersecretary (*müsteşar*), although the history of this post does not appear to have become continuous before the Crimean War.[87]

Below the minister and his undersecretary, and despite the tendencies toward a progressive shift of the traditional offices of the chief scribe to positions under the grand vezir, the Office of the Imperial Divan continued to occupy a central place in the Foreign Ministry. Still under the supervision of the *beylikçi*, this office included, by the end of the period, several new sections as well as its traditional ones, the responsibilities of the latter also having undergone some changes. Slightly to transgress the terminal date of this chapter, a set of regulations adopted in 1873 for what was then termed the Department of the Imperial Divan (*Divan-ı Hümayun Dairesi*) described it as being made up of six sections. These were the Section of the Imperial Divan (*Divan-ı Hümayun Kalemi*, corresponding to the *Beylik* Section of the traditional system), the Section for Important Affairs (*Mühimme Odası*) created in 1797, the traditional Sections for Appointments (*Rüus*) and Assignment of Benefices in Land (*Tahvil*), one new Section for Religious Affairs (*Mezahib Odası*), and another for the Drawing of the Imperial Cipher on appropriate documents (*Tuğrakeş Odası*).

Of these sections, the first four still retained functions much like those they had discharged before the founding of the Foreign Ministry. In addition to the official registration of laws and treaties, the duties of the Section of the Imperial Divan included receiving and responding to communications from the foreign ambassadors in Istanbul and comparing the questions that those communications raised with the relevant provisions of the international agreements and concessions then in force. The duties of the Section for Important Affairs, as they appear in the regulations of 1873, are similar and difficult to distinguish. The roles of the Sections for Appointments and Benefice Assignments still had to do with patronage, although the latter section appears to have been declining in importance, thanks to the episodic efforts to phase out the system of benefices in land. The Section for Religious Affairs appears to have inherited the function, traditionally discharged in the *Beylik* Section, of keeping records on the status of the non-Muslim communities inside the empire. Later in the 1870s, this responsibility would shift to the Ministry of Justice. The Section for the Drawing of the Imperial Cipher, its functions recalling those of the "affixer of the cipher" (*nişancı*) who had once been the chief scribe's superior, was a modest commentary on the magnitude of the changes that over the centuries had shaped the Sublime Porte and the position of the foreign minister within it.[88]

The Office of the Imperial Divan was the only one under the foreign minister to display such heterogeneity of responsibilities and the only one to have significant functions unrelated to foreign affairs. Perhaps for that very reason, it, too, would in another decade or so be classed as part of the staff of the grand vezir.[89] Lacking such a lengthy history, the other bureaus of the Foreign Ministry were more specialized and usually more fixed in their organizational affiliation with the ministry. Like the offices of earlier centuries, however, their emergence seems usually to reflect the subdivision of functions once performed in a single office, or in some cases the replication in already distinct departments of functions for which there might once have been but a single bureau or official.

The first of the new offices to emerge was the Translation Office of the Sublime Porte (*Bab-ı Âli Tercüme Odası*, 1821), founded to replace the old system of translators of the imperial Divan (*Tercüman-ı Divan-ı Hümayun*), a title that was nonetheless retained for the head of the new office. This nomenclature, referring to the Sublime Porte and the imperial Divan, is suggestive of the fact that there was at first no Foreign Ministry to which to relate the new office. With the nominal conversion of the chief scribe into a foreign minister, this Translation Office became in a sense the basic component of the emergent ministry, at least for the business that it conducted in languages other than Turkish. It is not surprising, then, that several of the other major offices of the ministry later emerged out of the Translation Office either directly or indirectly, or that its papers are probably the most comprehensive classification in the archives of the Ottoman Foreign Ministry.

Omitting several ephemeral organizational changes made in the traditional offices of the chief scribe in 1838-1839, perhaps the next component of the Foreign Ministry to appear was the *chef de protocole* (*hariciye teşrifatçısı*),[90] created in 1847, obviously on the model of the centuries-old office then serving with comparable title and functions under the grand vezir.

Another official mentioned in the yearbooks every year from the beginning is a "secretary for foreign affairs" (*hariciye kâtibi*). Perhaps a counterpart to the secretary for internal affairs (*dahiliye kâtibi*) mentioned earlier, he acquired two assistants in 1870 and a third some five years later. A document of the early 1870s indicates that the functions of this "secretary for foreign affairs" had to do with legal cases arising between Ottoman subjects and foreigners;[91] and in the yearbook for 1877, the title of the head of this office was in fact enlarged to secretary for foreign legal affairs (*deavi-i hariciye kâtibi*), the titles of his assistants being changed accordingly.[92] Assuming that the functions of this secretary and of the secretary for internal affairs lay entirely in this field would imply another comment on the rudimentary development of the "Ministry of Justice" during this period.

Also in existence by 1847-1848 was another official known from the early 1850s on as the corresponding secretary for foreign affairs (*mektubî-i hariciye*),[93] a title obviously copied from that of the corresponding secretary of the grand vezir. From a variety of sources, including the language skills of the clerks of this office as noted in the personnel records of the ministry, it is clear that the functions of this office were to conduct whatever correspondence the ministry had in Turkish.[94] Accordingly, to contrast this office with the next one to be discussed, we shall henceforth identify it, as we have in Figure V-2, as the Turkish Correspondence Office of the ministry.

Roughly at the end of the Crimean War, a parallel to the Turkish Correspondence Office appeared in what was termed the Foreign Correspondence Office (*Tahrirat-ı Ecnebiye Odası*), the Ottoman version of this title being replaced a few years later with the synonymous and thereafter more familiar *Tahrirat-ı Hariciye Odası*. Parallel in functions to the Turkish Correspondence Office, this new bureau was by origin an outgrowth of the Translation Office, founded to cope with the increasingly voluminous correspondence in French with foreign ambassadors in Istanbul and Ottoman representatives abroad.[95] From the end of the Crimean War, the role of the Translation Office thus appears to have been limited to the translation of documents coming into the ministry in languages other than Turkish,[96] while the Foreign Correspondence Office assumed responsibility for the correspondence of the ministry in French, as the Turkish Correspondence Office did for that in Turkish.

Up to the Crimean War, then, the Foreign Ministry developed in large part by a kind of modernization of the old document-oriented organizational patterns, now transposed into various forms of linguistic specialization: translation into Turkish, correspondence in Turkish, correspondence in French. The organization that had emerged by 1856 appears to have remained stable until about the time of Fuad Paşa's death (1869). Several more elements were then added, and with them the first signs of a different kind of organizational concept emerged.

First to appear in the government yearbooks was the Foreign Ministry records director (*Hariciye evrak müdürü*), mentioned in 1868-1869.[97] Since there were already special supervisory-level officials in the Turkish and Foreign Correspondence Offices to handle records problems there, the creation of this new office is another sign of the mounting demands that the control of official paperwork was beginning to make on Ottoman officials.

A set of regulations issued in 1869 called, in addition, for the creation in the Foreign Ministry of a Bureau of Nationality (*Tabiiyet Kalemi*). This had as its mission to determine the real nationality of individuals who claimed to be subjects or protégés of foreign powers. The bureau was thus clearly intended to play a key role in controlling an abuse at which the new law on nationality, promulgated earlier in the same year, was particularly aimed.[98] The fact that the new office does not appear in the government yearbooks before the end of the period implies, however, that the implementation of these regulations may only have occurred after some delay. With this reservation, the office nonetheless appears in Figure V-2.

Also noted for the first time in 1869 was what developed into the Foreign Ministry Press Office (*Hariciye Matbuat Kalemi*). Its role included supplying local and foreign newspapers with what would now be called press releases, as well as monitoring the rather considerable foreign-language press of the empire.[99]

Finally, in 1871, there appeared a special Accounting Office for the Foreign Ministry (*Hariciye Muhasebe Odası*).[100]

With this, the central organization of the Foreign Ministry assumed its final form for the period. As it did so, it began, especially in the Nationality and Press Offices, to display signs of a reorientation toward organizational concepts defined in terms of goals external to the *paperasseries* of the bureaucracy itself and directed sometimes at the provision of services to, sometimes at the exercise of controls over, the larger society. Growing organizational complexity was beginning to imply, however, that the ministry would have to develop improved mechanisms for coordinating the work of the new agencies if they were to perform their missions effectively.

The reorientation of organizational concepts was also evident in the offices and agencies outside Istanbul. Had the development of the provincial agencies of the Ministries of Justice and the Interior progressed further in this period, this would no doubt already be clear from those cases. As it was, two of the best illustrations appeared in the development of the Foreign Ministry.

One of these took the form of the provincial foreign affairs directors and their interpreters, appointed to cope with the increasing problems created in the provinces by foreign consular representatives, local residents with claims to foreign nationality, and the diplomatic crises always brewing over some part of the empire. The assignment of provincial foreign affairs directors became a matter of system with the laws of 1864 and 1871 on provincial administration, under which such officials, nominated by the Foreign Ministry but under orders of the local governor, were to be a regular part of the administrative staff of each province.[101] Documentation of the next period suggests that the directors in fact only appeared where the foreign presence was particularly consequential, and that the translators served sometimes under the directors and sometimes alone in provinces where no director was stationed.

The same kind of organizational reorientation was also implicit in the consular and diplomatic services. From the modest scale on which Mahmud II revived these in the 1830s, they grew by 1871 to the point of including embassies in Paris, London, Vienna, and Saint Petersburg, and legations in Berlin, Washington, Florence (still so listed in the yearbook, although Rome was already capital), Athens, and Tehran. There was also a host of consular officials, ranked as consuls general, consuls, vice-consuls, and—in places over which the empire still technically retained sovereignty—"commercial agents." The consular officials might be either careerists in the Foreign Ministry or individuals, often not Ottoman subjects, who held their titles on a purely honorary basis. On this account, there is no reliable way to determine the numbers of employees of the ministry serving in 1871 in consular posts. In one sense or another, however, the Ottoman consular network was beginning to extend around the world, to include North and South America and Africa as well as Europe and Asia.[102]

Thus the Foreign Ministry developed during the Tanzimat. On the basis of the personnel records of the ministry, it is possible to estimate that it had about two hundred salaried officials as of the end of this period.

To compare the Sublime Porte of 1871 with that of 1789 or of 1839 is thus to realize the magnitude of the changes resulting from the political imbalance and the reforms of the Tanzimat. Problems of resources and the inherent difficulties of projecting new concepts over the vast territories and heterogeneous populations of the empire impeded the changes in critical respects. Yet, in the development of the conciliar bodies, the formation of a new "chancery" under the grand vezir, the organizational development of the Foreign Ministry, or the emergence of new organizational conceptions, the reforms of this period made a profound difference. Of course, there were costs and unexpected problems associated with this kind of growth. The problems of coordination implied in the development of the Foreign Ministry are one example. Another, more vivid if less serious, appeared in the experiences of the official historiographer, Lûtfi Efendi. He learned the costs of growth the hard way as he found his access to the sources to which he was supposed to have a right denied in one office after another. He explained this in terms of civil-bureaucratic disrespect for his religious rank, which was equivalent to that of a vezir, and of what we would now call "getting the run-around."[103]

For better or for worse, the old and more intimately scaled bureaucratic structures were giving way to more modern but also bigger and more impersonal ones. To look now at the efforts made to systematize and regulate the new institutions is to gain a deeper insight into this transformation.

REFORM AND REGULATION OF THE CIVIL BUREAUCRACY

In discussing organizational and procedural patterns typical of the scribal service before the beginning of reform, we noted the craftsman-like emphasis on processes of document production, the guild-like organizational patterns, the limited scope of individual initiative, and the tendencies at all levels to indiscipline and self-service. We also noted the concept of official position as discretional within the limits of tradition and hierarchical subordination, rather than as a matter of legally defined rights and duties, and the consequently limited scope of rational processes of differentiation and specialization in the development of organizational and procedural patterns. Although a fundamental reorientation toward the creation of a rational-legal order was inherent in the very concept of reform, the limited progress of reform in the central offices before 1839 meant that these traditional patterns still formed a kind of matrix within which the transformation of the bureaucracy proceeded during the Tanzimat.

Thanks to the inherent incompatibilities between the new elements and the old, and to the conflicts that processes of change generated among the men who worked in this context, it becomes more difficult in this period to present idealized or stereotyped views of organizational and procedural patterns, as we did for the prereform period. It is certainly possible, however, to survey changes in organizational and procedural patterns in a topical way, noting survivals of traditional features and areas where rationalization and regularization did not occur as well as ones where they did. From this we may draw an understanding of how, and where, the reformers applied their regulatory powers in order to restructure the bureaucratic system over which they presided.

Since the regulatory documentation becomes so voluminous in this period as to require a selective approach, it will suffice here to look at documents of three types. These have to do, first, with routine questions of official discipline, then with broader aspects of personnel policy, and finally with regulations of an organic character, issued to govern the overall organizational and procedural patterns of new or existing agencies. Documents of the first two types, in particular, tend to apply to a broad range of central administrative agencies and not just to those of the Porte. The discussion in this section thus helps to illuminate the general corporate state of the civil bureaucracy, and not just the conditions found in specific agencies that it staffed.

Official Discipline

This documentation, usually taking the form of orders issued by the grand vezir, is extensive and quite repetitive. Its significance

comes partly from that very fact, although we must also acknowledge that the repetition was to a degree simply indicative
of instabilities built into official routine.

It was customary, for example, to change office hours season-
ally (*hasbe 'l-mevsim*) on account of the varying length of the
days.[104] The fast during the lunar month of Ramazan also upset
routine every year, although in ways that differed depending on
the season in which Ramazan fell and the urgency of the business in hand.[105] Changes of these types were enough to necessitate the repeated issue of documents on certain aspects of official
routine. The texts of the orders make clear, however, that the
reasons for their repetition went well beyond mere changes of
this kind.

The disciplinary problems that emerge from these orders assume even more significance in that the demands made of the
civil bureaucrats of the Tanzimat were by present-day standards
still relatively slight. The increase in the volume of official business had not yet reached the point where most officials were expected to devote more than seven or seven and a half hours a
day to their work. At times, not counting Ramazan, the number
of prescribed working hours was as low as four and a half.[106]
Officials living on the Asian side of the Bosphorus or on the is-
lands of the sea of Marmara were sometimes authorized to arrive late and leave early;[107] and everybody had one, or in certain
times and agencies more than one, day off per week.

Still, securing the compliance of the officials with whatever regime was in force was a chronic problem. In 1842, the weekly off
day was changed from Thursday to Friday, partly as a sign of
respect for the Friday congregational prayer, but mainly because many people had been taking both days off. In another fifteen years many had begun to take Sunday off—an expression,
no doubt, of the egalitarian spirit of the new era—and a special
order had to be issued to forbid that.[108] Probably the most common complaints in the orders are against coming to work late
and leaving early, absence without valid excuse (*özr-i şer'î, mani-i
hakikî*), and lack of promptitude in the dispatch of business. Various orders indicate that the supervisory personnel of the
bureaus were not the least offenders and threaten penalties.
Eventually, the orders on hours of work began to include the
stipulation that only clerks having nothing left to do might leave
at the time appointed for closing, while supervisors would be re-

quired to remain, on a rotational basis, until the departure of the ministers, to take care of any urgent business that might come up.[109]

Some of the disciplinary orders also give more specific ideas of what the officials were doing instead of attending to their duty. One problem still not under control was the crowd of visitors who distracted officials from their work.[110] The clerks of the Porte had to be told that they were to remain in their offices attending to their appointed tasks and not wander about outside mixing with people who came in on business (*erbab-ı masalih*), and that they were not to take into their hands any papers except ones having to do with the affairs of the offices. They were no longer to deal on the side in the old type of petty "legal practice" (*kâğıd haffaflığı*), they were to collect the fees that continued to be collected on a modified basis for many transactions, and any negligence in such matters was to be punished.[111] References such as these reinforce European reports of the limited extent to which things inside the offices of the Porte had changed with the beginning of reform,[112] while other types of sources make abundantly clear that the real interests of many officials still, as in the past, lay in avocations such as literature and mysticism.

In addition, of course, there were more serious abuses of discipline, which had to be taken up in the different setting of the new laws and codes promulgated following the Gülhane Decree of 1839 and superseding the penal code of 1838 for officials. For example, the codes of 1840 and 1858 included articles prohibiting offenses such as bribery, theft of government property, abuse of office, negligence, and mistreatment of the populace by officials. At times, other more specialized acts addressed questions such as bribery and the kinds of petty gifts that were harmless enough to be allowable.[113]

Overall, then, the documentation on official discipline establishes several basic facts. One is that kinds of indiscipline long familiar in scribal circles continued into the era of reform. The vezirial orders, repeatedly prohibiting the same forms of abuse and aimed mainly at the lower and middle echelons, are particularly reflective of the persistence of such behavior at those levels.

Another fact that the disciplinary orders demonstrate is the gradual propagation, through repetition, of the concept that the behavior of officials should, for specific reasons, be governed by rules. The reasons appear in the motives for compliance that the disciplinary orders invoke. Aside from various threats of punishment, the earlier orders reminded the officials that they were paid "ample salaries" (*müstevfa maaşlar*) for the proper performance of their duty. As if in acknowledgment of the failure of the fiscal policies of the period, later orders tended to fall back on less material considerations, such as the importance of the matters the clerks handled or the honor of their calling (*haysiyet, namus-i kitabet*). At the same time, the orders began to reiterate the idea of improvement in the efficiency and regularity of administration as indispensable for the proper functioning of the state. Speaking of delays in the conduct of business, for example, the orders denounced them as injurious to the interests of private individuals, especially of those who had to come to Istanbul on official business from the provinces, as harmful to the Treasury, and as inadmissible even at the lowest echelons of the local administrative hierarchy.[114]

Reflecting the spirit of the Gülhane Decree, then, the disciplinary rulings asserted the demand for a new regularity in administration and even, in an inchoate way, for respect of the public interest.

General Personnel Policy

From previous discussion of the political behavior of the reformers, it will already be clear that their ability to impose such concepts on their subordinates was restricted by their failure always to practice what they preached. Looking beyond the relatively narrow issue of official discipline to the broader question of general personnel policy, we find this point confirmed and amplified by the very limited extent to which the reformers applied their regulatory powers in this field at all. However startling it may seem in contrast to their influence on the reforms that shaped the civil bureaucracy in the 1830s, the fact is that the Tanzimat reformers really produced no coherent or comprehensive personnel policy going beyond those earlier measures.

A search through the record of the Tanzimat reforms for anything like a comprehensive system to govern appointments, promotions, and official compensation brings to light only a few fragmentary changes. There were occasional, rather weak measures, patterned after earlier ones, to reduce overcrowding in the offices.[115] As already discussed, there were efforts, ultimately of considerable significance despite immediate problems of discipline and institutional quality, to improve bureaucratic education. The development of the civil rank table continued into this period, as did that of rules to govern such ceremonial facets of official life as titulature, precedence, and the awarding of decorations.[116]

Where basic questions of appointment and promotion were concerned, a measure of 1863 transformed the appointment of the "agents of the gate" (*kapı kâhyası*) from a matter left to the discretion of the provincial governors general, and other local administrative officials who maintained such agents, into a prerogative of the central government.[117] In similar fashion, the Provincial Administration Law of 1864 considerably increased the extent to which the officials on the staff of the governor general were to be appointed from the center by imperial decree, thus asserting central control over appointments in one of the settings where the tradition of the patrimonial household had thus far prevailed in clearest form. One of the respects in which the subsequent law of 1871 increased the powers of the governor general was, however, in restoring much of the appointment power to him.[118] The rights of department heads in selection of their staffs also continued to be acknowledged.[119] By asserting the existence of regular patterns where there were at best elements of de facto system, an account that Âli Paşa penned in 1861 to explain the organization of the Ottoman diplomatic corps is misleading overall and mendacious at points, especially in affirming that "the only basis for promotion is capacity."[120] In bureaucratic recruitment and promotion and in the distribution of the rewards of office, the tradition of patrimonial discretionalism was still, as Âli Paşa knew, much more strongly entrenched than that.

The one really fundamental alteration in personnel policy in this period occurred with the promulgation of the Reform Decree of 1856. Going beyond the general concessions in the earlier Gülhane Decree to enumerate specifics, this document affirmed the eligibility of non-Muslims to hold government office in conformity with "rules to be generally applied."[121] In the wake of this decree, the numbers of non-Muslims in government service, at least in the civil bureaucracy, did increase significantly. Yet, the traditional pattern of their affiliation with official cadres did not change as much as the decree indicated, largely because the period ended without the promulgation—let alone general application—of the promised rules.

Why did the Tanzimat statesmen take such a piecemeal approach to the elaboration of a personnel policy for the civil-bureaucratic machine that they had created, especially when they were so active in efforts to maintain discipline among their subordinates? Perhaps the most basic reason lies in the problems that the Tanzimat statesmen faced in getting their policies enacted into law and in the related fact of their inability to legitimate their control of political power. Since their hold on power was solely de facto, any comprehensive regulation of conditions of bureaucratic service was not to be expected from them. In addition, the comprehensive regulation of career patterns, emphasizing proof of achievement as the criterion for appointment and advancement, that we associate with the concept of civil service today was an idea that was still just emerging, even in the most advanced Western states of the time. The wording of the Reform Decree of 1856 was enough to show that the Tanzimat statesmen had some awareness of this idea. Yet, the fact that they were so typically of diplomatic background, and that the diplomatic services of the major powers were so strongly elitist and aristocratic in character, suggests that the Tanzimat reformers really aspired not to regulate conditions of service overall so much as to acquire for themselves the privileges of an official nobility. Such an aspiration corresponded not only to the character of the European diplomatic elites, but also to the self-image implied in the grandee mentality noted in the upper echelons of the traditional ruling class. And it was an aspiration already perceptible in the reaction of the diplomatic elite to the bureaucratic reforms of the 1830s.

As a natural consequence of their political position, their tradition, and the weak development of alternative example in Western nations, the changes that the Tanzimat reformers made in personnel policy, at least after 1839, were thus limited. The proclamation of egalitarianism was their one really fundamental reform in this field, a measure which produced considerable practical effect even though the reformers failed to follow through with a general regularization of personnel policy, as promised. Where the reformers did attempt to define personnel policy in detail, as in their efforts to tighten discipline over subordinate echelons or to order ancillary points such as ranks and decorations, their use of the techniques of rational-legal reform was at best a secondary feature of an overall policy pattern that remained mostly unregulated and must by default have continued to follow the social patterns characteristic of the traditional ruling class. The employment of modern techniques of rationalization and regulation as if they were no more than tools or weapons to use in defense of a power position that remained exempt from their application was typical throughout the era of reform. Naturally, the Tanzimat statesmen also took the same approach to other types of organizational and procedural matters.

Regulations of Formal Organizational and Procedural Patterns

Measures of these types are particularly numerous and heterogeneous. In a sense, it is arbitrary to exclude questions of personnel policy from this category, even though the social implications of the personnel measures and a practical differentiation that appears in the original documentation make it worthwhile to do so. Even with this exclusion, however, it is easy to distinguish whole fields among the measures that remain.

In the field of finance, for example, despite the fact that the reformers never redeemed the failure of their initial effort at fiscal centralization, the process of rigging up the series of expedients by which the state attempted to keep going required the enactment of one systematizing measure after another. This is apparent in a variety of measures on taxation, such as the systems of stamped papers and revenue stamps in which the old practice of fee collection, not quite abolished after all, assumed a more modern guise.[122] In a symbolic sense, at least, a similar significance also attaches to the new kinds of budgets that began to be prepared in this period. In fact, the limited extent to which the Tanzimat statesmen had any grasp of financial affairs, their rapid slide into indebtedness, and the consequent erosion of the economic autonomy of the empire obviously divested the concepts of budgetary allocation and control of the meanings now normally associated with them. The process of budget preparation does seem to have included the gathering of information about the experience of previous years, however; and the budgets thus possess at least a retrospective documentary value.

A tabular summary of the budgetary data on the agencies of the Sublime Porte consequently appears in the Appendix, covering the years 1858-1918.[123] Yet it seems unwise, particularly in the present state of research, to place much reliance on the data contained in these documents.

Where the material obstacles to regularization were less massive, the achievements of the reformers could be much more substantial. Developments in official communications illustrate this point, even though that field presented some significant challenges of its own. Indeed, the reformers faced an unmistakable need to revolutionize both media and content if they were to project their policies intelligibly over the whole empire and keep track of the mounting volume and complexity of official business. The resulting efforts at such things as stylistic simplification,[124] development of conventions for drafting legal texts,[125] creation of controls over the circulation and security of official documents,[126] reduction of repetitive paperwork through the adoption of blank forms,[127] and publication of government actions through such media as the official newspaper (1831), yearbooks (1847), volumes of legal texts (1862), and diplomatic "color books" (1868)[128] form one class of reforms to which the success of all others was linked in a particularly intimate way.

Where the efforts of the reformers to give order and form to the evolving governmental apparatus begin to produce a pattern reflecting their motives and goals is in yet another class of measures. These are the regulatory acts of organic character, issued precisely for the purpose of defining the organizational structures and missions of specific agencies. A survey of documentation of this type yields results that are startling and yet confirm implications already drawn from the sources on personnel policy. This pattern emerges partly from the substantive content of the documents, partly from the limited range of agencies for which they exist.

Where organic regulations were drawn up, the extent to which they simply perpetuated traditional patterns is perhaps their most salient characteristic. This is not invariably the case, to be sure. One good example is the set of regulations that Mustafa Reşid Paşa prepared for the Supreme Council of Judicial Ordinances in 1839. Paralleling measures already adopted for the Military Council (*Şura-yı Askeriye*) created in 1832, these regulations attacked such obvious procedural problems of the old consultative assemblies as the deference in debate of lower-ranking members to their seniors, or the demand for unanimity in the making of decisions. The regulations provided that documents relating to matters to be discussed in the meetings should be distributed to the members in advance. Members wishing to speak on a given matter should sign up before the meeting and speak in the order of their signing. There was to be a fixed procedure for the right of rebuttal, the debates were to be recorded, decisions should be by majority vote, and so on.[129]

Not every comparable measure displayed this much good sense. The regulations of 1873 for the Office of the Imperial Divan still had not sorted out its traditional functions and bristle with old-fashioned job designations such as copy checkers (*mukabeleci*), summarizers (*hulâsa memuru*), register keepers (*defterci*), writers of formal letters (*namenüvis*), examining clerks (*mümeyyiz*), preparers of first drafts (literally, "blackeners," *müsevvid*), copyists ("whiteners," *mübeyyiz*, presumably so called after the fine white paper on which they wrote), as well as the ordinary clerks (*hulefa*) and supernumeraries (*mülâzım*).[130] The persistence in these terms of guild-like organizational concepts and of the craftsman-like fixation on the processes of document production is obvious.

Newer offices usually displayed from the start a greater specificity of functions and often had jurisdictional limits that were more or less clear. A set of regulations drawn up in 1869 for the Foreign Correspondence Office (*Tahrirat-ı Hariciye Kalemi*), however, describes its personnel only in such terms as chief clerk (*ser kalfa*), examining clerk (*mümeyyiz*), producers of rough drafts (*müsevvid*), copyists (*mübeyyiz*), and registrars (*mukayyıd*). While it is true that even the most modern of bureaucracies cannot dispense with their typists and file clerks, counterparts of the Ottoman types just named, these regulations do not delimit the responsibilities of the office at all, except as so many modes of paper-pushing. In the want of other sources, it would be impossible to tell how this office differed from either the Translation Office or what we have called the Turkish Correspondence Office, the Ottoman title of which literally identifies it only as the Office of the Corresponding Secretary (*Mektubî*) for Foreign Affairs. This kind of specification makes it easy to sense why Cevdet Paşa thought many of the laws and regulations of the period were poorly drafted.[131] Similarly, if traditional categories so dominated the thinking of the officials who disposed of the regulatory power, it is only too clear how strongly such ideas must have directed the behavior of lower-echelon officials, with their guild-like heritage, as they confronted the rising demands of a new era.

What gives these traditional traits even greater significance is the very fragmentary extent to which the reformers produced any kind of organic regulations for the agenices over which they presided. There were no organic regulatory documents to govern the Sublime Porte in entirety; nor does there appear to have been any for the grand vezirate or any of its subordinate offices except the humble Records Office (*Bab-ı Âli Evrak Odası*).[132] Regulations were issued for the Council of State and for the Council of Judicial Ordinances at their foundation in 1868.[133] But for the Ministries of Justice and the Interior, the reformers' efforts had to go first to the erection of the systems of courts and laws, on one hand, and the local administrative infrastructure, on the other. We find nothing at all to govern the central organs of the Ministry of Justice, and nothing on those of the Ministry of the Interior prior to 1869, when the post of minister was again separated from the grand vezirate and the ministry thus in a sense "recreated."[134]

Even in the Foreign Ministry, the regulatory activity of the reformers had not gone nearly as far as the ostensible organizational development of the ministry would imply. Indeed, for the period running through 1871, the only regulations of organic character thus far found for this ministry are the already cited ones of 1869 for the Foreign Correspondence Office and the Nationality Bureau (*Tabiiyet Kalemi*), the provisions on the provincial foreign affairs directors in the Provincial Administration Laws of 1864 and 1871, and—stretching the point—regulations on such aspects of the consular system as consular leaves and the fees to be collected in consular chanceries.[135] The regulations that we have used as the basis for our discussion of the Department of the Imperial Divan date, in fact, from 1873.[136] So far as can now be shown, just as there was no visible concern for the problems of coordination implied in the organizational growth of the ministry, there was no attempt to regulate it in entirety or in its other parts.

Thus, while the Tanzimat statesmen did make efforts to impose order on the evolving administrative system, traditional conceptions of bureaucratic roles and procedures continued to leave a strong imprint on such measures, and the extent to which the promulgation of laws and regulations kept up with the organizational growth of the period was, in fact, limited. This limitation provides a vivid indication of the difficulties that the reformers experienced in progressing from initial conceptualization of each new measure through full elaboration and practical implementation to supervision. But more was involved than that. Just as the reformers appear to have sought to use regulation as a means for the disciplinary control of the middle and lower echelons and for the ordering of peripheral details of personnel policy, in other types of organizational and procedural matters they again limited their efforts chiefly to workaday matters of routine and to the circumscription of subordinate elements of a bureaucracy in which the most important powers and relationships remained undefined. If we "map" the organic regulatory acts issued for the Sublime Porte against its overall structure, noting the agencies for which such acts were promulgated and those, including the most important, for which there were none, we have a picture of what Eisenstadt's pattern of "split-up modernization" meant for the development of the bureaucracy in this period.

To bring this picture into sharper focus, we need to look at changes in patterns of social organization among the officials then in service and at the gradual development of their reactions to this peculiar state of affairs.

THE SOCIOCULTURAL IMPACT OF THE TANZIMAT ON THE CIVIL BUREAUCRACY

Coming on top of the modifications already introduced under Selim III and Mahmud II, the reforms of the Tanzimat drastically transformed the sociocultural fabric of the civil bureaucracy and enlarged it greatly in size. Cumulatively, these changes introduced into the bureaucracy two new forces which, partly cutting along traditional lines and partly cutting across them, altered the differentiation and relative balance of the various groups previously discernible among scribal personnel. One of these forces was the cultural cleavage created in the civil bureaucracy, as throughout Ottoman society, by the rise of the new Westernist elite and the commitment of the state to policies of overtly innovative character. The second force was that of Ottomanism and egalitarianism. Within the civil bureaucracy, these forces shaped new sociocultural configurations that were to persist until the collapse of the empire.

To conclude our survey of bureaucratic reform during the Tanzimat, it is indispensable to discuss the new cleavages that developed with the bureaucratic growth of the period, the links between the new bureaucratic subgroups and the old, and the significance of the tensions resulting from these changes for the further transformation of the bureaucratic-political process. Given the greater complexity of the new social patterns and the fact that the available sources, vastly increased in volume for this period and much different in character, permit quantitative verification of many points about which it is possible for earlier periods to speak only in impressionistic terms, a thorough pursuit of these ends would require a discussion of larger scope than can find a place in this chapter. Here we shall therefore present only a summary, in primarily qualitative terms, of an analysis that we hope to present in detail in a later work.[137]

Traditionalistic Muslim Officials

In a period of such complex changes, it could hardly be expected that the new differentiating factors would neatly isolate all traditionalistic survivals in a single segment of the civil bureaucracy. Although knowledge of other languages, such as German or Russian, or of other types of technical skills, ranging from stenography to law, could give an official a modern aspect, the high degree to which mastery of French continued to be both symbol and substance of modernity in the eyes of Ottomans nonetheless marked off officials lacking this talismanic quality as the segment of the civil bureaucracy most likely to preserve traditional traits. Furthermore, since there had previously been no possibility for a non-Muslim to assimilate the culture of the ruling class fully without becoming Muslim, and since practically all the non-Muslims who entered official service in this period and later did claim proficiency in French, the traditionalistic officials of the later nineteenth century were all Muslim. Since lack of proficiency in French had an adverse effect on promotion prospects, finally, these men presented the aspect in many ways of a continuation of the old, lower scribal service.

How large a part of the civil bureaucracy fell into this group, and where were they to be found? At the Sublime Porte, they accounted at the end of this period for about thirty percent of those serving in the Foreign Ministry, or some threescore cases, the percentage declining slightly in the next period. In agencies where literacy in French made less difference, whether at the Porte or elsewhere, the percentage was probably higher. Naturally, men of this type continued to fill most of the offices surviving from the traditional scribal chancery. But in a bureaucracy that still operated for the vast majority of its purposes in Ottoman Turkish and that retained many elements of old patterns of procedure even as it created new and different patterns, traditional kinds of scribal skills were of use in many of the new institutions as well as the old. The continuing lack of any stratification of clerical and professional personnel probably helped to reinforce this point.

Even in the Foreign Ministry, the one ministry in which, under nineteenth-century conditions, command of French was surely most important, men lacking that qualification could serve in a variety of positions. The personnel records of the ministry show, for example, that the Turkish Correspondence Office (*Mektubî-i Hariciye Kalemi*), the one large office of the ministry in which duty required literacy only in Ottoman Turkish, was full of men whose traditionalistic character showed itself in their language skills and in many other ways as well. Even in the consular and diplomatic services, there was a marked difference between posts in major Western states and others located in the Aegean and Black Sea regions or in Iran and British India, where Ottoman interests were substantial. In Iran and India, indeed, Ottoman interests had an Islamic dimension which it required someone of strongly, if not exclusively, traditional cultural formation to serve.[138]

The traditionalism of the more conservative Muslim officials also appeared in a number of other characteristics that followed naturally from their confinement within the linguistic limits of the old culture, as well as from the fact that some of these men served in agencies predating the beginnings of reform. The fact that the education of these men was traditional tended to mean, for example, that they had less schooling prior to their entry into the offices and that their careers consequently began at slightly earlier ages—although the usual age at first appointment, even for this group, rose to between seventeen and eighteen by the last quarter of the century. Once in the offices, these men were the most apt to continue their training through traditional means, such as apprenticeship, study of Oriental languages or calligraphy with teachers retained in the offices,[139] or part-time attendance in the religious colleges. While literary interests ran high in some of the new offices as well as the old—the Translation Office of the Porte, in particular, is remembered as something of a literary club—among officials of this type such interests continued to find expression in the most traditional modes, particularly in old-fashioned types of versification. Furthermore, while only a minority of officials engaged in literary activity to the point of leaving verifiable evidence of their work, authorship and publication seem to have been most of all infrequent in this sector of the civil bureaucracy.

The conservatism of officials of this type also shows in their continuing association with the dervish orders. It would be going too far to assert that only officials lacking first-hand access to Western ideas took an interest in mysticism. But in an age when modernists such as Fuad and Âli were more apt to become Freemasons[140] than dervishes, dervish links were clearly becoming emblematic of cultural traditionalism. Among the literary sources on civil bureaucrats of this period, the memoirs of Aşçıdede Halil İbrahim provide unforgettable insights into the life of a man who was at once a lifelong bureaucrat and a passionate adherent of the Mevlevi and, at times, other dervish orders. Educated in part in the "School of Literary Studies" (*Mekteb-i Ulûm-ı Edebiye*), one of the very first of the new civil schools and thus, in fact, only marginally different from the traditional institutions, he spent all the time he could get away from his office and family in the meeting places of the mystics. In traveling between posts, he might shock more progressive colleagues by donning the garb of an itinerant dervish in preference to the frock coat and fez prescribed for officials. Faced with difficult decisions, he would take the advice of a dervish shaykh, or turn to divination with his rosary or a sacred text. Nonetheless a useful and, by the standards of the times, conscientious official, he served the Ministry of War for sixty years and eventually achieved the first rank second class of the civil hierarchy, the fourth grade from the top in a ladder of nine ranks.[141]

Aşçıdede Halil İbrahim's rank points to another distinguishing characteristic of men of his kind. Before the beginning of reform, there was nothing to stop such individuals, if they possessed ability and could form the right kind of connections, from rising to the highest offices. During the Tanzimat, however, the premium placed on a modernist cultural orientation created a new dissociation between proficiency in the traditional scribal literary culture and the kind of advancement to which it had once been a major entitlement. At the Porte during this period, there continued to be officials who were not too different from Aşçıdede Halil İbrahim in cultural terms and who did achieve such relatively high offices as *beylikçi* or director of the Department of the Imperial Divan, receiver (*amedî*), corresponding secretary (*mektubî*), or even undersecretary (*müsteşar*) of the grand vezir. The same individuals were at times also members of the major conciliar bodies. Outside the Sublime Porte, such persons might become provincial governors or perhaps even ministers in some of the smaller ministries. But in the era of reform, the most important civil-bureaucratic positions lay increasingly beyond their grasp.[142]

Comparing the situation of the traditionalist Muslims with that of the non-Muslims in official service, we begin to see something of the political tensions resulting from the sociocultural impact of bureaucratic reform.

Non-Muslims in the Civil Bureaucracy

While the traditional association of non-Muslims with the Ottoman ruling class did not come to a complete end with the abolition of the Greek Translatorship of the Imperial Divan in 1821, the number of non-Muslims in official positions over the next several decades appears to have been very small. When the non-Muslim presence began to grow again following the Reform Decree of 1856, it did so in ways reflective partly of traditional patterns, partly of the egalitarian provisions of the decree, and partly of the relative precocity with which non-Muslims had espoused the cultural westernism valued by the reformers.

Such a precocity had already been evident among the Greeks, long before the state itself became committed to reform. Stimulated by a variety of factors such as religious affinity, commercial ties, and movements of national revival, similar cultural orientations gradually spread to others of the non-Muslim peoples, as well.[143] While the Greek Revolution nearly destroyed the old position of the Phenariots in relation to the ruling class, as other crises would affect the positions of other groups at later dates, the increasing scope and tempo of innovative reform and the initially trifling numbers of Muslims with the technical qualifications required for new programs created a continuing need to draw on the skills of the non-Muslim peoples. This need was simply one more way in which the initial difficulties of creating a modernist bureaucratic elite led to a resort to "marginal men." Throughout the period between 1821 and the Reform Decree of 1856, small numbers of non-Muslims therefore continued to hold official or quasi-official positions as translators, engineers in the Imperial Powder Works, architects, physicians, or financiers (*sarrafs*). While some of these were Greek, Armenians were also prominent.

From 1856 on, the development of this non-Muslim presence accelerated considerably. The Armenians soon outstripped the Greeks to form the most numerous contingent,[144] while other groups, such as Ottoman Jews, Syro-Lebanese Christian Arabs, and even a few men of western European origin joined them in smaller numbers. In the Foreign Ministry, these non-Muslims, the ethnoreligious subgroups of which display numerous differences, came by the end of this period to account for just under forty percent of the personnel in service, or about seventy cases. In the succeeding period, however, the non-Muslim presence in that ministry fell to little over twenty percent, or not quite forty individuals. The decline was particularly sharp among the Armenians. Representation of some other non-Muslim communities grew, but not enough to compensate for a sharp increase in the proportional strength of the modernist Muslims. These changes presumably reflect both cultural developments among the Muslims and the effects of the political tensions of the 1890s on the position of the Armenians.

Even when the non-Muslim presence in the bureaucracy was at its height, the fact that claims to mastery of French were practically universal among the non-Muslims, while the Muslims were divided among those who could advance such claims and those who could not, indicates that a Westernist cultural orientation was still the factor of supreme importance in making the non-Muslims useful in official service. This was so true that numbers of them were unable to fill out their official personnel forms in correct Turkish, and a few did not even try to.[145] In any case, a variety of indicators, such as the total number of languages of which they claimed some knowledge and the relative frequency of study at European universities, suggest that the non-Muslims, in addition to being invariably Westernist in cultural orientation, were perhaps the best-educated officials of all. As usual, there are differences in this regard among the various non-Muslim communities; and for non-Muslims in general, as for their Muslim colleagues, to speak of having a good Western education in this period was seldom to claim more than a modest distinction.

Given their ethnoreligious identification and their educational qualifications, the non-Muslims of the civil bureaucracy appear mainly to have occupied official positions of two types. One type included positions for which a non-Muslim incumbent was particularly appropriate. Such, for example, were administrative posts in various regions of the empire that had important non-Muslim populations and had, for one reason or another, been placed in special administrative status. The best known of these regions was Lebanon, which under the special regulation of 1861 had to have a governor who was an Ottoman Christian but not a Lebanese.[146] Otherwise, the most salient characteristic of the positions that non-Muslims filled seems simply to have been that they were of the new types created by the reforms. Jobs that the traditionalistic Muslim segment of the civil bureaucracy often could not hold, these positions differed little from those associated with the rise of the Tanzimat statesmen themselves. In the Foreign Ministry, for example, non-Muslims appeared frequently as translators, consuls, and diplomats, and several of them enjoyed lengthy tenure as representatives of the Porte to Western states.[147]

In addition to being more numerous than their precursors in the traditional scribal service, the non-Muslim officials of the new civil bureaucracy thus appear to have been more fully integrated into its prevailing patterns of service and promotion. But this integration had its limits. The data contained in official personnel records indicate, for example, that the salary entitlements of the non-Muslim officials and their access to other forms of reward remained limited compared to those of the Western-oriented Muslims with whom this group compares in qualifications and types of service.[148] The Tanzimat statesmen also had some reluctance about the promotion of non-Muslim officials to high office. This is clear from Fuad Paşa's statement, made to the British ambassador at the time of the first appointment of a

non-Muslim minister, that some positions, including the ministries of war and foreign affairs and the grand vezirate, would
have to remain in Muslim hands.[149] Ultimately, there were to be
a number of non-Muslim ministers, including four in foreign
affairs,[150] but no retreat in principle from Fuad Paşa's statement.

This kind of reluctance, which the circumstances of the times
help to make understandable, was no doubt an added factor in
keeping the Tanzimat statesmen from developing the fully regulated personnel policy that they had promised in 1856. In the
want of such a thorough systematization, preexisting patterns
continued to characterize the position of non-Muslim officials as
much as that of Muslims. The evidence on the imperfect integration of non-Muslims into the bureaucracy thus includes traits
of the organizational models of both the autonomous confessional community and the patrimonial household. For example,
Cevdet Paşa blamed Âli Paşa for making the Foreign Correspondence Office of the Foreign Ministry into an Armenian enclave. The personnel records of the ministry substantiate this
observation, which surely reflects the consequences of the appointment of Sahak Abro Efendi, an able Armenian much in
favor with the leading Tanzimat statesmen, as chief of the
office.[151] The discernible patron-client networks and bureaucratic "dynasties" of the period also include cases attesting the
replication of these patterns among non-Muslims. This is especially true of the Greeks, above all of a few elite families that presented the aspect of, and to a degree literally were, survivors of
the old Phenariot elite.[152]

Despite their growth in numbers and relative prominence,
then, the non-Muslims in the civil bureaucracy continued to occupy a second-class position in relation to the modernist Muslim
elite and to display significant elements of the old patterns of en-
clavement and patrimonialism. If we assume that in this, as in
other respects, the implementation of the reforms within the
governmental systems was prerequisite to their taking root in
the larger society, then we must judge the attempts to implement the principles of equality and Ottomanism within the civil
bureaucracy a failure.

Yet it would misrepresent the commitment of Ottoman
statesmen to their principles to say no more than this. In fact,
the non-Muslim officials must be compared not only to the new

Muslim elite, but also to the more traditionalistic sector of Muslim officialdom. While non-Muslim officials may have been less well rewarded than the Muslim elite for performing similar functions, the non-Muslims on balance appear to have fared better than the traditionalistic Muslim officials in terms of both compensation and promotion.[153] Compared to their own precursors, who had been marginal to the norms of the old ruling class in terms of both ethnocultural characteristics and service patterns, the non-Muslim officials of the Tanzimat shared the cultural orientation valued by the Muslim elite and had clearly moved into a kind of intermediary position between upper and lower elements of the Muslims, now themselves differentiated in cultural terms. This kind of change could not fail to awaken doubts and resentments, which must be numbered among the obstacles to fuller realization of the egalitarian ideal. Indeed, given the impact that separatist nationalisms were producing in the empire, it is impossible to believe that the non-Muslim officials were not themselves of divided mind about their situation.[154]

In the acceptance of non-Muslim officials, as in other respects, the reforms of the Tanzimat were thus incompletely successful, but not without impact. Like the evidence on conditions in the First Ottoman Parliament (1876-1878),[155] information on conditions within official cadres indicates that the changes in intercommunal relations during the decades following the Reform Decree of 1856 were extensive, enough so to sustain comparison with changes over comparable periods in other societies where the bases of social cohesion and the effective force of the underlying principles are better established than they were in this moribund, multinational empire. The difference here was that the forces shaping the future would ultimately keep the ideal of a supranational Ottoman synthesis from becoming viable.

Modernist Muslim Officials

The emergence of this third major group, definable more precisely as Muslims claiming proficiency in French, was a continuation of the process that, starting with Selim III's experiments with permanent reciprocal diplomatic representation, had shaped the reformist elite. The growth of this group in numbers was a natural consequence of the influence that its members acquired. In the Foreign Ministry, the extent of growth was such that westernist Muslims accounted by the end of the period for almost exactly a third of the personnel of the ministry, or about sixty men. In the next period, the proportion rose to almost half, or about ninety men. In other agencies, the percentage of Western-oriented Muslims may, for obvious reasons of specialization, have been lower. Yet there is no question that this sector of civil officialdom increased sharply in relative size during the Tanzimat and continued to increase in subsequent periods.

As among the non-Muslim officials, the growth of this segment of the bureaucracy led to the appearance within it of internal subdivisions. In this case, the subdivisions resulted from differing responses to the new cultural dimension of the civil-bureaucratic elite, and thus implicitly from the difficulties of propagating new ideas. At least by the end of this period, there were essentially three subgroups distinguishable among the westernist Muslims of the civil bureaucracy. First came the serious modernizers in positions of power, that is, the leading statesmen of the period and their collaborators. Subsequently, there appeared another, and typically younger, group of serious modernizers. Differing from the leading reformers of the period in having a greater mastery of and more critical response to western ideas, the younger men experienced frustration in their official careers and consequently developed into the first Middle Eastern instance of the opposition intelligentsia that Eisenstadt describes in his concept of "split-up modernization."

Finally, there was among the westernist Muslims a residual category of men who were little more than casualties of cultural change. Addressed in the insouciant couplet of Hoca Tahsin Efendi—who was not one of their number—at the head of this chapter, these were men for whom modernity meant little more than glibness in French and the aping of Parisian manners and fashions. To all the serious-minded, whether modernist or traditionalist in orientation, such figures were *alafranga çelebiler*, a term literally meaning "Frankish-style gentlemen" but corresponding more in tone to something like "Frenchified playboys." In the literature of the period, as Şerif Mardin has shown, these playboys live on in ignominy, while more earnest modernists, noble in purpose and dashing in frock coat and crimson fez, stand before a society woefully short of heroes as little less than the beau ideal.[156]

The official careers of the modernist types obviously absorbed their interests to varying degrees. Indeed, the second and third of the three subgroups represent the beginnings of a process by which the traditionally almost complete identification of the educated Muslim segment of the population with government service would gradually break down—a process that would not, however, go beyond its incipient stages before the collapse of the empire.[157]

In office, it was only natural that modernist Muslims of all sorts be found in the new posts created by the reforms. On into the closing years of the century, the Translation Office of the Sublime Porte retained its reputation as the best place to start one's career. It was probably desirable, however, for those seriously interested in foreign affairs to move on after a few years to one of the western European consulates or embassies. Others could move on to positions in one of the more important of the other ministries, to one of the major conciliar bodies, or, if they had connections with provincial governors, to staff positions in provincial administration.[158] The lack of any comprehensive regulation of personnel procedures, the extent to which the patrimonial tradition still governed matters of appointment and promotion, and the disorderly growth of the administrative organization make it impossible to speak in more precise terms of a clearly marked *cursus honorum*.

Possessing in both ascriptive and prescriptive terms the characteristics most distinctive of the leading statesmen and most valued by them, westernist Muslim officials had, however, the best chances of promotion of any of the three major groups and enjoyed the highest levels of compensation. Since the distinctive qualifications of this group were not too difficult to attain, and since the leading statesmen continued in the traditional way to be on the lookout for talented young men, this was true even of the intellectuals of the opposition, to the extent that they were willing to sacrifice their principles, and of the playboy types, if sufficiently well connected. In this sense, the westernist Muslims displayed closest affinities both with the reformist oligarchy of the Tanzimat, who were after all the first of their kind, and with the upper echelons of the old scribal service.

And yet, so much had changed that it is misleading to make simplistic comparisons with a single element of the traditional scribal service. The westernist Muslims were no longer simply the upper echelon of a larger group, distinguishable in having risen above a relatively clearly marked rank frontier. With the proliferation of civil-bureaucratic ranks, there had ceased to exist any such neat frontier. The new force of cultural differentiation had created an entirely different kind of disjunction, which individuals crossed not as officials, but normally as students. At the same time, the force of egalitarian Ottomanism, however imperfectly realized in practice, had made it possible for non-Muslims in unprecedented numbers to assume a place intermediate in responsibilities and compensation between the Muslim elite and the other Muslims of the bureaucracy. Whatever their affinities with the groups distinguishable in the old scribal service, the major segments of the new civil bureaucracy were significantly different in the modes of their differentiation and in their positions in relation to one another.

Fully to appreciate the sociocultural changes that reform created in the civil bureaucracy, it is thus necessary to look at these major groups not just singly, but also in terms of the relations among them. In this respect, the most important changes of the Tanzimat had to do with the characteristic modes of upward mobility and political behavior.

Changing Patterns of Bureaucratic Mobility and Political Behavior

Eliminating the insecurities that had conditioned the "wheel-of-fortune mobility" characteristic of the traditional scribal service, Mahmud II's reforms of the 1830s substituted for the old pattern a new one of more typically pyramidal aspect,[159] yet one to which any static image of a pyramid was only partially appropriate. The pyramid of the new civil bureaucracy was still under construction, and it seems to have increased in size all the time, even despite the critical shortage of resources. It probably also changed in shape as it grew. The proliferation of ranks, the limited ability of the state to provide sufficient compensation to its servants, and the way in which the leading statesmen were now able to hold on to their positions suggest that this pyramid may have become attenuated toward the top and harder to scale, even as it broadened at its base.

To make things more complicated, the elements of which the pyramid was built were heterogeneous, and the engineering principles applied at different levels in its construction inconsis-

tent. More explicitly, this was a pyramid not of stones, but of
formal organizational structures filled with men, most of whom
aspired to move higher with time. Yet, the qualitative differences
among various categories of these men affected both their initial
placement in the structure and their ability to move upward.
These differences naturally created tensions; and the application by the engineer-statesmen, presiding over the erection of
this structure from their vantage point at its apex, of different
rules to the elaboration of different parts of the structure
heightened these tensions even more.

As the study of the regularizing and systematizing activities of
these "engineers" reveals, in the upper parts of the structure,
peopled more or less exclusively by men of modernist orientation, the reformers paradoxically still operated according to the
tradition of patrimonial factionalism and discretionalism. In the
lower or peripheral parts of the structure, most apt to be filled
by men whose traditionalistic cultural orientations denied them
access to the highest positions, the reformers tended to be most
vigorous in application of the new tools of rationalization and
regulation. There is little wonder, then, that the reformers
themselves sometimes confessed dismay at the results of their
efforts.

This pyramidal pattern, and the categories of men who
worked within it, persisted in general terms until the end of the
empire. During the Tanzimat, however, it was clear that the
growth of this structure, in power if not necessarily in size, could
go on only so long before being brought to a halt by the stresses
built up within it, by the outcry that its burgeoning evoked from
other parts of government and society, or by a combination of
the two.

Where bureaucratic mobility was concerned, the critical fault
in the structure lay in the effective limits of traditional techniques of patrimonial faction building when applied on such a
vastly enlarged scale among men lacking the sociocultural
homogeneity or the low consciousness of political issues characteristic of the traditional ruling class. Here, to a major extent,
lies the answer to a question often posed by contemporaries—
why Âli and Fuad failed to train successors to carry on their system after them.

Even under the conditions of the traditional system, their
preference for friends and kinsmen would have brought many

incompetents into their entourage and produced embarrass-
ments for them. Under the altered conditions of the Tanzimat,
the insidious way in which members of the opposition intelligentsia or "Frenchified playboys" emerged from even the best
households compounded these problems.

The practical necessity for the leading statesmen to demonstrate their commitment to the principles of equality and Ottomanism, given the imperfect extent to which those principles
gained acceptance, exerted a similar influence. The Tanzimat
statesmen accepted these principles to the extent of relying
heavily on non-Muslims, sometimes including foreigners, in
many capacities. Contemporaries, including European diplomats, were amazed at the extent of the reformers' trust even in
non-Muslims whose loyalties to the empire were known to be
suspect.[160] The criticisms raised by Ottoman Muslims were apt
to be more general, and it was not only traditionalists unable to
adapt to the new era who voiced such complaints. This is apparent from the way Cevdet linked Âli Paşa's failure to train successors to the latter's excessive reliance on Armenians,[161] or from
the comments on the promotion of non-Muslims that Ziya Paşa,
a leader of the opposition intelligentsia, inserted in his celebrated "Victory Eulogy" (*Zafername*), a satire directed, like Cevdet's remark, at Âli Paşa.[162]

The kinds of patrimonial faction-building techniques that had
worked under the conditions of the old scribal service could not,
under the altered conditions of the Tanzimat, integrate the
diverse human elements of the much-enlarged civil bureaucracy
in any satisfactory way. Nor would it ultimately work to use the
techniques of rational systematization only as a supplement to
the old methods. Anyone with sufficient power or resources
could make such a combination work in the short run. But
elimination of the internal absurdities of the bureaucratic
pyramid presupposed two things. One was resolution of the
doubts and ambiguities that hindered full acceptance of the
non-Muslim members of the bureaucracy. The other was the
removal, or at least minimization, of the opposition between
practice and principle and the creation of a more fully ra-
tionalized system, especially in the field of personnel policy. Attainment of the first of these desiderata would ultimately prove
impossible; progress toward the second did, in subsequent periods, gradually occur.

Meanwhile, for all those discontented with the way the civil-bureaucratic pyramid was developing, the increasing articulation of political issues provided new means for the expression of grievances, even as the persistence of traditional assumptions among the men at the top of the system made it difficult for them to know how to cope with such behavior. This change is clearest in the literary life of the officials, particularly in the sequence of events that brought forth the new opposition intelligentsia.

There are abundant examples to indicate that the old type of bureaucratic poetasting and the long-familiar use of satire and eulogy for the resolution of official grievances continued on into the last years of the empire. Some of the examples of this activity are both amusing and enlightening. One of the most celebrated satirists of the Tanzimat period was one Kâzım Paşa (1821-1889), who had somehow become a general officer (*ferik*) in the army. He once lampooned Mustafa Reşid Paşa's westernizing policies in a quatrain that compared Reşid to a doctor who set out to advance his own reputation by curing the state, which was healthy, of——the French pox (*frengi illeti*). Mustafa Reşid responded to this affront in the traditional way of a patrimonial grandee. He received his satirist in a personal interview and presented him with a gold watch.[163] It was certainly possible for satirists to overdo it and hurt themselves in the process,[164] but Mustafa Reşid's placation of Kâzım Paşa was thoroughly conventional.[165]

What Mustafa Reşid and his like were not prepared for was certain new types of activity that began to evolve out of this traditional pattern. For far-reaching changes in communications, especially the rise of journalism, created new outlets for the eulogists and satirists, giving them a new sense of their own importance and making them harder to tame by the conventional means. If we may accept an opinion attributed to Cevdet Paşa, a petty bureaucratic *littérateur* known as Hafız Müşfik Efendi (1825-?) played a central, but not unique, role in this development. At some time, probably in the late 1840s or early 1850s, he was employed in the Office of the Corresponding Secretary of the Grand Vezir and thus, under the assumptions of the day, was a candidate for promotion into the Office of the Receiver (*Amedî*). In Müşfik's place, Âli Paşa secured the appointment of his own son-in-law to the coveted position. It was the kind of thing that had happened many times before and had driven other men to drink, to mysticism, or to the composition of poetical attacks against their malefactors. Müşfik tried all those routes, and a new one as well. Leaving official service entirely, he went to work as a writer for the *Ceride-i Havadis*, the first non-official Ottoman newspaper, founded in 1840.[166] There he became the center of a coterie of like-minded poet-bureaucrats, which in turn began to attract persons of a somewhat different type, destined to develop, as Cevdet said, into what "is called in French the *opposition*."[167]

The roles of bureaucrat and *littérateur* were beginning to differentiate; and new types of literary expression, new media of communication, and new forms of political behavior were beginning to emerge. The opposition of which Cevdet Paşa spoke consisted of a small group of men whose motivation has upon occasion been explained in terms of frustrated bureaucratic aspirations analogous to those of Hafız Müşfik.[168] In fact, almost all of this group were of very high social status and were very well connected.[169] Those whose family connections were less gilt-edged had or could have had literary *intisab* connections with some of the leading statesmen of the period. The grandfatherly Yusuf Kâmil Paşa, one of the six major civil-bureaucratic grand vezirs of the Tanzimat, was particularly prominent as a protector of these and other literary talents.[170] But there was a factor that disinclined these young men to capitalize on their connections in traditional fashion. Instead, they opposed and criticized the leading statesmen and stood fast, at least to a degree, when the statesmen tried to buy them off. The Young Ottomans, as the new opposition came collectively to be known, were even ready to take the unprecedented step of going into voluntary exile in Europe in order to escape that kind of pressure.[171]

What made such a difference in the political behavior of the Young Ottomans was their response to the new western ideas. Almost all trained in the prestigious Translation Office of the Sublime Porte, they enjoyed what amounted practically to the best modern education then available for Young Ottoman gentlemen. Their intellectual formation was certainly not entirely westernist. But they possessed a better knowledge of the West than that with which the Tanzimat statesmen began their careers, and it was this knowledge that led the Young Ottomans to elaborate what amounted to the first identifiable political ideology of the modern Middle East.

While there were significant variations in their views, it is possible to summarize fundamental elements of the Young Ottomans' program in coherent fashion. Heavily under the imprint of European liberal thought, their principles included Ottoman patriotism, Namık Kemal (1840-1888) being particularly ardent in its advocacy, and demand for a constitutional, parliamentary system of government. The latter they intended as a restraint not so much on the sultan, whose office some of them—notably Ziya Paşa—rather idealized, as on the civil-bureaucratic elite of the Porte. The Young Ottomans opposed this elite not only as autocratic, but also as uncritically westernist in its policies. In contrast, the Young Ottomans insisted on a criterion that would become common among reformist intellectuals of the nineteenth-century Middle East. This was the implementation of only those reforms that could be justified in the light of the traditional value system.[172]

While the Young Ottomans reinterpreted this tradition somewhat loosely to fit their purposes, it provided them with a weapon by which to attack the Tanzimat statesmen at their weakest point—that of the legitimation of their policies and of their control of power. This use of tradition also gave the Young Ottoman program a moderate-conservative cast that had wide appeal. The leading literary lights of the movement capitalized on this appeal by developing the simple, direct style in which they found men like Hafız Müşfik already beginning to work. They also exploited new genres and media, such as popular journalism and Western-style theater, in which the poet Şinasi had already blazed a trail for them. Thus the Young Ottomans not only launched an appeal for the restoration of political balance and for a more reflective approach to reform, but also, despite their elite origin, did so in ways capable of producing tremendous resonance in the less favored segments of the bureaucracy and, to a degree, throughout Ottoman society.

With these developments, the patterns of social organization and political activity characteristic of the civil bureaucracy assumed forms much different from those traditionally known in the scribal service. As the image of the bureaucratic pyramid implies, the civil bureaucracy had entered a transitional state in which, as in the formal organizational and procedural apparatus of the Porte, elements of the patrimonial tradition continued to exist in discordant juxtaposition with new features representing the progress thus far made toward creation of a rational-legal order. The new subdivision of the civil bureaucracy into subgroups defined in terms of ethnoreligious identification, on one hand, and of cultural orientation and thus indirectly of educational achievement, on the other, is witness to this intermediate state of development. The way in which the traditional patterns clashed with the new in the minds of men who lived with the system is at the same time apparent in the tensions surrounding questions of bureaucratic mobility and in the emergence of ideological controversy.

In creating the conditions out of which the Young Ottoman movement emerged, in particular, the Tanzimat reformers wrought better than they knew. For from the nascent constitutional movement came the ideas that carried the empire forward from the attempt to develop a modern bureaucracy to the larger task of creating a modern polity, including not only the bureaucracy but also a new and effective set of controls over it.

CONCLUSION

This progression would not, however, occur in an easy or untroubled way. On the one hand, the traditional powers of the sultan had yet to be limited in principle. On the other, the possibilities of harnessing the new force of nationalism to the defense of the state, and thus the prospects for the redefinition of the locus of sovereignty—prerequisite for a modernistic restructuring of the polity—remained very much in doubt. These two facts alone were enough to assure that the remainder of the history of the empire would be a time of wrangling over how the political system should evolve and over whether it could survive at all.

During the Tanzimat, the central theme of Ottoman political life was the creation and operation of the bureaucratic-political system described in this chapter. In succeeding periods, the further development of this mechanism would gradually become a subsidiary issue in a political process of continually changing character and enlarging scope. Before going on to examine the Sublime Porte in its last phases, it is thus important to determine how, other than in calling forth their "antithesis" in the Young

Ottoman movement, the Tanzimat reformers contributed to the continuing development of the bureaucratic tradition.

The manifold problems and tensions growing out of the extreme political disequilibrium, and the somewhat improvised character of the new bureaucratic structures, obviously mean that this assessment cannot be unmixed. Nonetheless, there were many gains. This is especially true of the development of bureaucratic organization. The massive difficulties of creating needed kinds of infrastructure, empire-wide, in fields such as justice and internal administration mark obvious limitations of the reformers' achievements. The prominence of conciliar bodies in this period is, in its way, another sign of the difficulties of developing bureaucratic institutions of all the needed types, even though the conciliar bodies displayed a major development in terms of numbers, kinds, and roles within the limits of their own tradition. Nonetheless, the bureaucratic institutions associated with the Porte underwent significant changes. This is apparent in the formation of a new official suite—including some of the traditional chancery offices—under the grand vezir, in the organizational elaboration of the Foreign Ministry, and in the tentative appearance of new concepts of organization. To identify what were ultimately the most important organizational developments of this period, it is perhaps enough to point out that the history of the consular and diplomatic services of the Ottoman and later republican Foreign Ministry is essentially continuous from the 1830s to the present; that of the Council of State (*Şura-yı Devlet*) and its republican successor body (*Danıştay*), from 1868 on.

In the attempts of the reformers to regulate and systematize patterns of organization and procedure, the picture of partial but sometimes significant progress is similar. On the negative side of the balance sheet, it is necessary to note the dismal record of the period in finance, the persistence in some of the regulatory acts of traditional patterns, and the fact that the rate at which bureaucratic institutions grew far outstripped the rate at which they were brought under any kind of regulation at all. On the positive side, we note such advances as more effective techniques for the conduct of meetings in the councils and assemblies, or numerous innovations in the field of official communications. The leading officials of the period, and their younger critics even more, were also acquiring a capital of ideas and experience that would strengthen and improve subsequent regulatory efforts. Perhaps most important of all, they were coming to expect that such efforts should go on and that their imperfect success was a problem that required further action.

At the beginning of the Tanzimat, ideas of this type were to be found, even in inchoate form, among only a tiny handful of men. In some ways the greatest contribution of the Tanzimat to the development of political-bureaucratic life lay in the progressive enlargement of these modernist cadres, the attendant transformation in the sociocultural aspect of the civil bureaucracy, and gradually, through the generalization of new types of educational opportunities, the diffusion of the ideas distinctive of the new elite to larger and larger segments of the society. By 1871, as the altered aspect of the civil bureaucracy shows, what had been the scribal service was well advanced into a sociocultural transformation of almost revolutionary proportions, while the entire society was beginning to undergo a leavening process that would eventually provide the needed basis for a real restructuring of the political system.

How well would Ottoman statesmen be able to defend and extend their gains under the altered conditions of succeeding periods? This remained unclear, but one feature of the behavior of the Tanzimat elite had particularly disturbing implications in this regard. This was the way in which the leading statesmen of the period used the reasserted regulatory power of the state, not so much to create a fully developed rational-legal system, as to extend the range of control exercised by the kind of undefined, discretional powers typical of patrimonial tradition. Not unknown in the most law-bound of modern bureaucratic systems, this kind of behavior came in a particularly natural way to statesmen working in a context of "split-up modernization" and political imbalance. The gross extent of the reformers' indulgence in such behavior set a dangerous precedent, however. In fact, this kind of neopatrimonialism was to remain a leitmotiv of Ottoman bureaucratic and political history until the end, and the civil bureaucrats who came after the Tanzimat would more often bear the brunt of it than enjoy its benefits.

RESTORING POLITICAL BALANCE: THE FIRST CONSTITUTIONAL PERIOD AND RETURN TO SULTANIC DOMINANCE

Sadaretin inhilâli, Âli Paşa'nın irtihali iledir.

The death of Âli Paşa is the disintegration of the grand
vezirate.
> Yusuf Kâmil Paşa, on learning of Âli Paşa's death[1]

Her memuriyetin vazaifi nizam-ı mahsus ile tayin
olunacağından her memur kendi vazifesi dairesinde
mes'uldür.

Inasmuch as the duties of every official post will be determined by special regulation, every official is responsible
within the limits of his duty.
> Constitution of 1876, Article 40[2]

Milleti ikna ve müessesat-ı ahrarane ihdas edilerek ıslahat
icrasına çalışan pederim Abd ül-Mecid'in isrine iktifa etmek
istemekle meğer yanılmış imişim. Ba'dema ceddim Sultan
Mahmud'un isrini takib edeceğim. Onun gibi ben de şimdi
anlıyorum ki Cenab-ı Hakk'ın muhafazasını bana tevdi et-
tiği akvamı kuvvetten başka hiçbir şeyle yürütmek kabil ol-
mıyacak.

I made a mistake in wishing to content myself with the
example of my father, Abd ül-Mecid, who sought to carry
out reforms by persuading the people and creating liberal
institutions. From now on, I shall follow the example of my
grandfather, Sultan Mahmud. Like him, I now understand
that it is not possible to move the peoples whom God has
placed under my protection by any means other than force.
> Abd ül-Hamid to a delegation of Deputies, just prior
> to proroguing the Ottoman Parliament, 1878[3]

The death of Âli Paşa in 1871 marked not only a shift in the
locus of power, and thus the beginning of a new political period,
but also the first of a series of unsettling events that within a few
years brought the empire to a state of danger and uncertainty
even worse than the one in which the Tanzimat had opened almost forty years earlier. Âli's disappearance contributed to this
destabilization by making it easier for the erratic and unbal-
anced sultan, Abd ül-Aziz, and his favorites to reassert their influence. What this reassertion could mean became apparent
rather quickly with the two grand vezirates of Mahmud Nedim
Paşa (1871-1872, 1875-1876). A sometime protégé of Mustafa
Reşid Paşa, but usually excluded from important position—and
wisely so—during the Tanzimat, Mahmud Nedim now had his
day. Having won the favor of the sultan, he used his power to
break up the bureaucratic system of the Tanzimat by reorganiz-
ing key institutions and keeping personnel turnover in high
office at such a high rate that the bureaucracy became
paralyzed.[4]

Intellectual ferment and a variety of crises arising outside the
imperial "center" compounded the resulting confusion. Not
only was there mounting effervescence surrounding the Young
Ottoman movement, but more conservative kinds of opinion,
including an Islamicist current opposed to the cosmopolitan Ottomanism of the Tanzimat and a pan-Islamist strain, also made
themselves felt with increasing force. Underlying these developments was a serious deterioration of the economic situation. Agricultural crisis reached famine proportions in Anatolia
and other parts of the empire in 1873-1875, while the government of Mahmud Nedim Paşa found itself forced in 1875 to an-
nounce its inability to keep up the service of the immense
foreign debt that had by then accumulated. The outbreak in the
same year of a peasant revolt in Herzegovina and its subsequent
spread to other Balkan territories seriously aggravated the situation, raising the threat of foreign intervention and war.

Within the next several years, that threat and several others
materialized in fearful conjuncture. In 1876 alone, there were
three different sultans. Abd ül-Aziz was deposed, committing
suicide a few days thereafter. Murad V, focus of constitutionalist
hopes but badly shaken by the events then occurring, soon
proved mentally incompetent and was also deposed after only
three months. He was succeeded on 31 August 1876 by a little-
known prince named Abd ül-Hamid.

The Balkan troubles having continued to mushroom all the while, the new sultan soon found himself entangled in a disastrous war with Russia. As a direct or indirect consequence of this, he lost what remained in the way of practical control, and sometimes of formal sovereignty as well, over a list of territories that included Bessarabia, Rumania, Serbia, Bosnia, Herzegovina, Montenegro, parts of Bulgaria and Anatolia, Cyprus, and Tunis.[5] The British occupation of Egypt in 1882 further extended the list. Thanks in good measure to the economic consequences of the war with Russia, Abd ül-Hamid also saw his government lose control of a major part of its revenues with the creation in 1881 of the international Public Debt Administration, set up to serve the interests of investors in Ottoman government securities.

Never since 1839 so deeply in doubt, the survival of the empire would not again be so threatened before the Young Turk period. In the meantime, there would be some opportunity to work out the implications of two attempts, both inaugurated during the decade following the death of Âli Paşa, to bring the civil-bureaucratic pyramid of the Tanzimat back under effective political control. Both attempts represented responses to the threats that the empire had experienced, but both were also products of the politico-bureaucratic tradition of the empire and in particular of the reforms of the preceding period. One of these attempts aimed at creating controls of a characteristically modern type; one, at controls of a basically, but no longer totally, traditionalistic character. The first attempt appears in the constitutional movement in which the Young Ottomans figured so prominently; the second, in the resurgent sultanic despotism of Abd ül-Aziz in his last years and of Abd ül-Hamid II (1876-1909). Triumphing over the constitutionalists in the short run, Abd ül-Hamid in particular set the tone for the decades immediately following the catastrophes of the 1870s. Even under him, however, the constitutional experiment and the regulatory developments that lay behind it were never totally forgotten.

In the present chapter, we shall first characterize these two attempts at the restoration of political balance. Placing particular emphasis on their significance for the evolution of the bureaucracy, we shall devote special attention to the Hamidian system, since it produced the greater immediate effect down to 1908. We shall then analyze organizational changes at the Sublime Porte and the related regulatory issues, and thus assess the significance of this complex period for the development of the politico-bureaucratic tradition.

DIVERGENT TENDENCIES IN EFFORTS AT THE RESTORATION OF POLITICAL BALANCE

The First Constitutional Period

The constitutional movement, in a sense, marked the culmination of all that had happened in the development of the politico-bureaucratic institutions of the empire since Ottomans first began to sense the need for a general reordering of the governmental system. The reforms of the Tanzimat contributed to the demand for constitutional government not only in a general way, through the steps taken toward creation of a more rational and regulated administrative system and through the development of institutions with representative and legislative functions, but also in the sense that various of the empire's territories or populations received what were either implicitly or explicitly constitutions during that time. This was true in the tributary principalities, among which Rumania possessed what was officially designated as the Rumanian Constitution of 1866, while Tunisia was under a constitution of its own for a few years in the early 1860s. Constitution or no, four territories—Tunisia, Egypt, Serbia, and Rumania—acquired at least quasi-parliamentary bodies during the same years. Organic statutes were drawn up for the special administrative regimes created in certain provinces or districts, such as Crete and Lebanon,[6] as well as for the non-Muslim communities of the empire, which thus retained distinct communal institutions even as they began to enjoy the benefits of the newly proclaimed legal equality.[7] With the general reassertion of the legislative function of the state as background, the promulgation of organic statutes for parts of the imperial system naturally suggested the regulation in similar fashion of the system as a whole.

All the while, the growing awareness among Ottoman intellectuals of Western political ideas, and the continued demands from Western powers for reform as the price of political support, created added pressures for movement toward a constitutional system. With the Young Ottomans, in particular, there appeared an explicitly constitutionalist movement, capable of rousing a significant degree of popular support, if not yet of creating a genuine mass base. In the light of these facts, the promulgation of the Ottoman Constitution of 1876 seemed a natural response to the crisis of the times, much as the promulgation of the Gülhane Decree of 1839 had been to the Ottoman-Egyptian conflict of that day.

The parlous state of the empire and the still limited acceptance of constitutional principles nonetheless left their marks on the constitution in a variety of senses. First, it was not solely the work of the Young Ottoman intelligentsia. Limited in numbers and influence, they had to compromise with a number of other interests. Those who actually had a hand in the drafting of the final document, whether as members of the official Drafting Commission[8] or otherwise, included Namık Kemal and Ziya Bey (later Paşa) among the Young Ottomans; a variety of senior civil officials, most notably Midhat Paşa, distinguished by his record as a reformer in local administration and his constitutionalist convictions; a few generals; and high-ranking members of the religious establishment. There were also several anti-constitutionalists, of whom some of the most influential—the future Grand Vezir "Küçük" ("Little") Said Paşa or Ahmed Cevdet Paşa—could best be described as partisans of reform and legislation under the aegis of a sultanic enlightened despotism. Finally, there was the sultan himself. Not the least fateful circumstance attendant on the preparation of the constitution was the fact that the sultan under whom the Drafting Commission was finally formed was not the reputedly liberal Murad V, but rather Abd ül-Hamid, whose avowals of support for the constitution were no more than a ploy by which to reach the throne. In the event, the constitution also suffered in being drawn up in a hurry, the drafting being sandwiched between Abd ül-Hamid's order of 7 October 1876 for the formation of a Drafting Commission and the beginning on 23 December 1876 of the Constantinople Conference, convoked at British instance to defuse a Russian threat of unilateral intervention in the Balkan crisis. The promulgation of the constitution on the very day that the conference opened was a spectacular but futile attempt to convince the assembled delegates that the empire was capable of reforming itself without outside interference.[9]

Given these pressures and the general state of development of the Ottoman polity at the time, it was only natural that the constitution contain not only an element of vagueness and imprecision, but also certain provisions that would make it possible for the determined Abd ül-Hamid, eventually dropping his mask, to neutralize it and its partisans. In many ways, it is true, the constitution demonstrated the extent to which concepts such as equality, guaranteed individual rights, and the rule of law had become established in the thinking of Ottoman statesmen. It contained something like a Bill of Rights, a section defining the "general rights of subjects of the Ottoman State" (arts. 8-26). Succeeding sections dealt with the rights and duties of ministers of state, officials, the Parliament and its two houses, and a variety of other questions, regulating many points and, as in the case of article 40 quoted at the head of this chapter, promising that many others would be regulated subsequently.

Scattered through these provisions, however, were a number of critical loopholes. The most important had to do with the prerogatives of the sultan. His sovereignty remained unrestricted and his powers only partially defined. The constitution itself became law only by his sovereign decree.[10] The right to continue legislating by decree was nowhere denied him, and his freedom to veto laws passed in the Parliament, where the power to initiate bills remained essentially in the hands of his ministers, was without check. Most dangerous of all was a provision inserted into article 113 at Abd ül-Hamid's personal insistence. This allowed the sultan, on the basis of information furnished by the police, to exile anyone on grounds of danger to the security of the empire.[11]

Failing to restrict the sovereignty of the sultan, the constitution fell short of transforming the structural feature of the Ottoman polity that had been the fatal flaw in the system of the Tanzimat statesmen. The constitution did mark a new stage in the drive to create a rational-legal order. The Parliament also displayed a level of independence, capability, and procedural orderliness that astounded contemporary observers and subsequent historians—perhaps unduly, given the prominence among the deputies of the same sort of notables who had dominated the local assemblies created during the Tanzimat and were thus men of some political experience and awareness.[12] But the cards were stacked against the deputies and constitutionalists. Having used article 113 to get rid of Midhat Paşa as early as February 1877, Abd ül-Hamid exercised his right to dissolve the Chamber a year later without setting a date for new elections, which article 7 of the constitution called for in such cases. The constitution per se was never revoked, and the Senate continued to exist in a vestigial way; but what was to be remembered as the First Constitutional Period (*İlk Meşrutiyet*) was over.

Reassertion of Sultanic Dominance: The Palace System of Abd ül-Hamid

What took its place, though adumbrated in the last years of Abd ül-Aziz, was a system of Abd ül-Hamid's own creation. On a certain level, this system displayed a strong affinity with the constitutional regime, and thus with the reformist legacy. Particularly in his earlier years, Abd ül-Hamid was an avid reformer and legislator, intent in principle on improving the quality of administration. For example, in his Speech from the Throne at the opening of the first session of the Parliament, he identified an impressive series of issues on which bills were then being drafted in the Council of State for submission to the deputies. These included the internal regulations of the Houses of Parliament; the electoral law; a general regulation for the administration of provinces and communes (*nahiye*); a law on municipal organization; bills on civil court procedure, the organization of the courts, and procedures for the promotion and retirement of judges; and a bill on the duties and retirement rights of officials in general (*umum memurin*).[13]

In this as in other periods, it is not usually possible to tell exactly where the initiative for such measures came from. Many of them are attributed, in one source or another, not to Abd ül-Hamid but to such of his advisors as Küçük Said Paşa or Ahmed Cevdet Paşa.[14] It is nonetheless clear that Abd ül-Hamid took close interest, and in some cases actually did take the initiative, in policy matters of this kind. Again to cite the Speech from the Throne at the opening of the Parliament, he not only spoke repeatedly of changes in procedures for the selection of officials, but also announced that he intended to use the resources of the Privy Purse (*Hazine-i Hassa*) to found a school for training officials who would be drawn from all classes of the population and promoted on the basis of merit. The immediate sequel to this pronouncement appears not to have been the founding of a new school, but rather the expansion of an existing one, namely, the School of Civil Administration (*Mülkiye Mektebi*, 1859), whose growth in size and importance began at this time and on the Sultan's initiative.[15]

When we compare the short life and limited accomplishments of the Parliament[16] with the volume of legislation ultimately produced during the Hamidian years, we have a measure of the commitment of Abd ül-Hamid and those who worked under him to further elaboration of a rational-legal framework for the imperial system. In particular, the sultan's prompt action in the case of the School of Civil Administration, and the fact that he subsequently promulgated laws on most of the subjects mentioned in the Speech from the Throne, were clear indications that a new period in the regularization of administration was beginning. In the promised steps toward more precise regulation of the conditions of official service, indeed, the redefinition of the collective organizational aspect of the various branches of the bureaucracy again began to receive the kind of attention so conspicuously missing since the death of Mahmud II. The creation of the legislative outlines of something like a civil bureaucracy or civil service, in the sense that those terms were then beginning to acquire in the most up-to-date Western states, was to be a prominent feature of Abd ül-Hamid's efforts to bring the civil-bureaucratic pyramid back under effective political control.

Full appreciation of Abd ül-Hamid's impact on the bureaucracy requires recognition of this fact. This, however, was only one aspect of a reign marked by a disconsonance of practice and principle quite as serious as that noted during the Tanzimat. If the Sublime Porte then formed the central element of a politico-bureaucratic machine in which processes of rationalization and systematization were used to extend the power of an unregulated oligarchy, under Abd ül-Hamid the entire Porte and civil bureaucracy were subsumed into a similar but larger mechanism, centered in the palace. In this mechanism, the same kinds of processes were again used in much the same way; but since even the most important of the civil officials were now no more than subordinate members of the system, they felt the impact of this regulatory activity in a way that their predecessors had not. The spirit that dominated the legislative activity of this period was no more in harmony with any Weberian ideal of rational-legalism than was that of the leading figures of the Tanzimat.

Indeed, it was ultimately a great deal less so. While Abd ül-

Hamid was not always as violent as we might infer from some of his statements and actions, he was a strange, complex, and psychologically unsettled man. That he was intelligent, willful, and industrious enough to do as he promised in following the example of Mahmud II is clear. The methodical way he followed government business, his interest in legislation and in plans of reform, and his political survival all reflect this fact. Yet, thanks in part to the unwholesome palace environment in which he was reared, and in part also to the circumstances surrounding his accession, he was distinctly paranoid. Reportedly afraid to handle any documents that had not been specially "disinfected," to drink any coffee or smoke any cigarettes not specially prepared before his eyes by servants who did nothing else, or to eat any food but that prepared in a special kitchen that served him alone, Abd ül-Hamid used the tremendous powers that remained in his hands to protect himself from the objects of his fears. As a result, while major steps were taken during this period toward the creation of the outward forms of a rational-legal order, a quality of the mimetic and insubstantial continued to hang about these measures. As far as Abd ül-Hamid was concerned, indeed, what mattered most was not obedience to the law but obedience to a sovereign will superior to the law.[17]

A general description of the political system that Abd ül-Hamid built up to assert his personal dominance would go far beyond the bounds of this study; but it is indispensable to say something about the form that the palace service assumed in this period and about relations between it and its imperial chief, on the one hand, and the civil bureaucracy of the Porte, on the other.

If Abd ül-Hamid stood in personal control of this system, Yıldız Palace formed its center in a larger sense. This palace was not new, but no earlier sultan had used it as his principal residence. The ultimate form of the various compounds and buildings at Yıldız thus bore Abd ül-Hamid's own stamp. Halid Ziya Uşaklıgil has left an unforgettable, and perhaps overly negative, picture of what Yıldız was like. He describes the walls—so high that cats could not climb over them, he says—that separated the private part of the palace from the part that dealt with the outside world. An atmosphere of absolute secrecy surrounded all that happened in the former. The part of the establishment that outsiders could visit consisted of a series of nondescript buildings, among which considerable experience was required to know one's way.

In this part of the palace, the most important locale was for a long time the office of the marshal of the *Mabeyn* (*Mabeyn müşiri*), chief of the palace service. Gazi Osman Paşa, hero of the Battle of Plevna, held this post until his death in 1897, following which the position remained unfilled. The next most important component of the palace service after the marshal, and the real nerve center of that service after Osman Paşa's death, was what Uşaklıgil calls the "big *Mabeyn*." As opposed to the more traditional "little *Mabeyn*," consisting of the personal servants of the sultan, this was the palace secretariat. Charged with the transmission of communications to and from the sultan, this soon became the most important bureaucratic agency of the Hamidian system, the senior secretaries being among the most powerful officials and among the few with direct access to the sultan. Uşaklıgil depicts the offices of the "big *Mabeyn*" in ludicrous terms. They were furnished with a miscellany of odd pieces from the private apartments, and permeated by the odors emanating from the dinner trays always waiting in some corner to be carried away and from the coffee-making continuously in progress among the servants in the basement. Such was the setting in which Ottoman officials and foreign dignitaries alike formed their impressions of Yıldız Palace as they waited endlessly to see the sultan's secretaries.[18]

It was at Yıldız that the palace service reached the high point of its historic development. By 1908, the listing in the government yearbook of its more important members ran to almost forty pages. The listings include more than a score of palace secretaries (*Mabeyn kâtibi*), ten or so chamberlains (*kurena*), the traditional personal servants of the sultan, enough military aides-de-camp (*yaver*) to fill sixteen pages, and a Privy Treasury (*Hazine-i Hassa*) with an organization more complex than those of many ministries.[19] By one contemporary estimate, the palace organization included at least 12,000 people, not to mention 15,000 troops stationed in the vicinity for security.[20]

The policy for which Abd ül-Hamid sought to use this organization—a policy of which several sources name Küçük Said Paşa as originator and ultimately victim—was one of centralization, carried progressively to the point of "complete stultification of the Sublime Porte and . . . concentration of the entire work of the Administration in his [Abd ül-Hamid's] own hands."[21] Such was the degree of this centralization, in fact, that ambassadors, provincial governors, and military commanders[22] were ultimately corresponding as much with the palace secretariat as with the ministries to which they were nominally attached. Where the conduct of foreign relations was concerned, said the sultan, the Ottoman foreign minister in Istanbul and the diplomats stationed abroad were of slight importance, as he himself, guided by "fixed principles," would conduct the foreign relations of the empire in direct dealings with the foreign envoys accredited to his court.[23] It did not even matter who was the grand vezir, since, in the sultan's opinion, he was the real grand vezir. Abd ül-Hamid once also described the *Mabeyn* and the Porte as operating like two separate states.[24] It is not hard to tell which was the more powerful.

In such a system, the character of those close to the throne was of critical importance, especially in the later years, when the sultan no longer ventured outside the palace walls more than a few times a year.[25] At times, there were among the advisers of Abd ül-Hamid men of the ability and probity of Küçük Said or Ahmed Cevdet Paşa, or others of the tact and efficiency attributed to Tahsin Paşa, first secretary of the *Mabeyn* from 1894 to 1908.[26] The contrary was, however, more often the case, and a few examples will show how much what one ambassador called "the Palace ring"[27] ultimately did to discredit both the sultan and his system.

The second secretary in the *Mabeyn* during the later years of the reign was a Syrian known as "Arab" İzzet or İzzet Holo Paşa, who made himself so widely hated that he had to flee for his life at the outbreak of the Revolution of 1908. Once described as "the avatar of the 'Hamidian system,'" he owed his rise to a combination of corruption and cleverness. Repeatedly out of favor, he always found his way back. His greatest inspiration was reportedly the Hijaz Railway,[28] a project that combined spiritual with strategic utility in a way that Abd ül-Hamid found irresistible.

Not all "palace creatures" were so clever, and the misdeeds of several caught up with them in spectacular ways even before 1908. One notable case centered on the Bedir Han family, one-time Kurdish chieftains whom a succession of sultans had attempted to integrate into Ottoman officialdom. In 1906, a disagreement arose between the prefect of Istanbul, Rıdvan Paşa, himself a palace protégé, and two members of this family: Abd ül-Rezzak Bey, then on the staff of the *chef de protocole* of the palace, and his uncle, Ali Şamil Paşa, commander of the Selimiye garrison at Üsküdar. Before the matter was settled, two shoot-outs had occurred in Istanbul, Rıdvan Paşa being killed in the second. In response to the pleas of his ministers for legal action, the sultan simply exiled the entire Bedir Han family without following prescribed judicial processes at all.[29]

Even worse were the incidents that culminated in the fall of Fehim Paşa, one of Abd ül-Hamid's aides-de-camp and the chief of the secret police of the palace. Grandson of Abd ül-Hamid's former wet nurse and son of İsmet Bey, who was a "milk brother" and thus particular intimate of the sultan, Fehim commended himself most of all for what one observer called "hereditary loyalty." This ascribed quality enabled Fehim, a pudgy, baby-faced psychopath,[30] to rise rapidly to the rank of general of division (*ferik*) with special responsibility for maintaining the personal security of the sultan. Fehim placed a broad interpretation on this mission. Recruiting a "black band" of "agents" from the Istanbul underworld and turning his house into a prison where male "offenders" were tortured and females, as likely as not, were subjected to other abuses, Fehim instituted a system of terror and protection rackets. Borrowing a phrase from Sir Arthur Conan Doyle, Baron Marschall, the German ambassador, called Fehim the "Napoleon of Crime."

Fehim's greatest mistake was in bringing himself to the attention of Baron Marschall. One incident, known as *l'Affaire Marguerite*, had to do with a beautiful circus performer whom Fehim "married," and who was a German subject. A subsequent case arose over whether 10,000 railroad ties belonged to a German merchant who had contracted for them, or to Fehim. Baron Marschall decided to make an issue of the latter question, and confronting the sultan in special audience, extracted the promise of an investigation. This resulted in an outpouring of evidence from government agencies that had been powerless to do anything up to that point, the exile of Fehim, and the dispersion of the "black band." One of the most fearful linkages in the palace system was thus broken.[31] Among a number of disturbances that troubled the empire in 1906-1907,[32] this was one more warning of the upheaval that was about to destroy the Hamidian regime.

The enlarged palace organization at Yıldız, dominated in principle by the sultan, but in fact to a great degree by the "palace ring," was thus the core of the Hamidian machine. In addition, there were a number of mechanisms that served to buttress the sultan's position and extend his control over Ottoman society in general, and over the bureaucracy in particular.

As for mechanisms to control society in general, we can do no more here than allude to some of the more obvious. Clearly included among these was the regulatory activity that assorted so strangely with the real spirit of the system but was nonetheless useful as a means of implementing further reforms and tightening the sultan's grip. In addition, there was a strong reemphasis on the values basic to the legitimation of the sultan's position. With inherited claims to the sultanate and caliphate, Abd ül-Hamid was in a position to claim legitimacy for himself in a way impossible for the Tanzimat oligarchs. He did so very vigorously, but not simply in traditionalistic fashion. Rather, as the mounting volume of innovative legislation and the studied neglect of the official religious establishment indicate, his was a new use of the imperial tradition. In particular, the sultan's exploitation of the pan-Islamist theme was an attempt to appeal in new ways to Muslims everywhere, including non-Ottomans and even the heterodox.[33]

There is considerable evidence that this appeal was successful to some degree; but for those who did not respond to it, Abd ül-Hamid had means of coercion at his disposal. The regular military establishment figures less in this respect than might be expected. So great were the sultan's fears of a strong military force that, with the chief exception of the units assigned to the palace, he inhibited most efforts at military improvement.[34] Abd ül-Hamid did, however, institute rigorous controls in the field of communications. The extension during his reign of railroad and telegraph lines, the former of obvious strategic value and the latter of comparable utility for the rapid transmission of orders and intelligence,[35] was a notable feature of his efforts in this field. Also among the control mechanisms of the period was a rigorous system of press censorship, drawing for its implementation on a number of government agencies, and a system of spies and informers of which Fehim's band was only part. The reports of these spies, known as *jurnal* (from the French *journal*), occupied a great deal of the sultan's attention and, despite the manifest absurdity of many of them, greatly compounded his anxieties. After the 1908 Revolution, "cartloads" of *jurnal*s were found at Yıldız Palace, representing the work of a thousand informants or more, and ranging in subject as far afield as the alleged amours of a British ambassador.[36]

In many ways, then, the Hamidian system was a strange hybrid of the traditional and modern. It represents the most highly elaborated expression in Ottoman history of Eisenstadt's "split-up modernization" and thus also the clearest indication of the extent to which the patrimonial tradition could survive into the era of modernization and assume new forms. Still wedded, in its fundamental principles and its assumptions about the political process, to traditional concepts, the Hamidian neopatrimonialism was startlingly close in some of its methods to the totalitarian regimes of the twentieth century. The way in which Abd ül-Hamid sought to maintain his control over the bureaucracy provides added illustrations of this point.

To maintain this control, Abd ül-Hamid drew on the mechanisms discussed above and others as well. Here again, regulatory processes were of particular importance and will require considerable attention in this chapter. To avoid mistaking their role in the Hamidian system, however, it is essential to recognize how the neopatrimonialism of the period affected the bureaucracy in other ways. The most fundamental point here seems to be that Abd ül-Hamid was trying to seize control of the processes of social and political mobilization already established in the development of the bureaucratic pyramid and use them to maintain or restore the correspondence between polity and servile bureaucracy characteristic of the traditional state, thus eliminating any form of political activity not directly under his control.

The point is nowhere stated in so many words; yet the evidence that this was Abd ül-Hamid's chief goal in the handling of his bureaucracy is voluminous. For example, his approach to patronage and the distribution of honors clearly supports this interpretation. Significantly, the official personnel records accumulated during his reign—these being one of the modernistic controls then instituted—provide the basis for our estimate that 50,000 to 100,000 men held civil-bureaucratic positions, at least nominally, during the years 1876-1908. But that was clearly far more officials than the empire could put to productive use. By the late 1880s, for example, the Foreign Ministry alone was said to have 467 officials, counting unpaid apprentice clerks in the central offices but not honorary consuls. This was several times the number then serving in the Foreign Office of the German Empire.[37] While every office, as in the past, had its core of serious individuals, the rest were underemployed,[38] if they showed up at all. By 1908, for example, one of the offices of the Foreign Ministry, that of Legal Counsel, had fifty nominal officials, most of whom did not even know where at the Sublime Porte the office was located;[39] and many offices of the period were too small to accommodate all their supposed employees.[40]

As if deliberately to break down bureaucratic discipline and morale, Abd ül-Hamid had padded the payrolls to an unheard-of extent with secret agents, sons, sons-in-law, or protégés of men of influence, and actual or potential members of the opposition, whom he sought by such means to buy off and neutralize.[41] Matters reached the point where even a young man who had the traditionally optimal combination of assets— outstanding personal ability coupled with membership in a family of good and long-standing civil-bureaucratic connections— might encounter severe frustrations in his career.[42] Meanwhile, ranks and decorations rained in such profusion on those in favor at the palace that such honors gradually began to sink in popular esteem; and a young man who managed by some chance to land a good position was apt to find himself automatically suspect of being a palace agent.[43]

Having taken for himself the power concentrated at the apex of the bureaucratic pyramid during the Tanzimat, Abd ül-Hamid thus set about enlarging the organizations that composed that structure and filling them with those who had title to his favor or whom he wished to put in debt to himself. To maintain the subservience of all such persons was naturally one of his foremost objectives; and in addition to the means of coercion that he applied to all his subjects, there were a variety of techniques that served him specially, if not always successfully, for this end.

Particularly for those who came close to him, the threat of force was never far from the surface; and the legal guarantees of the security of official tenure, granted in the 1830s, afforded little if any protection. A senior official summoned to the palace never knew when he might be sent from there straight into exile without being allowed so much as to bid his family farewell.[44] No fewer than three of the men who served Abd ül-Hamid as grand

vezir became so harassed at various points in their careers that
they took refuge in European embassies or consulates. These
were Midhat Paşa in 1881, Küçük Said Paşa in 1895, and Kâmil
Paşa in 1907. In the case of Midhat, one of those whom Abd
ül-Hamid blamed for the deposition and death of Abd ül-Aziz,
consenting to leave this refuge was an ultimately fatal mistake.[45]

To a degree, this kind of high-handedness extended into the
lower reaches of the bureaucracy, as well. This was certainly apt
to be true for anyone who had the misfortune to be the subject
of an informant's *jurnal*, as it was in general for all those whom
the sultan regarded, for whatever reason, as his opponents.

In Abd ül-Hamid's treatment of such individuals, there was,
however, a recurrent inconsistency. At times, while ignoring
long and faithful service, he would heap honors and high positions on men whom he identified as opponents. Others he would
"appoint" to serve in "official posts," or simply to reside, in remote provinces under conditions of sometimes fatal hardship.[46]
In explanation of this behavior, Abd ül-Hamid once said of a
particular individual, "I know he is not a bad man, and no harm
comes to me from him. But I am good to the bad ones, so as to
escape their badness."[47] This was obviously not always true; but
it did create the possibility for men who had literary or polemical
interests—and usually no other means of support—to turn this
aspect of Abd ül-Hamid's behavior to account by fleeing to
places beyond the sultan's control and publishing, or threaten-
ing to publish, works hostile to the regime. Abd ül-Hamid's sen-
sitivity to the uses of the press made this into a conventional
form of blackmail, with which it became one of the chief duties
of the Ottoman embassies to cope.[48]

Various observers have noted, without being able to explain,
Abd ül-Hamid's vacillation between conciliation and persecution
of those of whom he disapproved.[49] In view of his apparent attempt to reintegrate all aspects of political life into the forms of
an enlarged but again servile bureaucracy, the two modes of behavior appear simply as alternatives offered by the patterns of
literary activity and of relations between sultanic master and
official slave in the patrimonial tradition of the ruling class.

As Abd ül-Hamid pursued his policy of turning the state once
again into a patrimonial household, the contrast between the
growth of the bureaucracy and the economic resources available
for its support added further irony to the fate of the officials of

this period. The state was officially bankrupt, although this did not mean that there were no resources available. The sultan had the reputation of being exceptionally astute in the management of financial affairs, and the Privy Treasury was a well-run as well as a large organization during this reign.[50] Simultaneously, developments in agriculture led to some increase in revenues, and the credit of the state improved to the point that it could again borrow abroad.[51] This hardly provided the means for solving all the problems of the official salary system; but it did, particularly given the added possibilities offered by nonmonetary forms of reward, enable Abd ül-Hamid to manipulate his officials in economic as well as other ways.

Some examples will illustrate how he did so. While attempts were ostensibly made in the 1880s to systematize salary levels, no large-scale or lasting effect resulted. Not only were officials with certain types of qualifications or ethnocultural characteristics discriminated against, but the range of nominal salaries remained phenomenally wide. For most of the period, even the median nominal salaries in the civil bureaucracy were probably barely above subsistence level for a small family, while the highest salaries were many times the median.[52] To compound this inequality, only the high-ranking officials received their salaries regularly and in gold, as opposed to the worn and barely identifiable coins of inferior metal that the less fortunate received, when they got anything.[53]

Nor was there much that the average official could do to protect his economic interests in the face of these problems. Those not close enough to the sultan to benefit directly from his munificence had to try to form "connections" with someone who was. In this sense, the economic policy of the state toward its officials assumed that they had personal and familial relations of the type implied in the model of the patrimonial household. Another thing that could make a difference was the specific agency in which the official served. Since collection and disbursement of revenues were still not centralized in the Ministry of Finance, the luckiest officials were those who worked in revenue-collecting departments such as Finance, Posts and Telegraphs, Customs, or Land Registry; for payment of the salaries of their own employees was one of the first priorities of those departments. For those who served in the provinces, the prosperity of the province made a corresponding difference.

Only in the richer ones, says Uşaklıgil, did the year have twelve months.[54]

There were some problems of the compensation system, however, that could not be escaped; for it is clear that Abd ül-Hamid not only knew about the malfunctional aspects of the system, but actually used them for his own ends. His prodigality with ranks and decorations was one form of legerdemain useful in stretching the available economic resources, especially as the recipients had to pay fees, if not also bribes, to get such honors. To officials whom he favored, Abd ül-Hamid often also assigned extra salaries, which were regularly paid, out of the Privy Treasury. The rare man whose conscience became troubled by the supplemental payments would not dare to decline them; for the sultan would regard such an act not as laudable, but rather as a sign of independence—exactly what the extra income was intended to eliminate.[55] Otherwise, when salary payments were made through normal bureaucratic channels, they were carefully orchestrated so as to have optimal effect in stimulating feelings of gratitude and loyalty. Usually coinciding with major religious festivals or other occasions when the government was anxious to have a show of good will, each payment was treated as "a special act of grace on the part of the Ruler, announced in the newspapers and celebrated almost like a national holiday."[56]

This futuristic use of salary payments as a form of "mood control" is one of the clearest expressions of the manipulative element in Abd ül-Hamid's compensation policy, but there were other expressions, as well. Unable or unwilling to pay his officials regularly, Abd ül-Hamid condoned peculation among the lower officials, condemning it even verbally only among those of high rank and large salaries.[57] In practice, as Arab İzzet or Fehim Paşa well knew, he condoned it among the latter, as well. Meanwhile, Abd ül-Hamid also widened the breaches in the traditional, but already battered, immunity of the official class to taxation. This he did through a variety of measures relating to revenue stamps and stamped papers, the use of which he commanded in such purely internal transactions of the bureaucracy as the compilation of personnel files or the issue to individuals of the vouchers (suret) used to acknowledge their entitlement to a certain sum by way of salary. At times, he also exacted special salary deductions for purposes such as the building of the Hijaz Railway.[58]

Ultimately, nothing makes the despotic character of Abd ül-Hamid's relationship with his bureaucrats more apparent than the economic plight in which they found themselves and the way he played on it. It was not reasonable to assume that the bureaucracy that had produced the Young Ottomans would endure this treatment indefinitely without protest. Yet, Abd ül-Hamid's triumph over the constitutionalists was sufficiently thorough that thirty years passed before his system could be overthrown.

As a result, while the years 1871-1908 were characterized by efforts to restore political balance, these efforts clearly displayed contradictory tendencies. Steps toward rational-legalism and modernization of the polity were more characteristic of the early years and culminated in the parliamentary episode. Efforts at implementation of a neotraditionalist conception of the polity were more typical after 1878. But since the effort at sultanic reassertion was already apparent in the last years of Abd ül-Aziz, and since the promulgation of new laws continued even under Abd ül-Hamid, the two tendencies cannot be neatly segregated out into chronologically distinct subperiods. Rather, as despotic and irrational tendencies became more pronounced under Abd ül-Hamid, legislative activity continued at the same time and began to display, on even grander scale than during the Tanzimat, the aspect of a means by which to tighten and extend the control of a dominant and unrestricted power.

Having thus far emphasized the negative side of the badly "split-up" Hamidian polity, we must now go on to a closer examination, first, of the organizational development of the Porte between 1871 and 1908 and, then, of the steps taken in the same period toward further regularization and systematization. The political patterns that we have discussed up to this point will provide us with a perspective for these analyses, which will have as their chief goal to assess the implications of the more rational developments of this period for the long-term evolution of the politico-bureaucratic tradition.

Organizational Development of the Sublime Porte during the First Constitutional Period and the Reign of Abd ül-Hamid

The way in which Abd ül-Hamid attempted to seize control of the bureaucratic pyramid and confine within it as nearly as possible the entire politically conscious segment of Ottoman society points to the essential qualitative difference between the growth in the civil bureaucracy during his reign and that which occurred under the bureaucratic empire builders of the Tanzimat. The organizational development of the Porte nonetheless continued after 1871 and to a degree represented one of the more positive aspects of the period. There were gains in the evolution of some of the formal organizational structures and in the growing prevalence of new kinds of organizational concepts first noted on a small scale in preceding decades. More significantly, while this process did not continue to the full extent that the constitution demanded, and while regulatory documents would not supplant the government yearbooks as the principal source from which to reconstruct bureaucratic organization until the Young Turk years, there was a perceptible increase in the extent to which there were formal laws and regulations to govern the structures and define the missions of the various agencies. Under Abd ül-Hamid, the growing elements of rationality had less and less to do with setting the overall tone of official life. Yet those elements formed valuable increments to the political and bureaucratic heritage left to later generations.

A survey of the Porte as it had come to be by 1908 will illustrate these points. Figure VI-1 provides a basic graphic reference for this discussion and, to set the Porte in larger perspective, again includes the palace and the other major civil-bureaucratic agencies.[59]

The Grand Vezir and His Staff

The constitutional episode and the reign of Abd ül-Hamid changed the grand vezirate to varying degrees in both theory and fact. Had the liberals among the drafters of the constitution had their way, the grand vezir as traditionally known would have passed into history and been replaced by a prime minister (*baş vekil*—the same title that Mahmud II used in his attack on the grand vezirate in 1838). This prime minister would then have selected the other ministers, who would collectively have disposed of extensive administrative powers.[60] As finally promulgated, however, the constitution still designated the highest bureaucratic office in traditional fashion as the grand vezirate (*sadaret*), although without mentioning the concept of "absolute delegacy" (*vekâlet-i mutlaka*). The appointment of the other

FIGURE VI-1. ORGANIZATION OF THE CIVIL BUREAUCRACY AND ITS RELATION TO THE PALACE, 1908

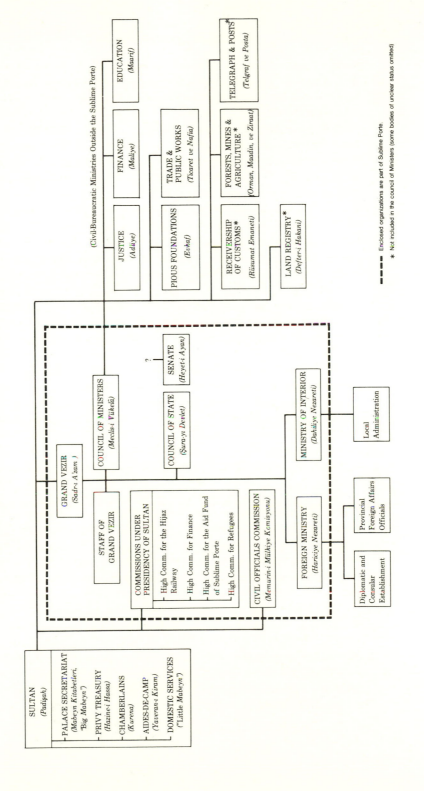

SULTAN
(Padişah)

- PALACE SECRETARIAT
  (Mabeyn Kitabetleri,
  "Big Mabeyn")
- PRIVY TREASURY
  (Hazine-i Hassa)
- CHAMBERLAINS
  (Kurena)
- AIDES-DE-CAMP
  (Yaveran-ı Kiram)
- DOMESTIC SERVICES
  ("Little Mabeyn")

GRAND VEZIR
(Sadr-ı A'zam)

COUNCIL OF MINISTERS
(Meclis-i Vükela)

STAFF OF
GRAND VEZIR

COMMISSIONS UNDER
PRESIDENCY OF SULTAN
- High Comm. for the Hijaz
  Railway
- High Comm. for Finance
- High Comm. for the Aid Fund
  of Sublime Porte
- High Comm. for Refugees

COUNCIL OF STATE
(Şura-yı Devlet)

SENATE
(Heyet-i A'yan)

CIVIL OFFICIALS COMMISSION
(Memurin-i Mülkiye Komisyonu)

FOREIGN MINISTRY
(Hariciye Nezareti)

MINISTRY OF INTERIOR
(Dahiliye Nezareti)

Diplomatic and
Consular
Establishment

Provincial
Foreign Affairs
Officials

Local
Administration

(Civil-Bureaucratic Ministries Outside the Sublime Porte)

JUSTICE
(Adliye)

FINANCE
(Maliye)

EDUCATION
(Maarif)

PIOUS FOUNDATIONS
(Evkaf)

TRADE &
PUBLIC WORKS
(Ticaret ve Nafia)

RECEIVERSHIP
OF CUSTOMS*
(Rüsumat Emaneti)

FORESTS, MINES &
AGRICULTURE *
(Orman, Maadin, ve Ziraat)

TELEGRAPH & POSTS*
(Telgraf ve Posta)

LAND REGISTRY*
(Defter-i Hakani)

▬ ▬ ▬ ▬ = Enclosed organizations are part of Sublime Porte.

* Not included in the council of Ministers (some bodies of unclear status omitted)

ministers was still to be by sultanic decree, with the result that there could be no collective ministerial solidarity; and the powers of the grand vezir and the other ministers were only vaguely described.[61]

The constitution thus failed to redefine the grand vezirate in any very thorough way. The liberals did not cease their efforts to effect fundamental changes, and Abd ül-Hamid did appoint prime ministers, rather than grand vezirs, on several occasions. But he lost no time in divesting the newer title of the significance that men such as Midhat Paşa aspired to give it. Abd ül-Hamid's first appointment of a prime minister occurred in February 1878. The Parliament had just been suspended, the Russians were at the gates of Istanbul, the wintry city was swarming with refugees, and Ahmed Vefik Paşa, offered the grand vezirate, would only accept it on condition of the change of title and the adoption of the principle of collective ministerial responsibility.[62] His successors, however, were unable to maintain either the title or the principle. For example, Hayr ül-Din Paşa, serving with the title of grand vezir, fell in 1879 over his attempt to defend the principle of collective ministerial responsibility. His successor received the title of prime minister, but the composition of his cabinet was largely spelled out, as Abd ül-Hamid was often to do, in the decree of appointment.[63] By 1882, when the title of prime minister passed out of use for the last time, it had ceased to make any difference; and the issue of collective ministerial responsibility, which had no basis in the constitution of 1876 anyway, was dead for the remainder of the reign.

These events heralded the progressive decline in the importance of the grand vezirate and of the Porte in general. One expression of this was changing patterns of tenure in the grand vezirate, as in many other offices. Between the death of Âli Paşa (1871) and the Young Turk Revolution (1908), there were thirty-two grand-vezirial incumbencies by nineteen men, most of them still civil bureaucrats.[64] For about a decade after the death of Âli Paşa, whose last grand vezirate had lasted over four years, turnover was very rapid. From Âli's death until the dismissal of Ahmed Vefik in 1882, there were twenty-three incumbencies by fifteen men. Thereafter, as the Hamidian system became more firmly established, turnover slowed dramatically, and there were only nine incumbencies by five individuals—of whom Küçük Said Paşa had already served as grand vezir before 1882—in the years before the 1908 revolution. During this interval, there were two grand vezirs with incumbencies of as much as six years each.[65] Yet length of tenure no longer entailed the kind of power Âli had enjoyed. The job had degenerated so much, indeed, that Ferid Paşa, grand vezir from 1903 to 1908, once said that his situation made him envious of the stevedores (*sırık hamalları*) working on the Istanbul wharves.[66]

As the grand vezirate declined in power, the accumulation of a bureaucratic staff directly subordinate to the grand vezir and distinct from any other ministry nevertheless continued along much the lines noted in the preceding period. By 1908, there were under the grand vezir a number of offices that had already emerged before 1871, some of them having undergone changes or reorganization since, plus one or two others that had either emerged or passed under his authority only more recently.

Of the offices already noted during the Tanzimat, the yearbooks continue to attest the existence through 1908 of the post of undersecretary (*müsteşar*) to the grand vezir; the receiver (*amedî*), supposedly presiding over almost fifty clerks divided into four classes; the Office of the Corresponding Secretary (*Mektubî*) of the grand vezir; a Cipher (*Şifre*) Office, presumably corresponding to the earlier Telegraph Office; the Records Office (*Bab-ı Âli Evrak Odası*); and the Archives (*Hazine-i Evrak*) of the Sublime Porte. Also still serving under the grand vezir were the master of ceremonies of the imperial Divan (*teşrifatî-i Divan-ı hümayun*) and several assistants of his in charge of decorations or medals (*nişan memurları*).

In the field of ceremonial, there had, however, also been a new development reflecting the shift in the locus of power and the consequent organizational elaboration of the palace. In the retinue of the grand vezir, there had emerged something like a supervisor general of protocol (*teşrifat-ı umumiye nazırı*). This post had existed more or less from the beginning of Abd ül-Hamid's reign,[67] although its relation to that of the master of ceremonies of the imperial Divan is not clear. From the late 1870s on, the new post was held by the same man who served as translator of the imperial Divan (*tercüman-ı Divan-ı hümayun*) and secretary for foreign correspondence in the Mabeyn (*Mabeyn-i hümayun tahrirat-ı ecnebiye kâtibi*). The need for a secretary for foreign correspondence in the palace, and the fact that the men who successively held this combination of posts had their actual offices there, are added reflections of the extent to which procedures for the conduct of official business, especially that of diplomatic character, had changed since the Tanzimat.[68]

In the way of recent additions to the grand vezir's suite, there
was now also a staff of military aides (*yaver*)[69] and a special translator to the grand vezir (*tercüman-ı sadaret-i uzmâ*).[70] The military
aides are a new sign of the old tendency toward imitation of the
sultan's household. The need for a translator must reflect the increasing organizational differentiation at the Porte.[71] For, although its nominal chief now served at the palace, the Translation Office of the Sublime Porte continued to exist where its
name implies. It remained under the foreign minister, however,
and was the only traditional chancery office that did not eventually become a part of the grand-vezirial entourage.

In contrast, the oldest of the scribal bureaus, referred to by
1908 in the plural as the Offices of the Imperial Divan (*Divan-ı
Hümayun Aklâmı*), had in the 1880s made precisely that shift.
There were also organizational changes within the office, or
group of offices, as it was ultimately more accurate to call it.
While all of the component sections remained under the supervision of the *beylikçi*, some of those noted in 1908 were new, at
least in form. These include a Registry Section (*Divan-ı Hümayun
Kuyud Odası*) and another for Provinces in Privileged Status
(*Vilâyat-ı Mümtaze Kalemi*).[72] In a way both sad and amusing,
İnal, who served in the latter, likened it to the colonial office of
another state. More nearly, it resembled a foreign ministry for
dealing with territories that had yet to consummate their break
from the empire.[73] Two others of the Offices of the Imperial
Divan were old ones: the Section for Important Affairs
(*Mühimme Odası*), created in 1797 and now including the officials
(*tuğrakeş*) charged with drawing the imperial cipher, and the
Office of the Imperial Divan proper.

Following a reorganization of 1900, the traditional subdivisions of this last office also survived within it, with some alterations and additions, as a number of "desks" or "tables." There
were six of these, their differentiation providing a measure of
the continuing influence in this office of the old, document-
oriented conceptions of organization. The roles assigned to the
six "desks" were the drafting of documents (*tesvid*, "blackening"); production of fair copies and registration (*tebyiz*, "whitening," and *kayd*); preparation of summaries (*hulâsa*); the keeping

of certain undefined types of registers (*defter*); preparation of brevets of appointment (*rüus*); and assignment of benefices in land (*tahvil*). The total number of clerks provided for in the order for this reorganization is forty-six, and the numbers assigned to the "desks" ranged from the twenty listed for fair copies and registration to the three still occupied at the opening of this century with the vestigial survivals of the traditional Ottoman system of benefices in land.[74]

The political eclipse of the grand vezirate thus did not halt the kinds of organizational development previously associated with that office.

Conciliar Bodies—The Council of Ministers

The same was true of a number of other organizations, including the major conciliar bodies. Among these, the continued convocation in times of stress of special, ad hoc consultative assemblies provided a striking reminder that the early form from which so many of the councils of the Tanzimat had derived was still not forgotten.[75] On balance, however, what was more characteristic was the further evolution of the conciliar bodies, as shown by the disappearance of some of the smaller ones into bureaucratic agencies, the emergence of the short-lived Parliament, and the adaptation of conciliar forms to serve the functions of control that the Tanzimat reformers had so much neglected.

To look first at the Council of Ministers, the uncertain state of its development during the Tanzimat and the determination of Abd ül-Hamid were enough to keep it from assuming anything like the form that the liberal constitutionalists sought to give it. Not only did Abd ül-Hamid make sure that the grand vezirs did not regain the control that the Tanzimat statesmen had exercised over ministerial appointments, but it has been said that he deliberately appointed ministers who would be unable to get along with one another and then encouraged them to spy and inform on their colleagues.[76] The degree of cohesion, power, or independence that the Council of Ministers enjoyed during this period thus had narrow limits. Yet, the council did develop in some ways, and it retained some degree of importance.

For one thing, the composition of the council stabilized to a considerable degree, at least after the accession of Abd ül-Hamid. The yearbooks from his reign are remarkably consistent in showing the council as consisting of the grand vezir or prime minister, the head of the religious establishment (*şeyh ül-İslâm*), the chairman (*reis*) of the Council of State, the ministers of foreign and internal affairs, and—from civil-bureaucratic departments outside the Porte—the ministers of justice, finance, education, pious foundations, and the combined portfolio of trade and public works. The undersecretary of the grand vezir was also regularly included. The ministers of the military departments—war (*Bab-ı Seraskerî*), artillery (*Tophane müşiriyeti*), and usually navy (*bahriye*)—were members, as well.[77] The old practice of swelling the council with ministers without portfolio died out in this period, the last person so mentioned being the elderly Ahmed Cevdet Paşa (d. 1895).[78] With this stabilization in the composition of the council, there appears also to have gone a reduction, at least after the accession of Abd ül-Hamid, in the rate of turnover in ministerial positions. We have already cited evidence of this in the grand vezirate. In the Ministries of Foreign and Internal Affairs, there were even longer incumbencies.

Given the altered political conditions of the Hamidian regime, this slowing of ministerial turnover was a sign of diminished political importance. Yet the Council of Ministers still had a role to fill. Cevdet Paşa, for example, blamed the fall of Abd ül-Aziz in part on the insistence of Mahmud Nedim Paşa as grand vezir on attributing all government acts, whatever reaction they were likely to provoke, to the sultan. In a way recalling d'Ohsson's comments of a century earlier about the *divan* of the grand vezir, Cevdet said that the Council of Ministers was like a curtain between the palace and the people. The sultan should appear behind decisions that would be well received by the populace; for others, this curtain should be the only visible backdrop.[79]

Abd ül-Hamid was intelligent enough to apply this reasoning, and the Council of State provided him with a procedural system ideally suited for doing so. According to a ruling of July 1872 on procedures for the enactment of new legislation, all laws and all later amendments were to be taken under study first in the Council of State, then in the Council of Ministers, and were subsequently to receive approval in the form of a decree of the sultan.[80] The constitutional system, had it lasted, would obviously have led to modification of this procedure. And it is no doubt true that Abd ül-Hamid decided the most important matters, as well as many trivial ones, by himself. But there were large volumes of time-consuming business that had to be left to some lower echelon. The format of the legal acts of the years between the suspension of the Parliament and the Young Turk Revolution makes clear that the system prescribed in 1872 was operative in case after case.[81] The ministers thus may not have enjoyed great power or independence under Abd ül-Hamid, but it does not follow that they had nothing to do or no role in shaping the voluminous legislation of the period.

The Council of State

Where their respective roles in legislation were concerned, the system of 1872 also indicates that the relationship of the Council of Ministers to the Council of State (*Şura-yı Devlet*) remained in this period much like that of the ministers to the earlier legislative councils of the Tanzimat. The chief difference was the locus of the higher power that dominated these bodies. Concurring in this interpretation, the British ambassador wrote of the Council of State in 1906 that it retained "almost the scope and functions of a Legislative Assembly," although in practical terms, the fact that it had no legislative initiative and that appointments to it were controlled by the sultan made its independence "very limited."[82]

Along with these elements of continuity, however, the Council of State also underwent substantial changes. Particularly during the interval between the death of Âli Paşa and the accession of Abd ül-Hamid, it became a political plaything of rival grand vezirs. Mahmud Nedim and others who were opposed to the legacy of the Tanzimat and the constitutional movement would attack the council and try to reduce it in size and functions. Midhat Paşa and other grand vezirs identified either with the Tanzimat elite or the constitutional movement would restore the council to something like its former state. The result was a good deal of thrashing about, but as the opening of the Parliament approached, the council began to assume the role of preparing the bills that were to be submitted for debate in its two houses.[83]

With the Parliamentary episode past and the Hamidian regime progressively more firmly consolidated, the Council of State began to take on that stability which, as with the Council of Ministers, hinted at loss of power, if not necessarily at a lack of work to do. Under its original regulations, the Council of State was divided into five sections (*daire*) for Civil Affairs (*Mülkiye*), Reform Legislation (*Tanzimat*), Public Works (*Nafia*), Finance (*Maliye*), and Adjudication (*Muhakemat*). In addition, there was a supporting staff that included a head secretary (*baş kâtib*), who was classed as a member of the council. Under him were a number of what Young refers to in French as *adjoints* (*muavin*) and *auditeurs* (*mülâzım*), as well as a staff of clerks divided into bureaus for purposes such as preparation of minutes and reports (*Mazbata Odası*) or keeping the files (*Evrak Odası*).[84] In 1880, in an effort at economy, the sections of the council proper were reduced to three for Internal Affairs (*Dahiliye*), Reform Legislation (*Tanzimat*), and Adjudication (*Muhakemat*).[85]

Of these, the Adjudication Section had a complicated list of responsibilities in the hearing of appeals from other tribunals and in administrative justice. These functions appear to have resulted over a period of time in the emergence of a series of Courts of First Instance (*Bidayet*), Appeal (*İstinaf*) and Cassation (*Temyiz*), although it is difficult to tell when these became fully differentiated from one another and from the Adjudication Section itself.[86]

A decree issued in 1897 gave the Council of State and its major component agencies what appears to have been their final form for the period. This provided again for three administrative sections, though not exactly the same three as before. One was to be a Section for Civil Affairs (*Mülkiye*). It corresponded essentially to the earlier Section for Internal Affairs (*Dahiliye*) and also assumed responsibility for investigating complaints about the conduct of administration and for resolving conflicts among administrative agencies. In addition, the Section for Civil Affairs had a kind of second-echelon review over the actions of the other two sections. The responsibilities of these sections were Finance (*Maliye*) and Reform Legislation (*Tanzimat*). The decree did not detail their functions very clearly, although it included indications that the mission of the Section for Finance lay in issuing concessions (*imtiyazat*), making contracts (*mukavelât*), and levying taxes, while that of the Section for Reform Legislation had to do with drafting laws and regulations.

As concerns administrative justice, the decree provided that the Adjudication Section (*Muhakemat Dairesi*) and the existing Court of First Instance (*Bidayet Mahkemesi*) were to become "entirely independent" (*bütün bütün mustakil*) from the council, and that courts of First Instance (*Bidayet*), Appeal (*İstinaf*), and Cassation (*Temyiz*) were to be organized separately. These were to be under the "supervision and administration" of the Ministry of Justice and under the presidency of the chairman of the Council of State. The decree promised the preparation of a special set of regulations for these courts, but nothing of the sort seems ever to have come to light. To judge from the evidence of the yearbooks, the net effect of these changes on the judicial side of the council was the disappearance of the Adjudication Section and the substitution for it of the three courts. Thus, for the remainder of Abd ül-Hamid's reign, the Council of State consisted of three sections for Civil Affairs, Finance, and Reform Legislation, and three administrative courts for each of the echelons of the normal process of trial and appeal.[87]

There were also a number of supporting agencies not mentioned in the decree of 1897. Along with Young's *auditeurs* (*mülâzım*) and the secretarial staff—the *adjoints* (*muavin*) seemingly having disappeared—these included several categories of specialized, technical personnel. Such were the public prosecutors (*müddei-i umumi*) and examining magistrates (*müstantık*) of the administrative courts.[88] In addition, there was a Conflict of Jurisdiction Council (*İhtilâf-ı Merci Encümeni*), which was made up of representatives of both the Council of State and the regular Court of Cassation and had as its mission the resolution of conflicts of jurisdiction between the regular courts (*mehakim-i âdiye*) and the administrative courts of the Council of State.[89] There was also a Grand Jury (*Heyet-i İttihamiye*).[90] Finally, there was an interesting body known as the Statistical Council of the Sublime Porte (*Bab-ı Âli İstatistik Encümeni*), presided over by the chairman of the Council of State and drawing its members from among his colleagues and from the Ministries of Foreign and Internal Affairs. More than its title implies, the Statistical Council had a part in the Hamidian system of controls in ways that will require further comment elsewhere.[91]

The Council of State thus continued its evolution as the chief legislative body of the empire and the central agency of administrative justice. Had its regulations been faithfully observed, it would still have been a relatively small organization. The decree of 1897 provided, for example, that the Section for Civil Affairs include eight members—soon increased to fourteen—with the chairman of the whole council as their head, that the Sections

for Finance and Reform Legislation each have a vice-chairman
(*reis-i sani*) and six members, and that the Courts of First Instance, Appeal, and Cassation have their own presidents (*reis*)
and four, six, and eight members, respectively. Such was the attitude of Abd ül-Hamid toward bureaucratic appointments that
these limits had been exceeded several-fold by 1908.[92] Even with
this featherbedding, however, the council remained a functioning organization, a fact affirmed by the tremendous volume of
legislation that emanated from it.

The Parliament

In a sense, the Parliament should have marked both a culmination to the historical evolution of the conciliar bodies and an important step toward fuller implementation of the representative
principle first introduced in the local consultative assemblies
created during the Tanzimat. Had the Parliament developed in
this way, however, both its houses would still have existed in
1908; and they would not have been listed as organizational
components of the Sublime Porte, from which they had originally been quite distinct, except perhaps to the extent of drawing secretarial support from that quarter.

In fact, the prorogation of the Chamber of Deputies (*Meclis-ı
Meb'usan*) in February 1878 meant that nothing of the Parliament existed thereafter except the Senate (*Heyet-i Ayan*), and
that in attenuated form. The constitution provided that the
members of the Senate were to be appointed for life by the sultan and were to receive a salary of 10,000 *kuruş* per month, a
handsome sum, though short of ministerial-level salaries. Following the prorogation of the chamber, Abd ül-Hamid continued to make appointments to fill senatorial vacancies until
1880. Since the Senate had nothing to do, however, senatorial
positions became mere sinecures for loyal servants of the sultanate. Fifty-one men were appointed to the Senate in all, but their
numbers began to dwindle after 1880, and by 1908 there were
only three left.[93] The listing of the Senate among the components of the Porte is thus a reflection of the atrophy of parliamentary institutions and is otherwise without practical significance.

The Ministry of the Interior

In the last chapter, we noted the discontinuities in the history of
the central organization of this ministry during the Tanzimat

and traced them partly to the determination of the reformers to concentrate as much power as possible in the smallest number of hands, partly to the concrete difficulties of projecting a new administrative system over the whole of the empire. After 1871, problems of the same sorts continued and in some cases worsened. The Ottomans saw their control ended, or threatened, in increasing numbers of provinces. The most serious of these problems, the Armenian troubles of the 1890s, created severe disruption not only on the imperial periphery, but in the Anatolian heart of the empire and in the capital itself. All the while, palace domination of internal administration made itself felt to such a point that the Ministry of the Interior ceased to have more than fragmentary authority over provincial administrative cadres.[94]

The extent to which this ministry, like others, became bent to its subordinate role is well symbolized in the character of Mehmed Memduh Paşa, who served Abd ül-Hamid as Minister of the Interior from 1895 to 1908. Author of a number of literary works, some still valued as historical sources, Memduh Paşa had previously been governor general (*vali*) of several provinces. Serving in this capacity at Sivas (1889-1892), he distinguished himself, according to a British account, for "shameless venality" and provocation of the Armenian issue. Memduh had reportedly won the favor of Abd ül-Hamid even before the latter's accession by submitting confidential reports, a practice that Memduh subsequently continued. One of the first of Abd ül-Hamid's informers, Memduh as minister was known for servility toward his superiors and for the hauteur he showed his subordinates. Thoroughly hated, he was persecuted in rare fashion after the Revolution of 1908 as part of the "wreckage of despotism" (*enkaz-ı istibdad*).[95]

The circumstances in which Memduh Paşa flourished naturally had their effects on the evolution of both the general system of local administration and the central organs of the Ministry of the Interior. In local administration, no change of such fundamental character as the Provincial Administration Law of 1871 reached the point of application during this period. The constitution of 1876 did provide for a new regulation of local administration on a basis of separation of powers and decentralization (literally, "broadening of discretion," *tevsi-i mezuniyet*, art. 108). The Chamber then passed a new provincial administration law during its first session, only to have the sultan return it for reconsideration during the second, which did not last long enough to perform this task. Reportedly, a mixed commission of Ottoman and foreign officials drafted a new provincial administration law in 1880, but it was neither applied nor published in the official series of Ottoman legal texts.

The only reforms actually applied dealt merely with facets of the local administrative system. These included measures on the provincial courts; the institutions to be set up at the fourth and lowest of the administrative echelons (the "commune" or *nahiye*); or the ways and means of eliminating common causes of complaint by the dispatch of judicial inspectors, the inclusion in the local gendarmerie of members from the various ethnoreligious communities, and the restraint of unauthorized fiscal exactions. Many measures had to do with the qualifications of local administrative personnel and the procedures for their appointment and promotion; such matters will require discussion in a later section on personnel policy. The field of municipal administration witnessed further refinements of the system set up for the city of Istanbul, as well as an attempt to create a pattern of urban administration for provincial cities. As time passed, necessarily, there were increasing numbers of acts aimed at the specific problems of such localities as Crete, eastern Rumelia, or the controversial provinces of eastern Anatolia. The irresponsibility of the palace system at the highest level, and the intractability of many of the local problems at the lowest, defined the narrow limits within which such efforts at administrative reform bore fruit in this period.[96]

Meanwhile, in Istanbul, the central organs of the ministry developed in ways reflecting the political tendencies and reformist emphases of the period. After an initial interval during which the post of minister again vanished, references to a minister of the interior reappeared in the yearbooks in 1878,[97] although the listing of his staff continued through the 1880s to be indicative of small numbers and limited organizational articulation. Of the elements that had emerged within the ministry during the Tanzimat, only the undersecretary (*müsteşar*) and corresponding secretary (*mektubî*) continued to exist, as did the traditional "agents of the gate" (*kapı kâhyası*) or representatives of the provincial governors general at the Porte. The roles of both the "agents" and the corresponding secretary pertained to communications between the ministry in Istanbul and the officials subordinate to it in the provinces. Given the still limited development of the central organizational structures of the ministry, the existence of two channels of communication between the provincial authorities and the center seems ironic. The weakly developed central agencies of the ministry must have been supplemented to some degree, however, by the Section for Civil or Internal Affairs, which continued to exist in the Council of State. And this is not to speak of the palace secretaries, whose tendency was to bypass the central organs of the ministry entirely and deal directly with provincial authorities.

Between the 1880s and 1908, the central organization of the Ministry of the Interior developed a good bit further, if in curious ways that show how it served the Hamidian system. The yearbook for 1908[98] lists a number of offices as forming parts of the ministry: the Office of the Corresponding Secretary, which by this time had one or more sections for correspondence by telegraph or cipher; other offices for filing (*Evrak Odası*) and accounting (*Muhasebe Kalemi*); and a branch of the system created in this period for the maintenance of official personnel records (*Sicill-i Ahval Şubesi*). There were also several special commissions, as well as other, miscellaneous institutions or groups of functionaries attached to the ministry. These categories include an otherwise unknown body called something like the Commission for the Expedition of Business and Reforms (*Tesri-i Muamelât ve Islahat Komisyonu*); a "Special Commission" (*Komisyon-ı Mahsus*), whose membership suggests that its mission lay in internal espionage; a Purchasing Commission for the ministry (*Dahiliye Nezareti Mubaayat Komisyonu*); the "agents of the gate" (*kapı kâhyası*); and the administrative and medical staff of a poorhouse (*Dar ül-Aceze*) that Abd ül-Hamid had founded. In particularly prominent positions were two other agencies of obvious importance in the Hamidian system of controls: the Domestic Press Directorate (*Matbuat-ı Dahiliye Müdiriyeti*) and what was called the General Administration of Population Registration (*Sicill-i Nüfus İdare-i Umumiyesi*).

Of these last two agencies, the Domestic Press Directorate included by 1908 a director with five assistants; five examining clerks (*mümeyyiz*); more than a dozen inspectors (*müfettiş*) responsible for supervision of newspapers, printing establishments, and theaters; and a couple of file clerks; as well, presumably, as an unlisted phalanx of secretaries. Clearly, this office exercised the responsibilities assigned to the Ministry of the Interior in the Draconian system of controls, interministerial in scope, set up by the Press Laws of the period.[99]

While it is not always possible to be certain from the yearbooks which offices are simply subsections of others, the General Administration of Population Registration appears to have been even larger than the Press Directorate. There was by this time a welter of legislation on matters of *état civil*,[100] the records-keeping demands of which are reflected in the size and organizational complexity of the agencies at work in that field. What appear to be the subordinate sections of the General Administration of Population Registration run to nine in number. Some of them had geographically defined responsibilities pertaining to Istanbul (*Der Saadet Kalemi*) or the provinces (*Vilâyat Kalemi*); others specialized in specific transactions such as the issue of travel permits (*Mürur Kalemi*),[101] passports (*Pasaport Kalemi*), or the compilation of population statistics (*İstatistik Kalemi*).

As of 1908, the central organization of the Ministry of the Interior, with its elaborate systems for population registration and control of the press, and its less-developed and overlapping systems for dealing with local administrative authorities through the Office of the Corresponding Secretary and the "agents of the gate," thus reflects the warping and inhibiting effect of the Hamidian despotism on the development of this branch of administration. Comparison with the even more rudimentary conditions of 1871 indicates, however, that limited progress had been made toward developing a central institutional core for the ministry. Even more significantly, although the Press Directorate and the General Administration of Population Registration were clearly parts of the Hamidian system of controls, they reflect the further progress of a new orientation in organizational development, already noticeable in a few cases in the preceding period. This amounted to a shift of emphasis away from the old document-oriented patterns and toward others defined more in terms of the roles of the bureaucracy in relation to the larger society. Although no really coherent and rational system of internal administration could come into existence until the palace despotism and the composite imperial structure had been replaced, the provincial administration law of 1871 and the small gains perceptible during this period in the Ministry of the Interior did provide some elements for such a system.

The Foreign Ministry

While the relative prominence that it had once enjoyed in comparison with other civil-bureaucratic agencies had declined in some respects, as of 1908 the Foreign Ministry was still the most highly evolved of the organizational components of the Sublime Porte. By the same token, the new kind of organizational orientation that we have just noted in the Ministry of the Interior, and that had already appeared in the Foreign Ministry to a limited degree during the Tanzimat, had asserted itself there much more strongly with the passage of additional decades. In the process, the central agencies of the ministry began to take on the aspect of a series of directorates, recalling those of modern, Western foreign ministries, with missions differentiated in terms of jurisdictional areas or goals external to the bureaucratic system as narrowly defined. As Figure VI-2 suggests, however, this change was still only partially complete at the time of the Young Turk Revolution, and there were other organizational problems that still awaited solution. Now, even more than during the Tanzimat, this was true of the working relationships among the various agencies of the ministry. Indeed, the proliferation of agencies had begun to imply a need to combine them into functionally related groups through which a more effective control of operations could be maintained. Of course, the ministry, and the Porte in general, would have to reemerge from the state of stagnation into which Abd ül-Hamid had plunged it before it would be possible to solve problems such as these.

Comparison of Figures V-2 and VI-2 shows that the central offices of the Foreign Ministry still included a number of organizations that had already existed in 1871, although changes of various sorts had occurred in all of them. This was true, first of all, of the posts of minister and undersecretary, as they settled into their appointed places in the Hamidian scheme of things.

After more than twenty changes of incumbent between 1871 and 1885, the post of minister was almost entirely monopolized from 1885 to 1909 by two men, Kürd Said Paşa (1885-1895)—so called to distinguish him from the grand vezir, Küçük Said—and Ahmed Tevfik Paşa (1895-1909).[102] Both of them could be described as men who managed to live with the Hamidian system without being tainted by it. With "no great diplomatic talent or profound knowledge of affairs, but possessing a complete com-

FIGURE VI-2. ORGANIZATION OF THE FOREIGN MINISTRY, 1908

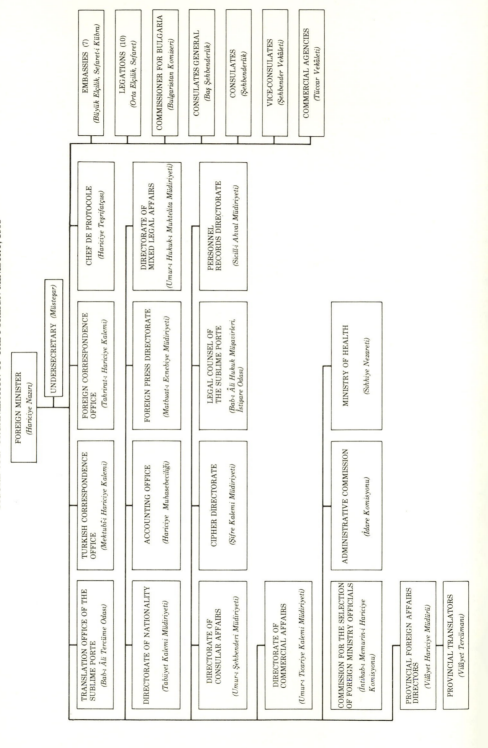

mand of his features, unruffled urbanity of manner, and a composure that no crisis has yet been known to disturb," Tevfik Paşa won praise of a sort as "an ideal Minister for Foreign Affairs under a régime which has reduced the rôle of that functionary to that of a buffer between the Palace, whence the foreign policy of the Empire is directed, and the representatives of the foreign powers." A former diplomat, Tevfik was also to serve as grand vezir on a number of occasions between 1909 and 1922.[103] An even longer tenure of office was to the credit of the perennial undersecretary of this period, Artin Dadian Paşa, who held that post first in 1875-1876, again in 1883-1885, and then continuously from 1885 until his death in 1901.[104]

Also surviving from the Tanzimat were the three bureaus that then bore basic responsibility for the written business of the ministry: the Translation Office of the Sublime Porte, the Turkish Correspondence Office, and the Foreign Correspondence Office. These, too, had undergone certain changes. For example, the fact that the translator of the imperial Divan now served at the palace meant that the nominal deputy chief of the office, the first translator (*mütercim-i evvel*), was now its effective head. The Foreign Correspondence Office, in turn, had changed in losing its old character as an Armenian enclave. In addition, Mehmed Nuri Bey, director there from 1892 to 1908, reportedly provided Abd ül-Hamid with what the minister and undersecretary did not, namely, "the window through which the Palace observes and controls all that goes on in the Ministry and, so far as his [Nuri's] influence extends, in the Diplomatic circles of Constantinople." Son of a French renegade named Château-neuf, Mehmed Nuri was by the same account: "a prominent centurion in the legions of Palace spies, amongst whom he ranks high for the quality of his reports, which he has the talent of making both interesting and agreeable to the taste of the Sovereign. Under an agreeable, cultivated and even refined exterior, he is corrupt and unscrupulous in the extreme."[105] In ways such as these, the Turkish and Foreign Correspondence Offices and the Translation Office of the Porte underwent the deforming effects of palace dominance. Nonetheless, their missions remained in principle unchanged; and they continued to grow not only in size but also in internal differentiation, as attested by the appearance in each of a director for important affairs (*mühimme müdürü*).[106]

In addition, of the offices known in 1871, those of the *chef de protocole* of the Foreign Ministry, of Nationality, and of Accounts also continued to exist, as did what had been the Foreign Press Office. Now styled a directorate, this last bureau performed functions that are not easy to distinguish from those of the Domestic Press Directorate in the Interior Ministry. An official description of the late 1880s does attribute a distinct mission to the Foreign Press Directorate, namely, to deny harmful statements in the European press and to inform foreign nations about the policies and progress of the Ottoman state.[107] This office nonetheless actually became a part of the Ministry of the Interior for a time in the 1890s, the Domestic and Foreign Press Directorates then being listed one after the other in the official yearbooks. The Foreign Press Office must thus have been useful to the sultan in his efforts to control the press, as the Domestic Press Directorate certainly was.[108]

Of the offices that formed parts of the ministry in 1871, two others had disappeared only in the sense of assuming other forms. What had been the Records Office (*Hariciye Evrak Odası*) had been replaced by separate sections in a number of other offices and therefore does not appear in Figure VI-2. The Turkish Correspondence Office had one section, headed by the Foreign Ministry records director (*Hariciye evrak müdürü*), the title borne by the head of the former Records Office of the ministry. There were also records directors, presumably with smaller staffs, in the Translation Office, Foreign Correspondence Office, Directorate for Consular Affairs, Foreign Press Directorate, Directorate of Nationality, and the Office of Legal Counsel. To judge from regulations issued for one of these records sections, their functions lay in controlling the flow, retrievability, and security of documents on current affairs.[109] The organizational decentralization of Foreign Ministry personnel working in records management hints again at the ongoing struggles of the government to cope with the mounting volume of official paperwork.

In one other case, an office mentioned in 1871 was abolished or reassigned to a different ministry, but then replaced by another bureau of seemingly similar character. The office in question was headed by a functionary known in 1871 as the secretary for foreign affairs (*hariciye kâtibi*) and later by the more explicit title of secretary for foreign legal affairs (*deavi-i hariciye kâtibi*). Evidence from the Foreign Ministry personnel files indicates that this office was either abolished or reassigned to the Ministry of Justice in 1880, but was replaced by something called the Office of Mixed Legal Affairs of the Foreign Ministry.[110] This acquired the status of a directorate by 1908. The details are not clear, but these changes are probably related in some way to a general reorganization of the judicial system in 1879.[111] In any case, the Foreign Ministry yearbooks describe the mission of the Office of Mixed Legal Affairs as production of legal opinions on certain types of cases arising between Ottoman subjects and foreign nationals—thus cases "mixed" in terms of the nationality of the contending parties—and certification and transmission of relevant documents.[112]

In addition to these offices, a number of others developed by 1908. To a degree, this occurred predictably by differentiation among the functions of a preexisting bureau, specifically the Foreign Correspondence Office, itself an offshoot of the Translation Office; and it is interesting to note the extent to which the new kind of organizational orientation, mentioned above, came into view as this subdivision of functions progressed.

Such were the origins of the Office, later Directorate, of Consular Affairs, created in 1873 and then described as "dependent on" the Foreign Correspondence Office, which presumably had handled the French-language correspondence of the ministry with both its consular and its diplomatic agencies up to that point. The new office was to be responsible for the correspondence of the ministry with the consular corps, receipt of consular reports, production of semiannual statistical reports on commerce and navigation based on the data contained in these reports, and a political information service. A document of 1880 makes clear that the office did not immediately live up to this program; yet the creation of the agency marked the start of a new effort to organize and regulate the workings of the consular system.[113] By 1908, the office, or directorate as it had become, had acquired a sizable staff, led by supervisory officials of long-familiar kinds. It also had its own records management section, and a special staff of consular inspectors, headed by a European known as Graziani Efendi.[114] The inspectors performed a function defined under a regulation for the Ottoman consular service first promulgated in 1881 and amended many times thereafter.[115]

Probably next in order of emergence among the offices of the Foreign Ministry was what appears in Figure VI-2 as the Cipher Directorate and is almost certainly to be identified with an earlier Telegraph Office. This, in turn, was yet another outgrowth of the Foreign Correspondence Office, in which as late as 1880 there had been simply a head clerk for telegraphy (*telgraf ciheti ser kalfası*).[116]

Several other offices also emerged at indeterminate points in the early 1880s. One such is the Office of Legal Counsel (*İstişare Odası*), under the dual headship of two senior jurisconsults known as the legal counsellors of the Sublime Porte (*Bab-ı Âli hukuk müşavirleri*). Under them were a number of assistants (*muavin*, presumably also supposed to have legal qualifications) and a staff of the more familiar clerical types (*hulefa*). In cases involving individuals of different nationalities, the Office of Legal Counsel had responsibilities that are difficult to distinguish from those of the Office of Mixed Legal Affairs. The basic responsibility of the legal counsellors, however, was to provide opinions, when requested, on legal problems arising in the relations of the empire with other states. The role of the legal counsellors thus recalled the traditional one of the *beylikçi* and the Office of the Imperial Divan in checking individual transactions for conformity to the terms of the applicable treaties or grants of concessions to foreign states.[117] In more modern terms, however, the legal counsellors were the advisors of the Ottoman government in international law. A good measure of the extent to which Ottomans perceived this as a new role is the fact that the first incumbents of the two legal counsellorships were foreigners. The "nationalization" of these posts only occurred in Abd ül-Hamid's last years, with the appointments of Gabriel Noradounghian, who was to become the empire's only Armenian minister of foreign affairs (1912-1913) and is now remembered as the compiler of a published collection of diplomatic documents, and İbrahim Hakkı Bey (later Paşa), a future grand vezir and a pioneer of modern legal studies among the Turks.[118]

More or less contemporaneous in origin with the Office of Legal Counsel was the Personnel Records Directorate, another branch of the system set up under Abd ül-Hamid to keep systematic personnel records.

Last to emerge of the offices and directorates that were part of the ministry by 1908 was the Directorate of Commercial Affairs, first mentioned in the yearbooks in 1896-1897.[119] This may have been an offshoot of the Directorate of Consular Affairs, and thus of the Foreign Correspondence Office and the Translation Office; but evidence on this point has yet to come to light.

In addition to these offices and directorates, finally, the central organs of the Foreign Ministry as of 1908 included two special commissions, as well as a body which, though nominally a separate "ministry" (*nezaret*), is perhaps best envisioned as a third organization of similar sort. The Commission for the Selection of Foreign Ministry Officials and the Administrative Commission, the membership of which consisted only of the directors or top supervisory officials of other offices of the ministry, evolved out of a Foreign Ministry Council (*Encümen-i Hariciye*). Created in 1885, this progressively acquired a miscellany of functions: monitoring the conduct of current business, purchasing, and supervision of appointments. About 1900, this council was subdivided into an Administrative Commission, which inherited responsibility for the first two functions of the former council, and the Commission for the Selection of Foreign Ministry Officials, which assumed responsibility for the third.[120] Like the Personnel Records Directorate, the Commission for the Selection of Foreign Ministry Officials and its counterparts in other ministries figured as branches of the system, centered in the Civil Officials Commission shown in Figure VI-1, for the control of appointments and other personnel actions in the civil bureaucracy.

In turn, what had come to be known as the "Ministry of Health" dated back, as did the history of its association with the Foreign Ministry, more or less to the creation of the quarantine system in 1838. From about 1880 on, the foreign minister also became the "minister of health," presiding in that capacity, at least nominally, over a Board of Health (*Meclis-i Umur-ı Sıhhiye*) made up of Ottoman officials and representatives of the other states that had diplomatic relations with the empire. Under this board, in turn, stood several clerical offices. The Board of Health was the scene of ongoing contention, thanks to the divergence of views among its international membership. The Ottomans wanted strict quarantine measures; the Europeans, animated by more up-to-date medical ideas and a keener sense of the economic costs of delays in quarantine, fought for more lenient terms. These differences gained in importance from the growth of trade and from the concerns raised, both among Muslims and among Europeans who controlled Islamic territory, by the annual pilgrimage to Mecca.[121]

By 1908, then, these were the elements that composed the central organization of the Foreign Ministry. There is no evidence that any particular effort had been made to pattern this structure after any European example. Indeed, there is no documentary evidence that the officials of the Ottoman Foreign Ministry made any close study of the organization of the corresponding agencies of European governments before 1908. This may help to explain both the continued prominence of long-familiar types of personnel—head clerks (*ser kalfa*), examining clerks (*mümeyyiz*), directors of important affairs (*mühimme müdürü*), and so on—and the lack of any discernible system for coordinating the work of the various departments. Yet, it is significant that the more recently created agencies had begun to assume a jurisdictionally defined or problem-oriented character, as opposed to the old pattern of specialization in production of particular types of documents, or, in this ministry, of working in a particular language. Alongside the old, there were now also new types of officials with new kinds of technical expertise and duties extending beyond the old paper-pushing routines. And the new bureaucratic roles were appearing at all levels, from humble cipher clerks, to consular inspectors, to the proud legal counsellors of the Porte. The lengthy evolution that lay behind this ministry makes it possible to see here with particular clarity how much the civil bureaucracy had begun to be oriented away from the traditional, introspective activities, centering on maintenance of the inherited cultural patterns of the imperial tradition, and toward varieties of administrative action that affected the world outside the offices with new intensity and in a variety of new ways.

As in the preceding period, this change should have found particularly clear expression in the agencies of the ministry outside Istanbul, although what was usually in fact more obvious was the subordination of these agencies to the workings of the Hamidian system. The provincial personnel, as before, were the provincial foreign affairs directors and their translators. While officials of this type still did not appear in every province, the Foreign Ministry yearbook for 1888-1889 lists both foreign affairs directors and translators in three provinces in the Aegean region, as well as translators in sixteen other provinces. Halid Ziya Uşaklıgil, who served for a time as assistant to the foreign affairs director in Izmir, has left his usual vivid picture of the job. Its duties dealt almost entirely with squabbles over the claims, then practically universal among the non-Muslims of the city, to foreign nationality.[122] From the standpoint of the foreign minister in Istanbul, a subject of almost equal disagreeableness was the relationship of the provincial foreign affairs directorships to his ministry, as opposed to that of the interior. Inadequately defined in the law of 1871 on provincial administration, this question gave rise to a feud that occupied the two ministries on into the Young Turk period.[123] The situation of the foreign affairs directors is thus instructive not only of the erosion of Ottoman sovereignty within the empire, but also of the increasing potential for jurisdictional conflicts as the government grew in size and organizational complexity.

Most important of the agencies outside Istanbul, obviously, were the diplomatic and consular missions, which had grown in number significantly by 1908. In the case of the embassies and legations, the reason for the growth was primarily the acquisition of independence by several of the Balkan states—Rumania, Serbia, Montenegro—as well as the accreditation of ministers to some of the smaller western European states—sometimes to more than one at a time. At various times during the period, there was also a variety of something like "commissioners" (*komiser*), representatives of the Porte in places of which it did not acknowledge the independence. The only one of these serving under the Foreign Ministry in 1908 was in Bulgaria.[124]

The diplomatic corps had thus grown, but it is no surprise to learn that the chiefs of some of the missions were really representatives of the palace and therefore neither professional diplomats nor career officials of the Foreign Ministry. These palace diplomats ranged from men of some ability and polish, like Salih Münir Paşa—a quondam associate of the Young Ottomans who for years was concurrently ambassador to France and minister to Switzerland and Belgium—to such unsavory secret agents as Nikola Gadban Efendi, or Necib Melhame—who won the disapproval of more than one of the governments to which he was accredited and eventually found himself ostracized by the *corps diplomatique* in Sofia.[125] Others represented the palace in the sense of being military men appointed to posts that had, from the sultan's point of view, largely military interest. This was the case in 1908 of Tevfik Paşa in Berlin, İbrahim Fethi Paşa in Belgrade, and Ahmed Fevzi Paşa in Cetinje.[126] All of these were general officers and titular aides-de-camp to the sultan. Still others "represented the palace" in spite of themselves, as virtual exiles. Such were the eccentric Keçecizade İzzet Fuad Paşa, minister in Madrid,[127] or the great poet Abd ül-Hak Hâmid, to whom European diplomatic posts for years provided suitable—and from the sultan's viewpoint, suitably remote—settings for indulging his tastes for wine, women, and song.[128]

Like the number of diplomatic posts, that of consular positions also increased over the years between 1871 and 1908. Although the impossibility of distinguishing honorary from salaried posts in the listings included in the government yearbooks usually precludes determination of the number of professional consular officials, a more detailed source of 1888-1889 mentions 76 salaried consular officials.[129] By 1908, the number had risen to over 100 in all grades from consul general down to chancery clerk. This does not count the commercial agents, who corresponded to the ordinary consular officials as the commissioners mentioned above did to the regular ambassadors, and were in 1908 found only in three Bulgarian towns.[130]

It may be questioned if Ottoman interests were adequate to support a consular establishment of this size, and it is clear from a variety of sources that padding had gone on in the consular service, as elsewhere. Still, most of the salaried consuls were in neighboring countries such as Greece, Rumania, Russia, and Iran, where the empire did have considerable interests of commercial and other kinds. These interests fueled a persistent official concern for the improvement of the consular service. One expression of this interest was a series of regulatory acts that will require closer scrutiny in the next section.

With the proliferation of bureaus and commissions at the Porte and the extension of the networks of agents in the provinces and abroad, the organizational development of the Foreign Ministry continued even during the years of sultanic reassertion. Under a sovereign intent on assuming most of its responsibilities for himself, the ministry could hardly reach a state of comprehensive structural rationalization. Yet here, perhaps more than in other agencies of the Porte, the elements required for any effort to achieve such a state had come into existence.

Commissions under the Presidency of the Sultan

Had the Sublime Porte continued to develop during this period simply along previously established lines, a description of the grand vezir and his staff, of the major conciliar bodies, and of the Ministries of the Interior and Foreign Affairs might well have provided an exhaustive portrayal of its organizational elements. In fact, however, the same force that interfered with the operation of these institutions and thwarted the development of the Parliament also affected the Porte in at least one other significant way, the result of which appears in Figure VI-1 as the Civil Officials Commission and the commissions under the presidency of the sultan. A discussion of these bodies, which, though ostensibly attached to the Porte, were directly subordinate to the sultan and not at all to the grand vezir,[131] must conclude our survey of the Porte as it had come to be in 1908.

To begin with the commissions under the presidency of the sultan: their regulations indicate that they were really interministerial in character and that the sultan himself appointed their members. The origin of all these bodies seems to have lain in the special importance that Abd ül-Hamid attached to their missions. This is most obviously the case of the Hijaz Railway Commission (*Hicaz Demir Yolu Komisyon-ı Âlisi*). The same must also be true of the Refugee Commission, the regulations of which identify it as the High Commission for Islamic Refugees (*Muhacirin-i İslâmiye Komisyon-ı Âlisi*), implying that its mission was resettlement of Muslims fleeing from lost provinces and, perhaps, from other lands under non-Muslim control. The importance of such a function for Abd ül-Hamid's religious policy, as for the maintenance of order, requires no comment.[132] The fact that İzzet Paşa, the infamous second secretary of the *Mabeyn*, was a member of both these commissions and also of the High Commission for Finance (*Maliye Komisyon-ı Âlisi*), said to have become a sort of headquarters of the abuses it was supposedly founded to eliminate, provides an added indication of how close these bodies really were to the sultan.[133]

The Aid Fund of the Sublime Porte (*Bab-ı Âli Teshilât Sandığı*), in turn, was one of the economic mechanisms through which the patrimonial sovereign manipulated his official servants. Perhaps the first form of this body was a commission set up in 1890 to administer a fund capitalized by deductions from salaries and used to make loans to officials who had suffered from hardships such as fire and earthquake. One hint of Abd ül-Hamid's attitude toward his bureaucracy and of his possibly special interest in maintaining good will among officials serving in the capital is that while all civil officials were subject to the deductions used to capitalize the fund, loan and repayment transactions could be conducted only in Istanbul.[134] To the extent that the fund became operative, here, surely, was one more disadvantage of assignment to remote localities.

The terms of two sets of regulations drawn up somewhat later for the Aid Fund of the Sublime Porte are somewhat different. The first of these regulations, dating from 1896, provides that the members and clerical assistants of the commission come only from among the personnel of the Council of State and the Ministries of Internal and Foreign Affairs, that only personnel serving at the Porte be eligible for the benefits of the fund, and that it draw its capital from a list of sources beginning with an ostentatious donation of 2,000 liras in gold by the Sultan. In these regulations, the role of the fund was to assure the making of salary payments. In the last set of regulations issued under Abd ül-Hamid, the fund, still administered and capitalized in more or less the same way, again appears as a loan fund.[135]

In any case, the loan fund resembled the other special commissions in performing a function of particular interest to the sultan. For patronage of the fund offered him a means by which to maintain his image as the benevolent protector of his official servants, even if he could not or would not make the salary system fully operative.[136]

Civil Officials Commission

The most important of the special commissions where the relations of Abd ül-Hamid with his officials were concerned, this body played a central role in the establishment of sultanic control over appointment and promotion in the civil bureaucracy.

Although it did not acquire the form shown in Figure VI-1 until 1896, the Civil Officials Commission was the end product of a development going back to the foundation around the year 1871 of a Commission for the Selection of Civil Officials (*İntihab-ı Memurin-i Mülkiye Komisyonu*). The yearbooks vary for several years as to whether this commission was simply "at the Sublime Porte,"[137] part of the staff of the grand vezir,[138] or under the Ministry of the Interior.[139] Regulations drawn up in the early 1880s and revised on a number of subsequent occasions make clear, however, that what appears to have been the same body was then under the supervision of the Ministry of the Interior and had as its mission the selection of certain types of officials to serve in the three lower echelons of the four-tiered local administrative system.[140]

The evolution of this commission seems to have had parallels in other ministries. At least in the Foreign Ministry, as we have seen, there was a Foreign Ministry Council (*Encümen-i Hariciye*) created in 1885 and given supervision of recruitment, among other things, and a more specialized Commission for the Selection of Foreign Ministry Officials, which emerged with the subdivision of the older council around the turn of the century.

In the meantime, efforts to systematize personnel procedures acquired another dimension with the creation of a modern system of personnel records (*sicill-i ahval*). Cevdet Paşa claimed credit for founding this system in 1877, while serving as minister of the interior. He alluded to what was rather obviously its true function in the Hamidian scheme of things by speaking of it, as do a number of other early sources, not as a "register of biographies" (*sicill-i ahval*) but rather as a register of morals or good conduct (*sicill-i ahlâk*).[141] A central commission to supervise this system came into existence at first as an element of the Ministry of the Interior,[142] and branch offices appeared in other departments. By 1891, there were fifty-seven branches, including those mentioned already as parts of the Ministries of Foreign and Internal Affairs.[143]

The Civil Officials Commission, created in 1896, became a central agency to supervise both appointments and the personnel records system. To the extent that the agencies previously in charge of these two functions survived in recognizable form—as the appointments commission of the Ministry of the Interior seemingly did not—they became subordinate elements of the new commission. Its stated purpose made its place in the Hamidian system of controls very clear. It was to process nominations of "civil and financial officials" appointed by imperial decree. As with the earlier commission in the Ministry of the Interior, there were to be cases excluded from the purview of the new body.

The most important of these were described rather vaguely as the higher central officials and the provincial governors general (*menasıb-ı divaniye ricali ve vilayât-ı şahane valileri*, art. 6), whom the sultan would appoint either on his own initiative or on the nomination of the grand vezir. The least important of the excluded cases were defined only by implication: those whose appointments did not require an imperial decree and were thus at the discretion of governors general or other comparable officials. In addition to its role in appointment making, the Civil Officials Commission was also to be responsible for analysis of reports submitted on officials by inspectors and for certain matters related to the trials of officials, although duties of this last kind overlapped powers of the Council of State and were shortly taken away for that reason.[144]

An expression in organizational form of the familiar tendency to create new systems, rationally structured and defined by law, to enlarge the span of control of a supreme power that continued to operate in terms of the traditional, patrimonial discretionalism, the Civil Officials Commission was thus clearly intended to enable Abd ül-Hamid to extend his direct control over personnel actions falling beyond the range of which he could otherwise have maintained cognizance. This characteristic of the commission forms a natural point of transition from discussion of formal organization to that of new developments in regulation and systematization, particularly in the field of personnel policy. But before we go on, it will be worthwhile to summarize the significance of the organizational changes that occurred at the Porte between 1871 and 1908.

The evolution of civil-bureaucratic institutions had in fact progressed in some noteworthy ways. Some changes were little more than regressive features of the sultanic reassertion, to be sure. These include the fate of the Parliament, the effacement of ministerial power, and the overelaboration of mechanisms for control of the press. In contrast, other changes sorted out previously unsolved problems, or further refined institutional mechanisms created in earlier periods. Here we note the completion of the reassignment of the offices of the traditional grand-vezirial chancery—with the Translation Office of the Sublime Porte as a lone but logical exception—from the staff of the foreign minister to that of the grand vezir. Also to mention are the progressive amendments in the organization of the Council of State and in its roles in legislation and administrative justice,

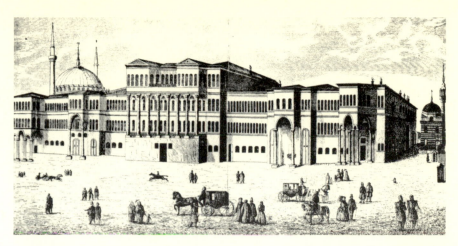

1. Façade of the Sublime Porte on the Side Facing the Golden Horn, an Ottoman View, c. 1867. The "Great Gateway" to the compound enclosing the Porte (Ill. 2) is just beyond the left extremity of the building as shown here. What appears over the left-hand wing of the building as a dome with two flanking minarets belongs to a large mosque in the vicinity, probably Aya Sofya. The small structure to the right is the little mosque known as the *Nallı Mescit*.

2. The *Bab-ı Kebir*, or "Great Gateway," to the Compound Enclosing the Buildings of the Sublime Porte, c. 1830s. The structure at the right is the *Alay Köşkü*, or "Parade Pavilion," built at an angle in the walls enclosing Topkapı Palace so that the sultan or other palace figures could easily observe parades and processions like that shown in the print.

3. Reception of a European Envoy by the Grand Vezir, c. 1790s

4. Interior Scene in the Residence of an Ottoman Dignitary (*Müsellim*) at Alaşehir in Anatolia, c. 1830s

5. Mustafa Reşid Paşa (1800-1858)   6. Keçecizade Fuad Paşa (1815-1869)

7. Mehmed Emin Âli Paşa (1815-1871)   8. Abd ül-Hamid II (1876-1909)

9. Crowd outside the Offices of the Grand Vezir Following the CUP Raid on the Sublime Porte, January 1913. This portico is on the uphill side of the Sublime Porte, the side facing away from the Golden Horn, and belongs to what appears in Ill. 1 as the right-hand wing of the building. This wing still survives and now houses the offices of the governor of Istanbul.

or the limited progress toward elaboration of a central structure for the Ministry of the Interior. Still other changes pointed toward a general modernization of organizational concepts. Lack of coordination among departments was becoming a problem in the Foreign Ministry; but what stood out more, to speak of the Porte as a whole, was the progressive substitution for the old, document-oriented organizational patterns of new ones expressed in terms of modes or areas of interaction between the bureaucracy and the larger society. Of greatest ultimate significance is a change implicit in the variety of regulatory texts which require discussion in consideration of the Council of State, the special commissions, or some of the components of the Ministries of Internal and Foreign Affairs. For what the growing numbers of these documents signify is the gradual closure of the time lag between conceptualization and initial implementation of new organizations and programs, on one hand, and their comprehensive regulation, on the other.

Further Steps toward Regulation and Systematization

Formal promulgation of laws and regulations was, of course, not enough to make a rational-legal order. Responding to this fact, Osman Nuri Bey, author of one of the more perceptive exposés of the Hamidian system to appear in the wake of the Revolution of 1908, gave succinct expression to a central problem in the evaluation of the laws and decrees of the fallen regime:

> Today, if the archives of the Sublime Porte were examined, such comprehensive and detailed decrees would appear on the measures to be taken for the reform and greater prosperity of the state and for the maintenance of order that one would suppose, upon reading them, that Abd ül-Hamid really thought day and night of nothing but assuring the perfect comfort and happiness of the state and its people. Yet, one would also suppose that his orders were not or could not be applied because of the ill will or inability of the authorities at the Porte and in the provinces.

Osman Nuri went on to blame the nonenforcement of these measures, not on the ministers at the Porte, but on the palace and on the practice of direct, secret communication between it and the agencies nominally subordinate to the ministers.[145]

Our survey of the workings of the Hamidian political system

indicates the substance behind these observations and enables us
to appreciate the resentments which this situation engendered
in men such as Osman Nuri. The interference of the palace secretaries and spies, coupled with the way the sultan sought to
dominate and use new organizational and procedural systems,
did a lot to project the traditional repression of bureaucratic initiative into a new era and, in general, to hamper efforts at more
effective administration. Nevertheless, the laws and decrees of
the Hamidian years produced a positive impact in some ways
that Osman Nuri's interpretation overlooks. As is already clear,
the laws and decrees did become at least partially effective where
they served the interests of the sultan. Even where they did not
become fully operative, they provided a conceptual basis for the
eventual transformation of the existing system and an implicit
critique of its internal contradictions.

A survey of the regulatory measures of the period, beginning
with those on personnel policy and going on to others that regulated and instituted controls over the workings of formal organizational and procedural systems, will yield a fuller idea of how
the laws and decrees of which Osman Nuri spoke served the interests of Abd ül-Hamid and, at the same time, contributed to
the longer-range development of the administrative tradition.
Again, as in the last chapter, it is appropriate to recall that such a
survey throws light not just on the condition of the Sublime
Porte, but also on the general state of the civil bureaucracy.

Legal Outlines of a Rational Personnel Policy

During this period, routine questions of official discipline
gradually ceased to receive as much attention as they did in the
personnel policy of the Tanzimat, and concern shifted to more
basic issues. Indeed, since Abd ül-Hamid's neopatrimonialism
and the liberalism of the constitutionalists shared the premise
that the bureaucracy needed to be brought under a kind of political control that had not existed during the Tanzimat, it is not
surprising that Abd ül-Hamid and his advisors contributed to
the collective restructuring of the civil bureaucracy more significantly than anyone since Mahmud II. It was during this
period that the general rules of official service, promised in the
Reform Decree of 1856, began to become law in significant
quantity; and many of these measures proved worthy of retention or elaboration after 1908. A survey of the civil-bureaucratic

personnel measures of the Hamidian years, including the system for keeping personnel records, the laws on promotion and retirement of civil officials, and those on the compensation system, quickly reveals their significance for the development of the bureaucratic tradition.

To govern the workings of the personnel records system, there were two sets of instructions, the first issued in 1879, the second in 1887.[146] These instructions began by dividing the civil officials of the empire into two imprecisely defined categories. The first consisted of "men of influence" (*sahib-i rey*), holding posts such as ministries, presidencies of councils or courts, or headships of departments. The second consisted of all other civil officials. Probably deriving from the differences in the procedures that Abd ül-Hamid intended to follow in appointment of officials of these two types, this distinction also had an effect on the records-keeping system. Records on officials of the first class were to be submitted directly to the central Personnel Records Commission at the Porte, where they would be examined, verified as necessary, and then registered in special registers. The files of officials of the second class would first be registered—or sometimes, in fact, conserved in the original—in the branches of the personnel records system set up in the various ministries and provinces. Those records would only subsequently go on to the central commission for registration and addition to its registers. The personnel files in the Foreign Ministry archives in Istanbul, and the almost two hundred large registers remaining in the prime ministers' archives from the central commission, give massive evidence of the generally faithful observance of these stipulations.

The instructions also specified the form of the questionnaire that was to be the basic document in each file. This questionnaire was a large sheet of paper divided into boxes. The column of boxes on the right contained the printed questions which the respondent was to answer in the wider boxes running down the middle of the sheet. To the left was another column of boxes intended for "observations" by the individual's superiors. The questions called for the names of the respondent and his father; the rank and position of the father, if an official; the family name if the respondent belonged to a well-known family (*sülâle*); the respondent's date of birth; an account of his education, with certified copies of his diplomas to be attached; a listing of the languages he knew, with self-rating as to whether he was capable of using the written form of the language for official purposes (*kitabet etmek*) or merely of reading or speaking the language; and a listing of any literary works he had written, with a note as to whether they were published or not. Following all this, there was to be a chronological account of the respondent's official service. This was to include dated entries for changes in salary or other forms of compensation as well as for changes of position. Periods out of office were to be listed, with the cause of the loss of the previous position and note of whether or not the respondent received an unemployment stipend (*mazuliyet maaşı*). Those who had worked in private business were to include that experience, as well. Each respondent was to note, appending all relevant documents, whether he had ever been subject to complaint or prosecution and, if the latter, what the outcome was. He was then to sign and seal his questionnaire.[147]

The regulations on the personnel records system further specified that utmost care was to be taken, as the records accumulated, to verify and register the information they contained. There were to be no erasures in the registers, and the officials authorized to make corrections were to sign them. The Personnel Records Commission was to undertake any correspondence necessary to verify doubtful points, a responsibility that sometimes generated twenty or more letters on a single file.[148] So that the files could be kept up to date, the Personnel Records Commission and its branches were also to receive notice of all personnel actions.[149]

This system was, of course, not without its flaws. So great was the concern for supervision of the records that signatures of up to nine officials sometimes appear below even banal additions to a dossier, whether there are deletions or not. In addition, the procedure for keeping the files current was never adequate for recording events—such as publication of additional literary works, or death—that did not result from initiatives taken within the bureaucracy. Where officials were dismissed or prosecuted for some offense, as occasionally happened, their records usually degenerated into an incomprehensible snarl.[150] Ottoman officials also tended to gloss over the reasons for their loss of position;[151] their superiors, to reduce their evaluative comments to a string of the laudatory adjectives that typically conclude the entries in old-fashioned, Ottoman biographical compendia.

Yet the importance of the personnel records is indisputable. Nothing like them had ever existed before. Operating in facilities so wretched that they could hardly even protect their records from the elements, and ultimately saddled with such other duties as the publication of the official yearbooks,[152] the officials of the Porte who were chiefly responsible for the personnel records system nonetheless produced one of the largest and most uniform collections of biographical data ever created in the Islamic Middle East. The value attributed to this system at the time is reflected in the volume of documentation concerning it in the Yıldız Palace Archives, as well as in the progressive creation of analogous systems for categories of officials not covered by the original one.[153]

For a more precise appreciation of the role of the personnel records in the making of personnel decisions, we must, however, consider another complex of regulatory acts that had as their ostensible purpose a comprehensive regulation of conditions of civil-bureaucratic recruitment and service. While measures of this type ultimately proliferated, the basic text in this field is a Decree on the Promotion and Retirement of Civil Officials (*Memurin-i Mülkiye Terakki ve Tekaüd Kararnamesi*), first promulgated in 1881. That version was superseded by another of 1884, of which various articles were amended on a number of subsequent occasions.[154]

This decree was, in fact, a curious document. It was divided into two sections, of which the first dealt summarily with conditions of appointment and promotion, while the second dealt with the creation of a modern kind of Retirement Fund (*Tekaüd Sandığı*), to be financed by deductions from salaries. Given the dual character of the decree, it will be profitable to consider the first section together with other measures of the period on related subjects and to discuss the second section later, in connection with other provisions on compensation systems.

The first section of the decree began by specifying basic requirements about the age, nationality, and education of applicants for appointment. Except in special cases, they were to be Ottoman subjects, aged at least twenty, or sixteen in the case of unsalaried apprentices (*mülâzım*), and they were either to present their diplomas or be examined by a board of officials. Part two of this section spelled out basic requirements of official discipline and concluded with articles explaining the personnel records system and forbidding ministers and governors general to appoint their relatives to serve under themselves. Part three of the first section went on to specify procedures for promotion. All officials, except graduates of the School of Civil Administration, were to begin at the lowest grade in their respective services and accomplish a specified amount of time in grade prior to promotion. The only exceptions were to be for provincial governors general, ambassadors, and secretaries of embassy—cases in which the sultan presumably intended to retain a discretional appointment-making power for himself. The various positions, the decree continued, were to be grouped in ranked classes, among which officials would have to work their way up. Parts four and five of the first section went on to specify the causes for which an official might be dismissed from his office and the conditions of eligibility for an unemployment stipend (*mazuliyet maaşı*), and then to refer to the regulations and laws that specified procedures to be followed when officials were suspected of offenses.

One of the laws promised in Abd ül-Hamid's speech from the throne at the opening of the first Ottoman Parliament, this decree, incompletely elaborated though many of its provisions were, was the closest the Ottomans would come before the collapse of the empire to the production of a single, comprehensive "civil service law." Through the promulgation of other laws and regulations, the development of a rational system of personnel administration nonetheless continued. Such measures covered a considerable range of topics. Among them, perhaps the most basic in importance were the regulations issued for the various boards and commissions for the selection of officials and those pertaining to educational qualifications for appointment.

In the first of these categories, instructions or regulations were issued in this period, as we have noted, for at least two of the appointment-making bodies then created: the Commission for the Selection of Officials in the Ministry of the Interior and the Civil Officials Commission, set up in 1896 to take charge of civil-bureaucratic appointments more generally. Both documents excluded certain categories of appointments from the cognizance of these commissions, but went on to prescribe orderly procedures to be followed within the zones of competence that remained.

The various instructions and regulations for the first of these two bodies, for example, went into considerable detail about how it was to conduct its business, keep its records, and prepare the documentation on those it nominated for appointment. Similarly, the regulations set out the qualifications for appointment, posing specific requirements for the cleanness of the candidate's previous record, his educational qualifications, and the accomplishment of specific amounts of time at one level of service prior to promotion to the next. The positions for which this commission was to select nominees were those of secretary (*tahrirat müdürü*) at the second highest local administrative echelon (*liva*, *sancak*) and chief administrative officer (*kaymakam*, *müdür*) at the next to lowest (*kaza*) and lowest (*nahiye*).[155]

The regulations of 1896 for the central Civil Officials Commission were less specific about some of these details. This is very likely a reflection of the broader competence of the new body, which, as may be recalled, was responsible for all civil-bureaucratic appointments that required an imperial decree and were not made directly at the initiative of the sultan or grand vezir. Its regulations nonetheless required that the Civil Officials Commission set up a fixed pattern of procedure. Appointments were to be proposed by the ministries within which they fell (presumably by the appointment boards of those ministries), then forwarded, after investigation of the candidates' dossiers, from the Civil Officials Commission to the palace, and finally ordered by imperial decree.[156]

Along with the copious evidence on patrimonial discretionalism and caprice in Abd ül-Hamid's use of bureaucratic patronage, there is evidence to indicate that these appointment-making systems did become operative. There is nothing contradictory about this, for the mission of the commissions was to select candidates who conformed to the sultan's expectations and whom the latter would then appoint as he saw fit. The opposition that liberals at times directed against the measures for systematizing appointments is surely best understood as a response to this kind of palace domination of recruitment and promotion.[157] In any case, the entries in the personnel records, from the creation of the Civil Officials Commission onward, reflect the more or less faithful application of its regulations.[158] Tahsin Paşa, long-time first secretary of the *Mabeyn*, also provides corroborating evidence on this point. He tells, for example, how the appointment commission would send its nominations to the palace, together with copies of the personnel dossiers on the nominees. Abd ül-Hamid would have the official biographies read to him and was especially keen to determine whether the nominees were graduates of the School of Civil Administration (*Mülkiye Mektebi*). Commenting to Tahsin on his role in the improvement of that school, Abd ül-Hamid once observed with pride that while persons of uncertain qualifications and affiliations had formerly been appointed to provincial posts, now only graduates of the school were.[159] This was an exaggeration. Yet, the interest of the sultan in improving the quality of administrative personnel and tightening his control over appointments is clear, as is the way in which the appointment commissions served him in these efforts.

Abd ül-Hamid's emphasis on the School of Civil Administration also underscores the importance of developments in education for the overall evolution of personnel policy. The School of Civil Administration was Abd ül-Hamid's pet educational institution; but this was a period of many important gains, including major extension of the systems of lower-level schools and the opening of such important higher-level institutions as the empire's first modern law school (*Hukuk Mektebi*, 1878) and university (*Dar ül-Fünun*, 1900).[160] In these developments, the close equivalency in Ottoman minds between education and government service found expression in a number of new ways.

Where the School of Civil Administration is concerned, what is most interesting in this connection is the clear preference given its graduates. The regulations of the school, which Abd ül-Hamid claimed to have dictated himself,[161] specified the eligibility of its alumni for appointment to a list of offices, including those of secretary of embassy, consul, and *kaymakam* or chief administrative officer at the next to lowest echelon of the local administration (*kaza*). These provisions were actually printed on the diplomas that the school issued its graduates. In an interesting reworking of the traditional terminology for brevets of appointment, the highest grade of these diplomas was termed *mülâzemet rüusü*. Literally suggesting the brevet (*rüus*) of a supernumerary (*mülâzım*), this was then translated into French as *baccalauréat*.[162]

There does not appear to have been any other school under Abd ül-Hamid of which the graduates had access to office on such privileged terms. Yet the state could not fill every office named in the regulations of the *Mülkiye* with one of its graduates

and had to make allowances for those who had won their qualifications in other schools or by experience. A number of measures
appeared on cases of such types. What is most striking about
these measures is the gradual but clearly discernible upgrading
of requirements. Ultimately, at least a secondary (*idadiye*) education was demanded from the chief administrative officers at
even the lowest of the four levels of the local administration
(*nahiye*), and an examination system was created for many types
of appointees. This system surely did not operate with full vigor.
Even in the best-ordered Western bureaucracies of the era, with
much more strongly developed educational systems to back
them up, examination systems did not always function rigor-
ously. Yet the documentation indicates that demand for promotion by examination was sufficient to permit the stiffening of the
formal requirements until they included much of the curriculum of the School of Civil Administration and a broad range
of information about governmental organization and law.[163]

Thus, while the Decree of 1884 on Promotion and Retirement
of Civil Officials was in many ways no more than a rudimentary
sketch for a general systematization of personnel policy, a variety of measures on related issues, particularly on the operations
of the selection boards and on the educational requirements for
appointment, helped to fill in needed details. More than that,
these measures became operative, at least to a degree, precisely
because they served the sultan in his efforts to dominate the bureaucracy.

Ultimately, of course, even the best-conceived personnel policy could not function effectively without a rational and operative compensation system to support it. The intractability of the
economic problems of the times, and the way in which it suited
Abd ül-Hamid to play on them, inhibited the development of
this dimension of personnel policy. Even here, however, there
are reforms, and to a degree practical improvements, to cite.

Reforms in this field began with a decree of 1880 on official
salaries. One of many attempts to economize by cutting salaries,
and presumably also a product of the financial maneuverings
leading up to the creation of the foreign-dominated Public Debt
Administration, this was perhaps the closest approach in this period to the general classification of official positions demanded
in the "Decree on the Promotion and Retirement of Civil Officials."[164] The decree on salaries ordered a twenty percent cut,

supposed to be compensated for by a contemporary reform of the coinage,[165] following which salaries were to be paid in sound money rather than the debased coin in use up to that time. The decree then went on to offer a comprehensive classification of bureaucratic positions, at least outside the palace, with specification of the salaries for the positions in each class.

The extent to which such a schematization could prevail against the realities of the economic situation and of the resurgent sultanic patrimonialism is well indicated by the fact that no more seems to have been heard of this kind of regulation, except for an amendment of 1884,[166] although there were additional salary cuts at later dates. At least in the civil bureaucracy, this was, however, the first attempt to elaborate something like the comprehensive salary table or *barem* (from the French *barème*) later created under the Republic.

In addition, there were subsequent attempts to regulate or refine various ancillary aspects of the compensation system. These included measures on the procedures for the assignment of unemployment stipends (*mazuliyet maaşı*)[167] and of travel pay and per diem.[168] Most important, however, was the creation under section two of the "Decree on the Promotion and Retirement of Civil Officials" of a modern system of retirement pensions.

The basic concept of this system was that anyone who served in the civil bureaucracy should, after thirty years, be entitled to retire with a pension determined on the basis of his salary over a given period and financed by a five percent salary deduction. The decree and its many subsequent amendments, all of which pertain to the pension system, also included a tangle of intricacies about persons who belonged to one branch of government service but served in another, those whose careers predated the creation of the system, retirement for reasons of illness, the entitlements of surviving dependents, the organization and administration of the fund, and the investment of its capital.

Like so many other measures, this pension system appears to have become operative to at least some degree but to have led a problem-ridden existence. The continued amendment of the articles of the decree is, in its way, a sign of the accumulation of experience in their implementation. Perhaps more ambiguously, the importance of the system found tangible expression in the growth of a separate *nezaret* to administer it. This was surely

a "supervisorship" rather than a "ministry," although the organization in question was quite large by 1908.[169] Whether this
size boded good or ill for the administration of the fund is unclear, but there were other developments that clearly meant no
good. It was not long, for example, before the Ministry of Finance was borrowing from the Retirement Fund.[170] The reasons
for this are none too clear, but the mere occurrence hints that
the salary deductions for the retirement fund were becoming no
more than another tax on the bureaucracy. This supposition
seems to find confirmation in the recollections of Aşçıdede Halil
İbrahim, whose experiences at earlier points in his lengthy
career have enlightened us on so many occasions. At a time
when he had passed retirement age "by leagues" (*fersah geçmişse
de*), he was still making his way to his office, half blind, bent over
his cane, and trusting in the dervish saints (*erenler*). It was well
known, he said, that the Retirement Fund could not pay its pensions.[171]

In the case of the pension fund, as in other respects, the attempt to create a modern system of official compensation indicated that the drive for systematization had exceeded what the
practical administrative capabilities and material resources of
the state could support. To survey the field of personnel policy
more generally, however, the last decades of the nineteenth century witnessed noteworthy developments. In addition to the
measures pertaining to compensation systems, these included
the creation of a modern system of personnel records and the
first steps toward a comprehensive regulation of conditions of
recruitment and promotion in the civil bureaucracy. For Abd
ül-Hamid, measures such as these could be no more than means
to the end of consolidating his control over an enlarged but
again servile bureaucracy. Like the lingering inequalities in conditions of service as encountered by the various bureaucratic
subgroups described in the last chapter, this primacy of sultanic
will over law points to the obvious limits of regularity in official
personnel policy during this period. Yet, even under the Hamidian neopatrimonialism, and partly to serve its ends, the concern
for rationality had gained new ground.

Steps toward Regulation and Control in Other Fields

That these developments in official personnel policy were part
of a larger pattern is already apparent from the growing extent
to which regulatory acts assume a place among the sources from

which we trace the evolution of the formal organizational apparatus of the Porte in this period. This fact means that we have
already introduced many of the organic regulatory documents
of these years and have begun to comment on the new trends in
organizational thinking that they imply. It remains only to add
certain points on the extent and limits of this kind of regulatory
activity, the qualitative change that it implied, and the way this
change expressed concern for the reinstitution of controls over
the actual operations of the bureaucracy.

One basic point deserving brief mention is that the drive for
overall regulation of the politico-bureaucratic system was in
some respects even stronger than the regulations that we have
specifically cited would indicate. Even after the parliamentary
episode, there were continuing efforts to produce the broad
range of administrative law promised in the constitution of
1876. Along with the innovations in personnel policy, there
were, for example, comprehensive regulations enacted for a
number of major agencies outside the Porte: the two Houses of
Parliament, and the Ministries of Justice, Finance, Public Works,
and Pious Foundations.[172] For the major agencies of the Porte,
with the exception of the Council of State and the special commissions, there seems to have been nothing of comparable
scope; but this was not for want of trying in certain quarters.

There was, for example, at least one ambitious attempt, undated but probably attributable to the years 1871-1878, to draw
up a comprehensive set of regulations for the Foreign Ministry.[173] That there were similar efforts to regulate the most important civil-bureaucratic institutions is also clear from a draft
law, dating from the brief grand vezirate of Hayr ül-Din Paşa
(1878-1879), on the duties of the various ministers and of the
Council of Ministers. Embodying the principle of collective responsibility, advocacy of which provoked Hayr ül-Din's fall, and
assigning vast but minutely defined responsibilities to the grand
vezir and his colleagues, this document assumed a resurrection
of the Parliament and a real limitation of the sultan's prerogatives.[174] The continuing struggle between Abd ül-Hamid and
the liberals, on into the 1880s, over the character of the grand
vezirate suggests that this ill-starred proposal must not have
been the only one of its kind. In any event, it is clear that the
demand for regularization was greater, at least in some circles,
than the measures actually promulgated would indicate.

This fact has to be weighed, of course, against the limits within which organizational and procedural patterns actually did undergo reform in this period. The clearest indication of these limits is in the vital field of finance, where any would-be reformers were still far from having sufficient power or knowledge to solve some of their most fundamental problems. As the empire slid into bankruptcy, circumstances did not help. Steps toward financial rationalization did occur, but their significance for the civil bureaucracy and the administrative tradition in general was often oblique or ironic.

Some of the efforts at fiscal rationalization grew out of the constitutional movement and Ottoman initiatives to forestall the official avowal of bankruptcy. To be noted here are the powers that the constitution gave the Chamber of Deputies over budgeting and other financial matters, the regulations of the Ministry of Finance, the attempt to create an independent Board of Audit (*Divan-ı Muhasebat*), and the attempt of 1880 at comprehensive systematization of official salaries.[175] Official bankruptcy led, in turn, to the establishment of the foreign-dominated Public Debt Administration, set up in 1881. Its powers a major breach of Ottoman sovereignty, the administration assumed control of six major revenues of the empire, applying them to the service of the foreign debt. Except insofar as they figured among the bondholders, as some did, Ottoman officials could have benefited from this agency only through the provisions requiring division of surplus revenues with the imperial government, or through observation of a new example of European-style administrative efficiency. However grudging Ottomans may have been to admit it, the debt administration must have exerted some such demonstration effect. For it ultimately employed several thousand Ottoman subjects, paying them regularly. The number of revenues the organization collected also increased over time for various reasons, partly because the Ottoman government elected on occasion to use the debt administration as its own collection agent.[176]

To translate the lessons that could be learned from the Public Debt Administration into Ottoman practice, however, was no easy matter. Not only did the debt administration control a large and growing share of the revenues, but Abd ül-Hamid created a split in what remained of the Ottoman economy. For himself, he developed a rationally run, personal financial empire within the empire. This was based on a vastly extended network of crown estates (*çiftlikât-ı hümayun*)—the reassertion of the sultan's claims to ownership of the land is another neopatrimonial motif—and was administered through the Privy Treasury (*Hazine-i Hassa*).[177] Only what was left of government finance fell within the purview of the minister of finance; but since there was still no progress toward centralized control of receipts and expenditures, his authority was negligible. The effect of this situation on the government budgets, which should have been among the most important instruments of rationalization and control, is self-evident (cf. the Appendix).[178] How this state of affairs affected individual officials is already clear from discussion of the compensation system.

Financial problems thus continued to figure as an almost insurmountable obstacle in the way of regulatory efforts. What makes this more unfortunate is that the drive for rationalization and control was gaining in other respects, not only in scope but also in sophistication. To be sure, some of the regulatory acts of the period continued to perpetuate traditionalistic organizational concepts[179] or to be incomplete or defective in composition.[180] But this was less typical than in the past. Good examples of the qualitative improvements in the regulatory acts of this period, and particularly of the growing emphasis on monitoring the actual performance of the bureaucracy, appear in two sets of documents, one pertaining to the consular service, the other to the field of official communications.

Including organic regulations for the service, a set of instructions detailing consular responsibilities, tables listing the fees to be collected for various transactions, and a ruling on leaves, the consular regulations display an innovative character which becomes quite clear if we recall the traditional scribes or the consular and diplomatic officials of Selim III. The consul envisioned in these documents was a salaried professional and either an alumnus of the School of Civil Administration or a graduate of another school who had proven his qualifications by examination. He did not engage in trade. He performed specified services for a defined geographical area and was subject to periodic inspection. He knew how to perform the social and ceremonial obligations of his post correctly and tactfully and to conduct his official business and correspondence, not only according to Ottoman conventions, but also according to those spelled out in de Clerq's *Guide des consulats*.[181] The consul kept his files in pre-scribed order and reported periodically to the ministry on specific matters relating to commerce and public hygiene. Most importantly, he provided an intricately detailed list of services to Ottoman subjects in his district. These services included aid to and repatriation of the indigent, a lengthy list of functions hav-ing to do with shipping, and performance of all the transac-tions—delivery of passports and visas, registration of births, marriages, deaths, and so forth—required under the Ottoman laws on population registration.[182]

It does not require a great speculative leap to conclude that this image of the consular official was made in Europe, and measurement against these standards of most of the Ottoman consuls in the Aegean region, around the Black Sea, or in Iran would probably have produced a sad contrast. To judge from the complaints of a man who was clearly one of the better con-sular officials of the time, it was also true that Abd ül-Hamid had a hand in preventing the implementation of these measures by turning the chief function of the consuls, as of the diplomats, into "police surveillance" of the Ottoman subjects in their dis-tricts.[183] Yet, enough correspondence passed between the Foreign Ministry and the consulates over matters relating to these regulations to indicate that they did have some effect.[184] Indeed, it is possible to document at least a few cases in which consular officials lost their positions for abuse of office.[185] To judge from the memoirs of Pâker and Söylemezoğlu, we must conclude, too, that there were beginning to be consular and dip-lomatic agents who set out for their posts with an image of them-selves much like the one projected in the regulations.

A new concept of the bureaucratic professional was emerging, and it was emerging in a context that demanded an unprece-dented degree of control and accountability in the working of bureaucratic institutions. At times, this new emphasis appears in the controls included among the range of functions that officials were to perform for the larger society. This is implicitly true of the system of population registration, which made demands on the consuls as well as on many officials of the Ministry of the In-terior. More importantly for present purposes and for the gen-eral effort at restoration of political balance, there was a new emphasis on controls, taking such forms as inspections and re-ports, over the way officials behaved and over the conduct of administrative business. Like some of the new institutions in the field of personnel policy, the consulates could be used in ways that had little justification except in terms of an exaggerated concern for maintenance of the sultan's dominance. But this kind of diversion could not occur without inviting attack from those who responded to the spirit of the new measures.

Similar implications also emerge from the reforms of this period in the field of official communications. Whatever the extent of bureaucratic featherbedding and underemployment, the volume of paperwork continued to grow and to be perceived as unmanageable. Extreme centralization did nothing to diminish this problem; no more did the lack of any idea that certain types of documentation were of temporary utility and ought not to be retained permanently in the files. The number and scale of the archival collections remaining from these years acquaint every researcher with these facts.

Contemporary officials responded to such problems in part through various attempts at improvement in records management. The organizational evolution of the various records offices and archives is one sign of this effort. There was also a variety of procedural changes, including extension of the use of standardized forms for certain types of transactions, adoption of systems for the numbering of documents,[186] and substitution of filing in dossiers for the old practices of registering documents in chronological order or storing them in sacks.[187] One set of regulations prescribed procedures, resembling some of those in the consular regulations, by which embassies should register and secure their correspondence.[188] Another set demanded monthly examination of the registers of the Records Office of the Porte, the sending out of inquiries about documents that had not been returned from other offices on time, and the reporting to the grand vezir of officials or offices that did not respond to these inquiries within a set interval.[189]

Other measures indicate the connection between concern for the control of official paperwork and the growing centralization of administration. An order of 1882, for example, said that since many of the documents issued by the Office of the Imperial Divan were prepared in response to imperial decrees, they need no longer be submitted for the seal of the grand vezir. Since the types of documents named had mostly to do with appointments, this order is clearly a sign of the loss of patronage by the grand vezir and its reconcentration in the hands of the sultan.[190] Yet centralization did not necessarily imply that the sultan did not want ideas and recommendations from lower echelons. On more than one occasion, orders went out to all offices and ministries to the effect that they were not to refer problems to higher echelons without including supporting documentation and recommendations for solutions.[191] Under Abd ül-Hamid, as in the traditional system, officials had reason not to be forward in expression of their opinions; but he, like some of his ancestors, demanded that they be so, anyway.

As the procedures for document control became more rigorous, special attention also had to be given to the registration and promulgation of laws, regulations, treaties, and other such acts. The principal change of the period in this regard occurred with a decree of July 1872, which we have already mentioned as defining the roles of the Council of State and the Council of Ministers in the legislative process. The same decree provided, in addition, that each new law would become executory at a date specified in the law or, in want of specification, fifteen days following publication of the law in the official newspapers of the capital (*Takvim-i Vekayi*) and of the provinces. In provinces that had no such newspapers, the fifteen days would be counted from the public proclamation of the law.[192] In fact, one of the saddest victories of despotism under Abd ül-Hamid was that the official newspaper of the capital fell victim to the censor, supposedly for nothing more than a typesetter's error, while publication of the volumes of legal acts, the *Düstur*, also lapsed for most of the reign. Care was still taken to maintain the traditional system for registration of laws and diplomatic agreements in the Office of the Imperial Divan.[193] Similarly, legal acts continued to appear in special printings or in the newspapers that did remain in circulation. But regular publication of the official newspaper of the central government or of the legal volumes would only resume under the Young Turks.[194]

Where the connection between reform in the field of official communications and the increasing emphasis on control and monitoring of bureaucratic performance ultimately became clearest was in the so-called "statistical system." This appears to have been founded in 1879 on the recommendation of Küçük Said Paşa, then prime minister (*baş vekil*), as a means by which to provide the central administration with sound information on which to base policy.[195] An ambitious set of regulations ordered the formation in various local and central agencies of special bodies to gather the statistical information. The regulations went on to define the procedures by which the information should be aggregated as it passed to higher echelons, made available to the interested ministries in Istanbul, and published. The system was an elaborate one; yet the publication of official economic statistics, beginning in the 1880s, indicates that it produced tangible results.[196]

The uses of this statistical system for control of the civil bureaucracy became obvious with the creation in 1891 of the Statistical Council of the Sublime Porte, attached to the Council of State. Some details are not clear, but this seems to have amounted to a revised version of the earlier system. Its regulations specifically charged this Statistical Council with collecting information on everything that happened in the provinces— births, deaths, the presence of foreigners, crime, the building of roads and schools, the numbers of documents sent and received—"down to the smallest detail." The governors general (*vali*) of the provinces, and also the governors (*mutasarrıf*) of *sancak*s that did not come under the authority of a governor general, were to submit this information to Istanbul in annual reports. Whenever such an official was transferred, a special report of the same type was to be submitted. One copy of it would go to the palace, where it would presumably serve as a report on the official's performance. There were again articles in the regulations to specify how statistical information should be collected at the lower echelons of the local administration, how information of some of the same types should be collected through the Foreign Ministry from the embassies, and how the information gathered should be published.[197]

A set of reports submitted from the embassies in 1905 provides a measure of the practical workings of this system. The reports typically took the form of a tabulation of the number of documents received and dispatched during a given period of time, sometimes with breakdowns as to the source or destination of the documents or the matters with which they dealt. Such statistics may be criticized as a crude measure, at best, of the volume of business handled or the efficiency of the agency in question. Yet the compilation of this kind of statistics appears to conform to the practice of the Western bureaucracies of the day,[198] and the resulting data are not totally useless. In this case, the reports varied widely, those of some of the less professional ambassadors being slovenly or incomplete enough to elicit criticism from the Statistical Commission. The better reports, in contrast, were quite informative. These included one from the embassy in Berlin, beginning with an account of the "constant" correspondence between that post and the palace, or the report of Galip Kemali Söylemezoğlu, by then first secretary in Bucharest. He produced a handsome tabular summary of the correspondence of that legation, not just for one year but for all nine since the appointment of the then minister, Kâzım Bey.[199]

As documentation of such types confirms, developments of this period in the conceptualization of other types of organizational and procedural patterns paralleled and amplified those that had reshaped the ostensible personnel policy of the civil bureaucracy. Not only was there significant progress toward organic regulation of bureaucratic structures—despite frustrated aspirations and plans that never reached the point of enactment—but a desire for reactivation and reassertion of the bureaucracy, a desire already discernible by the end of the eighteenth century, had also begun to find fulfillment in the displacement of old concepts of official roles and procedures by new ones emphasizing service and control. As long as the Hamidian system survived, the new concepts of organization and procedure would remain subject to its deforming influence. The consequences of the financial situation of the government were equally grave and even harder to deal with. Yet the increasing prominence of new ideas about how the administrative system should operate indicated a movement toward closer approximation of the rational-legal ideal. Some measures, such as the consular instructions or the use of "statistical" data to monitor official performance, even began to anticipate the emphasis on efficiency that, in the thinking of some students of the most advanced of modern bureaucratic systems, begins to assume primacy over the Weberian emphasis on law.[200] If the Hamidian palace system were to be eliminated, surely the scope for such developments would be vastly increased.

CONCLUSION

Between 1871 and 1908, then, the Sublime Porte achieved a new degree of organizational elaboration and articulation. The general outlines of a rational personnel policy were adopted for the

entire civil bureaucracy and in some respects made operative.
Increasingly modern conceptions of official roles and procedures also became current, along with a new concern to monitor
the actual performance of the bureaucracy. Most importantly,
this effort to build controls into the bureaucratic system was part
of a larger concern for the restoration in some form of the political equilibrium that had been so profoundly disturbed during
the Tanzimat.

As concerns the long-term development of the politico-
bureaucratic tradition, it was chiefly in this last respect—finance
aside—that this period was one of frustration and conflict. For
the failure of the constitutional movement and the creation of
the Hamidian machine, although a *tour de force*, was in too many
ways a journey into the past. As long as this machine remained
operative, its workings vitiated the practical improvements that
might otherwise have been expected from the reforms of the
period and compounded, rather than diminished, the problems
of maintaining the imperial system.

There was, however, to be one more major effort to solve all
these problems. Since this attempt forms another phase in the
history of the opposition intelligentsia, the first phase of which
we have already discussed in connection with the Young Ottomans and the constitutional movement, it is appropriate in concluding this chapter to say something about how the Hamidian
system helped to call forth this effort.

So successful was Abd ül-Hamid at first in creating his political
system and in neutralizing those who opposed him that the history of the opposition was very nearly discontinuous from soon
after the termination of the parliamentary experiment until the
end of the 1880s.[201] It was not possible, however, to enroll larger
and larger numbers in official cadres, demanding more and
more from them in the way of education, and at the same time
expect them to abjure the ideas of culture heroes such as Namık
Kemal or Ziya Paşa, or to remain undisturbed by the absurdities
of the domestic order or the contradictions between it and the
world outside. When the diverse elements of what would become known as the Young Turk movement began to emerge,
they did so in ways that took up the Young Ottoman legacy but
also signified a broadening of both the social basis of the opposition and its intellectual horizons.[202]

Reflecting the growth of pressure for enlargement of the

scope of political participation, the leadership of the new opposition emerged from not one but several social settings. Spreading at first among the cadets of the military schools and then among the students of the School of Civil Administration, the movement gradually won recruits in various branches of official service and outside the bureaucracy, as well. The elements of the empire's populations represented among the early activists of the movement also presented a picture of much greater diversity, in terms of both ethnicity and social status, than had the blue-blooded founders of the Young Ottoman movement. Ultimately, however, it was to be the military officer corps, and within it men whose frustrations were at least partly linked to their relatively obscure origins, who would provide the actual leadership for the Revolution of 1908.

Like their social origins, the ideas of the Young Turks displayed a new diversity. Some of the ideas recalled the Young Ottoman program. For example, the thought of the Young Turks focused on a demand for restoration of the constitution and was still strongly influenced by the liberal political philosophy. The Young Turks—the conventional name for whom is in this sense a misnomer—also resembled the Young Ottomans in continuing to emphasize the Ottomanist supranationalism and the preservation of the empire. But Young Turk political thought also included new elements incompatible with the Young Ottoman legacy. For example, Turkish nationalist tendencies, having emerged in other circles, gradually began to influence the Young Turks, especially after 1908. Other contradictions derived from the fact that the Young Turks' awareness of Western thought was broader and more up to date than that of their ideological predecessors had been for its day. Şerif Mardin, the leading student of the Young Turks' ideas, has found them responding to such diverse intellectual trends as positivism and social Darwinism and to contemporary developments in fields ranging from philosophy to economics, sociology, psychology, and the physical sciences. With this increase in the breadth and currency of awareness of Western ideas—itself a major indicator of the impact of the educational reforms and literary innovations of this and the preceding period—went a growing secularization of world views and, in some quarters at least, a new emphasis on deliberate and thoroughgoing westernization. Simultaneously, the concern, typical of the Young Ottomans, to justify each intended reform in the light of Islamic religious-legal tradition began to disappear.

As of 1908, Young Turk political ideas were still evolving, and there were among those ideas several that implicitly contradicted the general constitutional emphasis of the movement or had otherwise explosive potentials. Since the survival of the cosmopolitan empire was the paramount political concern of the Young Turks, this was most obviously true of Turkish nationalism, especially as it began to influence policy following the revolution.[203] Scarcely less disquieting in its implications for the long-term development of the polity was a tendency to elitism and authoritarianism. This emerged among the Young Turks for several reasons, including military training and the character of some of the Western ideas—such as emphasis on bureaucratic expertise and efficiency—to which the new opposition responded. Coupled with their concern for the preservation of the empire, this tendency led the Young Turks in practice to display a sort of modernized version of the elitism and the "statist-secularist" orientation so long prominent in the tradition of the ruling class, and thus to couple their overt liberalism with yet another kind of neopatrimonial behavior.

Even had it not been for the international situation, ideas and tendencies such as these might have led the Young Turks, once in power, into serious trouble. As matters developed in fact, the international problems assumed precedence in overwhelming the new leadership and precipitating the final collapse of the empire. Before that happened, however, the Young Turks not only overthrew the Hamidian machine, but also carried out reforms that gave unequivocal proof both of the continuing vitality of the ancient administrative tradition and of the momentum that had accumulated behind the newer drive for achievement of a rational-legal order.

Chapter Seven

ONCE MORE TOWARD REDEFINITION
OF THE POLITICAL BALANCE

Tanzimat-ı hayriyenin te'sisinden mebde-i saltanatımıza
kadar geçen müddet zarfında terbiye-i umumiyece hasıl
olan terakki masalih-i umumiyenin usul-ı meşrutiyete rab-
tını ihtar eylemekle kariha-ı zatiyemizden olarak Kanun-ı
Esasi i'lân olunmuş iken ağraz-ı muhtelife menafi-i
umumiye fikrine takaddum ettiğinden kanun-ı mezkûrun
ta'tili hakkında ihtarat tekessür etmiş ve nihayet . . . bu ta'til
devletçe karargir olmuştu. O vakitten şimdiye kadar geçen
ahval ile efkâr ve temayülât-ı umumiyenin neticesinde
memleketin idare-i meşrutaya kabiliyeti meşhud olmasiyle
Kanun-ı Esasi'nin kâffe-i ahkâmı mer'i ül-icra olmasına ve
Meclis-i Meb'usanın her sene ictimaına irademiz taallûk
ederek . . . Kanun-ı Esasi'nin tatbikatına ba'dema hiç bir
vechle ve hiç bir surette asla ve kat'a halel gelmiyeceğini . . .
beyan eyledim.

The progress achieved in the general level of culture in the
period between the inauguration of the Tanzimat and the
beginning of our reign having suggested the conduct of
public affairs according to constitutional principles, we of
our own free inspiration promulgated the constitution.
Nonetheless, as particular interests gained precedence over
the concept of the general good, signs urging suspension of
the constitution multiplied; and finally . . . this suspension
was decided on by the state. As a result [of the evolution]
between that time and the present of circumstances, ideas,
and general inclinations, the readiness of the country for
constitutional government is now evident; and therefore,
our sovereign decree having been issued . . . for the respect
in practice of all the provisions of the constitution and for
the annual meeting of the Chamber of Deputies, I have
proclaimed that no interference shall ever or in any way
come to the application of the constitution.

Decree of Abd ül-Hamid to Grand
Vezir Said Paşa, August, 1908[1]

Eski zamanlarda benim vaziyetime düşen sadr-ı a'zamların kafasını padişahlar, binek taşında kesdirirlerdi. Ben, o haldeyim.

In the old days, the Sultans would have grand vezirs who got into my situation beheaded on their mounting block. That's the fix I'm in.

Grand Vezir İbrahim Hakkı Paşa,
in dismay at the outbreak of
the Italo-Turkish War, 1911[2]

As the character of the Young Turk movement implied, the development of the civil bureaucracy continued after 1908 in the context of a political process of broader scope than had ever before been known. On occasion, with civil-bureaucratic old-timers like Küçük Said or Kâmil Paşa as grand vezir, the Porte was still to be a contender for political dominance. But the civil-bureaucratic elite was now only one group of aspirants to such preeminence. Others included not only the Young Turk leadership, concentrated in the revolutionary Committee of Union and Progress (CUP), but also the restored Parliament and the parties that formed within it, other individuals or groups in the military, and ultimately the sultan once again.[3] The old identity between polity and bureaucracy was now gone forever.

Not only were political and bureaucratic life increasingly differentiated, but both were more plagued with crisis in this period than ever before. On the international scene, first, the distraction that the revolution of 1908 created in Istanbul served as a signal to Austria for the annexation of Bosnia and Herzegovina, to Bulgaria for the proclamation of its independence, and to Greece for the annexation of Crete. With scarcely an interlude, the sequence of troubles continued with the Italo-Turkish War of 1911-1912, the First and Second Balkan Wars, the First World War, and then the Turkish War of Independence. As on earlier occasions, the new period thus opened with an exceptional series of disturbances. This time, they did not end before the six-hundred-year-old empire had finally collapsed.

To make matters worse, the revolution of 1908 also provoked serious tensions in the internal life of the empire. Less than a year after the libertarian outburst of 1908, there occurred, in April 1909, an unsuccessful attempt at a rightist coup. The upshot of this was the deposition of Abd ül-Hamid and the progressive restriction of various of the freedoms proclaimed the preceding year.[4] With the condescension typical of his profession and his social class, Baron Marschall, still German ambassador, likened the freedoms of 1908 to new toys given to children, who had played with them too hard and broken them.[5] April 1909 did leave many Turks with the feeling that restraint was needed. The continuous warfare from 1911 on heightened this feeling, setting up a political drift within the Young Turk leadership toward military dictatorship and thus bringing neopatrimonial tendencies again to the fore in place of liberal principle, even as the empire drifted toward its ultimate catastrophe.

Despite all these problems, internal and external, the revolutionary ardor of 1908 was not immediately or totally lost. As it expressed itself generally in practical policy and intellectual life, this fact has found vivid illustration in the accounts of Bernard Lewis and Niyazi Berkes.[6] Here, we shall see that it also expressed itself with vigor in the evolution of the Sublime Porte and the civil bureaucracy during these years.

To demonstrate this point, we shall look first at the efforts made following the revolution of 1908 to dismantle the Hamidian system. We shall then examine the organizational development of the Sublime Porte through the beginning of World War I, as well as the evolution of personnel policy and other types of procedural patterns. This analysis will make apparent that the more rational innovations of the Hamidian years proved almost as valuable to the reformers of this period as did the achievements of the First Constitutional Period. More than that, our analysis will show that even as political circumstances degenerated, the extent to which rational-legalism became a reality in the workings of the administrative system, as well as an ideal in the minds of officials, continued to grow. In this respect, the gains that ensued, during the brief decade between the Young Turk Revolution and the catastrophic denouement of World War I were, if anything, greater than those observed in earlier and lengthier periods.

DISMANTLING THE HAMIDIAN SYSTEM AND
PURGING THE CIVIL BUREAUCRACY

The dismantling of the Hamidian system and the inauguration of the new regime occurred in two stages. The first came with the revolution of July 1908, the return to implementation of the constitution of 1876, which had never formally been revoked, and the transformation of Abd ül-Hamid into a constitutional monarch. The second followed the attempted counter-coup of April 1909, with the deposition of Abd ül-Hamid, the accession of his half brother Mehmed Reşad, and the closing of Yıldız Palace.

That the new period would be one of fundamental political changes quickly became apparent. In early August 1908, the sultan issued an imperial rescript (*hatt-ı hümayun*) addressed to, and indeed drafted by, the grand vezir, Küçük Said Paşa. Beginning with a doctored view, quoted at the head of this chapter, of the prior history of the constitution, this not only promised that the constitution and all the laws on the conduct of administration would henceforth be scrupulously observed, but also went on to list a fifteen-point program. The topics ranged from the security of the individual in his home to procedures to be observed by the police and the courts, freedom of the press, improvement of the army, review and emendation of existing legislation on the various branches of administration, and the requirement that officials respect the official chain of command. The rescript also returned various responsibilities relating to the appointment and shifting of officials to the grand vezir, giving him the right to nominate all ministers but the *şeyh ül-İslâm* and those of war and the navy. İnal, who assisted Said Paşa in drafting this document and also witnessed its ceremonial, public reading at the Sublime Porte, recounts advising Said Paşa against the exception of appointments to the military ministries. At the public reading, this point raised an uproar that led to Said Paşa's fall and the concession to his successor, Kâmil Paşa, of the right to nominate all ministers except the *şeyh ül-İslâm*.[7]

With the opening of the Parliament in 1908, changes of the type demanded in the rescript began to assume the form of constitutional amendments, of which a number became law in August 1909. Among these was an amendment reducing the sultan to a constitutional monarch, bound to swear before the Parliament that he would uphold the constitution (art. 3). The sultan's prerogatives were defined more carefully than in the past, while his role in the appointment of ministers was reduced to the choice of the grand vezir and the *şeyh ül-İslâm* and approval of the grand vezir's nominees for the other ministries (arts. 7, 27). The sultan's right arbitrarily to exile any individual on grounds of danger to the security of the state disappeared (art. 113). Simultaneously, the principle of the individual and collective responsibility of the ministers to the Parliament gained acknowledgment (art. 30), while other changes strengthened the deputies' right to interpellate the ministers (art. 38) and gave legislative initiative to the deputies and the senators as well as to the ministers (art. 53).[8]

These changes were extensive enough that they have been described as a vigorous affirmation of the "sovereignty of parliament."[9] In fact, if we distinguish practical political power, which the Parliament certainly gained from the amendments, from sovereignty viewed as the legitimate source of such power and the right of control over the exercise of power, then it does not appear that the Young Turks really attempted any definition of the locus of sovereignty, at least no explicit one, in their amendments. Unless they could produce a solution to the nationality problem, this was a question they really could not face; for the only redefinition that could command ultimate credence in the twentieth century would have been the sovereignty, not of the Parliament, but of the people it represented.

Indeed, subsequent events underscored this point. For at a time when its influence in the Parliament had waned, the CUP began pressing for further constitutional changes to strengthen the power of the executive—thus nominally the sultan—once again. By the time the CUP collapsed in 1918, enough such amendments had passed that the sultan reemerged as the most powerful figure in the political system, except that there was no real power left. For the Young Turks, much as for the men of the Tanzimat, the power of the sultan proved an indispensable resource; and the problem of redefining the bases of sovereignty had to await a later revolution, the leaders of which had turned their backs to the imperial ideal and decided for themselves who "the people" were.[10]

The Young Turks were thus unable to solve the most basic constitutional problem left over from the First Constitutional

Period. Nonetheless, they introduced not only the changes conveyed through the constitutional amendments, but also a number of other measures aimed at a fundamental alteration of the political climate. Concentrated in 1908 and 1909, these included a general pardon of political prisoners and persons "appointed" to hold office or reside in remote provinces, abolition of the system of spies and informers, a law on the mode of appointment of palace officials, and subsequent measures on the rehabilitation of political victims of the Hamidian period.[11] With each of these measures, the Young Turks smashed another mechanism of the Hamidian system.

Where the civil bureaucracy is concerned, as in the case of the constitutional amendments, it is not always easy in logical terms to distinguish measures aimed at the destruction of the old regime from those aimed at creation of the new. Most officials of the day would have seen things in a different light, however. For with the measures which we have just discussed went a series of others aimed specifically at the bureaucracy and referred to somewhat euphemistically as "reorganizations" (tensikat). Accompanied for a time by the suppression of Abd ül-Hamid's Civil Officials Commission (Memurin-i Mülkiye Komisyonu),[12] these "reorganizations" were in one sense the start of an ongoing series of changes in bureaucratic organization and personnel policy. First of all, however, the "reorganizations" meant a drastic purge of the bureaucracy and the elimination in particular of the spies and palace creatures.

While this purging of undesirables began in the summer of 1908,[13] the law that gave final form to the process was not passed until 1909. Under its terms, there was to be in each ministry or department a special commission consisting of three members of that department under the chairmanship of a member of the Senate and the vice-chairmanship of a member of the Chamber of Deputies. These commissions were to examine the service records and abilities of each official, determine the number of officials actually needed in the department, and fill all vacancies, giving preference to the best qualified of those who either were serving or had served in that department. Those who were "excluded from the cadres" and judged "fit for employment" (caiz ül-istihdam) were eligible to receive an unemployment stipend on condition that they accepted, unless they had a legitimate excuse, any position subsequently offered to them (art. 7).

They might also elect to accept a lump sum determined on the basis of their prior salary and sever their connections with official service. Those whom the commissions found to be at fault were to be excluded from office without any right of further employment and without either unemployment stipend or indemnification (art. 10). Persons found improperly qualified for official service were to be excluded with a meager gratuity (art. 11); and those over age sixty-five were, with limited exceptions, to be retired (art. 12).[14] The clarification of points not covered in this legislation and the continuing budgetary needs created by the obligation to cover the stipends of former officials—an obligation that could not always be promptly met—gave rise to a continuing series of additional enactments, extending into the last days of the imperial government.[15]

For many officials, the purges marked the end of their careers and thus, in a personal sense, the fundamental meaning of the revolution. There is no doubt that the effects of the law were felt far and wide and had a great deal to do with souring the initial enthusiasm evoked by the overthrow of the Hamidian system. The British ambassador's annual report for 1909 indicates that by then some 27,000 officials had already been removed from the payrolls of the various branches of service, with or without unemployment stipends. The political implications of such an upheaval were underscored by the fact that this number included many "whose only offense was their inutility," by the smallness of the unemployment stipends and indemnities, and by the fact that for those who remained in office, increased regularity in the payment of salaries was offset by simultaneous reductions in amount.[16] Both the real distress and the histrionics to which the purges gave rise emerge clearly in İnal's account of the times. In addition to threats of "strikes," he mentions one man who was killed by bandits following reassignment to a provincial post, and another who lost his mind after similar reassignment and threw himself off a mountain.[17] The Parliament soon found much of its session time taken up with the petitions that dissatisfied victims of the "reorganization" were allowed, under the law of 1909 (art. 15), to address only to it. A supplementary law of 1910 consequently shifted the processing of appeals to a special administrative commission, while a later law simply suspended those of 1909-1910 and forbade further appeals.[18] By then, experience had yielded a kind of oblique tribute to the success of Abd ül-Hamid's patronage policy, for the revolutionaries had only been able to reverse it at the cost of fundamental political harm to themselves.

It was inevitable, however, that the new period begin with some such measure. The fact that the Ministry of Finance had over a thousand officials by 1908, while the Foreign Ministry supposedly had six hundred, marked the reductions as indispensable to the new rulers of a bankrupt empire.[19] The volume of reports that emerged from the attempt to verify the extent of multiple salary holding pointed a similar moral.[20] These were problems that had to be faced before the "reorganizations" could progress to the positive phase that the restoration of constitutional government implied.

THE ORGANIZATIONAL DEVELOPMENT OF THE SUBLIME PORTE TO THE BEGINNING OF WORLD WAR I

One of the fifteen points mentioned in the imperial rescript that Abd ül-Hamid sent to the grand vezir, Küçük Said Paşa, in August 1908 was the review and emendation of existing legislation on the administrative system. Following the fall of Said Paşa, his successor, Kâmil Paşa, sent out a circular to the various ministries and agencies ordering the formation in each of a commission of knowledgeable specialists to review the preexisting laws and regulations, which were "mostly not in keeping with present requirements." Since all aspects of administration, central and provincial, needed to be brought into conformity with the provisions of the constitution, the parliamentary system, and "uniform rules" (*kavaid-i muttaride*), the commissions were to examine those laws and regulations, consult experts, and prepare any necessary new measures in time for them to be examined in the Council of State prior to submission to the Parliament at its opening.[21]

There was hardly time for any such comprehensive review prior to the opening of the Parliament, which occurred only a few months later, in December 1908. Indeed, to judge from the befuddled reaction that Kâmil Paşa's circular roused from Ahmed Tevfik Paşa, who had been foreign minister since 1895, there were obstacles to the rapid reorientation of the civil bureaucracy more fundamental than shortage of time. For Tevfik

Paşa, perhaps because of long habituation to the Hamidian system, did not seem to know anything about the regulations supposed to govern his ministry.[22]

It quickly became apparent, however, that the new period was
to be one of considerable change in the organizational apparatus
of administration. Increasingly, bureaucratic reform was, as the
term *tensikat* implied, becoming a matter of "reorganization" or
further refinement of already existing institutions; and this was
a process to which Ottoman officials applied an unprecedented
degree of sophistication. In the Foreign Ministry, for example,
the next several years witnessed the solicitation for the first time,
so far as can now be determined, of reports on the organization,
functions, and needs, of all departments of the ministry.[23] With
this, the reformers linked their efforts to a review of prior experience. Simultaneously, they made systematic efforts, again for
the first time, it appears, to gather information on the organizational patterns and personnel policies of the corresponding
agencies of all the other governments with which the empire had
diplomatic relations.[24]

In the light of inquiries such as these, or, in the case of the
grand vezirate and Council of Ministers, as a result of interaction with the revived Parliament and other political interests,
bureaucratic institutions began, in fact, to undergo a general
transformation. As they did so, they achieved an unprecedented
degree of regulation. With reform more and more a matter of
reorganization of existing institutions, the lag once so obvious
between the organizational emergence of bureaucratic agencies
and their formal regulation began to be a thing of the past. Indeed, all major agencies of the Porte were either regulated or
regulated anew in these years. As this occurred, the processes of
organizational development, regulation of organizational and
procedural patterns, and installation of control mechanisms also
began to be sufficiently integrated with one another that regulatory documents at last became the principal sources for the
analysis of bureaucratic structure and to a great degree of procedural patterns, as well.

These changes are not solely attributable to the Young Turk
leadership, any more than to the civil-bureaucratic grand vezirs
of 1908. Yet the fact that a disproportionate number of the
major regulatory acts reached the point of promulgation between the coup of January 1913,[25] by which the CUP reestab-

lished its political dominance, and the outbreak of World War I is significant in demonstrating that it was the Young Turk leadership who pushed the regulatory drive of 1908 to fruition. Given the character of the coup and the growing prominence of a neopatrimonial style in the political behavior of the CUP, this is a heartening sign that the Young Turks did not forget the rational-legal ideal, even in the midst of the political and military troubles that were about to overwhelm the empire.

Since this period ended in the collapse of the empire, the best way to appreciate the results of the bureaucratic reorganization will be to examine the Sublime Porte, not at the end of the period, as in previous chapters, but rather as of the beginning of World War I. Where noteworthy developments occurred at later dates, they will receive comment in the text, and the notes will include references to the documentation on later changes of all kinds. Yet the discussion that follows will focus on organizational patterns of 1914. Figure VII-1 provides an overview of these patterns, based chiefly on contemporary regulatory acts and secondarily on the governmental yearbooks. In a way reflecting the alteration and enlargement in scope of the political process, this table differs from the corresponding ones in earlier chapters in showing the Sublime Porte in relation not to the palace, but rather to both the Parliament, to which the ministers were in principle responsible, and the Committee of Union and Progress, then in fact the dominant political power.

The Grand Vezir and His Staff

As in preceding periods, the grand vezirate underwent changes in terms of both the character of the office and the organization of the bureaus attached directly to it. In the months preceding the deposition of Abd ül-Hamid, Küçük Said Paşa (grand vezir, 22 July-5 August 1908) and Kâmil Paşa (6 August 1908-13 February 1909) attempted to resume something like the former power of the office. Both were distinguished by age, experience, and long histories of bad relations with Abd ül-Hamid. Kâmil, in particular, had liberal leanings and links with the British that made him useful to a Committee of Union and Progress, the members of which were still relatively young and inexperienced in politics. For his part, Kâmil attached little political importance to the CUP and doubted its ability to muster a parliamentary majority. His attempt of February 1909 to change the ministers

FIGURE VII-1. ORGANIZATION OF THE CIVIL BUREAUCRACY AND ITS RELATION TO
THE PARLIAMENT AND THE COMMITTEE OF UNION AND PROGRESS, 1914

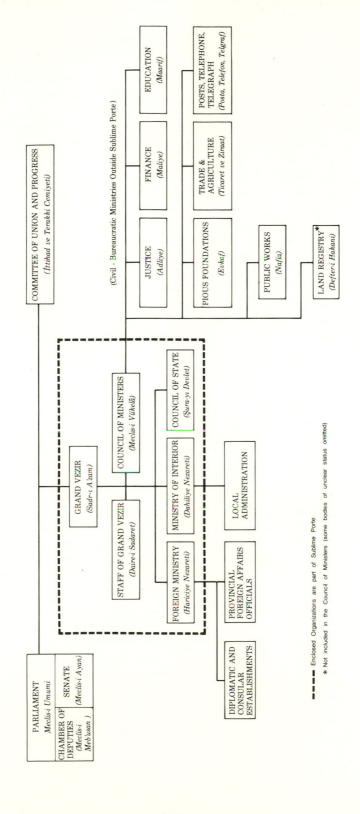

of war and the navy without prior concurrence from either the CUP or the members of his cabinet precipitated a crisis that proved him wrong and resulted in his fall.[26]

From that point until July 1912, the grand vezirate continued to be held by men who had made their careers principally or entirely as civil bureaucrats. During this interval, there were six incumbencies by four different men, of whom the jurist İbrahim Hakkı Paşa and, once again, Küçük Said were the most able.[27] In the wake of the attempted coup of April 1909, however, the CUP began to take a more forward position in politics, installing members in such sensitive positions as the secretaryships of the palace and certain Cabinet posts.[28] The CUP's ability to control the political life of the empire was anything but assured at this time—indeed, it declined sharply. But the rival contenders for dominance were henceforth not in the civil bureaucracy so much as in the Parliament, or in the kind of "military opposition" that appeared in the wake of the 1909 coup with Mahmud Şevket Paşa and his Army of Deliverance or in the Savior Officers' Group formed in May-June 1912 to oppose the CUP and restore "legal government."[29]

The outbreak of the Italo-Turkish and the First and Second Balkan Wars inevitably provoked a further destabilization of the political situation. Signs of this appear in the despairing statement of İbrahim Hakkı Paşa, quoted at the beginning of this chapter, or in Said Paşa's explanation to the sultan in July 1912 of why he had resigned upon *winning* a vote of confidence: "they have confidence in me, but I have no confidence in them."[30]

One result of the growing uncertainty was the appearance of military heroes in the grand vezirate. This began with the appointment on 22 July 1912 of Gazi Ahmed Muhtar Paşa, a senior figure considered to stand above politics.[31] Kâmil Paşa succeeded him once again in October 1912 but was forced to resign the following January, when the CUP, in response to a catastrophic military situation and a drastic ebbing of its political influence, mounted a daring raid on the Sublime Porte. This culminated in a shootout in which the minister of war and several other people were killed,[32] and a new government was formed with Mahmud Şevket Paşa as grand vezir and minister of war. Not a member of the CUP, although in sympathy with its patriotic principles, he was a renowned military commander and one of the most dynamic figures of the period.

In an atmosphere made tense by the loss of virtually all that had been left of the European provinces and by the threat of a counter-coup, Mahmud Şevket was soon murdered, leaving the way open for the CUP to crack down on the opposition and consolidate its position behind the façade of a Cabinet headed by Mehmed Said Halim Paşa, an Egyptian "prince" whose links with the Ottoman official elite and whose qualifications for office did not go much beyond his pedigree and his membership in the CUP.[33] This time the CUP maintained its control sufficiently well that Said Halim Paşa was able to remain in office, though with little power of his own, from June 1913 until February 1917, the longest grand vezirial incumbency of the Young Turk period.

At his resignation in 1917, Said Halim was succeeded for most of the rest of the war by Tal'at Paşa, a member of the so-called Young Turk "Triumvirate" of the war years. Tal'at had begun his career as a provincial postal clerk, achieved prominence through revolutionary activity, served after 1908 as president of the parliamentary party of the CUP, held several ministerial posts, and enlisted during the Balkan Wars, before emerging as grand vezir. He was thus a living symbol both of the far-reaching processes of social mobilization that had grown out of the reform of the bureaucracy, and of the changing forms of political life.[34]

Tal'at's resignation in October 1918 and the armistice that followed shortly thereafter signaled the political collapse of the CUP and cleared the stage for a series of other incumbents. Three were generals, none of whom held office for long.[35] Another, Damad Ferid Paşa, had tenuous links to the civil bureaucracy; but his main qualification for office was his marriage to an Ottoman princess.[36] The last was that hardy perennial of the civil bureaucracy, Ahmed Tevfik Paşa, whose sad honor it was to be the last grand vezir of the empire.[37]

As the grand vezirs of the period succeeded one another, the character of their office changed in a number of important respects. The long-standing civil-bureaucratic hold on the position obviously weakened, and it became subordinate, not so much to the sultan, as to a new range of political powers operating either within or outside the parliamentary system. As this happened, the grand vezirate began, if imperfectly, to take on an institutional character more like that of the premierships of Western, liberal polities. The right of the grand vezir to form his own cabinet had been fought out in 1908 and incorporated in one of the constitutional amendments of 1909, as had the principle of ministerial responsibility. The sultan's choice of grand vezir still had no necessary connection with electoral processes. Yet various of the grand vezirs of the period were members or affiliates of specific parties or factions;[38] and in Tal'at the empire acquired its first grand vezir who could reasonably be regarded as a politician more than a bureaucrat. Significantly, he was the first deputy (*meb'us*) or former deputy to become grand vezir.[39]

Ultimately, however, the degeneration of the political and military situation thwarted this metamorphosis of the grand vezirate into an essentially political office, and some peculiar patterns began to emerge. Most notably, there were no fewer than five incidents in which various grand vezirs resigned, only to be reappointed to succeed themselves. The first such case occurred in December 1911 in connection with an unsuccessful effort of Said Paşa to secure passage of a constitutional amendment that would increase the powers of the sultan, and thus in effect of the CUP, at the expense of the Parliament.[40] All other cases of this type fell in the armistice period following World War I and appear to have represented protests against the demands of the occupying powers, or at least attempts to achieve greater degrees of ministerial solidarity in the face of the terms imposed on the defeated empire.[41] There is no doubt, too, that this kind of succession pattern in the grand vezirate was attributable to the "shortage of men" that contemporary European observers continually noted. Traceable as far back as the purges of 1908-1909, this problem was compounded by the collapse of the CUP and the flight of its top leadership at the end of World War I.[42]

The evolution of the grand vezirate during the Young Turk Period was thus impeded by the imperfect development of the parliamentary system and by the circumstances of war and imperial collapse. Nevertheless, the period saw appreciable steps toward the readjustment of this office to the organizational forms and needs of the parliamentary, constitutional system on which Turkish political hopes had come in large part to center.

Simultaneously, the bureaucratic staff attached to the grand vezirate also underwent changes, which we may follow conveniently on the basis of a set of regulations issued for these offices in March 1914.[43]

Leaving aside the undersecretary of the grand vezir, who was omitted from these regulations but was mentioned in all the yearbooks of the period, the most conspicuous alteration indicated in 1914 appeared in the core of offices subordinate in the traditional system to the chief scribe (*reis ül-küttab*) and by 1908 almost entirely to the grand vezir. Of these, the Office of the Receiver (*Amedî*), transformed following the revolution into something like an "Office for the Council of Ministers and [Its] Reports" (*Meclis-i Vükelâ ve Mâruzat Kalemi*), had reappeared by 1914 under its old name.[44] What had once been the Office of the Imperial Divan now appeared as the Office of the *Beylikçi* of the Imperial Divan (*Divan-ı Hümayun Beylikçiliği Kalemi*). The number of sections into which it was divided had dwindled to two, one specializing in preparation of rough drafts and fair copies (*tesvid ve tebyiz*), the other discharging the long-familiar responsibilities of this office in the registration (*kayd*) of laws, decrees, and other such documents. The entourage of the *beylikçi* no longer included any section known specifically as the Office or Section of the Imperial Divan; but two of what had been the sections of this office had become separate bureaus in their own right. One of these was known by 1914 as the Office for Privileged or Autonomous Provinces (*Eyalat-ı Mümtaze ve Muhtare Kalemi*), headed for much of the Young Turk period by Mahmud Kemal İnal. The other was the Office for Important Affairs (now referred to as the *Umur-ı Mühimme Kalemi*), the same bureau being identified slightly later in the last of the government yearbooks as the Directorate of Important Affairs and of the Private Secretarial Staff of the Grand Vezir (*Mühimme ve Kalem-i Mahsus Müdiriyeti*).[45] The former Office of the Corresponding Secretary (*Mektubî*) of the Grand Vezir had meanwhile turned into an Office of Administrative Affairs (*Umur-ı İdariye Kalemi*), which reverted to its traditional title by September 1919.[46]

Aside from these changes in the traditional chancery offices, the list of bureaus subordinate to the grand vezir was little different in 1914 from what it had been in 1908. There was something called the Protocol Office of the Imperial Divan (*Teşrifat-ı Divan-ı Hümayun Kalemi*), a Records Office (*Evrak Kalemi*, corresponding to the earlier Records Office of the Sublime Porte), the Archives (*Hazine-i Evrak Kalemi*), and a Cipher Office. The Decorations Officers (*Nişan Memurları*) present in 1908 had disappeared, a fact perhaps attributable to the way in which Abd ül-Hamid's use of such honors had destroyed their prestige. The translator of the grand vezir (*sadaret-i uzmâ tercümanı*) still appeared in the last of the government yearbooks,[47] though not in the regulations of March 1914. In addition, there was also one office not known in earlier periods. This was a Directorate of Legal Compilation (*müdevvenat-ı kanuniye*), the duties of which included the publication of the official series of legal volumes, the *Düstur*, and of the official gazette, *Takvim-i Vekayi*, both suspended under Abd ül-Hamid but resurrected under the Young Turks.[48] Briefly attached to the grand vezirate in 1918-1919, finally, was the Directorate General of Statistics, seeming successor to the Statistical Council linked under Abd ül-Hamid to the Council of State.[49]

Thus the staff of the grand vezirate continued to evolve as that office began to adjust to the larger transformation of the political system.

The Council of Ministers

As the CUP began to place men of its own in ministerial positions, and still more with its direct domination from 1913 to 1918 of the grand vezirate, the Cabinet also began to display the effects of this transformation. As this happened, however, the composition of the Cabinet remained much as before 1908; and its functions gained, at least to a degree, in clarity of definition.

To speak first of organization, the list of officials included in the Cabinet consisted more or less invariably, at least through World War I, of the grand vezir, the head of the religious establishment, the chairman of the Council of State, and the ministers of foreign affairs, internal affairs, justice, finance, education, pious foundations, trade and agriculture, public works, war, the navy, and the triple portfolio of posts, telephones, and telegraphs. This last post was a new addition to the Cabinet since 1908. In contrast, two other posts previously included were subsequently dropped or abolished: the undersecretary of the grand vezir and the separate portfolio for the artillery (*Tophane müşiriyeti*).[50]

While the composition of the Cabinet thus changed relatively little, the restoration of parliamentary government led to substantial alterations in the way the Council operated and in the procedures for legislation. A number of these alterations, such as those on ministerial appointments and responsibility, appeared in the constitutional amendments of 1909. In addition, there were also efforts to define and systematize procedures for making decisions in the Cabinet and for keeping its records. These efforts took the form of a set of "internal regulations" drawn up in March 1909 and modified in June 1912.[51]

As promulgated in 1909, these first defined the procedures for cabinet meetings, which were to be convoked by the grand vezir, were to begin with old business and then go on to new, were to take up each item on the agenda only if the minister in whose jurisdiction it fell was present, and so forth. Minutes were to be prepared on each decision and signed by all the ministers; and a special procedure was set up for the numbering and registration, to permit ready recovery, of all documents coming to the council from the various ministries. The offices of both the corresponding secretary (*mektubî*) of the grand vezir and, still more, the receiver (*amedî*) were made responsible for various parts of the secretarial business of the council.

The revised regulations of 1912 aimed at both further streamlining the procedures for the paperwork of the council and narrowing the scope of its initiative. According to these provisions, the ministers were to discuss only matters that pertained to general policy (*siyaset-i umumiyeye müteallık*), were placed under their collective responsibility by the express provisions of the constitution, or were made dependent on their decision by other laws. The regulations added that matters that had to be submitted to the palace to receive the commands of the sultan should be forwarded only with a draft decree (*irade*) already signed by the ministers, and then went into further details about responsibilities for preparation of the records on the proceedings of the council.

Any attempt to apply the confusing criteria that these regulations advanced for definition of the matters to be left to the discretion of the cabinet would surely have generated conflict. Since only a few more months passed before the coup of 1913, what resolved such problems was presumably not regulatory specifications but rather the political realities then transforming the character of ministerial office.

The Council of State

In the Council of State, meanwhile, these same political realities, as well as the pressures of wartime, had pronounced but sometimes perplexing effects.

Here, changes began with the purges and reorganizations of

1908. A decree of September 1908 restored the council, grossly inflated in size in the later Hamidian years, to much the size and form decreed for it in 1897. The main difference was that there were now to be not three but four sections (*daire*), with responsibilities in the fields of civil affairs (*Mülkiye*), finance (*Maliye*), reform legislation (*Tanzimat*), and education and public works (*Maarif ve Nafia*). As before, there were also to be a set of administrative courts. Each of the four sections of the council was to have a vice-chairman and six members. The Courts of First Instance (*Bidayet*), Appeal (*İstinaf*), and Cassation (*Temyiz*) were each to have a president and four, six, and eight members, respectively, each of the two lower courts also including some sort of deputy member (*aza mülâzımı*). There were also supposed to be three public prosecutors (*müddei-i umumi*), three assistants (*muavin*) to the public prosecutors, one examining magistrate (*müstantık*), and a Grand Jury (*Heyet-i İttihamiye*). This decree did not mention the council to resolve conflicts of jurisdiction among the various courts (*İhtilâf-ı Merci Encümeni*), but it nonetheless continued to exist. A clerical staff divided into various offices supported both the sections of the council and its courts; and there was provision for membership on the council, as in the past, of the *damad*s or sons-in-law of the sultans, but henceforth only on an honorary basis.[52]

Available evidence suggests that these provisions were at first followed rather closely and then modified progressively in practice. For example, the volume of business in the courts led within a month to the addition of two extra officials to each of them.[53] On what came to be referred to as the administrative side of the council, the Finance Section was soon merged with the Section for Education and Public Works.[54] Within a couple of years, the triple mission of this new section had proven unwieldy. At that point, the Section for Civil Affairs was underworked—a fact probably relating to the institutional development of the Ministry of the Interior in this period. Consequently, in 1912, matters relating to education were taken away from the overloaded section and shifted to what thenceforth became a Section for Civil Affairs and Education (*Mülkiye ve Maarif*).[55]

Probably about the same time, although the particulars remain unclear, much more fundamental changes occurred in the administrative courts. These changes may have had to do with the recurrent proclamations of martial law and the suspension, following the outbreak of the Balkan Wars, of the right of appeal of court-martial decisions.[56] The changes would certainly have had to do with a new law of February 1914 on the trial of officials. This limited the role of the Council of State, as of the various local administrative assemblies (*Meclis-i İdare*), to the preliminary investigation of charges and countercharges, a duty to be performed on the administrative side of the Council of State, and shifted actual prosecution of the cases into the courts of the Ministry of Justice.[57]

The cumulative effect of these changes was such that the last of the government yearbooks shows nothing left on the judicial side of the Council of State except the Council on Conflicts of Jurisdiction (*İhtilâf-ı Merci Encümeni*). Even this had undergone a change of mission. No longer dealing with conflicts between the "ordinary" and the administrative courts, this body now had the mission of resolving conflicts between the courts subordinate to the Ministry of Justice and the courts-martial (*mehakim-i adliye ile divan-ı harplar*). The membership of the Council on Conflicts of Jurisdiction changed accordingly, to consist of three members each from the civil and military Courts of Cassation.[58]

A product at once of the ancient tradition of *divan*s as encountered in the Ottoman Empire and of the models offered by the corresponding agencies of several Western states, the Ottoman Council of State thus evolved into the last days of the empire. The shearing off of the administrative courts, and the fact that the changes of organization and role in the council are only incompletely covered in regulatory acts, suggest that the Young Turk period must have been a time of troubles for this agency more than others. Under the Republic, for example, the successor body (*Danıştay*) clearly regained a major role in administrative justice.[59] The questions that surround the evolution of the Council of State in this period thus go beyond what can now be answered and suggest the need for a detailed study of its extensive archives.[60]

The Ministry of the Interior

For this ministry, in contrast, the Young Turk period was perhaps the most fruitful of the entire era of reform. The elimination of the Hamidian system, and particularly of the direct interference of the palace in local administration, opened the way both for the revision of the law of 1871 on provincial administration and for an unprecedented development of the central organs of the ministry. The tensions aroused by such policies of the Young Turks as their emphasis on Turkification, and especially the crises that developed in the non-Turkish parts of the empire during World War I,[61] are enough to indicate how far these reforms were from taking full effect at the time. The significance of these measures for the elaboration of the administrative legacy that remained to the postimperial order is nonetheless immense.

The new General Law on Provincial Administration of 26 March 1913, replacing that of 1871, has been described as providing "the basic framework for local government" as it has remained in Turkey to the present day.[62] The law of 1913 does include provisions—such as those on tax-farming—that by now have surely long been obsolete. Yet it was a major innovation in a number of respects, as comparison with the corresponding act of 1871 makes clear.

As concerns local administration per se, the most striking feature of the new law is probably the measure of decentralization that it allowed. This had been foreshadowed in the provincial administration law of 1871 and called for in article 108 of the constitution of 1876. But it is a matter of the first importance for the history of Ottoman legislation that the law granted the new degree of decentralization by attributing to the provincial government a dual character: as an element of the imperial administration, on the one hand, and as a distinct local entity, endowed with legal personality, on the other.[63] In keeping with the principle of legal personality, thus introduced for the first time into Ottoman law, the province was to have its own budget, for example, and assume considerable responsibilities in the management of revenues and expenditures, to include paying official salaries and raising surtaxes and loans within certain limits (art. 98). What was, at least implicitly, to assure the compatibility of this degree of decentralization with maintenance of the interests of the central government was another feature that clearly marks the importance of the law of 1913 for the general modernization of administration in the Ottoman Empire. This is the emphasis that numerous articles of the law placed, either expressly or obliquely, on functions of service and control.

To begin with the provisions on local governmental institutions, the new law retained the basic concept of four echelons of territorial subdivisions, but also introduced certain organizational modifications. The law preserved the institutional forms elaborated in 1871 in the general sense that the provincial governor general (*vali*) was to be assisted by a permanent cadre of administrative officials of prescribed types (art. 5), an administrative council (*Meclis-i İdare*) consisting of the higher provincial officials together with the local heads of the various religious communities and various elected members (art. 62), and a general council (*Meclis-i Umumi*). Meeting once yearly, the general council was to consist of representatives elected from the various districts (*kaza*) of the province by an indirect system based on that used for election of deputies to the Parliament in Istanbul (arts. 103-105). The conditions that were to exist at the lowest of the four administrative echelons, the *nahiye*, were left for separate specification; but the law provided that the second and third echelons were to have institutions patterned after those at the province level (arts. 5, 37-61, 69, 71).

In other respects, meanwhile, the law of 1913 went beyond this retention and elaboration of already familiar forms. One decentralizing innovation was a provision for neighboring provinces to create joint committees to deal with certain matters of common interest (arts. 145-46). Another new feature, reflecting the emphases on both control and decentralization, was the provision for a new Province Council (*Encümen-i Vilâyet*), a permanent standing committee elected out of the General Council of each province at its annual meeting to perform certain advisory and control functions, particularly in connection with the budget and financial affairs (arts. 136-44).

The emphasis on control became even clearer in the procedures that the new law created for appointment and dismissal of local officials. Here decentralization appeared in the more guarded form of a redistribution of power, a change requiring increased specificity as to how appointments of different types were to be made. The new law still allowed provincial governors general and even the chief administrators of the next two echelons below them (*mutasarrıf, kaymakam*) to make appointments to some of the administrative positions on their staffs and to advise the responsible agencies on appointments to others (arts. 8-10, 48, 61, 102). But the law also turned over lengthy lists of local positions to the Ministry of the Interior or to other ministries to which the responsibilities of the positions in question corresponded. This was a contrast, in one sense, to the hazy way in which the provincial administration law of 1871 left local appointments to the governor general. In a different sense, the provisions of 1913 also contrasted with Hamidian policy. At least from the creation of the Civil Officials Commission (1896) on, this had carved out a large but ill-defined category of appointments—ones requiring sanction in the form of an imperial decree—and concentrated the making of them in a central commission dominated by the sultan. Under the law of 1913, there were still a few appointments that required confirmation by imperial decree, but that was no more than a formality. More importantly, the spirit of discretionalism that had pervaded earlier appointment procedures faded, as the law not only defined various appointment-making systems, but also explicitly listed the positions to which each applied. That this change was only part of a more general systematization of conditions of service in the provinces was also clear from the provisions of the new law on dismissals (arts. 11-19). Without counterpart in the provincial administration law of 1871, and only partly anticipated in the regulations of Abd ül-Hamid's Civil Officials Commission, these provisions required the furnishing of "legally valid reasons" (*esbab-ı mücibe-i kanuniye*) for dismissal and maintained the right of any subject to complain against any official.[64]

In addition, the law of 1913 included many other provisions that dealt expressly with the services that local government was to perform and the way this performance was to be monitored. Tours of inspection, for example, were a traditionally familiar control device, on which some provisions had been included in the local administration law of 1871.[65] Upgrading requirements, the law of 1913 demanded that the chief administrative officers of the province and of the next two echelons (*vilâyet, sancak* or *liva, kaza*) spend stated proportions of their time making tours of this kind (arts. 30, 42, 54). Partly in connection with these tours, the same officials were also to file certain types of reports. The provincial budget, which the governor general had to submit not only to the General Council of his province but also to the Ministry of the Interior, was in effect such a report. There was, in addition, to be a regular system of inspectors general, separate from the provincial administrative cadres.[66] All the while, the provincial administrative authorities were to provide an impressive list of services in fields as diverse as public works, develop-

ment of commercial and credit institutions, education, and public health (art. 78). This list indicates with new clarity what many
efforts of preceding periods had hinted, namely, that the Ottoman government had begun to have development policies, but
did not yet have that name to apply to them.

Thus the Young Turks attempted to place the local administration of the empire on a new footing, emphasizing decentralization in certain respects, but also public service and accountability. With this effort went certain related measures, including the creation of a special province of Istanbul[67] and a law,
which we shall discuss in a later section, on the officials of the
ministry. Most important in the development of formal bureaucratic organization was a set of regulations, dating from December 1913, for the organization of the central offices of the ministry.[68] Considering the prior state of these offices, the regulations
seemed, indeed, to create a central organizational core for the
ministry for the first time.

At the head of this organization stood the minister, his undersecretary (*müsteşar*), and the minister's private secretarial staff
(*Kalem-i Mahsus*). Attached to the *Kalem-i Mahsus* were the
Cipher Office, responsible for the telegraphic communications
of the ministry, and the Translatorship of the Two Holy Cities
(*Haremeyn-i Muhteremeyn Tercümanlığı*), the title of which implies
that it was responsible for the Arabic-language correspondence
with the Sharif of Mecca (art. 3).

In addition to these offices, the ministry included eleven directorates or other agencies of equivalent status and had two
other directorates general simply attached (*merbut*) to it. Several
of the eleven directorates were, or appear to have been, modified forms of agencies that existed in the preceding period.
Such were the Directorate of Accounts (*Muhasebe Müdiriyeti*, art.
4) and the Population Directorate (*Nüfus Müdiriyeti*), in charge
of population registration and compilation of the relevant statistics (art. 12). Such, too, were the Personnel Records Directorate (*Sicill-i Ahval Müdiriyeti*, art. 11) and the Records Directorate (*Evrak Müdiriyeti*, art. 14).

Two other new directorates appear to have replaced agencies
known in preceding periods. The superseded institutions were
the Office of the Corresponding Secretary (*Mektubî*) of the
Ministry of the Interior and the "agents of the gate" (*kapı kâhyası*)
or representatives of the provincial governors general at the

Porte, a traditional function evidently abolished in 1909.[69] In place of these two institutions, the responsibilities of which had been somewhat difficult to distinguish, the regulations of 1913 called for a Directorate of General Internal Administration (*İdare-i Umumiye-i Dahiliye*) and another for Local Provincial Affairs (*Umur-ı Mahalliye-i Vilâyat*). The duty of the former was to supervise all business entrusted to this ministry by law or regulation and not performed by others of its agencies, and to conduct all related correspondence passing between this ministry and the other ministries or the various provinces (art. 6). The role of the Directorate of Local Provincial Affairs lay in analysis and approval of the provincial budgets, and in monitoring the functions that the law on provincial administration entrusted to the provinces in the fields of public works, education, agriculture, manufacturing, and commerce (art. 7). The apparent redivision of the functions traditionally discharged by the agents of the gate and the corresponding secretary is of course also another example, certainly where the corresponding secretary is concerned, of the creation of more modern organizational forms through the subdivision of agencies whose responsibilities had been defined in terms of the traditional, document-oriented specifications.

The regulations of 1913 also provided for agencies that had no counterparts in the ministry in 1908. One of these, the Personnel Directorate (*Memurin Müdiriyeti*, art. 10), appears to have emerged, following the abolition in October 1908 of the central Civil Officials Commission created in 1896, as an appointment-making body for the Ministry of the Interior. With the restoration of the Civil Officials Commission in 1912, this Personnel Directorate, like the Personnel Records Directorate that we have already mentioned, must effectively have become a branch of that commission in the Ministry of the Interior, although the documentation is not totally clear on this point.

The situation of the remaining directorates of the ministry is more certain. One of these was the Directorate of Public Security (*Emniyet-i Umumiye Müdiriyeti*, art. 5), created in August 1909.[70] This directorate replaced the former Ministry of Police (*Zabtiye Nezareti*). The functions of the Directorate of Prisons (*Hapishaneler Müdiriyeti*, art. 13) are self-explanatory, and its attachment to the Ministry of the Interior follows naturally from the presence there of the Directorate of Public Security. Finally, the Ministry of the Interior included a Directorate of Tribal and Refugee Affairs (*Umur-ı Aşair ve Muhacirin Müdiriyeti*, art. 8),[71] heir as far as the refugees were concerned to Abd ül-Hamid's High Commission on Refugees, and an Office of Legal Counsel (*Hukuk Müşavirliği*, art. 9). The duties of this office, presumably patterned in a sense after the comparable one in the Foreign Ministry, included drafting laws and regulations, advising the ministry on legal problems, and representing the ministry in legal actions. The legal counsellor also had as an additional duty to assist the undersecretary of the ministry; his staff, to serve as that of the undersecretary (art. 2).

Along with these directorates, which formed the central organization of the Ministry of the Interior as narrowly defined, there were two other directorates general attached, according to the regulations of 1913, to the same ministry, as well as a commission that appears to have been in similar status. The attached directorates general were those of Inspection (*Heyet-i Teftişiye*) and of Public Health (*Sıhhiye*, art. 15). Of these, the former corresponds to the inspectorate general already mentioned in connection with the local administration; the latter, presumably to the Ministry of Health formerly associated with the Foreign Ministry. No doubt on account of war-related necessity, this by 1917-1918 had become an organization of considerable size, headed by the man who was concurrently grand vezir and minister of the interior, Tal'at Paşa.[72]

Finally, though it is not mentioned in the regulations of 1913 on the organization of the Ministry of the Interior and thus has to be traced from other sources, we must also mention the Civil Officials Commission (*Memurin-i Mülkiye Komisyonu*). The abolition in 1908 of this commission, one of the most constructive innovations of the Hamidian years, soon proved more a matter of revolutionary ardor than of administrative prudence. The commission was consequently resurrected in 1912 and linked to the Ministry of the Interior. Why the commission was not mentioned in the regulations promulgated for the ministry a year later is unclear. In any case, other documentation indicates that the Civil Officials Commission became once again, as between 1896 and 1908, the central agency to coordinate the work of the offices found in the Ministry of the Interior, as in other ministries, for keeping personnel records and supervising appointments.[73]

Thus the Ministry of the Interior at last acquired a more or less fully elaborated central organization. The relationships among its various agencies were yet to define, but the agencies were at least structured in terms of the relatively modern kinds of organizational concepts that had gradually begun to appear in the civil bureaucracy during the two preceding periods. Indications of the total number of men serving in this ministry in 1914 are lacking. As in the past, the fact that many of the local administrative officials were subordinate to it must have made it the largest of the civil-bureaucratic ministries. To speak only of the central offices, an estimate based on the organization tables included in the regulations of 1913 for six of the directorates would indicate that the ministry had something like 250 officials in Istanbul. Comparison with the yearbooks of the later Hamidian years suggests that here, as elsewhere, the improved levels of regularity and efficiency to which the statesmen of the day aspired had to be reached with considerably fewer men than had once been on the rolls.

The Foreign Ministry

Along with the offices of the grand vezir and the Ministry of the Interior, the Foreign Ministry also received general regulations in the months immediately preceding World War I. Here, as in the case of the vezirial staff, it was the first such document to be promulgated; and it was in many ways a sketchy document. Together with such other references as the yearbooks and a series of reports on organization and staffing prepared within the ministry, the regulations of February 1914 nonetheless make it possible to assess the remarkable state that this ministry, long the most highly elaborated of the component agencies of the Porte, ultimately assumed.

Perhaps the most striking trait of the regulations is the extent to which they answered a need which had become increasingly apparent in this ministry over the two preceding periods and was now beginning to appear in the Ministry of the Interior as well. For there were explicit provisions on some, if not yet all, of the operational and hierarchical links that were to exist among the component organizations of the ministry. Since the regulations did not resolve all problems of this type, some of the hierarchical relationships shown in Figure VII-2 are conjectural and are accordingly marked with question marks. As the figure shows, however, the regulations did combine the agencies of the ministry into groups, functionally coherent in at least some cases, and specify the attachment of some of the groups to either the minister or the undersecretary. Thus the regulations began to create means for maintenance of order and control in the workings of the ministry as it grew in organizational complexity.[74]

Even with this organizational development, however, the Foreign Ministry failed to regain the political prominence once so much associated with it. Considering the growing scope and complexity of the political process, if not also the antipathy of some of the leading figures of the ministry for the new regime,[75] this was perhaps as much a part of the modernization of politico-bureaucratic life as the organizational changes that appear in Figure VII-2.

As in the case of the Ministry of the Interior, the organization defined for the Foreign Ministry began, in the immediate entourage of the minister, with the undersecretary, the minister's private secretarial staff (*Kalem-i Mahsus*), and a Cipher Office. The last two elements were described as directly attached (*merbut*) to the minister.

Attached in the same way to the undersecretary, in turn, was a larger grouping of agencies. Their functions were heterogeneous but mostly familiar from preceding periods. Along with the assistant to the undersecretary, this grouping included the Directorates of Personnel Records, the Press, Nationality Affairs, Records, Translation, and Accounts, as well as two other bureaus whose functions are not so clear. The first of these is what we have shown in Figure VII-2 as the Reception Office; the second, the Superintendency of the Offices. If our interpretation of their titles is correct, the Reception Office would have represented chiefly a means for limiting the access of outsiders, particularly embassy dragomans, to the offices of the ministry,[76] while the superintendency would have been responsible for the security or perhaps simply the menial services of the ministry.

Of the agencies directly attached to the undersecretary, some were, in turn, divided into subsections. This was true, for example, of the Directorate of the Press, into which the former Domestic Press Directorate or Administration (*Matbuat-ı Dahiliye İdaresi*) had been integrated in April 1913.[77] Responsible for enforcing the laws on the press and on printing establishments,

FIGURE VII-2. ORGANIZATION OF THE FOREIGN MINISTRY, 1914

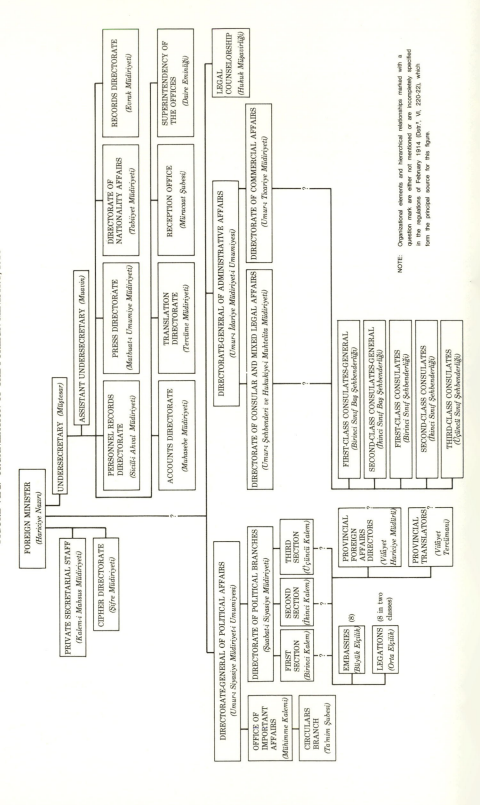

NOTE: Organizational elements and hierarchical relationships marked with a question mark are either not mentioned or are incompletely specified in the regulations of February 1914 (Dstr.², VI, 220-22), which form the principal source for this figure.

reimposed following the attempted coup of 1909,[78] this Press Directorate was to have a director, assistant to the director, and three branches. One of these was something like a Public Information Office (*İstihbarat Kalemi*), its role being the diffusion of information about the Ottoman government and—a long-standing item of concern—the denial of harmful reports in the foreign press. Another branch (*Tedkikat Kalemi*) was charged with analyzing the press, foreign and domestic, and translating items of interest to the imperial government. The third section, that of administration (*İdare Şubesi*), was responsible for the application of the laws on the press and on printing establishments and, incidentally, for keeping statistics on the Ottoman press. The report that provides these details indicates that the Press Directorate then had twenty-six men working in it.[79]

The Directorate of Nationality Affairs, in its turn, was subdivided into what the regulations of 1914 identified as the Nationality Office (*Tabiiyet Kalemi*) and the Verification of Nationality Office (*Tasdik-i Tabiiyet Kalemi*). The difference between the two is not clear, although verification of nationality in doubtful cases is precisely where the mission of this directorate lay. A report that the Director of Nationality Affairs submitted in 1912 indicates that his agency then had a total staff of ten. Alleging a growth in the volume of business since the restoration of constitutional government, this report argues for additional appointments to the office.[80]

Two others of the directorates subordinate to the undersecretary were subdivided internally in terms of different kinds of records-keeping processes. In the case of the Accounts Directorate, these were for Investigation of Accounts (*Tedkik-i Hesabat Kalemi*) and Balance Sheets (*Muvazene Kalemi*). In the case of the Records Directorate, clearly formed by reintegration of the separate records sections attached as of 1908 to various other departments of the ministry, the divisions were for registration of documents and maintenance of dossiers (*Kayd ve Dosya Kalemi*), keeping the archives (*Hazine-i Evrak*), and receipt and dispatch of communications (*Mersulat ve Mevrudat Şubesi*).

The Records Directorate thus combined archival functions with control over the flow of current documents, such as was discharged for the Porte in general by what was in 1908 the Records Office of the Sublime Porte, later known as the Records Directorate (*Evrak Müdiriyeti*) of the grand vezirate. The magnitude of the archival function appears from a report of 1913, which speaks of fifty or sixty years' accumulation of documents then lying about the offices of the ministry helter-skelter (*perakende*). According to the same report, the directorate had a staff of thirty, which the director considered adequate. Compared to the smaller numbers then serving in some other agencies whose missions might logically be deemed more important, this number is an impressive tribute to the impression that records-control problems then made on the minds of Ottoman statesmen.[81]

One final point about the entourage of the undersecretary leads to a comparison that makes this point clearly. The Translation Directorate shown in Figure VII-2 is the successor of the Translation Office of the Sublime Porte, once the most important central agency of the Foreign Ministry and practically the only civil-bureaucratic agency of its kind. Organizational changes during the Young Turk period make it difficult to trace the size of the directorate with assurance, but it may have fallen as low as five or six—a decline surely due to the continued diffusion of the skills once concentrated there.[82]

Moving on beyond the entourage of the undersecretary, we come to two other organizational groupings, designated as directorates general. The regulations of 1914 (art. 5) fail to specify exactly where these stood in terms of either formal hierarchical subordination or working relationships with the consular and diplomatic establishments. Nonetheless, what the two directorates general clearly represent is the regroupment of the elements of the central organization of the ministry dealing with diplomatic business, on the one hand, and consular affairs, on the other. In the process of this regroupment, some of the previously familiar agencies of the ministry became subordinate elements of one or another of the new directorates general. Others, such as the Turkish Correspondence Office (*Mektubî-i Hariciye*) and Foreign Correspondence Office (*Tahrirat-ı Hariciye*) ceased to exist as such.

Clearly discharging primary responsibility for diplomatic business was the Directorate General of Political Affairs. This included an Important Affairs Office (*Mühimme Odası*), created in 1913 to conduct correspondence that possessed special importance or required special handling.[83] The regulations of 1914 also mention a Circulars Section (*Ta'min Şubesi*) as attached to this office. The directorate general also included a Directorate of Political Branches, under which fell three sections that the regulations of 1914 identify only as first, second, and third. Since other sources of the period throw no light on the differences among these, we can only infer that they corresponded to something like the geographically designated offices or "desks" in the foreign ministries of some other states. In 1912, the Directorate General of Political Affairs, then differently organized, contained twenty officials.[84]

The second of the directorates general, shown in Figure VII-2 as responsible for administrative affairs (*umur-ı idariye*, art. 5), corresponds to what had been known earlier in the Young Turk years as the Directorate General of Consular, Commercial, and Mixed Legal Affairs (*Umur-ı Şehbenderi ve Ticariye ve Hukuk-ı Muhtelita Müdiriyet-i Umumiyesi*). This grouped together three agencies, separate until 1908, with responsibilities in the three fields indicated in the lengthy title.[85] Indeed, the tripartite character still persisted inside the organization as described in the regulations of 1914, the subordinate Directorate of Consular and Mixed Legal Affairs there being assigned two component offices, presumably one for each of the two functions mentioned in its name.

A report submitted in 1912 by the head of what was then the Directorate General of Consular, Commercial, and Mixed Legal Affairs gives insights into the actual operations of this agency.[86] The Consular Affairs Branch had its own director (*müdür*), two examining clerks (*mümeyyiz*) and sixteen clerks. The branch had two sections with geographically designated responsibilities. The central agency responsible for corresponding with the consulates, for sending out to them all the various stamps, forms, and other papers they needed to do their jobs, and for receiving documentation from the consuls on the civil status of Ottoman subjects residing in the various consular districts, the Consular Affairs Branch appears from this account to have been a busy place. The Commercial Affairs Branch, in turn, had its own director, two examining clerks and ten clerks, the staff being divided into two sections, one operating in Turkish and one in French. The duties of this branch lay in drafting commercial treaties, supervising their application, and following other matters relating to public hygiene and international trade. The duties of the Office of Mixed Legal Affairs lay, finally, in disposing of the various types of international legal problems that could arise in connection with individuals. In this office there were one examining clerk and five clerks. This was only one-third or one-fourth of the staff that had been assigned to the Directorate of Mixed Legal Affairs (*Umur-ı Hukuk-ı Muhtelita Müdiriyeti*) up to 1908. The report of 1912 indicated that the office now needed to be upgraded to a directorate, and that it should have a director and a couple of additional officials with legal training added to it. A new set of regulations issued for the Directorate General of Administrative Affairs in 1916 indicates that some such expansion may have occurred by then, although their late date argues against attributing much force to those regulations in want of confirmation from other sources.[87]

Last among the central agencies of the Foreign Ministry as defined in the regulations of February 1914 (art. 6) was the Legal Counsellorship (*Hukuk Müşavirliği*), which resembled the two directorates general in the lack of specification of its hierarchical relations with other parts of the ministry, as well, presumably, as in its relative importance. As before 1908, there were still two men holding the title of legal counsellor, with an Office of Legal Counsel (*İstişare Odası*) attached to them.[88] Although the Ministry of the Interior, if not also other ministries, had now acquired legal counsellors of its own, the counsellors in the Foreign Ministry were still responsible for serving the entire Ottoman government, and not just the Foreign Ministry, with respect to international law. While these posts had begun as a matter of course to be held by Ottoman subjects, there was also a special, additional post of First Legal Counsellor in existence between December 1913 and October 1915. This had as its incumbent a distinguished European legal expert, Count Leon Ostrorog, who had served the Ottoman government for some years before 1913 in similar capacities.[89]

On account of the prestige of its mission, the Office of Legal Counsel had been one of the most padded offices under Abd ül-Hamid. In contrast to the fifty officials nominally attached to it then, after 1908, not counting the special position held by Ostrorog, there were only the two legal counsellors, a director (*müdür*) of the Office of Legal Counsel, seven assistants (*muavin*), and a couple of secretaries. Since here, as in other offices dealing with legal affairs, the volume of business had increased considerably with the restoration of constitutional government, a need was expressed in 1912 for two extra officials with legal qualifications and as many again for additional secretarial support. It does not appear that these requests were filled, although the appointment of Ostrorog would certainly have alleviated the need for additional legal expertise.[90]

Complementing the central agencies of the ministry were those outside Istanbul. These perhaps still included the provincial foreign affairs officers and translators, although there is evidence to indicate that the Foreign Ministry had by 1915 lost its long-standing feud with the Ministry of the Interior over control of those posts.[91] As for the consular and diplomatic establishments, they had been pruned considerably in the purges of 1908-1909[92] and were further reduced with the closures of mission necessitated by war. The closure of the missions in the former German and Austro-Hungarian Empires following the armistice reduced these services almost to nothing, although the empire did attempt to revive its diplomatic representation during the armistice years.[93] In the meantime, the regulations of February 1914 gave the Ottoman consular and diplomatic services what was to be their final, officially defined form prior to World War I.

As indicated in Figure VII-2, the regulations (arts. 7-11) provided for a diplomatic corps consisting of eight embassies (*büyük elçilik*) and eight legations (*orta elçilik*). The embassies were to be in Berlin, Paris, Saint Petersburg, Rome, Tehran, London, Washington, and Vienna. The legations, graded in two classes depending on the ranks of the incumbents, were to be in Athens, Stockholm, Brussels, Bucharest, Belgrade, Sofia, Madrid, and The Hague. The consular service, as in the past, was to include both honorary and salaried consuls, the latter divided into first- and second-class consuls general and three classes of consuls. As in other cases, the regulations failed to specify the exact hierarchical relations of the consular and diplomatic officials to the senior officials of the ministry in Istanbul. Presumably, consuls and diplomats addressed their correspondence to the minister and normally dealt, in fact, with the two directorates general whose responsibilities corresponded to their own. The regulations of 1914 were equally uninformative on the exact composition of the diplomatic missions and on the numbers and locations of consular posts of the different types, simply identifying these as points to be regulated by further special instructions, which must never have appeared.

Thus the Ottoman Foreign Ministry reached the climax of its historic evolution. To judge from the fragmentary indications quoted in preceding paragraphs, its central offices would now have included something in excess of 150 men.[94]

Miscellaneous

Having now surveyed the state of the Sublime Porte as of 1914, it is perhaps appropriate to say something about what had happened to the agencies which, forming parts of that organization in 1908, no longer did so six years later.

In the case of the Senate, the change in status was a consequence of the restoration of the constitution and the revival of parliamentary government. In the case of the commissions formerly under direct control from the palace, the changes also reflected the abolition of the Hamidian system, but in different ways. Two of these had become parts of the Ministry of the Interior. These were the former High Commission for Refugees, now seemingly subsumed into the Directorate of Tribal and Refugee Affairs, and the Civil Officials Commission, abolished in 1908 but apparently restored in 1912. The High Commission for the Hijaz Railway had, meanwhile, turned into a directorate general in the Ministry of Pious Foundations.[95]

Only the Aid Fund of the Sublime Porte seems to have retained any sort of independent position there. With its mission essentially unchanged, it was placed by a set of regulations issued in May 1914 under the administration of a commission, membership in which was honorary and was reserved to officials drawn from the departments that the fund served. Subsequent revisions of the regulations attest the continued existence of the fund into the last years.[96] In contrast to the commissions of the Hamidian period that, like so many other such bodies before them, evolved into permanent bureaucratic agencies, the Aid Fund still appears to have remained a small, conciliar organization, basically ancillary to the bureaucratic functions of the Porte. Accordingly, there is no need to show it in Figure VII-1.

As one of the agencies of the Porte to receive new regulations in 1913-1914, the Aid Fund in its modest way nonetheless reflects the significance of the Young Turk Period for the overall development of civil-bureaucratic institutions. For during this period, the Offices of the Grand Vezir and the Ministries of Internal and Foreign Affairs all underwent organic regulation, while the Council of Ministers and the Council of State all received regulations in at least some form. Thus the agencies of the Sublime Porte finally approached full compliance with the constitutional demand for enactments of this kind.

In a sense, this fact sums up the significance of this period for the development of the civil bureaucracy. At the same time, however, there are certain additional points that also require note. First, while traditional concepts of organization and procedure never entirely vanished, they continued, as the measures on the Ministry of the Interior showed with particular clarity, to yield ground to newer ones emphasizing goals and responsibilities external to the bureaucratic system per se. While this kind of organizational reorientation was still associated at times simply with a proliferation of bureaus, in the Foreign Ministry we can see the new agencies being regrouped into larger and at least sometimes coherent groupings through which operational control could be maintained in the midst of organizational growth.

This organizational regroupment in the Foreign Ministry was, in fact, only a single expression of the growing emphasis on control and accountability, and many others appeared with the increasing integration of the various phases of institutional development and regulation and with the larger drive for achievement of a modern kind of political balance. The emphasis on control had, of course, already found expression in the preceding period in phenomena such as the mechanisms for the selection of officials, in Abd ül-Hamid's use of statistics, or in the consular inspectorates and reports. After 1908, requirements of such kinds multiplied, a fact perhaps best illustrated by the intricate counterpoise of control and decentralization in the provincial administration law of 1913. Simultaneously, in a way expressed more in practical fact than in regulatory specification, the increasing demand for the responsiveness of bureaucratic institutions to political interests external to themselves also began to affect the grand vezirate and the cabinet posts in the sense of transforming them for the first time into political more than bureaucratic offices. More and more oriented away from the formalistic and introspective patterns of the old scribal service, the institutions of the Sublime Porte were becoming increasingly subject to law and to requirements of service to a polity of broadened scope.

REGULATION IN OTHER FIELDS OF POLICY AND PROCEDURE

In view of the changing extent and character of regulatory activity during these years, an analysis of organizational development leaves less to discuss in the way of other regulatory issues than in earlier periods. Nonetheless, the field of personnel policy included important sequels to the Hamidian innovations. There were also developments worthy of comment in other fields, such as official communications. A discussion of measures of these types will provide added insights into the growing rationalization of the Sublime Porte, and to a degree of the civil bureaucracy more generally, during the Young Turk years.

Personnel Policy

The statesmen of this period did not succeed in solving all the problems apparent in the Hamidian personnel measures. Nonetheless, especially if we may consider measures that did not reach the point of formal promulgation, they continued the development of civil-bureaucratic personnel policy in all three of the phases that had come to characterize it: the system for the maintenance of personnel records, the laws on conditions of recruitment and service, and those on compensation systems.

The purges and reorganizations that marked the beginning of the Young Turk Period appear to have had a particularly devastating effect on the personnel records system. On the one hand, the purges generated vast quantities of data that needed to be integrated into the records. On the other hand, the purges surely reduced the numbers of officials available for this task. The result was that the personnel records could no longer be kept up to date. Most files stop, in fact, just short of the Young Turk Revolution, mentioning neither the purges nor, where appropriate, the individual's further service.

Contemporary statesmen nonetheless realized the value of the records and tried to keep the system going. Even in 1908, when they suppressed the central Civil Officials Commission (*Memurin-i Mülkiye Komisyonu*) and returned the making of appointments to the various ministries, they explicitly retained a separate Personnel Records Administration (*Sicill-i Ahval İdaresi*), subordinate up to that point to the commission that had just been abolished and from then on to the Ministry of the Interior. To judge from the yearbooks, there were also branch offices for personnel records in at least some other ministries. Following the restoration of the Civil Officials Commission in 1912, these various elements seem again to have figured as its branches.[97]

Part of the problem with the maintenance of the personnel records may, in fact, have derived precisely from a growing awareness among the reformers of the utility of those records for other aspects of personnel administration. To judge from what happened in the Foreign Ministry, the previously evident trend to increase the work required of such offices continued in this period. Including the processing of records on official attendance, of leave requests and applications for retirement pensions or unemployment stipends, and of the documentation required for award of decorations,[98] the new requirements chart the gradual evolution of the personnel records offices into bureaus for general personnel administration.

In view of this continuity of interest, it is not surprising to observe that new regulations for the personnel records system appeared in May 1914. Supposed to replace all preexisting guidelines on the workings of the system, the regulations were, in fact, very complicated, much more demanding than earlier guidelines as concerns the information to be included in the records, the documentation to be provided in substantiation of certain types of statements, and the procedures for conservation of the records.[99] The result of a conscientious attempt at application of these regulations would thus probably have been anything but a practical improvement in the efficiency with which the records-keeping system operated. In fact, while it is clear that the personnel records offices continued to function to some degree at least as late as 1918,[100] there is little evidence of compliance with the new regulations. If they had any impact at all, it would thus have been on the personnel records system that the Nationalists created very shortly in Ankara.[101]

The chief effect of the reforms of this period on general personnel policy, meanwhile, seems to have been to dissociate the system for retirement pensions from that for recruitment and promotion, the two having been treated together in the major

legislation of the Hamidian years. To look first at the provisions
on recruitment and promotion, leaving retirement rights for
consideration with other questions of compensation, there is no
indication that the earlier legislation was abrogated or replaced
by other measures of comparable generality. What the reformers of the Young Turk years did try to do was to flesh out
the sketchy terms of the provisions of 1884 on promotion and
retirement with more detailed regulations on conditions of service in specific ministries, as well as other measures modifying
specific points of detail in general personnel procedure.

For the major agencies of the Sublime Porte, we find two attempts during these years to regulate conditions of service in
specific ministries. One of them, actually enacted into law, is a set
of regulations of December 1915 for officials of the Ministry of
the Interior. This is a sort of complement to the other major
provisions pertaining to that ministry—the Provincial Administration Law and the regulations for the central offices, both dating from 1913. The other attempt, which never reached the
point of enactment, appears in a group of drafts prepared in the
Foreign Ministry to provide a comparable kind of specification
for its officials. Preparation of these drafts began soon after the
1908 revolution and continued at least through 1912, the date of
a particularly well-developed example that provides a convenient basis for discussion.[102]

The regulations issued in 1915 for the officials of the Ministry
of the Interior[103] attempted first to provide something that had
been called for in the Hamidian legislation but never provided,
except to an imperfect extent through the decree of 1880 on
official salaries. This was a general classification by salary, at least
for this ministry, of all the positions subordinate to it. While the
table that presented this classification was not very clearly con-
structed and did not integrate officials serving in provincial posts
with those in the central offices, subsequent articles went on to
specify how appointments were to be made to the various
categories of positions (arts. 2-11). By mentioning holders of
specific provincial posts as eligible for appointment to a given
central position or vice versa, these articles did at least imply the
beginnings of a common grading system for central and provincial posts. Acknowledging the role that the Provincial Administration Law of 1913 left to provincial authorities in the making
of appointments of certain types (art. 17), the regulations of

1915 also elaborated in greater detail the procedures to follow in appointments that were controlled from the ministry in Istanbul. Some such appointees were to be designated by the minister; some, by an appointment-making body now called the Council of Directors (*Encümen-i Müdiran*). This would presumably have superseded the Personnel Directorate mentioned in the regulations of December 1913 on the organization of the central offices of the ministry and, to judge from its name, would have consisted of the directors of the various departments of the ministry. The regulations of 1915 also distinguished certain appointments as requiring the sanction of an imperial decree (*irade*); the order of the minister sufficed for others.

These regulations further specified that applicants to enter the service of the Ministry of the Interior were to meet certain qualifications of age, character, and education and were, in addition, to pass a competitive examination. Where the educational requirements are concerned, the most notable innovation since the Hamidian years is the elimination of the preference accorded to graduates of the School of Civil Administration (*Mekteb-i Mülkiye*), as opposed to others of the modern schools. Seniority first, and ability second, were to be the determining factors in promotion (art. 18), while certain types of officials were required to spend certain amounts of time in grade before they could be promoted (art. 13).

The draft regulations of 1912 for the officials of the Foreign Ministry,[104] in turn, included a number of analogous ideas. Again, there was an attempt to classify all the positions under the ministry in a comprehensive hierarchical scheme (art. 2). As before, there were to be set qualifications for admission into the service of the ministry. Resembling those in the regulations for the Ministry of the Interior but also at points imitating the conventions of the aristocratic European foreign services, these included being of "good family," proficiency in both Ottoman and French, education in the Schools of Law (*Mekteb-i Hukuk*) or Civil Administration or in equivalent foreign institutions, and passage of a competitive examination. There was also to be some variation in procedures for appointments at different levels. Most were to depend on a special Commission for the Selection of Foreign Ministry Officials (*İntihab-ı Memurin-i Hariciye Komisyonu*), a title familiar since Hamidian days but not mentioned in the regulations of February 1914 on the organization of the ministry; other appointments were simply at the discretion of the minister (arts. 11-13). Here, too, seniority was to be the basic factor in promotion, although "ability would also be taken into account" (art. 15), and time in grade was to be a requirement for advancement in grade (art. 20).

In other respects, however, the draft regulations for Foreign Ministry officials differed significantly from those for the Ministry of the Interior. Due perhaps to the special importance of the diplomatic function, certainly to the conviction that the Foreign Ministry should have a distinct personnel policy, and probably also to the fact that Abd ül-Hamid's innovations in appointment-making procedures related chiefly to local administration, the sense of a prior lack of any orderly personnel policy was particularly strong in this ministry. There was also a feeling that the diplomatic personnel of the ministry had heretofore received greater compensation for their efforts than those of its central offices.[105] In reaction to these problems, the draft regulations of 1912 proposed that all officials of the ministry be classified into distinct services. To get around the inequities in compensation, there were to be only two services, the consular and the diplomatic, and even those officials serving in Istanbul would belong to one or the other. This kind of classification would also facilitate transfers of officials between Istanbul and the foreign posts.

To make it possible to transfer individuals without harm to their careers, the draft proposed the creation of a new status, intermediate between appointment and dismissal. Heretofore it had been impossible to change officials without either swapping two (becayiş) or arbitrarily dismissing one. Henceforth, there was to be a status referred to as being à la disposition du Ministère (Nezaret'in emrine muntazır, art. 4). This would make it possible to shift officials to meet the administrative needs of the service without placing the stigma of dismissal on their records.

Since these provisions never became law, the Ottoman Foreign Ministry ended its history without acquiring a rationally regulated personnel system. There was thus never any way to assure, for example, that all those appointed to diplomatic posts really were what one minister picturesquely referred to as "export goods."[106] The nonenactment of the Foreign Ministry personnel regulations, and even more the fact that reform of general personnel procedure was now occurring within each ministry without further attention to the kind of basic legal framework first sketched out under Abd ül-Hamid, made clear how much still needed to be done for the thorough regularization of civil-bureaucratic conditions of service.

In the event, completion of this task would remain for the Republic. In addition to the measures just discussed, however, there were in the meantime also some others of detail. One of these, reflecting an added dimension of the concern over the quality of the diplomatic corps, was a decree of 1909 requiring officials of the Foreign Ministry to request official permission prior to marrying.[107] The measure was aimed specifically at marriages with foreigners and derived from a feeling that some unions of this type had been undesirable.[108] Likewise applying to the Foreign Ministry was a measure of 1910 modifying an earlier decree on consular leaves.[109] Applying to officials of all types, in a sense, though more specifically a part of the educational history of the period, there was also a set of regulations, drawn up in May 1913 and extended or modified on a number of occasions thereafter, for the standardization of the examinations to be taken by students who had completed the lycée-level schools (*mekâtib-i sultaniye*) and were candidates for the diploma that was still known as the *mülâzemet rüusü* and now, under this examination system, became an imitation indeed of the French *baccalauréat*.[110]

With the outbreak of the Italo-Turkish and later wars, there were other personnel measures reflecting the gravity of wartime. In this category were instructions of October 1911 on the duties of civil officials in time of mobilization,[111] a decree of the same month prescribing penalties for officials who did not observe the prescribed hours for attendance in their offices,[112] other decrees of 1912 and 1913 prohibiting membership by officials and teachers in political parties,[113] and regulations of 1915 on the granting of honorary military ranks to statesmen (*rical-ı devlet*) serving with the armed forces or rendering other extraordinary services.[114]

As they set about the further regulation of conditions of recruitment and promotion, the statesmen of the period also began early on to address their attention to the various aspects of the official compensation system. While they still produced no comprehensive salary table for the entire civil bureaucracy, they did draw up a number of tables of smaller scope. The various reorganization schemes on the basis of which they conducted the

purges of 1908-1909 bore this character, at least in part.[115] The
hierarchical systems of salary grades incorporated into the regulations of 1915 for the officials of the Ministry of the Interior
and the draft regulations of 1912 for those of the Foreign Ministry were also of this kind. Simultaneously, there seems to have
been a tendency to abolish the deductions through which Abd-
ül-Hamid had, in effect, taxed his captive bureaucrats for the
benefit of his pet projects.[116]

Ancillary aspects of the compensation system came under renewed scrutiny, as well. There was a whole series of measures on
unemployment stipends and travel allowances. In part, these
measures aimed at keeping the unemployment stipends from
turning into salaries for doing nothing, a character they often
bore under Abd ül-Hamid.[117] In August 1909, there was also a
new law on the retirement pensions of civil officials, teachers,
and various other categories of government employees. Replacing the corresponding provisions of the Hamidian Decrees on
Promotion and Retirement of Civil Officials, this revised and
simplified the preexisting provisions and initiated the process of
abolishing the receipt of multiple pensions by officials who had
spent parts of their careers in different branches of service. As in
the past, the basic concept of the pension system was that pensions should be funded by a deduction of five percent from
salaries, a rate effectively increased in May 1914, when deductions to cover pensions and unemployment stipends were combined and placed at twelve percent.[118]

Beginning in 1914, finally, there was also a long string of
measures having to do with war-related problems of inflation,
shortage of goods, and the handling of salaries and other entitlements of officials who were either returning from provinces
that had been lost or who, in the armistice years, ran afoul of the
imperial government for political reasons. One such measure
was a decree of 1920 cutting off the salaries of officials whom the
Occupation authorities had exiled to Malta. Acts of these kinds
record the final agonies of the collapsing empire and otherwise
require no comment.[119]

Before matters reached this point, the Young Turk years witnessed some gains in all fields of personnel policy, if not yet a
comprehensive systematization. The system of personnel records at least continued to exist and received new regulations, if
ones of excessive complexity. The personnel records offices, de-

spite the practical impediments to their effective operation, also began more and more to resemble the personnel directorates of modern bureaucratic organizations. General systems for recruitment and promotion of officials, on one hand, and for retirement pensions, on the other, were taken up in separate acts and revised. Not all the measures on conditions of service reached the point of promulgation, but acts on all major phases of the compensation system did so. It was these changes, despite their limits, that made it possible for the early development of official personnel policy under the Republic to display the character that a recent student has described as "evolutionary, rather than revolutionary."[120]

Systematization and Control in Other Procedural Fields

As the formal organizational structures of the Sublime Porte and the personnel procedures of the civil bureaucracy came increasingly under law and regulation, the workings of the bureaucracy also began to assume a new degree of systematization in other ways. The brevity of the period seemed to limit the range of accomplishment, however, and some previously intractable problems remained beyond solution. To illustrate this point, we may appropriately take up two topics that have engaged our attention in earlier chapters: the management of government finance, and official communications.

At various dates, the Young Turk period brought ostensible relief from a number of the most serious problems noted during earlier periods in Ottoman government finance. First, Abd ül-Hamid's estates were confiscated, turned over to the Ministry of Finance, and auctioned off. Serious efforts were then made to achieve order in the affairs of that ministry and to make the budgets more accurate and reliable. In 1914, between the outbreak of World War I and the Ottoman entry into the war, the government unilaterally abolished the capitulatory privileges enjoyed by foreigners in the empire. Finally, with Ottoman entry into the war and the departure from Istanbul of subjects of the Entente powers, the Public Debt Administration remained under the control of the German, Austrian, and Ottoman delegates, who used it to support the Ottoman government financially for the remainder of the war.[121]

By 1914, however, it was clear that not all hopes of improvement in government finance would be realized. Reporting in

1909 on the financial effects of the bureaucratic purges and reorganizations, Baron Marschall had affirmed that officials and officers were being regularly paid, that the old independence of individual ministries had at last been done away with, and the entire financial system centralized in the Ministry of Finance.[122] In the early years of the period, there were also other reforms, including a partial reordering of the system of taxation, which produced fiscal benefits. But the improvements that Baron Marschall described were not lasting ones. By 1910, for example, efforts at fiscal centralization had encountered serious problems in the opposition of Mahmud Şevket Paşa, as minister of war, to the attempts of the minister of finance, Cavid Bey, to exert a power of review over the military budget.[123] Budget laws did continue to be passed in such unprecedented number and detail that much expert research would be required to evaluate them thoroughly. It seems clear, though, that the very bulk of the documentation signified ongoing trouble. For amendments and supplements to budgetary acts continued to be passed in some cases for several years after the end of the financial year to which those measures were supposed to apply, and large deficits appeared in every one of the general budgets (*muvazene-i umumiye*) published after 1908 (cf. the Appendix).[124] World War I meant the resumption of the issue of paper money, its drastic depreciation, and eventually economic chaos.[125] For officials who had survived the purges at the beginning of the period and had their hopes raised by the attempts then made at financial reform, this situation must have been cause for despair, indeed.

The field of official communications, in contrast, illustrated what could still be accomplished where economic constraints were less pressing. Some of the changes in this field dealt, to be sure, only with minor problems of government paperwork. Such were a decree of December 1913 placing restrictions on giving out originals, rather than copies, of imperial decrees (*irade*) from the archives to other offices that had need of them.[126] Another measure of similar character, though of considerable importance for financial administration, was a law of 1917 shifting the dates of the month in the solar calendar that the Ottomans used for financial purposes to conform with those of the Gregorian calendar used in the West.[127]

Of more basic significance, particularly considering that the volume of legislation produced during this period appears to have exceeded all that enacted between 1839 and 1908, were measures pertaining specifically to the publication of laws and regulations. While there were improvements of various sorts, including gains in clarity of language and organization, perhaps the most important changes in this area came with a revision of the processes for official registration and promulgation of laws.

Under a new system set up by law in May 1911 and amended in February 1914,[128] each new law, upon receipt of the sultan's formal assent, was still to go to the Directorate of the Imperial Divan or Office of the *Beylikçi* of the Imperial Divan, as it was variously called during these years, for registration in the long-customary way. That agency was also to prepare as many certified copies as were needed and send them to the agency or agencies responsible for enforcement of the law. Under the revised system of 1914, the *beylikçi* was then to send the original documents to the Directorate of Legal Compilation, another of the bureaus in the staff of the grand vezir. The Directorate of Legal Compilation was without fail to see to the publication of the law in the official gazette, the *Takvim-i Vekayi*, and in the published volumes of legal texts, the *Düstur*. This done, the original documents would go back to the *beylikçi* and from him to the Archives.

Upon receipt of the text, the agencies responsible for enforcement would prepare additional copies for distribution to their subordinate agencies, to include those of the local administration whenever appropriate, and the latter would in turn see to the publication of the law in the local newspapers or by other suitable means. Each law would then take effect at the date specified in it or, barring specification, from the date of its publication in the official gazette. These measures of 1911 and 1914 were the first attempt since 1872 to define a comprehensive system for publishing new laws and placing them in effect.

Even if contemporary efforts at fiscal reform foundered as ignobly as had those of the two preceding periods, these measures on official communications and legislation provide a fitting final comment on what we have seen of the growing emphasis on law and regularity in all phases of administration in this period. It was an emphasis clearly perceptible at the time to Count Ostrorog, whom we have already mentioned as first legal counsellor at the Porte. As he saw it, while there were competing concepts deriving from Islamic tradition, one of the central ideas in the political life of the period was the concept that the empire should be a state ruled by law, a *Rechtsstaat* of the sort described by Western theorists.[129] The regulatory acts discussed in this chapter were perhaps not all well inspired or adequate to the problems they addressed; yet they provide concrete evidence on impressive scale of the persistence with which Ottoman statesmen pursued this idea.

CONCLUSION

As the years passed, the situation in which the officials and statesmen of the Young Turk years found themselves was such as to reduce this pursuit more or less to an impossibility. After the Armistice in 1918, the circumstances of defeat and the Allied occupation of Istanbul diminished what was left of the Ottoman bureaucracy to the condition of wretchedness documented in the memoirs of Galip Kemali Söylemezoğlu, one of the few still trying to maintain the diplomatic representation of the empire, or in the biographical accounts of Mahmud Kemal İnal, the last *beylikçi* of the empire and one of the last and greatest exponents of the scribal literary tradition. The magnitude of İnal's achievement in memorializing the intellectual and bureaucratic elites of the former empire becomes all the clearer as we learn, from his account of his own life, of the hardships he endured during these years, particularly when his home was taken over by the occupying forces and his collection of books and papers largely destroyed.[130]

İnal, of course, was not the only one who suffered; and indeed, as the city filled with refugees and displaced persons, those in official position were surely not the worst off. Still, the lot of the officials was not an enviable one. Most of them had been left by the virtual destruction of the state with little to do, and by the disruption of the economy and the decline of the public revenues with little or nothing to live on.[131]

Particularly as the Nationalist movement emerged and began to win successes, the loyalties of these men began to shift to the new force that was emerging in the Anatolian heartland. Certainly, there were those who found it impossible for one reason or another to make the shift of allegiance. Yet, down to the point when the costs and growing difficulties of their mission persuaded the Occupation authorities to give up the city, they watched with concern as nationalist sentiment spread into Ottoman official circles in Istanbul. By 1921, the British High Commissioner was reporting that the "Constantinople Government are practically the self-constituted mouthpiece of the Angora Government."[132] The following year, when the Grand National Assembly voted the abolition of the sultanate (1 November 1922), the last Ottoman Cabinet resigned, and the Nationalists ordered the termination of activity in all the agencies of the imperial government, the difficulties of the former Ottoman officials who remained in Istanbul naturally increased. By then, however, many had already gone to Ankara, and others were ready to go.[133]

Having helped to create a complex of institutions very different from anything known to their ancestors of a century before, the men who journeyed thus to an unknown future carried with them a stock of ideas and expectations that did much to facilitate the formation of a new state in the Anatolian interior. By the same token, they played a major part in making possible the surprise that the Nationalists gave to a world grown accustomed to think not only that the Ottoman Empire was finished as a state, but also that the Turks were finished as a people.

The reforms of the Young Turk years had a great deal to do with preparing the bureaucratic tradition for its continuing life in the new, republican setting. Fully to appreciate the significance of these reforms requires considering them not just in the context of their own time, however, but rather in the deeper perspective of the entire era of reform.

Chapter Eight

ONE AND ONE-THIRD CENTURIES OF CIVIL-BUREAUCRATIC REFORM

The differences between the Sublime Porte of the early twentieth century and that of the late eighteenth, like those between the civil bureaucracy in its last phases and the earlier scribal service, were all but revolutionary in extent. A look back at the Porte and the scribal service as they were at the end of the eighteenth century, followed by a review of the forces that contributed to the ensuing transformation and an assessment of the contrasts that had appeared by the end of Ottoman imperial history, will bring into view the full extent and significance of the changes that had occurred in these institutions.

On the eve of reform, the Sublime Porte was still a relatively small and in some ways unclearly structured organization. It included the grand vezir's household as well as his *divan* and the bureaus immediately attached to him. Of these, the Offices of the Steward of the Grand Vezir (*Kâhya Bey*) and the Chief Bailiff (*Çavuş Başı*) were still only imperfectly identified with the scribal service. Indeed, the real scribal element of the Porte was practically limited to the chief scribe (*reis ül-küttab*) and his staff, found in the Office of the Imperial Divan and several other bureaus that had appeared alongside it by the end of the eighteenth century.

The aptness of the designation scribal service expressed itself clearly in both the organizational and the procedural patterns found inside these offices. Personnel designations and concepts of scribal functions, in particular, displayed a fixation on the details of routines for the production of documents. As a natural consequence both of this fact and of the assumption that officials served the ruler rather than the subjects, there were few signs of any concern for the impact of scribal routines on the world outside the offices. Still less was there any means by which to enforce such a concern. The scribal service did have a great literary tradition behind it, and the political utility of this found tangible expression as scribal officials began to rise to the highest offices of the state. Most scribes of the Porte were distinguished, however, by little more than a craftsman-like approach to their work, and remained within a range of experience that did not extend even as far afield as the scribal offices of the Treasury. Even those who rose to high office had little real preparation for service as administrators or statesmen and were well qualified only by comparison with other segments of the ruling class.

Analysis of the social state of the scribal service of the late pre-reform period reinforces these points and provides insights into the underlying characteristics of the imperial system, as well. Here the most basic fact to note is the differentiation of the scribal service into subgroups structured along the lines of models of social organization encountered elsewhere in the society. In reflection of the Islamic character of the state and the principles that governed intercommunal relations within it, non-Muslims appeared in the scribal service or on its flanges only in small enclavements recalling the autonomous confessional communities of the subject classes. Among Muslim officials, in turn, there was a differentiation in terms of rank, with variant patterns of social organization appearing above and below the line of division. At the lower levels, in ways ranging from its method of training by apprenticeship to its personnel designations and the outlook of its members, the scribal service was practically a craft-guild. For Muslims who managed to gain promotion into the upper echelons, in contrast, the guild-like pattern yielded to a different one. Present to some degree among the other groups and corresponding to the most widely encountered principle of Ottoman social and political organization, this is what we have referred to as the model of the patrimonial household. Among the grandees of the ruling class, replication of this pattern not only signified use of the material perquisites of high station for imitation of the sultanic style, but also provided the organizational basis for the political factionalism so characteristic of upper bureaucratic life.

Overall, the points that stand out most strongly about the scribal service of the late eighteenth century, as about the imperial system in general, are this patrimonial motif, on one hand, and the effects of imperial decline, on the other. The organizational patterns observable at the Porte illustrate the patrimonial character of the system through a coexistence of divergent tendencies, at once toward differentiation and specialization of functions, and toward simultaneous concentration of disparate and essentially undefined powers in the hands of key functionaries. The difficulty of explaining some of the organizational forms noted on the eve of the reform era surely derives from this coexistence and highlights the limited extent to which the differentiation of functions could progress in such an environment. Characteristic procedural patterns reveal, meanwhile, how effectively the concentration of unregulated powers at the top of the system diminished, or even repressed, the initiative of officials at other levels. One consequence of this repression was the quickness of the officials to resort to extreme forms of indiscipline, when they could, in defense of personal interests. Such indiscipline was apparent both at the lower echelons and among the bureaucratic elite, for whom the politicization of office and the insecurity of the sultan-slave relationship made such behavior a vital necessity.

The processes of imperial decline were also clearly of critical importance in aggravating the weaknesses of the patrimonial system and in determining the developmental patterns of the scribal service. The contrast between the systems of recruitment and training developed in the branches of the ruling class that flourished when the state was at its height and those that served the same purposes for the later scribal service illustrates this point vividly. Indeed, this contrast provides not only a measure of the effects of decline, but also an insight into the probable reasons for the prominence of guild-like traits in lower scribal echelons. Another significant indicator of faltering administrative capabilities is the regression over a period of centuries from compensation by salary, at least for some officials, into generalized prebendalism. As it affected the scribal elite through the systems of annual appointment and fee-collection, imperial decline was also of major importance in compounding the incentives for an extreme orientation to self-service and for replication of the model of the patrimonial household. It is thus paradoxical that the system of annual appointment, in conjunction with the decay of the military-administrative establishment, was also a key factor in creating the efendi-turned-paşa pattern and thus sending forth the scribal officials to play roles of new variety and importance in the upper levels of the administrative system. Imperial decline fostered the growth of the scribal service in some respects, then, even while inhibiting it in others.

As the empire entered the era of reform, the desire to reassert the control of the central government over the whole empire created a necessity to upgrade the quality and regularity of administration. Such an upgrading amounted to launching the empire generally on a transition from traditionalism toward the creation of a rationally structured and legally defined order; and this necessitated a major transformation of the ruling class, in which the scribal service was becoming the most prominent branch. As long as the sultans retained their traditional powers without formal restriction, one implication of this reassertion of the center was conflict between them and the most influential of their official servants. For most if not all of the era of reform, the shifting state of this conflict was the decisive factor in differentiating the successive political periods. But there were also other factors that interacted to heighten this conflict and to complicate the transition toward rational-legalism in other ways.

In the opening phases of the reform era, the most conspicuous of these factors was the shortage of official manpower qualified to provide leadership in reform movements. As a new elite began to form, it was at first very small in size; and the response of its members to the new ideas to which they were exposed tended to be uncritical and narrowly self-interested. The magnitude of the unforeseen consequences that could ensue when circumstances placed power abruptly into the hands of such men is clear—at least in hindsight—from the results of the virtual adoption of free trade in 1838 or even the move toward egalitarianism in 1839.

The subsequent growth in the sophistication of Ottoman reformers was rapid. Yet, the necessity to contend with various forms of foreign interference and domestic opposition narrowed their freedom of action. The incongruity of the reforms with the setting into which they were introduced also hampered reformist efforts, as did the basic but at first unrecognized need to develop effective techniques for carrying new measures through from initial formulation to implementation and supervision.

The greater the resource requirements of a given measure, or the greater the extent to which it required the creation of new infrastructure on an imperial scale, the more clearly these problems appeared. It is important to note, however, that the ability of the Ottomans to raise the resources required to support their reforms varied greatly, depending on whether it was a question of economic resources or human. In the former respect, the Ottomans never overcame the fiasco of the reforms enacted at the beginning of the Tanzimat; indeed, the incorporation of the empire into a European-dominated economic system was far advanced before the era of reform began and simply continued thereafter. The development of new kinds of manpower was ultimately a different story; although here, too, there were shortages and unexpected ironies.

Bureaucratic expansion and related educational reforms in fact launched processes of social, cultural, and political change that eventually affected not just the ruling elite but all of Ottoman society. In terms of meeting bureaucratic manpower needs, the results obtained were significant, though never fully adequate; but other consequences of these changes soon proved more important. For the elements of the society that had some awareness of, and presumed to speak on, current affairs began to grow in number and diversity. At the same time, of course, innovative reform was creating increasingly evident dissonances in the socio-political order and loosening it more and more from the sanctions of tradition. The growth of the politically conscious segment of the population thus coincided with a growing articulation of politically arguable issues and policies, and the result was the emergence of political ideology in the modern sense.

The problem of finding a basis on which to legitimate innovative reform, together with the lack of any cohesive social basis for the redefinition of the locus of sovereignty, compounded the problems surrounding the development of ideological controversy, rendering them insoluble within the framework of the imperial system. Particularly since the ideologues of the reform era were not ready to contemplate destroying the imperial order, one consequence of this insolubility was to maintain the political importance of certain elements of the traditional imperial center, above all the office of the sultan. Thus, even as demand for modernization of the polity grew, it became apparent that elements of patrimonial tradition could survive in symbiosis with the newly created elements of a rational-legal order. The course that reform followed, as it progressed through the initial period of sultanic reassertion, the radical political imbalance of the Tanzimat, the first abortive effort at creation of a constitutional regime, the despotism of Abd ül-Hamid, and the revolutionary years of the Young Turks showed how varied the manifestations of this neopatrimonial symbiosis could be. The same course of events also showed how difficult it would be not only to restore, but also to modernize the political equilibrium.

The aspect that the Sublime Porte and the civil bureaucracy assumed during the Young Turk period illustrates, nonetheless, how much successive generations of Ottoman reformers were able to accomplish under the circumstances in which they labored. To speak first of formal organization, even after the purges of 1908-1909, the Sublime Porte remained a much larger and more complex organization than in 1789. Its major organizational components had taken on a more consistently civil-bureaucratic aspect, although a few in fact began, after the restoration of parliamentary government, to acquire a political more than a bureaucratic character. The major component agencies of the Porte increasingly presented an aspect like that of other modern bureaucracies, although in fact each had its roots in agencies of the traditional imperial system.

The grand vezir, for example, had in some respects begun to resemble the prime minister of a liberal polity—a development that the presidential system of the early Republic would for a time deprive of sequel. Still, despite a few experiments with an alternate designation, the post represented a historical continuity of which its title was a clear indicator. The Council of Ministers and Council of State, along with numbers of other conciliar bodies, some of which had now become regular bureaucratic departments or even ministries, were heirs to the old *divan*s and ad hoc consultative assemblies. Indeed, nothing sounds a clearer or more appropriate caution against equating all the organizational developments of the nineteenth century with westernization than the dual pedigree of the Cabinet and Council of State, tracing back in one direction into the dim antiquity of Islamic tradition, and in another to the corresponding institutions of the major European states. In the Ministry of the Interior, despite the discontinuities in its history, the old steward of the grand-vezirial household had found his logical counterpart in modern bureaucratic terms. The Foreign Ministry, of course, derived from the ancient office of the chief scribe (*reis ül-küttab*), an evolution that led, as the organizational apparatus of a specialized Foreign Ministry emerged, to the shift of most of the traditional chancery offices to the new entourage then forming in immediate subordination to the grand vezir. The old chief bailiff (*çavuş başı*) alone had no institutional progeny at the Porte in 1922. His were to be found instead in the separate Ministry of Justice.

These changes in the differentiation and designation of the various major agencies of the Porte had as a natural accompaniment a profound reorientation in their internal organizational and procedural patterns. Within the larger agencies just named, the growing numbers of component organizations were now structured increasingly in terms of rational specialization, a fact reflected in their very names and in the growing specificity with which it is possible to speak of their functions. At least in the Foreign Ministry, the need to create mechanisms through which to coordinate the operations of different bureaus was also beginning to find recognition. Throughout the various departments, personnel designations continued to include document-oriented or guild-like terms such as examining clerk (*mümeyyiz*) or the usual designation of the ordinary clerks as *hulefa*. Yet, conceptions of bureaucratic roles were beginning increasingly to reflect functions of service and control and to emphasize interaction between the officials inside the bureaucracy and the society outside. Thus, the relatively limited variety of traditional scribal roles extended to include such new ones as the consuls and ambassadors, the public prosecutors and examining magistrates of the Council of State, the local administrators under the Ministry of the Interior, the various types of inspectors, or the jurists serving in the Office of Legal Counsel at the Sublime Porte. Alongside or in place of the old procedural patterns there were new ones relating to such varied functions as the compilation of statistics, the delivery of passports and identity papers, control of the flow of current documentation, and the drafting and publication of laws. Regulations and controls were at times over-elaborated to the point of precluding efficient administration and perpetuating the old repression of official initiative. Yet the old image of the official as a slave of the sultan was at least beginning to yield to a new conception of the official as a public servant, performing his duties under legally defined conditions and within the limits of an operative system of accountability.

As before, the social patterns now characteristic of the civil bureaucracy amplify and clarify the significance of these changes in formal organization and procedure. The changes that these patterns display were very extensive and in fact merit consideration from two different points of view.

In one perspective, the best way to assess these changes is in terms of differences from the patterns of social organization evident within the scribal service on the eve of reform. What stands out here is the opening of new cleavages in the civil bureaucracy and the shifting in the relative balance of the various discernible groups. The efforts at elite formation in progress since the early years of the reform era had brought forth a new, Westernist elite among the Muslims. Egalitarianism and the new demand for officials of Westernist cultural orientation had also given the non-Muslims, who almost invariably displayed the qualifications of the Muslim elite, greater prominence and greater integration into the civil bureaucracy. The same factors were beginning to relegate Muslims of exclusively traditional formation to a sort of residual category recalling the old, lower scribal echelons. Naturally, these changes did not occur without setting up social tensions, which were linked directly to the emergence of ideological controversy and helped to create a broad response to the appeals of the opposition intelligentsia. As concerns the general social ordering of the civil bureaucracy, however, what is most significant is the way the new diffentiations reflect both ascriptive and prescriptive criteria—ethnoreligious identity, on the one hand, and cultural orientation, implicitly even educational achievement, on the other. The shift from traditional to characteristically modern concepts of social order was incomplete but in progress.

In another perspective, at the same time, the best way to appreciate the transformation in the social fabric of the bureaucracy is in terms of those changes of legal principle that first made the difference between scribal service and civil bureaucracy and then began to produce the kind of rationally defined and legally regulated personnel policy that the latter term implies. Changes of this kind began with the reforms of the 1830s—the development of the civil-bureaucratic rank table, the abandonment of the practice of annual appointment, the attempted institution of official salaries, the abolition of nonjudicial punishments, and the steps that the Gülhane Decree of 1839 represented toward inauguration of legal equality. During the

Tanzimat, extreme political imbalance had as one of its natural costs the inability of the civil-bureaucratic beneficiaries of the imbalance to achieve a general regularization of their status. Yet the Reform Decree of 1856 did specify more clearly what egalitarianism should mean, and it is significant that the provisions of this decree on official service by non-Muslims at least alluded to rules to be generally applied in the bureaucracy. With the efforts of the succeeding period at the restoration of political equilibrium came the first attempt to provide such rules by superimposing on the reforms of the 1830s the outlines of a rational system of personnel administration. The social realities apparent among the different groups of officials indicate that this policy never became entirely operative; yet the continuity in its development, from the 1870s on into the Young Turk period, proves that its desirability was one point on which autocrats and constitutionalists could see eye to eye.

The new personnel policy was simply one conspicuous element of a pattern that by 1914 had emerged as the most important point of contrast to the patrimonialism and the various processes of decay so characteristic of the imperial system at the end of the eighteenth century. This new pattern is most readily identified in terms of rational-legalism and the way in which it had begun not just to coexist with, but actually to supplant the traditional patrimonialism of the imperial system. In progress to some degree since the days of Selim III, this transition had advanced to a really remarkable extent following the return to constitutional government in 1908. The transition was obviously not yet complete, and events of the Young Turk period showed that the processes of rational regulation were still not totally safe from neopatrimonial forms of abuse. Still, by the outbreak of World War I, rational-legalism had grown into a powerful reality not just in the minds of the more liberal Ottoman statesmen, but also in the body of concepts, principles, and laws that exerted an increasing hold over the structure of the administrative apparatus and over its actual operations. The extent of progress toward realization of the rational-legal ideal is nowhere more apparent, indeed, than in the marked extent to which the development of administrative law and regulation—the chief means for the practical implementation of the new concepts of bureaucratic roles and procedure—had by 1914 at last come abreast of the proliferation of new programs and institutions.

By the time of its collapse, then, the Ottoman Empire had acquired a unique position among the historic states of the Islamic world in a sense that went beyond the mere fact of its longevity. Now, it was unique as well in the extent to which it had acquired the legal and administrative apparatus of a modern polity.[1] The patent archaism of the overall imperial framework was obviously something that even the most extensive progress of this kind could not change. Yet, the Ottomans had made tremendous strides in creating a rationally regulated bureaucratic apparatus of a sort that could, with appropriate restructuring of the larger socio-political framework, provide the means for the kind of credible and effective administration to which they had by then aspired for a century and more.

The near-revolutionary transformation that we have seen in the Sublime Porte and the branch of Ottoman officialdom that staffed it would thus have to await its consummation in a revolutionary reconstitution of the polity along lines of popular sovereignty and mass consensualism. In terms of direct and obvious continuities, the struggle to continue this modernist transformation of the politico-bureaucratic tradition forms part of the political and administrative history of the Turkish Republic. In subtler and sometimes indirect ways, the story of this struggle also forms part of the history of the other successor states. The further evolution of the administrative tradition in the successor states is, however, only the latest chapter in a history that began in the last decade of the eighteenth century and comprises one of the most significant parts of an even larger story, that of the struggle to create effective, modern administrative systems in all the nations of the Third World.

BUDGETARY "ALLOCATIONS" FOR AGENCIES OF THE SUBLIME PORTE IN SELECTED YEARS

As indicated in the text, the Ministry of Finance had no effective control of the receipt and disbursement of government funds for most, if not all, of the years shown. For this reason, it is appropriate to treat the concept of budgetary "allocations" (*tahsisat*) with reservation. As noted here, some of the budgets indicate that the sums shown were only estimates or requests, or were determined by sultanic fiat. The almost invariable deficits are also to be noted in attempting to evaluate the reliability of the budgetary figures.

ALL SUMS STATED IN MILLIONS OF KURUŞ[a]

	Offices of Grand Vezirate	Council of State	Ministry of Interior	Foreign Ministry	Total Budgeted Expenditures	Apparent Budgetary Deficit (Surplus)
1858[b] (BBA, Meclis-i Mahsus 529, fin. yr. 1274)	—	—	265.9[c]	16.5	1,200.7	—
1864[b] (BBA, Yıldız 18. 525/212. 128. 25, fin. yr. 1280)	—	8.4[d]	184.1[c]	13.2	1,602.8	(18.3)
1869[b] (BBA, Yıldız 18. 525/229. 128. 26, fin. yr. 1285)	—	—	256.2[c]	15.4	2,036.1	50.7
1871 (BBA, Mal. Müd. 11,777, fin. yr. 1287)	9.2	7.1	229.8[c]	17.5	—[e]	—
1873 (BBA, Mal. Müd. 11,777, fin. yr. 1289)	5.5	6.3	185.6[c]	16.5	—[e]	—

ALL SUMS STATED IN MILLIONS OF KURUŞ[a]

	Offices of Grand Vezirate	Council of State	Ministry of Interior	Foreign Ministry	Total Budgeted Expenditures	Apparent Budgetary Deficit (Surplus)
1880 (*Dstr.*[1], v, 1078ff., fin. yr. 1296)	2.3	1.9	57.1[f]	12.7	1,704.0	88.3
1888 (*Dstr.*[1], v, 1078ff., fin. yr. 1304)	4.6	3.6	68.0[f]	16.5	1,922.2	173.3[g]
1892-1895 (*Dstr.*[1], vii, 129ff., fin. yr. 1308-1311: "average of actual annual allocations")		90.2		19.2	1,980.0	?[g]
1897 (*Dstr.*[1], vii, 891ff., fin. yr. 1313: "allocated per imperial decree." cf. ibid., vii, 129ff.)		90.4		19.0	1,844.9	def.?
1902 (*Dstr.*[1], vii, 891ff., fin. yr. 1318: projected allocations)		102.6		25.4	2,183.6	207.2
1905 (*Dstr.*[1], viii, 476ff., fin. yr. 1321: "allocated per imperial decree")		110.6		25.0	2,196.2	(33.0)
1906 (*Dstr.*[1], viii, 476ff., fin. yr. 1322: requested allocations)		115.6		24.9	2,536.5	52.3
1909[h] (*Dstr.*[2], i, 438ff., fin. yr. 1325)	3.4	5.2	108.5[i]	21.8	3,054.0[j]	546.1
1910[h] (*Dstr.*[2], ii, 435ff., fin. yr. 1326)	2.7	3.3	131.1[i]	25.9	3,299.8[j,k]	698.3
1911[h] (*Dstr.*[2], iii, 479ff., fin. yr. 1327)	3.6	3.3	135.6[i]	24.5	3,623.3[j]	775.6
1912[h,l] (*Dstr.*[2], iv, 174ff., fin. yr. 1328)	2.6	3.3	122.4[i]	23.6	3,399.7[j]	348.3

ALL SUMS STATED IN MILLIONS OF KURUŞ[a]

	Offices of Grand Vezirate	Council of State	Ministry of Interior	Foreign Ministry	Total Budgeted Expenditures	Apparent Budgetary Deficit (Surplus)
1913[m] (*Dstr.*², v, 108-109, fin. yr. 1329)	—	—	—	—	—	—
1914[h] (*Dstr.*², vi, 1077ff., fin. yr. 1330)	7.1	2.4	102.7[n]	26.0	3,401.2[j]	140.5
1915[h] (*Dstr.*², vii, 253ff., fin. yr. 1331)	3.1	2.4	97.6[n]	25.8	3,565.8[j]	882.1
1916[h] (*Dstr.*², viii, 485ff., fin. yr. 1332)	3.1	2.4	84.9[o]	36.4	3,972.5[j]	1,471.2
1917[h] (*Dstr.*², ix, 314ff., fin. yr. 1333)	3.3	2.6	118.8[o]	35.9	5,330.5	2,972.0
1918[h] (*Dstr.*², x, 179ff., fin. yr. 1334)	3.7	2.7	127.9[o]	41.7	5,197.0	1,795.3

[a] In the early budgets, *kise* ("purses") have been converted to kuruş at 1:500; in the budget for 1918, liras have been converted to kuruş at the nominal rate of 1:100. The figures in all other budgets are stated in kuruş.

[b] The absence of certain entries for the years through 1869 is a consequence of inconsistent budgeting categories or incomplete research notes.

[c] It is not clear why the figures shown for the Ministry of the Interior through 1873 are so high. Is it a question of inconsistent budgeting categories or extraordinary expenditures? Is it a function of the fact that the ministry was really subsumed for most of these years into the grand vezirate, which then dominated all affairs of state?

[d] This entry predates the creation of the Council of State, but is the most nearly corresponding budget entry, namely, that for salaries of the ministers without portfolio and the members of the Supreme Council of Judicial Ordinances.

[e] General totals are missing in the register cited.

[f] This entry excludes personnel in medical and public health services.

[g] The data in the budgets do not check.

[h] Published budgets for these years also include detailed breakdowns by department.

[i] These entries exclude the separate budget for the Directorate of Public Security.

[j] These entries are headed "Total Allocations to the Departments" (*devaire verilen tahsisat*).

ᵏ This total does not include extraordinary appropriations.

ˡ This budget was published with a temporary law ordering continued application for the time being of the budget for the preceding year, but with some changes in allocations.

ᵐ The source cited is an imperial decree of 18 RA 1331/1913 for application in financial year 1329 of the general budget (*muvazene-i umumiye*) of 1328, but the decree is not followed by the usual detailed tables of income and expenditure.

ⁿ These entries exclude the separate budgets of the Directorate of Public Security and the Directorate General of Health.

ᵒ These entries exclude the separate budgets of the two agencies mentioned in the preceding note, as well as that of the Directorate General of Tribal and Refugee Affairs.

CHAPTER ONE

1. Quoted in Sabri F. Ülgener, *İktisadî İnhitat Tarihimizin Ahlâk ve Zihniyet Meseleleri* (Istanbul, 1951), 99.

2. For example, see William L. Cleveland, *The Making of an Arab Nationalist: Ottomanism and Arabism in the Life and Thought of Sati' al-Husri* (Princeton, 1971). Other examples among the graduates of the Ottoman School of Civil Administration are included in Mücellidoğlu Ali Çankaya, *Son Asır Türk Târihinin Önemli Olayları ile Birlikde Yeni Mülkiye Târihi ve Mülkiyeliler (Mülkiye Şeref Kitabı)*, 8 vols. (Ankara, 1968-1969).

3. Niyazi Berkes, *The Development of Secularism in Turkey* (Montreal, 1964), 418-19.

4. Tayyib Gökbilgin, "Bâbıâli," *IA*, II, 174-77; J. Deny, "Bâb-ı 'Alî," *EI*[2], I, 836; Hamilton A. R. Gibb and Harold Bowen, *Islamic Society and the West: A Study of the Impact of Western Civilization on Moslem Culture in the Near East*, 1 vol. in 2 parts (London, 1950-1957), I, i, 44 n. 1; 113.

5. Edward A. Shils, "Centre and Periphery," in *The Logic of Personal Knowledge: Essays Presented to Michael Polanyi on his Seventieth Birthday, 11 March 1961* (London, 1961), 117-30.

6. Max Weber, *Economy and Society: An Outline of Interpretive Sociology*, 3 vols., edited by Guenther Roth and Claus Wittich (New York, 1968), I, 226-41; III, 1006-1110. The extensive development of "patrimonial officialdom" would also suggest that the Ottoman Empire conforms to the type that Eisenstadt defined in his *Political Systems of Empires* (New York, 1963) as the "historical bureaucratic empire." Indeed, Weber specifically refers to the Ottoman Empire in his discussion of patrimonialism; Eisenstadt refers to it in *Political Systems*. Eisenstadt argues, however, for drawing a distinction between "patrimonial" and "imperial" systems and has developed this idea increasingly in his more recent works. To an important degree, the distinction as now defined has to do with the greater extent to which the "center" of an "imperial" system was differentiated structurally and symbolically from the "periphery," attempting to maintain this differentiation and to impose its own goals and values on the "periphery," in addition to extracting resources from it. See Eisenstadt, *Political Systems*, 22-24; id., *Traditional Patrimonialism and Modern Neopatrimonialism*, Sage Research Papers in the Social Sciences, I, series no. 90-003 (Beverly Hills, California, 1973), 30-37, 60; id., *Tradition, Change, and Modernity* (New York, 1973), 173-76; id., *Revolution and the Transformation of Societies: A Comparative Study of Civilizations* (New York, 1978), 86ff. Particularly as concerns the imposition by the "center" of its own goals and values on the "periphery," the conformity of the Ottoman Empire to the "imperial" as distinct from the "patrimonial" type would seem to vary in different periods and respects. Indeed, the way in which Eisenstadt himself speaks of the Ottoman state in his latest work reflects this ambiguity: *Revolution and the Transformation of Societies*, 74, 84, 136-38, 232. Given this fact, the importance of the "model of the patrimonial household" to be discussed later in this chapter, the way in which decline reinforced the patrimonial elements in the Ottoman system, and the emergence in the era of reform of what Eisenstadt and

others now term neopatrimonialism, we shall treat the Ottoman Empire in the remainder of this study as a patrimonial system. How and when the empire conformed to Eisenstadt's concept of an "imperial" regime is an appropriate subject for investigation in another setting. I am indebted to Professor Eisenstadt for personal discussion of these matters, Jerusalem, June 1978.

7. Halil İnalcık, *The Ottoman Empire: The Classical Age, 1300-1600* (London, 1973), 85.

8. Weber emphasized the way in which patrimonialism anticipates the welfare state; *Economy and Society*, III, 1107. The welfare orientation of the Ottoman sultans appears in such things as their emphasis on public works and pious foundations, their concern for the provisioning of Istanbul, and their maintenance of a relatively extensive system of pensions (the *duagû vazifesi*, for example; Pakalın, *OTD*, I, 479).

9. İnalcık, "Pâdişah," *IA*, IX, 492-94; id., "Appendix: The Ottomans and the Caliphate," in *The Cambridge History of Islam*, 2 vols., edited by P. M. Holt et al. (Cambridge, 1970), I, 320-23.

10. In addition to the references cited in the preceding note, see Erwin I. J. Rosenthal, *Political Thought in Medieval Islam: An Introductory Outline* (Cambridge, 1962); Marshall G. S. Hodgson, *The Venture of Islam: Conscience and History in a World Civilization*, 3 vols. (Chicago, 1974), II, 42-57, 391-410, 424-28; III, 99-111; Osman Turan, "The Ideal of World Domination among the Medieval Turks," *Studia Islamica*, IV (1955), 77-90; Ann K. S. Lambton, "Quis Custodiet Custodes: Some Reflections on the Persian Theory of Government," *Studia Islamica*, VI (1956), 125-46; id., "Justice in the Medieval Persian Theory of Kingship," *Studia Islamica*, XVII (1962), 91-119; George Makdisi, "Les rapports entre Calife et Sultân à l'époque saljûqide," *IJMES*, VI (1975), 228-36.

11. Uriel Heyd, *Studies in Old Ottoman Criminal Law*, edited by V. L. Ménage (Oxford, 1973), 2, 167-83, 208-21, 317-18; Ömer Lûtfi Barkan, "Kanûn-nâme," *IA*, VI, 185-95; İnalcık, "Pâdişah," *IA*, IX, 494-95.

12. Albert Hourani, "The Changing Face of the Fertile Crescent in the XVIIIth Century," *Studia İslamica*, VIII (1957), 106-107.

13. İnalcık, *Ottoman Empire*, 179-85; Lewis V. Thomas, *A Study of Naima*, edited by Norman Itzkowitz (New York, 1972), 24-27, 106-10.

14. Halil İnalcık, "Ghulām: iv.—Ottoman Empire," *EI²*, II, 1085-91; Barnette Miller, *The Palace School of Muhammad the Conqueror* (Cambridge, 1941), ch. iv.

15. Halil İnalcık, "Reis-ül-Küttâb," *IA*, IX, 679.

16. Halil İnalcık, "On the Secularism in Turkey," *Orientalistische Literaturzeitung*, LXIV (1969), col. 439-42; id., "Reis-ül-Küttâb," *IA*, IX, 678-79.

17. Under the Ottomans, the term *divan* no longer referred, as it had in earlier Islamic states, to government bureaus; Gibb and Bowen, *Islamic Society*, I, i, 115-16.

18. Weber, *Economy and Society*, I, 271-82; III, 994-98, 1025-31, 1088-90.

19. For an overview of the current state of knowledge on these institutions and an important contribution to their study, see Stanford J. Shaw (with Ezel Kural Shaw as coauthor of vol. II), *History of the Ottoman Empire and Modern Turkey*, 2 vols. (Cambridge, 1976-1977).

20. V. L. Ménage, "Devshirme," *EI²*, II, 210-13; Basilike Papoulia, *Ursprung und Wesen der "Knabenlese" im Osmanischen Reich* (Munich, 1963).

21. The virtual bureaucratization of the religious scholars was another respect

in which the Ottomans added a new dimension to the organizational patterns inherited from earlier Islamic states. Gibb and Bowen, *Islamic Society*, I, ii, 83ff.; Richard Repp, "Some Observations on the Development of the Ottoman Learned Hierarchy," in *Scholars, Saints, and Sufis: Muslim Religious Institutions in the Middle East since 1500*, edited by Nikki Keddie (Berkeley and Los Angeles, 1972), 29-32; Uriel Heyd, "The Ottoman 'Ulemâ and Westernization in the Time of Selîm III and Maḥmûd II," *Scripta Hierosalymitana*, IX: *Studies in Islamic History and Civilization* (1961), 63-96; Richard W. Bulliet, "The Shaikh al-Islām and the Evolution of Islamic Society," *Studia Islamica*, XXXV (1972), 53-67; Michael M. Pixley, "The Development and Role of the Şeyhülislam in Early Ottoman History," *JAOS*, XCVI (1976), 89-96.

22. Gibb and Bowen, *Islamic Society*, I, i, 43-45; İnalcık, "Ghulām," *EI²*, II, 1090; M. Cavid Baysun, "Musâdere," *IA*, VIII, 669-73; Halil Sahillioğlu, "The Position of Slaves in the Social and Economic Life of Bursa in the Late 15th and Early 16th Centuries," unpublished paper; Metin Kunt, "Kulların Kulları," *Boğaziçi Universitesi Dergisi, Hümaniter Bilimler*, III (1975), 28-29.

23. Weber, *Economy and Society*, III, 956-58, 1028-31.

24. On this "grandee mentality" (*ağalık ve efendilik şuuru*), see Ülgener, *Zihniyet Meseleleri*, 45ff., 68, 96ff., 155ff.

25. S. N. Eisenstadt, *Traditional Patrimonialism and Modern Neopatrimonialism*, 34, 44-45; id. "Convergence and Divergence of Modern and Modernizing Societies: Indications from the Analysis of the Structuring of Social Hierarchies in Middle Eastern Societies," *IJMES*, VIII (1977), 12, 16; cf. Ülgener, *Zihniyet Meseleleri*, 150ff., 170ff. Here we need not take account of the "political power" that notables of the non-Muslim subject classes could enjoy within their own communities.

26. In extending the term "bureaucracy" to all branches of government service, we are following a usage general among social scientists. While a sociologist, for example, would apply the term to many settings even in the business world, there are still historians who associate it exclusively with government personnel in the field of civil administration, a setting for which we shall use more specific terms. Cf. Weber, *Economy and Society*, III, 956; Anthony Downs, *Inside Bureaucracy* (Boston, 1967), ch. iii.

27. Fred W. Riggs, "Bureaucratic Politics in Comparative Perspective," in *Frontiers of Development Administration*, edited by Fred W. Riggs (Durham, North Carolina, 1970), 388-90. Cf. id., "Bureaucrats and Political Development: A Paradoxical View," in *Bureaucracy and Political Development*, edited by Joseph LaPalombara (Princeton, 1967), 127ff.; Riggs, *Administration in Developing Countries* (Boston, 1964), 222-37; Şerif Mardin, *The Genesis of Young Ottoman Thought: A Study in the Modernization of Turkish Political Ideas* (Princeton, 1962), 119 and n. 35, citing Carl Friedrich; Eisenstadt, *Political Systems of Empires*, ch. x.

28. Mardin, *Genesis*, 94-102; Thomas, *Naima*, 78.

29. Weber, *Economy and Society*, I, 231-35; III, 1104-1109.

30. Eisenstadt, "Convergence and Divergence," 10-27. There is no need for serious discussion here of a philosophical view that depicted the society as consisting of four estate-like elements (*erkân*, "pillars"): soldiers, religious scholars, merchants, and cultivators. Borrowed by Islamic political philosophers from those of ancient Greece, and appearing in various permutations, this concept is suspect as a picture of actual social organization in Islamic societies. Ottoman

statesmen sometimes used it for purposes of special pleading, and it has sometimes led recent scholars into error. Cf. Rosenthal, *Political Thought*, 229; Mardin, *Genesis*, 98-100; Klaus Röhrborn, *Untersuchungen zur osmanischen Verwaltungsgeschichte* (Berlin, 1973), 84-86; Kemal Karpat, "The Transformation of the Ottoman State, 1789-1908," *IJMES*, III (1972), 243-44; C.A.O. van Nieuwenhuijze, *Social Stratification and the Middle East* (Leiden, 1965), 10.

31. As often noted, Islamic law dealt mainly with the responsibilities of the individual in relation to God and as a member of the overall Muslim community, was thus strongly egalitarian in character, and accorded little recognition to associational or corporative forms of organization intermediate between the individual and the entire collectivity of the faithful.

32. Cf. Gibb and Bowen, *Islamic Society*, I, i, 159.

33. Şerif Mardin, "Power, Civil Society and Culture in the Ottoman Empire," *Comparative Studies in Society and History*, XI (1969), 271-72; id., "Historical Determinants of Social Stratification: Social Class and Class Consciousness in Turkey," *Siyasal Bilgiler Fakültesi Dergisi*, XXII (1968), 117ff.

34. Claude Cahen, "Dhimma," *EI²*, II, 227-31.

35. The old interpretation of the communal system is particularly associated with Gibb and Bowen, although they were dissatisfied with the sources at their disposal; Gibb and Bowen, *Islamic Society*, I, ii, 207ff. The new interpretation is particularly linked to the Ph.D. dissertation of Benjamin Braude, "Community and Conflict in the Economy of the Ottoman Balkans" (Harvard, 1978), and the proceedings of the Conference on the Non-Muslim Communities in the Ottoman Empire and its Successor States, held at Princeton University in June 1978. The account of the new interpretation as given here is based on papers that Dr. Braude presented at the annual meeting of the Middle East Studies Association, November 1977, and at the Princeton conference, as well as on papers presented at that conference by Amnon Cohen, Halil İnalcık, Kevork Bardakjian, Hagop Barsoumian, Mark Epstein, and Richard Clogg. The interpretation given here is subject to emendation as these and other related works are revised and published. Cf. also Karl Binswanger, *Untersuchungen zum Status der Nichtmuslime im Osmanischen Reich des 16. Jahrhunderts, mit einer Neudefinition des Begriffes "Dimma"* (Munich, 1977).

36. Roderic H. Davison, *Reform in the Ottoman Empire, 1856-1876* (Princeton, 1963), 119 n. 17.

37. Halil İnalcık, "Imtiyāzāt," *EI²*, III, 1180.

38. Robert Mantran, *İstanbul dans la seconde moitié du XVIIe siècle* (Paris, 1962), 350-51; Gabriel Baer, "Monopolies and Restrictive Practices of Turkish Guilds," *JESHO*, XIII (1970), 156-59.

39. Cahen, "Dhimma," *EI²*, II, 228-29; Gibb and Bowen, *Islamic Society*, I, ii, 217-18, 259; Steven Runciman, *The Great Church in Captivity: A Study of the Patriarchate of Constantinople from the Eve of the Turkish Conquest to the Greek War of Independence* (Cambridge, 1968), 370-77.

40. Roderic H. Davison, "Turkish Attitudes Concerning Christian-Muslim Equality in the Nineteenth Century," *American Historical Review*, LIX (1954), 844-64; id., *Reform*, 55-56, 114-35.

41. Gabriel Baer, "Guilds in Middle Eastern History," in *Studies in the Economic History of the Middle East, from the Rise of Islam to the Present Day*, edited by M. A. Cook (London, 1970), 12, 16, 27; Claude Cahen, "Y a-t-il eu des corporations professionnelles dans le monde musulman classique?" in *The Islamic City: A Col-*

loquium, edited by Albert H. Hourani and S. M. Stern (Philadelphia, 1970), 51-63; cf. Bernard Lewis, "The Islamic Guilds," *Economic History Review*, VIII (1937), 20-33.

42. Hodgson, *Venture*, II, 125-31, 279-86.

43. Speros Vryonis, Jr., *The Decline of Medieval Hellenism in Asia Minor and the Process of Islamization from the Eleventh through the Fifteenth Century* (Berkeley and Los Angeles, 1971), 397.

44. S. D. Goitein, *A Mediterranean Society: The Jewish Communities of the Arab World as Portrayed in the Documents of the Cairo Geniza*, II: *The Community* (Berkeley and Los Angeles, 1971), 61-65.

45. Claude Cahen, "Mouvements populaires et autonomisme urbain dans l'Asie musulmane du Moyen Age," *Arabica*, V (1958), 225-51; VI (1959), 25-56, 233-65; id., "Futuwwa," *EI²*, II, 961-65.

46. Hodgson, *Venture*, II, 282; Claude Cahen, *Pre-Ottoman Turkey: A General Survey of the Material and Spiritual Culture and History, c. 1071-1330*, translated by J. Jones-Williams (New York, 1968), 197; Franz Taeschner, "Futuwwa, eine gemeinschaftbildende Idee im mittelalterlichen Orient und ihre verschiedenen Erscheinungsformen," *Schweizerisches Archiv für Volkskunde*, LII (1956), 128-30, 136-39; Neşet Çağatay, *Bir Türk Kurumu olan Ahilik* (Ankara, 1974), 23ff.; Angelika Hartmann, *An-Nāṣir li-Dīn Allāh (1180-1225): Politik, Religion, Kultur in der späten 'Abbāsidenzeit* (Berlin, 1975), 92-108, 233-54.

47. Franz Taeschner, "Akhī," *EI²*, I, 322; cf. Irène Mélikoff, "Ghāzī," *EI²*, II, 1043-45; Taeschner, "Idee," 131; for a speculative interpretation of the *ahi* groups, see Çağatay, *Ahilik*, 55-57.

48. Taeschner, "Idee," 144-49; Gibb and Bowen, *Islamic Society*, I, ii, 183, 188-90; Vryonis, *Decline*, ch. 5. Cf. Neşet Çağatay, "Fütüvvetçilikle Ahiliğin Ayrıntıları," *Bell.*, XL (1976), 423-38.

49. Cahen, *Pre-Ottoman Turkey*, 196-200; Hamilton A. R. Gibb, trans., *The Travels of Ibn Battuta, A.D. 1325-1354: Translated with Revisions and Notes from the Arabic text edited by C. Defrémery and B. R. Sanguinetti*, 3 vols. (Cambridge, 1958-71), II, 418-22, 426-65; Vryonis, *Decline*, 398-400.

50. Franz Taeschner, "War Murad I Grossmeister oder Mitglied des Achibundes?" *Oriens*, VI (1952), 23-31; id., "Idee," 149-50; id., "Akhī," *EI²*, I, 322.

51. Paul Wittek, *The Rise of the Ottoman Empire* (London, 1938), 49-50.

52. Gibb and Bowen, *Islamic Society*, I, ii, 189, 192-93, 195, 199-200; Abdülbâkî Gölpınarlı, "Mevlevîlik," *IA*, VIII, 166-67, 169; John K. Birge, *The Bektashi Order of Dervishes* (London, 1937), 15-16, 57; Suraiya Faroqhi, "The Tekke of Haci Bektaş: Social Position and Economic Activities," *IJMES*, VI (1976), 183-208, citing Ömer Lûtfi Barkan, "Osmanlı İmparatorluğunda bir İskân ve Kolonizasyon Metodu olarak Vakıflar ve Temlikler, I: İstilâ Devirlerinin Kolonizatör Türk Dervişleri ve Zâviyeler," *Vakıflar Dergisi*, II (1942), 279-353; personal discussion with Irène Mélikoff-Sayar, Ankara, July 1977.

53. Gabriel Baer, "The Administrative, Economic and Social Functions of Turkish Guilds," *IJMES*, I (1970), 28-50; id., "Monopolies and Restrictive Practices," 145-65; id., "Guilds in Middle Eastern History," 17-30; Mantran, *İstanbul*, 357, 361-62, and 391-93 (military guilds); İsmail Hakkı Uzunçarşılı, *Osmanlı Devleti Teşkilâtından Kapukulu Ocakları*, 2 vols. (Ankara, 1943-44), I, 368-73 (also on military service by guilds).

54. Ülgener, *Zihniyet Meseleleri*, 52-57; Robert W. Olson, "The Esnaf and the

Patrona Halil Rebellion of 1730: A Realignment in Ottoman Politics?" *JESHO*, xvii (1974), 329-44.

55. Çağatay, *Ahilik*, 28-35; Taeschner, "Idee," 146-56; id., "Futuwwa: Post-Mongol Period," *EI²*, ii, 966-68.

56. Birge, *Bektashi*, 96-101.

57. Taeschner, "Akhī," *EI²*, i, 322-23; Vryonis, *Decline*, 400. There was also another kind of three-grade ranking found in the *futuwwa* and the *ahi* groups: that of *kavlî* or "verbal" affiliate, *seyfî* or member invested with a "sword," and *şürbî* or member who had "drunk" from the common cup. These rankings probably overlapped with those mentioned for the *ahi*s in the text; Taeschner, "Idee," 140, 147, 153.

58. Baer, "Functions," 36; id., "Guilds in Middle Eastern History," 24; id., "The Structure of Turkish Guilds and its Significance for Ottoman Social History," *Proceedings of the Israel Academy of Sciences and Humanities*, iv (1969-1970), 183-95; Mantran, *Istanbul*, 368-71; Ülgener, *Zihniyet Meseleleri*, 83.

59. Gölpınarlı, "Mevlevîlik," *IA*, viii, 171; cf. Birge, *Bektashi*, 162-66.

60. Baer, "Guilds in Middle Eastern History," 30; id., "Structure of Turkish Guilds," 187-88, 195-96.

61. İsmail Hakkı Uzunçarşılı, *Osmanlı Devletinin Saray Teşkilâtı* (Ankara, 1945), 189-200; Abdülbâkî Gölpınarlı, "Şedd," *IA*, xi, 378-81; Pakalın, *OTD*, iii, 383-85, "Taklid-i Seyf" (his argument contradicts, but his evidence supports, the argument made here).

62. Gibb and Bowen, *Islamic Society*, i, i, 56-66.

63. İnalcık, *Ottoman Empire*, 85-86, on harem women. On school children: İnal, *Şair.*, ii, 1187; Aşçıdede Halil İbrahim, *Geçen Asrı aydınlatan Kıymetli Vesikalardan bir Eser: Hatıralar*, edited by Reşad Ekrem Koçu (Istanbul, 1960), 18; cf. M. L. Bremer, *Die Memoiren des türkischen Derwischs Aşçı Dede İbrahim* (Walldorf-Hessen, 1959), not available to me. Older pupils were assigned as *kalfa*s to younger ones, who became their *çırak*s. The teacher, of course, was not an *usta* but a *hoca*, a terminological substitution found also in the scribal bureaus.

64. Metin Kunt, *Sancaktan Eyalete: 1550-1650 Arasında Osmanlı Ümerası ve İl İdaresi* (Istanbul, 1975); id., unpublished studies entitled "Social Origins of the Ümera" and "The Structure of the Military-Administrative Career." See also Rifaat Ali Abou-el-Haj, "The Ottoman Vezir and Paşa Households, 1683-1703: A Preliminary Report," *JAOS*, xciv (1974), 438-47.

65. For indications of marriages by members of the slave-military establishment who had achieved high position, see A. D. Alderson, *The Structure of the Ottoman Dynasty* (Oxford, 1956), 97.

66. For example, İnal, *Şair.*, i, 590, 791; ii, 964-68, 1446; iii, 1804; Nermin Menemencioğlu, "Namık Kemal Abroad: A Centenary," *Middle Eastern Studies*, iv (1967), 29, for information on specific bureaucratic marriages. For recent discussions in the anthropological literature on marriage preferences among Turks, see Wolfram Eberhard, "Change in Leading Families in Southern Turkey," in *Peoples and Cultures of the Middle East*, edited by Louise Sweet (New York, 1970), ii, 255-56; Paul Stirling, *Turkish Village* (New York, 1965), 189-92, 201-208; Jean-Paul Roux, *Les traditions des nomades de la Turquie méridionale* (Paris, 1970), 321-24; J. Cuisenier, "Parenté et organisation sociale dans le domaine turc," *Annales: Économies, Sociétés, Civilisations*, xxvii (1972), 924-48; Paul Magnarella, *Tradition and Change in a Turkish Town* (New York, 1974), 87-90; Daniel

G. Bates, "Normative and Alternative Systems of Marriage among the Yörük of Southeastern Turkey," *Anthropological Quarterly*, xlvii (1974), 270-87; Ayşe Kudat, "Institutional Rigidity and Individual Initiative in Marriages of Turkish Peasants," *Anthropological Quarterly*, xlvii (1974), 288-303; Michael E. Meeker, "Meaning and Society in the Near East: Examples from the Black Sea Turks and the Levantine Arabs," *IJMES*, vii (1976), 243-70, 383-422. Meeker provides significant insights into the lack of a strongly marked preference for endogamy of the sort associated with other Middle Eastern societies. The work of others, such as Roux and Bates, suggests, however, that nomadic Turkish populations display such preferences.

67. Şerif Mardin, "Super Westernization in Urban Life in the Ottoman Empire in the Last Quarter of the Nineteenth Century," in *Turkey: Geographic and Social Perspectives*, edited by Peter Benedict et al. (Leiden, 1974), 410.

68. Elias J. W. Gibb, *A History of Ottoman Poetry*, 6 vols. (London, 1904), iii, 333.

69. Cf. Meeker, "Meaning and Society," 383ff., especially 393-94.

70. Alderson, *Structure of the Ottoman Dynasty*, 94-98; cf. the jests in the folk culture about the *iç güvey*, or man living with his wife's parents.

71. Aşçıdede Halil İbrahim, *Hatıralar*, 56ff.

72. Ibid., 36ff.

73. Halil İnalcık, "Husrev Paşa," *IA*, v, 613; Avigdor Levy, The Officer Corps in Sultan Mahmud II's New Army, 1826-39," *IJMES*, ii (1971), 28-29.

74. Metin Kunt, "Kulların Kulları," 27-42; id., *Sancaktan Eyalete*, 98-109; id., "Social Origins of the Ümera"; id., "The Structure of the Military-Administrative Career"; İnalcık, "Ghulām," *EI²*, ii, 1090; Herbert L. Bodman, Jr., *Political Factions in Aleppo, 1760-1826* (Chapel Hill, N.C., 1963), ch. 2.

75. In view of the fact that a non-Muslim could not become fully integrated into the traditional ruling class without conversion, one sign of these difficulties is that several of the most prominent Muslim scribal officials of the late eighteenth or early nineteenth century, having failed to form the contacts needed to launch their careers, had to form "connections" with prominent non-Muslims, and thus work their way indirectly into the more normal channels of advancement. The officials in question were Halil Hamid Paşa (Ahmed Cevdet, *Tarih-i Cevdet*, 12 vols. [Istanbul, 1309/1891-1892], iii, 133-34); Halet Efendi (ibid., x, 115); and Keçecizade İzzet Molla (İnal, *Şair*, i, 735-36).

76. Metin Kunt, "Ethnic-Regional (*Cins*) Solidarity in the Seventeenth-Century Ottoman Establishment," *IJMES*, v (1974), 233-39.

77. Cevdet, *Tarih*, iv, 328-29; x, 115; Ahmed Lûtfi, *Tarih-i Lûtfi*, 8 vols. (Istanbul, 1290-1328/c. 1873-1910), iv, 164; Ahmed Cevdet, *Tezâkir 40—Tetimme* (Ankara, 1967), 18-20, İnal, *Şair.*, i, 296, 735-36; ii, 819, 918, 1033, 1079, 1320, 1351-52, 1382, 1424-25; iv, 1972, 2149-50.

78. Röhrborn, *Verwaltungsgeschichte*, 66-67; Mantran, *İstanbul*, 102-103; İnal, *Şair.*, ii, 971-72,description of an exceptionally grand provincial household of the early nineteenth century; Mustafa Nuri, *Netayic ül-Vukuat*, 4 vols. (Istanbul, 1294-1327/1877-1909), iii, 92-94, description of household of a typical vezir of the eighteenth century.

79. Although born into a commercial family at later date, Halid Ziya Uşaklıgil gives quite a feeling for life in such settings in the early chapters of *Kırk Yıl* (Istanbul, 1969).

80. İsmail H. Uzunçarşılı, *Osmanlı Devletinin Merkez ve Bahriye Teşkilâtı* (Ankara, 1948), 264-66; Joseph von Hammer-Purgstall, *Constantinopolis und der Bosporos, örtlich und geschichtlich beschrieben* (Osnabrück, 1967; reprint of edition of 1822), I, 327-29.

81. İsmail H. Uzunçarşılı, *Saray*; Barnette Miller, *Beyond the Sublime Porte* (New Haven, 1931); id., *The Palace School of Muhammad the Conqueror* (Cambridge, Mass., 1941); Gibb and Bowen, *Islamic Society*, I, i, 71-88; Hammer, *Constantinopolis*, I, 220-321.

82. Lady Mary Wortley Montagu, *The Complete Letters of Lady Mary Wortley Montagu*, 3 vols., edited by Robert Halsband (Oxford, 1965-1967), I, 347-52, 380-87.

83. Ahmed Cevdet, *Tezâkir 13-20* (Ankara, 1960), 17-18; İnal, *Şair.*, II,793-97. 971-72; III, 1744.

84. İnal, *Şair.*, II, 1006.

85. A late example is in Kemal Karpat, "The Memoirs of N. Batzaria: The Young Turks and Nationalism," *IJMES*, VI (1975), 290.

86. Reşat Kaynar, *Mustafa Reşit Paşa ve Tanzimat* (Ankara, 1954), 44, marriage of M.R. to a concubine of his deceased patron and uncle, Seyyid Ali Paşa; Aşçıdede Halil İbrahim, *Hatıralar*, 60, marriage to nursemaid of son of patron, Derviş, Paşa; İnal, *Şair.*, III, 1804, marriage of poet Şinasi to slave of one of Mahmud II's favorite harem women (*ikbal*).

87. Aşçıdede Halil İbrahim, *Hatıralar*, 11-13, describes his family and says most of the Muslims of Kandilli were related to him.

88. Weber, *Economy and Society*, I, 228.

89. Ogier Ghiselin de Busbecq, *The Turkish Letters of Ogier Ghiselin de Busbecq*, edited and translated by Edward Seymour Forster (Oxford, 1927), 22-23, 59-61.

90. Aşçıdede Halil İbrahim, *Hatıralar*, 13-15.

91. A. Ubicini, *La Turquie actuelle* (Paris, 1855), 170; on Rıza, cf. Ahmed Cevdet, *Tezâkir 1-12* (Ankara, 1953), 6.

92. İnal, *Şair.*, I, 117.

93. Mardin, "Power, Civil Society, and Culture," 272.

94. G. E. Aylmer, *The King's Servants: The Civil Service of Charles I, 1625-1642* (London, 1961), 10-12; Eisenstadt, *Political Systems*, 233-34; id., *Traditional Patrimonialism and Modern Neopatrimonialism*, 35.

95. Cf. comments of Walter G. Andrews, Jr., *An Introduction to Ottoman Poetry* (Minneapolis and Chicago, 1976), 148-50 and 158-59 on the *kaside* and on satire.

96. Thomas, *Naima*, 35.

97. İnal, *Şair.*, I, 751; II, 814ff., 831, 1011, 1021-22, 1211-13, 1272-73; III, 1569; id., *Sadr.*, I, 24-25, 31ff., 187 n. 1.

98. Cevdet, *Tarih*, VIII, 131-32; XII, 55-59, 109-15.

99. Ibid., x, 122-16, 184-86, 235; XI, 25; XII, 55-59; other accounts of the factional politics of this period appear in Stanford J. Shaw, *Between Old and New: The Ottoman Empire under Sultan Selim III, 1789-1807* (Cambridge, Mass., 1971), ch. 20; and Avigdor Levy, "Sultan Mahmud II's New Army," 36-39; İnal, *Şair.*, II, 1301-12.

CHAPTER TWO

1. Mustafa Nuri, *Netayic*, II, 104.

2. BBA, Buy. 1, entry of 3 CA 1240/1824.

3. The chief exceptions to this lay in the field of military technology and in the short-lived "silhouette of a Renaissance" at the beginning of the eighteenth century; Berkes, *Secularism*, 23-50.

4. Weber, *Economy and Society*, 1, 215ff.; S. N. Eisenstadt, *Modernization: Protest and Change* (Englewood Cliffs, N.J., 1966), v, 15-16; id., *Traditional Patrimonialism and Modern Neopatrimonialism*, 43-44. For stimulating my awareness of these points and of the contrast between the patrimonial tradition and rational-legalism, I am indebted to Metin Heper, *Türk Kamu Bürokrasisinde Gelenekçilik ve Modernleşme: Siyaset Sosyolojisi Açısından bir İnceleme* (Istanbul, 1977), ch. 2, and to discussions with him and Şerif Mardin in Istanbul in the spring of 1976. As to Weber's charismatic authority, this of course became a major factor in Turkish history with Atatürk, but never on comparable scale in the nineteenth century. The remainder of this chapter is an adaptation, in the light of the ideas referred to here, of substantive arguments first presented in my paper, "The Evolution of the Ottoman Ruling Class, from Traditionalism to Reform," presented at a conference on "Polity, Society, and Economy in the Nineteenth and Twentieth Centuries in Turkey and North Africa." The conference was held in Istanbul in May 1975 under the sponsorship of the Joint Committee on the Near and Middle East of the Social Science Research Council and the American Council of Learned Societies.

5. Albert H. Lybyer, *The Government of the Ottoman Empire in the Time of Suleiman the Magnificent* (Cambridge, Mass., 1913).

6. Gibb and Bowen, *Islamic Society*, 1, i, 43-45, 173ff.

7. Thomas, *Naima*, 22-24; Norman Itzkowitz, "Eighteenth Century Ottoman Realities," *Studia Islamica*, XVI (1962), 73-94.

8. The pioneering works of Uzunçarşılı, on institutional history imply an overall schematization, but without bringing it or its development over time into full focus; İsmail H. Uzunçarşılı, *Osmanlı Devleti Teşkilâtından Kapukulu Ocakları*, 2 vols. (Ankara, 1943-1944); id., *Osmanlı Devletinin Saray Teşkilâtı* (Ankara, 1945); id., *Osmanlı Devletinin Merkez ve Bahriye Teşkilâtı* (Ankara, 1948); id., *Osmanlı Devletinin İlmiye Teşkilâtı* (Ankara, 1965). Although he alludes to "civil service" once, İnalcık implicitly accepts the dichotomous interpretation for the prereform periods in "The Nature of Traditional Society: B. Turkey," in *Political Modernization in Japan and Turkey*, edited by Robert E. Ward and Dankwart A. Rustow (Princeton, 1964), 43-44. Yet, he speaks of "men of the pen," "men of the sword," and "men of religion" in *Ottoman Empire*, 100. Attempting to describe the "political leadership groups" of the late sixteenth and early seventeenth century, Röhrborn, *Verwaltungsgeschichte*, 13-26, speaks more of individual positions than of branches of the ruling class or other groups of any size. Josef Matuz, *Das Kanzleiwesen Sultan Süleymâns des Prächtigen* (Wiesbaden, 1974), 19-20, comments on the inapplicability to the sixteenth century of descriptions of the organization of the grand vezir's chancery as of the eighteenth, but does not make reference to broader organizational patterns or changes in them over time.

9. Matuz, *Kanz.*, 13-14; Uzunçarşılı, *Merkez*, 48 n. 5, 50, 158-63. On the later history of this practice, see Joseph von Hammer-Purgstall, *Des osmanischen Reichs Staatsverfassung und Staatsverwaltung* (Vienna, 1815; reprinted Hildesheim, 1963), II, 96-97, 136-37; Cevdet, *Tarih*, v, 114-15; VIII, 103-104, 271. On the general concept of the ruling class as "military," see Hodgson, *Venture*, II, 562-63.

10. Thomas, *Naima*, 24; Itzkowitz, "Realities," 80, 82, 85; cf. Gibb and Bowen, *Islamic Society*, I, i, 45, 120 n. 5, 127 n. 9. On personnel movements between the

religious and military-administrative establishments, cf. İnalcık, "Ghulām," *EI²*, II, 1087. For an example from the political-philosophical tradition (al-Dawwânî) of the identification of the "men of the pen" with the religious scholars, see Rosenthal, *Political Thought*, 220.

11. Itzkowitz, "Realities," 77.

12. Heyd, *Criminal Law*, 152-57. Cf. R. C. Repp, "The Altered Nature and Role of the Ulema," in *Studies in Eighteenth Century Islamic History*, edited by Thomas Naff and Roger Owen (Carbondale, Ill., 1977), 277-87.

13. Uzunçarşılı, *Saray*; Gibb and Bowen, *Islamic Society*, I, i, 71-88, 329-62.

14. İnalcık, "Ghulām," *EI²*, II, 1086. On the changing social character of the palace service, cf. Itzkowitz, "Realities," 84-85.

15. Ignatius Mouradgea d'Ohsson, *Tableau général de l'Empire othoman*, 7 vols. (Paris, 1788-1824), VII, 54-62; Uzunçarşılı, *Saray*, 172-83, 354-57; Gibb and Bowen, *Islamic Society*, I, i, 76, 82, 332-33; İnalcık, "Ghulām," *EI²*, II, 1088.

16. Uşaklıgil, *Kırk Yıl*, 497-99.

17. Matuz, *Kanz.*, 16.

18. D'Ohsson, *Tableau*, VII, 34-35, 59-61, and Hammer, *Staats.*, II, 13-14, did not yet clearly perceive this emergence of the sword-bearer. Cf. Cevdet, *Tarih*, III, 127-28; IX, 258; Uzunçarşılı, *Saray*, 342-48; Gibb and Bowen, *Islamic Society*, I, i. 80-82, 338-40; Şerafeddin Turan, "Silâhdâr." *IA*, X, 640-41.

19. Gibb and Bowen, *Islamic Society*, I, i, 80, 333; Hammer, *Constantinopolis*, I, 220.

20. İnalcık, "Reis-ül-Küttâb," *IA*, IX, 672-73; cf. Matuz, *Kanz.*, 18 n. 2, 23. The *tuğra* consists of the name of the reigning Sultan with that of his father and the phrase "ever victorious"—e.g., *Mahmud Han bin Abd ül-Hamid Han, muzaffer daima*—the letters being arranged in a complex pattern of which the general contours varied only marginally over centuries. The uses of this motif generally correspond to those of the great seal of a Western government. The *tuğra* of Abd ül-Mecid (1839-1861), who was the son of Mahmud II (1808-1839), appears as the frontispiece of this volume.

21. Matuz, *Kanz.*, 22-24; Heyd, *Criminal Law*, 171, 189; Uzunçarşılı, *Merkez*, 214-27; M. T. Gökbilgin, "Nişancı," *IA*, IX, 299; Nejat Göyünç, "Tevki," *IA*, XII, 217-19.

22. Matuz, *Kanz.*, 45-48.

23. Ibid., 21; Uzunçarşılı, *Merkez*, 96-110; Gibb and Bowen, *Islamic Society*, I, i, 124-28. Pakalın, *OTD*, I, 418-19, "Defter Emini," "Defterhane."

24. Matuz, *Kanz.*, 33-45; İnalcık, "Reis-ül-Küttâb," *IA*, IX, 671-83.

25. Uzunçarşılı, *Merkez*, 319-37; id., "Defterdâr," *IA*, III, 506-508; Gibb and Bowen, *Islamic Society*, I, i, 128-37.

26. Uzunçarşılı, *Merkez*, 71-76; Cengiz Orhonlu, "Tercüman," *IA*, XII, 176-77; Matuz, *Kanz.*, 21; id., "Die Pfortendolmetscher zur Herrschaftszeit Süleymâns des Prächtigen," *Südostforschungen*, XXIV (1975), 26-60.

27. Uzunçarşılı, *Merkez*, 58-64; Matuz, *Kanz.*, 21.

28. İnalcık, *Ottoman Empire*, 101.

29. Ömer Lûtfi Barkan, "H. 933-934 (M. 1527-1528) Malî Yılına ait bir Bütçe Örneği," *IFM*, XV (1953-1954), 323-26, cf. 314 n. 1 for date. Matuz makes heavy use of this document in *Kanz*. It is, however, only one piece of documentary evidence on a subject about which much more unpublished material should exist.

30. Barkan, "H. 933-934 (M. 1527-1528) Malî Yılına ait bir Bütçe Örneği,"

300, figures of c. 1527, cited by İnalcık, "Ghulām," *EI²*, II, 1089. Cf. Röhrborn, *Verwaltungsgeschichte*, 78 n. 128.

31. Matuz, *Kanz.*, 52.

32. Ibid., 28, 39, 53-54.

33. Ibid., 55; this was the case of Ahmed Feridun, compiler of the *Münşeat ül-Selâtin*, and one of the most noted scribal intellectuals of the sixteenth century.

34. İnalcık, "Reis-ül-Küttâb," *IA*, IX, 676-77, 679; cf. Klaus Röhrborn, "Die Emanzipation der Finanzbürokratie im Osmanischen Reich (Ende 16. Jahrhundert)," *Zeitschrift der Deutschen Morgenländischen Gesellschaft*, CXXII (1972), 130-37, on the development of collective self-awareness among the scribes.

35. Matuz, *Kanz.*, 19-20, 51, 55, 61.

36. Matuz, *Kanz.*, 59; Röhrborn, *Verwaltungsgeschichte*, 20-22, 144-49; id., "Emanzipation," 118-39.

37. Uzunçarşılı, *Merkez*, 136-38, 262-64; B. Lewis, art. "Dīwān-ı humāyūn," *EI²*, II, 339.

38. Itzkowitz, "Realities," 89-91.

39. Thomas, *Naima*, 35-42; cf. Uzunçarşılı, *Merkez*, 64-68, treating this post as part of the Office of the Imperial Divan. As an official post, the office of historiographer was an eighteenth-century creation.

40. Rifa'at A. Abou-El-Haj, "Ottoman Diplomacy at Karlowitz," *JAOS*, LXXXVII (1967), 498-512.

41. TPK, D3208, including enumeration of officials serving in the Treasury (*Bab-ı Defteri*) and at the Sublime Porte (*Bab-ı Âli*). The document can be dated only on the basis of internal evidence. Since the listings for the Porte include the Office of the *Amedî*, which İnalcık believes to have come into existence about 1777 (İnalcık, "Reis-ül-Küttâb," *IA*, IX, 674-75) but not the Section for Important Affairs (*Mühimme Odası*) founded in the Office of the Imperial Divan in 1797 (BBA, Kal. Niz., 4-7, entry of 1 Ş 1211/1797), TPK, D3208, should date from the years between 1777 and 1797.

42. Itzkowitz, "Realities," 86; cf. Thomas, *Naima*, 51.

43. For present purposes, we may overlook some questions that would require treatment in a comprehensive study of this question. One important example is the relatively low levels of development of nonmilitary governmental institutions in most of the successor states, as opposed to the Ottoman Empire itself or the Turkish Republic.

44. Berkes, *Secularism*, 47-48, 58ff.

45. Stanford Shaw, *Old and New*, pt. iii.

46. Howard A. Reed, "The Destruction of the Janissaries by Mahmud II in June, 1826," Ph.D. dissertation, Princeton, 1951; Avigdor Levy, "The Military Policy of Sultan Mahmud II, 1808-1839," Ph.D. dissertation, Harvard, 1968.

47. Osman Ergin, *İstanbul Mektepleri ve İlim, Terbiye ve San'at Müesseseleri dolayısile Türkiye Maarif Tarihi* (Istanbul, 1939-1943), II, 264ff.; Levy, "Sultan Mahmud's New Army," 21-39.

48. Findley, "Sir James W. Redhouse (1811-1892): The Making of a Perfect Orientalist?" forthcoming in *JAOS*; Bernard Lewis, *The Emergence of Modern Turkey* (Oxford, 1968), 87.

49. Mardin, *Genesis*, 130-31; id., *Jön Türklerin Siyasî Fikirleri, 1895-1908* (Ankara, 1964), ch. 2; FO 371/548, File 29285, Memorandum by Colonel Surtees on "The Turkish Empire as a Military Factor," included in the ambassador's "Gen-

eral Report on Turkey for the Year 1906" (Conf. Pr. 8982), 16. Cf. Kemal Karpat, "The Transformation of the Ottoman State, 1789-1908," *IJMES*, III (1972), 277-79.

50. Heyd, "The Ottoman 'Ulemâ and Westernization," 92.

51. The inability of the military to provide the kind of leadership needed in 1839 was dramatically illustrated by the shift of power from Husrev Paşa, a military reformer, to Mustafa Reşid Paşa, first of the great civil-bureaucratic statesmen of the mid-nineteenth century. On this transition, see İnalcık, "The Nature of Traditional Society: B. Turkey," 54-55; id., "Husrev Paşa," *IA*, v, 614.

52. E.g., Cevdet, *Tarih*, IV, 261-62; V, 27-35, 231; XII, 82-83.

53. Ibid., IV, 195.

54. Ibid., III, 38.

55. Heyd, "The Ottoman 'Ulemâ and Westernization," 90-96. See also Avigdor Levy, "The Ottoman Ulema and the Military Reforms of Sultan Mahmud II," *Asian and African Studies*, VII (1971), 13-39.

56. Lewis, *Emergence*, 92-94.

57. Halil İnalcık, "Application of the Tanzimat and its Social Effects," *Archivum Ottomanicum*, V (1973), 100ff.; İlber Ortaylı, *Tanzimattan Sonra Mahalli İdareler (1840-1878)* (Ankara, 1974), 95-96.

58. Richard L. Chambers, "The Education of a Nineteenth-Century Ottoman Âlim, Ahmed Cevdet Paşa," *IJMES*, IV (1973), 459-60, 464.

59. Mardin, *Jön Türk.*, 41-42.

60. Hammer, *Staats.*, II, 103; Cevdet, *Tarih*, VIII, 146.

61. Lûtfi, *Tarih*, III, 166; Şerafeddin Turan, "Silâhdâr," *IA*, x, 641.

62. Cf. the memoirs of Halid Ziya Uşaklıgil, *Saray ve Ötesi* (Istanbul, 1965), appointed first secretary to Sultan Mehmed Reşad in 1909.

63. Cevdet, *Tarih*, IV, 195.

64. *Salname-i Devlet-i Aliye-i Osmaniye* (Istanbul, 1326/1908), 160, 204, 228, 554, 562, 586, 602.

65. Estimate based on BBA, DSA. This collection includes almost two hundred registers, of which each may contain up to five hundred biographies. Cf. Midhat Sertoğlu, *Muhteva Bakımından Başvekâlet Arşivi* (Ankara, 1955), 81-82. The identification of the collection with the Interior (*Dahiliye*) Ministry signifies no more than that the commission mainly responsible for keeping the records was located there. The collection covers essentially the whole civil bureaucracy, but not other branches of the ruling class: *Dstr.*[1], IV, 63, instructions of March 1879, art. 1. A later reference identifies the system as applying specifically to civil officials (*memurin-i mülkiye*) and members of other branches of service when employed in civil-bureaucratic posts: ibid., v, 965-71, instructions of May 1887, arts, 1, 25. The extent to which it is meaningful to think of all these people as active civil officials will require consideration in Chapter Six.

66. Mardin, *Genesis*, 127-28; Lewis, *Emergence*, 374. Enver Ziya Karal, *OT*, VIII, 320ff., uses the term as if it meant "provincial administration," a practice that must derive from the original name of the Interior Ministry as the *Mülkiye Nezareti*, also from the fact that most civil officials probably served in the provinces. Ottoman usage was never fully consistent and often seemed to take *mülkiye* as a residual category in contrast to others more precisely named. See, for instance, *Dstr.*[1], VI, 488-90, regulation of January 1890 on the duties and responsibilities of civil and financial officials (*mülkiye ve maliye memurları*) at the provin-

cial level; ibid., VI, 1105, regulations of September 1891 for the Statistical Council of the Sublime Porte, art. 3, reference to "matters pertaining to civil, financial, judicial, public-works, educational, and municipal affairs" (*ahval-i mülkiye ve maliye ve adliye ve nafia ve maarif ve belediyeye aid hususatı*); ibid., VII, 133, instructions of December 1896 for the Civil Officials Commission, art. 6, reference again to "civil and financial officials" (*memurin-i mülkiye ve maliye*). In other cases, the use of the term *mülkiye* clearly encompasses the cases seemingly distinguished in the passages just cited; e.g., ibid., *zeyl* IV, 13, decree of May 1884 on promotion and retirement of civil officials, art. 19, definition of eligibility for civil retirement pensions; ibid., VI, 1143-45, decree of December 1891 on unemployment stipends for civil officials. That *mülkiye* referred to the civil bureaucracy in general is also clear in any situation where there is reference to official ranks, as in the tables of correspondence of civil, military, and religious ranks regularly published in the government yearbooks (e.g., *Saln.* [1297], 84; [1326], 38).

67. In using terms such as civil bureaucracy or civil service, we assume in a general way the concept of modern bureaucracy as described by Weber, *Economy and Society*, III, 956-58, or more recently by Downs, *Inside Bureaucracy*, ch. 3. In more specific terms, we refer to those government officials employed in civil-administrative affairs (as contrasted in the Ottoman case to religious or military affairs or those of the palace) in proportion as the conditions of recruitment, service, and advancement under which those officials worked began to be brought under rules and regulations embodying such distinctive traits of modern bureaucracy as promotion on the basis of achievement and performance. In the nineteenth century, regulatory patterns of this kind emerged only gradually, not only in the Ottoman Empire, but also in the Western states that served as the chief models for the Ottoman reforms. Cf. E. N. Gladden, *Civil Services of the United Kingdom* (London, 1967), 1-5; id., *A History of Public Administration*, 2 vols. (London, 1972), II, ch. 9.

CHAPTER THREE

1. From the *Hayriye* of the poet Nabi (1630-1712); E.J.W. Gibb, *Poetry*, III, 343-44; VI, 231; with modifications of Gibb's translation.

2. Uzunçarşılı, *Merkez*, 113. On the problem of dating the so-called *Kanunname* of Mehmed the Conqueror, quoted there, see Konrad Dilger, *Untersuchungen zur Geschichte des Osmanischen Hofzeremoniells im 15. und 16. Jahrhundert* (Munich, 1967), 14-34.

3. Thus according to Hammer, *Staats.*, II, 82, 137, and d'Ohsson, *Tableau*, VII, 191, both of whom were contemporary observers. Cf. the account in İnalcık, *Ottoman Empire*, 95-96, on sixteenth-century conditions.

4. Hammer, *Staats.*, II, 79-101; d'Ohsson, *Tableau*, VII, 151-59; Gibb and Bowen, *Islamic Society*, I, i, 107-13.

5. Uzunçarşılı, *Merkez*, 136-40, 262-63; Heyd, *Criminal Law*, 224-26; d'Ohsson, *Tableau*, VII, 213-32.

6. Hammer, *Staats.*, II, 119-29; d'Ohsson, *Tableau*, VII, 166-69; Gibb and Bowen, *Islamic Society*, I, i, 118-20; for the sixteenth century, Matuz notes only one *tezkereci*, then subordinate to the affixer of the cipher (*nişancı*), *Kanz.*, 45-47. Cf. Uzunçarşılı, *Saray*, 408-19.

7. TPK, D3208; Hammer, *Staats.*, II, 102-108, 132-33; d'Ohsson, *Tableau*, VII, 159, 170-72; Gibb and Bowen, *Islamic Society*, I, i, 120, 363-64; Uzunçarşılı, *Merkez*, 256-59.

8. Hammer, *Staats.*, II, 112-13; d'Ohsson, *Tableau*, VII, 159-66; Gibb and Bowen, *Islamic Society*, I, i, 121-24; İnalcık, "Reis-ül-Küttâb," *IA*, IX, 671-83.

9. Hammer, *Staats.*, II, 109-10; d'Ohsson, *Tableau*, VII, 160; Gibb and Bowen, *Islamic Society*, I, i, 121-22; Uzunçarşılı, *Merkez*, 40-43; İnalcık, "Reis-ül-Küttâb," *IA*, IX, 674-75; Sertoğlu, *Başvekâlet*, 14-29; the account of the offices of the chief scribe in Jan Reychman and Ananiasz Zajaczkowski, *Handbook of Ottoman-Turkish Diplomatics*, translated by Andrew S. Ehrenkreutz (The Hague, 1968), 165-68, is highly inaccurate.

10. Hammer, *Staats.*, II, 110-11; Uzunçarşılı, *Merkez*, 43-45.

11. On the contrast of fief and benefice, see Weber, *Economy and Society*, III, 966-67, 1031-38, 1073-77. We shall use the term "benefice" to refer to various kinds of remuneration, other than salaries, to which members of the ruling class might be entitled by virtue of their occupancy of specific offices, but not, in principle, if they ceased to hold those offices. As a general term to signify compensation by such means, as opposed to the payment of salaries from a central treasury, we shall speak of "prebendalism." The essential difference between the prebendal forms of income and salaries is that the latter presuppose a money economy and centralized fiscal administration. Prebendalism arises when those conditions are not entirely fulfilled and means that officials are assigned certain perquisites, often in kind, or allowed to collect specific revenues directly for their compensation. We shall not follow Weber in assuming the assignment of prebends or benefices to be for life (ibid., III, 966).

12. Hammer, *Staats.*, II, 111; d'Ohsson, *Tableau*, VII, 160; Uzunçarşılı, *Merkez*, 45-48; Pakalın, *OTD*, III, 71-72, "Rüus" and "Rüus-i Hümayun Kalemi."

13. Uzunçarşılı, *İlmiye*, 77, 183; cf. Cevdet, *Tarih*, VI, 195.

14. D'Ohsson, *Tableau*, VII, 160.

15. T. Gökbilgin, "Nişancı," *IA*, IX, 299; Pakalın, *OTD*, I, 418, "Defter Emini."

16. Röhrborn, *Verwaltungsgeschichte*, 39ff., 49-52, 59-61, 68-69, 77-84.

17. Nejat Göyünç, "XVI. Yüzyılda Ruûs ve Önemi," *Tar. Der.*, XVII, no. 22 (1967), 20-23; Nedim Filipović, "O izrazu 'tahvil,' " *Prilozi za Orijentalnu Filologiju i Istoriju Jugoslovenskih Naroda pod Turskom Vladavinom*, II (1951), 239-47.

18. TPK, D3208 (tabulation itemized by office and summing to 90, but including *kâtibs* only); Hammer, *Staats.*, II, 111-12 (gives total of 120, which he says includes *kâtibs*, *şagirds*, and *şerhlis*); d'Ohsson, *Tableau*, VII, 160 (indicating a total of 150, again including *kâtibs*, *şagirds*, and *şerhlis*); Uzunçarşılı, *Merkez*, 45-46, attributes 150 to the *Rüus* Office alone, but that is a misreading of d'Ohsson.

19. Matuz, "Pfortendolmetscher," 32, 40.

20. Ibid., 36; Runciman, *Great Church*, 364-69.

21. Hammer, *Staats.*, II, 117-19; Orhonlu, "Tercüman," *IA*, XII, 177-78; Uzunçarşılı, *Merkez*, 75.

22. TPK, D3208; Hammer, *Staats.*, II, 129-31; d'Ohsson, *Tableau*, VII, 169-70; Gibb and Bowen, *Islamic Society*, I, i, 120; Uzunçarşılı, *Merkez*, 260. Cf. Itzkowitz, "Realities," 88: of twenty-six men who served as chief scribe, 1697-1774, ten were promoted to that post from the position of corresponding secretary. Sertoğlu, *Başvekâlet*, 46, mentions registers from this office dating as far back as 1696.

23. TPK, D3208; Hammer, *Staats.*, II, 113; d'Ohsson, *Tableau*, VII, 166; T. Gökbilgin, "Âmedci," *IA*, I, 396-97; id., Âmeddji," *EI²*, I, 443; İnalcık, "Reis'ül-Küttâb," *IA*, IX, 675; Uzunçarşılı, *Merkez*, 55-58; Sertoğlu, *Başvekâlet*, 13-14.

24. Weber, *Economy and Society*, III, 1028-29, 1088-90.

25. Gibb and Bowen, *Islamic Society*, I, i, 122 n. 4; Findley, "The Legacy of Tradition to Reform: Origins of the Ottoman Foreign Ministry," *IJMES*, I (1970), 339; Joel Shinder, "Career Line Formation in the Ottoman Bureaucracy, 1648-1750: A New Perspective," *JESHO*, XVI (1973), 231-35.

26. BBA, Müh. 165, 30, *hüküm* of Et RA 1180/August 1766 to Chief Scribe; cf. BBA, Rüus 217, *ilm-ü-haber* of same date, addressed to *Beylikçi*, but seemingly identical in text; BBA, Müh. 165, 44, *hüküm* of El R 1180/September 1766 to Keeper of the Registers; Uzunçarşılı, *Merkez*, 49 n. 5, quoting a document of Et Ş 1144/February 1732. The number of *gedik*s varies in different references.

27. Pakalın, *OTD*, I, 656-61, "Gedik," "Gedikli," etc., indicating application of *gedik* system in a number of settings in ruling class; cf. Mantran, *İstanbul*, 368-70; Baer, "Monopolies and Restrictive Practices," 159-65.

28. For published budgetary documents containing information on payment of salaries to scribal officials, see Barkan, "H. 933-934 (M. 1527-1528) Malî Yılına ait bir Bütçe Örneği," *IFM*, XV (1953-1954), 309, salary list of 1494-1495, dated on 308 n. 1, and 323-26, list of c. 1530s, dating discussed on 314 n. 1; M. Belin, "Essais sur l'histoire économique de la Turquie," ch. 4, sect. 1, "Budgets particuliers," *Journal asiatique*, 6e série, IV (1864), 256-57, list of 1592; Barkan, "1070-1071 (1660-1661) Tarihli Osmanlı Bütçesi ve Bir Mukayese," *IFM*, XVII (1955-1956), 316, list of 1660-1661; id., "1079-1080 (1669-1670) Mâlî Yılına âit bir Osmanlı Bütçesi ve Ek'leri," *IFM*, XVII (1955-1956), 230, list of 1669-1670. Some sixteenth-century sources also include indications of a different type of salaries paid on an annual basis (*salyane*). See Barkan, "954-955 (1547-1548) Malî Yılına Âit Bir Osmanlı Bütçesi," *IFM*, XIX (1957-1958), 263-64; id., "H. 974-975 (M. 1567-1568) Malî Yılına Âit Bir Osmanlı Bütçesi," *IFM*, XIX (1957-1958), 309. At least for scribal personnel of the Porte, however, there is no known record of the payment of salaries in the eighteenth century.

29. BBA, Müh. 165, 44, *hüküm* of El R 1180/September 1766 to Keeper of Registers.

30. Cf. Uzunçarşılı, *Merkez*, 83.

31. J. Deny, "Tîmâr," *EI¹*, IV, 771.

32. See document of 1799, associating the term *pervazi* with the *şerhli*s, in Tevfik Temelkuran, "Divân-ı Hümâyûn Mühimme Kalemi," *İstanbul Üniversitesi Edebiyat Fakültesi Tarih Enstitüsü Dergisi*, no. 6 (1975), 151, and Pakalın, *OTD*, II, 772, "Pervazi."

33. See sources cited in Findley, "Legacy," 339 n. 4; Temelkuran, "Mühimme Kalemi," 151; Pakalın, *OTD*, II, 611-12, "Mülâzım."

34. Hammer, *Staats.*, II, 114-17; d'Ohsson, *Tableau*, VII, 161; Uzunçarşılı, *Merkez*, 40, 42, 47; Pakalın, *OTD*, II, 249, "Kesedar" (an alternate spelling). On filing documents in sacks, cf. Matuz, *Kanz.*, 89-90.

35. BBA, Kal. Niz., 18-19, regulations of 2 Ş 1211/January 1797 for Office of the Corresponding Secretary (*Mektubî*), the more usual and morphologically more parallel terms for the document-producing processes being *tesvid*, *telhis*, and *tebyiz*; ibid., 30-31, regulations of same date for Office of Receiver (*Amedî*).

36. Hammer, *Staats.*, II, 113-14.

37. E.g., İnalcık, "Reis-ül-Küttâb," *IA*, ıx, 674; followed by Matuz, *Kanz.*, 19-20.

38. James W. Redhouse, *A Turkish and English Lexicon* (Constantinople, 1921), 339, under "bitik" and "bitikji." Cf. Gerard Clauson, *An Etymological Dictionary of Pre-Thirteenth-Century Turkish* (Oxford, 1972), 304; and İnalcık, "Reis-ül-Küttâb," *IA*, ıx, 672, on these terms in pre-Ottoman usage. Despite the apparent antiquity of its name, the office of *beylikçi* is not noted for the period of which Matuz wrote.

39. TPK, D3208, relevant passage translated in L. Fekete, *Die Siyâqat-Schrift in der türkischen Finanzverwaltung* (Budapest, 1955), ı, 68 n. 2.

40. For further information on the processing and formal properties of different types of documents, as well as bibliography on Ottoman diplomatics, see Matuz, *Kanz.*, 64ff. and bibliography. For a convenient work in English on one facet of Ottoman diplomatics, see Uriel Heyd, *Ottoman Documents on Palestine, 1552-1615: A Study of the Firman according to the Mühimme Defteri* (Oxford, 1960).

41. George Larpent, *Turkey; Its History and Progress: From the Journals and Correspondence of Sir James Porter* . . . , 2 vols. (London, 1854; reprinted 1971), ı, 268-69.

42. Hammer, *Staats.*, ıı, 115-17.

43. D'Ohsson, *Tableau*, vıı, 228-32; cf. account of an assembly of 1789 in Shaw, *Old and New*, 73-75.

44. For example, Cevdet, *Tarih*, ııı, 35-47, an account of c. 1784; x, 17-20, account of 1812.

45. Ibid., ıv, 156-57, events of 1788-1789; vıı, 28, events of 1799.

46. Ibid., ııı, 37, account of 1775; ıx, 302, order of the sultan to an assembly convened June 1810 (cf. ıx, 180).

47. Ibid., ıı, 243-44, account of an assembly of c. 1783; ııı, 35-37, discussions of 1784 on the Crimea (the grand vezir informed the sultan that he thought the Russians were trying to force the convening of a council, knowing that whatever was discussed there would leak out); ıv, 360, assembly of 1788-1789; ıx, 302, discussion of 1810.

48. Ibid., ııı, 38; v, 270, events of 1792; vı, 6, events of c. 1792; x, 19, assembly of January 1812.

49. Kaynar, *Mustafa Reşit*, 206.

50. Cevdet, *Tarih*, ııı, 332, decree of Abd ül-Hamid I, c. 1784, denouncing the sorry wretches (*yâdıgâr*) who served the empire for not being of use to it, as the statesmen of the Christian governments were to them.

51. Like diplomatics, the ritual or ceremonial life of the state goes beyond what we can discuss here. Relevant references include Dilger, *Hofzeremoniell*; Hammer, *Staats.*, passim, e.g., ı, 87ff., 434ff.; ıı, 131f., 412ff.; Uzunçarşılı, *Merkez*, 58-64, 289-317.

52. Runciman, *Great Church*, 360-84.

53. Cevdet, *Tarih*, v, 63-64.

54. Traian Stoianovich, "The Conquering Balkan Orthodox Merchant," *Journal of Economic History*, xx (1960), 269-73.

55. In addition to Runciman and Stoianovich, see Orhonlu, "Tercüman," *IA*, xıı, 176-78; Ergin, *Maarif*, ı, 56-59; ıı, 613-17, Turkish summary of Epaminondas I. Stamatiadis, *Biographiai ton Helēnon Megalon Diermineon tou Othomanikou Kratous* (Athens, 1865); Joseph Gottwald, "Phanariotische Studien," *Leipziger Vierteljahrsschrift für Südosteuropa*, v (1941), 1-58; Théodore Blancard, *Les Mav-*

royéni: histoire d'Orient (de 1700 à nos jours), 2 vols. (Paris, 1909); Alexandre A. C. Stourdza, *L'Europe orientale et le role historique des Maurocordato, 1660-1830* (Paris, 1913).

56. BBA, Kal. Niz., 5, reference in regulations of 17 N 1211/March 1797 for Office of Imperial Divan.

57. Itzkowitz, "Realities," 93; Temelkuran, "Mühimme Kalemi," 142; cf. Findley, "Legacy," 346.

58. TPK, D3208.

59. Cf. Ergin, *Maarif*, I, 51-60.

60. Lûtfi, *Tarih*, IV, 115-16.

61. M. Fuad Köprülü, "Hâce," *IA*, V, 20-24; Ira Lapidus, *Muslim Cities in the Later Middle Ages* (Cambridge, Mass., 1967), 128; Mantran, *İstanbul*, 466, citing Evliya Çelebi; H. İnalcık, "Bursa and the Commerce of the Levant," *JESHO*, III (1960), 133ff.

62. İnalcık, "Reis-ül-Küttâb," *IA*, IX, 679.

63. Ergin, *Maarif*, I, 53; BBA, Kal. Niz., 11, entry of 27 M 1255/April 1839; Thomas, *Naima*, 34-35.

64. For example, Cevdet, *Tarih*, III, 133-34, on Grand Vezir Halil Hamid Paşa (d. 1784); İnal, *Şair.*, II, 1301-1302 on Pertev Paşa (1785-1837), on whom cf. Ş. Turan, "Pertev Paşa," *IA*, IX, 554. More generally, see Ahmed Resmi, *Halifet ül-Rüesa* (Istanbul, 1269/1853), passim; my thanks to Professor Halil Inalcık for assisting me in obtaining photocopies of this work.

65. Ahmed Resmi, *Halifet*, 191-93, biography of Chief Scribe Hâmid Bey Efendi; Cevdet, *Tarih*, VII, 93-94 on Abd ül-Şekûr Efendi, including quotation of a satirical couplet. Cf. Cevdet, *Tarih*, XII, 112, on difficulties of Canib Efendi, able (*iş eri*) but lacking connections.

66. D'Ohsson, *Tableau*, VII, 176-77; BBA, Kal. Niz., 9, undated entry, preceded by an entry of 1248/1832-1833 and followed by one of 1234/c. 1819, referring to this kind of petty "legal practice."

67. Matuz, *Kanz.*, 120; Temelkuran. "Mühimme Kalemi," 140.

68. For example, a study of one type of register from the Appointments Section (*Rüus Kalemi*) of the Office of the Imperial Divan showed the entire text of each brevet copied in, one after the other, often with no differences from the preceding entry but the date and the name of the recipient (BBA, Rüus 163, 168, 175, 184 of c. 1256-1272/1840-1856). The same kind of repetition appears in the earliest records of consular appointments (BBA, Şehb. 1, entries beginning 1217/1802-1803). Such labor-saving techniques as blank forms appear to have been unknown until later.

69. BBA, Tahvil 30, entry of 23 N 1238/1823.

70. Eisenstadt, *Political Systems*, 276ff.

71. Temelkuran, "Mühimme Kalemi," 151, citing BBA, HH 4470, İrade D 1571 of c. 1799.

72. Cf. Weber, *Economy and Society*, III, 963ff., 1014.

73. Stanford J. Shaw, *The Financial and Administrative Organization and Development of Ottoman Egypt, 1517-1798* (Princeton, 1962), 346-48.

74. Pakalın, *OTD*, III, 68, "Rütbe." There was also a rank of *baş muhasebeci* ("chief accountant") given to certain officials, including ambassadors. Uzunçarşılı, *Merkez*, 68ff.; d'Ohsson, *Tableau*, VII, 191-97; Hammer, *Staats.*, II, 112.

75. Itzkowitz, "Realities," 87-88.

76. For example, Ahmed Resmi, *Halifet*, passim.

77. Uzunçarşılı, *Merkez*, 70; cf. Cevdet, *Tarih*, II, 129-30, appointments of 1779; II, 177, appointments of 1782; VI, 157, appointments of 1795; X, 86-87, appointments of 1812.

78. Mustafa Nuri, *Netayic*, III, 85-86; Cevdet, *Tarih*, II, 160. Cf. Kunt, "The Structure of the Military-Administrative Career."

79. D'Ohsson, *Tableau*, VII, 182, 188-89; the sum mentioned does not include comparable exactions that the grand vezir also got from tax farmers. Conversion rate from FO 78/18, Spencer Smith to Lord Grenville, 10 April 1797.

80. Pakalın, *OTD*, I, 255, "Caize"; Uzunçarşılı, *Merkez*, 157.

81. K. W. Swart, *Sale of Offices in the Seventeenth Century* (The Hague, 1949), 99-111; Röhrborn, *Verwaltungsgeschichte*, 114-53; cf. Shaw, *Egypt*, 346; Matuz, *Kanz.*, 56.

82. Heyd, *Criminal Law*, 213; Matuz, *Kanz.*, 81-82.

83. Barkan, "Avârız," *IA*, II, 13-19; Avdo Sućeska, "Die Entwicklung der Besteuerung durch die 'Avâriz-i dîvânîye und die Tekâlîf-i 'örfîye im Osmanischen Reich während des 17. und 18. Jahrhunderts," *Südostforschungen*, XXVII (1968), 89-130.

84. Cevdet, *Tarih*, III, 129-36.

85. Ibid., VI, 195-96, 230-31; VII, 45-46.

86. For example, İngiliz Mahmud Raif Efendi, a former diplomat and chief scribe: ibid., VIII, 155-57.

87. Ibid., XII, 55-60; cf. Şihâbeddin Tekindağ, "Hâlet Efendi," *IA*, V, 123-25.

88. Lûtfi, *Tarih*, II, 76-77; cf. Orhan Köprülü, "Gâlib Paşa," *IA*, IV, 710-14.

89. Lûtfi, *Tarih*, V, 91-92, 99-102; Şerâfeddin Turan, "Pertev Paşa," *IA*, IX, 554-56; İnal, *Şair.*, II, 1302-12; FO 78/329B, Ponsonby to Palmerston, 31 January 1838, secret, with details on fall of Pertev.

90. Cevdet, *Tarih*, IV, 261, on security of religious establishment. On scribes: Gibb, *Poetry*, III, 333, citing Nabi; İnalcık, "Reis-ül-Küttâb," *IA*, IX, 681.

91. Kunt, *Sancaktan Eyalete*, 104.

92. Uzunçarşılı, *Merkez*, 54 n. 4; 244.

93. Har., TKE 1151, register on rations (*tayinat*) for officials of Sublime Porte, 1233/1817-1818.

94. Cevdet, *Tarih*, VI, 154-55.

95. Findley, "Legacy," 355.

96. BBA, Müh. 166, 100-101, entries of Er C 1182/November 1768; Pakalın, *OTD*, III, 579-80, "Vakıf."

97. TPK, D3208; Uzunçarşılı, *Merkez*, 47; İnalcık, "Reis-ül-Küttâb," *IA*, IX, 675.

98. To the comparisons in Findley, "Legacy," 349 n. 3, add Gladden, *History of Public Administration*, II, 313, and Ray Jones, *The Nineteenth-Century Foreign Office: An Administrative History* (London, 1971), e.g., 148-64, conditions of 1850.

99. Eisenstadt, *Political Systems*, 160-65.

100. Matuz, *Kanz.*, 55.

101. Cevdet, *Tarih*, V, 114; cf. VI, 157-58.

102. Itzkowitz, "Realities," 86.

103. Matuz, *Kanz.*, 29-33, 41-44.

104. İsmail Hami Danişmend, *İzahlı Osmanlı Tarihi Kronolojisi*, 4 vols. (Istanbul, 1961), III, 609-15; IV, 629-37. This count ignores all incumbencies after the first

in the case of men who held the office more than once, and ends with the man in office at the conclusion of the Treaty of Küçük Kaynarca.

105. İnalcık, "Reis-ül-Küttâb," *IA*, ıx, 671.

106. Itzkowitz, "Realities," 86-87; cf. 89 re date 1703. The one who had never been chief scribe but who had ambassadorial experience was Yirmi Sekiz Çelebizade Mehmed Said; see Dilâver Ağazade Ömer, *Zeyl* to Osmanzade Taib Ahmed, *Ḥadīqat ül-vüzerâ (Der Garten der Wesire)* (Freiburg, 1969; reprint of Istanbul edition of 1271/1854-1855), 84-86 (there are three *zeyl*s, paginated separately).

107. Dilâver Ağazade Ömer, *Zeyl* to *Ḥadīqat*, 76-77: Divitdar Mehmed Emin.

108. The two former chief scribes are Halil Hamid Paşa: Cevdet, *Tarih*, ııı, 133-34, cf. Ahmed Cavid, second *Zeyl* to *Ḥadīqat*, 34-36; and Mehmed Said Galib Paşa: Ahmed Rif'at, *Werd ül-Ḥadâ'iq (Die Rose der Gärten)* (Freiburg, 1970; reprint of Istanbul edition of 1283/1866-1867), 22-24, cf. Orhan Köprülü, "Gâlib Paşa," *IA*, ıv, 710-14. The former corresponding secretary was Mehmed Emin Rauf: Ahmed Rif'at, *Werd*, 11-15. The former steward is Derviş Mehmed: Ahmed Cavid, second *Zeyl* to *Ḥadīqat*, 27-28. The former chief bailiff is Arnavud Memiş: Bağdadî Abd ül-Fettah Şevket, third *Zeyl* to *Ḥadīqat*, 17-18.

109. Danişmend, *Kronoloji*, ııı, 521-22; ıv, 471-96 on grand vezirs; ııı, 613-15; ıv, 629-51 on chief scribes.

110. Ibid. Cf. Cevdet, *Tarih*, ıv, 247, on Silahdar Seyyid Mehmed Paşa.

111. Mustafa Nuri, *Netayic*, ııı, 95-96.

112. Hazinedar Şahin Ali Paşa, grand vezir 1785-86: Cevdet, *Tarih*, ııı, 257-58; Danişmend, *Kronoloji*, ıv, 487. Cf. comments by Cevdet on marginally literate individuals who rose to other high positions: *Tarih*, vııı, 165; xıı, 87-88.

113. Cevdet, *Tarih*, v, 18-19, 102-106; Shaw, *Old and New*, 28-36, 91, 101-104, 106, 127-28, 369.

114. Cevdet, *Tarih*, vıı, 83-84.

CHAPTER FOUR

1. Cevdet, *Tarih*, vı, 221.

2. Text in Reşat Kaynar, *Mustafa Reşit*, 296 (transcription slightly amended).

3. *Dstr.*[1], ı, 4-5.

4. Shaw covers the reforms comprehensively (*Old and New*, pt. iii), but gives Selim little credit for innovation (ibid., 71, 167, 199, 405-407); cf. id., *History*, ı, 260-66. Other comprehensive accounts: Asım, *Tarih*, 2 vols. (Istanbul, n.d.); Cevdet, *Tarih*, vı-vııı.

5. Avigdor Levy, "Power Politics at the Center, 1808-1812: Resurgence of the Ottoman Sultanate," paper presented at the First International Congress on the Social and Economic History of Turkey, 1071-1920, Hacettepe University, Ankara, July 1977. On the political and military neutralization of the provincial magnates see also Cevdet, *Tarih*, x, 87ff.

6. Cevdet, *Tarih*, vı, 7.

7. Ibid., ıv, 156.

8. Ibid., ıv, 156-60 (events of 1788-1789); vııı, 279 (1804-1805); x, 17-20 (1811).

9. For a recent work throwing light both on late Ottoman fiscal methods and

on the undermining of Ottoman manufactures by European competition even before the beginning of the Industrial Revolution in Europe, see Mehmet Genç, "A Comparative Study of the Life-Term Tax-Farming Data and the Volume of Commercial and Industrial Activities in the Ottoman Empire during the Second Half of the Eighteenth Century," paper presented to the Symposium on South Eastern European and Balkan Cities and the Industrial Revolution in Western Europe, Hamburg, March 1976; or id., "Osmanlı Maliyesinde Malikâne Sistemi," in Osman Okyar et al., eds., *Türkiye İktisat Tarihi Semineri* (Ankara, 1975), 231-96.

10. Halil İnalcık, "Imtiyâzât," *EI²*, III, 1185-89.

11. Cevdet, *Tarih*, VI, 194-95 (events of 1790-1791).

12. Ibid., III, 270 (events of 1785-1786); VIII, 73 (1806-1807). Cf. Thomas Naff, "Ottoman Diplomatic Relations with Europe in the Eighteenth Century: Patterns and Trends," in *Studies in Eighteenth Century Islamic History*, edited by Naff and Owens, 88-107.

13. Cevdet, *Tarih*, XI, 132.

14. Ibid., XI, 25-27, 32-33 (events of c. 1819-1820).

15. Ibid., IX, 2-3 (c. 1808). Cf. Halil İnalcık, "Centralization and Decentralization in Ottoman Administration," in *Studies in Eighteenth Century Islamic History*, edited by Naff and Owen, 27-52.

16. Uriel Heyd, *Criminal Law*, 152-57. His view may be overstated; cf. H. İnalcık, "Adaletnameler," *Belgeler*, II (1965), 49-142, and Y. Özkaya, "XVIIIinci Yüzyılda Çıkarılan Adalet-nâmelere göre Türkiye'nin İç Durumu," *Bell.*, XXXVIII (1974), 445-91. The role of the *kanuncu* (legal expert) in the Office of the Imperial Divan should also be borne in mind.

17. B. Lewis, "Dustūr, ii.—Turkey," *EI²*, 640-41.

18. Cevdet, *Tarih*, II, 97-98 (events of 1778).

19. Ibid., II, 129-30 (1779).

20. Ibid., III, 115 (c. 1784), 256 (c. 1786).

21. On this and the question of reactions to the French Revolution, see Lewis, *Emergence*, 65-73, including significant quotations from Asım, *Tarih*. For a significant discussion of the European situation and its implications, written by the chief scribe, Atıf Efendi, on the eve of the French invasion of Egypt, see also Cevdet, *Tarih*, VI, 394-401.

22. F. R. Unat, *Osmanlı Sefirleri ve Sefaretnameleri* (Ankara, 1968), 43-168; of the 27 envoys he discusses for the period 1655-1793, at least 17 had some identification with the scribal service.

23. Niyazi Berkes, *Secularism*, 23ff.

24. Shaw, *Old and New*, 12-17.

25. Unat, *Sefaretnameler*, 154-62; Cevdet, *Tarih*, V, 232ff.; Shaw, *Old and New*, 95-98; Karal, *Selim III'ün Hat-tı [sic] Hümayunları, Nizam-ı Cedit, 1789-1807* (Ankara, 1946), 31-34.

26. Cevdet, *Tarih*, V, 79-80, 346-69; Unat, *Sefaretnameler*, 149-54.

27. Şerif Mardin, *Genesis*, 179ff.; Lewis, *Emergence*, 132.

28. Shaw, *Old and New*, 91ff.; Lewis, *Emergence*, 57-58; E. Z. Karal, "Nizâm-ı Cedid'e dair Lâyihalar," *Tar. Ves.*, I (1942), 414-25; II (1942-1943), 104-11, 342-51, 424-32.

29. Unat, *Sefaretnameler*, 168ff.

30. Cevdet, *Tarih*, v, 115-16; vi, 57-59, 150-55, 221; Shaw, *Old and New*, 167-74.

31. BBA, Kal. Niz., 4-7, regulations for Office of the Imperial Divan; 18-19, for Office of Corresponding Secretary; 30-31, for Office of Receiver. Each set of regulations bears an order for execution (*hatt-ı hümayun*) dated 1 or 2 Ş 1211/1797.

32. BBA, Kal. Niz., 18-19.

33. Ibid., 5.

34. Ibid., 5, 19, 30.

35. Ibid., 19, 31.

36. Cevdet, *Tarih*, vi, 235-36.

37. BBA, Kal. Niz., 5; Tevfik Temelkuran, "Mühimme Kalemi," 139ff.; C. Findley, "The Foundation of the Ottoman Foreign Ministry: The Beginnings of Bureaucratic Reform under Selim III and Mahmud II," *IJMES*, iii (1972), 391 n. 2.

38. BBA, Kal. Niz., 5-7; Temelkuran, "Mühimme Kalemi," 148-50.

39. Lûtfi, *Tarih*, v, 99; Temelkuran, "Mühimme Kalemi," 143.

40. Matuz, *Kanz.*, 77-78; Temelkuran, "Mühimme Kalemi," 155-61; Sertoğlu, *Başvekâlet*, 24.

41. BBA, Kal. Niz., 5; cf. Findley, "Legacy," 346.

42. BBA, Kal. Niz., 8, entry of 19 R 1216/1801.

43. Ibid., 8, entry of 16 C 1248/November 1832; 9, entry of 20 R 1234/February 1819; 10, entry of 15 C 1254/September 1838.

44. Ibid., 21, entry of 13 N 1222/November 1807. "Examination papers" (*imtihanname*) of such a sort from later dates demonstrate no more than the candidates' ability to write a few lines, not necessarily expressing a complete thought, but in good penmanship and a "high style"; BBA, İrade D 1066 and D 1289 of 7 Ş (?) and 15 L 1256/1840.

45. Temelkuran, "Mühimme Kalemi," 153-54, text of BBA, HH 23969.

46. BBA, Kal. Niz., 34-39, entry of 27 ZA 1254/February 1839; published by İhsan Sungu, "Mekteb-i Maarif-i Adliyyenin Tesisi," *Tar. Ves.*, I (1941), 212-25; cf. Findley, "Foundation," 394.

47. J. C. Hurewitz, "The Europeanization of Ottoman Diplomacy: The Conversion from Unilateralism to Reciprocity in the Nineteenth Century," *Bell.*, xxv (1961), 455-66; id., "Ottoman Diplomacy and the European State System," *Middle East Journal*, xv (1961), 141-52.

48. Bertold Spuler, "Die Europäische Diplomatie in Konstantinopel, bis zum Frieden von Belgrad (1739)," *Jahrbücher für Kultur und Geschichte der Slaven*, Neue Folge, xi (1935), 183ff.; T. Naff, "Reform and the Conduct of Ottoman Diplomacy," *JAOS*, lxxxiii (1963), 306-307; id., "Ottoman Diplomatic Relations," 88-107. Cf. Cevdet, *Tarih*, vi, 128-30; viii, 102, recounting abandonment of the imprisonment of ambassadors (1806-1807).

49. Cevdet, *Tarih*, vi, 257-61; Ercümend Kuran, *Avrupa'da Osmanlı İkamet Elçiliklerinin Kuruluşu ve İlk Elçilerin Siyasi Faâliyetleri, 1793-1821* (Ankara, 1968), 14.

50. Cevdet, *Tarih*, vi, 88-89, 231-32; Naff, "Diplomacy," 303-304; Kuran, *İkamet Elçilikleri*, 13-22; İsmail Soysal, *Fransız İhtilâli ve Türk-Fransız Diplomasi Münasebetleri (1789-1802)* (Ankara, 1964).

51. Kuran, İkamet Elçilikleri, 52 n. 19.

52. Traian Stoianovich, "The Conquering Balkan Orthodox Merchant," Journal of Economic History, xx (1960), 296.

53. Ibid., 272; Pakalın, OTD, ı, 782, "Hayriye Tüccarı"; Baer, "The Administrative, Economic and Social Functions of Turkish Guilds," 34, 43.

54. Redhouse, A Turkish and English Lexicon, 388, under "bender"; cf. Julius Zenker, Türkisch-Arabisch-Persisches Handwörterbuch (Leipzig, 1866; reprinted Hildesheim, 1967), ıı, 537, under "şah-bender," giving "chef de la douane/Ober-Zolleinnehmer" as his first definition.

55. BBA, Şehb. no. 1, early entries, beginning 1217/1802-1803; cf. Stoianovich, "Balkan Orthodox Merchant," 267ff.; M. Tayyib Gökbilgin, "Konsolos," IA, vı, 839-40.

56. Naff, "Diplomacy," 305, 313; id., "Ottoman Diplomatic Relations," 88-107.

57. Kuran, İkamet Elçilikleri, 20, 27, 36.

58. Ibid., 26; Herbette, Une ambassade turque sous le Directoire (Paris, 1902), 1-2, 191-99; Karal, Halet Efendi'nin Paris Büyük Elçiliği (Istanbul, 1940), 52, 89.

59. Kuran, İkamet Elçilikleri, 42.

60. Ibid., 40.

61. The importance of this aspect of Ottoman diplomacy is evident as far back as the mission of Yirmi Sekiz Çelebi Mehmed Efendi to Paris in 1720-1721; cf. Unat, Sefaretnameler, 56; Berkes, Secularism, 33ff.

62. Kuran, İkamet Elçilikleri, 64; FO 78/18, Spencer Smith to Lord Grenville, 10 April 1797, followed by various communications from Ottoman Embassy in London.

63. Naff, "Diplomacy," 305; Herbette, Une ambassade turque, 257-61; Karal, Halet, 18ff.

64. For example, Sıdki Efendi in London: Shafik Ghorbal, "The Missions of Ali Effendi in Paris and of Sedki Effendi in London. 1797-1811; A Contribution to the Study of the Westernisation of Ottoman Institutions," Bulletin of the Faculty of Arts, University of Egypt, ı (1933), 125-27.

65. Lewis, Emergence, 105; cf. Karal, Halet, 31ff., 89.

66. Naff, "Diplomacy," 305; Kuran, İkamet Elçilikleri, 31; Unat, Sefaretnameler, 190.

67. Ercümend Kuran, "Türkiye'nin Batılılaşmasında Osmanlı daimî Elçiliklerinin Rolü," VI. Türk Tarih Kongresi: Kongreye Sunulan Bildiriler (Ankara, 1967), 491; Cevdet, Tarih, vııı, 155-56.

68. Mardin, Genesis, 161; Lûtfi, Tarih, ıı, 155-57; O. Köprülü, "Gâlib Paşa," IA, ıv, 710-14.

69. İnal, Şair., ı, 107-108; ııı, 1564; Mardin, Genesis, 229-30.

70. BBA, Buy. no. 3, entry of 8 S 1255/1839. Along with numerous works in traditional genres, the library included two works on mathematics (hendese), a mineralogical treatise of some sort (Risale fi Beyan Maadini 'l-Nafia), a "Frankish" dictionary (lûgat-i efrenc), miscellaneous "Frankish" books (kütüb-i efrenciye, 8 vols.), plus a large map, and two Gospels or New Testaments (incil), one in Arabic and the other described simply as a translation.

71. FO 78/18, Spencer Smith to Lord Grenville, 10 April 1797.

72. Théodore Blancard, Les Mavroyéni, ıı, 133ff.; Findley, "Foundation," 398; Kuran, İkamet Elçilikleri, 52-65.

73. Hurewitz, "Europeanization of Ottoman Diplomacy," 462; FO 78/104,

Chargé Antonaki Ramadani to Marquis of Londonderry, 6 August 1821, giving notice of orders to return to Istanbul and enclosing copies of relevant correspondence.

74. The existence in some sense of Ottoman consuls during the revolutionary years is apparent from a letter, in Har., TKE 708, dated 6 August 1824 and addressed in Italian from Angelo de Cazzaiti, Ottoman consul at Livorno, to the *Gloriosissimo Reis Efendi!* Cazzaiti's seal makes clear that he was an Ottoman subject. He was probably Greek despite the Italianized name. The letter reports a naval engagement off the Algerian coast.

75. Findley, "Foundation," 400-401; C. Orhonlu, "Tercüman," *IA*, XII, 178; Şanizade, *Tarih*, 4 vols. (Istanbul, 1290-1291/1873-1874), IV, 20-22, 33-35; Cevdet, *Tarih*, XI, 166; XII, 43-44.

76. FO 78/107, Strangford's no. 52 of 25 April 1822, dating fall of Aristarchi to "the 16th instant."

77. Şanizade, *Tarih*, IV, 35.

78. FO 78/107, Strangford's no. 52 of 25 April 1822; cf. Y. Çark, *Türk Devleti Hizmetinde Ermeniler* (Istanbul, 1953), 135ff.

79. FO 78/108, Strangford's no. 65, 10 May 1822.

80. Additional details in Findley, "Foundation," 402-403.

81. F. R. Unat, "Başhoca İshak Efendi," *Bell.*, XXVIII (1964), 89-115.

82. Cevdet, *Tarih*, XII, 191-94; E. Z. Karal, "Mehmed Namık Paşa'nın Hal Tercümesi, 1804-1892," *Tar. Ves.*, II (1942), 220-27; Şehabeddin Akalın, "Mehmed Namık Paşa," *Tar. Der.*, IV, no. 7 (1952), 127-46; Levy, "Sultan Mahmud's New Army," 32-34. Namık Paşa was one of the conservatives appointed to the commission that drafted the Constitution of 1876.

83. C. Findley, "Sir James W. Redhouse (1811-1892): The Making of a Perfect Orientalist?" forthcoming in *Journal of the American Oriental Society*.

84. BBA, Buy. no. 2, entry of 11 S 1249/30 June 1833. Information on the previous compensation of employees of the office comes from BBA, Buy. no. 2, entry of 22 ZA 1243/1828, and Cev. Har. 41, 57, 1159, 1177, 2222, 2326, 2481. The fact that the office, previously so obscure, was substantially upgraded at this time no doubt accounts for the impression conveyed in many works (starting with Lûtfi, *Tarih*, IV, 99, 176) that it was only founded about 1833.

85. BBA, Cev. Har. 441, salary receipt of 28 Z 1256/1841.

86. Lewis, *Emergence*, 118; cf. Lûtfi, *Tarih*, VI, 67.

87. T. Blancard, *Les Mavroyéni*, II, 185ff.; Lûtfi, *Tarih*, III, 86-88; TPK, E2825 and E4057.

88. Unat, *Sefaretnameler*, 210-14; Şinasi Altındağ, ed., "Mehmed Ali İsyanında Yardım Talebinde Bulunmak üzere 1832 Tarihinde Namık Paşa'nın Hususi Elçi olarak Londra'ya Gönderilmesi," *Tar. Ves.*, II (1943), 441-51; III (1944-1949), 127-36, 200-205.

89. For example, Mustafa Reşid's problems with his nephew, Nuri Efendi: Findley, "Foundation," 406; Kaynar, *Mustafa Reşit*, 63.

90. Lûtfi, *Tarih*, V, 99-101; İnal, *Şair.*, I, 69-77; II, 1301-12; Şerafettin Turan, "Pertev Paşa," *IA*, IX, 554-56; Kaynar, *Mustafa Reşit*, 30-37; Mardin, *Genesis*, 158ff.

91. HHS, Türkei, VI/66, Stürmer's no. 242A-B, 2 August 1837.

92. For example, Mustafa Reşid studied the language during his first embassy in Paris (c. 1834); Kaynar, *Mustafa Reşit*, 64.

93. Charles Webster, *The Foreign Policy of Palmerston, 1830-1841; Britain, the Liberal Movement and the Eastern Question* (New York, 1969), II, ch. 8.

94. Lûtfi, *Tarih*, IV, 158-59; V, 6-7; Kaynar, *Mustafa Reşit*, 63ff.; HHS, Türkei, VI/64, Stürmer's no. 171, 20 April 1836; VI/70, Stürmer's no. 363C, 26 September 1839.

95. Findley, "Foundation," 407, with citations from Joseph von Hammer-Purgstall, *Erinnerungen aus meinem Leben, 1774-1852*, edited by Reinhart Bachofen von Echt (Vienna, 1940), 318, 322, 324-25.

96. Mardin, *Genesis*, 179ff.; cf. Frederick S. Rodkey, "Reshid Pasha's Memorandum of August 12, 1839," *Journal of Modern History*, II (1930), 251-57.

97. On the writings of Sadık Rif'at, see Mardin, *Genesis*, 169-95, based chiefly on Sadık Rif'at, *Müntahabât-ı Âsar*. For ideas of Mustafa Reşid, the most inclusive source is Kaynar, *Mustafa Reşit*; cf. Cavid Baysun, ed., "Mustafa Reşid Paşa'nın Paris ve Londra Sefaretleri Esnasındaki Siyasî Yazıları," *Tar. Ves.*, II (1942-1943), 41-55, 208-19, 452-61; III (1944-1949), 51-59, 206-21; continued as Baysun, ed., "Mustafa Reşid Paşa'nin Siyasi Yazıları," *Tar. Der.*, XII (1961), 43-62; XIII (1963), 175-90.

98. Lûtfi, *Tarih*, V, 29-30, 147; *Har. Saln.* (1302), 162-63, *hatt-ı hümayun* dated as taking effect on 23 ZA 1251/11 March 1836.

99. HHS, Türkei, VI/65, Stürmer's no. 206A-B, 30 November 1836. An undersecretaryship also came into existence in the Ministry of Civil Affairs (i.e., of the Interior) at the same time.

100. Lûtfi, *Tarih*, V, 108-109; FO 78/330, letter of F. Pisani to Ponsonby, 21 March 1838; FO 78/331, page from *Moniteur ottoman* of 5 May 1838, enclosed in Ponsonby's no. 117 of 9 May 1838; Kaynar, *Mustafa Reşit*, 107-10. The creation of the other ministries will be discussed in the next section of this chapter.

101. Joseph von Hammer-Purgstall, *Geschichte des osmanischen Reiches*, 10 vols. (Pest, 1835), X, 695, commenting on *Staats*. (1815).

102. Lûtfi, *Tarih*, V, 29-31, 147; Kaynar, *Mustafa Reşit*, 107ff.; Uzunçarşılı, *Merkez*, 259; HHS, Türkei, VI/64, Stürmer's no. 166 of 16 March 1836.

103. Pakalın, *OTD*, I, 338, art. "Çavuşbaşı."

104. Lûtfi, *Tarih*, V, 104-105.

105. Ibid., V, 113-14; Uzunçarşılı, *Merkez*, 177-78.

106. Lûtfi, *Tarih*, V, 123; Uzunçarşılı, *Merkez*, 264.

107. Avigdor Levy, "Military Policy of Mahmud II," 479-89.

108. Lûtfi, *Tarih*, V, 106-108, 178-79.

109. HHS, Türkei, VI/67, Stürmer's no. 277B, 4 April 1838.

110. Kaynar, *Mustafa Reşit*, 198ff. That Mahmud in fact *divided* his "ministers" between the two councils is another indication of his aspiration to dominate.

111. S. J. Shaw, "The Central Legislative Councils in the Nineteenth Century Ottoman Reform Movement before 1876," *IJMES*, I (1970), 54-57.

112. Mardin, *Genesis*, 131, citing Murad Efendi [Franz von Werner], *Türkische Skizzen* (Leipzig, 1878), 65.

113. Pakalın, *OTD*, III, 68-71, "Rütbe."

114. Ibid., I, 695, "Hacegân Rütbesi"; Lûtfi, *Tarih*, V, 102; for specific cases that may indicate the cheapening of the rank, or at any rate its assignment to individuals at extremely early ages, see İnal, *Şair.*, I, 352; II, 918.

115. Findley, "Foundation," 411.

116. Lûtfi, *Tarih*, V, 30; Pakalın, *OTD*, II, 613, "Mülkiye."

117. Tables of these styles of address normally figured in the government

yearbooks (*salname*), which began to be issued in 1846-1847.

118. Sadık Rif'at advocated the creation of the rank table for precisely this reason; Mardin, *Genesis*, 185.

119. Lûtfi, *Tarih*, IV, 113-14; V, 114-16.

120. S. J. Shaw, "The Nineteenth-Century Ottoman Tax Reforms and Revenue System," *IJMES*, VI (1975), 422.

121. Lûtfi, *Tarih*, V, 121-22, 180-81, text of a vezirial letter of 7 S 1254/2 May 1838; İlber Ortaylı, *Mahalli İdareler*, 22-24.

122. HHS. Türkei, VI/67, von Klezl's no. 279C, 18 April 1838.

123. AAE, Turquie 276, Roussin's no. 77, 16 July 1838.

124. HHS, Türkei VI/67, von Klezl's no. 283A-C, 16 May 1838.

125. Lûtfi, *Tarih*, V, 132-34; VIII, 86.

126. Text in Kaynar, *Mustafa Reşit*, 295-301, citing BBA, HH 48294.

127. English text in Hurewitz, *MENA*, I, 269-71. The hesitant wording of parts of the decree is doubtless due in some measure to the uncertain political position of Mustafa Reşid and his friends at the time; Lûtfi, *Tarih*, VI, 60-64, eyewitness account of promulgation of decree.

128. S. N. Eisenstadt, *Modernization: Protest and Change*, 67-75; id., *Traditional Patrimonialism and Modern Neopatrimonialism*, passim; id., *Revolution and the Transformation of Societies*, ch. 9. Eisenstadt does not discuss "split-up modernization" in the last two of these works. Thus the discussion that follows is intended to relate the specific concept of "split-up modernization" to the general one of "neopatrimonialism" as we shall use the two in this study. I am indebted both to Şerif Mardin and to S. N. Eisenstadt for opportunities to discuss these and other related subjects with them.

CHAPTER FIVE

1. *Dstr.*[1], I, 8. Interesting as an example of the official promotion of the concepts of equality and Ottoman nationalism, this passage is not one of the finest in the annals of Ottoman prose and has been somewhat rearranged in the translation.

2. İnal, *Sadr.*, I, 77. Fuad Paşa is making a pun on *sadr*, which by itself means something like the "heart" or "forepart" of anything, but in the phrase *sadr-ı a'zam* (literally "greatest prominence") was perhaps the most common title for the grand vezir. Written at a point when the foreign minister, Mustafa Reşid Paşa, was more powerful than the grand vezir of the moment, the verse alludes specifically to that situation. More generally, the verse evokes the close association in this period of the Foreign Ministry with the grand vezirate and the heavy emphasis of the times on diplomatic affairs.

3. İnal, *Şair.*, III, 1834.

4. HHS, Türkei VI/69, copy of private letter of Ponsonby to Beauvale in Vienna, 8 July 1839, enclosed in Stürmer's no. 347 A-C of same date, describing the young sultan as "governed by Eunuks & silly girls & his mother." Cf. İnal, *Sadr.*, I, 594; II, 1264; III, 2095; AAE, Turquie 328, Thouvenel to Walewski, 17 November 1856, on weaknesses of Abd ül-Mecid; FO 78/1366, Bulwer to Malmesbury, 18 August 1858, quoting Abd ül-Mecid as saying "Ah, oui, l'influence des parens est bien mauvaise, j'en sais quelque chose!"

5. İnal, *Sadr.*, I, 594-99.

6. Davison, *Reform*, ch. 9.

7. For reasons having to do with our concern with the locus of power, we are applying the term Tanzimat to the period 1839-1871; but other writers have used it in varying ways. At times, it has been applied only to the Gülhane Decree and the reforms introduced directly in consequence of it (e.g., Redhouse, *Lexicon*, 600, under "tanzimat"). Often, the term is applied to all the reforms prior to the accession of Abd ül-Hamid. Sometimes, since similar reforms continued under him, the term is applied to all or part of his reign. Cf. A. Cevad Eren, "Tanzîmât," *IA*, XI, 709-65.

8. İnalcık, "The Nature of Traditional Society: B. Turkey," 54-55; id., "Husrev Paşa," *IA*, v, 614; cf. Levy, "Sultan Mahmud's New Army," 28-29, 36-39; Lûtfi, *Tarih*, VI, 38.

9. Lewis, *Emergence*, 111-12.

10. İnal, *Sadr.*, I, 59-82.

11. Ercümend Kuran, "Reşid Paşa," *IA*, IX, 701-705.

12. İnal, *Sadr.*, I, 83-148, 196-263.

13. *Har. Saln.* (1302), 164ff.; Danişmend, *Kronoloji*, IV, 496-507; Stanford J. Shaw and Ezel K. Shaw, *History of the Ottoman Empire and Modern Turkey*, II: *Reform, Revolution, and Republic: The Rise of Modern Turkey, 1808-1975* (Cambridge, 1977), 62.

14. Davison, *Reform*, 36-37, 83-84, 90; id., "Ottoman Diplomacy at the Congress of Paris (1856) and the Question of Reforms," *VII. Türk Tarih Kongresi: Kongreye Sunulan Bildiriler*, 2 vols. (Ankara, 1973), II, 580-86.

15. Davison, *Reform*, 239-44.

16. B. Lewis, "Baladiyya," *EI²*, I, 972-73; Ortaylı, *Mahalli İdareler*, 116.

17. Hıfzı Veldet, "Kanunlaştırma Hareketleri ve Tanzimat," *Tanzimat I, Yüzüncü Yıldönümü Münasebetile* (Istanbul, 1940), 196ff.

18. Harold Temperley's adulation of Canning as the "Great Elchi" extorts from the Ottomans a tribute they never paid. The title *büyük elçi* ("great envoy") applied in Ottoman usage to any ambassador and conveys no acknowledgment of greatness except in comparison with the *orta elçi* or minister ("middling envoy"). Harold Temperley, *England and the Near East: The Crimea* (London, 1936); id., "Last Phase of Stratford de Redcliffe, 1855-58," *English Historical Review*, XLVII (1932), 216-59. Cf. W. E. Mosse, "The Return of Reschid Pasha: An Incident in the Career of Lord Stratford de Redcliffe," *Eng. Hist. Rev.*, LXVIII (1953), 546-73; Allan Cunningham, "Stratford Canning and the Tanzimat," in *Beginnings of Modernization in the Middle East: The Nineteenth Century*, edited by William R. Polk and Richard L. Chambers (Chicago, 1968), 245-64; A. Henry Layard, *Autobiography and Letters*, 2 vols. (London, 1903), II, 63-66.

19. İnal, *Şadr.*, I, 34.

20. FO 78/2177, Elliot to Granville, 7 September 1871.

21. Ortaylı, *Mahalli İdareler*, 20; Roderic H. Davison, "The Advent of the Principle of Representation in the Government of the Ottoman Empire," in *Beginnings of Modernization in the Middle East*, edited by Polk and Chambers, 93-108.

22. Berkes, *Secularism*, passim.

23. Ergin, *Maarif*, II, 324-41.

24. Ibid., II, 321-23.

25. Ibid., II, 315ff.; Richard L. Chambers, "Notes on the *Mekteb-i Osmanî* in Paris, 1857-1874," in *Beginnings of Modernization in the Middle East*, edited by Polk and Chambers, 313-29; Shaw and Shaw, *History*, II, 106-13.

26. This document in Ergin, *Maarif*, II, 399; discussion here based on BBA, Rüus 163, 168, 175, 184, entries dated 1256-1282/1840-1865; fuller treatment in Findley, "From Reis Efendi to Foreign Minister: Ottoman Bureaucratic Reform and the Creation of the Foreign Ministry," Ph.D. dissertation, Harvard, 1969, 143-47.

27. Kaynar, *Mustafa Reşit*, 283-84; Davison, "Ḳā'ime," *EI²*, IV, 460-61; A. Du Velay, *Essai sur l'histoire financière de la Turquie, depuis le règne du Sultan Mahmoud II jusqu'à nos jours* (Paris, 1903), 120ff.; Shaw, "Nineteenth-Century . . . Tax Reforms," 421-59; Shaw and Shaw, *History*, II, 95-105, 155-56.

28. Hurewitz, *MENA*, I, 265-66; İnalcık, "Imtiyāzāt," *EI²*, III, 1187; Frank E. Bailey, *British Policy and the Turkish Reform Movement: A Study in Anglo-Turkish Relations, 1826-1853* (Cambridge, Mass., 1942); Mübahat S. Kütükoğlu, *Osmanlı-İngiliz İktisâdî Münâsebetleri, II: (1838-1850)* (Istanbul, 1976).

29. HHS, Türkei VI/71, Stürmer's no. 371A-C, 6 November 1839.

30. This, of course, is to use "rational-legalism" as a Weberian synonym for Yaney's "systematization": George Yaney, *The Systematization of Russian Government: Social Evolution in the Domestic Administration of Imperial Russia, 1711-1905* (Urbana, Illinois, 1973), ch. 1.

31. İnal, *Şair.*, II, 1302-1303.

32. During the Tanzimat, this was especially true of Yusuf Kâmil Paşa, one of the grand vezirs of the period: İnal, *Şair.*, II, 795; id., *Sadr.*, I, 106-107, 223-24, 229-30, 233-35.

33. İnal, *Şair.*, II, 1002, quoting Ebu 'l-Ziya Tevfik on Mehmed Tahir Münif Paşa.

34. Cf. Davison, *Reform*, 395-402; İnal, *Sadr.*, I, 360-94.

35. İnalcık, "Husrev Paşa," *IA*, V, 614-15.

36. İnalcık, "Application of the Tanzimat and its Social Effects," *Archivum Ottomanicum*, V (1973), 104-105.

37. On Mustafa Reşid Paşa, see Cevdet, *Tezâkir 1-12*, 19-20, 26-27, and id., *Tezâkir 40*, 63; on Fuad, see İnal, *Sadr.*, I, 185; on Âli, ibid., I, 35-36. Questionable activities include nominal holding of provincial governorships at the same time as high positions in Istanbul (Lûtfi, *Tarih*, IX, 72); retention of benefice-incomes that should have been relinquished on leaving other, lower offices (Uzunçarşılı, *Merkez*, 54 n. 4); accepting money or gifts from the governors of Egypt (İnal, *Sadr.*, I, 35-36); and various "speculations" (FO 78/1358, Canning to Malmesbury, 9 April 1858).

38. Kaynar, *Mustafa Reşit*, 199; cf. Cevdet, *Tezâkir 13-20*, 21.

39. For indications of nepotism and favoritism on the part of Mustafa Reşid, see Kaynar, *Mustafa Reşit*, 145-48, 404-405; Cevdet, *Tezâkir 13-20*, 22; Davison, *Reform*, 82; İnal, *Sadr.*, I, 76, 265; Lûtfi, *Tarih*, IX, 50, 117-18; X, 51. On Fuad, see Lûtfi, *Tarih*, X, 126. On Âli, İnal, *Sadr.*, I, 20; id., *Şair.*, II, 1019-20. On Kıbrıslı Mehmed, see İnal, *Sadr.*, I, 87. Miscellaneous other incidents in İnal, *Şair.*, II, 1314, 1424-25; IV, 1971.

40. Cevdet, *Tezâkir 1-12*, 45, 87; Lûtfi, *Tarih*, IX, 46: "The great preoccupations of those times were as if three in number: the first was to drive out one's rivals; the second was to bring in one's friends; the third was to silence the tongues of the people by paying close attention to the price of bread and other necessities. The occurrence of frequent changes and appointments was mostly the result of the first and second factors" (vol. IX of Lûtfi covers events of 1849-1860).

41. Cevdet, *Tezâkir 40*, 61-62.

42. Ibid., 72-73, 84; cf. id., *Tezâkir 13-20*, 21.

43. İnal, *Sadr.*, I, 138; cf. Davison, *Reform*, 9, quoting a jest of Fuad Paşa.

44. Kaynar, *Mustafa Reşit*, 104, on his preference for "absolute government" (*hükûmet-i mutlaka*) as opposed to "limited" (*hükûmet-i meşruta*); Mardin, *Genesis*, 186-89; Davison, *Reform*, 41-42, 87, 90-91.

45. Cevdet, *Tezâkir 13-20*, 54-59; İnal, *Sadr.*, I, 27, 32, 177, 222; cf. Mardin, *Genesis*, 108. Diplomatic correspondence includes many indications of the deterioration of relations between Abd ül-Aziz and Fuad Paşa from 1867 to the death of the latter in 1869: FO 78/2018, Elliot to Stanley, 12 January and 27 (?) January 1868; FO 78/2073, Elliot's no. 82, 21 February 1869; AAE, Turquie 377, Bourée to de Moustier, 16 September and 14 October 1868; HHS, PA XII/91, Prokesch-Osten to Beust, 17 January 1868; AA, 856/3 (?), Schriftwechsel mit der . . . Gesandtschaft zu Constantinopel . . . über die innere Zustände . . . der Türkei, Brassier von St.-Simon's no. 11 of 15-16 January 1868, Uebel's no. 146 of 29 September 1868 and no. 154 of 14 October 1868 (T 139, mf. roll 354).

46. The government yearbooks (*Saln.*, 1263-1288/1847-1871) are one of the most important single sources for our discussion of formal organizational patterns. They are, however, difficult to use correctly. Since they do not ordinarily list any officials below the supervisory level (*mümeyyiz, ser kalfa*, and the like), it is extremely rare that they give any indication of the total number serving in any agency. In addition, it is only in the next period that their listings begin to be organized in a way corresponding very closely to government organization. For the Tanzimat, bodies such as the Council of Ministers or the other major councils have separate listings, but the organization of the various ministries and their component agencies usually has to be reconstructed by picking out the appropriate entries from long lists included under such vague or anachronistic headings as "Senior Officials of the Offices" (*Zâbıtan-ı Aklâm*) or even "Divan Positions" (*Menasıb-ı Divaniye*). This was the method followed in preparation of this section.

47. Lûtfi, *Tarih*, VI, 39.

48. Aristarchi, *LO*, II, 14-15. I have not been able to find a text in Ottoman that preserves all the honorific titulature used in addressing the grand vezir in the prologue to this document. It seems probable that the phrase "alter ego" is a translation for *vekil-i mutlak* (absolute delegate).

49. İnal, *Sadr.*, I, 50-51.

50. FO 78/2177, Elliot to Granville, 7 September 1871.

51. Lûtfi, *Tarih*, V, 122; Mehmed Süreyya, *Sicill-i Osmani*, 4 vols. (Istanbul, 1308-1315/1891-1897), IV, 806-807; AAE, Turquie 325, Thouvenel's no. 32 of 31 March 1856.

52. Lûtfi, *Tarih*, X, 62-63; *Saln.* (1284), 54-55; (1286), 57.

53. T. Gökbilgin, "Âmedci," *IA*, I, 397; id., "Âmeddji," *EI²*, I, 433. This prestigious office was one of the few whose clerks (*hulefa*) were listed fully in the yearbooks of this period; see *Saln.* (1263-1288), under "Amedî-i Divan-ı Hümayun Hulefası."

54. *Saln.* (1288), 60, 66.

55. Lûtfi, *Tarih*, VIII, 120-22.

56. *Dstr.*¹, IV, 58-60, regulations of 1861; cf. Sertoğlu, *Başvekâlet*, 59-61.

57. *Saln.* (1286), 55.

58. Weber, *Economy and Society*, I, 281-82; III, 994-98, 1089.

59. This list was determined by checking *Saln.* (1263, 1266, and subsequent even years through 1288) under "Vükelâ-yı Saltanat-ı Seniye ve A'za-yı Meclis-i Has," "A'za-yı Meclis-i Mahsus," and corresponding headings; cf. Cevdet, *Tezâkir 1-12*, 17.

60. Shaw and Shaw, *History*, II, 81-82; anecdotal evidence on ministerial deliberations in İnal, *Sadr.*, I, 231-32; cf. Roderic H. Davison, "Ottoman Diplomacy at the Congress of Paris (1856) and the Question of Reforms," 583-86; id., "The Nature of Ottoman Foreign Policy in the Nineteenth Century," paper presented at the conference on State, Society, and Economy in Nineteenth Century Iran and the Ottoman Empire, held in Babolsar, Iran, in June 1978 under joint sponsorship of the Reza Shah Kabir University and the Joint Committee on the Near and Middle East of the American Council of Learned Societies and the Social Science Research Council.

61. Shaw, "Central Legislative Councils," 51-84; Shaw and Shaw, *History*, II, 76-81; principal sources, with others as cited, for discussion of these councils.

62. İnalcık, "Application of the Tanzimat," 101, 104, 111; M. A. Ubicini, *Letters on Turkey*, translated by Lady Easthope, 2 vols. (London, 1856; reprinted, New York, 1973), I, 170-72.

63. Cevdet, *Tezâkir 1-12*, 27, 36-37; id., *Tezâkir 13-20*, 153; cf. id., *Tezâkir 40*, 72-74.

64. Original regulations in *Dstr.*[1], I, 703-18; cf. Young, *CD*, I, 3-5; Aristarchi, *LO*, II, 38-41; Davison, *Reform*, 241ff.; id., "Advent of Representation," 104.

65. Regulations in *Dstr.*[1], I, 325-42; Aristarchi, *LO*, II, 42-55; FO 78/2020, Elliot to Stanley, 12 May 1868, enclosing a contemporary Ottoman printing of the French text.

66. Lûtfi, *Tarih*, v, 128.

67. *Har. Saln.* (1318), 436-71 on history of the Quarantine Board; legislative role on 448; Young, *CD*, III, 125ff.

68. *Saln.* (1263), n.p., listings immediately following those for Council of Ministers and Supreme Council of Judicial Ordinances; cf. *Saln.* (1288), 45ff.

69. *Saln.* (1288), 59.

70. HHS, Türkei VI/65, Stürmer's no. 206A-B, 30 November 1836.

71. Lûtfi, *Tarih*, v, 123; cf. a work by a different author with the same names: Ahmed Lûtfi, *Mir'at-ı Adalet, yahut Tarihçe-i Adliye-i Devlet-i Aliye* (Istanbul, 1306/1889), 105ff., a sketchy account. The only thing that could be called a court of justice at the Porte during the years 1839-1868 was the Supreme Council of Judicial Ordinances, when functioning as a high court of appeal, and its successor councils. These had presidents (*reis*) of their own; yet the *divan-ı deavi nazırı* may have had some role in them.

72. *Saln.* (1265), 29, 39, 41, 44; (1286), 37, 50, 51, 52, 55; Shaw and Shaw, *History*, II, 36-37.

73. *Dstr.*[1], I, 352-63; Aristarchi, *LO*, II, 273-319; Ortaylı, *Mahalli İdareler*, 49, 71-73; Davison, *Reform*, 255-56; Shaw and Shaw, *History*, II, 118-19.

74. Veldet, "Kanunlaştırma Hareketleri," 175-99; Berkes, *Secularism*, 160ff.; Cevdet, *Tezâkir 1-12*, 63-64; id., *Tezâkir 40*, 72-74.

75. *Saln.* (1287), 37, 52, 53. Handwritten emendations in the copy of this yearbook that is now shelved in the reading room of BBA and almost certainly was once kept for reference in one of the offices of the Porte indicate (p. 37) that the supervisor of judicial affairs (*deavi nazırı*) died on 19 ZA 1287/February 1871.

The names of his two assistants (*muavin*) are also crossed out, but no names of successors were written in for any of these officials. Subsequent yearbooks no longer mention these posts. Cf. Cevdet, *Tezâkir 40*, 84-85; Young, *CD*, I, 159-60; Aristarchi, *LO*, v, 26-28. Shaw and Shaw, *History*, II, 75-76, 217, date the creation of the Ministry of Justice to 1870.

76. Cf. *Saln.* (1289), 39, on *Havale Cemiyeti* and *İcra Cemiyeti*, regulations for which, dated November-December 1870, appear in *Dstr.*[1], I, 343-51; Young, *CD*, I, 197-210.

77. Fevziye A. Tansel, "Ahmed Vefik Paşa," *Bell.*, XXVIII (1964), 119, 125; İnal, *Sadr.*, I, 654. M. Kaya Bilgegil, *Ziyâ Paşa üzerinde bir Araştırma* (Erzurum, 1970), 44.

78. Shaw and Shaw, *History*, II, 72, 167 n. 8; *Saln.* (1288), 39, 60-61, 65-66.

79. İnalcık, "Application of the Tanzimat," 99 ff.; Ortaylı, *Mahalli İdareler*, 15ff.; Moshe Ma'oz, *Ottoman Reform in Syria and Palestine, 1840-1861: The Impact of the Tanzimat on Politics and Society* (Oxford, 1968), 34-38; Davison, *Reform*, 46-49; id., "Advent of Representation," 98; Shaw and Shaw, *History*, II, 83-87.

80. Davison, *Reform*, 47-48, 107-108; Hans-Jürgen Kornrumpf, *Die Territorialverwaltung im östlichen Teil der europäischen Türkei vom Erlass der Vilayetsordnung (1864) bis zum Berliner Kongress (1878) nach amtlichen osmanischen Veröffentlichungen* (Freiburg im Breisgau, 1976), 13-22; Pakalın, *OTD*, II, 172-73, "Kapu Kethüdası"; BBA, Buy. 5, entry of 28 R 1280/October 1863.

81. Mark Pinson, "Ottoman Bulgaria in the First Tanzimat Period—The Revolts in Nish (1841) and Vidin (1850)," *Middle Eastern Studies*, XI (1975), 113-18; Albert Hourani, "Ottoman Reform and the Politics of Notables," in *Beginnings of Modernization in the Middle East*, edited by Polk and Chambers, 41-68.

82. Ma'oz, *Syria and Palestine*, 87-95, on local assemblies; Shaw, "Central Legislative Councils," 60, 67, 69, 74, 76, 83, 84, on committees of Supreme Council of Judicial Ordinances and successor bodies.

83. In addition to references already cited: E. Z. Karal, "Zarif Paşa'nın Hatıratı, 1816-1862," *Bell.*, IV (1940), 443-94; Andrew G. Gould, "Lords or Bandits? The Derebeys of Cilicia," *IJMES*, VII (1976), 485-506; Kenan Akyüz, *Ziya Paşa'nın Amasya Mutasarrıflığı Sırasındaki Olaylar* (Ankara, 1964); Bilgegil, *Ziya Paşa*, 33-67, 268ff.

84. Ortaylı, *Mahalli İdareler*, 107ff.; Davison, *Reform*, 136-45; Kornrumpf, *Territorialverwaltung*, 31-37, 39-74; Shaw and Shaw, *History*, II, 91-95.

85. *Dstr.*[1], I, 608-51; Young, *CD*, I, 36-69; Aristarchi, *LO*, II, 273-89; III, 7-39; Davison, *Reform*, 146-71; id., "Advent of Representation," 102-103; Ortaylı, *Mahalli İdareler*, 42-86; Kornrumpf, *Territorialverwaltung*, 22-26, 74-115; Shaw and Shaw, *History*, II, 87-95; Lewis, *Emergence*, 387ff. On the French system, cf. Bernard Le Clère and Vincent Wright, *Les préfets du Second Empire* (Paris, 1973), 35ff.

86. This in connection with the Sections for Appointments and Benefice Assignments in the Office of the Imperial Divan.

87. The post was abolished in 1841: BBA, Cev. Har. 7257, 12-15 ZA 1257. It existed again but was combined with that of *beylikçi* in 1845: BBA, Irade D 5736, 16 Z (?) 1261. The undersecretary for foreign affairs was first mentioned in the yearbooks in 1855: *Saln.* (1271), 49, being noted each year thereafter.

88. Temelkuran, "Mühimme Kalemi," 143, 161-75; for the original assign-

ment (c. 1838) to the Porte of the official who drew the imperial cipher, see Lûtfi, *Tarih*, v, 124. Cf. Shaw and Shaw, *History*, ii, 72-73.

89. *Saln.* (1298), 108; Said Paşa, *Said Paşa'nın Hâtıratı*, 3 vols. (Istanbul, 1328/ 1910), i, 210.

90. Lûtfi, *Tarih*, viii, 132.

91. Aristarchi, *LO*, ii, 427-28.

92. *Saln.* (1294), 112. That it is the same office is clear from the carryover, with appropriate change of titles, of three assistants attributed to the "secretary for foreign affairs" in *Saln.* (1293), 62, and (1294), 107, but to the "secretary for foreign legal affairs" in *Saln.* (1294), 112.

93. First mention in *Saln.* (1264), 15 (pagination of the ms. copy in the reading room of BBA). Known at first as the *tahrirat-ı hariciye müdürü*—a title that later became permanently associated with a quite distinct office—this office first appears with the title *hariciye mektubcusu* (same as *mektubî-i hariciye*) in *Saln.* (1268), 52, same incumbent.

94. For later confirmation, see *Har. Saln.* (1306), 244.

95. Lûtfi, *Tarih*, x, 63; cf. *Saln.* (1273), 48; (1281), 45. The career of the first important chief of the office, and thus the continuity of the office despite changes in title, can be followed in BBA, DSA, iv, 178, personnel file of Sahak Abro Efendi.

96. Cf. *Har. Saln.* (1306), 245.

97. *Saln.* (1285), 53; (1286), 52, 55.

98. Young, *CD*, ii, 226-29, 238-40; Aristarchi, *LO*, i, 7-8, 12-13; *Dstr.*[1] 16-18; Davison, *Reform*, 262-63.

99. *Saln.* (1286), 51; İnal. *Şair.*, iii, 1587, comments on Mehmed Said Bey, deputy director and later director of the office in the mid-1870s.

100. *Saln.* (1288), 65.

101. Young, *CD*, i, 38, art. 10, and 53, art. 22. For an example of the appointment of a similar kind of official at an earlier date, see Ma'oz, *Syria and Palestine*, 220.

102. *Saln.* (1285), 118ff.; (1286), 147ff.; (1287), 162ff.; (1288), 177ff.

103. İnal, *Şair.*, ii, 898-99; cf. ibid., ii, 1373-74: resignation of another historiographer in 1848 on account of similar problems.

104. BBA, Buy. 3, entries of 11 S 1257/1841, 15 RA 1258/1842, 28 L 1258/ 1842, 23 RA 1259/1843, 23 M 1262/1846, 6 CA 1262/1846, 7 L 1262/1846, 25 CA 1264/1848, 6 L 1264/1848, 24 C 1265/1849, 1 B 1269/1853, 24 Ş 1259/1853, 23 RA 1271/1854, 19 L 1271/1855, 17 C (?) 1272/1856, 16 R 1275/1858; Buy. 5, entries of 20 CA 1280/1863, 13 M 1281/1864, 21 R 1288/1864, 22 CA 1293/1876, and so on. In these registers, the entries often include indications that they originated as circulars from the grand vezir to various agencies.

105. BBA, Buy. 3 entries of 25 Ş 1255/1839 and 17 Ş 1260/1844; Buy. 5, entry of 2 N 1294/1877.

106. BBA, Buy. 3, entries of 25 CA 1264/1848 (7.5 hours per day), 5 C 1265/ 1848 (7 hours), 1 B 1269/1853 (7 hours); Buy. 5, entries of 5 C 1279/1862 (4.5 hours), 13 M 1281/1864 (4.5 hours). Did the bureaucratic workday decline in length with the passage of years?

107. BBA, Buy. 3, entry of 24 Ş 1269/1853.

108. BBA, Ayn. 767, entry of 6 Z 1257/1842; Buy. 3, entry of 5 R 1273/1856.

109. BBA, Buy. 5, entries of 5 C 1279/1862, 20 CA 1280/1863, 2 Ş 1281/1864.

110. Lûtfi, *Tarih*, VIII, 92; cf. references to exclusion of beggars from the Records Office of the Porte in *Dstr.*[1], IV, 60.

111. BBA, Buy. 5, entry of 15 C 1279/1862; identical text in Rüus 217 under same date.

112. Davison, *Reform*, 35-36.

113. Kaynar, *Mustafa Reşit*, 303-13; *Dstr.*[1], I, 551-62; cf. Aristarchi, *LO*, II, 225-37; E. Z. Karal, "Rüşvetin Kaldırılması için Yapılan Teşebbüsler," *Tar. Ves.*, I (1941), 45-65.

114. BBA, Buy. 3, entries of 11 S 1257/1841 and 21 Z 1265/1849; Buy. 5, entries of 15 C 1279/1862, 2 Ş 1281/1864, 22 M 1294/1877.

115. BBA, Buy. 3, entry of 21 Z 1265/1845 for the *Meclis-i Vâlâ Tahrirat Odası*.

116. Lûtfi, *Tarih*, VIII, 92-93, 114-15, 139, 155-56, 176; IX, 45-46, 62, 116; BBA, Rüus 217, entry of 13 CA 1263/1847; Buy. 3, entries of 13 CA 1263/1847 (same as preceding), 20 S 1265/1849, and 13 ZA 1268/1852 (published in *Dstr.*[1], I, 725-30); Buy. 5, entry of 6 C-26 L 1278/1861-1862 (cf. *Dstr.*[1], I, 731-35); Buy. 6, entry of 6 C 1286/1869.

117. Pakalın, *OTD*, II, 172-73, "Kapu Kethüdası."

118. Young, *CD*, I, 37-38, arts. 6-12, law of 1864; 49, art. 5, law of 1871. The later reference does say that the governor general will exercise his appointment powers in conformity with special regulations, but no systematic regulation of appointment-making procedures appears to have occurred before the next period.

119. BBA, Buy. 5, entry of 19 CA 1296/May 1879.

120. Har., Müt. 8, in dossier headed "Diverses nominations, 1864," Âli to Bulwer, 5 Feb. 1861, written at Bulwer's request.

121. Hurewitz, *MENA*, I, 315-18, especially 317.

122. For example, Lûtfi, *Tarih*, VIII, 12; BBA, Buy. 5, entries of 17 ZA 1281/1865 and 15 S 1283/1866; many *tarifes* (fee-tables) in *Dstr.*[1].

123. Budgets for this period are available as follows in various collections of BBA: Mesail-i Mühimme 419, enclosure 3 (1840); Mesail-i Mühimme 451 (1846); Maliye deft. 8989, p. 27 (1849); Irade Meclis-i Mahsus 338 (1856); Maliye deft. 18858 (1857); Irade Meclis-i Mahsus 529 (1858); Yıldız 18. 525/208. 128. 25 (1862-1863); Yıldız 18. 525/212. 128. 25 (1863-1864); Yıldız 18. 525/223. 128. 26 (1868-1869); Yıldız 18. 525/229. 128. 26 (1869-1870); Mal. Müd. 11177 (1870-1873). A detailed budget of 1859 for the Foreign Ministry is in Har., TKE 763. I am indebted to Mehmed Genç for the references for 1840-1858. Cf. Shaw, "Nineteenth-Century . . . Tax Reforms," 448-52; Du Velay, *Essai*, 174ff.

124. Cevdet, *Tezâkir 40*, 21, 58; Şerif Mardin, "Some Notes on an Early Phase in the Modernization of Communications in Turkey," *Comparative Studies in Society and History*, III (1961), 252ff.

125. In terms of simplification of language, reduction of justificatory verbiage, and achievement of clarity of organization through articulation of the text into numbered articles and sections and the grouping of related provisions, the contrast between early regulatory acts such as the code of 1838 for officials (Kaynar, *Mustafa Reşit*, 295-301) or even the Gülhane Decree (*Dstr.*[1], I, 4-7; Hurewitz, *MENA*, I, 269-71) and much of the later legislation found in *Dstr.*[1] is like night and day.

126. *Dstr.*[1], IV, 58-60, regulations of 1861 for Records Office of Sublime Porte.

127. Kaynar, *Mustafa Reşit*, 109.

128. Cevdet, *Tezâkir 40*, 74; Lûtfi, *Tarih*, III, 156-60; XII, 4, 141-42.

129. FO 78/392, Ponsonby to Palmerston, 7 January 1840, enclosing "Régle-ment ayant pour objet de déterminer la marche à suivre dans les délibérations de Grand Conseil; publié vers la fin de Décembre 1839" (*sic*) Kaynar, *Mustafa Reşit*, 206-209; cf. Levy, "Military Policy of Mahmud II," 480-81. For a later revision, see Shaw and Shaw, *History*, II, 79.

130. Temelkuran, "Mühimme Kalemi," 161-68.

131. Cevdet, *Tezâkir 1-12*, 89.

132. *Dstr.*[1], IV, 58-60.

133. *Dstr.*[1], I, 325-42, 703-18; Young, *CD*, I, 3-5; Aristarchi, *LO*, II, 38-55.

134. Shaw and Shaw, *History*, II, 72, 167 n. 8.

135. Aristarchi, *LO*, IV, 7-14.

136. Cf. also Uzunçarşılı, *Merkez*, 45, on regulations of 1872 for Section for Benefice Assignment (*Tahvil Kalemi*).

137. Including the personnel files in BBA and Har., as well as the published biographical works, such as İnal, *Şair.*, and id., *Sadr.*, the sources for such a study are voluminous enough by themselves to indicate why it cannot be included in entirety here.

138. BBA, Şehb. 1, entries of Er RA & El C 1264/March-May 1848: the earliest Ottoman representatives in Calcutta and Bombay were appointed on the rec-ommendation of the governor of Jidda and bore the title *Hicaz Tüccar Vekili* ("agents of the Hijaz merchants"). Through the work of Abd ül-Hak Hâmid, who was no traditionalist except, perhaps, in his literary education, consular service in India also had an influence on the development of late Ottoman litera-ture (İnal, *Şair.*, I, 561-70).

139. For cases where this kind of teaching within the offices continued as late as 1913, see İnal, *Şair.*, II, 1382, 1412, 1483; III, 1562; cf. BBA, Buy. 6, decision of Council of Ministers, 12 Ş 1311/February 1894, to appoint a teacher of *celi divani* script in the Office of the Imperial Divan.

140. Davison, *Reform*, 90.

141. Aşçıdede Halil İbrahim, *Hatıralar*, 13-24, 33-35, 50-51, 66-71, 94-101.

142. Outstanding bureaucrats of exclusively traditional cultural formation in-clude Mehmed Besim Bey (BBA, DSA III, 164), *beylikçi* in 1860-1861 and mem-ber of various councils; Mustafa Münir Bey (Har., SA 418), *mektubî* of the Foreign Ministry, c. 1895-1908; Abdullah Niyazi Efendi (BBA, DSA I, 550), *beylikçi*, 1871-1885; and Ali Şefkati Efendi (BBA, DSA I, 558, and İnal, *Şair.*, III, 1742-46), undersecretary to the grand vezir, 1873-1874, *amedî*, 1878-1885, etc.

143. See, for example, Avedis Sanjian, *The Armenian Communities in Syria under Ottoman Dominion* (Cambridge, Mass., 1965), ch. 4; Louise Nalbandian, *The Armenian Revolutionary Movement: The Development of Armenian Political Parties through the Nineteenth Century* (Berkeley and Los Angeles, 1963), ch. 2; Ergin, *Maarif*, II, 602-73, on non-Muslim schools.

144. Çark, *Türk Devleti Hizmetinde Ermeniler*, 39ff.; Mesrob K. Krikorian, *Arme-nians in the Service of the Ottoman Empire, 1860-1908* (London, 1977), passim.

145. For example, Dakes Efendi (Har., SA 6) summed up his knowledge of Turkish better than he knew when he wrote, "ifade-i merama tahriran muktedir olabilirim" ("I am able to be capable of explaining my meaning in writing"); Dé-mètre Mavroyeni (Har., SA 129) filled out his personnel questionnaire entirely

in French; Pozik Yusuf Azarian (Har., SA 725) made various errors of grammar and spelling; and Henri Armaon (Har., SA 258) lost a position in 1892 for being unable to read and write Turkish.

146. Hurewitz, *MENA*, I, 346-49; Young, *CD*, I, 135ff.; Ortaylı, *Mahalli İdareler*, 37ff.

147. E.g., Kostaki Musurus Paşa, ambassador in London, 1851-1885: Sinan Kuneralp, "Bir Osmanlı Diplomatı, Kostaki Musurus Paşa," *Bell.*, xxxiv (1970), 421-35; succeeded there by his son in 1902: BBA, DSA I, 684, İstefanaki Musurus Paşa. "Etienne" Karatheodory, minister in Brussels for many years, beginning in 1875: Har., SA 30. Rüstem Paşa headed diplomatic missions, c. 1870-1895, in Russia, Italy, and England: BBA, DSA II, 100. Rüstem was an Italian "renegade," but there seems to be no indication of actual conversion to Islam.

148. Some of the quantitative data on this point is in Findley, "The Acid Test of Ottomanism: The Acceptance of Non-Muslims in the Late Ottoman Bureaucracy," paper presented at the conference on The Non-Muslim Communities in the Ottoman Empire and its Successor States, Princeton University, June 1978. I intend to include a more extensive discussion of the same subject in a later study.

149. FO 78/2019, Elliot to Stanley, 10 March, 1868, commenting on appointment of Agathon Efendi, an Armenian, as minister of public works.

150. The non-Muslim foreign ministers were Alexander Karatheodory (1878-1879), Sava Paşa (1879-1880), Gabriel Noradounghian (1912-1913), and Yusuf Franco Paşa (1919); *Dışişleri Bakanlığı Yıllığı, 1964-65*, edited by Hâmid Aral (Ankara, 1965?), 14.

151. İnal, *Sadr.*, I, 38; BBA, DSA IV, 178; Çark, *Türk Devleti Hizmetinde Ermeniler*, 130-31.

152. For example, several members of the Aristarchi family continued to serve in the Foreign Ministry, including Aleko Aristarchi (Har., SA 504) as well as at least one who held ambassadorships (*Dışişleri Yıllığı*, 297, 365); from the Karatheodory family, aside from the Alexander who became foreign minister, there was at least one other Alexander (Har., SA 42), as well as his brother "Etienne" (Har., SA 30).

153. For the years 1860-1908, non-Muslim officials of the Foreign Ministry outranked the traditionalistic Muslims more or less consistently and had higher median salaries in all but twelve years.

154. Davison, *Reform*, 132-35.

155. Robert Devereux, *The First Ottoman Constitutional Period: A Study of the Midhat Constitution and Parliament* (Baltimore, 1963), 216-26.

156. Davison, *Reform*, 33-34; Mardin, "Super Westernization," 403ff.

157. In his biography of Âli Efendi, a collaborator of Hafız Müşfik, whom we shall discuss below, İnal, *Şair.*, I, 95, sums up this association of education and government service thus: "He—like his counterparts without number—entered government service, which was supposed to be the only place for the application of learning and the only source of subsistence."

158. For an especially vivid example of how a chance encounter on a Bosphorus ferry led to such an appointment (c. 1869), see ibid., II, 1424-25.

159. Şerif Mardin, "Historical Determinants of Social Stratification," 139-40; cf. id., *Genesis*, 110.

160. Ubicini, *La Turquie actuelle*, 164-65; FO 78/2177, Elliot's no. 350 of 28 September 1871, reporting appointment of Alexander Karatheodory as under-

secretary for foreign affairs and commenting on the "Hellenic tendencies" of the family.

161. İnal, *Sadr.*, I, 38.

162. E.J.W. Gibb, *Poetry*, V, 105-106; VI, 374.

163. İnal, *Şair.*, II, 815.

164. İnal, *Şair.*, I, 751-52, on problems of Keçecizade İzzet Molla.

165. Other, similar cases ibid., II, 1021-22, 1211-13; III, 1569. For advice on literary sources on the bureaucracy, I am indebted to Mehmed Kaplan, Professor of Modern Turkish literature at the University of Istanbul, and to his associate Dr. İnci Enginün, as well as to Professor Fahir İz of the University of Chicago.

166. Lewis, *Emergence*, 95, 146-47.

167. İnal, *Şair.*, II, 1018-19; cf. Mardin, *Genesis*, 124-27, 258-59.

168. Mardin, *Genesis*, 121-32; cf. id., "Power, Civil Society and Culture," 277; id., "Super Westernization," 407, 416, 425.

169. İnal, *Şair.*, I, 139ff., on background of Ayetullah Bey (cf. ibid., III, 1622-24, on boyhood acquaintance between his grandfather, Abd ül-Rahman Sami Paşa, and Mustafa Reşid); ibid., II, 945, 1165ff., on background of Mehmed Bey and his uncle, Mahmud Nedim Paşa; Mardin, *Genesis*, 72 n. 128 on Mehmed Bey as "milk-brother" of Sultan Abd ül-Hamid; Mardin, *Genesis*, 28 on Mustafa Fazıl Paşa as brother of Khedive Ismail of Egypt.

170. İnal, *Şair.*, I, 139; II, 794, 1183, 1211; III, 1542, 1544; on the need of literary figures for this kind of protection, cf. Mardin, *Jön Türk.*, 94.

171. Nermin Menemencioğlu, "Namık Kemal Abroad: A Centenary," *Middle Eastern Studies*, IV (1967), 29-49.

172. This summary based on Mardin, *Genesis*, passim, and Findley, "Ideological Change in the Late Ottoman Empire," paper presented at the conference on State, Society, and Economy in Nineteenth Century Iran and the Ottoman Empire, held in Babolsar, Iran, in June 1978 under joint sponsorship of the Reza Shah Kabir University and the Joint Committee on the Near and Middle East of the American Council of Learned Societies and the Social Science Research Council.

CHAPTER SIX

1. İnal, *Sadr.*, I, 313; id., *Şair.*, II, 1175.

2. *Dstr.*[1], IV, 8.

3. Hakkı Tarık Us, ed., *Meclis-i Meb'usan 1293:1877 Zabıt Ceridesi*, 2 vols. (Istanbul, 1939-1954), II, 401; quoted in Devereux, *First Constitution*, 244, transcription and translation altered. In the Turkish text, I have amended *irs* to *isr* on the suggestion of Professor Halil İnalcık.

4. Davison, *Reform*, 280-88, 307-26; Cevdet, *Tezâkir 40*, 146; İnal, *Şair.*, II, 1168; AAE, Turquie 390, de Vogüé to de Rémusat, 24 October 1871, mentioning friends of Âli Paşa and lower-ranking Christian officials as targets of the dismissals; cf. HHS, PA XII/98, Mayr to Beust, 12 and 15 September 1871; FO 78/2177, Elliot to Granville, 28 September and 6 October 1871. Cf. the Appendix on budgetary fluctuations in these years.

5. William L. Langer, *European Alliances and Alignments*, 2nd ed. (New York, 1962), 155, 164.

6. Davison, *Reform*, 365; Hurewitz, *MENA*, I, 346-49; Aristarchi, *LO*, II, 56-211; Young, *CD*, I, 113-58.

7. Davison, *Reform*, 114-35; Young, *CD*, II, 12ff.

8. Devereux, *First Constitution*, 46-51, 259-60.

9. Ibid., 80-82, 91-97; Davison, *Reform*, 382-83.

10. İnalcık, "Pâdişah," *IA*, IX, 495; B. Lewis, "Dustūr," *EI²*, II, 642; Devereux, *First Constitution*, 81.

11. Text of constitution in *Dstr.*¹, IV, 2-20, and Aristarchi, *LO*, V, 1-25. Cf. Devereux, *First Constitution*, 60-79; Davison, *Reform*, ch. 10.

12. Davison, "Advent of Representation," 103, 106-108 on mode of election; Devereux, *First Constitution*, 138-53, 255-56, 261-75.

13. Devereux, *First Constitution*, 113; Us, *Zabıt*, I, 11. Cf. Stanford J. Shaw, "A Promise of Reform: Two Complementary Documents," *IJMES*, IV (1973), 359-65.

14. On Said, see E. Kuran, "Sa'id Paşa," *IA*, X, 82-86; id., "Küçük Said Paşa (1840-1914) as a Turkish Modernist," *IJMES*, I (1970), 124-32; İnal, *Sadr.*, II, 1232-37; and Said Paşa, *Hâtırat*. Cf. Ali Ölmezoğlu, "Cevdet Paşa," *IA*, III, 114-23; Cevdet, *Tezâkir 40*, passim.

15. Us, *Zabıt*, I, 11-12; Ergin, *Maarif*, II, 502; Tahsin Paşa, *Abdülhamit ve Yıldız Hatıraları* (Istanbul, 1931), 36-37.

16. Devereux, *First Constitution*, 186-215.

17. So said Tahsin Paşa, *Hatıralar*, 139; cf. İnal, *Sadr.*, II, 1264-1306; Osman Nuri, *Abd ül-Hamid-i Sani ve Devr-i Saltanatı*, 3 vols. (Istanbul, 1327/1909), II, 477ff.

18. Uşaklıgil, *Kırk Yıl*, 359-60, 497-510; cf. Tahsin, *Hatıralar*, 18ff.; Osman Nuri, *Abd ül-Hamid-i Sani*, II, 449-76; Pakalın, *OTD*, III, 635-37, "Yıldız sarayı."

19. *Saln.* (1326), 120-57; cf. Shaw and Shaw, *History*, II, 213-15.

20. Osman Nuri, *Abd ül-Hamid-i Sani*, II, 449, 452, 496-527.

21. FO 371/548, File 29285, "General Report on Turkey for the Year 1906" (Conf. Pr. 8982), 36; Tahsin Paşa, *Hatıralar*, 25-33, 92; cf. Said Paşa, *Hâtırat*, I, 17.

22. FO 78/4608, Currie to Kimberley, 4 February 1895. BBA contains regular series of correspondence between the palace secretaries and the embassies. Quite extensive, the correspondence was usually transcribed into small, bound registers. Some scores of these are in the Yıldız papers, usually under *Kısım* no. 36, *Karton* nos. X-XIX, and variable *Evrak* and *Zarf* nos.

23. AA, Türkei 161, Bd. 1, Radowitz to Caprivi, 4 September 1891 (T 139, mf. roll 394); cf. FO 371/532, O'Conor to Grey, 7, 9, and 26 February 1908.

24. Sultan Abdül Hamid, *Siyasî Hatıratım* (Istanbul, 1974), 118, translation of *Pensées et souvenirs de l'ex-Sultan Abdul-Hamid*, ed. Ali Vahbi Bey (Neuchâtel, 1909?); Mehmet Hocaoğlu, ed., *Abdülhamit Han'in Muhtıraları (Belgeler)* (Istanbul, n.d.), 79.

25. İnal, *Sadr.*, II, 1277-79.

26. FO 371/548, File 29285, "General Report for 1906," 25-26.

27. FO 78/4343, White to Salisbury, 27 February 1891.

28. FO 371/548, File 29285, "General Report for 1906," 26; FO 371/544, File 23627, G. Barclay to Grey, 28 July 1908 and Lowther to Grey, 2 August 1908; Osman Nuri, *Abd ül-Hamid-i Sani*, II, 501-509, 513.

29. İnal, *Sadr.*, III, 1611-12; Har., SA 315, official personnel file of Bedirhan Paşazade Abd ül-Rezzak Bey (incomplete); FO 371/548, File 29285, "General Report for 1906," 28; Rakım Ziyaoğlu, *İstanbul Kadıları, Şehreminleri, Belediye Reisleri ve Partiler Tarihi, 1453-1971* (Istanbul, 1971), 140-47 on Rıdvan Paşa.

30. İnal, *Sadr.*, III, 1608-11; Osman Nuri, *Abd ül-Hamid-i Sani*, II, 483, 545 (photograph), 554-61.

31. AA, Türkei 134, Bd. 21, Marschall to Bülow, 8 February 1907 (T 139, mf. roll 392), a detailed account of the affair; cf. Edwin Pears, *Forty Years in Constantinople: The Recollections of Sir Edwin Pears, 1873-1916* (New York, 1916), 206-208.

32. Ernest E. Ramsaur, *The Young Turks: Prelude to the Revolution of 1908* (Princeton, 1957), 130.

33. Berkes, *Secularism*, 253ff.; Nikki R. Keddie, *Sayyid Jamâl ad-Dîn "al-Afghani," a Political Biography* (Berkeley and Los Angeles, 1972), ch. 13.

34. Karal, *OT*, VIII, 352-75; Mardin, *Jön Türk.*, 39-40.

35. Berkes, *Secularism*, 256-57; Shaw and Shaw, *History*, II, 226-30.

36. İnal, *Sadr.*, II, 1272-74, 1279-81, 1365-66; Karal, *OT*, VIII, 265-68; FO 371/776, File 20279, Lowther to Grey, 29 May 1909, recounting statement of Mahmud Şevket Paşa about the "cartloads"; BBA, Yıldız 18. 553/548. 93. 38, document of 26 Z 1309/July 1892 on British ambassador.

37. *Har. Saln.* (1306), 631. On the German Foreign Office, see Lamar Cecil, *The German Diplomatic Service, 1871-1914* (Princeton, 1976), 19.

38. Uşaklıgil, *Kırk Yıl*, 332-33, 605. A novelistic account of conditions in the Translation Office of the Sublime Porte appears in Mizancı Murad, *Turfanda mı yoksa Turfa mı*. In the modernized version published by M. Ertuğrul Düzdağ under the title *Mansur Bey* (Istanbul, 1972), this is ch. 8.

39. Har., Müt. 249, dossier on reorganization of Foreign Ministry, report of Münir and Hrand Beys, Legal Counsellors, 19 Mayıs 1328/June 1912.

40. Esat Cemal Pâker, *Siyasî Tarihimizde Kırk Yıllık Hariciye Hatıraları* (Istanbul, 1952), 7.

41. İnal, *Şair.*, III, 1587, recounting efforts of Abd ül-Hamid to get one Mehmed Said, who had published criticisms of a prominent palace figure, to accept an official position so that Mehmed Said's publishing activity could then more easily be hampered. Influence was also exerted on Mehmed Said's father, Ahmed Kemal Paşa, a former ambassador (cf. ibid., II, 819ff.).

42. Ibid., IV, 2149ff., İnal's comments on himself.

43. Ibid., II, 1315 n. 2; IV, 2151, 2170; Uşaklıgil, *Kırk Yıl*, 327, 355.

44. İnal, *Şair.*, II, 999.

45. İnal, *Sadr.*, I, 385ff.; II, 1027ff., 1381ff.; cf. Abdül Hamid, *Siyasî Hatıratım*, 102-103; Said Paşa, *Hâtırat*, I, 325ff.; II, 4ff.

46. Uşaklıgil, *Kırk Yıl*, 330; Tahsin Paşa, *Hatıralar*, 146ff.

47. İnal, *Sadr.*, II, 1281.

48. Osman Nuri, *Abd ül-Hamid-i Sani*, II, 542-48; same account in Paul Fesch, *Constantinople aux derniers jours d'Abdul-Hamid* (Paris, 1907), 79-87; cf. Tahsin Paşa, *Hatıralar*, 130; Mardin, *Jön Türk.*, 126. There is a great deal on such matters in the correspondence that passed between the *Mabeyn* and the embassies: for example, BBA, Yıldız 36. 139/24. 139. XVIII, notebook containing copies of correspondence with Berlin embassy, passim, or Yıldız 15. 74/40. 74. 15, on Keçecizade İzzet Fuad Paşa, minister in Madrid, c. 1901. Cf. AA, Türkei 162, Bd. 2, Radowitz to Caprivi, 23 March 1891 (T 139, mf. roll 394); Türkei, 162, Bd. 5, Alvensleben to Bülow, 19 November 1900 (T 139, mf. roll 395); Türkei

159, Bd. 3, Ahmed Rif'at Bey, son of late Grand Vezir Halil Rif'at Paşa, to Bülow, 21 May 1904, and Stodman (?) to Bülow, 9 July 1904 (T 139, mf. roll 394).

49. Ramsaur, *The Young Turks*, 34-35; also Uşaklıgil, İnal, et al.

50. Tahsin Paşa, *Hatıralar*, 10-12; Young, *CD*, v, 15 n. 2, describing Abd ül-Hamid as the largest landowner in the world.

51. Donald Quataert, "Ottoman Reform and Agriculture in Anatolia, 1876-1908," Ph.D. dissertation, University of California, Los Angeles, 1973; Du Velay, *Essai sur l'histoire financière*, 644-48.

52. The basis for these observations lies in my analysis of the data contained in Har., SA, and BBA, DSA, on the salaries of Foreign Ministry officials and in comparison of these data with available information on prices. I hope to publish these statistics in a later work and have presented some in Findley, "Acid Test," Table 6.

53. After about fifty years of service, Aşçıdede Halil İbrahim went on the Pilgrimage. When he returned, he was promoted in rank, his salary was tripled, and began to be paid in gold (*Hatıralar*, 103).

54. Young, *CD*, v, 15 n. 3; Uşaklıgil, *Kırk Yıl*, 311-12.

55. Tahsin Paşa, *Hatıralar*, 136-38; Said Paşa, *Hâtırat*, II, 145; cf. Cevdet, *Tezâkir 40*, 275, 280.

56. AA, Türkei 134, Bd. 18, Wangenheim to Bülow, 26 August 1901 (T 139, mf. roll 392).

57. Abdül Hamid, *Siyasî Hatıratım*, 77-79, 113-14; cf. Hocaoğlu, *Abdülhamit Han'ın Muhtıraları*, 114-16.

58. *Dstr.*[1], VII, 947-48, *irade* of 1903; 1168-69, *irade* of 1903; VIII, 625-27, *irade* of 1906. Miscellaneous other measures for the benefit of the Hijaz Railway, ibid., VII, 929-30, 949-52, 1041-45; VIII, 69-70, 132-35.

59. Unless otherwise noted, the source for all observations about the organizational state of the Porte in 1908, as well as for Figures VI-1 and VI-2, is *Saln.* (1326), 160-245. For a nearly contemporary, Western-language account, obviously based on Ottoman yearbooks and on *Dstr.*[1] but not entirely accurate, cf. Loytved, "Grundriss der allgemeinen Organisation der Verwaltungsbehörden der eigentlichen Türkei," *Mitteilungen des Seminars für Orientalischen Sprachen zu Berlin*, II. Abteilung, *Westasiatische Studien*, VII (1904), 25-52.

60. Davison, *Reform*, 372, Midhat Paşa's draft.

61. *Dstr.*[1], IV, 67, arts. 27ff.; Aristarchi, *LO*, v, 10-12; cf. Karal, *OT*, VIII, 268-69; Devereux, *First Constitution*, 67-69, 173.

62. İnal, *Sadr.*, I, 670-71.

63. Ibid., II, 909-11, 967-68. On the political ideas of Hayr ül-Din, see Mardin, *Genesis*, 385-95, and Leon Carl Brown, *The Surest Path: The Political Treatise of a Nineteenth-Century Muslim Statesman* (Cambridge, Mass., 1967).

64. Exceptions or partial exceptions are Ahmed Es'ad (İnal, *Sadr.*, I, 415-35, rose through military service), Şirvanizade Mehmed Rüşdi (ibid., I, 436-82, training and first decade of career in religious establishment), Hüseyin Avni (ibid., I, 483-593, military), İbrahim Edhem (ibid., I, 600-35, military), Hayr ül-Din (ibid., II, 895-960, rose in service of Bey of Tunis and not of Istanbul government), Abd ül-Rahman Nur ül-Din (ibid., II, 1320-46, originally military, followed by civil positions, but mostly in provinces), Ahmed Cevad (ibid., II, 1473-1534, military). *Mütercim* Mehmed Rüşdi began in military service, but became thoroughly identified with the civil bureaucracy before 1871 (ibid., I, 101-48). Küçük Said's

service as a palace secretary (1876-1877) was an anomaly in an otherwise civil-bureaucratic career (ibid., II, 989-1263).

65. Mehmed Kâmil Paşa (1885-1891) and Halil Rif'at Paşa (1895-1901); Danişmend, *Kronoloji*, IV, 507-19.

66. İnal, *Sadr.*, III, 1604.

67. *Saln.* (1294), 108.

68. Mahmud Münir Paşa (Har., SA 167) acquired all three of these posts in the 1870s and retained them until 1899. He was succeeded in all three by one İbrahim Rasih Paşa and then, in 1906, by Mehmed Galib Paşa (Har., SA 426). Cf. Uşaklıgil, *Kirk Yıl*, 500; id., *Saray ve Ötesi*, 59-60.

69. Noted at least as early as 1892-1893: *Saln.* (1310), 158-59.

70. Noted at least as early as 1888: *Saln.* (1305), 134.

71. Cf. comments of Said Paşa, *Hâtırat*, II, 161-62.

72. Both noted at least as early as 1888: *Saln.* (1305), 136.

73. İnal, *Şair.*, IV, 2155.

74. BBA, Buy. 8, undated entry flanked by entries of 14 and 29 S 1318/1900.

75. Devereux, *First Constitution*, 37-38, 45-46, 96-97, 243-44, on "Grand Councils"; Davison, *Reform*, 348-49, 354, 356, 363, 368, 393-94; Pakalın, *OTD*, III, 361, "Şûra-yı Saltanat"; FO 371/548, File 29285, "General Report for 1906," 22, on the holding of special sessions (*encümen*) of the Council of Ministers at the palace.

76. Karal, *OT*, VIII, 272.

77. *Saln.* (1289-1326) under headings "Vükelâ-yı Fiham ve Meclis-i Has," "Heyet ve Meclis-i Vükelâ-yı Fiham," etc.

78. *Saln.* (1312), 156.

79. Cevdet, *Tezâkir 40*, 151.

80. *Dstr.*[1], I, 16, *irade* of July 1872; Young, *CD*, I, xiv n. 8.

81. For example, *Dstr.*[1], V-VIII, passim: many of the acts published in these volumes appear as sets of documents, including a report drawn up in the Council of State, a covering memorandum from the Council of Ministers, and the decree (*irade*) conveying the approval of the sultan.

82. FO 371/548, File 29285, "General Report for 1906," 23.

83. Shaw, "Central Legislative Councils," 82-84; Devereux, *First Constitution*, 71, 113, 171-72, 212. Cf. the Appendix, changes in ostensible budgetary allocations of Council of State, 1871-1880.

84. Shaw, "Central Legislative Councils," 76ff.; *Dstr.*[1], I, 703-18; Young, *CD*, I, 3-11. The *mülâzım*s of the Council of State were salaried officials of some importance, not to be confused with the unpaid supernumeraries or apprentices to which this term applies in other civil-bureaucratic settings. Information on the clerical staff of the council in BBA, TDvM, 10/30-35, documents of 30 B-10 N 1294/August-September 1877; *Saln.* (1297), 126.

85. BBA, TDvM, 10/39-40, documents of 2-7 CA 1297/April 1880.

86. *Saln.* (1305), 139-40; (1310), 166-69; *Dstr.*[1], V, 519-20, *irade* of 1886; 1076-77, *irade* of 1888 (original documents in BBA, TDvM, 10/43-47); VI, 209-10, *irade* of 1888; 1459-60, *irade* of 1894 (originals in BBA, TDvM, 10/50-53); 1474-75, *irade* of 1894 (original in BBA, TDvM, 10/54).

87. BBA, TDvM, 10/58-62, of which 10/60 is the decree of 11 Ş 1314/January 1897, published in *Dstr.*[1], VII, 146; Young, *CD*, I, 6-7. Cf. *Dstr.*[1], VII, 405-406, *irade* of 1900; *Saln.* (1315), 118-23; earlier evidence for the existence of the courts appears in the *Saln.* references in n. 86.

88. Former noted at least by 1880: *Saln.* (1297), 104; latter, at least by 1892-

1893: *Saln.* (1310), 170-73. On public prosecutors, see Abd ul-Rahman Şeref, *Tarih Musahabeleri* (Istanbul, 1339/1920-1921), 342-47.

89. *Dstr.*[1], v, 519-20, *irade* of 1886.

90. *Saln.* (1305), 140.

91. *Dstr.*[1], *Mütemmim*, 160-62, regulations of 1891; same text ibid., vi, 1105-1107.

92. *Dstr.*[1], vii, 146, 150, decree and amendment of 1897; cf. *Saln.* (1326), 182-99.

93. Devereux, *First Constitution*, 227-30, 276-77; *Saln.* (1326), 170.

94. Osman Nuri, *Abd ül-Hamid-i Sani*, ii, 591-92.

95. FO 371/548, File 29285, "General Report for 1906," 32; İnal, *Şair.*, ii, 918-31.

96. Kornrumpf, *Territorialverwaltung*, 26-30, 35-37, 115-40; Ortaylı, *Mahalli İdareler*, 87ff., 154ff., 186ff.; Shaw and Shaw, *History*, ii, 243-45; Lewis, *Emergence*, 390-91; relevant provisions of Constitution of 1876 in *Dstr.*[1], iv, 18. Additional regulatory acts in *Dstr.*[1], v, 191-96, 947; vi, 397, 404-405, 488-90; vii, 116-18; viii, 712-37, as well as many others in same volumes on territories in special status (see indices). Cf. Young, *CD*, i, 69-112, 119-34, 150-54.

97. For several years following the death of Âli Paşa in 1871, the yearbooks show the Council of Ministers as including an undersecretary to the grand vezir, but no minister of the interior: *Saln.* (1289), 35; (1290), 36; (1291), 35; (1292), 35; (1293), 36; (1294), 102-103. This suggests that the undersecretary of the grand vezir continued for some time after 1871 to function, as he had previously, as a kind of alternate for the minister of the interior. In 1878, however, an entry for a minister of the interior appears, together with one for the undersecretary to the grand vezir: *Saln.* (1295), 98-99.

98. *Saln.* (1326), 204-26.

99. *Dstr.*[1], v, 992-1000, regulations of 1885 on printing establishments; vi, 1247, amendment to preceding; 1544-55, regulations of 1894 on printing establishments and booksellers; vii, 712-13, *irade* of 1901 on examination of all works in Domestic Press Directorate prior to publication. Cf. Young, *CD*, ii, 351ff.

100. *Dstr.*[1], viii, 143-45, document of 1905, with appended table of references to earlier legislation; cf. Young, *CD*, ii, 261ff. See also Kemal Karpat, "Ottoman Population Records and the Census of 1881/82-1893," *IJMES*, ix (1978), 246ff.

101. *Dstr.*[1], v, 861-65, regulations of 1887 on these permits.

102. *Har. Saln.* (1306), 72-77; *Dışişleri Yıllığı* (1964-1965), 13-14.

103. FO 371/548, File 29285, "General Report for 1906," 29; Har., SA 429, personnel file of Ahmed Tevfik Paşa; İnal, *Sadr.*, iii, 1704-62.

104. Galip Kemali Söylemezoğlu, *Hariciye Hizmetinde Otuz Sene*, 4 vols. (Istanbul, 1949-55), i, 54-55; Çark, *Türk Devleti Hizmetinde Ermeniler*, 147-50; Har., SA 435, personnel file of Artin Dadian Paşa.

105. FO 371/548, File 29285, "General Report for 1906, 30; cf. Söylemezoğlu, *Otuz Sene*, i, 55; Har., SA 420, personnel file of Mehmed Nuri Bey.

106. *Saln.* (1326), 228-33. Regulations drawn up in this period, still in very traditionalistic terms, for the Turkish Correspondence Office and Translation Office are to be found in Har., Niz. Kav., 36/40, "Mektubî-i Hariciye Kalemi Nizamnamesidir," with order for execution dated 27 S 1296/1877, and BBA, Meclis-i Tanzimat deft. for 1298-99, 283-86, "Bab-ı Âli Tercüme Odasına mahsus Kararnamedir," with order for execution dated 7 C 1300/1883.

107. *Har. Saln.* (1306), 248.

108. *Saln.* (1312), 190-91, (1313), 192-93; (1314), 194-95; (1315), 134-35; (1316), 144-45. Biographical sources recording the shift to the Ministry of the Interior and then back to the Foreign Ministry include Har., SA 124, personnel file of Neşan Saferian Efendi, foreign press director throughout these years; Har., SA 204, Avnik Maksud Bey; Har., SA 768, Emil Rosenfeld Efendi. Cf. Tahsin Paşa, *Hatıralar*, 15, 22-23.

109. *Har. Saln.* (1302), 238-39; Meclis-i Tanzimat deft. for 1298-1299, 285-86, decree on Records Section of Translation Office, 7`C 1300/1883.

110. Har., SA 25, İsmail Fuad Bey; Har., SA 555, Ahmed Faik Bey, entries of RA-R 1297/1880.

111. Young, *CD*, I, 159-80.

112. *Har. Saln.* (1302), 239-40; (1306), 246-47.

113. Har., İdare 180, circular of Foreign Minister to diplomatic missions and "Notice sur l'institution du Bureau des consulats," 9 December 1873; cf. BBA, A.AMD 1297.6.9, memorandum of 9 C 1297/1880. I am indebted to Eşref Eşrefoğlu for enabling me to examine the latter document.

114. *Saln.* (1326), 234-35; Har., SA 443, Edouard Graziani Efendi.

115. Har., Niz. Kav., Âsar-ı Matbua, 27/1, printed text in Ottoman and French, with handwritten note at end saying the text had been sanctioned by an *irade* of 15 B 1298/1881; cf. Young, *CD*, III, 1-10.

116. *Saln.* (1297), 116; *Har. Saln.* (1302), 236-37.

117. *Har. Saln.* (1302), 241-42; (1306), 247-48, cf. Temelkuran, "Mühimme Kalemi," 137-38, 162; Said Paşa, *Hâtırat*, I, 213.

118. İnal, *Sadr.*, III, 1764; FO 371/548, File 29285, "General Report for 1906," 31; A.A.A., "İbrahim Hakkı Paşa," *IA*, v, ii, 892-94; Çark, *Türk Devleti Hizmetinde Ermeniler*, 153-56.

119. *Saln.* (1314), 212-13.

120. *Har. Saln.* (1302), 224-25, 604; (1306), 230-31, 243-44; (1318), 220-21; *Dstr.*[1], v, 201-202, *irade* of 1885.

121. *Saln.* (1297), 117-18; *Har. Saln.* (1302), 334-35; (1306), 304-305; (1318), 248-59, 436-71; *Saln.* (1326), 598-601; Young, *CD*, III, 125ff.; *Dstr.*[1], zeyl iv, 54-86; Said Paşa, *Hâtırat*, I, 145-46.

122. *Har. Saln.* (1306), 313-15; Uşaklıgil, *Kırk Yıl*, 307-12.

123. Young, *CD*, I, 53, art. 22; Har., Müt 156, dossier entitled "Vilâyat-ı osmaniye umur-ı ecnebiye müdürüyle tercümanlarının suret-i tayinleri hakkında, 1913."

124. *Har. Saln.* (1302), 336; (1306), 312; *Saln.* (1326), 992-93. Whether or not actual conflict developed over the matter, there was at least implicit confusion over whether these commissioners should come under the Foreign Ministry or under the Section for Provinces in Privileged Status (*Vilâyat-ı Mümtaze Kalemi*) of the Office of the Imperial Divan, now part of the staff of the grand vezir. Perhaps for this reason, the official yearbooks do not mention Gazi Ahmed Muhtar Paşa, Ottoman Commissioner in British-occupied Egypt, 1885-1908 (İnal, *Sadr.*, III, 1811), among the commissioners attached to the Foreign Ministry, although much correspondence from his mission is in the Foreign Ministry archives.

125. On Münir, see Har., SA 438; Pâker, *Kırk Yıllık*, 37-38; Fesch, *Derniers jours*, 79-87. On Gadban, Har., SA 332. On N. Melhame, FO 371/548, File 29285, "General Report for 1906," 35-36; Said Paşa, *Hâtırat*, II, 101-103.

126. *Saln.* (1326), 1008-1009, 1012-13, 1028-29. The Tevfik Paşa here men-

tioned is Saraylızade Ahmed Tevfik Paşa (Har., SA 723), to be distinguished from the Ahmed Tevfik Paşa who was then foreign minister and was later grand vezir (Har., SA 429; İnal, *Sadr.*, III, 1704-62).

127. *Saln.* (1326), 1030-31. Rather strangely, correspondence on İzzet's problems in Madrid is to be found in Har., Müt. 8, dossier labeled "Corps diplomatique et consulaire ottoman. Démissions. 1862."

128. İnal, *Şair.*, I, 561-70.

129. *Har. Saln.* (1306), 631.

130. *Saln.* (1326), 992-93, 1008-33 (counting all consular agents not designated *fahri*, i.e., "honorary"). On the commercial agents, cf. *Dstr.*[1], v, 759, instructions of 1887.

131. Osman Nuri, *Abd ül-Hamid-i Sani*, II, 453, speaks of the Commissions for Finance and the Hijaz Railway as actually meeting at the palace.

132. *Dstr.*[1], VIII, 309-13, regulations of 1905; other related documents ibid., 313-23, 333-37, 498-99, 657-58. For existence of a comparable commission at earlier dates, cf. Shaw and Shaw, *History*, II, 115-18, 217, 241-42, and *Saln.* (1297), 91.

133. *Saln.* (1326), 162-69; cf. Tahsin Paşa, *Hatıralar*, 136-38; and *Dstr.*[1], VIII, 90-92, instructions of 1904 for High Commission for Finance.

134. *Dstr.*[1], VI, 566-70, regulations of 1890.

135. Ibid., VII, 100-103, regulations of 1896; VIII, 645-47, regulations of 1907, with table of other references, including acts promulgated in the next period.

136. Cf. Aşçıdede Halil İbrahim, *Hatıralar*, 89, for his experience with the Aid Fund.

137. *Saln.* (1289), 49; (1290), unlisted?; (1291), 45; (1292), 46; (1293), 50, listed but without reference to the Sublime Porte. The yearbooks also vary in the titles they assign this body.

138. *Saln.* (1294), 108; (1295), 110. I do not now have access to the volume for 1296.

139. *Saln.* (1297), 110; (1305), 147-48; (1310), 178-79.

140. *Dstr.*[1], *zeyl* iii, 56-61, instructions of 1882; *zeyl* iv, 321, addition to preceding; VI, 224-30, regulations of 1888; 570-71, amendment of 1890 to art. 14 of preceding; 1275-80, new regulations of 1892. Cf. Young, *CD*, I, 19-23, partial translation of regulations of 1888. Cf. also *Dstr.*[1], VI, 350-51, decree of May 1889.

141. Cevdet, *Tezâkir 40*, 168-69; cf. *Dstr.*[1], IV, 775, art. 11; *zeyl* iv, 10, art. 11.

142. *Dstr.*[1], IV, 63-66, instructions of 1879; V, 965-71, instructions of 1887; 1001, document of 1888; VI, 3-8, instructions of 1887 again; *Saln.* (1305), 148; (1310), 192-97; Young, *CD*, I, 19-23.

143. BBA, Yıldız 14. 1339. 126. 10, report of 21 S 1309/1891 by Rıza Efendi, Director of the General Personnel Records Commission.

144. *Dstr.*[1], VII, 132-36, regulations of 1896; cf. Young, *CD*, I, 17-19. *Dstr.*[1], VII, 173-75, *irade* of 1897 resolving conflict of attributions in favor of Council of State; this corresponds to BBA, TDvM, 10/66-68. On other, comparable appointment-making bodies, see *Dstr.*[1], *zeyl* iii, 101-102; v, 1058-62; VI, 1367-68, 1476; VIII, 128-32, 431-34.

145. Osman Nuri, *Abd ül-Hamid-i Sani*, II, 591-92.

146. Cf. references in n. 142 above. A contemporary printing of the regulations of 1887 appears in pamphlet form in BBA, BEO 232401. Two unpromulgated draft regulations for the personnel records system are also in BBA, Yıldız, 37. 47/35-36. 47. 113, along with more or less all the published references.

147. This is a synthetic account based on the references in n. 142 and Har., SA, where the questionnaire normally forms the basic document in the file on each individual. The questionnaires actually varied somewhat from printing to printing.

148. BBA, Yıldız 14. 1339. 126. 10, report of 21 S 1309/1891 by Rıza Efendi, director of the General Personnel Records Commission.

149. *Dstr.*¹, IV, 65-66, art. 16; V, 970, art. 19-21.

150. For example, Har., SA 6, 170, 180, 212; cf. Har., SA 193, an orderly, clearcut case of trial, conviction for embezzlement, exclusion from service, and imprisonment.

151. Cf. comment of İnal, *Şair.*, II, 1020.

152. *Har. Saln.* (1306), 235-36; BBA, Yıldız, 14. 1339. 126. 10, report of 21 S 1309/1891; BEO 220980, Mehmed Tevfik Paşa, Chairman of Civil Officials Commission, to Grand Vezir, 6 L 1324/1906; BEO 223626, Mehmed Tevfik Paşa to Grand Vezir, 27 ZA 1324/1907; BEO 235983, Mehmed Tevfik Paşa to Grand Vezir, 1 Ş 1325/1907, with enclosures.

153. For example, *Dstr.*¹, V, 1062-64, regulations of 1888 for recrods on judicial officials.

154. Versions of 1881 in *Dstr.*¹, IV, 773-89; *zeyl* iii, 62-81. Version of 1884 ibid., *zeyl* iv, 8-31; cf. Young, *CD*, I, 23-26. Later amendments in *Dstr.*¹, V, 545-46, 597-98, 933-34; VI, 95-96, 327, 458, 471, 1179, 1385. For a comparable regulation on retirement of members of the religious establishment, cf. ibid., VI, 1500-11; amendments ibid., VI, 1544; VII, 151-53.

155. Cf. n. 140 above.

156. *Dstr.*¹ VII, 132-36; cf. Young, *CD*, I, 17-19.

157. Cf. Shimon Shamir, "The Modernization of Syria: Problems and Solutions in the Early Period of Abdülhamid," in *Beginnings of Modernization in the Middle East*, ed. Polk and Chambers, 355, 357-58.

158. In Har., SA, for example, we find innumerable entries, beginning c. 1896, that spell out in more or less invariable language that a given appointment occurred on the "communication" (*iş'ar*) of the Foreign Ministry (i.e., of the Commission for the Selection of Foreign Ministry Officials), the decision (*karar*) of the Civil Officials Commission, and the issuance of an imperial decree in response to its request (*bi 'l-istizan . . . irade*).

159. Tahsin Paşa, *Hatıralar*, 36-37. By "persons of uncertain qualifications and affiliations," we are translating Abd ül-Hamid's *ağalar*, a term with variable applications ranging—depending on which were current at the time—from provincial landowners to certain military personnel to eunuchs to illiterate servants.

160. Ergin, *Maarif*, III, 677-715, 890-918, 997-1041.

161. Tahsin Paşa, *Hatıralar*, 36-37.

162. Ergin, *Maarif*, II, 517; cf. Har., SA 260, file of Fahr el-Din Reşad Bey, including certified copies, made on printed forms filled out in both Ottoman and French, of two diplomas from this school.

163. *Dstr.*¹, VII, 212-13, *irade* of 1899; 287-89, *irade* of 1899; 658-59, *irade* of 1901; 939-41, *irade* of 1903; VIII, 4-15, *irade* of 1903 and examination program. On examination systems in contemporary, Western bureaucratic agencies, cf. Cecil, *German Diplomatic Service*, 26ff.; Zara S. Steiner, *The Foreign Office and Foreign Policy, 1898-1914* (Cambridge, 1969), 16ff.

164. *Dstr.*¹, *zeyl* i, 36-58, decree of 1880; cf. Har., Niz. Kav., 34/32, contempo-

rary printing in the form of a bilingual pamphlet with title "Traitements des fonctionnaires."

165. For example, *Dstr.*[1], *zeyl* i, 57, art. 62 of decree of 1880; cf. C. A. Schaefer, "Geldwesen und Staatsbankfrage in der Türkei," in *Das Türkische Reich: Wirtschaftliche Darstellungen*, ed. Josef Hellauer (Berlin, 1918), 29ff.; Young, *CD*, v, 1-12.

166. *Dstr.*[1], v, 103-104.

167. Ibid., vi, 1143-45, decree of 1891; viii, 744, amendment of 1907. Was there no earlier regulation on unemployment stipends? They already existed during the Tanzimat.

168. Ibid., iii, 10-22, decree, appendix, and rate table of 1873-1874; v, 392, *irade* of 1886; vi, 999, amendment of 1891; vii, 199-203, *irade* of 1898.

169. *Saln.* (1305), 148; (1326), 660-63.

170. *Dstr.*[1], vi, 93-95, contract of 1888.

171. Aşçıdede Halil İbrahim, *Hatıralar*, 114-17; cf. Said Paşa, *Hâtırat*, ıı, ii, 31-32.

172. *Dstr.*[1], iv, 20-58, internal regulations of 1877 for Chamber of Deputies and Senate; 125-31, regulations of 1879 for Ministry of Justice and Religious Affairs; 674-92, regulations of 1880 for Ministries of Finance, Public Works, and Pious Foundations.

173. BBA, TDvM, undated draft regulations for Foreign Ministry. A reference in art. 4 implying the existence of a special relationship between the Ottoman Empire, on one hand, and the Rumanian Principalities and Serbia, on the other, indicates that this document dates from before the recognition of the independence of Serbia and Rumania in the Treaty of Berlin, 1878. The text does not indicate a clear *terminus a quo*, but it is difficult to imagine that such an attempt at comprehensive regulation of the Foreign Ministry could have been made before the death of Âli Paşa in 1871.

174. BBA, Yıldız 31. 1800. 97. 80, draft law on duties of the ministers and of the Council of Ministers, with covering memoranda dated 1-8 RA 1296/ February-March 1879.

175. Shaw and Shaw, *History*, ıı, 177, 224-25; Karal, *OT*, viii, 415ff.; Young, *CD*, v, 14-18; cf. *Dstr.*[1], iv, 602-603; regulations of 1879 for Board of Audit.

176. Donald C. Blaisdell, *European Financial Control in the Ottoman Empire: A Study of the Establishment, Activities, and Significance of the Ottoman Public Debt* (New York, 1929), 88ff., 147-53; cf. Robert G. Landen, *The Emergence of the Modern Middle East: Selected Readings* (New York, 1970), 173, comments on integrity of Ottoman employees of the debt administration in excerpts from Adam Block, *Special Report on the Public Debt Followed by the Translation of the Annual Report of the Council of Administration for the Twenty Fourth Financial Period* (Istanbul, 1906).

177. The growth of the crown estates and Privy Treasury under Abd ül-Hamid needs research and would make an excellent dissertation topic; cf. Pakalın, *OTD*, ı, 786-88, "Hazine-i Hassa"; Young, *CD*, v, 15 n. 2.

178. Karal, *OT*, viii, 419-34; Young, *CD*, v, 17-18, with budget table for 1897 and 1901. Other budgetary documents of the period in BBA, Mal. Müd. 11177 (1870-1873); Mal. Müd. 14506 (1875, 1877); *Dstr.*[1], v, 1078-91 (report on budget for 1888, also including data for 1880 and 1887); *Dstr.*[1], vii, 129-32 (budget for 1897, including data for 1892-94); *Dstr.*[1], viii, 476-93 (budget for 1906, with data also for 1905). Budgetary information for 1906 also appears in FO 371/549, File 37954, "Memo by Sir A. Block on the Present Financial Condition of the Otto-

man Empire" (1908), 10-11. There are also contemporary Ottoman publications of some of the budgets; e.g., *Budget des recettes et des dépenses de l'exercice 1288 (1872-73)*, pamphlet published by Ministry of Finance (Istanbul, 1872), or *Bin İki Yüz Doksan Altı Sene-i Maliyesi Muvazene-i Umumiyesi* (Istanbul, n.d.), budget of 1880. Other references in Shaw, "Nineteenth Century . . . Tax Reforms," 449-50.

179. Cf. the order for the reorganization of 1900 in the Office of the Imperial Divan, cited in n. 74, and the regulations cited in n. 106 for the Turkish Correspondence Office (*Mektubî-i Hariciye*), and Translation Office (*Bab-ı Âli Tercüme Odası*), dating from 1877 and 1883, respectively.

180. This was true in certain respects of the decree of 1897 on the Council of State; cf. n. 87.

181. Cf. Ministère de l'Instruction Publique et des Beaux-Arts, *Catalogue général des livres imprimés de la Bibliothèque Nationale, Auteurs* (Paris, 1907), XXIX, 1174-75, entry for A.-J.-H. de Clerq, *Guide pratique des consulats*, 2 vols., four editions from 1851 to 1898, plus other similar works by same author.

182. Young, *CD*, III, 1-40. Har., Niz. Kav., Âsar-ı Matbua 27/1, bilingual printed text of "Règlement organique pour les Consulats ottomans," with handwritten note at end giving date of *irade* as 15 B 1298/1881; cf. *Dstr.*[1], *zeyl* ii, 192-202; *zeyl* iii, 123, modification of art. 45; v, 696, *irade* of 1886 amending art. 12; 731-32, additional amendments of 1886; VII, 907-908, amendments of 1902. Cf. *Dstr.*[1], *zeyl* iv, 39-51, instructions of 1883 to Ottoman consuls; v, 105-20, additional articles of the instructions. Ottoman texts also in *Har. Saln.* (1318), 362-433.

183. Har., Müt. 249, dossier on "Réorganisation du Service consulaire, 1908," Consul-General Necib in Bucharest to Foreign Minister, 18/31 January 1909.

184. Har., İdare 324, dossier on "Règlements, instructions, et modifications sur le service Consulaire ottomane, 1877 à 85" [*sic*].

185. Har., İdare 322, Consul-General Feyzi Bey, Batum, 30 September 1902, to Foreign Minister on abuses of previous incumbent; Har., SA 68, file of Krikor Hakimoğlu, entry of 8 Z 1304/1887: dismissal as vice-consul at Poti on ground of collecting unauthorized sums by way of fees; Har., SA 531, file of Mehmed Mazhar Bey, entry of c. 1320/1902 on loss of position as vice-consul at Poti upon verification of abuses in issue of passports and *passavants*.

186. BBA, Nizamat deft. 6, 85, entry of 21 M 1310/1892; *Dstr.*[1], VIII, 15-16, instructions of 1904 on use of blank forms in awarding of decorations.

187. The practical effects of this change appear in BBA in the changes observable over the years in the organization of collections such as the *hatt-ı hümayun*s (imperial decrees), *irade*s (imperial decrees issued through the palace secretaries), or later the papers of the *Bab-ı Âli Evrak Odası* (Records Office of the Sublime Porte).

188. *Dstr.*[1], v, 459-62, instructions of 1886.

189. BBA, Buy. 6, entry of 16 RA 1302/1885.

190. BBA, Buy. 6, entry of 21 B 1299/1882.

191. *Dstr.*[1], *zeyl* i, 12-13, circular of grand vezir, 1880; BBA, Nizamat deft. 8, 50-51, *irade* of 29 N 1316/1899; cf. Said Paşa, *Hâtırat*, I, 28.

192. Young, *CD*, I, xiv n. 8; cf. *Dstr.*[1], I, 16, *irade* of 1872.

193. BBA, Buy. 6, entry of 8 R 1301/1884; also in BBA, Nizamat deft. 1, 12-13 (?), same date; cf. Said Paşa, *Hâtırat*, I, 200-202.

194. Stanford J. Shaw, "Ottoman Archival Materials for the Nineteenth and

Early Twentieth Centuries: The Archives of Istanbul," *IJMES*, VI (1975), 99-100, on publication history of *Dstr.*[1] of which V-VIII were not published until 1937-1943. Cf. İnal, *Sadr.*, II, 1273; *Dstr.*[1], VI, 933-36, *irade* of 1901 on official newspaper.

195. Said Paşa, *Hâtırat*, I, 29; BBA, TDvM, folder on İstatistik Müdiriyet-i Umumiyesi, Prime Minister Said Paşa to Ministry of Trade, 23 ZA 1296/1879.

196. *Dstr.*[1], IV, 670-72, regulations of 1880; related documentation in BBA, TDvM, folder on İstatistik Müdiriyet-i Umumiyesi. Commercial statistics began to appear in this period in publications such as the *Journal de la Chambre de commerce de Constantinople.* On published economic statistics, see Vedat Eldem, *Osmanlı İmparatorluğunun İktisadi Şartları Hakkında bir Tetkik* (Ankara?, 1970), 19-21.

197. *Dstr.*[1], *Mütemmim*, 160-62, regulations of 1891; same text in ibid., VI, 1105-1107.

198. For example, Cecil, *German Diplomatic Service*, 20, Table 3; Steiner, *Foreign Office*, 3-4.

199. BBA, BEO 191242, report of the Statistical Council, 30 M 1323/1905, with enclosures from the embassies. For the same kind of statistics at earlier dates, cf. *Har. Saln.* (1306), 647-57.

200. Heper, *Türk Kamu Bürokrasisinde Gelenekçilik ve Modernleşme*, 47-53.

201. Mardin, *Genesis*, 76-78; id., "Libertarian Movements in the Ottoman Empire, 1878-1895," *Middle East Journal*, XIV (1962), 169-82.

202. The remainder of this discussion is based primarily on Mardin, *Jön Türk.*; Ramsaur, *The Young Turks*; Shaw and Shaw, *History*, II, 263-67; and Findley, "Ideological Change."

203. Berkes, *Secularism*, 326ff., 343ff., 359ff., 373ff.; Uriel Heyd, *Foundations of Turkish Nationalism, The Life and Teachings of Ziya Gökalp* (London, 1950); Lewis, *Emergence*, ch. 10; David Kushner, *The Rise of Turkish Nationalism, 1876-1908* (London, 1977).

CHAPTER SEVEN

1. *Dstr.*[2], I, 11.

2. İnal, *Sadr.*, II, 1085; cf. III, 1771-76.

3. Feroz Ahmad, *The Young Turks: The Committee of Union and Progress in Turkish Politics, 1908-1914* (Oxford, 1969); cf. Yusuf Hikmet Bayur, *Türk İnkilâbı Tarihi*, 3 vols. in numerous parts (Ankara, 1940-   ).

4. Victor R. Swenson, "The Military Rising in Istanbul 1909," *Journal of Contemporary History*, V (1970), 171-84; Sina Akşin, *31 Mart Olayı* (Ankara, 1970).

5. AA, Türkei 134, Bd. 27, Marschall to Bethmann Hollweg, 7 October 1909: "Als diese Verfassung im vorigen Jahre wiederhergestellt wurde, hat sich über die Türken ein ganzes Füllhorn von Rechten ergossen. Presse, Vereine, Versammlungen, Wort und Schrift, alles war schrankenlos frei geworden. Aber die Türken haben, wie auch andere Kinder es zu tun pflegen, das neue Spielzeug so intensiven Kraftproben unterzogen dass es bald kaput war. Auf den Freudentaumel folgte die allgemeine Verhetzung der Geister, die Streiks, das Revolvertum, die allgemeine Unsicherheit, mit einem Worte die Anarchie . . ." (T 139, mf. roll 392).

6. Lewis, *Emergence*, 210-38; Berkes, *Secularism*, 325ff.

7. *Dstr.*², I, 11-14; İnal, *Sadr.*, II, 1066ff.; B. Lewis, "Dustūr," *EI²*, II, 643; Said Paşa, *Hâtırat*, II, ii, 457ff.

8. *Dstr.*², I, 638-44; cf. Ahmad, *Young Turks*, 58-60; Shaw and Shaw, *History*, II, 284-85.

9. Lewis, "Dustūr," *EI²*, II, 643.

10. Ibid., 644.

11. *Dstr.*², I, 5-6, 9-10, *irade*s of 1908; 230, law of 1909; III, 422-23, law of 1911; VI, 531, amendment of 1914 to preceding.

12. Ibid., I, 90-92, *irade* of 1908; cf. A. Biliotti and Ahmed Sedad, *Législation ottomane depuis le rétablissement de la Constitution*, I, *du 24 Djemazi-ul-ahir 1326-10 Juillet 1324/1908 au 1er Zilcadé 1327-1er Novembre 1325/1909* (Paris, 1912), 55.

13. *Dstr.*², I, 55-56, *irade* of 1908; cf. Biliotti and Sedad, *Législation*, I, 43-44.

14. *Dstr.*², I, 326-33, law of 1909; II, 264-66, supplementary law of 1910; cf. Biliotti and Sedad, *Législation*, I, 183-94.

15. For example, *Dstr.*², IV, 79-80; V, 631; VI, 107; VII, 482-83; VIII, 402, 725-26, 936, 1169; X, 495-96; XII, 539.

16. FO 424/250, "Turkey. Annual Report for 1909" (Conf. Pr. 9624), 6, 58-59. Same report also in FO 371/1002, File 4235.

17. İnal, *Şair.*, IV, 2153.

18. *Dstr.*², II, 264-66, supplementary law of 1910; VI, 107, temporary law of 1913. (Art. 36 of the constitution, as amended in 1909, allowed the enactment of "temporary laws" under certain circumstances when the Parliament was not in session. The laws originated as decisions of the Council of Ministers, were promulgated by sultanic decree, and had to be submitted to Parliament at its next session. Cf. ibid., I, 641-42.)

19. FO 424/250, "Annual Report for 1909," 58; AA, Türkei 134, Bd. 27, Marschall to Bethmann Hollweg, 7 October 1909 (T 139, mf. roll 392).

20. BBA, BEO 252830, minute of Cabinet (*Meclis-i Mahsus*), 13 B 1326/1908, with enclosed reports. I am indebted to Donald H. Quataert for this reference.

21. Har., Müt 249, dossier on "Réorganisation du Ministère Impérial des A. E." (referred to in subsequent notes as "F. M. reorg. dossier"), Kâmil Paşa to Foreign Minister, 22 B 1326/August 1908, circular character of communication clear from contents. Cf. Shaw and Shaw, *History*, II, 273-74.

22. Har., Müt. 249, F. M. reorg. dossier, other documents enclosed with Kâmil Paşa's circular, dates through 7 ZA 1326/December 1908.

23. Har., Müt. 249, F. M. reorg. dossier, envelope containing reports solicited by the minister from the various departments, c. 1912. This dossier also contains two drafts for comprehensive regulations on the organization of the ministry. Cf. Har., Müt. 249, dossier on "Réorganisation du service consulaire, 1908," including various reports and reclassification schemes.

24. Har., Müt. 249, dossier on "Avancement des fonctionnaires," enclosing reports and sometimes actual personnel regulations for the foreign services of France, Austria-Hungary, the United States, Belgium, Spain, Italy, Russia, Sweden, Great Britain, Germany, Greece, Holland, Serbia, Bulgaria, Rumania. Cf. Har., Müt 255, dossier on organization of various foreign ministries, including a typewritten report of about a hundred pages on the French Foreign Ministry (c. 1913) and a report in Ottoman comparing the organization of the German and Austro-Hungarian Foreign Ministries. Cf. also AA, Türkei 162, Bd. 7, Miquel to Bethmann Hollweg, 11 April 1910, on Ottoman interest in adopting a Japanese

system of using senior military officers for diplomatic posts (T 139, mf. roll 395).

25. Ahmad, *Young Turks*, 119.

26. Ibid., 27, 31-36, İnal, *Sadr.*, II, 1399-1400; Shaw and Shaw, *History*, II, 279.

27. Danişmend, *Kronoloji*, IV, 519-22.

28. Ahmad, *Young Turks*, 50-54.

29. Ibid., 106ff.

30. Ibid., 107.

31. Ibid., 108ff., 174.

32. Ibid., 116, 119; Danişmend, IV, 397-401; İnal, *Sadr.*, II, 1411; Shaw and Shaw, *History*, II, 290-92, 295-96; AA, Türkei 134, Bd. 31, report of Dr. Weber, first dragoman of German embassy, present at the Sublime Porte when the raid occurred, enclosed in Wangenheim to Bethmann Hollweg, 21 January 1913 (T 139, mf. roll 392).

33. Ahmad, *Young Turks*, 130, 171; İnal, *Şadr.*, III, 1893-1932; FO 424/250, "Turkey. Annual Report, 1912" (Conf. Pr. 10280), 18; FO 424/250, "Turkey. Annual Report, 1913" (Conf. Pr. 10523), 39-40; AA, Türkei 161, Bd. 5, Kühlmann to Bethmann Hollweg, 5 February 1917 (T 139, roll 394).

34. Ahmad, *Young Turks*, 90, 97, 159, 179-80; İnal, *Sadr.*, III, 1933-72; FO 424/250, "Annual Report, 1913," 40; Shaw and Shaw, *History*, II, 298-300.

35. Ahmed İzzet (İnal, *Sadr.*, III, 1973-2028), Ali Rıza (ibid., III, 2105-17), Salih Hulûsi (ibid., III, 2118-31); cf. Danişmend, *Kronoloji*, IV, 525-27.

36. İnal, *Sadr.*, III, 2029-94.

37. Ibid., III, 1732-43; cf. Shaw and Shaw, *History*, II, 332-34.

38. Grand vezirs with links of some kind to the CUP were Hüseyin Hilmi (Ahmad, *Young Turks*, 172), Said Halim (ibid., 171), and Tal'at (ibid., 179-80). Kâmil Paşa had an alliance with the Liberal Union (ibid., 28, 36, 172-73), and Damad Ferid was onetime chairman of the Hürriyet ve İtilaf party (ibid., 169).

39. İnal, *Sadr.*, III, 1938.

40. Ahmad, *Young Turks*, 101-102; Lewis, "Dustūr," *EI²*, II, 643.

41. İnal, *Sadr.*, III, 1721, 2039-40, 2046-48, 2063-64.

42. AA, Türkei 183, Bd. 5, Kühlmann to Bethmann Hollweg, 5 February 1917, noting this dearth especially in diplomatic corps (T 139, mf. roll 394); FO 424/250, "Turkey. Annual Report, 1910" (Conf. Pr. 9811), 11: "The committee régime, since it rid itself of men of experience, is constantly complaining of the 'dearth of men.' "

43. *Dstr.²*, VI, 238-39, law of March 1914; cf. *Saln.* (1327), 106-107; (1328), 102-103; (1333-1334), 122-24. I am indebted to Turgut Işıksal of the Başbakanlık Arşivi, Istanbul, and to Karl Stowasser of the University of Maryland for assistance in procuring photocopies from the yearbooks for 1328 and 1333-1334.

44. M. Tayyib Gökbilgin, "Âmedci," *IA*, I, 397; id., "Âmeddji," *EI²*, I, 433, where the term *mâruzat* is incorrectly translated as a reference to interpreters. Cf. *Saln.* (1328), 102.

45. *Dstr.²*, VI, 238, art. 4; *Saln.* (1327), 107; (1333-1334), 123-24.

46. *Dstr.²*, XI, 367, a salary table of 1919.

47. *Saln.* (1333-1334), 134.

48. *Dstr.²*, VI, 227, art. 1, part 2, of temporary law of 1914 on procedures for promulgation of laws. Cf. İnal, *Şair.*, IV, 2161-62, on his service as head of this office, c. 1919-1922.

49. On changes in the status of this organization during this period see *Dstr.²*,

IV, 12-13, *irade* of 1911; VIII, 1187, law of 1916; X, 163-64, law of 1918 attaching Directorate General of Statistics to grand vezirate; XI, 309, decree of 1919 abolishing the agency; 366-67, a more detailed decree of 1919.

50. *Saln.* (1327), 92; (1328), 94. The photocopies which I have from *Saln.* (1333-1334) do not include the page showing the Council of Ministers, but the composition of the council is readily traceable from the titles of the officials shown as signers of many of the acts published in *Dstr.*²

51. *Dstr.*², I, 143-45, regulations of 1909; IV, 547-48, revised regulations of 1912.

52. *Dstr.*², I, 71-72, *irade* of 1908; cf. Biliotti and Sedad, *Législation*, I, 49-50; original documents in BBA, TDvM, 10/72-74. Cf. also *Saln.* (1327), 110-14.

53. *Dstr.*², I, 82-83, *irade* of 1908; original in BBA, TDvM, 10/77-79.

54. *Saln.* (1327), 111; (1328), 107.

55. BBA, TDvM, 10/84-85, documents of 6-11 ZA 1330/1912; cf. *Saln.* (1333-1334), 126-27.

56. *Dstr.*², II, 668-74, temporary law of 1910 on martial law; VI, 573, 658-59, temporary laws of 1914 on appeals from military courts.

57. Ibid., VI, 207-12, temporary law of 1914; VII, 124-25, temporary law of 1914 modifying art. 5 of preceding.

58. *Saln.* (1333-1334), 128.

59. C. H. Dodd, *Politics and Government in Turkey* (Berkeley and Los Angeles, 1969), 47 (referring to *reestablishment* of the council under the Republic), 239-44; Robert V. Presthus with Sevda Erem, *Statistical Analysis in Comparative Administration: The Turkish Conseil d'Etat* (Ithaca, N.Y., 1958).

60. Sertoğlu, *Başvekâlet*, 82.

61. For example, in Syria and in the Armenian-inhabited areas in the east. Available accounts include George Antonius, *The Arab Awakening: The Story of the Arab National Movement* (New York, 1946, 1965), 150ff., 184ff., 201ff.; C. Ernest Dawn, *From Ottomanism to Arabism: Essays on the Origins of Arab Nationalism* (Urbana, Ill., 1973), ch. 1; Richard G. Hovanissian, *Armenia on the Road to Independence, 1918* (Berkeley and Los Angeles, 1967), 48-55.

62. Dodd, *Politics and Government*, 18. A temporary law of 1912 replaced parts of the law of 1871; see *Dstr.*², IV, 421-38. The version of 1913 then replaced those of 1871 and 1912; see *Dstr.*², V, 186-213, the basis of our discussion. A contemporary British analysis of this law is in FO 424/250, "Annual Report, 1913," 24-25.

63. Lewis, *Emergence*, 391. The reference in the law of 1913 to the province as a legal person (*şahs-ı manevi*) is in art. 75 (*Dstr.*², V, 200). Cf. Davison, *Reform*, 391.

64. Provisions on governor general's appointment powers in provincial law of 1871 in Young, *CD*, I, 49, art. 5; cf. *Dstr.*¹, I, 626. Responsibilities of the Hamidian commissions for selection of officials discussed in Ch. VI. Cf. *Dstr.*¹, VII, 134, art. 13, regulations for Civil Officials Commission, provisions on dismissal of officials.

65. Young, *CD*, I, 49, art. 7; cf. *Dstr.*¹, I, 627.

66. *Dstr.*², II, 171-75, instructions of 1910; V, 561-65, temporary law and instructions of 1913; VII, 73-74, regulations of 1913; VII, 772-74, regulations of 1915.

67. Ibid., I, 410-11, law of 1909. Later measures pertaining to administration

of Istanbul ibid., vi, 52-57, regulations of 1913; ix, 263, law of 1917; xii, 40, 48, 277, various measures of 1920.

68. Ibid., vi, 130-35. Article numbers mentioned below in the text in discussion of the offices of the Ministry of the Interior refer to this source.

69. Abolition of these posts is to be inferred from a law of 1909 (ibid., i, 603-604) on salaries to be paid to those excluded from the Istanbul police and to the "agents of the gate," mentioned in art. 2 of that law as having been excluded from the organization of the Ministry of the Interior.

70. The same law created both the Province of Istanbul and this Directorate of Public Security: ibid., i, 410-16, law of 1909; cf. iii, 433-34, amendment of 1911.

71. Cf. ibid., viii, 891, *irade* of 1916.

72. *Saln.* (1333-1334), 343-54; cf. *Dstr.*², viii, 666-70, 769-70, laws of 1916; ix, 577-79, law of 1917; xii, 364, decree of 1921. For all or part of the Young Turk period, the Directorate of Public Security, the Directorate of Tribal and Refugee Affairs, and the Directorate General of Public Health had budgets of their own, separate from that of the Ministry of the Interior; cf. the Appendix, entries for 1909-1918 and nn. i, n, and o.

73. *Dstr.*², iv, 637, *irade* of 1912; v, 517, *irade* of 1913; vi, 5, *irade* of 1912.

74. Ibid., vi, 220-22, regulations of February 1914; article numbers cited in the discussion of the organization of the ministry refer to this text.

75. AA, Türkei 161, Bd. 5, Kühlmann to Bethmann Hollweg, 5 February 1917 (T 139, mf. roll 394).

76. On the struggles of Rif'at Paşa (foreign minister, 1909-1911) to cope with this problem and the related one of document security, see Çankaya, *Mülkiye Tarihi*, iii, 95; cf. AA, Türkei 134, Bd. 29, Marschall to Bethmann Hollweg, 20 April 1911, recounting Rif'at's concerns over theft of documents, involvement of an assistant dragoman of the Russian embassy in the thefts, and consequent attempts to close four doors in the Foreign Ministry to foreigners (T 139, mf. roll 392).

77. *Dstr.*², v, 308-309, temporary law of 1913; cf. ibid., xii, 386-88, decree of 1921.

78. Ibid., i, 395-406, laws of 1909; iv, 365-66, temporary law of 1912; v, 111, 181-85, temporary laws of 1913; vi, 49, temporary law of 1913; 984-85, law of 1914; xii, 494, decree of 1921.

79. Har., Müt. 249, F. M. reorg. dossier, report on Foreign Ministry Press Directorate, unsigned and undated but datable from internal evidence to sometime after April 1913.

80. Har., Müt. 249, F. M. reorg. dossier, report of 20-27 Mayıs 1328/June 1912 on what was then the *Tabiiyet Kalemi.*

81. Har., Müt. 249, F. M. reorg. dossier, report of 13 Mart 1329/March 1913 on what was then called the *Evrak Müdiriyet-i Umumiyesi.*

82. Har., Müt. 249, F. M. reorg. dossier, report of Mehmed Agâh, director of Translation Branch of Directorate General of Political Affairs, 23 Haziran 1328/July 1912, attached to report of the Director-General.

83. Har., Müt. 249, F. M. reorg. dossier, draft of circular to embassies, with dates indicating an order to prepare fair copies (*tebyiz*) on 4 Mart 1329/March 1913.

84. Har., Müt. 249, F. M. reorg. dossier, report of Mehmed Salih, director general of political affairs, 22 B 1330/July 1912; cf. *Saln.* (1327), 169; (1328), 163; (1333-1334), 188-89.

85. *Saln.* (1327), 170; (1328), 163-64; cf. ibid. (1333-1334), 189.

86. Har., Müt. 249, F. M. reorg. dossier, report of Director General Nikolaki Efendi, 29 Mayıs 1328/11 June 1912.

87. Har., Müt. 249, F. M. reorg. dossier (?), document entitled "Umur-ı İdariye Müdiriyet-i Umumiyesi Şuabatının Vazaifi," with cover letter of Suad Bey, director general of administrative affairs, 10 February 1916, this having an order written on it for the printing and application of the document.

88. *Saln.* (1327), 171-72; (1328), 165; (1333-1334), 189-90.

89. *Dstr.*[2], vi, 135, temporary law of 1913 on creation of this post; vii, 732, temporary law of 1915 abolishing it and annulling Ostrorog's contract. Ostrorog's position was presumably a casualty of World War I.

90. Har., Müt. 249, F. M. reorg. dossier, report of Legal Counsellors Münir and Hrand Abro, 19 Mayıs 1328/June 1912.

91. *Dstr.*[2], viii, 181, regulations of 1915 on officials of Ministry of Interior, art. 16, provision for appointment of provincial foreign affairs directors and translators by a council in the Ministry of the Interior.

92. Har., Müt. 249, dossier labeled "Réorganisation du service consulaire, 1908," circular of Foreign Minister Tevfik Paşa, 19 October 1908, on reorganization of consular corps, enclosing a document headed "İcrası makrun-ı müsaade-i seniye olan tensikat mücebince teşekkül eden Heyet-i Şehbenderi." Cf. Har., Müt., 249, F. M. reorg. dossier, lithographed pamphlet entitled "Tensikat üzerine teşkil [for teşekkül?] edecek Heyet-i Şehbenderi," undated.

93. BBA, TDvM, folder on Foreign Ministry, Foreign Minister Mustafa Reşid Paşa to Grand Vezir, 30 RA 1338/December 1919 on closing of consulates in Austria and Germany; and Foreign Minister Safa Bey to Grand Vezir, 11 RA 1339/November 1920, with enclosures. Cf. Söylemezoğlu, *Otuz Sene*, iii-iv, passim; Pâker, *Kırk Yıllık*, passim.

94. For attempts at reorganization of the ministry during the Armistice years, see *Dstr.*[2], xii, 75-82, 345-50, decrees of 1920.

95. Ibid., vi, 161-62, temporary law of 1914; other later provisions in viii, 679-81, 1097.

96. Ibid., vi, 733-37, regulations of 1914; later revisions of art. 3, on the governance of the fund, ibid., viii, 1288-89; ix, 303-304; xi, 253-54.

97. Ibid., i, 90-92, *irade* of 1908; cf. Biliotti and Sedad, *Législation*, i, 55. Cf. *Saln.* (1327), 168, 206; (1328), 162, 196; (1333-1334), 186, 202.

98. Har., Müt 249, F. M. reorg. dossier, report of Ali Rıza, director of the Personnel Records Directorate of the Foreign Ministry, 19 Mayıs 1328/June 1912.

99. *Dstr.*[2], vi, 820-49, regulations of 1914.

100. Har., İdare 663, "Etats de service des fonctionnaires ottomans," including copies of correspondence about specific individuals, dating at least as late as 21 October 1918. Some files in Har., SA, include entries of later date; e.g., Har., SA 429, file of Ahmed Tevfik Paşa, entries as late as 17 Kanun-ı Evvel 1337/ December 1921.

101. That a personnel records directorate existed in Ankara, c. 1922-1923, is apparent from a reference in Söylemezoğlu, *Otuz Sene*, iv, 141-42.

102. Har., Müt. 249, F. M. reorg. dossier, various drafts, including one by Galip Kemali Söylemezoğlu, dated Bucharest, 19 Haziran, 1325/July 1909, and two others, one in French and one in Ottoman. Söylemezoğlu published his draft in *Otuz Sene*, i, 201-204. The draft of 1912 is in Har., Niz. Kav., 27/3, printed pamphlet entitled "Memurin-i Hariciyenin İntisab ve Tayin ve Terfilerine aid

Lâyiha-ı Kanuniye," with prefatory note signed by Ohannes Kuyumcıan, under-secretary of the Foreign Ministry, 5 Kanun-ı Evvel 1328/December 1912.

103. *Dstr.*², VIII, 178-86, regulations of 1915.

104. Har., Niz. Kav., 27/3, "Memurin-i Hariciyenin İntisab ve Tayin ve Terfilerine aid Lâyiha-ı Kanuniye," 1912.

105. Ibid., 11, 13.

106. Çankaya, *Mülkiye Tarihi*, III, 95, on Rif'at Paşa.

107. *Dstr.*², I, 725-26, *irade* of 1909; cf. Biliotti and Sedad, *Législation*, 452.

108. Çankaya, *Mülkiye Tarihi*, III, 95.

109. *Dstr.*², II, 647-48, addendum, dated 1910, to a decree of 1901.

110. Ibid., V, 498-501, regulations of 1913. Later measures, either modifying these regulations or extending their application, ibid., VIII, 897; X, 588; XI, 446; XII, 713.

111. Ibid., III, 742-47, instructions of 1911; IV, 568-69, addendum of 1912.

112. Ibid., III, 753-54, *irade* of 1911; cf. V, 370, *irade* of 1913 on same subject.

113. Ibid., IV, 648-49, *irade* of 1912; V, 99-100, *irade* of 1913.

114. Ibid., VII, 574-75, regulations of 1915; cf. XI, 611, *irade* of 1920 repealing the preceding.

115. Ibid., I, 62-64, *irade* of 1908 on salaries of various high officials; cf. Biliotti and Sedad, *Législation*, I, 46-47; cf. salary tables included in measures on reorganization of consular service, mentioned in n. 92.

116. *Dstr.*², I, 101-103, *irade* of 1908 abolishing a certain type of deduction made from civil-bureaucratic salaries to turn over to the financial administrators of the Hijaz Railway.

117. Ibid., I, 634-37, law of 1909 on unemployment stipends. Various measures on travel allowances ibid., VII, 88-89, 597; VIII, 700; IX, 614-18, 653-54, 744; X, 51, 570; XI, 126, 261-74, 303, 338-39, 541.

118. Ibid., I, 666-73, law of 1909; cf. Biliotti and Sedad, *Législation*, I, 386-95. Other, later provisions on same subject in *Dstr.*², III, 14-15; VI, 322, 338-39, 640-42; VII, 595; VIII, 315-16; IX, 206-207, 582; X, 14-15, 57-58, 81, 351-53; XI, 223.

119. Relevant texts in *Dstr.*², VI, 160-61, 901-02; VIII, 1290-92, 1362-63; 1373; IX, 116-17, 139-41, 152-53, 163-65, 209-11, 292-93, 299-300, 593, 736-37; X, 12, 427-31, 558-63; XI, 82, 109-10, 113-15, 136, 149-51, 159, 174, 179-82, 225, 259, 354, 368, 376, 395, 488-91, 518-19, 529-32; XII, 90-92, 98-99, 176-78, 373, 421-22, 493, 636-39, 681-82.

120. Dodd, *Politics and Government*, 47.

121. Pakalın, *OTD*, I, 788, "Hazine-i Hassa"; Blaisdell, *European Financial Control*, 177ff. *Dstr.*², VI, 1273, *irade* on abolition of capitulatory privileges; 1336-37, 1340, other related measures; cf. J. C. Hurewitz, *Diplomacy in the Near and Middle East: A Documentary Record*, 2 vols. (Princeton, N.J., 1956), II, 2-3.

122. AA, Türkei 134, Bd. 27, Marschall to Bethmann Hollweg, 7 October 1909 (T 139, mf. roll 392).

123. Ahmad, *Young Turks*, 70-74.

124. Budgetary legislation for the Young Turk period can be located through the indices in *Dstr.*², where the entries under the heading *Bütçe* often fill several pages. Precise references for the general budgets for the years 1908-1918 appear in the Appendix. For examples of the passage of supplemental budgetary legislation well after the end of the financial year to which it pertains, see *Dstr.*², VIII, 1078-90, laws of 1916 on addition of various items to budget of 1913.

125. Roderic H. Davison, "Ķā'ime," *EI²*, IV, 461.

126. *Dstr.²*, VI, 47-48, *irade* of 1913.

127. Ibid., IX, 185-86, law of 1917.

128. Ibid., III, 417-18, law of 1911; VI, 227, temporary law of 1914.

129. Quoted in Ahmad, *Young Turks*, 89.

130. Söylemezoğlu, *Otuz Sene*; İnal, *Şair.*; id., *Sadr.*, passim, especially *Şair.*, IV, 2158ff.

131. There is considerable documentation on these problems in British correspondence of the period. For example, FO 371/4140, File 13, High Commissioner Webb to Curzon, 29 September 1919, enclosing letter of Grand Vezir Damad Ferid to Webb, 18 September 1919 and memorandum on economic situation of Istanbul government; FO 371/6542, E 6212/201/44, High Commissioner Rumbold to Curzon, 24 May 1921; FO 371/6542, E 6440/201/44, Rattigan to Curzon, 28 May 1921; FO 371/7947, E 4988/4988/44, "Annual Report, 1921," 2.

132. FO 371/6468, E 4613/1/44, Rumbold to Curzon, 13 April 1921; cf. FO 371/6468, E 4612/1/44, Rumbold to Curzon, same date, and FO 371/6536, E 13327/143/44, Rumbold to Curzon, 29 November 1921.

133. Danişmend, *Kronoloji*, IV, 467-68; İnal, *Şair.*, IV, 2162ff. George S. Harris has studied carry-over of personnel from the imperial to the republican Foreign Ministry in "The Ataturk Revolution and the Foreign Office, 1913-1931: A Preliminary Study" (unpublished, 1972).

CHAPTER EIGHT

1. For a study of the very different circumstances in which the ideal of rule of law began to acquire influence in another Middle Eastern setting, see Farhat J. Ziadeh, *Lawyers, the Rule of Law, and Liberalism in Modern Egypt* (Stanford, 1968).

This is a selective listing of the sources used in preparation of this study. In the case of archival sources, the listing is exhaustive to the extent of naming all archives and all archival collections consulted. The listing of published works, in contrast, normally includes only those cited frequently. The chief exception is in favor of works on bureaucracy and modernization, theoretical or comparative in interest, which have influenced the development of this study in ways that at times go beyond what can be shown directly in the notes.

I. Turkish Archival Sources

A. *Başbakanlık* (formerly *Başvekâlet*, i.e., "Prime Ministers' ")
Archives, Istanbul

Ayniyat Defterleri, registers containing copies of certain grand-vezirial correspondence; sampled and found of secondary value (Sertoğlu, *Başvekâlet*, 46-50).

Bab-ı Âli Evrak Odası, Records Office of the Sublime Porte; consulted for papers on the Foreign Ministry, Council of State, and Civil Officials Commission; used index volumes 157, 164, 184, 634, 713, 741-42 (Sertoğlu, *Başvekâlet*, 59-61; Stanford J. Shaw, "Ottoman Archival Materials for the Nineteenth and Early Twentieth Centuries: The Archives of Istanbul," *IJMES*, VI [1975], 100-106).

Buyuruldu Defterleri, registers of grand-vezirial orders, 8 registers (Sertoğlu, *Başvekâlet*, 46).

Cevdet Tasnifi, Hariciye Kısmı, Cevdet Collection, Section on Foreign Affairs (Sertoğlu, *Başvekâlet*, 70-71; Shaw, "Archival Materials," 95-96).

Dahiliye Sicill-i Ahval Tasnifi, registers of the Personnel Records Commission, the central place of record for official biographies of civil-bureaucratic officials (Sertoğlu, *Başvekâlet*, 81-82).

Hatt-ı Hümayun Tasnifi, sultanic decrees, usually written onto reports from the Grand Vezir; the collection runs through c. 1839 (Sertoğlu, *Başvekâlet*, 51; Shaw, "Archival Materials," 95).

İrade Tasnifi, sultanic decrees, issued through the palace secretaries. This collection in a sense forms a continuation of the preceding. Used for early Tanzimat period (Sertoğlu, *Başvekâlet*, 51-52; Shaw, "Archival Materials," 96-99).

Kalem Nizamnamesi, a register of regulatory documents for the offices of the chief scribe, classified as no. 37 of the *Divan-ı Hümayun Muhtelif ve*

Mütenevvi Defterleri, or Miscellaneous Registers of the Imperial Divan (Sertoğlu, *Başvekâlet*, 32).

Maliyeden Müdevver Defterler, treasury registers; used selected ones containing budgetary data.

Meclis-i Tanzimat Defterleri, registers of the High Council of Reforms, 7 registers, including entries of c. 1271-1300/1854-1883. The *Nizamat Defterleri* are a continuation of this series, the two together comprising the source from which the laws published in the *Düstur* were selected (Sertoğlu, *Başvekâlet*, 15; Shaw, "Archival Materials," 108).

Mühimme Defterleri, registers of important affairs, used selected volumes for c. 1760-1825 (Sertoğlu, *Başvekâlet*, 15-22; Shaw, "Archival Materials," 108).

Nizamat Defterleri, registers of laws and regulations, 37 registers (Shaw, "Archival Materials," 99).

Rüus Defterleri, registers of brevets of appointments; consulted nos. 163, 168, 175, 184, 217, 221-23, 228-29, 234-35, 250 (Sertoğlu, *Başvekâlet*, 30).

Şehbender Defteri, register of consular appointments; used the first register, including appointments for c. 1217-1300/1802-1883 (Sertoğlu, *Başvekâlet*, 28; Shaw, "Archival Materials," 110).

Tahvil Defterleri, registers of the Section for the Assignment of Benefices in Land in the Office of the Imperial Divan, nos. 26, 30, 57, 58, 66-69, pertaining to assignment of benefice-incomes to employees in government offices (Sertoğlu, *Başvekâlet*, 30).

Teşkilât-ı Devair ve Mecalis, papers on organization of major bureaucratic and conciliar agencies, from about the 1870s on.

Yıldız Tasnifi, Yıldız Palace Archives. The four numbers included in footnote citations of documents from this collection are those designated in the catalogues of the collection as referring to *kısım*, *evrak*, *zarf*, and *karton* (Sertoğlu, *Başvekâlet*, 74-78; Shaw, "Archival Materials," 110-12; id., "The *Yıldız* Palace Archives of Abdülhamit II," *Archivum Ottomanicum*, III [1971], 211-37).

B. *Hariciye* (Foreign Ministry) Archives, Istanbul

İdare Kısmı, Administrative Section, various dossiers dating from the 1870s and later.

Mütenevvi Tasnifi, Miscellaneous Collection, the most valuable source on the reform of the ministry during the Young Turk Period.

Nizamat ve Kavanin, Regulations and Laws, mostly in printed form.

Sicill-i Ahval, personnel files, including the original questionnaires filled out by the individuals themselves, for some 771 officials who served in the Foreign Ministry at various points between the late 1870s and c. 1908. Examined all files.

Tercüme Kalemi Evrakı, Papers of the Translation Office; several thousand bundles in file boxes; consulted on selective basis. Whether in topical or chronological terms, this collection is broader than its name would imply and is in fact one of the most important collections in the Foreign Ministry Archives.

C. Topkapı Palace Archives, Istanbul

Here there were only a few useful documents for the years running through the 1830s.

II. Non-Turkish Archival Sources

A. *Auswärtiges Amt*, Papers of the Imperial German Foreign Office

I consulted German diplomatic correspondence pertaining to the Ottoman Empire (Türkei series) for the years 1868-1922 on the basis of the microfilms now held in the U.S. National Archives, Washington, D.C. The subseries used, with the appropriate microfilm roll numbers, are as follows:

Allgemeine Angelegenheiten der Türkei, General Affairs of Turkey (T 139, mf. roll 392).
Diplomatische Vertretung der Türkei im Auslande, Diplomatic Representation of Turkey Abroad (T 139, mf. roll 394-95).
Schriftwechsel . . . über die innere Zustände . . . der Türkei, Correspondence on Internal Conditions in Turkey (T 139, mf. roll 354).
Türkische Militärs, The Turkish Military (T 139, mf. roll 394).
Türkische Ministerien, Turkish Ministries (T 139, mf. roll 394).

B. *Archives du Ministère des Affaires étrangères*, Paris

I used the Istanbul Embassy correspondence for 1838-1839, 1856, 1858, 1861, 1868, 1871-1872, and 1876 (Turquie, 276-404, selected volumes).

C. Foreign Office Papers, The Public Record Office, London

I have examined large numbers of volumes in the series including Istanbul Embassy Correspondence for the period 1797-1922 (FO 78/18-4615, selected volumes for 1797-1895, followed by FO 371/355-7908, selected volumes for 1907-1922).

D. *Haus-, Hof-, und Staatsarchiv*, Vienna

I used the diplomatic correspondence included in the papers of the *Staatskanzlei* for the years 1835-1839 (Türkei, VI/63-71) and the subsequent correspondence in the *Politisches Archiv* for 1849-1850, 1858-1859, 1868-1869, and 1870-1872 (Türkei, XII/39-100, selected volumes).

III. Published Sources

Abou-el-Haj, Rifa'at Ali. "Ottoman Attitudes toward Peace Making: The Karlowitz Case." *Der Islam*, LI (1974), 131-37.

———. "Ottoman Diplomacy at Karlowitz." *JAOS*, LXXXVII (1967), 498-512.

———. "The Ottoman Vezir and Paşa Households, 1683-1703: A Preliminary Report." *JAOS*, XCIV (1974), 438-47.

Ahmad, Feroz. *The Young Turks: The Committee of Union and Progress in Turkish Politics, 1908-1914.* Oxford, 1969.

Ahmed Resmî. *Halîfet ül-Rüesâ.* Istanbul, 1269/1852-1853 (a compendium of biographies of holders of the office of chief scribe [*reis ül-küttab*]).

Aḥmed Rif'at. *Werd ül-ḥadā'iq (Die Rose der Gärten).* Freiburg, 1970. Reprint of Istanbul edition of 1283/1866-1867 (a compendium of biographies of grand vezirs).

Aristarchi Bey, Grégoire. *Législation ottomane, ou recueil des lois, règlements, ordonnances, traités, capitulations et autres documents officiels de l'Empire ottoman.* 7 vols. Constantinople, 1873-1888.

Armstrong, John A. *The European Administrative Elite.* Princeton, 1973.

Aşçıdede Halil İbrahim. *Geçen Asrı Aydınlatan Kıymetli Vesikalardan bir Eser: Hatıralar.* Edited by Reşad Ekrem Koçu. Istanbul, 1960 (memoirs of Aşçıdede H. İ.).

Aylmer, G. E. *The King's Servants: The Civil Service of Charles I, 1625-1642.* London, 1961.

Bakhash, Shaul. "The Evolution of Qajar Bureaucracy, 1779-1879." *Middle Eastern Studies*, VII (1971), 139-68.

Bareilles, Bertrand. *Un turc à Paris, 1806-1811: Relation de voyage et de mission de Mouhib Effendi, ambassadeur extraordinaire du Sultan Selim III.* Paris, 1920.

Berger, Morroe. *Bureaucracy and Society in Modern Egypt.* Princeton, 1957.

Berkes, Niyazi. *The Development of Secularism in Turkey.* Montreal, 1964.

Biliotti, A., and Ahmed Sedad. *Législation ottomane depuis le rétablissement de la Constitution.* I, *24 Djemazi-ul-Ahir 1326-10 juillet 1324/1908 au 1er Zilcadé 1327-1er novembre 1325/1909.* Paris, 1912.

Blancard, Théodore. *Les Mavroyéni: Histoire d'Orient (de 1700 à nos jours).* 2 vols. Paris, 1909.

Blau, Peter M. *The Dynamics of Bureaucracy.* 2d ed., Chicago, 1963.

Bozdağ, İsmet. *Abdülhamid'in Hatıra Defteri (Belgeler ve Resimlerle).* Istanbul, 1975 ("Journal" of Abd ül-Hamid).

Çark, Y. *Türk Devleti Hizmetinde Ermeniler.* Istanbul, 1953 ("Armenians in the Service of the Turkish State").

Cecil, Lamar. *The German Diplomatic Service, 1871-1914.* Princeton, 1976.

Cevdet, Ahmed, Paşa. *Tarih-i Cevdet.* 12 vols. 2d ed. (*tertib-i cedid*), Istanbul, 1309/1891-1892 (the "History" of Cevdet Paşa).

———. *Tezâkir 1-12, 13-20, 21-39, 40-Tetimme.* 4 vols. Edited by Cavid Baysun. Ankara, 1953-1967 (forty "Memoranda" on historical subjects and his own experiences).

Crozier, Michel. *Le phénomène bureaucratique.* Paris, 1963.

Danişmend, İsmail Hami. *İzahlı Osmanlı Tarihi Kronolojisi.* 4 vols. Istanbul, 1961 ("Explanatory Chronology of Ottoman History").

Davison, Roderic H. "The Advent of the Principle of Representation in the Government of the Ottoman Empire," in William R. Polk and Richard L. Chambers, eds., *Beginnings of Modernization in the Middle East: The Nineteenth Century.* Chicago, 1968, 93-108.

———. "Ottoman Diplomacy at the Congress of Paris (1856) and the Question of Reform," *VII. Türk Tarih Kongresi, Kongreye Sunulan Bildiriler.* 2 vols. Ankara, 1973, II, 580-86.

———. *Reform in the Ottoman Empire, 1856-1876.* Princeton, 1963.

———. "Turkish Attitudes Concerning Christian-Muslim Equality in the Nineteenth Century." *American Historical Review,* LIX (1954), 844-64.

Devereux, Robert. *The First Ottoman Constitutional Period: A Study of the Midhat Constitution and Parliament.* Baltimore, 1963.

Dodd, C. H. *Politics and Government in Turkey.* Berkeley and Los Angeles, 1969.

Downs, Anthony. *Inside Bureaucracy.* Boston, 1967.

Düstur. First Series (*Birinci Tertib*). 4 vols. plus 4 appendices (*zeyl*) and a later "Completion" volume (*Mütemmim*), Istanbul, 1289-1335/1872-1917, as well as 4 additional vols. published as vols. V-VIII, Ankara, 1937-1943.

———. Second Series (*İkinci Tertib*). 12 vols. Istanbul, 1329-1927 [*sic*; i.e., 1911-1927]. (The official series of laws and regulations published by the Ottoman government.)

Eisenstadt, S. N. "Bureaucracy and Political Development," in Joseph LaPalombara, ed., *Bureaucracy and Political Development.* Princeton, 1967, 96-119.

———. "Convergence and Divergence of Modern and Modernizing Societies: Indications from the Analysis of the Structuring of Social Hierarchies in Middle Eastern Societies." *IJMES,* VIII (1977), 1-27.

———. *Essays on Comparative Institutions.* New York, 1965.

———. *Modernization: Protest and Change.* Englewood Cliffs, N.J., 1966.

———. *Political Systems of Empires.* New York, 1963.

———. *Revolution and the Transformation of Societies: A Comparative Study of Civilizations.* New York, 1978.

———. *Tradition, Change, and Modernity.* New York, 1973.

———. *Traditional Patrimonialism and Modern Neopatrimonialism.* Sage Research Papers in the Social Sciences, vol. I, series no. 90-003

(Studies in Comparative Modernization Series). Beverly Hills, California, 1973.

Encyclopaedia of Islam. London and Leiden, 1st ed., 1913-1938; 2nd ed., 1954-.

Ergin, Osman. *İstanbul Mektepleri ve İlim, Terbiye ve San'at Müesseseleri Dolayısile Türkiye Maarif Tarihi.* 5 vols. Istanbul, 1939-1943 ("The Educational History of Turkey, with Special Reference to the Schools and Cultural Institutions of Istanbul").

Findley, Carter V. "The Acid Test of Ottomanism: The Acceptance of Non-Muslims in the Late Ottoman Bureaucracy." Paper presented at the conference on "The Non-Muslim Communities in the Ottoman Empire and its Successor States," Princeton University, June 1978.

————. "The Evolution of the Ottoman Ruling Class, from Traditionalism to Reform," a paper presented at a conference on "Polity, Society, and Economy in the Nineteenth and Twentieth Centuries in Turkey and North Africa," May 1975. The conference was sponsored by the Joint Committee on the Near and Middle East of the Social Science Research Council and the American Council of Learned Societies, and proceedings are in process of publication.

————. "The Foundation of the Ottoman Foreign Ministry: The Beginnings of Bureaucratic Reform under Selim III and Mahmud II." *IJMES*, III (1972), 388-416.

————. "From Reis Efendi to Foreign Minister: Ottoman Bureaucratic Reform and the Creation of the Foreign Ministry." Ph.D. dissertation, Harvard, 1969.

————. "Ideological Change in the Late Ottoman Empire." Paper presented at the conference on "State, Society, and Economy in Nineteenth Century Iran and the Ottoman Empire," held in Babolsar, Iran, in June 1978 under joint sponsorship of the Reza Shah Kabir University and the Joint Committee on the Near and Middle East of the American Council of Learned Societies and the Social Science Research Council.

————. "The Legacy of Tradition to Reform: Origins of the Ottoman Foreign Ministry," *IJMES*, I (1970), 334-57.

————. "Sir James W. Redhouse (1811-1892): The Making of a Perfect Orientalist?" *JAOS*, forthcoming.

Frey, Frederick. *The Turkish Political Elite.* Cambridge, Mass., 1965.

Ghorbal, Shafik. "The Missions of Ali Effendi in Paris and of Sedki Effendi in London, 1797-1811; A Contribution to the Study of the Westernisation of Ottoman Institutions." *Bulletin of the Faculty of Arts, University of Egypt*, I (1933), 114-29.

Gibb, Hamilton A. R., and Harold Bowen. *Islamic Society and the West: A Study of the Impact of Western Civilization on Moslem Culture in the Near East.* 1 vol. in 2 parts. Oxford, 1950-1957.

Gladden, E. N. *Civil Services of the United Kingdom, 1855-1970.* New York, 1967.

———. *A History of Public Administration.* 2 vols. London, 1972.

Gould, Andrew G. "Lords or Bandits? The Derebeys of Cilicia." *IJMES*, VII (1976), 485-506.

Hammer-Purgstall, Joseph von. *Des osmanischen Reichs Staatsverfassung und Staatsverwaltung.* 2 vols. Vienna, 1815; reprinted, Hildesheim, 1963.

Heper, Metin. *Bürokratik Yönetim Geleneği: Osmanlı İmparatorluğu ve Türkiye Cumhuriyetinde Gelişimi ve Niteliği.* Ankara, 1974 ("The Tradition of Bureaucratic Administration: Its Development in the Ottoman Empire and the Turkish Republic and Its Character").

———. "Political Modernization as Reflected in Bureaucratic Change: The Turkish Bureaucracy and a 'Historical Bureaucratic Empire' Tradition." *IJMES*, VII (1976), 507-21.

———. *Türk Kamu Bürokrasisinde Gelenekçilik ve Modernleşme: Siyaset Sosyolojisi Açısından Bir İnceleme.* Istanbul, 1977 ("Traditionalism and Modernization in Turkish Public Bureaucracy: A Study from the Viewpoint of Political Sociology").

Herbette, Maurice. *Une ambassade turque sous le Directoire.* Paris, 1902.

Heyd, Uriel. "The Ottoman 'Ulemâ and Westernization in the Time of Selîm III and Maḥmûd II." *Scripta Hierosalymitana.* IX: *Studies in Islamic History and Civilization* (1961), 63-96.

———. *Studies in Old Ottoman Criminal Law.* Edited by V. L. Ménage. Oxford, 1973.

Ho, Ping-ti. *The Ladder of Success in Imperial China.* New York. 1964.

Hocaoğlu, Mehmet, ed. *Abdülhamit Han'ın Muhtıraları (Belgeler).* Istanbul, n.d. (c. 1975) ("Memoranda of Abd ül-Hamid").

Hurewitz, J. C. *Diplomacy in the Near and Middle East: A Documentary Record, 1914-1956,* 2d of 2 vols. Princeton, 1956.

———. "The Europeanization of Ottoman Diplomacy: The Conversion from Unilateralism to Reciprocity in the Nineteenth Century." *Bell.,* XXV (1961), 455-66.

———. *The Middle East and North Africa in World Politics: A Documentary Record.* I: *European Expansion, 1535-1914.* 2d ed., revised and enlarged, New Haven, 1975.

———. "Ottoman Diplomacy and the European State System." *Middle East Journal,* XV (1961), 141-52.

İnal, Mahmud Kemal. *Osmanlı Devrinde Son Sadrıazamlar.* 14 fascicles in 3 vols. 3rd printing, Istanbul, 1964-65 (biographies of the grand vezirs of the late periods).

———. *Son Asir Türk Şairleri.* 10 fascicles in 4 vols. Istanbul, printing of 1969 ("Turkish Poets of the Last Century"—biographies of members of the literary-bureaucratic intelligentsia).

İnalcık, Halil. *The Ottoman Empire: The Classical Age: 1300-1600*. London, 1973.

————. "Application of the Tanzimat and its Social Effects." *Archivum Ottomanicum*, v (1973), 97-127, revised English version of id., "Tanzimat'ın Uygulanması ve Sosyal Tepkileri," *Bell.*, xxvııı (1964), 623-49.

İslâm Ansiklopedisi, more than 125 fascicles to date, now in vol. xıı. Istanbul, 1940-   ("Encyclopedia of Islam," differs from European prototype in expanded treatment of Turkish subjects).

Itzkowitz, Norman. "Eighteenth Century Ottoman Realities." *Studia Islamica*, xvı (1962), 73-94.

Jones, Ray. *The Nineteenth Century Foreign Office: An Administrative History*. London, 1971.

Kâmil, Mehmed, Paşa. *Hâtırat-ı Sadr-ı Esbak Kâmil Paşa*. 1: *Hâtırat-ı Siyasiyat, der Ahd-ı Sultan Abd ül-Hamid Han-ı Sani*. Istanbul, 1329/1910 ("Memoirs of the Former Grand Vezir, Kâmil Paşa").

Karal, Enver Ziya. *Halet Efendinin Paris Büyük Elçiliği (1802-1806)*. Istanbul, 1940 ("The Embassy of Halet Efendi to Paris").

————. *Osmanlı Tarihi*. Vols. v-vııı. Ankara, 1947-1962 ("Ottoman History").

————. *Selim III'ün Hat-tı [sic] Hümayunları: Nizam-ı Cedit, 1789-1807*. Ankara, 1946 ("Decrees of Selim III: The 'New Order,' 1789-1807").

Karpat, Kemal. "The Transformation of the Ottoman State, 1789-1908." *IJMES*, ııı (1972), 243-81.

Kaynar, Reşat. *Mustafa Reşit Paşa ve Tanzimat*. Ankara, 1954 ("Mustafa Reşid Paşa and the Tanzimat").

Kornrumpf, Hans-Jürgen. *Die Territorialverwaltung im östlichen Teil der europäischen Türkei vom Erlass der Vilayetsordnung (1864) bis zum Berliner Kongress nach amtlichen osmanischen Veröffentlichungen*. Freiburg im Breisgau, 1976.

Kunt, Metin. "Ethnic-Regional (*Cins*) Solidarity in the Seventeenth-Century Ottoman Establishment." *IJMES*, v (1974), 233-39.

————. "Kulların Kulları." *Boğaziçi Üniversitesi Dergisi, Hümaniter Bilimler*, ııı (1975), 27-42 ("Slaves of the Slaves").

————. *Sancaktan Eyalete: 1550-1650 Arasında Osmanlı Umerası ve İl İdaresi*. Istanbul, 1975.

Kuran, Ercümend. *Avrupa'da Osmanlı İkamet Elçiliklerinin Kuruluşu ve İlk Elçilerin Siyasi Faâliyetleri, 1793-1821*. Ankara, 1968 ("The Foundation of Permanent Ottoman Embassies in Europe and the Political Activities of the First Ambassadors").

————. "Küçük Said Paşa (1840-1914) as a Turkish Modernist." *IJMES*, ı (1970), 124-32.

————. "Türkiye'nin batılılaşmasında Osmanlı daimî elçiliklerinin rolü." *VI. Türk Tarih Kongresi, Kongreye Sunulan Bildiriler*. Ankara,

1967, 489-96 ("The Role of Permanent Embassies in the Westernization of Turkey").

Levy, Avigdor. "The Military Policy of Sultan Mahmud II, 1808-1839." Ph.D. dissertation, Harvard, 1968.

――――. "The Officer Corps in Sultan Mahmud II's New Army, 1826-39." *IJMES*, II (1971), 21-39.

――――. "The Ottoman Ulema and the Military Reforms of Sultan Mahmud II." *Asian and African Studies*, VII (1971), 13-39.

Levy, Marion J., Jr. *Modernization and the Structure of Societies: A Setting for International Affairs*. Princeton, 1966.

Lewis, Bernard. *The Emergence of Modern Turkey*. 2d ed., London, 1968.

Loytved. "Grundriss der allgemeinen Organisation der Verwaltungsbehörden der eigentlichen Türkei." *Mitteilungen des Seminars für Orientalischen Sprachen zu Berlin*. II. Abteilung, *Westasiatische Studien*, VII (1904), 25-52.

Lûfti, Ahmed, Efendi. *Tarih-ı Lûtfi*, 8 published vols., the 8th edited by Abd ul-Rahman Şeref. Istanbul, 1290-1328/1873-1910. Additional volumes exist in ms., of which viii-xii and xiv-xv are in the Library of the Turkish Historical Society, Ankara (TTK Mss. 531/1-7). Professor S. J. Shaw kindly made available to me photocopies of these volumes (The "History" of Lûtfi Efendi).

Lybyer, Albert Howe. *The Government of the Ottoman Empire in the Time of Suleiman the Magnificent*. Cambridge, Mass., 1913.

Ma'oz, Moshe. *Ottoman Reform in Syria and Palestine, 1840-1861: The Impact of the Tanzimat on Politics and Society*. Oxford, 1968.

Mardin, Şerif. *The Genesis of Young Ottoman Thought: A Study in the Modernization of Turkish Political Ideas*. Princeton, 1962.

――――. "Historical Determinants of Social Stratification: Social Class and Class Consciousness in Turkey." *Siyasal Bilgiler Fakültesi Dergisi*, XXII (1968), 111-42.

――――. *Jön Türklerin Siyasî Fikirleri*. Ankara, 1964 ("Political Ideas of the Young Turks").

――――. "Libertarian Movements in the Ottoman Empire, 1878-1895," *Middle East Journal*, XIV (1962), 169-82.

――――. "Power, Civil Society and Culture in the Ottoman Empire." *Comparative Studies in Society and History*, XI (1969), 258-81.

――――. "Some Notes on an Early Phase in the Modernization of Communications in Turkey." *Comparative Studies in Society and History*, III (1961), 250-71.

――――. "Super Westernization in Urban Life in the Ottoman Empire in the Last Quarter of the Nineteenth Century," in Peter Benedict, Erol Tümertekin, Fatma Mansur, eds., *Turkey: Geographic and Social Perspectives*, Leiden, 1974, 403-46.

Matuz, Joseph. *Das Kanzleiwesen Sultan Süleymâns des Prächtigen*. Wiesbaden, 1974.

Matuz, Joseph. "Die Pfortendolmetscher zur Herrschaftszeit Süleymâns des Prächtigen." *Südostforschungen*, xxxiv (1975), 26-60.

Meeker, Michael E. "Meaning and Society in the Near East: Examples from the Black Sea Turks and the Levantine Arabs." *IJMES*, vii (1976), 243-70, 383-422.

Naff, Thomas. "Ottoman Diplomatic Relations with Europe in the Eighteenth Century: Patterns and Trends," in Thomas Naff and Roger Owen, eds., *Studies in Eighteenth Century Islamic History*, Carbondale, Ill., 1977, 88-107.

———. "Reform and the Conduct of Ottoman Diplomacy in the Reign of Selim III, 1789-1807." *JAOS*, LXXXIII (1963), 295-315.

van Nieuwenhuijze, C.A.O. *Social Stratification and the Middle East: An Interpretation*. Leiden, 1965.

Nuri, Mustafa, Paşa. *Netayic ül-Vukuat*. 4 vols. Istanbul, 1294-1327/ 1877-1909 (the "History" of Mustafa Nuri Paşa).

Nuri, Osman, Bey. *Abd ül-Hamid-i Sani ve Devr-i Saltanatı: Hayat-ı Hususiye ve Siyasiyesi*. 3 vols., completed by A.R., Istanbul, 1327/1909 ("Abd ül-Hamid II and His Reign: Private and Public Life").

d'Ohsson, Ignatius Mouradgea. *Tableau général de l'Empire othoman*. Vol. vii. Paris, 1824.

Ortaylı, İlber. *Tanzimattan Sonra Mahalli Idareler (1840-1878)*. Ankara, 1974 ("Local Administration after the Tanzimat, 1840-1878").

Pakalın, Mehmet Zeki. *Osmanlı Tarih Deyimleri ve Terimleri Sözlüğü*. 17 fascicles in 3 vols. Istanbul, 1946-53 ("Dictionary of Historical Expressions and Terms").

Pâker, Esat Cemal. *Siyasi Tarihimizde Kırk Yıllık Hariciye Hatıraları*. Istanbul, 1952 (Memoirs of forty years in the Foreign Service).

Pinson, Mark. "Ottoman Bulgaria in the First Tanzimat Period—The Revolts in Nish (1841) and Vidin (1850)." *Middle Eastern Studies*, xi (1975), 103-46.

Quataert, Donald. "Ottoman Reform and Agriculture in Anatolia, 1876-1908." Ph.D. dissertation, University of California at Los Angeles, 1973.

Ramsaur, Ernest Edmondson, Jr. *The Young Turks: Prelude to the Revolution of 1908*. Princeton, 1957.

Riggs, Fred W. *Administration in Developing Countries, the Theory of Prismatic Society*. Boston, 1964.

———. "Bureaucratic Politics in Comparative Perspective," in Fred W. Riggs, ed., *Frontiers of Development Administration*, Durham, N.C., 1971, 375-414.

———. "Bureaucrats and Political Development: A Paradoxical View," in Joseph LaPalombara, ed., *Bureaucracy and Political Development*, Princeton, 1967, 120-67.

Röhrborn, Klaus. "Die Emanzipation der Finanzbürokratie im Osmanischen Reich (Ende 16. Jahrhundert)." *Zeitschrift der Deutschen Morgenländischen Gesellschaft*, CXXII (1972), 118-39.

———. *Untersuchungen zur osmanischen Verwaltungsgeschichte.* Berlin, 1973.

Rosenberg, Hans. *Bureaucracy, Aristocracy, and Autocracy, the Prussian Experience (1660-1815).* Cambridge, Mass., 1966.

Runciman, Steven. *The Great Church in Captivity: A Study of the Patriarchate of Constantinople from the Eve of the Turkish Conquest to the Greek War of Independence.* Cambridge, 1968.

Said, Mehmed, Paşa. *Said Paşa'nın Hâtıratı.* 2 vols. in 3 parts. Istanbul, 1328/1910 ("Memoirs of Said Paşa").

Salname (title later expanded to *Salname-i Devlet-i Aliye-i Osmaniye*). 67 vols. Istanbul, 1263-1334/1847-1918. (Official "Yearbooks" of the Ottoman government; published annually through 1908 and irregularly thereafter. Cited by year of publication, the years being *hicrî* in all cases through 1326/1908 and *malî* or "financial" for the three later volumes.)

Salname-i Nezaret-i Hariciye (title varies). 4 vols. Istanbul, 1302, 1306, 1318, 1320/1884-1885, 1888-1889, 1900-1901, 1902-1903 ("Yearbooks" of the Ottoman Foreign Ministry; only four published).

Sertoğlu, Midhat. *Muhteva Bakımından Başvekâlet Arşivi.* Ankara, 1955 (Guide to the collections of the *Başvekâlet* or *Başbakanlık* Archives, Istanbul).

Shamir, Shimon. "The Modernization of Syria: Problems and Solutions in the Early Period of Abdülhamid," in William R. Polk and Richard L. Chambers, eds., *Beginnings of Modernization in the Middle East: The Nineteenth Century*, Chicago, 1968, 351-81.

Shaw, Stanford J. *Between Old and New: The Ottoman Empire under Sultan Selim III, 1789-1807.* Cambridge, Mass., 1971.

———. "The Central Legislative Councils in the Nineteenth Century Ottoman Reform Movement Before 1876." *IJMES*, I (1970), 51-84.

——— (with Ezel Kural Shaw as coauthor of vol. II). *History of the Ottoman Empire and Modern Turkey.* 2 vols. Cambridge, 1976-77.

———. "The Nineteenth-Century Ottoman Tax Reforms and Revenue System." *IJMES*, VI (1975), 421-59.

Shils, Edward A. "Centre and Periphery," in *The Logic of Personal Knowledge: Essays Presented to Michael Polanyi on his Seventieth Birthday, 11 March 1961*, London, 1961, 117-30.

Shinder, Joel. "Career Line Formation in the Ottoman Bureaucracy, 1648-1750: A New Perspective." *JESHO*, XVI (1973), 217-37.

Silberman, Bernard. *Ministers of Modernization: Elite Mobility in the Meiji Restoration.* Tucson, 1964.

Söylemezoğlu, Galip Kemali. *Hariciye Hizmetinde Otuz Sene* (title varies). 4 vols. Istanbul, 1949-1955.

Spuler, Bertold. "Die Europäische Diplomatie in Konstantinopel bis zum Frieden von Belgrad (1739)." *Jahrbücher für Kultur und Geschichte der Slaven*, Neue Folge, xi (1935), 53-115, 171-222, 313-66; *Jahrbücher für die Geschichte Osteuropas*, 1 (1936), 383-439, 229-262(?).

Stoianovich, Traian. "The Conquering Balkan Orthodox Merchant." *Journal of Economic History*, xx (1960), 234-313.

Suleiman, Ezra N. *Politics, Power, and Bureaucracy in France: The Administrative Elite*. Princeton, 1974.

Swenson, Victor R. "The Military Rising in Istanbul 1909." *Journal of Contemporary History*, v, no. 4 (1970), 171-84.

Szyliowicz, Joseph S. "Changes in the Recruitment Patterns and Career-Lines of Ottoman Provincial Administrators during the Nineteenth Century," in Moshe Ma'oz, ed., *Studies on Palestine during the Ottoman Period*, Jerusalem, 1975, 249-83.

Tahsin Paşa. *Abdülhamit ve Yıldız Hatıraları*. Istanbul, 1931 ("Memoirs of Abd ül-Hamid and Yıldız Palace").

Tâ'ib Ahmed, 'Osmânzâde. *Hadîqat ül-vüzerâ (Der Garten der Wesire), mit den Fortsetzungen (zeyl) des Dilâver Ağazâde Ömer Efendi, Ahmed Gâvîd und Bağdâdî 'Abd ül-fettâh Şevqet*. Freiburg, 1969. Reprint of Istanbul edition of 1271/1854-1855 (biographies of grand vezirs).

Tanzimat I: Yüzüncü Yıldönümü Münasebetile. Istanbul, 1940 (a collection of essays commemorating the hundredth anniversary of the Tanzimat).

Temelkuran, Tevfik. "Divân-i Hümâyûn Mühimme Kalemi." *Tar. Der.*, no. 6 (1975), 129-75 ("The Section for Important Affairs in the Office of the Imperial Divan").

Thomas, Lewis V. *A Study of Naima*. Edited by Norman Itzkowitz. New York, 1972.

Ülgener, Sabri F. *İktisadî İnhitat Tarihimizin Ahlâk ve Zihniyet Meseleleri*. Istanbul, 1951 ("Problems of Morality and Mentality in the History of our Economic Decline").

Unat, Faik Reşit. *Hicrî Tarihleri Milâdî Tarihe Çevirme Kılavuzu*. Expanded 4th printing, Ankara, 1974. (Date conversion tables; used in this study for all dates in the *hicrî* and financial [*malî, rumî*] calendars.)

―――. *Osmanlı Sefirleri ve Sefaretnameleri*. Completed and published by Bekir Sıtkı Baykal, Ankara, 1968 ("Ottoman Ambassadors and Embassy Narratives").

Us, Hakkı Tarık. *Meclis-i Meb'usan 1293:1877 Zabıt Ceridesi*. 2 vols. Istanbul, 1939-1954 ("Proceedings of the Chamber of Deputies, 1877").

Uşaklıgil, Halid Ziya. *Kırk Yıl*. İstanbul, 1969 ("Forty Years"—memoirs).

―――. *Saray ve Ötesi*. Istanbul, 1965 ("The Palace and Beyond," continuation of his memoirs).

Uzunçarşılı, İsmail Hakkı. *Osmanlı Devletinin İlmiye Teşkilâtı*. Ankara, 1965 ("The Organization of the Religious Establishment in the Ottoman Empire").

———. *Osmanlı Devletinin Merkez ve Bahriye Teşkilâtı*. Ankara, 1948 ("The Central and Naval Organizations of the Ottoman Empire"—includes discussion of the scribal service).

———. *Osmanlı Devletinin Saray Teşkilâtı*. Ankara, 1945 ("The Palace Organization of the Ottoman Empire").

———. *Osmanlı Devleti Teşkilâtından Kapukulu Ocakları*. 2 vols. Ankara, 1943-1944 (Organization of the military units attached directly to the palace).

Weber, Max. *Economy and Society: An Outline of Interpretive Sociology.* Edited by Guenther Roth and Claus Wittich. 3 vols., New York, 1968.

———. *From Max Weber: Essays in Sociology.* Edited and translated by H. H. Gerth and C. Wright Mills. Oxford, 1946.

Yaney, George L. *The Systematization of Russian Government: Social Evolution in the Domestic Administration of Imperial Russia, 1711-1905.* Urbana, Ill., 1973.

Young, George. *Corps de droit ottoman: Recueil des codes, lois, règlements, ordonnances et actes les plus importants du droit intérieur, et d'études sur le droit coutumier de l'Empire ottoman.* 7 vols. Oxford, 1905-1906.

Ziadeh, Farhat J. *Lawyers, the Rule of Law, and Liberalism in Modern Egypt.* Stanford, 1968.

Library of Congress Cataloging in Publication Data

Findley, Carter V   1941-
Bureaucratic reform in the Ottoman Empire.

(Princeton studies on the Near East)
Bibliography: p.
1.   Turkey—Politics and government—19th century.
2.   Bureaucracy—Turkey.   I.   Title.   II.   Series:
Princeton studies on the Near East.
JQ1806.Z1F55   354'.561'01   79-22162
ISBN 0-691-05288-3